The *Doctor Who* Error Finder

The *Doctor Who* Error Finder

Plot, Continuity and Production Mistakes in the Television Series and Films

R. H. LANGLEY

McFarland & Company, Inc., Publishers
Jefferson, North Carolina, and London

Library of Congress Cataloguing-in-Publication Data

Langley, R.H., 1948–
The *Doctor Who* error finder : plot, continuity and production
mistakes in the television series and films / R.H. Langley.
p.   cm.
Includes index.

ISBN 0-7864-1990-3 (softcover : 50# alkaline paper)

1. Doctor Who (Television program)—Miscellanea.   I. Title.
PN1992.77.D6273L36   2005   791.45'72—dc22   2005006382

British Library cataloguing data are available

©2005 R.H. Langley. All rights reserved

*No part of this book may be reproduced or transmitted in any form
or by any means, electronic or mechanical, including photocopying
or recording, or by any information storage and retrieval system,
without permission in writing from the publisher.*

On the cover: background ©2005 Wood River Gallery;
telephone booth ©2005 clipart.com

Manufactured in the United States of America

*McFarland & Company, Inc., Publishers
Box 611, Jefferson, North Carolina 28640
www.mcfarlandpub.com*

To Veronica

Acknowledgments

This book could not exist without the hard work and dedication of all people concerned with the production of *Doctor Who*. Pointing out bloopers may not seem the best way of thanking these people, but the book could not have been created if these people had not done such an excellent job.

I would like to thank Ally Winford for supplying me with several important bits of useful information.

I would also like to thank Daniel O'Malley. He provided many useful suggestions when I was starting this project. His website, timelash.com, was an excellent source of additional information throughout the course of this project.

R.H. Langley

Table of Contents

Acknowledgments	vii
Preface	1

I. THE FIRST DOCTOR

Pilot: An Unearthly Child	9
(A) 100,000 BC	11
(B) The Mutants	13
(C) Inside the Spaceship	15
(D) Marco Polo	16
Pause to Consider: Missing Stories	17
(E) The Keys of Marinus	18
(F) The Aztecs	20
(G) The Sensorites	21
(H) The Reign of Terror	23
(J) Planet of Giants	24
(K) The Dalek Invasion of Earth	25
Pause to Consider: Anachronisms	29
(L) The Rescue	29
(M) The Romans	30
(N) The Web Planet	32
(P) The Crusade	34
(Q) The Space Museum	35
(R) The Chase	36
(S) The Time Meddler	41
(T) Galaxy 4	42
(T/A) Mission to the Unknown	43
(U) The Myth Makers	44
(V) The Daleks' Master Plan	45
(W) The Massacre of St. Bartholemew's Eve	48
Pause to Consider: The First Doctor and His Lines	49

(X)	The Ark	49
(Y)	The Celestial Toymaker	51
(Z)	The Gunfighters	52
(AA)	The Savages	53
(BB)	The War Machines	54
(CC)	The Smugglers	56
(DD)	The Tenth Planet	57

II. THE SECOND DOCTOR

(EE)	The Power of the Daleks	61

Pause to Consider: Audio Tapes — 63

(FF)	The Highlanders	63
(GG)	The Underwater Menace	64
(HH)	The Moonbase	65
(JJ)	The Macra Terror	68
(KK)	The Faceless Ones	69
(LL)	The Evil of the Daleks	70
(MM)	The Tomb of the Cybermen	72
(NN)	The Abominable Snowmen	75
(OO)	The Ice Warriors	76
(PP)	The Enemy of the World	79
(QQ)	The Web of Fear	80
(RR)	Fury from the Deep	82
(SS)	The Wheel in Space	83
(TT)	The Dominators	86
(UU)	The Mind Robber	88
(VV)	The Invasion	90
(WW)	The Krotons	93

Pause to Consider: Accents — 95

(XX)	The Seeds of Death	95
(YY)	The Space Pirates	98
(ZZ)	The War Games	100

III. THE THIRD DOCTOR

(AAA)	Spearhead from Space	107
(BBB)	Doctor Who and the Silurians	110
(CCC)	The Ambassadors of Death	111
(DDD)	Inferno	114
(EEE)	Terror of the Autons	116
(FFF)	The Mind of Evil	118
(GGG)	The Claws of Axos	120
(HHH)	Colony in Space	122
(JJJ)	The Daemons	125
(KKK)	Day of the Daleks	127

(MMM)	The Curse of Peladon	129
(LLL)	The Sea Devils	130
(NNN)	The Mutants	133

Pause to Consider: CSO 135

(OOO)	The Time Monster	136
(RRR)	The Three Doctors	138
(PPP)	Carnival of Monsters	141
(QQQ)	Frontier in Space	143
(SSS)	Planet of the Daleks	145
(TTT)	The Green Death	148
(UUU)	The Time Warrior	151
(WWW)	Invasion of the Dinosaurs	152
(XXX)	Death to the Daleks	154
(YYY)	The Monster of Peladon	155
(ZZZ)	Planet of the Spiders	157

IV. The Fourth Doctor

(4A)	Robot	161
(4C)	The Ark in Space	162
(4B)	The Sontaran Experiment	164
(4E)	Genesis of the Daleks	164
(4D)	Revenge of the Cybermen	166
(4F)	Terror of the Zygons	168
(4H)	Planet of Evil	169
(4G)	Pyramids of Mars	170
(4J)	The Android Invasion	173
(4K)	The Brain of Morbius	175
(4L)	The Seeds of Doom	176
(4M)	The Masque of Mandragora	178

Pause to Consider: The "Time Lords' Gift" 179

(4N)	The Hand of Fear	180
(4P)	The Deadly Assassin	181
(4Q)	The Face of Evil	182
(4R)	The Robots of Death	184
(4S)	The Talons of Weng-Chiang	185
(4V)	Horror of Fang Rock	187
(4T)	The Invisible Enemy	188
(4X)	Image of the Fendahl	190
(4W)	The Sun Makers	191
(4Y)	Underworld	193
(4Z)	The Invasion of Time	194

The Search for the Key to Time [stories 5A through 5F]

(5A)	The Ribos Operation	196
(5B)	The Pirate Planet	197

- (5C) The Stones of Blood — 199
- (5D) The Androids of Tara — 200
- (5E) The Power of Kroll — 201
- (5F) The Armageddon Factor — 203

- (5J) Destiny of the Daleks — 204
- (5H) City of Death — 206
- (5G) The Creature from the Pit — 208
- (5K) Nightmare of Eden — 209
- (5L) The Horns of Nimon — 210
- (5M) Shada — 212
- (5N) The Leisure Hive — 213
- (5Q) Meglos — 214

The E-Space Trilogy [stories 5R through 5S] — 216
- (5R) Full Circle — 216
- (5P) State of Decay — 217
- (5S) Warrior's Gate — 218

- (5T) The Keeper of Traken — 220
- (5V) Logopolis — 221

V. THE FIFTH DOCTOR

- (5Z) Castrovalva — 225
- (5W) Four to Doomsday — 227
- (5Y) Kinda — 229
- (5X) The Visitation — 231
- (6A) Black Orchid — 233
- (6B) Earthshock — 233
- (6C) Time-Flight — 236

Pause to Consider: Boom Mike Shadows — 237

- (6E) Arc of Infinity — 238
- (6D) Snakedance — 239

The Guardian Trilogy [stories 6F through 6H] — 240
- (6F) Mawdryn Undead — 240
- (6G) Terminus — 241
- (6H) Enlightenment — 242

- (6J) The King's Demons — 244
- (6K) The Five Doctors — 245
- (6L) Warriors of the Deep — 247
- (6M) The Awakening — 249
- (6N) Frontios — 249
- (6P) Resurrection of the Daleks — 251
- (6Q) Planet of Fire — 252
- (6R) The Caves of Androzani — 254

VI. THE SIXTH DOCTOR

- (6S) The Twin Dilemma — 259
- (6T) Attack of the Cybermen — 261
- (6V) Vengeance on Varos — 263
- (6X) The Mark of the Rani — 264
- (6W) The Two Doctors — 266
- (6Y) Timelash — 268

Pause to Consider: Astronomy — 271

- (6Z) Revelation of the Daleks — 272
- (7A/7B/7C) The Trial of a Time Lord: — 273
  - *The Mysterious Planet* — 273
  - *Mindwarp* — 276
  - *The Ultimate Foe* — 277
  - *Time Inc.* — 280

VII. THE SEVENTH DOCTOR

- (7D) Time and the Rani — 285
- (7E) Paradise Towers — 287
- (7F) Delta and the Bannermen — 288
- (7G) Dragonfire — 289
- (7H) Remembrance of the Daleks — 291
- (7L) The Happiness Patrol — 293
- (7K) Silver Nemesis — 294
- (7J) The Greatest Show in the Galaxy — 296
- (7N) Battlefield — 297
- (7Q) Ghost Light — 299
- (7M) The Curse of Fenric — 300
- (7P) Survival — 302

VIII. THE EIGHTH DOCTOR

Dr. Who [1996 TV movie] — 307

IX. THE FORGOTTEN DOCTOR: THE PETER CUSHING MOVIES

- Dr. Who and the Daleks — 315
- Daleks — Invasion Earth 2150 A.D. — 316

X. RELATED PROGRAMS

- K-9 and Company — 321
- Dimensions in Time — 321
- The Curse of Fatal Death — 322

Index — 325

Preface

This book chronicles the broadcast episodes of *Doctor Who*. Other books have done the same. However, this book offers unique information that will lead you to view the series from a different perspective.

This book lists and describes the errors (many people call them bloopers) that appear in the *Doctor Who* stories. Similar lists are incomplete and contain errors of their own. This book offers significantly more information than other lists and corrects many mistakes in those lists. In addition, it comments on many other details (besides the out-and-out errors) that are of interest to fans of the show.

While researching this book I found that errors cited in other lists were sometimes difficult to locate in the shows. This book solves that problem by listing not only the episode title but also the approximate time at which the error occurs within the episode.

More than over 4000 errors are listed in this book, many for the first time. Also listed are nearly 1500 other items of interest, such as the first use of a sonic screwdriver and other facts of interest to serious fans. Readers beware: This list contains many "Spoilers," or information that reveals a surprise in the plot. If you feel you must use this book while viewing an adventure for the first time, you should resist the urge to read ahead.

What Kinds of Errors Are Listed?

Most people have seen one or more "blooper" reels — simple collections of outtakes removed from a television show before transmission of the story. In these reels, actors walk into doors, stumble over their lines, or utter the wrong lines. Outtakes are untransmitted bloopers. This book consists of items *actually transmitted*, and not items purged before transmission. Examples include, among other things, the following:

shadows visible in a shot
microphones or other equipment visible in a shot
persons other than the actors appearing on the set
obvious strings or supports
anachronisms (primarily from stories in the Earth's past)
errors in continuity (normally within the same story)
actors having trouble with their lines
actors having trouble walking or with inanimate objects
unsteady sets or props
problems with the laws of nature or common sense

Despite the large amount of information it contains, this book is not an exhaustive list. Many minor bloopers are not listed. Minor problems include items such as small fleeting shadows.

This book lists broadcast errors from every season of the television episodes of *Doctor Who*. In addition, there are errors from the untransmitted parts of the pilot episode and *Shada*. The two Peter Cushing movies and the one spinoff, *K9 and Company*, are likewise covered. Finally, there are special entries for *Dimensions in Time* and *The Curse of Fatal Death*. In some cases, extended versions of the stories are available. This book does not cover extended versions unless they are also broadcast versions.

Errors involving more than one story present a special problem. It would not be fair to simply point out inconsistencies between the First Doctor and the Seventh Doctor (though in a few cases they are noted in order to make a particular point). Problems from sequential stories (for example, *The Enemy of the World* and *The Web of Fear*) and from sequels (for example, *The Curse of Peladon* and *The Monster of Peladon*) are worth noting. Problems involving more than one story are "multi-story errors." Here's an example: At the end of *The War Games,* only a few seconds pass between the erasure of Jamie and Zoe's memories, and the Second Doctor becoming the Third Doctor. How can the Second Doctor know this when he sees Jamie and Zoe in *The Five Doctors*?

Many items that could be considered errors involve something taking place offscreen. For example, how do Daleks manipulate things with their "hands"? One of the Daleks searches Marat's body (*Planet of the Daleks*) and finds a map, which the searcher holds up for the other Daleks to see. How does a Dalek search a body? Since this action occurred offscreen and was not transmitted, it is not listed in this book as an error.

In *The Masque of Mandragora*, Sarah Jane Smith wonders why she can understand what people and aliens say when they cannot be speaking in English. The Doctor replies, "It's the Time Lords' Gift I allow you to share." Logically, then, any actor's speaking in any language other than English should constitute a blooper. For the most part this list does not include these errors.

The Time Lords' Gift extends to units of measure. For example, the Cybermen have their own distance units, but the Doctor, the companions, and the viewers "hear" the units translated into miles, hours, or weeks. The situations where non–Earth units are present should be the problems.

Appearances of actors' underwear are not listed. Perhaps some more voyeuristic viewers should create lists of their own.

It was difficult to decide how to deal with the appearance of the Doctor and companions in out-of-period clothing. Some fans feel that an actor commenting on out-of-period clothing is an inconsistency with the story line. Others feel that *not* commenting is the real inconsistency. In this book I have noted occurrences of out-of-period clothing that are at variance with other stories. Note: When one of the Doctor's companions changes into period clothing through precognition, this is also a blooper; all such instances are listed here.

For the most part, a "multiple blooper" (the same error occurring more than once) gets only one listing in this book (rather than being listed each time it occurs). In such cases I have tried to list the best, but not necessarily the first, instance of the error. In other cases, I have listed multiple appearances of a blooper in order to keep this book consistent with other lists that do the same. Finally, certain errors are so blatant that they deserve being listed every time, and have been.

Boom mike and light fixture shadows are quite common. In some sets, the position of the mikes or lights causes these shadows to appear more than once. In this book, such shadows are usually noted only once regardless of how often they appear in a scene. Exceptions have been made, however, when additional appearances are particularly obvious or especially interesting. When the actual boom mike or light fixture appears on screen, this is a major error, and every such appearance is listed.

Certain sets, such as jungle sets, tend to produce multiple shadows that are not due to misplaced boom mikes or light fixtures. These shadows are not errors, though they are sometimes misinterpreted as such.

Other shadows may be errors. It is not always possible to tell. In this book I have chosen not to list small shadows if they do not have definite shapes to allow their identification as specific objects. Large shadows do appear on this list, even if their cause is uncertain. Any size shadow is an error if it distracts one or more of the actors.

Certain terms cause errors. One example is the mixing of the terms star system, galaxy, and constellation. These are distinctly different terms, but in many cases one is incorrectly used in place of another. Another example of incorrect terminology is the reference to meteors as meteorites in *The Wheel in Space*. Meteors travel in space; they become meteorites only when they hit a planet's surface. Technically, every use of an incorrect term is an error. To list them all, however, would produce something like this:

> **Episode 1**, 21:47; **Episode 1**, 22:15; **Episode 2**, 7:09; **Episode 2**, 15:20; **Episode 3**, 6:00; **Episode 3**, 7:42; **Episode 3**, 8:11; **Episode 3**, 10:57; **Episode 3**, 11:03; **Episode 3**, 13:10; **Episode 3**, 13:25; **Episode 3**, 21:16; **Episode 3**, 21:48; **Episode 4**, 6:07; **Episode 4**, 6:12; **Episode 4**, 6:43; **Episode 4**, 15:34; **Episode 4**, 16:12; **Episode 4**, 17:03; **Episode 4**, 17:39; **Episode 4**, 19:37; **Episode 5**, 6:47; **Episode 5**, 7:58; **Episode 5**, 9:51; **Episode 5**, 12:30; **Episode 5**, 15:16; **Episode 5**, 16:50; **Episode 5**, 21:06; **Episode 6**, 0:40; **Episode 6**, 1:56; **Episode 6**, 5:19; **Episode 6**, 8:26...

Clearly, listing every instance of a multiple error is not useful.

Technobabble, in general, is not blooper material — not even redundant terms like "microvirologist" (*The Ark*) and pseudoscientific terms like "light neutrons" (*The Chase*). This is especially true for stories set in the future. There is no way of predicting what words will retain their current meaning or what new meanings could develop when converting alien terms into English. Technobabble items reported as errors in other sources are listed here with the explanation that they *are* technobabble, not bloopers.

Some of the listed items are anachronisms. It's easy to spot an anachronism when something from the present appears in a story set in the past. "Anachronisms" in futuristic stories, especially after the Dalek invasion of Earth, require a different consideration. Anachronisms involving the past are listed, but this book avoids listing "Future Anachronisms."

Note: Exceptions to any of the above may occur if the error in question is especially funny, prolonged, blatant, or otherwise interesting.

In the *Doctor Who* fan community, rumors about bloopers are always circulating. Many of the alleged errors are rumored to occur in the "lost" episodes involving the First and Second Doctors — programs destroyed by the BBC but circulated among collectors on poor-quality audio tapes. There is no way to confirm or refute these rumors. The recordings of the missing episodes give only audio bloopers. Though not confirmed, all of these rumored bloopers are listed in this book.

I have attempted to include all errors previously reported on other lists — even "false bloopers," that is, reports that have been discredited. False bloopers appear in this list with an explanation of why they are not actually errors. I chose to include, and refute, these false reports because the elimination of false entries without an explanation would only fuel continued rumors.

Some of these false bloopers may occur in edited versions of the stories that I have not seen. I assume the good faith reporting of all items, and I make no judgments concerning the submitters. I do not list the source of these false entries, partly because some sources are unknown and partly to avoid inviting judgments against the submitters.

One fun aspect of this project was developing rational explanations for some well-known "errors." You may accept these explanations or not. You may wish to find your own explanation. For example, many error lists include the "Last Name blooper" from *The Reign of Terror*. This is an interesting case, but we have an explanation of why it is not really an error.

Note: In no case should the reader assume that incompetence, lack of professionalism, or foolishness on the part of anyone associated with the BBC caused an error. Bloopers result from little things that happened unnoticed, the lack of time to do a scene over, tired people, and the simple fact that people make mistakes.

A Note About Time Listings

In each episode, I have noted the time at which each error appears. I have made every attempt to ensure an accurate listing of these times, but variations in VCRs and in editing may cause discrepancies. I observed the greatest differences in timing when playing a CD on a multi-format unit.

The stories were, for the most part, originally broadcast as individual episodes (what I call the episodic version). Later editing produced a movie version of many of the stories. For this reason, many of the stories exist as both episodic and movie versions. The episodic version, if available, is the one chosen for this list.

The editing of the episodes into a movie requires the removal of all the opening credits except for the first episode, and all the closing credits except for the last episode. There is normally a modification of the closing credits. Cliffhanger or reprise segments are excised. Thus, there is an increasing discrepancy between the times in the episodic and movie versions as one nears the end.

Sources

The following sources of *Doctor Who* episodes were important to this work. I list them in order of decreasing reliability:

DVD— Recent releases of some of the stories are in DVD format. These are the best sources. Reported times are very accurate.

Commercial Tapes— The BBC produces and sells, directly or indirectly, these tapes. Commercial products also include tapes such as *The Hartnell Years* and *Daleks—The Early Years*. These are all very good sources of information. A few of the commercial tapes are in movie format; this format alters some of the times reported from the original. When watching episodes edited into movie format, the viewer must determine which original episode contained the blooper. Reported times normally vary by less than 5 seconds in nonmovie versions.

Collector's Tapes— These are tapes recorded by collectors from TV broadcasts in the United States in the 1980s to present. The quality is not always good. In most cases, these are movie versions. Editing was necessary to convert the episodes into a movie. Sometimes the editing into a movie is good, and sometimes it is poor. I viewed these tapes and noted discrepancies with the episodic versions. It was necessary to estimate the episode in which the blooper appeared. Additional errors may be due to the transmitting stations.

Commercial CD— The BBC is releasing some of the "lost" episodes in CD format. These are important for those episodes with little or no available video. The times are very accurate; however, the method of listing each scene separately may result in some confusion. Many of these are from collectors' audio recordings (see below).

Commercial Audio Tapes—At one time, the BBC released some of the "lost" episodes on audiotape. Editing for length occurred in a few of the episodes, so the times are not very accurate. I consulted these to locate discrepancies.

Collectors Audio Recordings—Among collectors there are audio recordings of all the "lost" episodes. I used these recordings as a last resort. The times are questionable on these, as some of the episodes are over 27 minutes long. Times may differ from other sources by as much as 10 seconds. Apparently, many background noises were added during the recording of these episodes. There are cases where there is tape print-through. Tape print-through occurs when the sound is transferred from one portion of the tape to an adjacent portion, allowing both portions to be heard simultaneously. The resulting confusion of sounds makes the tape difficult to understand.

Books—In some cases, there are changes in the stories. Books are not a reliable source.

Photographs—Many photographs are available. Unfortunately, some of these are publicity photographs and may not be part of the actual story. Most photographs do not contain bloopers. It is very difficult to determine the timing of an error from a photograph. No errors in this book's listings came from a photograph.

Reconstructions—Over the years, many of the missing episodes have been reconstructed. Reconstructions are made up of pieces of film, photographic stills, and other visual material combined with the soundtrack. Because only a limited amount of material exists, the creation of a reconstruction is arduous. Reconstructions are the best way of visualizing many of the missing adventures, but the absence of some of the material causes many problems. It would not be proper to formally list errors created by the reconstruction process. This book lists a few errors in the last episode of *The Tenth Planet*. These are included to illustrate the problems of reconstruction, not to find fault with the process itself.

Complications

In some cases the commercial release of a story is different from the original transmitted version. There are many reasons why the stories were reedited. This book specifies which version was actually viewed in the construction of the error list, and which version was the source of the reported times. Differences in editing are present in many cases.

Broadcast Order

The BBC assigned each of the stories a code number. The first story (*100,000 BC*) was A, the second story was B, and so on. The process ran through the alphabet (skipping some letters) with single letters; the sequence continued with double letters (AA, BB, CC...). After working their way through ZZZ, the BBC changed the coda to a number and a letter: 4A through 4Z, 5A through 5Z, and so on. The last story was 7Q. These codas reveal the sequence of recording. The order of recording is not always the order of broadcast.

Mostly, the order of broadcast is not significant, but there are exceptions. The best-known exception is the "Flowerchild's Earring" error from *Silver Nemesis*. Ace is wearing Flowerchild's earring in *Silver Nemesis*, even though she did not find the earring until *The Greatest Show in the Galaxy* (broadcast later). This "error" arises because of the order of broadcast; had the shows been broadcast in the order of recording, there would be no error. The inclusion of the codes will allow readers to pick out similar errors.

Arrangement of Entries

The following arrangement is used throughout this book. Not all of the categories appear in every entry.

(Code) Title   The code is a letter designation assigned by the BBC to reflect the order in which the stories were produced (not the order of transmission).

The title here is the official (BBC) title. Some stories are better known by other names.

Alternate Titles: Fans know some of the stories by different titles. Some of these titles arise from sources other than official *Doctor Who* materials.

Writer: and Director: The writer(s) and director(s) of record are present. Pseudonyms are deciphered.

Media: Here I list the form(s) viewed or listened to for errors. The form(s) leading to the reported times is designated as "used." If times from more than one source are present, there is a letter designation.

Highlights: This section lists one or more noteworthy items about the story.

Questions: Questions have arisen concerning some stories. Some sources list these as bloopers, but this book considers them merely points worth pondering.

Errors and Other Points of Interest: This list contains errors and other important moments in chronological order. If multiple times are involved (because of different formats), the earliest time is usually the one listed. The names of the actors who were not regulars in the series are given.

Some bloopers encompass multiple episodes, or do not have defined times. Such bloopers appear in this "Errors and Other Points of Interest" section, before the first episode is covered.

Coverage of errors in each individual episode begins with the episode title and first date of transmission. (Until May 1966, the end of *The Gunfighters*, individual episodes had names; these are given here.) Following this information is a list of errors, including the approximate time where each error occurs. The time is at or just before the beginning of the blooper. The times do not necessarily refer to the first instance of the blooper.

This format is repeated for each episode.

Comments: Additional information, if any, will be included here.

References

Two very important reference works are:

Paul Cornell, Martin Day and Keith Topping. *The Discontinuity Guide*. Doctor Who Books. Virgin Publishing Ltd.: London, 1995.

David J. Howe and Stephen James Walker. *The Television Companion*. Telos Publishing Ltd.: Surrey, 2003.

I
THE FIRST DOCTOR

Pilot: An Unearthly Child

Writer: Anthony Coburn; **Director:** Waris Hussein

Media: Commercial tapes — Pilot 1 (25 minutes) packaged in *The Hartnell Years*, and Pilot 2 (36 minutes) packaged with *The Edge of Destruction*. The two versions are edited differently (both used)

Highlights: It is interesting to note the numerous changes made between the Pilot and the first transmitted episode. The opening theme of the Pilot includes an explosion.

Questions: The name TARDIS is an acronym that Susan made up from "Time And Relative Dimension In Space." This means that the word TARDIS is essentially an English word. If, for example, Susan had used German, she would need to make an acronym for *"Zeit Und Verwandte Dimension In Raum,"* meaning that the Doctor would be traveling in a ZUVDIR. The acronym will depend upon the language of the traveler. Why do the Time Lords not use an acronym derived from their own language? On the other hand, is English the language of the Time Lords?

Errors and Other Points of Interest

Pilot 1

First Transmitted: August 26, 1991

1:04 The sign says, "I. M. FOREMAN" (76 Totter's Lane). **5:03** Notice that Barbara is carrying thin books. **5:31** Barbara's shoe becomes stuck in the doorway as she and Ian enter the room to ask Susan if she would like a lift home. Barbara must struggle for some time to get her shoe free. **5:47** Susan, when talking about John Smith and the Common Men, corrects a mistake she made when trying to say, "nineteen to two in hit parade." At first Susan says, "Two to nineteen." There are misquotes claiming Susan says, "Nineteen to two on the hit parade." **6:11** The book that Barbara hands Susan has the same dimensions as the ones she was carrying — except for thickness. The book on the French Revolution that Barbara hands Susan is very thick. **6:56** Ian pulls the door to the room shut behind him, but the door bounces back open and then shut. **7:53** Ian pulls the handbrake on his car. **8:00** Some viewers report, incorrectly, that a stagehand moves past the car as Ian and Barbara are driving. However, it could be a "pedestrian," since Ian has already stopped the car and he has set the brake. **8:30** Barbara has trouble with the line "That a fifteen year old girl...." **10:18** Ian and Susan define time as the fourth dimension and space as the fifth dimension. **13:20** The camera operator stumbles and causes a clatter when approaching the TARDIS. **13:53** The Doctor enters too early and must wait until Ian and Barbara hide. This allows the Doctor to enter without "seeing" the teachers. **14:10** The Doctor removes the lock from the TARDIS so he can enter. **15:02** A light shines between the TARDIS doors; therefore, the doors are open, not closed. Ian should be able to open the doors. **16:26** The Doctor tells Ian and Barbara, "You imagine you heard music." Neither Ian nor Barbara mentioned anything about music. This is a slip on the Doctor's part; however, Ian and Barbara miss it. **17:24** Susan is standing to the left rear of the console. **17:50** A shadow appears on the TARDIS doors after Ian and Barbara enter the TARDIS. Apparently, someone is walking by outside the TARDIS. **18:55** Susan says, "Time And Relative Dimension In Space." **19:31** Unlike Susan, the Doctor refers to space AND time as the fourth dimension. He does not describe the two as the fourth and fifth dimensions. **20:24** Susan says she was born in the forty-ninth century — this fact does not appear in subsequent stories. **20:52** Ian claims that Susan pushed something when they entered. Susan was not near the console when Ian entered. **20:56** Ian goes to a part of the console that is nowhere near where Susan was standing earlier. **21:35** There are claims reporting that a PA may be heard calling shots during some scenes. An example supposedly occurs while the Doctor is preparing the TARDIS console to "zap" Ian. This version contains no definite sounds of this type. **24:36** The man's shadow entering from the lower right does not match the direction or the length of the other shadows.

Pilot 2
First Transmitted: See above

1:04 The sign says, "I. M. FOREMAN" (76 Totter's Lane). **5:20** Notice that Barbara is carrying thin books. **5:48** Barbara's shoe becomes stuck in the doorway as she and Ian enter the room to ask Susan if she would like a lift home. Barbara must struggle to get her shoe free. **6:06** Susan, when talking about John Smith and the Common Men, corrects a mistake she makes when trying to say, "nineteen to two in hit parade." At first Susan says, "Two to nineteen." Some reports misquote Susan. These reports claim Susan says, "nineteen to two on the hit parade." **6:28** The book that Barbara hands Susan has the same dimensions as the ones she was carrying — except for thickness. The book on the French Revolution that Barbara hands Susan is much thicker than the books seen earlier. **7:14** Ian pulls the door to the room shut behind him, but the door bounces back open and shut. **8:11** Ian pulls the handbrake on his car. **8:19** Some viewers incorrectly report that a stagehand moves past the car as Ian and Barbara are driving. However, it could be a "pedestrian," since the car has already stopped and the brake set. **8:49** Barbara has trouble with the line "That a fifteen year old girl...." **10:37** Ian and Susan define time as the fourth dimension and space as the fifth dimension. **13:38** The camera operator stumbles and causes a clatter when approaching the TARDIS. **14:10** The Doctor enters too early and must wait until Ian and Barbara hide, so the Doctor can enter without "seeing" the teachers. **14:29** The Doctor removes the lock from the TARDIS so he can enter. **15:20** A light appears between the TARDIS doors; therefore, the doors are open, not closed. Ian should be able to open the doors. **16:43** The Doctor tells Ian and Barbara, "You imagine you heard music." Neither Ian nor Barbara mentioned anything about music. This is a slip on the Doctor's part; however, Ian and Barbara miss it. **17:37** There are reports that a PA may be heard calling shots during some scenes. An example occurs as Barbara sticks her head through the TARDIS doors. **17:38** There is a break leading to a new start. Most of the preceding material is in Pilot 1. The material between here and the second restart is not in Pilot 1. **18:18–19:00** The TARDIS doors will not shut; listen to the repeated sound also. **19:43** Susan explains, "Time And Relative Dimension In Space." **20:18**

Unlike Susan, the Doctor refers to space AND time as the fourth dimension. He does not describe the two as the fourth and fifth dimensions. **21:13** Susan says she was born in the forty-ninth century — this is not the same in any of the regular stories in the series. **22:57** What is the Doctor holding in his right hand? **25:37** The man's shadow entering from the lower right does not match the direction and length of the other shadows. **26:33** Restart **27:08** Restart — the material from here to the end is in Pilot 1. **27:36** Susan is standing to the left rear of the console. **28:02** After Ian and Barbara enter the TARDIS, you can see a shadow moving along the TARDIS doors. **29:08** Susan explains, "Time And Relative Dimension In Space." **30:37** Susan says she was born in the forty-ninth century. **31:05** Ian claims that Susan pushed something when they entered. Susan was not near the console when Ian entered. **31:11** Ian goes to a part of the console that is nowhere near where Susan was standing earlier. **34:49** The man's shadow entering from the lower right does not match the direction and length of the other shadows.

Comments: The problem with the TARDIS doors not closing is a problem in the Pilot. During the narration in *The Hartnell Years*, we learn that the problem with the TARDIS doors only occurred during the first taping, not during the re-take shown in Pilot 1.

Pilot 1 (from *The Hartnell Years*) and Pilot 2 (with *The Edge of Destruction*) are very similar. Pilot 2 contains some re-shot scenes. Some bloopers reported in both Pilots are only in Pilot 2, other bloopers are only in *100,000 BC*.

(A)   100,000 BC

Alternate Titles: *An Unearthly Child* and *The Tribe of Gum*
Writer: Anthony Coburn; **Director:** Waris Hussein

Media: Commercial tape — episodic version — 96 minutes (used); Collector's tape — movie version — 90 minutes; Excerpts also appear on the commercial tape — *The Hartnell Years*

Highlights: The Doctor (William Hartnell) and his granddaughter, Susan Foreman (Carole Ann Ford), leave London with Barbara Wright (Jacqueline Hill) and Ian Chesterton (William Russell) to begin the adventures of Doctor Who.

Questions: Is a police box the appropriate camouflage inside a building in a junkyard? Is this adventure in the Earth's past or on another planet?

Errors and Other Points of Interest

There are reports that transmission of Episode 1 was about ten minutes late due to the assassination of President Kennedy. It was a little over one minute late. The transmission of the second episode was late due to a re-transmission of the first episode.

No one addresses the character listed in the closing credits as Old Mother (Eileen Way) by this "name" during the story. The other characters call her "Old Woman."

Episode 1: An Unearthly Child
First Transmitted: Nov. 23, 1963

0:52 The sign says, "I. M. FOREMAN" (76 Totter's Lane). **4:37** Barbara is carrying thin books. **5:30** Barbara hands

Susan a larger and thicker book than she was carrying previously. This book, on the French Revolution, is not as thick as the book used during the pilot. This book has a dust jacket with no adornment other than the title. Apparently, there was no author. **6:18** Susan comments on an "error" in the text instead of examining inkblots as she did in the Pilots. **8:33** Ian and Susan define time as the fourth dimension and space as the fifth dimension. **12:20** The camera shakes as the Doctor is saying, "not the police then." **14:32** Susan is on the far side of the console as everyone else enters. **14:44** Susan closes the TARDIS doors. **14:44** The switch Susan uses to close the TARDIS doors has a light next to it, which shifts from off to on with the switch Susan is using. The Doctor uses a switch without a shining light next to it. Some viewers claim the Doctor electrocutes Ian. According to the dictionary "electrocute" means to kill by means of electricity — Ian clearly did not die. **15:32** The Doctor and Ian manage to interrupt each other as they are examining the TARDIS clock. **15:52** There is a voice in the background after the Doctor finishes discussing the filament. This sound occurs at other times. There is a report that there is someone using a PA to call the camera shots. **16:57** Susan explains, "Time And Relative Dimension In Space." Susan specifically says that she made up the name from the initials. **18:47** Susan says she "was born in another time — another world," instead of in "the forty-ninth century." **19:01** Ian claims the Doctor closed the door (or so the some viewers claim). Ian actually says "he" or "she," but a sound effect partially covers this, and a few seconds later Ian says what seems to be "him"; however, the sound effects also make this uncertain. If Ian indeed says, "he" and "him," this is a blooper. Later Ian says, "I saw you." **19:06** Ian first goes to the near side of the console, and then he goes to the far side (Susan closed the doors to the right of where Ian is standing). **22:26** The man's shadow entering from the lower right does not match the direction and length of the other shadows. This also occurs in the reprise.

Episode 2: The Cave of Skulls
First Transmitted: Nov. 30, 1963

5:11 The Doctor answers, "Doctor Who" (in response to "Dr. Foreman"). **6:46** The Doctor uses a different switch to open the door. Susan did not use this switch earlier. **7:44** There is a boom mike shadow on Susan's left arm as she, Barbara, and Ian are walking away from the TARDIS. **10:02** Ian says, "Dr. Who" in response to Barbara calling the Doctor, "Doctor Foreman." **11:44** Ian puts his hand on the sand and says that it is strange that it is cold. Everyone bundles up as if the group is very cold. So, why is Ian surprised about the sand being cold? **23:33** Pay close attention to the skulls referred to by the Doctor. Notice how this arrangement changes in the reprise.

Episode 3: The Forest of Fear
First Transmitted: Dec. 7, 1963

0:47 Only one skull is present at this point. The cliffhanger had two skulls. **5:28** Birds are chirping in the middle of the night as Za (Derek Newark) and Hur (Alethea Charlton) leave the cave. **10:40** A boom mike appears in the upper left as the Doctor and Susan begin talking. **11:16** The camera "jerks" as Ian and the Doctor are talking.

Episode 4: The Firemaker
First Transmitted: Dec. 12, 1963

8:21 As Za enters the Cave of Skulls apparently Kal (Jeremy Young) is already there (much too soon); Kal is at the left edge of the screen. **16:57** Barbara stumbles over "a stone with a hole in it." **20:35** As the travelers are running back towards the TARDIS, they are obviously running in place against a moving background. There are claims that this occurs in Episode 3. **23:11** There are reports that a stagehand is visible through a wide gap in one of the corners of the TARDIS. This does not appear in this version. There is a shadow in a large gap. This shadow might be mistaken for a stagehand.

Comments: The first episode of this story and the two versions of the pilot episode have led to many problems. A blooper may appear in any one of these and be attributed to one or both of the others.

(B)   THE MUTANTS

Alternate Titles: *The Daleks.* The commercial tape lists the first four episodes as *The Dead Planet* and the last three episodes as *The Expedition.*
Writer: Terry Nation; **Directors:** Christopher Barry and Richard Martin

Media: Commercial two-tape set — *The Dead Planet* and *The Expedition* — episodic version — 171 minutes (used); Excerpts are present in the tape *The Missing Years* packaged with *The Edge of Destruction*; Collector's tape — movie version — 162 minutes; Commercial tape — *Daleks — The Early Years* — excerpts
Highlights: The Daleks join Doctor Who.
Questions: If a group of cows is a herd, a bunch of crows is a murder, and a collection of dogs is a pack, what do you call a gathering of Daleks? (See the comments for the answer; hints appear in Episode 2 and Episode 6.)

Errors and Other Points of Interest

Some viewers report the following blooper in this story: While Ian and the Doctor are examining the clock in the TARDIS, both of them manage to interrupt each other. This occurs in *100,000 BC* (Episode 1); it is not present here.

Episode 1: The Dead Planet
First Transmitted: Dec. 21, 1963
1:54 Ian brings it to everyone's attention that the branches are not moving in the breeze. In the next shot, there is movement; it appears that someone is moving a backdrop towards the left rear. **4:14** The Doctor moves some branches and they wave like normal branches instead of being brittle and breaking. This problem appears at other times also. **4:46** Some viewers find fault with the Doctor's description of the lizard as being "setisolified." **11:53** There are lights reflected on the glass in front the Doctor and Ian. Later the Doctor stands directly behind the reflection. **15:52** The camera operator has trouble tracking the Doctor after he stands and Barbara begins talking.

Episode 2: The Survivors
First Transmitted: Dec. 28, 1963
1:19 A boom mike shadow appears on the wall behind Ian, and later on Ian's head. The shadow is in the upper left corner. **2:41** There is an assumption that radiation levels, when dangerous to Daleks, are equally dangerous to Humans. This may or may not be a valid assumption. **6:15** There are claims that the presence of a bed in the Dalek City is a blooper. A Dalek cell would have two possible purposes — to imprison Daleks or to imprison Thals. Daleks clearly do not need beds, but Thal prisoners would need a bed. **7:12** Barbara mentions, "There wasn't any furniture." What does she think she is sitting on? **8:14** The camera shakes after the Doctor says "die." **11:09** We learn that the

Thal-Dalek war "ended" about 500 years before this story. **13:06** The Doctor, before he corrects himself, refers to the drugs they found outside the TARDIS as "anti-radiation gloves." **18:15** There are many Daleks speaking simultaneously. This is a hint to the question posed earlier. **20:00** This is the first of many Episode 2 shots with Susan running in place in front of a scrolling background. There are claims that this is in Episode 3. **23:28** When Susan pushes the door switch, the entire TARDIS console wobbles.

Episode 3: The Escape
First Transmitted: Jan. 4, 1964

2:21 Susan leans against the TARDIS doors and the doors are not closed. **6:08** We find out that the Thals are wandering the land because there was no rain two years before. **9:45** The seated Dyoni (Virginia Wetherell) suddenly jumps. **10:54** At this point, we learn that the Thals have been traveling for four years. Some fans question inconsistencies in the time the Thals have wandered. It is possible that the Thals traveled about the plateau for a time before leaving the plateau. **12:24** We find that the Daleks can read Gallifreyan. This is as logical as reading English. It is also possible that the Doctor's comment in *The Masque of Mandragora* applies to written languages. **16:24** There appears to be a mouse hole behind Ian's knee. We can see this "hole" many times. **18:12** The Thals can also read Gallifreyan or English. **22:42** When the Doctor and Ian open the Dalek, we see a relatively small empty chamber with a bottom. There is obviously not enough room for Ian. **24:27** This is the first time we get to see part of a real Dalek. The creature appears during the reprise also.

Episode 4: The Ambush
First Transmitted: Jan. 11, 1964

10:09 The Doctor opens a magnetically sealed door by himself. It should be easier to open this door if there were no power. **15:05** Ian's only purpose for staying in the city is to warn the Thals about an ambush by the Daleks. Why does he just stand a few feet away from Temmosus (Alan Wheatley) and watch? This lack of action is a blooper. **22:09** The Doctor says the Daleks originated as the Dals, and not Kaleds.

Episode 5: The Expedition
First Transmitted: Jan. 18, 1964

3:22 The Doctor "intentionally" calls Ian "Cheshireman." This makes all later mispronunciations of Ian's name by the First Doctor questionable. **20:58** We learn it has been over a year since the Thals left the plateau. This does not necessarily mean they first began wandering at this time, only that this is when the group left the plateau. **21:59** The Thal does not seem to be pointing in the right direction.

Episode 6: The Ordeal
First Transmitted: Jan. 25, 1964

3:24 One of the Daleks in the Control Room turns around and we hear it crashing into one of the control consoles. **5:27** Where did Ganatus (Philip Bond) learn the Earth custom of "ladies first"? **5:58** When the shot shifts from Ganatus entering the cave to Barbara, there is a single misaligned frame of Barbara. **8:35** Another of the Daleks in the Control Room turns around and apparently crashes into one of the control consoles (based on the sound). **9:14** A classic Doctor quote—"We mustn't diddle about here." **11:05** As Ganatus is attempting to convince Antodus (Marcus Hammond) into going on instead of going back, Ganatus incorrectly exclaims, "You must go back." **13:53** The TARDIS key looks like a normal key. **14:14** When the Doctor shorts the Dalek electrical system, the flash occurs too soon. **17:27** Ian grabs the "rock" wall and a piece of the polystyrene breaks off in his hand leaving a white patch on the wall. **20:28** Two Daleks attempt to say the same thing at the same time. Their words are slightly different, and their rates of delivery are drastically different. This is another hint concerning the question posed earlier. **21:45** Barbara pulls a piece of the "rock" wall polystyrene off, leaving a white patch.

Episode 7: The Rescue
First Transmitted: Feb. 1, 1964

2:20 The Dalek lights are not coordinated. This also occurs at other times. **8:27** One of the wheels on a Dalek is out of correct balance and considerable noise results. **9:24** The camera jumps as the two Daleks talk. **11:03** A boom mike shadow appears above the closing door. **11:06** The Thals prove that it is possible to open a powered Dalek door. The door should be easier to open when there is no power. **13:12** The Dalek's head jerks to the side as its light catches on the edge of the door. **14:51** Some fans report the presence of blow-up Dalek photographs. **15:30** There are reports claiming that it would not be possible for the Thals to leave the City after the power loss. This would not be a problem. We know that the powered doors are not a problem — so un-powered doors should be easy to open. **19:18** There is a boom mike shadow on Barbara's head.

Comments: Answer to the question: A Babble of Daleks.

This is the first time that the Doctor saves a race from extinction.

The Doctor defeats the Daleks on Skaro. This story appears to be so far in the future that the Daleks have forgotten who the Doctor is. If this story were in the distant future, this would indicate another Dalek-Thal war.

(C)   INSIDE THE SPACESHIP

Alternate Titles: *The Edge of Destruction* and *Beyond the Sun*
Writer: David Whitaker; **Directors:** Richard Martin and Frank Cox

Media: Commercial two-tape set with the *Pilot* episode and *The Missing Years* — episodic version — 47 minutes (used); Collector's tape — movie version — 46 minutes
Highlights: This story is the only one that takes place entirely within the TARDIS and it is the only story with no additional cast.

Errors and Other Points of Interest

Episode 1: The Edge of Destruction
First Transmitted: Feb. 8, 1964

1:42 A boom mike shadow appears on the wall. **1:57** The reflection of some of the production crew and equipment appears in the TV monitor. This occurs at other times also. **4:23** Ian does not detect the double heart of a Time Lord. **5:23** The "white void" outside the TARDIS has a floor. **6:39** The TARDIS doors have trouble opening. **9:27** The camera operator has trouble keeping the camera aligned. **11:20** The Doctor mutters, "It's not very logical" twice. He does not say, "It's not very likely," as reported by some viewers. **15:57** The shadow of one of the BBC crewmembers appears and runs away before we see the Doctor. **17:06** The TARDIS doors do not close smoothly. **18:42** The Doctor has trouble saying, "You knocked both Susan and I unconscious."

Episode 2: The Brink of Disaster
First Transmitted: Feb. 15, 1964

3:57 The fault locator alarm predates the cloister bell. **7:54** There is a boom mike shadow on the TARDIS console. **10:37** The Doctor exclaims, "You'd be blown to atoms by a split second!" **15:06** The "Fast Return" switch label looks hand printed. **18:11** Apparently, the Doctor forgot to explain the melted clocks. **18:43** The Doctor intentionally mispronounces Ian's name.

Comments: Richard Martin directed the first episode, and Frank Cox directed the second episode.

(D) Marco Polo

Writer: John Lucarotti; **Directors:** Waris Hussein and John Crockett

Media: Commercial audio recording — episodic version — 173 minutes (used); Collector's audio recording — episodic version — 173 minutes

Highlights: This story takes place over a longer period than any other story. Marco Polo's (Mark Eden) commentary in the original story is an interesting innovation. William Russell narrates the commercial version.

Errors and Other Points of Interest

Many bloopers are visual, and so audio stories, such as this one, will have fewer bloopers reported.

During many of the early stories, the characters sometimes call the Doctor's ship "TARDIS" and sometimes call it "The TARDIS." Examples of these two uses by the major characters appear in the following listings. Eventually this settles down to "The TARDIS."

Episode 1: The Roof of the World
First Transmitted: Feb. 22, 1964

8:41 (CD-1, track 6, 1:40) As the Doctor introduces everyone to Marco Polo, he introduces Ian as Charlton. **9:40 (CD-1, track 6, 2:39)** According to Marco Polo, the year is 1289. **9:42 (CD-1, track 6, 2:41)** Some fans claim that Marco Polo's presence on the Pamir Plateau causes a blooper. If Marco Polo is on the plateau, why does he not escape and return to Europe? **9:42 (CD-1, track 6, 2:41)** Some viewers claim that the absence of Marco Polo's father and uncle is another blooper. This, and the preceding "blooper," explains each other. Marco Polo will not try to escape without his family, and Kublai Khan keeps Marco's family away from the plateau so escape together is not possible. However, this does not explain the later absence of his father and uncle. **11:29 (CD-1, track 8, 0:11)** Marco Polo notes that the clothes of the Doctor and companions are different. Many observers claim no one ever notices unusual clothing during the Doctor Who stories. **19:27 (CD-1, track 12, 2:18)** This is one of several references to the city "Peking." Marco Polo uses this name as he tells the Doctor and the others about how he first came to Peking. The setting of this story is in the thirteenth century. This is before the use of the name Peking. The name was "Khan-balik." **22:06–22:37 (CD-1, track 12, 4:56)** The Doctor has a strange hysterical laughing fit (this may have begun earlier — maybe at Episode 1, 21:39). Some fans claim this to be a blooper. Susan and Barbara, at least, seem to go along with the laughter as if it were intentional.

Episode 2: The Singing Sands
First Transmitted: Feb. 29, 1964

3:59 (CD-1, track 18, 0:00) While talking to Susan, Barbara tells her, "We'll get the TARDIS Susan." Note "the TARDIS." **4:38 (CD-1, track 18, 0:39)** Later, while still talking to Susan, Barbara mentions "TARDIS is the only home we have at the moment." Note "TARDIS."

Episode 3: Five Hundred Eyes
First Transmitted: Mar. 7, 1964

1:19 (CD-2, track 3, 0:29) The Narrator announces the title of the episode as "Five Hundred Eyes." At the end of Episode 2, the preceding episode, we "see" the title *The Cave of Five Hundred Eyes* instead of the correct title *Five Hundred Eyes*. Obviously, there is no way to confirm this blooper through an audio recording. **9:23 (CD-2, track 12, 0:24)** The Doctor tells Ian he will "sneak into the TARDIS." Note "the TARDIS."

Episode 4: The Wall of Lies
First Transmitted: Mar. 14, 1964

17:47 (CD-2, track 37, 1:32) Why is Marco Polo so strongly convinced that an emissary of an enemy is so trustworthy? Marco Polo should show some suspicion. **20:26 (CD-2, track 38, 1:51)** After Marco Polo confiscates the second TARDIS key, the Doctor again has another laughing "fit." This repeated laughing "fit" makes the preceding "fit" a questionable blooper.

Episode 5: Rider from Shang-tu
First Transmitted: Mar. 21, 1964

3:07 (CD-3, track 6, 0:37) When talking to Marco Polo, the Doctor says, "Use TARDIS" instead of, "Use the TARDIS." **13:13 (CD-3, track 12, 1:24)** The Doctor asks Marco Polo "and the TARDIS?" Why does the Doctor use "the TARDIS" this time? **19:14 (CD-3, track 19, 0:15)** We hear a cough off-stage. The Collector may have introduced this during the recording of this episode.

Episode 6: Mighty Kublai Khan
First Transmitted: Mar. 28, 1964

1:12 (CD-3, track 25, 0:26) We hear the theme music. The music may have begun earlier. This may be due to a transfer of the sound from part of the Collector's tape to another part (print-through). Apparent print-through occurs at other times. **11:30 (CD-3, track 31, 1:47)** Ian, in an aside comment, tells the audience, "The TARDIS has been stolen." **19:27 (CD-3, track 35, 3:50)** The Doctor explains to Kublai Khan (Martin Miller) that he, the Doctor, is "not a doctor of medicine."

Episode 7: Assassin at Peking
First Transmitted: Apr. 4, 1964

7:00 (CD-3, track 41, 0:13) While talking to Barbara and Susan, Marco Polo says, "caravan ... has won back TARDIS." **8:15 (CD-3, track 41, 1:27)** Susan interjects, "Grandfather is going to win back the TARDIS." **8:36 (CD-3, track 41, 1:49)** After losing the TARDIS to Kublai Khan, the Doctor again repeats his uncontrollable laughter. This has happened each time the Doctor has "lost" the TARDIS. Either all of these laughing bouts are bloopers, or none of the occurrences qualifies as a blooper. **12:15 (CD-3, track 43, 2:27)** Kublai Khan refers to backgammon as a game of chance. Some viewers claim that he said a game of cards.

Pause to Consider: Missing Stories

The BBC destroyed many First and Second Doctor episodes. Fortunately, fans of the series taped the audio portions of these programs. These audio tapes have passed from collector to collector over the years. The quality of many of the original tapes was not good, and copying the tapes did not help. There are current releases, on CD, of the audio versions of many of these stories. When collectors first recorded the stories off-air, new background sounds entered the soundtrack. Thus, there are minimal blooper claims of "unknown" sounds in these stories.

(E) THE KEYS OF MARINUS

Writer: Terry Nation; **Director:** John Gorrie

Media: Commercial tape — episodic version — 147 minutes (used); Collector's tape — movie version — 144 minutes — in some cases part of the cliffhanger along with the reprise are present

Errors and Other Points of Interest

Episode 1: The Sea of Death
First Transmitted: Apr. 11, 1964

0:55 There is no TARDIS landing sound. **1:03** The radiation meter has moved to the opposite side of the TARDIS console from that in *The Mutants*. **1:25** Some viewers claim the following words, spoken by the Doctor, constitute a blooper: "Yes, I don't think. I don't see why not." There is a definite pause between the two sentences, just as anyone would normally do when changing their mind. **2:31** In answer to Barbara's query about the sea being frozen, the Doctor says, "Impossible in this temperature, besides it's too warm." **3:36** Barbara "trips" and nearly knocks a "rock" over. **5:34** The Doctor says to Ian, "And if you'd had your shoes on, my boy, you could have lent her hers." **9:06** As the Voord falls through the wall panel, the swinging panel shows a stagehand hiding behind the panel. **10:24** It is possible to see the hand of someone rotating the panel. **10:28** A stagehand enters from the left too soon after the Doctor falls into the pyramid. Some fans have incorrectly reported that this occurs after Susan falls into the pyramid. **12:20** The shot of Ian, immediately after Barbara "enters" the pyramid, shows a stagehand ducking for cover. Some viewers claim that this is Barbara and not a stagehand. **13:54** The Voord falling into the pit is obviously a cardboard cutout. **14:22** Arbitan (George Colouris) uses Voord as the singular and the plural form of the noun. **14:27** If Arbitan is afraid of the Voord, why does he not lock the doors? Ian says he thought the place was impregnable. **15:22** The camera jumps while the Doctor and Arbitan are talking. **16:15** Arbitan now uses Voords as the plural for Voord. **18:54** Susan walks around the TARDIS to measure the extent of the force field. When Susan walks in front of Ian, she must walk inside the impenetrable barrier. There are incorrect reports that Ian was the person walking around the TARDIS. **20:58** The travel dials make a distinct sound when activated. **21:58** After the Voord stabs Arbitan, Arbitan turns and the knife "comes out." Once the knife is clearly out, the Voord remembers to jerk the knife out — too late.

Episode 2: The Velvet Web
First Transmitted: Apr. 18, 1964

3:35 Barbara has time to meet Altos (Robin Phillips), change clothes, and settle into her new environment before the Doctor, Ian and Susan catch up with her. Unfortunately, she is only a few seconds ahead of the rest of the group. **6:45** The shadow of a camera passes over the sleeping body of Susan. **7:56** Barbara is asleep as Sabetha (Katharine Schofield) places the disks on the sleepers' heads. **12:59** Barbara's struggle with the door shakes the entire wall to the left side of the door. **13:17** The door closing behind Altos bounces back open. **14:19** Barbara recognizes Sabetha as the person who put the disks on their foreheads. However, Barbara was asleep when Sabetha came into the sleeping chamber. **14:34** Barbara tells Sabetha, "I believe you are under some deep form of deep hypnosis." **17:28** Morpho (Heron Carvic) informs Altos that the Doctor is "to work on the scheme to increase man powers." **20:53** Barbara supposedly kills all of the Controllers of Morphoton, but she only manages to break one of the protective globes.

Episode 3: The Screaming Jungle
First Transmitted: Apr. 25, 1964

2:28 The camera jerks and a thump sounds off-stage. **6:07** The camera jerks as Ian runs to help Barbara. **10:02** When Ian walks past the small statue, someone coughs off-stage. **13:22** As Ian prepares to pry the bars apart, it is obvious that one of the bars is not secure. **16:05** The camera jerks as we hear the camera hit something. **18:07** Ian twice attempts to open the safe. In both cases, he continuously turns the knob in one direction instead of left and right. **22:14** Some viewers report, incorrectly, that the key was in a bottle labeled De_3O_2; the actual label reads DE_3O_2. This may be a code and not a chemical formula. The sample in the bottle is obviously not a pure chemical. **22:38** Unlike other times, the travel dials make no sound as Ian and Barbara leave.

Episode 4: The Snows of Terror
First Transmitted: May 2, 1961

0:26 When Barbara and Ian are freezing to death — why do they not use their travel dials? **4:55** Considering the importance of the travel dials — Why is Ian so willing to trade his travel dial for furs from Vasor (Francis de Wolff)? **12:14** Vasor touches the "ice" walls and it is obvious that the walls are cellophane. **14:05** The "frozen" warriors keep moving. **14:21** When Ian starts across the bridge, the wall sways. This happens because the wall, in part, supports the bridge. **19:10** Some viewers claim that Sabetha slipping while escaping from the de-iced warriors is a blooper. Ian's very quick response makes this a questionable call. There are erroneous reports that this occurs in Episode 3. **20:11** One of the "icicles" falls as Susan is crossing the bridge, but the ice never hits bottom. **21:52** Why did they leave the travel dials and the keys with Vasor? **23:20** The blow to Ian's head does not even come close to hitting him. **23:24** Ian falls into one position here and into a different position in the reprise.

Episode 5: Sentence of Death
First Transmitted: May 9, 1964

0:25 Ian and the others were all standing together when they left for Millennius; however, only Ian appears inside the vault. **0:46** Ian now falls into a different position from that in the cliffhanger of the preceding episode. **7:59** The motion of the camera is wobbly as it pans back from Ian. **13:45** The Doctor says, "I can't improve at this very moment, I can't prove...." **15:13** After Aydan (Martin Cort) enters the room, he sees Barbara and Susan, and then he says, "You are one of the people with Chesterton." **16:39** The arrows appear painted onto the dials of the "telephone." **19:29** The camera shakes as Aydan begins to confess.

Episode 6: The Keys of Marinus
First Transmitted: May 16, 1964

13:19 When one of the Voord and Sabetha enter the control room, the Voord stumbles over his own feet, or he trips on the bottom edge of the door. Some observers have incorrectly stated that he stumbled over to Yartek (Stephen Dartnell). **24:01** There is no TARDIS take-off sound.

Comments: The Doctor saves the people of the planet Marinus.

(F) THE AZTECS

Writer: John Lucarotti; **Director:** John Crockett

Media: Commercial DVD — episodic version — 99 minutes (used); Commercial tape — episodic version — 99 minutes (used); Collector's tape — movie version — 93 minutes
Highlights: The Doctor's engagement.
Questions: Where does the light come from in Yetaxa's tomb?

Errors and Other Points of Interest

Some people have reported that a Welch Ixta (Ian Cullen) is a blooper. This and other accents in the Doctor Who stories are not problems.

Some fans believe the Aztec costumes are not sufficiently brief. This may not be entirely true, as it can get cool during the winter months.

Episode 1: The Temple of Evil
First Transmitted: May 23, 1964

0:30 The TARDIS takes off with no sound. **6:00** Tlotoxl (John Ringham) utters, "No more talk against us that the gods were against us." **7:32** A few moments after the Doctor corrects Ian's pronunciation, the Doctor appears to have a little trouble with his lines. This may not be a real blooper. **15:58** The Doctor, then Ian, have trouble with this scene. This trouble begins with the Doctor introducing Ian to Cameca (Margot van der Burgh). There are incorrect reports attributing this to Episode 2. **21:03** The camera jerks as it bounces into the altar during the sacrificial scene.

Episode 2: The Warriors of Death
First Transmitted: May 30, 1964

0:38 As the camera approaches Tlotoxl for a close-up, it jerks as if it hits something. **7:03** It is hard to hear the Perfect Victim (André Boulay) as he is too far from the boom mike.

Episode 3: The Bride of Sacrifice
First Transmitted: June 6, 1964

8:19 There is a loud click and the picture goes out of focus. **9:48** There is a loud sound offstage. **13:33** The Doctor learns he proposed to Cameca.

Episode 4: The Day of Darkness
First Transmitted: June 13, 1964

2:35 The light on the door is not where Ian is pointing. **5:41** Ixta has trouble saying "Seven warriors…." **6:33** The Doctor exclaims, "My dear Susan, oh how glad … I'll tell how glad I am to see you later on!" **9:40** The camera jerks and a squeak sounds as the camera moves in on Autloc (Keith Pyott). This is not obvious on the DVD. **16:52** Shortly after Cameca says, "The handmaiden must come to the temple with me," the audio engineer accidentally plays part of the story's incidental music. There is a partial correction of this mistake, so only a split second of music is present. This is not present on the DVD. **20:05** There is no crowd gathering in the square to see the sacrifice. **20:19** "Ian" and "Ixta" are obviously stunt doubles. **20:20** Ixta's shadow falls on the backdrop painting of the city square. **20:47** It is possible to see the edge of the stage and the bottom of the painted backdrop. This is at the right edge of the screen. This only appears in the DVD version.

(G) The Sensorites

Writer: Peter R. Newman; **Directors:** Mervyn Pinfield and Frank Cox

Media: Commercial Tape — episodic version —150 minutes (used); Collector's tape — movie version — times indicated with an "M"—146 minutes (used)
Highlights: This story has the first *Doctor Who* visual effect showing a ship flying in space.

Errors and Other Points of Interest

Some fans question the transmission of sound through the vacuum of space by the Sensorites. This is a technobabble problem and not a true blooper. An explanation is present in this listing.

This story is supposedly the first attempt to show a completely alien culture in a Doctor Who story. Does this mean that Dalek culture is not alien?

Episode 1: Strangers in Space
First Transmitted: June 20, 1964

2:28 The TARDIS door opens directly into the spaceship's cabin. **4:06** The Doctor, on examining the watches, says, "These are the non-winding time." **8:10** The TARDIS doors are immediately next to the ship's cabin. No one could stand by the doors and not be seen by people in the cabin. How can the Sensorites examine and later remove the TARDIS lock? **8:14** A cough sounds offstage as the Sensorite hand reaches for the TARDIS lock. **10:29** The Sense-Sphere must be an extremely small planet. On the view screen, the Sense-Sphere appears smaller than the Moon appears from the Earth. When the ship appears as if it is going to crash, Ian says, "Nineteen miles to nearest point of impact," thus the Sense-Sphere appears smaller than the Moon at a distance of only nineteen miles. **11:53** The Doctor says, "I rather fancy that's settled that little bit of solution." **15:15** The opening sound for the door takes place much later than it should. **20:14** Captain Maitland (Lorne Cossette) makes marks on the door as he tries to cut through it. There are no other marks on the door at this time. **20:41** Some fans claim the Sensorites transmit sound through the vacuum of space. This may not be sound but mental communication sent by the Sensorites to scare the crew. The Doctor and Companions hardly seem to notice the "sound." It is also possible that the Sensorites placed radio receivers on the spacecraft during one of their earlier visits. Real sound is a blooper, mental "sound" or sound from a receiver is not a blooper. **22:01** As the camera approaches the Doctor while he is pondering their fate, the camera crashes into the control console. **22:59** The Doctor says, "My dear Cheston" to Ian. **23:52** It is possible to see both hands of the Sensorite looking in the window.

Episode 2: The Unwilling Warriors
First Transmitted: June 27, 1964

0:54 Unlike the cliffhanger — it is not possible to see either hand of the Sensorite outside the window. **2:59** Some viewers claim that when Captain Maitland begins to cut the lock from the door there are marks already present before the work has begun. This is not the case, as the original marks appeared in Episode 1. This scene starts with work in progress. The earlier scene ends with the larger marks noted later. **4:53** One of the Sensorites manages to step on the other's foot. It has been claimed that they step on each other's toes, but Sensorites have no toes. **9:44** Susan says, "Isn't it better to travel hopefully than ... arrive?" **11:34** The Sensorites "sound" only affects the ship's crew. This supports the argument that the "sound" is mental and not true sound. **12:57** As Barbara and Ian enter the room a wall section to the right of the door pops out and then back into position. **22:15** The eyes of the Sensorites dilate in bright light and contract in the dark. This does not really work. If their eyes dilate in the bright light it would be the same as when you turn on a very bright light after being in a dark room — you cannot see. The opposite effect would occur when their eyes contract in the dark.

Episode 3: Hidden Danger
First Transmitted: July 11, 1964

8:31 There are claims that in Episode 2, the Doctor says, Molybd ... Molb ... Minerals...." The actual quote is here, and it sounds more like, "Molbd ... Minerals." **15:42** The Sensorites know that five visitors were coming down from the spaceship. Why do they only reserve three seats? It is possible that they know one (John (Stephen Dartnell)) would be going for treatment, but the decision for Carol (Ilona Rodgers) to accompany him was not made until after the reservation of three seats for the five visitors. **17:23** The Sensorites now learn that fewer seats will be necessary as John and Carol leave. **22:22** The First Elder (Eric Francis) explains about the sashes and other items used to identify the Sensorites. The "ordinary" people do not have any insignia. The First Elder goes on to say they "are contented with their similarity." Apparently, the lack of insignia does not lead to misidentification of other non-official Sensorites. Thus, the successful impersonation of one Sensorite by another is questionable.

Episode 4: A Race Against Death
First Transmitted: July 18, 1964

7:08 In response to Carol's comment, the City Administrator (Peter Glaze) says, "I had never thought of that." Why have the Sensorites never faced the problem that only sashes, collars, and the like may identify them? It would look like this would have been a common problem. **10:40** The Doctor says that atropine poisoning is responsible for the deaths. **13:04** The studio lights reflect in the Doctor's glasses. **16:33** A boom mike creeps into the upper left of the screen. **1:27:33M** A boom mike appears in the upper right as Susan stands up to go to the laboratory. This reappears later. This only occurs on the Collector's tape. **24:03** The Doctor identifies the plant he finds as Deadly Nightshade (an Earth plant). How can an Earth plant grow in the dark?

Episode 5: Kidnap
First Transmitted: July 25, 1964

1:32:00–1:37:12M This segment is a repeat from the end of the preceding episode. The editing of the climax occurred, but this additional repeated material is still present. This is only present in the Collector's tape. This may be the fault of the television station when transmitting this story. **2:52** The Doctor says, "Something hit me under the heart." He does not say hearts. **6:10** One of the Sensorites says, "I heard them over ... over ... talking." **23:46** Susan says, "I wonder where they're up to ... where they're gone to...."

Episode 6: A Desperate Venture
First Transmitted: Aug. 1, 1964

2:34 A cough sounds offstage as Barbara says, "And I think we are being used by one of the Sensorites." **8:32** The Doctor and Ian are looking at the shoulder flash they found. The remaining letters read "INEER," but the Doctor reads "INNER." **8:48** The sound operator accidentally leaves the underground sound on until partway through the scene. This happens again later. **13:43** Why do Barbara and John not take a copy of the map with them?

Comments: The Sensorites probably

did not simply leave and return to the spaceship. Carol would detect this movement. The Doctor saves the planet known as the Sense-Sphere (also Sensesphere).

(H) THE REIGN OF TERROR

Writer: Dennis Spooner; **Directors:** Henric Hirsch and John Gorrie

Media: Commercial tape — episodes 1-3 and 6 — 98 minutes (used); Collector's audio recording — episodic version — 147 minutes (used); Collector recording of episodes 1–3 and 6 — 98 minutes

Errors and Other Points of Interest

Episode 1: A Land of Fear
First Transmitted: Aug. 8, 1964

0:20 The first part of this episode is very wobbly. **0:44** The hum of the TARDIS interior is present before the TARDIS arrives. **0:54** The TARDIS appears without the characteristic landing sound. **0:54** In addition to the light on the top, there is an internal light flashing in the TARDIS. **6:36** As the camera pans across the set, there is a sound in the background and the camera shakes. **9:08** Ian leans over and peers through the window to the cottage. As the camera approaches from behind Ian, there is a clunk as the camera hits something. The camera also shakes at this time. **10:38** Some viewers raise the blooper question, "How do they find the right size clothes?" At the point, Barbara says, "There's a whole wardrobe here! They are all different sizes too." As a post for escaping persons, many changes of clothing should be there.

Episode 2: Guests of Madame Guillotine
First Transmitted: Aug. 15, 1964

5:19 The Doctor is wearing a ring on each hand. The small ring on his left hand disappears later. **10:48** The blooper question has been posed — how does Webster (Jeffry Wickham) know of "Jules Renan" and "Le Chen Gris?" Apparently, the person(s) posing this question assumes the first competent British spy to be James Bond. **19:14** The Road Works Overseer (Dallas Cavell) drops one of his coins and does not notice. This is out of character.

Episode 3: A Change of Identity
First Transmitted: Aug. 22, 1964

6:40 There is a prisoner in the cart with Barbara and Susan. **7:38** When Jules (Donald Morely) and Jean (Roy Herrick) are planning their attack, one of them (Jean?) says, "I'll take the one on the right." The problem is that there are two soldiers on the right and one on the left. **8:03** One of the attackers, Jean, turns around (by the wheel on the right) in only one frame. This is not one of the soldiers standing as reported by some viewers. **8:18** The other prisoner in the cart simply disappears, and the rescuers do not seem to notice. **10:13** Why would the Shopkeeper (John Barrard), or anyone unofficial, have an "official" uniform? The shopkeeper did not state that he had anything at all to do with supplying uniforms or other official regalia. **11:30** The Doctor's small ring is missing. **11:32** The Doctor trades his "special" ring and his clothes for his new clothes. **12:48** One of the most often quoted bloopers concerns

Jules Renan's claim that the people helping others to escape should only use Christian names. Jules tells Barbara of the use of Christian names at this point. This is the basis for the Name Blooper. **16:32** Jules refers to Rouvray (Laidlaw Dalling) and D'Argenson (Neville Smith) by last name and not their Christian names. However, this may not be a blooper. Jules Renan tells Barbara that he rescued Rouvray and D'Argenson like Barbara and Susan. As escapees and not one of the people helping them to escape, the authorities would have known their full names, and there would have been no need to avoid their last names. This is the Name Blooper.

Episode 4: The Tyrant of France
First Transmitted: Aug. 29, 1964

12:51 In spite of "Christian names only," Barbara learns Jules Renan's name from Ian. Jules is not upset about this. This indicates that the Name Blooper is not a real blooper. **15:23** To help explain an earlier question of how Webster knew about Jules, Jules Renan states that the English have been giving his name as a contact. **19:48** The Physician (Ronald Pickup) says he needs to collect some leeches to treat Susan. Then he says he will be out all day (so he cannot treat Susan). Barbara does not catch his mistake.

Episode 5: A Bargain of Necessity
First Transmitted: Sept. 5, 1964

11:36 During their discourse, both the Doctor and the Jailer (Jack Cunningham) refer to Lemaitre (James Cairncross) by name. The Jailer always pronounces Lemaitre's name with three syllables, whereas the Doctor uses only two syllables. **12:54** During Lemaitre's and Robespierre's (Keith Anderson) conversation, we learn that the next day is July 27, 1794. **13:24** Robespierre tells Lemaitre about "Barass (John Law) leaving for Paris," instead of "Barass leaving from Paris." **18:33** The Doctor has trouble with his lines as he tells Lemaitre, "I must insist that you reason ... release that child immediately." **19:16** Lemaitre returns the Doctor's ring.

Episode 6: Prisoners of Conciergerie
First Transmitted: Sept. 12, 1964

4:03 We find that Webster also knew of "The Sinking Ship" and Barrass. Even though Webster was no James Bond. **5:39** Lemaitre sometimes addresses Jules as "Ju." **13:27** The Doctor again has his small ring. **16:50** The Doctor tells the Jailer, "I see you haven't heard the naa the news yet, my man." **18:02** The Jailer now appears to pronounce Lemaitre's name with only two syllables.

Comments: As with most Doctor Who historical adventures, the historical accuracy is, at best, questionable.

(J) PLANET OF GIANTS

Writer: Louis Marks; **Directors:** Mervyn Pinfield and Douglas Camfield

Media: Commercial tape — episodic version — 73 minutes (used); Collector's tape — movie version — 71 minutes
Highlights: The giant fly scares Barbara.
Questions: Forester (Alan Tilvern) tells Smithers (Reginald Barratt) that Farrow (Frank Crawshaw) was going on holiday in a boat, thus an overturned boat and a body would be a cover for the murder. How does Forester expect this to explain the bullet wound? When the group reunites at the bottom of the sink, why do they not immediately go down the drain instead of climbing back to the bench top?

Errors and Other Points of Interest

Episode 1: Planet of Giants
First Transmitted: Oct. 31, 1964

1:56 There is no TARDIS landing sound. **3:57** The monitor "blowing out" appears to be a picture on the monitor screen of a blown out screen instead of an actual screen blowing out. No pieces of glass or smoke leave the screen. **12:32** Some fans complain that Susan uses the term "TARDIS" instead "the TARDIS."

Episode 2: Dangerous Journey
First Transmitted: Nov. 7, 1964

1:16 The Doctor and Ian explain to Susan why they cannot communicate with the "giants." **14:49** After the fly takes off, the shadow of one of the fly's legs is still moving behind and to Ian's left. **19:07** The Doctor again explains to Susan why they cannot communicate with the "giants." **21:30** Susan drops into what should be the open top of the drainpipe, but instead of falling, she stands and walks. **22:26** Smithers (Reginald Barratt) reaches into a white porcelain sink, instead of the gray sink the Doctor and Susan were in. **23:02** Some viewers claim a blooper because at the end of this episode the plug is on the bench top and not in the sink. Then at the start of the next episode, the plug is back in the sink. This blooper, to a certain extent, is from the movie version. The episodic version refutes this blooper. An explanation appears in the "next episode" of the movie version when the Doctor states that the plug is back in the sink.

Episode 3: Crisis
First Transmitted: Nov. 14, 1964

0:51 In the reprise, Smithers does not pull the plug entirely out of the sink. The plug remains in the sink. This negates the claimed blooper. Much of this does not appear in the movie version. It does not create a new blooper. **0:59** The Doctor observes that the plug is back in the sink. **4:48** This is for anyone who has ever taken organic chemistry — find the carbon atom with only three bonds. **7:11** Even though the Doctor has explained the impossibility of communicating with the "giants," now he suggests using the telephone. **9:54** Where is the cork Susan is about to place under the receiver? The receiver is apparent in the top view, but there is no cork on either side of it. Later, the second cork is still invisible. **10:57** The entire group attempts to communicate with the "giants" using the telephone. **21:51** The side of the can blowing out, without the can itself moving, contradicts Newton's Third Law. In the next shot of the can, it has simply fallen over. This does not correct the blooper — the can should fly entirely across the room. **23:22** There is no TARDIS take-off sound. **25:24** The blown out monitor has regenerated — there is still no picture, but the screen no longer seems exploded. **25:32** The TARDIS has regained its landing sound.

Comments: This is the first Doctor Who story to explore environmental issues.

(K) THE DALEK INVASION OF EARTH

Alternate Titles: *The Daleks*
Writer: Terry Nation; **Director:** Richard Martin

Media: Commercial 2 DVD set — episodic version — 148 minutes (used); Commercial 2-tape set — episodic version — 149 minutes; Commercial tape — *Daleks — The Early Years —*

excerpts; Collector's tape—movie version—142 minutes—part of some of the cliffhangers are present along with part of some of the reprises

Highlights: The title of the first episode is a pun alluding to the devastation caused by the Daleks.

Susan Foreman (Carole Ann Ford) leaves the series at the end of Episode 6. Susan is the first character to leave the series.

The Doctor's final speech is to appear again in the series.

Errors and Other Points of Interest

Early in the story some, not all, of the Daleks have a rod in the center of the parabolic dishes on their backs. By the end of the story, none of the Daleks has a rod present. Two examples appear on this list.

Some fans cite many aspects of the reason behind the invasion of the Earth as bloopers. Much of this comes from a mixture of what the Daleks say, Phil's theory, and the Doctor's supposition. There may be a little mixing of facts with those in the Peter Cushing movie. The reason for the invasion is technobabble. The Daleks never give a reason why they picked the Earth. In Episode 5, the Daleks explain that for Project Degravitate they wish to release the molten core to eliminate the gravitational and magnetic forces in Earth's core. They then wish to replace the hollow core with a power system to pilot the planet anywhere in the Universe. Since most, if not all, planets have magnetic cores, there must be something special about Earth's—maybe it is easier to reach because of the fissure, maybe is has the right size for their power system, maybe the ratio of the planet radius to core radius is ideal.... The reason is technobabble, and open to infinite maybes. In Episode 3, Ian is told by Larry Madison (Graham Rigby) of a *theory* proposed by his brother Phil that "The Daleks want the magnetic core of the Earth." As a theory, it may not be true. The Daleks do not confirm this. In Episode 5, the Doctor supposes that the Daleks are on Earth because Earth has something no other planet has. Many people have extended this to mean that the Doctor was talking about the magnetic core. Some of the discrepancy is from the Peter Cushing movie.

Episode 1: World's End
First Transmitted: Nov. 21, 1964

0:40 The first scene illustrates why the Daleks test the potential robomen; they wish to prevent the loss of workers. There are claims that the later test of the Doctor's is a blooper. **1:03** There is no TARDIS landing sound; however, the TARDIS interior sound is present outside the TARDIS. **2:23** The side windows on the TARDIS are open. **2:30** Barbara trips while she is walking away from the TARDIS. **3:38** The Doctor exclaims, "You take this bridge now.... Isn't easy task, is it?" **4:19** It is possible to look through the open side windows and see that there is no back wall on the TARDIS. **5:03** Ian trips on a brick. **8:52** Notice Barbara's location relative to the sign. Then watch her exit. **9:06** Barbara enters the set from a direction that does not correspond to her previous exit. **11:16** While the Doctor and Ian are exploring an abandoned warehouse, they find a calendar dated 2164. The date appears taped onto the calendar page. This is not necessarily the year; there is no way of telling when the last people visited the warehouse. This is an unusual calendar in that only the year is given. **12:11** The "dead" roboman must force the box to fall over and then the roboman crawls out of the box. **14:12** During the hanging scene, you can see the face of Ian's stunt double. **16:04** The Dalek saucer looks like it is a prop from *Plan 9 from Outer Space* (strings and all, but the strings are not in the same position). **20:14** "A dead human body in the river? I should say that's near murder. Isn't it?" says the Doctor. **22:31** Some fans question the presence of the Dalek in the river.

Episode 2: The Daleks
First Transmitted: Nov. 28, 1964

0:50 Note the stalk in the center of the dish on the Dalek's back. **5:41** There are claims that there are two stagehands present outside the saucer — they are not obvious in this version. **5:41** The two Daleks in the background are cardboard cutouts. **5:45** The shadow of someone quickly hiding appears at the edge of the opening saucer door. **6:04** A clang sounds offstage. **6:15** A member of the production crew quickly ducks out of sight in the left rear of the screen. **7:20** The dish on this Dalek's back has no center stalk. **10:57** The commanding Dalek has a multi-colored vertical panel on its base with "bumps." **13:14** A person must step out of the way by the opening door. **14:26** The commanding Dalek clears his throat as it enters the control room to make a speech. **16:47** The rod needed to move the bar in the case is visible to the left of the case. Later, it is possible to see the rod push the bar. **18:55** Ian responds to the Doctor's inquiry about three-dimensional graph geometry with "No Doctor, only Boyle's Law." Boyle's Law concerns the relationship between the volume of a gas and its pressure. What does geometry have to do with gases?

Episode 3: Day of Reckoning
First Transmitted: Dec. 5, 1964

0:04 The on-screen notes for the DVD report that this episode was first broadcast on 2 October 1964. This is when filming ended for this episode. **1:37** One of the bombs explodes on the floor before the attacker actually throws the bomb. **2:24** Some viewers claim a blooper about pushing a Dalek down the ramp during the attack on the saucer. This Dalek falls over in one position, but appears in a different position later. There appears to be no such blooper. No one pushes a Dalek down the ramp during the attack. The attackers overturn one Dalek (not on a ramp), but since it was moving when it fell, it could have moved to a different position. This blooper actually occurs in the Peter Cushing movie *Daleks—Invasion Earth 2150 A.D.* **3:42** The commanding Dalek is now black with silver "bumps." **5:45** The man cowering on the floor simply disappears. He does not leave with the fleeing group. **13:58** The appearance of pleasure boats on the Thames seems questionable with the Daleks controlling the Earth; however, the boats appear deserted. **15:16** Moving vehicles appear in the background in the abandoned London. **15:31** A pedestrian is calmly walking along the street in the background. **15:45** Cars drive along the street behind the Daleks in Trafalgar Square. **17:09** Someone appears to be riding a bicycle along the street. **17:39** Dortmun (Alan Judd) refers to the metal encasing the Daleks as "Dalekenium." **18:18** There is a boom mike shadow on the manikin. **23:54** Larry (Graham Rigby) tells Ian about Phil's theory: "The Daleks want the magnetic core of Earth."

Episode 4: The End of Tomorrow
First Transmitted: Dec. 12, 1964

0:44 The shadow, apparently of a camera, moves across the set. **1:24** Note the position of the pointer on the timer during the next few shots. **2:56** David (Peter Fraser) explains to Susan that the Daleks will be gone because of the expected explosion. Since the destruction of London is imminent, there should be no Daleks left in London. Jenny (Ann Davies) and Barbara discuss the possibility of the Dalek hearing them starting the truck, even though there should be no Daleks. **4:29** This is the first use of a quarry in a Doctor Who story. **7:58** Someone drops what sounds like a piece of wood on the floor offstage. **12:30** Jenny asks Barbara if the Dalek saw them. Why is a Dalek still in the city? **12:55** There is a Dalek patrol close to London. Why did they not evacuate? **17:53** Someone coughs offstage after Ashton says, "Are you one of these Brotherhood of Man kind of people?" **19:09** We learn that Daleks have pets. **19:42** David causes the wall to shake as he climbs through the opening. **22:14** Notice how the slither looks.

Episode 5: The Waking Ally
First Transmitted: Dec. 19, 1964

0:21 What does the title mean? **0:30** The slither has apparently regenerated. **0:42** When Ian jumps into the bucket, he nearly knocks the top off the bucket. The top continues to rock back and forth. The bucket does not behave as an object suspended from the top. **15:46** The Doctor wonders if the Daleks are digging for something no other planet has. **18:45** The lights on the Dalek do not flash while it is talking to Barbara. **20:46** The lights on the Black Dalek do not match its talking. **20:54** Some fans question why the mine is in Bedfordshire. They consider this a blooper because the Daleks should pick a thinner part of the Earth's crust. This is a technobabble problem, and not a true blooper. The explanation appears on the Dalek diagram; the mine is a "fissure shaft." The Daleks picked a site with a readily available fissure. **22:13–22:47** The Daleks discuss their plan. **22:20** The Daleks wish to remove the Earth's core and replace it with a power system to pilot the planet anywhere in the Universe.

Episode 6: Flashpoint
First Transmitted: Dec. 26, 1964

0:39 There is no Dalek visible on the structure. **0:45** A Dalek is now present on the structure. **5:55** It is obvious that both Jenny and Barbara are holding their neck restraints in place. **6:56** The top edge of the quarry is not too stable. **7:39** The Dalek's "motor" is creaking. **10:28** The Doctor and Tyler (Bernard Kay) are hiding on opposite sides of the doorway while the two are attempting to sneak into the Dalek base. Several Daleks file past them and the last Dalek has its eyepiece turned directly at the Doctor as it passes. This Dalek continues past the Doctor. Some viewers claim that the rebels were attempting to ambush the Daleks at this point; this is not true. **11:10** The Doctor says the Daleks' plan will "upset the entire constellation." This is one of the many cases where the writers assume that the solar system–constellation–galaxy–universe. **11:23** The reflection of a boom mike appears in the lower panel to the left of the Doctor. **13:15** The sign from under the bridge in Episode 1 is visible to the right of the doorway through which the rebels are entering. **14:56** More than one person's shadow appears on the "sky" behind them. **15:26** The countdown sound effect continues after the explosion. This is not obvious on the DVD version. **17:00** A boom mike shadow appears on the side of the TARDIS between the Doctor and Susan. **18:12** Near the end, when the Doctor is preparing to open the TARDIS door, there is the sound of a Dalek in the background. Apparently, introduction of this sound occurred during duplication of the master tape.

Other Observations: In the tape, *Daleks—The Early Years*, and on the DVD — the BBC trailer for this story makes the announcement: "The year is 2000..."

Comments: This is the first time the Doctor saves the planet Earth. This is not directly due to the Doctor's actions.

> **Pause to Consider: Anachronisms**
>
> This story provides the justification for ignoring many later "anachronisms." In general, this list only includes anachronisms for some stories. Anachronisms are possible bloopers when they occur in the past or near future. "Anachronisms" in futuristic stories, especially after the Dalek invasion of Earth, require a different consideration. This list avoids "Future Anachronisms." The bombardment of the Earth, and the subsequent plague, resulted in the loss of many aspects of science and technology. The later occupation of the Earth probably caused the loss of additional knowledge. During the years after the destruction of the Daleks, many items would need re-inventing or re-thinking. In addition, even a remembered technology might require facilities that are no longer present. Re-discovery of some things may occur in a sequence different from the past. For example, just because in our past the development of the external combustion engine preceded the development of the internal combustion engine, it does not mean that the same sequence will occur during the recovery period. Finally, the lack of need may slow down the re-development of an invention. Re-discovered technology might include tape recorders. Tape recorders may be much more important in the future than they are today, and used for a much longer time after their "re-discovery" than their present use would indicate. Future anachronisms may be bloopers, but until the stories become part of the past, this is uncertain. We will revise this list as necessary during the recovery period after the Dalek invasion.

(L) The Rescue

Writer: David Whitaker; **Director:** Christopher Barry

Media: Commercial 2 tape set — *The Rescue/The Romans* — episodic version — 49 minutes (used); Collector's tape — movie version — 49 minutes

Highlights: Vicki (Maureen O'Brien) joins the series with this story. Vicki is not short for Victoria.

Questions: What is Vicki's last name?

Errors and Other Points of Interest

Episode 1: The Powerful Enemy
First Transmitted: Jan. 2, 1965

0:42 The radio antenna dish is moving. **1:42** Bennett (Ray Barrett) tells Vicki that the rescue ship cannot find Dido unless they guide the ship. This explains the often-posed question of why the destruction of the radio set occurs at the end of the story. This is a technobabble answer. **4:40** Ian and Barbara wake the Doctor after the TARDIS has landed. Barbara tells the Doctor the trembling (movement of the ship) has stopped. The Doctor tells Barbara, "Oh my dear, I'm glad you're feeling better." This may only be an attempt at humor on the Doctor's part, or it may mean that the Doctor has just awoken from a deep sleep. **6:34** The TARDIS light is still flashing. **6:34** It is possible to see the cave wall through the open doors of the TARDIS. This model of the TARDIS has no back wall. **8:13** Koquillion ("Sydney Wilson") apparently came into the cave by the "back way," since he did not pass Ian and Barbara. **8:44** When Barbara and Ian first see the ship the radio antenna dish is no longer moving. **13:10** Ian, with the Doctor's help, describes a Dido native (they are never called Didonians in the story), and the description sounds like Koquillion. The Doctor does not mention that he is describing a ceremonial costume. **14:22** Ian comments on the Doctor's "medical" exam. The Doctor replies, "It's a pity I didn't get that degree, eh?" Some fans cite this as a blooper in view of the Doctor's comments in *The Moonbase*. Not getting a degree does not mean he has no training towards a degree. **16:10** Koquillion tells Vicki about trapping the crew in a cave, and that the travelers may be dead. He knows there is a second entrance, so why does he assume the travelers trapped or dead? **17:59** Vicki has trouble with the word "invited" as she tells Barbara what happened to the ship's crew. **18:46** Barbara starts to ask Vicki "Why did he kill you?" but Barbara corrects herself in mid-sentence to say "doesn't" instead of "did." Some viewers incorrectly attribute this misstatement to Vicki. **20:52** Some fans claim the sight of Vicki's underwear is a blooper. This supposedly occurs as she bends over the cabinet and pulls out the flare gun. Considering the fact that Vicki is wearing leotards it is impossible to see her underwear. **21:37** Bennett, not Koquillion, enters the main cabin of the spaceship. Vicki is relieved to see him. Vicki does not wonder how Koquillion left, when she did not see him leave. Vicki does not know about the secret exit. **24:50** The name "Sydney Wilson" is present to disguise the fact one actor played both Bennett and Koquillion.

Episode 2: Desperate Measures
First Transmitted: Jan. 9, 1965

5:06 Just before Barbara kills Vicki's "pet" (Sandy) a stagehand is visible to the left and behind the pet. **5:33** When Barbara fires the flare-gun at Sandy, a firework simply drops off the end of the gun. **7:07** Ian pronounces Koquillion as "Cockylickin." This is not a true blooper as Ian is trying to be funny. There are claims that this is a blooper. **11:48** Vicki says she left Earth in "2493." She has spent time in space and on Dido. This may conflict with the report that the story occurs in 2493. **12:32** Vicki's assertion, "they didn't have time machines in 1963," implies that sometime between 1963 and 2493 time machines appeared on Earth. **14:03** The Doctor discovers the secret exit from Bennett's room. **15:56** Barbara, Ian and Vicki wonder where the Doctor and Bennett went. They do not wonder how the two missing people got past them, and there is no mention of the trapdoor. **18:25** The supporting columns are not supporting anything. **19:12** The shadow of a camera appears on the back of the native on the right.

Comments: This is the first time the addition of a new "permanent" character occurs in the series.

(M) The Romans

Writer: Dennis Spooner; **Director:** Christopher Barry

Media: Commercial 2-tape set — episodic version — 97 minutes (used) — *The Rescue/The Romans*; Collector's tape — movie version — 92 minutes

Highlights: This is one of the more comedic stories (especially Episode 3), though there is much more to it.

Errors and Other Points of Interest

This is a "historical" story. However, the history is at best questionable. Historical inaccuracies are part of the writers' artistic license. Historical "bloopers" are not part of this listing. For example, Nero was not in Rome when the fire started. Some historical items have crept into various blooper lists. These are included here. Blatantly erroneous items (such as telling the viewers that discovery of North America was in 1875) are bloopers, and would be present in this list.

There is a claim that the Doctor tells a guard to "sod off."

Episode 1: The Slave Traders
First Transmitted: Jan. 16, 1965

1:40 The Doctor has an interesting line "There's a great deal of difference between resting and being sort of ... bone idle." **1:52** In order to aid the Doctor in this stimulating dialogue, Ian begins "Where Barbara and Vicki." **10:37** The Doctor calls Ian "Chesterfield"; Barbara and the Doctor's further comments indicate this was intentional. **13:20** This is one of the many appearances of a fountain with a plastic liner.

Episode 2: All Roads Lead to Rome
First Transmitted: Jan. 23, 1965

Reportedly, the Doctor has trouble saying "disastrous" during this episode.

1:38 Some fans find fault with the Doctor's speech ending in "fisticuffs." This appears to be more artistic license than fumbling. **2:59** The Doctor has trouble with his lines as he begins "My dear, it was a vasecte...." It is possible that the Doctor knew that more than the assassin's tongue suffered. **10:24** The sea "rushing in" the ship is obviously buckets of water. **17:09** The Doctor apparently forgets his lines when he first meets Tavius (Michael Peake). He remembers his line and interrupts Tavius who has gone on with the script. **17:30** During the time of this story, Nero (Derek Francis) was in his mid-twenties. The actor does not appear to be in his mid-twenties. This is a historical inaccuracy, and not a true blooper. **19:04** Nero is obviously not playing the lyre; his finger movements do not match the music. However, much worse "playing" has made it to the screen. **19:16** During the Doctor's conversation with Nero, the Doctor says, "That, your Excellency, would be an impossibissibility."

Episode 3: Conspiracy
First Transmitted: Jan. 30, 1965

0:58 The lyre Nero is holding does not have normal strings; it has filaments so there will be some resistance when hitting the servant over the head. **2:50** When Nero turns and begins to walk away from Poppaea (Kay Patrick) a boom mike appears. **2:58** Nero has trouble saying, "Naturally I appreciate the feelings of my fellow artists." **5:31** The pedestal Barbara sets the tray on is not very stable. **18:49** Flavius serves the Doctor wine. This is in variance with the Doctor's drinking habits in other stories. **24:36** Another historical inaccuracy, cited as a blooper by some, is that the swords are the wrong shape, and sword versus net competitions never occurred.

Episode 4: Inferno
First Transmitted: Feb. 6, 1965

1:12 Ian's friend Delos (Peter Diamond) kills one of the guards. Nero kicks the body of the dead guard off the stage. When the guard lands we find that the first time Doctor Who viewers get to see a moon was not in *The Moonbase*. **5:44** The Doctor informs the viewers that it is July 64 AD. **8:26** Notice how the Doctor is holding his glasses. It is unlikely they would be able to focus the Sun's rays. **8:35** This shot of the Doctor's glasses, from a different angle, shows the glasses in a different position. **12:23** Nero pays the "torch bearers" with metal washers. **13:53** A boom mike shadow adorns Barbara.

(N) THE WEB PLANET

Writer: Bill Strutton; **Director:** Richard Martin

Media: Commercial tape — episodic version — 147 minutes (used); Collector's tape — movie version — 138 minutes

Errors and Other Points of Interest

There is a blooper in many blooper lists. In several places these lists perpetuate the myth that the returning inhabitants are the Menoptera. The correct name (see the closing credits) is Menoptra.

In many cases, the wooden supports for the rock formations are present. The claimed appearances of the wooden supports for the mountains are not present.

Episode 1: The Web Planet
First Transmitted: Feb. 13, 1965

2:17 There is a power cord on the floor leading to the TARDIS console. **6:51** Barbara asks the Doctor for a sedative, and he sends her to the first aid box. **7:38** Ian has trouble fastening his respiratory compensator. **7:56** In one scene, the Doctor forgets his line. This begins after Ian says, "How do we open the doors? We have no power?" Ian tries to signal the Doctor by repeatedly looking at the object the Doctor is supposed to describe. Finally, the Doctor says, "This is not merely a decorative object," and goes on to finish the scene without ever telling Ian the purpose of the object. **8:35** We learn one of the purposes of the "object" mentioned earlier. The object is the Doctor's ring. **8:43** Just after the TARDIS doors open, the face of a man appears at the edge of the open door. **9:04** Barbara gives Vicki some pills that will "make her sleep." Vicki reads the label on the vial and learns that the sleep inducing sedative is aspirin. **12:12** A wire is present above and to the left of Ian. The purpose of this wire becomes apparent a few seconds later as it whisks Ian's pen away. **14:01** Just before Ian follows the Doctor off the set, a boom mike shadow appears on Ian's coat. **14:51** You can see people moving about outside through the crack beside the TARDIS doors. **15:33** Barbara goes into the bedroom to check on how Vicki is feeling. When Barbara sets down in front of a reflective wall, there is the reflection of a spotlight. In the next view, the reflection disappears, because the spotlight is in a different position. **16:29** As the Doctor and Ian are walking across the landscape, the wooden support of one of the rock formations juts out of the lower front. **16:54** You can see through the Doctor and Ian to the rocks surrounding the pyramid. **18:04** The Doctor dips Ian's tie into the pool and destroys it. Later the Doctor says that the pool contained an acid with "similar properties to formic acid." Formic acid does not behave in this manner to any cloth available to Ian. Formic acid has a very definite odor, but neither the Doctor nor Ian notices any odor. Thus, neither the reactivity nor the odor is similar to those properties of formic acid. To which properties was the Doctor alluding? **21:15** When Barbara leaves the TARDIS, the doors close. **21:56** When Vicki goes to look for Barbara, the TARDIS doors are no longer closed. **23:00** The Doctor returns at the end of the episode to find the TARDIS missing. For some reason, there is a dubbed line. This occurs when we hear the Doctor say, "My ship ... My TARDIS." The dubbing is very poor, as the sound does not come close to the Doctor's lip movements.

Episode 2: The Zarbi
First Transmitted: Feb. 20, 1965

0:30 During the reprise at the beginning of the episode, the Doctor mouths "My ship," and then says, "My TARDIS" in sync with the sound. **6:40** The Menoptra throw Barbara's bracelet into a pool of acid to destroy it. Earlier in the story the Doctor says it is similar to formic acid. Formic acid has no effect on gold. Neither does any other common acid. The only way to destroy gold with common acids is to use a mixture of nitric acid and hydrochloric acid called *aqua regia*. This acid mixture is only stable for a short time, so it could not be in pools on the planet's surface. **7:12** Immediately after the Menoptra throw Barbara's bracelet into the acid, Ian and the Doctor walk onto the set and cast giant shadows on the "distant" mountains. This is one of many instances — it is not the first or last time. **8:50** Some viewers claim the Doctor has trouble with his lines. Supposedly, the Doctor pauses after saying, "I didn't want to...." Ian's question about the galaxy brings the Doctor back on track. This does not occur in this story. The true problem occurs a few seconds later. **8:56** During their discussion, the Doctor tells Ian they are "many light Earths ... light years from Earth." **11:36** As Barbara escapes from the Menoptra, she pulls down a rock formation on leaving the cave. The "rocks" make a very un-rocklike sound as they fall. **14:21–14:36** There is no action in the headquarters. Some fans consider this a blooper. These fans also report this lack of action lasts for five seconds. **14:58** As Ian and the Doctor walk onto the set in the scene immediately after Vicki exits the TARDIS, a camera, complete with the camera operator's head, casts a shadow on the back of Ian's coat. **16:51** As Barbara sits contemplating the pool, it is possible to see supports under one of the formations behind her. **19:27** On their way to attack the Menoptra, the abdomen of one of the Zarbi "clunks" on the floor. **19:52** When one of the Menoptra dies, its wings fall off. This is a reported blooper. If the wings fell off every time, it would not be a blooper, but a general consequence of Menoptra death. **21:54** In the room with the TARDIS, there is a boom mike shadow on the wall behind the Doctor.

Episode 3: Escape to Danger
First Transmitted: Feb. 27, 1965

3:05 The Zarbi cast shadows on the starry sky. **5:30** One of the Zarbi runs into a camera with a definite cluck, this causes the camera to shake. **10:03** A Zarbi jumps up as Ian begins to escape. When the Zarbi turns, it is obvious what caused it to jump — it has lost the right side of its jaw. **10:20** Before there were jelly babies, there was chocolate. **11:08** Reflections in the lower part of the Astral Map on which the Doctor and Vicki are working show various things happening offstage; for example, someone is turning pages of the script. **14:08** As Ian is escaping, a Menoptra lands near him. It is possible to see the rope supporting the "flying" Menoptra. **14:10** A Larvae Gun is pursuing Ian. The "animal" sounds as if it is on casters. There are reports that a rope can be seen towing the Larvae Gun. **16:30** The large shadow of a spotlight falls on Vicki's back as she starts to take the box back to the TARDIS. **16:34** Some viewers consider the Zarbi's fear of spiders to be a blooper. This would imply that grown humans never ever show any fear of spiders. **21:21** As one of the larvae guns comes off a ledge at the very left of the screen, the legs of the operator jut from underneath the creature. **21:42** Ian causes a problem as he tries to fit into the crevice. The right side (and later the left side) of the set begins to rock back and forth.

Episode 4: Crater of Needles
First Transmitted: Mar. 6, 1965

0:33 During the scene where the rocks

are burying Ian, it sounds as if someone is laughing. **2:40** The camera shakes during Barbara's close-up. **4:02** One of the Menoptra is apparently having an extended conversation with a Zarbi guard. **8:55** Vrestin's (Roslyn de Winter) hands are "glued" together. **9:14** Some fans consider Hetra's (Ian Thompson) acting as a French bandit to be a blooper. **21:15** Vrestin's hands come unglued as her wings open. **22:04** Nearly all the landing Menoptra have easily seen supporting ropes.

Episode 5: Invasion
First Transmitted: Mar. 13, 1965

3:09 We learn that the Doctor's ring has other powers. Later Doctors do not use this ring. The last time the ring appears is in the first Second Doctor story. **9:16** A large boom mike shadow adorns the front of Barbara's sweater. **11:53** Viewers have noted the shadows of the Doctor, Vicki, and the Zarbi on the "distant" landscape at this and other times. These are increasingly obvious. The Zarbi do not appear in all cases. This problem occurs in other places (not listed). **19:18** The camera shakes as the Doctor says, "I see."

Episode 6: The Centre
First Transmitted: Mar. 20, 1965

1:15 The Animus asks the Doctor, "You attempted escape?" The Doctor replies, "We have been on a slight ... exploitation." It is possible that the Doctor had trouble reading the cue cards through the plastic dome. **2:04** When we first see Barbara, you can still hear the Doctor moaning loudly from the preceding scene. Barbara must ignore this and go on with the scene. Some viewers claim, incorrectly, that Barbara was on the opposite side of the planet. The Crater of Needles was only two hours away, and she and the Menoptra have been approaching to attack, so they are closer. **3:14** Some viewers consider the Menoptra line "Zarbiiiiii!" to be a blooper. **3:58** A Menoptra reaches down to grab a string dangling from the Zarbi. **6:08** One of the Zarbi bumps the right wall and it waves, as a backdrop should. **12:23** Someone is moving behind the background screen as Barbara discovers the isotope in the Astral Map. **15:37** A string supports the top of the Animus. This string appears in more than one scene. **16:45** One of the Zarbi discovers water. Then the actors grouping around causes the wooden set to creak and groan loudly. **20:01** At least one viewer appears to object to the Optera jumping around, casting shadows on the "distant" landscape and saying, "Light is good." **21:23** One of the claimed bloopers is the open window (broken?) as the TARDIS takes off. Through most of the preceding stories, one or more of the TARDIS windows have been open at times. **21:52** The story ends on a blooper — the cast casts shadows on the "distant" landscape. **24:10** Some viewers consider Howard King's lighting to be a blooper.

Comments: This is the first story where none of the other characters appears human.

The Doctor again helps save the planet Vortis.

(P) THE CRUSADE

Writer: David Whitaker; **Director:** Douglas Camfield

Media: Commercial DVD—*Lost in Time*—Episodes 1 and 3 with audio only for episodes 2 and 4—97 minutes (used); Commercial tape—episodic version—97 minutes (used), with *The Space Museum* and CD of episodes 2 and 4; Commercial tape—*The Hartnell Years*—episode 3 only—25 minutes

Errors and Other Points of Interest

Episode 1: The Lion
First Transmitted: Mar. 27, 1965

0:56 The landing sound of the TARDIS is different; also, there is no flashing light. **8:26** The Doctor tells Vicki and Ian that they must find some clothes to wear. Either there is no TARDIS wardrobe, or it is missing clothing from this period in time. **8:50** Ian seems to step in a hole. **9:28** Sir William des Preaux (John Flint) notes Barbara's strange clothing. This refutes the claims of some viewers who claim no one ever notices the unusual clothing of the travelers. **13:12** Meet Ben Daheer (Reg Prichard) and remember him. (See *The Daleks' Master Plan*.)

Episode 2: The Knight of Jaffa
First Transmitted: Apr. 3, 1965

6:50 (CD-1, track 1, 6:53) El Akir (Walter Randall) becomes angry with Barbara but not with Sir William des Preaux. El Akir should be angrier with Sir William. **13:26 (CD-1, track 1, 13:26)** Ian becomes "Sir Ian." **19:27 (CD-1, track 1, 19:27)** Saladin (Bernard Kay) and Saphadin (Roger Avon) seem overly willing to accept the kidnapping of one of their prisoners. No matter what the explanation of Barbara's leaving, there is the principle involved.

Episode 3: The Wheel of Fortune
First Transmitted: Apr. 10, 1965

4:34 A large shadow pans over Vicki and the Doctor. **24:00** You can hear someone yell, "Cut!" after El Akir tells Barbara "And death is very far away." This is not in the DVD version.

Episode 4: The Warlords
First Transmitted: Apr. 17, 1965

13:26 (CD-1, track 2, 13:27) Barbara learns about the balcony and the tree in the garden. The balcony is where Ian enters to save Barbara in the novelization, but not in the broadcast version. Some fans claim that Ian entering through the balcony is a blooper. Since Ian only enters through the balcony in the book, this cannot be a blooper in the broadcast version. **22:12 (CD-1, track 2, 22:13)** Many viewers object to the Doctor's comment to Ian: "I think you've earned a good knight's sleep."

Comments: The Doctor helps King Richard. There are video problems in episode 1 on the DVD.

(Q) The Space Museum

Writer: Glyn Jones; **Director:** Mervyn Pinfield

Media: Commercial tape — episodic version — 92 minutes (used), with *The Crusade*; Collector's tape — movie version 85 minutes
Questions: Vicki's hand passes through one of the museum exhibits. Later Ian's hand does the same thing. What keeps the group from sinking through the floor?

Errors and Other Points of Interest

Episode 1: The Space Museum
First Transmitted: Apr. 24, 1965

2:10 Ian mentions that they are wearing 13th century clothes when they were actually wearing 12th century clothes. Of course, we must remember that he was a science teacher and not a history teacher. **6:22** Soon after leaving the TARDIS, Vicki casts a shadow on the "distant" mountains. **7:20** The presence of shadows on the mountains occurs at various times. There are reports that shadows appear at the point where the Doctor bends over to examine the footprints on the ground. This is an example of a blooper in blooper lists; the Doctor never bends over to examine any footprints. The Doctor bends over to examine the *lack* of footprints, after Ian tells everyone that the TARDIS crew is not leaving footprints. **8:53** Watch as Ian begins to walk forward. The ground "lights up" as if someone just remembered to turn on a light. **9:35** The camera bobbles around for several seconds. **10:16** The Doctor has trouble saying "fluorescent." **11:26** Vicki tells everyone that she read about the Dalek Invasion of the Earth in history books. Vicki goes on to say the invasion was about 300 years before. Thus, in variance to other stories, the Dalek Invasion is in books. People, in many other stories, claim no knowledge of the Daleks. *The Power of the Daleks* is a good example. **14:52** Barbara bumps into the space-suited manikin, and instead of passing through it, she causes it to rock.

Episode 2: The Dimensions of Time
First Transmitted: May 1, 1965

3:24 Some fans find fault with the Moroks using "ray guns." **4:33** As the group is starting up the steps to leave the room there is a "honk" offstage. **9:38** Tor (Jeremy Bulloch) has trouble talking about capturing the Doctor or Vicki. **13:12** When two Morok guards begin walking down the corridor there is a loud "squeak" offstage. **19:41** Before Paul was the walrus, the Doctor claimed to be a walrus.

Episode 3: The Search
First Transmitted: May 8, 1965

9:02 Dako (Peter Craze) learns Barbara's name but not Vicki's name. **12:47** Dako tells Barbara that Vicki has gone with his friends. When did Dako learn Vicki's name? **18:23** Only the top left reel on the computer is moving. At least two reels should be moving. **19:34** All four reels on the computer are now moving.

Episode 4: The Final Phase
First Transmitted: May 15, 1965

12:41 The Morok Commander (Ivor Salter) has trouble saying "guerrilla." **12:46** Some fans have trouble repeating the line "Have any arms fallen into Xeron hands?" without laughing. It is surprising that the Commander was able to say it. **14:28** Barbara has trouble saying, "I wish I had thought of it." **16:19** Dako says that Vicki "found her friends," but he only knows about her finding a friend (Barbara). **19:33** The question has been posed, as a blooper, how does the Time and Space Visualizer (also referred to as the Space-Time Visualizer) fit through the TARDIS doors? We do not see the unit in this story, thus this is a questionable blooper. Dismantling and reassembly of the unit is possible. **21:00** The Dalek reports, "They are once again in time and space." Apparently, the Doctor and his fellow travelers were not in either of these dimensions while on Xeros. This line is also present at the beginning of the next story.

Comments: The Doctor helps save the planet Xeros.

(R) THE CHASE

Writer: Terry Nation; **Director:** Richard Martin

Media: Commercial tape — episodic version — 148 minutes (used); Collector's tape — movie version — 138 minutes; Commercial tape — *Daleks — The Early Years* — excerpts

Highlights: Ian Chesterton (William Russell) and Barbara Wright (Jacqueline Hill) leave the series at the end of this story. In the last episode, Steven Taylor (Peter Purves) joins the series.

Questions: Why should a haunted house exhibit, the Frankenstein Monster, attack Daleks?

Errors and Other Points of Interest

Some viewers claim that in the fifth episode a problem results when a Dalek appears in the background of the jungle before the Daleks land on Mechanus. This cannot be a problem in this episode since the Daleks arrived at the end of the preceding episode. There is only one shot of the jungle given before the Daleks land. There is a form in the background, which could be mistaken for a Dalek, but it is something else.

In Episode 5, the Daleks gather to attack, and as they go to attack, they pass the cave where the TARDIS crew are hiding, and continue on to come to the same cave. See if you can note the exact time and place.

There are reports of the jostling of the camera as the Mechanoids capture the Doctor and crew.

Episode 1: The Executioners
First Transmitted: May 22, 1965

0:37 The Dalek reports, "They are once again in time and space." Apparently, the Doctor and his fellow travelers were not in either of these dimensions while on Xeros. This is in the reprise from the preceding episode. **1:10** If the Time-Space Visualizer can "look" anywhere, why are only the planets of one solar system listed on the front? **1:44** As Vicki leaves, she puts down a pair of pliers. These immediately fall onto the floor with appropriate clatter. Some viewers claim, incorrectly, a screwdriver fell instead of a pair of pliers. **9:41** How does Ian know the words to the Beatles' song? Release of this song occurred about eighteen months after Ian left the Earth. **10:54** The Doctor and the others exit to the left. This may or may not be in the direction of the console. This leads into a possible blooper relating the relative positions of the console, doors and the Visualizer. **11:15** It is possible to see the studio ceiling and lights above the TARDIS set. **13:07** Vicki's shadow appears on the backdrop. **14:46** There is a claimed discrepancy in the position of the TARDIS doors relative to the Space-Time Visualizer. When Barbara re-enters the TARDIS she does not come from the direction the Doctor went when he said, "We're about to materialize!" It is possible that the Doctor went to the console and not the door. Thus, the TARDIS doors are not necessarily in the direction viewers assume. The relative positions of the console, doors and Visualizer are unknown. The Doctor enters the set from the same direction as Barbara. **16:12** One of the Daleks reports, "The Doctor and the three humans delayed our conquest of Earth." This implies that after the events in *The Dalek Invasion of Earth*, the Daleks finished taking over the Earth after a delay. **17:03** When the Daleks are entering their time machine one of them must lift itself up to get over the bottom edge of the door. **17:33** The Doctor turns the Visualizer "off," but it takes several seconds for the picture to disappear. **20:38** It is possible to see part of the drop cloth under the sand. **21:56** Ian's yell and its echo do not match.

Episode 2: The Death of Time
First Transmitted: May 29, 1965

0:54 The Dalek is obviously walking,

not "gliding" over the sand. **1:01** There are footprints on the sand behind the second Dalek. **1:26** The speeches of the two Daleks interfere with each other. **2:17** People claim that the Dalek moving over the sand is leaving footprints. This may be the case, but he manages to do a good job staying in front of his footprints. **2:54** As one of the Aridians tops the sand dune, his shadow falls on the "distant" mountains and upon the sky. **4:35** Hair often appears to be sticking out from under the Aridian's masks. However, the backs of all the masks appear to be parts of helmets, and even the fronts appear to be parts of helmets molded to the actor's heads. This problem appears at many points. **6:04** When the Aridian prepares to detonate the explosives, the explosives detonate prematurely. **8:11** While one Dalek is saying, "There it was buried by last night's storm." The lights on both Daleks are flashing. **12:10** The second Dalek lifts himself up so he can move across the set. **15:38** When Vicki enters the set, she runs into one of the Aridians. He seems a little confused, and then he looks about before sneaking off the set. **16:49** In order for Barbara to fall into the clutches of the Mire Beast, she must run over to the wall and allow the beast to grab her. **19:06** Ian tells everyone that the TARDIS is 20 yards away. **21:56** The Doctor and Crew appear to be looking into the hole the Dalek just fell into, and then they turn around and quickly run into the TARDIS that is only a few feet away, not 20 yards from them. **21:58** The Doctor enters the TARDIS without his coat.

Episode 3: Flight Through Eternity
First Transmitted: June 5, 1965

1:15 A boom mike shadow passes over the Time Rotor. **1:28** Vicki's movements and facial expressions suggest that she needs to go to the ladies room. At least this is what some fans claim. **1:46** The Doctor says they gave the Daleks "a very good hiding." **1:57** The Doctor refers to the fact that he built the TARDIS. **2:40** The motionless Daleks standing on each side of the ramp are ex-movie Daleks. After their return to the BBC, there was no time to completely convert their appearance from the movie to TV form. Look at the bases and dome lights. **3:04** One of the Daleks orders the others to compute time by "Earth Scale." No reason is given, but this is why some fans claim both the use of Earth time and distance units are bloopers. **3:07** One of the Daleks has apparently forgotten how to talk. **3:16** The TARDIS has a fifteen-minute lead. Some fans suggest that it is not possible to have a lead when moving through the Space-Time continuum. (The same seekers attribute this incorrectly to Episode 2.) This would be true if the pursuers knew the destination of the TARDIS. If the Daleks knew the destination, they could simply program their ship to reach the destination before, or at the same time, the TARDIS landed. The Doctor explains part of this later. **3:21** The Daleks overlapping speeches are hard to follow. **4:09** The Doctor says it takes twelve minutes for the computers to "reorientate and gather power," thus some "catch-up" time is to be expected; especially if it takes the Daleks less than this amount of time to adjust to a course change by the TARDIS. **4:25** Some fans propose a questionable blooper about Vicki pointing and saying, "Doctor! The rotor is slowing down!" Supposedly the Doctor responds with, "No, but I'm not ready!" Vicki appears to be pointing to the side of the console instead of the central column. These fans claim that she pointed towards two strobe lights. There are no lights. Vicki's actual quote is "Doctor! It's slowing down!" The reported response by the Doctor is much later, thus it is incorrectly attributed to being part of this blooper. The Doctor's later response was in response to Barbara's comment about the TARDIS landing. **5:10** At the upper right of the screen, you can see the person who could be married to Steven's great, great,

great ... grandmother. (Alternatively, is he the person who lived next door to Steven's great, great, great ... grandmother?) **5:42** The Tour Guide (Arne Gordon) needs to get his facts straight. If it took thirty seconds for someone the hit the ground after jumping from the Empire State Building, then the building must be over 4400 meters high. The actual height is 443 meters. The tour guide gives the height as 1473 feet (449 meters). The actual time to fall would be less than ten seconds. Some viewers attribute this incorrectly to Episode 2. **7:35** Morton Dill (Peter Purves), the tourist, says the time is "three after twelve." However, he responds to Vicki's "Good afternoon," with "Morning." **13:31** This is the second part of the previously reported erroneous blooper. This is the point where the Doctor responds to Barbara's comment (not Vicki's) with, "I'm not ready. I'm not ready." **16:15** We hear the sound of Vicki hitting the crewmember on the head before she delivers the blow. **18:52** The ability of the Daleks to get a clear picture of the *Marie Celeste* while they were some distance away has been listed as a blooper. (This fault attributed incorrectly to Episode 2.) The presence of a Dalek Time-Space Visualizer could explain the ability of the Daleks seeing the ship. **23:53** After the Doctor says "close on our track," someone talks off set. **23:57** The TARDIS lead is now eight minutes, a value repeated in the reprise.

Episode 4: *Journey Into Terror*
First Transmitted: June 12, 1965

1:08 Just before the TARDIS materializes, it is possible to hear what may be the materialization of the Dalek time machine. **1:14** The shadow of a person appears on the doors of the materializing TARDIS. The person quickly runs away. **1:30** The Doctor's coat, left on Aridius, returns after being dry-cleaned. **1:52** Some viewers cite the presence of visible wires on the bats as a blooper. Wires should be present for "Haunted House" bat, unless the owners used trained bats instead of props like the other "exhibits." **5:29** The camera responsible for Ian's close-up comes through the door as Ian descends the stairs. **5:29** A Dalek appears just above the top step behind Ian. **5:31** There is a Dalek in the back of the room containing the Frankenstein Monster (John Maxim). It does not say nor do anything the first time the Doctor and Ian enter the room. The Dalek's time machine is not in the Haunted House at the time of the first appearance of the Dalek. **5:42** The Frankenstein Monster is not wearing a coat. The Creature is wearing only bandages. **5:43** The Doctor says, "I say, I think we'd better go and check where Vicki and Barbara is!" **5:58** As the Frankenstein Monster lies down after the Doctor and Ian rush out of the room, you can hear Vicki's next line, "What's that in aid of?" This is her line from the next scene. **6:07** There are claims that it is a blooper when Barbara quotes, "Ask not for whom the bell tolls...." This implies that there was a bell sound. We do not hear any bells. **6:39** At first, Count Dracula has trouble answering Barbara's question. **10:11** A cough sounds off-stage as the Doctor and Ian walk towards the stairway. **10:12** Normally when someone steps on the bottom step we hear a creak and the flutter of wings. This happens several times. This does not happen at this time. There seems to be a delay. It is possible to climb the stairs immediately after someone triggers the effort and before the system has re-set. This happens some times, and not at others. **10:17** The Daleks arrive in the Haunted House. **11:27** The Dalek previously hiding in the "laboratory" now sweeps into action. In this case, it is not a blooper since this is after the arrival of the Daleks. **11:56** The Dalek fires on the Frankenstein Monster. If this caused damage to the creature's circuitry, it could explain the later behavior of the monster. **12:13** See if you can find the operator in the shadows with a boom mike as the Doctor and Ian come down the stairs. **13:08** The fashion conscious Frankenstein Monster is now wearing a coat. Why does he change clothes? **13:19** Some fans find fault with Frankenstein Monster actually attacking. The monster does not actually attack people; it attacks Daleks. **14:24** The Doctor says, "that house was neither tame ... time nor space." He probably means that the house was neither IN time nor IN space. **15:56** When one of the Daleks moves in front of the machine with the three-digit numbers showing, the numbers appear on the Daleks for an instant. **18:02** You can see the reflection of a man in the replicator door. He stands and walks away before the "Doctor" enters. **18:21** The robot "Doctor" walks into the chamber just before Vicki walks over to the chamber. **19:25** The Doctor says that it will take months — maybe years to repair the TARDIS. Why would this make any difference to their going back to rescue Vicki? No matter what time they start back, they can always return to a specific time. **20:01** As the Doctor, Ian and Barbara are discussing the capture of the Dalek time machine a large shadow of a light fixture falls across Barbara. **20:47** In the Dalek time machine, someone quickly runs across the bottom of the screen. **20:48** One of the Daleks appears to have trouble with his voice circuits, "Uh-uh aah in Earth time uh-h four minutes." **21:35** The "Doctor" (Edmund Warwick) (who is supposed to be "indistinguishable from the original") does not look very much like the Doctor. A better solution is in *The Massacre of St. Bartholomew's Eve*. **21:42** Some viewers claim the Daleks are present on Mechanus before they actually arrive. The TARDIS crew looks out onto Mechanus, no Daleks are present, but there is a blurred image. This may be mistaken for a Dalek. This is the only shot of the jungle before the Daleks land. **22:27** The Daleks arrive on Mechanus. **23:02** There is a bad dub of the Doctor's voice for the "Doctor." **23:24** The credits list Frankenstein's Monster as just "Frankenstein."

Episode 5: The Death of Doctor Who
First Transmitted: June 19, 1965

There is a claim that the massing Daleks go past the entrance to the cave the Doctor and the other travelers are hiding more than once.

4:12 The Doctor, Ian and Barbara walk right past the Daleks' machine. Ian even stops and looks directly at the machine without seeing it. **7:01** An "unseen" Dalek is in the jungle as you look out the cave entrance. **7:52** Soon after Vicki finds the TARDIS on Mechanus, she runs to the lighted path. It is possible to see a boom mike in the background along the path. **8:00** You can see someone's hand reach out of the "bushes" along the path and pick up something from the ground. **10:58** Ian carries Vicki past the Dalek's time machine, and neither, Steven, nor Vicki, nor the Doctor notices the craft. **15:43** We no longer need to look at the robot that is "identical" to the Doctor or listen to bad dubs. **16:35** As Ian exits the cave to talk to the Doctor, a boom mike shadow shows itself, this continues off and on until the end of the scene. **21:10** A BBC camera is present in the background, as the Daleks are getting ready to attack. The camera has a "5" painted on the side. There are reports that the number is a "3." **22:03** The cave wall teeters as the Doctor rushes back into the cave.

Episode 6: The Planet of Decision
First Transmitted: June 26, 1965

There is a claim that the camera shakes noticeably as the Mechanoids capture the Doctor and the others.

4:09 The door to the cell bounces when it drops shut. **8:46** The Dalek in the lift calls the Mechanoids "the Mechans" or "the Mechons." **9:19** Steven flubs his line and starts to say the distance from the city roof is 15 feet. He quickly corrects himself and says it is 1500 feet. **11:09** Steven walks around his construction to talk to the Doctor and Ian. The camera follows Steven until it suddenly jerks, followed by a "thud" and someone saying "oooh!" A cough also sounds. **14:16** The 1500+ feet of cable is very slack. The cable's own weight should make it taunt. Some viewers incorrectly refer to the cable as a rope; a rope that long would break under its own weight. It is also supporting Vicki's weight at this point. **14:17** Barbara nearly falls off the roof of the Mechanoid city. When Ian saves her, he nearly pulls her pants off. **15:02** The top of the second Dalek "jumps." **15:58** Some of the explosions are obviously cartoons. **17:05** The explosion of the Mechanoid City is obviously the explosion of a cliff superimposed on the jungle behind the city. **19:17** As the Doctor is arguing with Ian and Barbara about using the Dalek time machine, the Doctor tells the pair, "you'll end up as a couple of burnt cinders flying around in Spain."

Comments: The Doctor slips past the Daleks again.

(S) THE TIME MEDDLER

Writer: Dennis Spooner; **Director:** Douglas Camfield

Media: Commercial tape — episodic version — 96 minutes (used); Collector's tape — movie version — 90 minutes (used)
Highlights: Another Time Lord and another TARDIS.

Errors and Other Points of Interest

There is no mention of the words Gallifrey or Gallifreyan in this story. This is contrary to what some fans report.

Episode 1: The Watcher
First Transmitted: July 3, 1965

6:20 Vicki tells Steven that TARDIS stands for "Time And Relative Dimensions In Space." **8:23** Many fans claim a blooper because Steven keeps saying 10th century when the Doctor "clearly" told him it was the 11th century. The Doctor's comment was to Vicki as they were examining Viking helmet. The Doctor says that it must be the "10th—11th century." Steven does not appear to be listening very well to what the Doctor is saying. **10:45** When Steven suggests they climb off the beach, the Doctor says, "But I'm not a mountain goat and I prefer walking to any day — and I hate climbing." **11:40** When the Monk (Peter Butterworth) tries to open the TARDIS doors they do not budge, but when he lightly leans against the doors they almost open. **14:48** The Doctor accepts and drinks mead. Normally, the First Doctor does not drink anything containing alcohol. **21:25** Steven mentions the 10th century on finding the watch, and in the next episode he again mention the 10th century after checking the time.

Episode 2: The Meddling Monk
First Transmitted: July 10, 1965

3:54 Steven throws the blackberries in his right hand away so he can eat those in his left hand. Why not eat all the berries? **4:18** Steven mentions the 10th century after checking the time. **8:01** The Monk wears a ring similar to the Doctor's ring. Is this supposed to be a Time Lord device? **24:27** Pay attention to what Steven does to the door. **24:42** Pay attention to the rug on the bed.

Episode 3: A Battle of Wits
First Transmitted: July 17, 1965
   0:27 Steven does not handle the door the same way he did during the cliffhanger. **0:40** There is a different rug on the bed. **1:16** Just before Steven and Vicki leave the cell, the Doctor's dark cloak is on the bed (Vicki lifted the cloak and then replaced it). **2:51** When the Monk enters, there is a sheepskin, not a dark cloak on the bed. **11:59** The Monk brings many modern devices with him, but only brings a slide rule to do his calculations. **13:53** Some people have trouble with the Doctor's line as he utters, "Well, as it happens I happen to be a very curious fellow" to the Monk.

Episode 4: Checkmate
First Transmitted: July 24, 1965
   2:44 Dodo reads to Steven that the Monk placed £200 in a London bank. The Monk did this in 1968. He then traveled 200 years and collected "a fortune in compound interest." Apparently, the Dalek invasion did not interfere with banking or that the Dalek invasion was after 2168. **18:21** The Doctor has trouble saying, "Personnel correspondence."

   Comments: The Doctor saves the Earth.

(T) GALAXY 4

Writer: William Emms; **Director:** Derek Martinus

> *Media:* Commercial 2 CD set — episodic version — 98 minutes (used); Commercial tape — an excerpt (nearly 6:00 minutes) in the tape *The Missing Years* packaged with *The Edge of Destruction* (used)
> *Highlight:* Peter Purves narrates the CD version.
> *Questions:* Why does it take Maaga (Stephanie Bidmead) so long to decide to steal the TARDIS?

Errors and Other Points of Interest

Episode 1: Four Hundred Dawns
First Transmitted: Sept. 11, 1965
   0:44 (CD-1, track 2, 0:09) The Narrator mentions trees and plants are growing. **1:59 (CD-1, track 3, 1:02)** The Doctor checks the readings and finds nothing unusual about the planet's atmosphere. **2:16 (CD-1, track 3, 1:19)** The Doctor observes that there is no life. What are trees and plants? **11:28** This is the approximate starting time of the existing six-minute excerpt. **14:14 (CD-1, track 9, 2:31)** Steven has trouble when he tries to say "women." This may not be a true blooper. This occurs at 2:46 from the beginning of the video excerpt. **17:39 (CD-1, track 13, 0:52)** The Doctor says he must return to his ship. Maaga does not immediately realize that she could use the TARDIS to escape.

Episode 2: Trap of Steel
First Transmitted: Sept. 18, 1965
   4:35 (CD-1, track 22, 1:10) Maaga is worried about the Doctor, Vicki, and Steven escaping. Maaga still has not thought to use the TARDIS to escape. **8:49 (CD-1, track 24, 3:11)** When Maaga asks for help the Doctor says, "I don't seem to have much

chance." The Doctor should have said "choice" not "chance." **14:39 (CD-1, track 26, 2:53)** Maaga finally realizes she can escape in the TARDIS.

Episode 3: Air Lock
First Transmitted: Sept. 25, 1965
  2:06 (CD-2, track 5, 0:29) The Doctor explains that the machine is "to convert air into ammonia gas." Normal air does not have sufficient hydrogen for this to work, and it would be too difficult to get hydrogen directly from the water vapor. If, upon first landing, the Doctor found the air to be unusual, there could be other explanations. This is bad technobabble. **4:28 (CD-2, track 6, 0:56)** Maaga reminisces that she would need soldiers to "conquer space." Maaga apparently began with four soldiers to accomplish this task. Conquering space would seem a lot for five people to do. **18:11 (CD-2, track 15, 1:22)** The Doctor appears to say, "I wust ... I must...." **20:55 (CD-2, track 17, 0:29)** It sounds as if the Rill Voice (Robert Cartland) refers to the Chumblies by the name "comely machines."

Episode 4: The Exploding Planet
First Transmitted: Oct. 2, 1965
  5:24 (CD-2, track 30, 0:09) Vicki refers to "ammoniak gas" instead of ammonia gas. **6:13 (CD-2, track 30, 0:59)** The Doctor has trouble speaking after telling Steven to get some rest. **10:50 (CD-2, track 32, 0:27)** The Doctor's description of the planet's destruction is bad technobabble. **17:11 (CD-2, track 40, 0:58)** Steven joins Vicki as he refers to "ammoniak gas."
  Comments: This is one of the few cases where the excerpt is sufficiently long for good placement.

(T/A) MISSION TO THE UNKNOWN

Alternate Titles: *Dalek Cutaway*
Writer: Terry Nation; **Director:** Derek Martinus

Media: Commercial CD — 25 minutes (used) — part of a 5 CD set *The Daleks' Master Plan*; Collector's audio recording — 24 minutes
Highlights: No member of the regular cast appears in this episode. The CD Narrator is Peter Purves.
This is the shortest story (other than the Pilot).
Question: Why, other than in *The Daleks' Master Plan*, are there no Varga plants in the Dalek stories?

Errors and Other Points of Interest

Episode 1: Mission to the Unknown
First Transmitted: Oct. 9, 1965
  7:09 (CD-1, track 4, 0:56) Lowery (Jeremy Young) tells Cory (Edward de Souza), "Daleks invaded Earth — thousand years ago." This allows an estimate of the date of this story. However, the events in *The Daleks' Master Plan* take place in the year 4000. **7:12 (CD-1, track 4, 0:59)** Cory tells Lowery that Daleks were not in our galaxy for some time. This indicates that either the Daleks left Skaro for a time or the Earth and Skaro are in different galaxies. **13:05 (CD-1, track 9, 0:08)** The Daleks know there are aliens on Kembel. **13:46 (CD-1, track 10, 0:20)** Cory explains that

the recorder is like an ordinary tape recorder. The recorder is apparently not a true tape recorder. This may explain the appearance of devices observers call anachronistic tape recorders. **18:02 (CD-1, track 15, 0:44)** The Daleks know the aliens are from the Earth. This gives the Daleks an even better reason not to announce their plans over loudspeakers. **21:04 (CD-1, track 18, 0:38)** Cory reports that he heard the Dalek's "secret" plan over the loudspeaker. Since the Daleks already knew that aliens from Earth were on the planet it is unlikely that the Daleks would announce their secret plans so openly. This would be true even if they assumed they would capture the aliens before they could pass on the information. **21:46 (CD-1, track 18, 1:21)** The message that Marc Cory records is: "This is Marc Cory, Special Security Service, reporting from the planet Kembel. The Daleks are planning the complete destruction of our Galaxy. Together with the powers of the outer galaxies, a war force is being assembled." **22:26 (CD-1, track 20, 0:04)** Marc Cory finishes his message with "...our Galaxy is to be saved. Whoever receives this message must relay this information to Earth immediately. It—it is vital that defense mechanisms are put into operation at once. Message ends."

Comments: There are erroneous reports that the names of all members of the alliance appear in this story. Only Malpha (Robert Cartland) receives credit on screen. Other names reported in this story are either from *The Daleks' Master Plan* or from other stories.

(U) THE MYTH MAKERS

Writer: Donald Cotton; **Director:** Michael Leeston-Smith

Media: Commercial 2 CD set—episodic version—100 minutes (used); Collector's audio recording—102 minutes
Highlights: Vicki (Maureen O'Brien) leaves the series at the end of this story to be replaced (temporarily) by Katarina (Adrienne Hill). The Narrator of the CD version is Peter Purves.

Errors and Other Points of Interest

Episode 1: Temple of Secrets
First Transmitted: Oct. 16, 1965

6:41 (CD-1, track 5, 0:16) To refute problems claimed by some viewers, Steven looks for suitable clothes. **17:39 (CD-1, track 11, 1:27)** The Doctor has some trouble with his lines. **18:30 (CD-1, track 11, 2:18)** Agamemnon (Francis de Wolff) does not catch the Doctor's mistake. If the Doctor is Zeus, why should he worry about dying? **22:05 (CD-1, track 14, 0:08)** Odysseus (Ivor Salter) claims Steven is a Trojan spy.

Episode 2: Small Prophet, Quick Return
First Transmitted: Oct. 23, 1965

1:07 (CD-1, track 17, 0:18) Odysseus claims that both Steven and the Doctor are Trojan spies. Odysseus is so certain of this he wants to kill the two travelers. **6:41 (CD-1, track 19, 0:03)** Again, to refute problems claimed by some viewers, a traveler, Vicki this time, looks for appropriate clothing. **12:28 (CD-1, track 21, 3:16)** Vicki becomes Cressida. **15:41 (CD-1, track 22, 1:30)** Steven suggests to Odysseus that he, Steven, should go to Troy. Earlier, Odysseus suspected Steven of being a Trojan spy. Why would Odysseus allow a suspected spy (Steven) to go to Troy?

Episode 3: Death of a Spy
First Transmitted: Oct. 30, 1965
11:22 (CD-2, track 5, 1:18) The Doctor describes the horse as 40 feet tall. **13:11 (CD-2, track 7, 0:28)** Odysseus describes the horse as 40 feet tall. This proves Odysseus knows the actual size of the horse. **24:38 (CD-2, track 16, 2:01)** Some viewers consider the exchange at the end of this episode to be a blooper. Cassandra (Francis White) begins with "Woe to the Trojans." Paris (Barrie Ingham) follows with "I'm afraid you are a bit late to say 'Whoa' to the horse."

Episode 4: Horse of Destruction
First Transmitted: Nov. 6, 1965
1:43 (CD-2, track 20, 0:48) King Priam (Max Adrian) has trouble saying "better view." **6:37 (CD-2, track 25, 1:05)** King Priam has more trouble with his lines as he attempts to say "Square of Oratory." **8:02 (CD-2, track 26, 0:48)** Odysseus tells the Doctor if he tries to leave the horse, the Doctor will fall 40 feet. How is this possible unless the Doctor climbs from the horse's "stomach" to the very top of the horse before leaping? The top of the horse is 40 feet, not the bottom of the "stomach."

(V) The Daleks' Master Plan

Writers: Terry Nation and Dennis Spooner; **Director:** Douglas Camfield

Media: Commercial DVD — *Lost in Time* — Episodes 2, 5, and 10 (used); Commercial 5 CD set — 293 minutes (used) (including a 2 minute prolog connecting to *The Myth Makers*), with *Mission to the Unknown*; Commercial tape — *Daleks — The Early Years* — excerpts, and Episodes 5 and 10; Collector's audio tape — 292 minutes; Excerpts are present in the tape "*The Missing Years*" packaged with "*The Edge of Destruction.*"
Highlights: The "Brigadier" first appears as Bret Vyon. Katarina steps out of the series in the fourth episode. Sara Kingdom (Jean Marsh) becomes a temporary companion. The Narrator of the CD set is Peter Purves.
Questions: Why does the Monk (Peter Butterworth) not escape when he returns to his ship after the Daleks threaten him?

Errors and Other Points of Interest

Episode 1: The Nightmare Begins
First Transmitted: Nov. 13, 1965
5:37 (CD-2, track 5, 2:49) The year is 4000. According to *Mission to the Unknown* this is 1000 years after the Dalek Invasion. **15:11 (CD-2, track 10, 0:17)** Bret Vyon's (Nicholas Courtney) leaving the key in the TARDIS door is a stretch.

Episode 2: Day of Armageddon
First Transmitted: Nov. 20, 1965

0:59 (CD-2, track 21, 0:28) The Daleks inform Base Security about the TARDIS. **4:10 (CD-2, track 22, 2:06)** Zephon (Julian Sherrier) tells Mavic Chen (Kevin Stoney) that the Solar System is much more influential than its size would indicate. This is to refute the question posed by some viewers on how a single solar system is equal to entire galaxies. **5:30 (CD-2, track 23, 0:23)** The Daleks discuss the fact that they will eliminate all members of the alliance after they have served their purpose. They need Mavic Chen for the taranium, so they do not want to kill him until they get the mineral. **10:53 (CD-2, track 28, 0:17)** The Doctor refers to the Dalek invasion in the year 2157. This is the wrong year, based on *The Dalek Invasion of Earth*.

Episode 3: Devil's Planet
First Transmitted: Nov. 27, 1965

8:31 (CD-2, track 49, 1:18) The Doctor asks Bret Vyon for something to play magnetic tape. There is a claim that the use of magnetic tape is an anachronism. This is a future anachronism, and, therefore, is not a true problem. **9:50 (CD-2, track 49, 2:37)** The message on the tape recording is not the message recorded in *Mission to the Unknown*. The recording goes, "This is Marc Corey, Special Security Agent, reporting from the planet Kembel. The Daleks are planning the complete destruction of our Galaxy together with the powers of the outer Galaxies a war force is being assembled...." There are incorrect reports attributing this to Episode 1. **11:55 (CD-2, track 52, 0:56)** The Daleks seem to have forgotten about the TARDIS when they question Mavic Chen.

Episode 4: The Traitors
First Transmitted: Dec. 4, 1965

2:47 (CD-3, track 3, 0:53) The Daleks destroy the pursuit ship when the crew failed in their mission. A Dalek makes the comment, just after we hear the order to destroy the ship, "We will not tolerate mistakes." **4:11 (CD-3, track 4, 1:14)** The Doctor yells to Bret Vyon, "Take him back to Kendal!" The Doctor corrects this to "Kembel." **4:45 (CD-3, track 5, 0:00)** Katarina leaves the series. She is the first companion to die.

Episode 5: Counter Plot
First Transmitted: Dec. 11, 1965

3:25 Some fans have trouble with the fact that during cellular dissemination the Doctor gurns. **12:24 (CD-3, track 35, 1:05)** Ford Prefect might find exception to the Doctor's comment, "The mice couldn't have done that." **13:49** The Visians on Mira are apparently relatives of the "Creatures from the Id" on *Forbidden Planet* (Altair IV). **20:41** The camera shakes as Sara and Steven are talking.

Episode 6: Coronas of the Sun
First Transmitted: Dec. 18, 1965

2:30 (CD-3, track 49, 1:20) The Narrator notes that the Visians become visible when hit by the Daleks' fire. This is another similarity to the Creatures from the Id. **9:24 (CD-3, track 53, 1:52)** The Daleks send a rescue ship to Mira to save the stranded Daleks who were unsuccessful in capturing the Doctor. Why save the second group of failures?

Episode 7: The Feast of Steven
First Transmitted: Dec. 25, 1965

1:17 (CD-4, track 3, 0:14) Some fans have trouble with the TARDIS appearing outside the Police Station. They feel it would look out of place. No one comments on it being out of place, and the Narrator even comments that the TARDIS looks at home outside the Police Station. **4:50 (CD-4, track 8, 0:30)** In the police station, the Doctor says to one of the people, "Haven't I seen your face before somewhere...? Yes, of course, I remember now, yes, the Market Place at Jaffa." This in reference to the actor (Reg Pritchard) being in an earlier story, *The Crusade*. **7:53 (CD-4, track 13, 0:13)** The Doctor says, "Time And Relative Dimensions In Space." **23:46 (CD-4, track 30, 0:34)** Some viewers consider the Doctor's Christmas greeting a blooper. It is not. If it were not intentional, significant editing would be present.

Episode 8: Volcano
First Transmitted: Jan. 1, 1966

10:05 (CD-4, track 39, 0:02) After the TARDIS takes off from the cricket field, the Doctor refers to what they saw as "some sporting event." Apparently, the Doctor does not know what cricket is. **18:29 (CD-4, track 46, 0:41)** The Doctor uses his ring to help open the TARDIS doors. After many stories, the ring is again important. **23:29 (CD-4, track 52, 0:05)** The Dalek time machine is now traveling. This repeats in the reprise.

Episode 9: Golden Death
First Transmitted: Jan. 8, 1966

3:02 (CD-4, track 57, 0:26) Steven notes that the other time machine is still registering. Apparently, they do not detect both the Monk's TARDIS and the Dalek's machine. There are claims that this is a blooper, but the explanation comes later. **4:54 (CD-4, track 59, 0:00)** The Dalek time machine materializes. **5:29 (CD-4, track 59, 0:34)** Continuing with the earlier false blooper, Sara reports that the ship following them no longer appears on the time curve indicator. This is as the Dalek's ship lands, and the Monk's TARDIS is still traveling, undetected. **10:24 (CD-4, track 65, 0:57)** The Monk's TARDIS lands in Egypt. **20:59 (CD-4, track 73, 1:25)** The Monk explains why the Doctor could not detect him. This "eliminates" the earlier blooper claim. However, the explanation is technobabble.

Episode 10: Escape Switch
First Transmitted: Jan. 15, 1966

1:46 The studio lights reflect from the sarcophagus lid. **6:12** There is a boom mike shadow on top of the Dalek on the right. **9:06** The relative sizes and positions of the pyramids appear to be incorrect. **12:18 (CD-5, track 10, 1:28)** The Doctor arranges a rendezvous at the west angle of the Great Pyramid. One of the interesting facts about the Great Pyramid is its nearly perfect alignment with respect to compass directions. There is a west side, a southwest angle, and a northwest angle. **12:32** The Dalek entering the machine bumps into the stationary Dalek. **17:36 (CD-5, track 16, 0:15)** The Doctor goofs saying, "Magic ... Mavic Chen."

Episode 11: The Abandoned Planet
First Transmitted: Jan. 22, 1966

8:31 (CD-5, track 27, 0:23) Why did the Varga plants go? Are the Daleks such considerate gardeners? **12:36 (CD-5, track 31, 0:07)** The Dalek Supreme announces that it is time to eliminate the alliance. The Daleks needed an alliance so they could infiltrate the other powers in the Universe. After they have all the leaders in their control, they plan to kill the leaders to eliminate any organized opposition. Some viewers have a problem with the elimination of the Alliance. These viewers feel that if the Daleks planned to eliminate the alliance, why create it? **14:02 (CD-5, track 33, 0:25)** Some viewers ask — what is the logic behind the Daleks abandoning their base on Kembel? This abandonment not only includes the base, but also the Daleks' time machine. A simple firing squad could eliminate the Galactic Council. The problem with this question is that it imposes Earth psychology onto an alien species.

Episode 12: Destruction of Time
First Transmitted: Jan. 29, 1966

11:27 (CD-5, track 51, 0:14) The alarm starts. **11:35 (CD-5, track 52, 0:00)** The considerate Daleks turn the alarm down so it will be easier to hear the Doctor and Sara talking. **12:56 (CD-5, track 54, 0:00)** Why is the alarm no longer sounding? **15:16 (CD-5, track 59, 1:16)** Sara dies. Some fans consider Sara to be a full-fledged companion. If Sara is a companion this is the first time the Doctor caused a companion to die. (The Doctor did not have any control over Katarina's death.) Sara lasted longer than Katarina.

Comments: The Doctor defeats the Daleks again. The Doctor saves the Earth along with the Universe.

(W) THE MASSACRE OF ST. BARTHOLOMEW'S EVE

Alternate Title: *The Massacre*

Writer: John Lucarotti and Donald Tosh; **Director:** Paddy Russell

Media: Commercial 2 CD set — episodic version —100 minutes (used); Collector's audio recording —100 minutes
Highlights: Dodo Chaplet (Jackie Lane) joins the series at the end of the last episode. William Hartnell, as the Abbot of Amboise, refutes those people who say he always has trouble with his lines. The Narrator of the CD is Peter Purves.
Questions: Are Dodo and Anne Chaplet (Annette Robertson) related?

Errors and Other Points of Interest

There is noticeable tape print-through at various points. This is especially noticeable in the last episode.

There are incorrect reports that the tocsin bell sounds at the beginning and end of each episode. Proof of this error is in this listing.

Episode 1: War of God
First Transmitted: Feb. 5, 1966

0:44 (CD-1, track 2, 0:00) There is no tocsin bell at the beginning of this episode. **3:01 (CD-1, track 2, 2:17)** The Doctor and Steven reenter the TARDIS to get appropriate clothes. Finally, the TARDIS has a wardrobe. **6:17 (CD-1, track 3, 3:04)** The Doctor has trouble talking. **10:48 (CD-1, track 4, 1:37)** The Doctor, while talking to Preslin (Erik Chitty), refers to the microscope as a machine; all true scientists would refer to it as an instrument. **22:55 (CD-1, track 14, 2:28)** The tocsin bell sounds before the end of this episode.

Episode 2: The Sea Beggar
First Transmitted: Feb. 12, 1966

0:40 (CD-1, track 17, 0:00) There is no tocsin bell. **13:26 (CD-1, track 23, 0:00)** Many viewers object to Anne's accent. **21:38 (CD-1, track 27, 0:52)** The tocsin bell sounds one scene before the end of this episode.

Episode 3: Priest of Death
First Transmitted: Feb. 19, 1966

0:43 (CD-2, track 2, 0:00) There is no tocsin bell. Anne mentions that she already heard the bell. **9:51 (CD-2, track 7, 0:02)** William Hartnell's performance at this point demonstrates that he can get through a scene without having problems with his lines. This refutes the claim by some viewers that everything Hartnell said was a blooper. **22:47 (CD-2, track 15, 0:00)** There is no tocsin bell in the last scene.

Episode 4: Bell of Doom
First Transmitted: Feb. 26, 1966

0:44 (CD-2, track 17, 0:00) It is late morning, thus, it is too late for the tocsin bell to sound at the beginning of this episode. **2:46 (CD-2, track 17, 2:02)** Why does Steven believe the Doctor must have changed his clothes before going to the Abbott's house? The Doctor already was already wearing period clothes. **14:36 (CD-2, track 23, 1:07)** The tocsin bell sounds long before the end of the episode. **19:10 (CD-2, track 24, 2:56)** The Doctor's speech near the end supposedly terminated because the Doctor forgot his lines. This occurrence is not obvious in this version of the story. The problem may be obvious on viewing. **20:04 (CD-2, track 24, 3:50)** The Doctor refers to Chesterton as "Checkerton." Some fans claim the Doctor said "Chatterton." **22:02 (CD-2, track 26, 0:55)** The Doctor uses the phrase "Time And Relative Dimensions In Space." **24:15 (CD-2, track 26, 3:09)** Steven asks the Doctor if Dodo Chaplet is a descendent of Anne Chaplet. The Doctor says that it is "very possible." We never learn if the two are related. This avoids the problem of last names — if Anne had a child, would the infant have the same last name.

Pause to Consider: The First Doctor and His Lines

There are many Hartnell "bloopers" attributed to his missing his lines. Some of these "mistakes" may be, in reality, part of his characterization of the Doctor. Compare Hartnell's portrayal of the Abbot of Amboise in *The Massacre* to his normal character of the Doctor. The "mistakes" have disappeared. In *The Three Doctors*, after being out of character for a time, he does not use the same characterization of the Doctor as he did during his time as the Doctor, and he still has no trouble with his lines. Viewers should realize, all the Doctors flub more lines than their companions do because the Doctors always have more lines. Comparison of the First Doctor to later actors may be unfair for another reason. By the 1970s, if not earlier, the actors learned to follow a flubbed line with something that would require the scene to be reshot. Thus, later actors were able to get their flubs replaced, but the First Doctor flubs remained.

(X) THE ARK

Writers: Paul Erikson and Lesley Scott; **Director:** Michael Imison

Media: Commercial tape — episodic version — 98 minutes (used); Collector's tape movie version — 92 minutes

Questions: The travelers in the Ark are wearing the same clothing styles after 700 years. How are we supposed to believe the people on the Ark are Earthlings?

Errors and Other Points of Interest

Episode 1: The Steel Sky
First Transmitted: Mar. 5, 1966

1:52 The light on top of the TARDIS does not flash during the landing. **4:53** These are some examples showing the Commander (Eric Elliott) apparently wearing bad dentures. **5:21** The badly fitting dentures may explain why the Commander has trouble saying, "approximately." **9:35** When the Doctor notices Dodo's unusual choice of clothing, he says, "Have you been fruiting about in my wardrobe?" **12:03** The camera shakes significantly. **14:55** The Commander asks the Doctor, "You travel in that black box?" This implies that the TARDIS is black and not blue. **17:49** The Commander knows about the Trojan War, Nero, and the Daleks. **18:44** It seems unusual that the Commander knows about Nero and the Trojan War, but has never heard of the Ark. **20:04** As the Monoid begins backing through the doorway, someone inside quickly moves a box out of view. **20:49** After the Monoid drives into the room, a boom mike shadow appears on the right wall. **22:50** For the climax of the episode, Zentos (Inigo Jackson) says, "Take them into custody and later they will be made to suffer for the crime that they have committed." The wording is different in the reprise at the beginning of the next episode.

Episode 2: The Plague
First Transmitted: Mar. 12, 1966

0:28 Between the fading of the opening credits and the appearance of Zentos, there is a spoken cue. **0:30** Zentos gives a slightly different speech in the reprise. "Take them into custody and later they will be made to answer for the crime that they have committed." His "new" speech includes "...they will be made to *answer* for the crime...." **3:53** The operator misjudges the position as the camera moves in for the close-up. **7:20** We hear a loud crack as Mellium's (Kate Newman) picture jumps on the monitor. **14:17** Some fans claim, that Baccu (Ian Frost) tried to put his hands into his pants pockets before he realizes that he has no pants. He may just be resting his hands on his hips. **16:10** Mellium, and others, pull down their protective masks to speak their lines. Obviously talking is more important than protecting their lives. **16:12** The Doctor incorrectly advises the people to keep the fever patients (beginning with Steven) warm. **17:29** A loud screech sounds offstage; it even startles the actors. **17:49** A large squarish object, perhaps another camera, makes an abbreviated appearance at the right edge of the screen. **20:25** When Steven begins to get better the Doctor says, "The fever's down and the temperature's dropped." This is a little redundant.

Episode 3: The Return
First Transmitted: Mar. 19, 1966

4:43 The reflection of part of the studio crew appears on the monitor. You can see at least one of the production crew move his hand. **5:44** As Dodo defends their past actions to Monoid 1 (Edmund Coulter), a loud crash sounds as she says, "find a cure." **11:38** Before an observant fan reports this — the "dead" man is still breathing. **12:56** The string supporting the launcher is obvious. **14:28** The Refusian demonstrates the operation of the door. Moving the center lever down will close the door. Moving the center lever up will open the door. **14:52** A studio light reflects off Monoid 2's (Ralph Carrigan) collar. **16:23** Monoid 2 stumbles down the step when entering the room.

Episode 4: The Bomb
First Transmitted: Mar. 26, 1966

1:58 Monoid 4 (John Caesar) is talking to another Monoid at the right of the screen. The Monoid on the right does not look like Patrick McGoohan. **5:02** A boom mike appears above Maharis (Terence Woodfield) as Monoid 1 dismisses him. **7:55** The strings on the launchers are obvious. **7:56** The reflection of a camera appears in the monitor. **13:02** There is a large boom mike shadow on the back wall. **17:49** Unlike the earlier demonstration, moving the center lever down opens the door. **19:37** Now, when the lever moves down the door closes. **20:00** There is a boom mike shadow on the wall as the Refusian offers to help move the statue. **21:13** The explosion takes place near the head, but not within the statue where the bomb was located. **21:37** The center Monoid has a boom mike shadow on its chest.

Comments: Indirectly the Doctor saves the Earth. However, this time it is not the planet, but the people.

(Y) The Celestial Toymaker

Writers: Brian Hayles and Donald Tosh; **Director:** Bill Sellars

Media: Commercial DVD — *Lost in Time* — Episode 4 only — 24 minutes (used); Commercial 2 CD set — episodic version — 98 minutes (used) (there is an additional prolog (nearly 2 minutes) segment covering the end of the preceding story.); Commercial tape — *The Hartnell Years* — episode 4 only — 24 minutes (used) (times include an M); Collector's audio recording — 97 minutes
Highlight: The Narrator of the CD is Peter Purves.
Questions: Is the Toymaker an Eternal?

Errors and Other Points of Interest

Episode 1: The Celestial Toyroom
First Transmitted: Apr. 2, 1966

4:07 (CD-1, track 7, 1:07) The Doctor has difficulty saying Celestial Toymaker. **7:54 (CD-1, track 7, 4:54)** The Toymaker (Michael Gough) has trouble with his line as he utters, "have you have you."

Episode 2: The Hall of Dolls
First Transmitted: Apr. 9, 1966

1:28 (CD-1, track 14, 0:58) The Narrator (Peter Purves) describes the set. He notes that there is a sign on the door reading, "Pull to Open." **2:00 (CD-1, track 15, 0:27)** Steven cannot open the door. Dodo suggests, "Let's pull instead." Apparently, they had been pushing on a door with a sign saying pull.

Episode 3: The Dancing Floor
First Transmitted: Apr. 16, 1966

2:15 (CD-2, track 4, 0:41) Why do the dolls follow Steven and Dodo if they are just going to stop? **20:13 (CD-2, track 13, 0:15)** The Toymaker says there will be one or two more games. How can the Toymaker not know exactly how many games remain?

Episode 4: The Final Test
First Transmitted: Apr. 23, 1966

2:17 Note the position of the game pieces. **2:29 (2:28 M)** The alignment of the game pieces varies in different scenes. The game pieces are in line with the black triangles when the Doctor's hand plays the Trilogic game. The speeded-up sequences no longer have the pieces aligned with the triangles. This occurs at other times in the story, but only the occurrences in this episode remain. **8:17 (CD-2, track 22, 1:42)** After Cyril (Peter Stephens) finishes his turn, Dodo asks whose turn is it, and Steven says it is his, but Dodo's turn comes after Cyril's turn. **11:14** The camera suddenly changes position after Dodo says, "That's red ink!" **11:18 (CD-2, track 24, 1:30)** Cyril flubs his line when telling Dodo to go back to the start. **11:33 (CD-2, track 24, 1:46)** Cyril falls off one of the pedestals and dies. It has been argued that this should not occur because he was not grounded (this is why birds can sit on power lines without being killed). This would be true if Cyril fell directly onto the floor. We do not see exactly how Cyril falls. If he landed directly on the floor (we only see where he fell after the electric shock) this is a blooper; however, grounding would occur if he touched anything else while he was touching the floor. **15:54** There is a plethora of shadows in nearly every scene in the game room. In this case, there is an obvious boom mike shadow on the front of the monitor. **18:11** As the camera shifts to show the Doctor's entrance — the column of the TARDIS moves down. The column moves later even though the TARDIS is not in flight.

(Z) THE GUNFIGHTERS

Writer: Donald Cotton; **Director:** Rex Tucker

Media: Commercial tape — episodic version — 96 minutes (used); Collector's tape — movie version — 90 minutes (used)
Highlights: Mr. Wearp.

Errors and Other Points of Interest

Some fans have problems with the song, in particular the line "earning your gunfighter's wings." This line came from World War I (airplanes). This line is an anachronism.

Episode 1: A Holiday for the Doctor
First Transmitted: Apr. 30, 1966

0:30M In general, the movie versions include the name of the story. In this case, the title of the first episode (*A Holiday for the Doctor*) is present, but instead of the story title. **1:07** Some fans find fault with the amazing accents of the actors. **2:59** After learning that they have landed in the Old West, the Doctor mutters, "Fat chance I've got of finding a dentist in the Middle West ... Wild West." **6:36** Seth Harper (Shane Rimmer) is sitting wrong. No gunfighter, especially one expecting Doc Holliday, would ever sit with his back to the door. Just ask Wild Bill Hickok. **6:46** The "western" accents could be better. Combined with remembering their lines, the actors have additional difficulties. For example, when Phineas Clanton (Maurice Good) says, "Now let's get this straight. You mean you don't know where Holliday ... y-you never met Holliday either?" **10:30** The Doctor introduces himself to Bat Masterson (Richard Beale) as Dr. Caligari. Bat replies "Doctor Who?" to which the Doctor answers, "Yes, quite right." Apparently, the TARDIS is the cabinet of Dr. Caligari. **14:46** "I never touch alcohol," says the Doctor. This did not stop him in earlier stories, such as his enjoyment of mead in *The Time Meddler*. **20:47** To Doc Holliday's farewell "Goodbye and good luck," the Doctor replies, "The same to you and many of them!" If the Doctor is still suffering from having his tooth pulled, this could give an explanation. **21:32** Some observers claim the first two episodes have the quietest gunshots. This is an example of one. The Commercial version seems to have this problem partially fixed.

Episode 2: Don't Shoot the Pianist
First Transmitted: May 7, 1966

6:05 The camera shakes and there is a squeak as Steven starts the get the Clanton gang's guns. **12:50** The reflection of a camera appears in the window. **14:12** After Wyatt Earp (John Alderson) sits in the chair, the camera focusing on him bobs up and down.

Episode 3: Johnny Ringo
First Transmitted: May 14, 1966

3:55 The camera shakes as Charlie (David Graham), the bartender, tells Ike (William Hurndall) and Billy (David Cole) Clanton about the death of Seth Harper. **14:54** When Doc Holliday (Anthony Jacobs) is explaining his change of plans to Kate (Sheena Marshe), he has trouble with his lines: "For the first time in my life, I have just been taken — beaten ... to the draw." **17:53** When the Doctor tells of Steven's sojourn with Ringo (Laurence Payne), Mr. Wearp says to the Doctor, "You mean

Regret has gone after Holliday alone?" The Doctor replies, "No, no, my dear marshal, no, she's gone with a young man by the name of Ringo." **22:35** The light outside the door blows out as the Clantons enter the jail.

Episode 4: The O.K. Corral
First Transmitted: May 21, 1966

3:51 There is a boom mike shadow on Wyatt Earp's shirt. **15:35** Johnny Ringo tells the Clantons to begin firing before the Earps get into range. This would lead to a large number of missed shots. This would explain the fault many people have claimed about the number of shots fired. **17:09** The Earps are obviously not on the Earth. Wyatt casts three shadows, so there must be three suns in the sky. **17:19** The Clantons begin firing—and missing. **22:43** The final credits list "Next Episode: *Dr. Who and the Savages*," instead of *The Savages*.

Comments: This is the last story to use separate titles for each of the episodes.

For those who are interested in historic accuracy, Johnny Ringo, and Ike, Billy and Phineas Clanton were not the group at the O.K. Corral. The people killed were Billy Clanton, and Frank and Tom McLaury.

(AA) THE SAVAGES

Writer: Ian Stuart Black; **Director:** Christopher Barry

Media: Commercial 2-CD set—episodic version—101 minutes (used); Collector's audio recording—episodic version—93 minutes
Highlights: Steven Taylor (Peter Purves) leaves the series at the end of this story. Peter Purves narrates the CD version this story.

Errors and Other Points of Interest

Episode 1
First Transmitted: May 28, 1966

5:18 (CD-1, track 5, 1:22) Captain Edal (Peter Thomas) explains to the Doctor that the Elders have been "plotting the course of your space-time vehicle for many light years." Apparently, they are using "light years," incorrectly, as a time unit instead of a distance unit. **8:19 (CD-1, track 7, 0:26)** Jano (Frederick Jaeger) mentions "charts of space and time." This appears to be technobabble. **8:44 (CD-1, track 7, 0:50)** Jano tells the Doctor that they charted the TARDIS voyages in space and time. Many viewers, in later stories, cite that it is not possible to track the TARDIS.

Episode 2
First Transmitted: June 4, 1966

11:42 (CD-1, track 42, 0:52) Why are Jano and Edal so concerned if they know they are "right"? **14:06 (CD-1, track 43, 2:03)** One of the often-cited errors in this story is, why do the savages remain near the city when it would be safer for them to move? At this point Edal states that the savage the Doctor had been helping "should be on the Reserve...." This implies that the movements of the savages are restricted so they cannot simply move out of the area.

Episode 3
First Transmitted: June 11, 1966

5:20 (CD-2, track 7, 0:13) Chal (Ewen Solon) informs Steven and Dodo another reason why the Savages do not leave the vicinity of the city. He tells the companions that they are on an island. Do not forget that the ability to create things, such as boats, has been removed from the Savages minds over the years. **20:25 (CD-2, track 18, 0:54)** Compare Jano's impersonation of the Doctor to the "impersonation" of the Doctor in *The Chase*.

Episode 4
First Transmitted: June 18, 1966

9:42 (CD-2, track 40, 1:08) The Doctor and Steven discuss the destruction of the apparatus. Are we to believe that it would not be possible to rebuild the apparatus? Is this the only machine on the entire planet? This story is on an island. Are there no other islands or continents? **22:29 (CD-2, track 51, 1:49)** Jano also makes the mistake of using "light year" as a time unit instead of a distance unit when tells the Doctor, "for many light years we looked forward to your arrival."

Comments: The Commercial version is significantly longer than the Collector's version. This is apparently due to additional time used for the linking narration.

In both movies and in TV stories many writers incorrectly use "light years" as time units. The occurrences in this story are not as bad as many others; the incorrect usages almost fit. As a check for appropriateness, it should be possible to replace "light year" with any other distance unit and have the line make sense. Try replacing "light years" with a time unit, such as hours or minutes. If the line still makes sense, then "light years" is incorrect.

Comments: The Doctor "saves" an unnamed planet.

(BB)   THE WAR MACHINES

Writer: Ian Stuart Black; **Director:** Michael Ferguson

Media: Commercial tape — episodic version — 94 minutes (used); Collector's tape movie version — 87 minutes
Highlights: Dodo leaves the series after the second episode. Polly (Anneke Wills) and Ben Jackson (Michael Craze) join the series in the first episode.
Questions: Why are there so many explosives? They are never used.

Errors and Other Points of Interest

There have been many explanations as to why Wotan uses the name Doctor Who. There will be no attempt to discuss all of them here.

Episode 1
First Transmitted: June 6, 1966

2:05 On seeing the Post Office Tower, the Doctor says, "There's something about that tower — I can scent it." Dodo's reply is "Smells okay to me." Some observers consider the Doctor's statement to be a blooper. Dodo's reply makes the Doctor's comment an unlikely blooper. **5:54** Wotan prints out the square root of 17422 as 131.993 instead of 131.992, the correct value. **6:23** Dodo reads Wotan's printout: "Time And Relative Dimensions In Space." **6:45** As Dodo says, "just a buzzing in the ears," the camera bobs up and down. **10:44** The Post Office Tower opened in 1966, and the story supposedly takes place in that year. In a news conference,

Sir Charles Summer (William Mervyn) gives the date of Monday 16 July. This date would refer to 1962 or 1973. In 1966, July 16 was a Saturday. **23:03** Not a true blooper, but this (and a numerous later times) is where WOTAN first refers to the Doctor as Doctor Who. Some of the controlled people also say Doctor Who.

Episode 2
First Transmitted: July 2, 1966

4:30 As the Tramp (Roy Godfrey) searches his pockets for the taxi fare, the camera shakes; this occurs again after the cab leaves. **6:58** The crates brought into the "secret" warehouse have a large "W" on them (presumably referring to WOTAN). If the work is supposed to be a secret, why announce it with conspicuous labels on the boxes? **8:14** When the Tramp enters the warehouse, his detection is very quick, an alarm sounds, and his exact location is given. **10:56** The Doctor apparently has trouble with his lines. This begins with "I wonder, Sir Charles, do you suppose...." **21:00** After the Doctor explains, "I don't think you will arouse so much suspicion as the police might," there is a loud sound offstage. **21:50** Ben is able to enter and wander about, no alarm sounds, and he is detected only by accident. What happened to the alarms tripped when the Tramp entered?

Episode 3
First Transmitted: July 9, 1966

0:22 During the reprise from the preceding episode the number on the war machine keeps changing number "9" to number "3." This could be an attempt to show that tests were taking place in more than one location, but the locations do not look different. **6:07** Why allow Ben to live without being hypnotized? **21:21** As the soldiers start to run away after throwing their grenades, a door on the side of the War Machine starts to open.

Episode 4
First Transmitted: July 16, 1966

4:02 A proposed blooper begins here. As the Doctor passes his cloak over to Ben, something falls out and we hear it hit the ground. Some people incorrectly claim that the Doctor's cloak knocks the end off the war machine's gun. Other people claim the TARDIS key accidentally fell out of the cloak pocket. Supposedly, Ben tries to give the object back to the Doctor, but cannot get his attention and simply puts the object on the gun arm. However, what really happens is that it is not clear exactly what the item is that falls on the ground. Ben picks it up and then starts to put the object on the gun; however, he stops and keeps it. This may not be a blooper. **5:55** As the Doctor stands after examining the war machine, he hits his head on the machine. **16:46** Someone was late in remembering to turn on the antenna on the top of the war machine. **18:46** Some people have cited the appearance of the war machine at the top of the tower to be a possible blooper. From the presence of some of the equipment in the room, there must be a large freight lift somewhere. **21:46** We see that Ben is putting something in his pocket earlier — now we find that it was not a blooper, but a plot device. Ben needs to have the TARDIS key to return it to the Doctor at this time. If Ben did not have the key at this point, Polly could not take it and let the two new companions into the TARDIS. **22:15** The light on top of the TARDIS does not flash during takeoff.

Comments: The Doctor saves the Earth again.

Unlike previous companions, Dodo simply disappears.

(CC) The Smugglers

Writer: Brain Hayles; **Director:** Julia Smith

Media: Commercial 2-CD set — episodic version — 99 minutes (used); Collector's audio recording — episodic version — 98 minutes; Excerpts are present in the tape *The Missing Years* packaged with *The Edge of Destruction*.
Highlight: The Narrator of the CD version is Anneke Wills.

Errors and Other Points of Interest

Episode 1
First Transmitted: Sept. 10, 1966
1:57 (CD-1, track 2, 0:59) The Doctor tells Ben and Polly, "…you see that scanner? That's what I call a scanner, up there!" The Doctor is very irked because of Ben and Polly entering the TARDIS; thus it is not surprising that he is talking down to them. This explanation is an alternative to the simple blooper of the Doctor having trouble with his lines. **3:08 (CD-1, track 3, 0:21)** After they have left the TARDIS, Ben turns back and asks the Doctor what he is doing. To this the Doctor replies, "I never leave it unlocked." **7:07 (CD-1, track 6, 0:12)** When offered brandy the Doctor utters, "No, we don't touch it." This is in accord with the Doctor refusing to drink alcoholic beverages at other times. **10:26 (CD-1, track 7, 0:42)** Joseph Longfoot (Terence de Marney), the Churchwarden, gives the initial rhyme: "This is Deadman's secret key. Smallwood, Ringwood, Gurney." This is the only time we hear this version of the rhyme. Some viewers claim that the Doctor changed the rhyme each time he repeated it. This is not true; in addition, the Doctor's rhyme, not this one, is consistent with the rest of the story. **24:36 (CD-1, track 23, 0:30)** The Narrator describes Pike (Michael Godfrey) raising his right arm to reveal a barbed hook. This refutes the claims by some fans that it is Pike's left hand.

Episode 2
First Transmitted: Sept. 17, 1966
6:05 (CD-1, track 28, 1:32) The Doctor answers Captain Pike's comment, "Let us talk together like gentlemen — eh Doctor," with "Thank you no." **6:52 (CD-1, track 28, 2:19)** The Doctor drinks and enjoys the wine (Madeira). In earlier stories, and earlier in this story, he stated that he does not touch alcohol.

Episode 3
First Transmitted: Sept. 24, 1966
20:22 (CD-2, track 20, 0:20) According to the Doctor, the rhyme is "…Deadman's secret key. Ringwood, Smallbeer, and Gurney." The Doctor, Ben and Polly go on to find grave markers in the crypt with these three names. This rhyme is consistent with the story." **21:04 (CD-2, track 20, 1:01)** Polly, Ben, and the Doctor find, in order, Ringwood, Gurney, and Smallbeer. This confirms the names. There is no Smallwood, so apparently, the blooper was with the first telling of the rhyme, and Longfoot, not the Doctor, created the blooper.

Episode 4
First Transmitted: Oct. 1, 1966
2:12 (CD-2, track 26, 0:14) The Doctor uses the same rhyme: "… Deadman's secret key. Ringwood, Smallbeer, and Gurney." Cherub (George A. Cooper) confirms each of the names. **15:18 (CD-2, track 38,**

0:06) The Doctor repeats the names from the rhyme (no attempt is made to repeat the rhyme), and the markers are found in the crypt.

(DD) The Tenth Planet

Writers: Kit Pedler and Gerry Davis; **Director:** Derek Martinus

Media: Commercial tape — episodic version with a reconstruction of episode 4 — 94 minutes (used); Commercial 2-CD set — Episodic version — 96 minutes (used); Collectors' audio recording — 94 minutes; Excerpts are present in the tape "*The Missing Years*" packaged with "*The Edge of Destruction.*" Excerpts also appear in *Cybermen — The Early Years.*

Highlights: The First Doctor (William Hartnell) becomes the Second Doctor (Patrick Troughton). Anneke Wills narrates the CD version.

Meet the Cybermen, but do not try to read their lips.

Errors and Other Points of Interest

People have reported some concern about blizzards in Antarctica (one example listed). Blizzards are very rare near the South Pole. Only the outside scenes with actors show anything approaching blizzard conditions. When models are used, there is no blowing snow. The explanation could be in the American Sergeant's (John Brandon) comments on the blowing snow — he does not say it is snowing. This could mean that no new snow is falling, therefore no blizzard is occurring.

Some viewers report that in either the closing credits for the first or the third episode the music credits read "THEME MUSIC BYRON GRAINER," instead of crediting the music to Ron Grainer. This blooper does not appear in any of the closing credits. In all cases, the closing credits read "TITLE MUSIC BY RON GRAINER...." The other credit errors were present, thus it is unlikely that this is the only one corrected for this release. Apparently these viewers missed the space between "BY" and "RON."

Episode 1
First Transmitted: Oct. 8, 1966

0:50 Some viewers incorrectly report that the credits at the end of the episode misspell Kit Pedler's name as Kitt. The error, besides the misspelling, is that Kit Pedler's incorrect name appears in the opening credits. This only occurs in the first episode. **1:56 (CD-1, track 3, 0:53)** Doctor Barclay (David Dodimead) says there is a blizzard. This is the only actual mention of a blizzard. **2:50 (CD-1, track 6, 2:55)** The American Sergeant comments on the blowing snow. He does not mention a blizzard. **2:59** There is a substantial amount of blowing snow. This may or may not represent a blizzard. **3:23 (CD-1, track 7, 0:24)** There is no TARDIS landing sound. It is possible that the wind covers the sound. **4:06** The TARDIS light does not stop flashing. **4:42** A boom mike appears in the upper part of the screen. **8:34 (CD-1, track 13, 0:55)** The calendar shows December 1986. Thus, it is late spring or early summer. **10:32 (CD-1, track 14, 0:57)** The Astronauts, Williams and Schultz (Earl Cameron and Alan White), discover a "new" planet between Venus and Mars. Later they say that it looks familiar. There is currently a familiar looking planet between Venus and Mars; its name is the Earth. **16:26** Based on the time between the appearances of "South America," the length of a day on Mondas is seventeen seconds. If Mondas were the size of the Earth, a point at the equator would be moving at over five million miles an hour. **20:12** You should carefully note where the Cyberman spaceship lands. You should also note the lack of blowing snow. **21:51** The Cybermen wear parkas to pass for human. The units on their head make this a stretch in reality. **22:02** The Cybermen have "human" hands. **22:48** The closing credits correctly list "TITLE MUSIC BY RON GRANIER."

Episode 2
First Transmitted: Oct. 15, 1966

1:04 A boom mike appears in the top center of the screen. **2:33** There are no stars in space beyond Mondas. **4:31** The Cybermen begin talking before their mouths open. This continues throughout the story. **9:47** Someone's head enters the screen next to Ben's arm. **14:10 (CD-1, track 36, 3:02)** The discussion at this point, in part, refutes the claim by many that the Cybermen attack the Earth to get its energy. The energy drain is a natural phenomenon; the Cybermen wish to destroy the Earth before the energy transfer destroys Mondas. **15:27 (CD-1, track 37, 0:31)** There is a loud noise just after Ben turns off the light. **22:55** The closing credits correctly list "TITLE MUSIC BY RON GRANIER."

Episode 3
First Transmitted: Oct. 22, 1966

0:39 Gerry Davis appears in the opening credits as "Gerry Davies." **1:05** A boom mike shadow infects Ben's arm and hand. **3:19 (CD-2, track 4, 1:02)** The third of General Cutter's (Robert Beatty) points includes, "The Earth is being drained of its energy by this so-called planet Mondas — whatever it's called." **3:50** The camera shakes twice. **13:15 (CD-2, track 10, 0:34)** Barclay says that he cannot fit into the ventilation shaft, but as Ben goes through the shaft, it is obviously very large. It is possible that there are narrow sections not shown. **14:08** By repeating the footage, both Cyberman spaceships land in the same place (with the first ship having disappeared when the second ship lands). **14:44** During the first attack of the Cybermen outside the base, watch the Cyberman nearest the camera. As he looks around — one of his "earmuffs" dangles about wildly. Some fans claim, erroneously, that this occurs in Episode 1. **23:18** The closing credits correctly list "TITLE MUSIC BY RON GRANIER."

Episode 4
First Transmitted: Oct. 29, 1966

4:41 (CD-2, track 25, 4:22) The Doctor tells Ben, "We have no chance" instead of "We have no choice." **6:10** Polly enters the Cyberman spaceship. **17:15** One of the stills shows Polly in the Control Room — even though she is supposed to be a prisoner aboard the Cyberman ship. This is a problem with reconstructions and not a real blooper. **18:42 (CD-2, track 41, 2:13)** Barclay asks, "What is your fuel position?" **22:09 (CD-2, track 45, 0:38)** This is the first time we see the regeneration of a Time Lord. The sound of the TARDIS taking off accompanies the regeneration. **23:22** The closing credits correctly list "TITLE MUSIC BY RON GRANIER."

Comments: The fourth episode is a reconstruction. This is a more interesting product than the CD's. The audio only CD of this story is excellent like similar CD versions. The audio only recording apparently has a few additional sounds, which are probably not from the original transmission, so they are not present here as bloopers.

The Doctor meets and defeats the Cybermen. The Doctor saves the Earth.

II
THE SECOND DOCTOR

(EE) THE POWER OF THE DALEKS

Writer: David Whitaker; **Director:** Christopher Barry

Media: Commercial CD — episodic version — 150 minutes (used); Commercial audio tape — episodic version — 132 minutes (used) A "T" indicates times from this tape; Commercial tape — *Daleks — The Early Years* — Excerpts; Collector's audio recording — episodic version — 145 minutes

Highlights: The new Doctor appears, and continues the series. The Fourth Doctor's (Tom Baker) first person narration of the Commercial audio tape is an interesting approach. Anneke Wills narrates the CD version.

Questions: Do Daleks have the Time Lords' ability to recognize regenerated Time Lords? With all the mercury, why are there no "Mad Hatters"?

Errors and Other Points of Interest

The narration may cover or explain some of the bloopers.

There are reports that one of the Daleks has trouble passing through the arched doorway. This problem occurs in an excerpt. The exact position in the story cannot be determined.

There are attempts to disguise the fact that there are only four Daleks on the set. When a group of Daleks passes through a door, there is a break between the fourth Dalek and the "fifth." This sequence appears in *Daleks — The Early Years*, but the time and episode are uncertain.

There is an unconfirmed report that the use of a photograph of Daleks covers for the fact that there are only four Daleks available. This is not confirmable because of the loss of the video portion of these episodes.

Episode 1
First Transmitted: Nov. 5, 1966

4:09T The Narrator of the commercial tape mentions that the Doctor is now wearing checked pants; thus the Doctor's clothes, at least some of them, have regenerated. Some fans report this as a blooper; however, the First Doctor was wearing checked trousers at the end of *The Tenth Planet*. The descriptions both here, and later, imply that Patrick Troughton is shorter and slimmer than William Hartnell is. If the first regeneration includes clothing, then all regenerations where the Doctor's clothing does not change are bloopers. This time is for the Commercial audio tape. **5:28 (CD-1, track 2, 4:56)** The Doctor's ring no longer fits. This ring was important in *The Web Planet* and in *The Dalek's Master Plan*. **10:35 (CD-1, track 3, 2:49)** The Doctor mentions the name Vulcan, but it is not obvious, at this point, that the name refers to a planet. **13:03 (CD-1, track 5, 0:53)** As Quin (Nicholas Hawtrey) and Bragen (Bernard Archard) are talking, the first mention of the planet's name, Vulcan, is given. Some viewers incorrectly report that this story used the planet name Vulcan before *Star Trek*. *Star Trek* first aired on September 8, 1966, nearly two months before this story. **17:59 (CD-1, track 7, 2:27)** Hensell (Peter Bathurst) tells Bragen to get the Doctor and the companions some clothes. This refutes the claim by many viewers that no one ever notices the travelers' unusual clothing.

Episode 2
First Transmitted: Nov. 12, 1966

5:30 (CD-1, track 17, 1:34) Apparently, no one on Vulcan knows who or what the Daleks are. Thus, the story would seem to occur before *The Dalek Invasion of Earth*; however, the colony seems to be more advanced than the civilization indicated by the ruins in that story. **22:45 (CD-1, track 26, 1:54)** The Dalek recognizes the regenerated Doctor. Ben and Polly were unable to do this. Apparently, Daleks, like the Time Lords, can recognize regenerated individuals.

Episode 3
First Transmitted: Nov. 19, 1966

8:26 (CD-1, track 33, 0:27) Lesterson (Robert James) tells Janley (Pamela Ann Davy) that the Dalek has a positronic brain. This is one of David Whitaker's salutes to Isaac Asimov. **9:28 (CD-1, track 33, 1:09)** It is possible to hear coughing in the background while the Doctor and Lesterson are talking. This may not be a blooper, but a problem introduced by the Collector during the off-screen recording.

15:51 (CD-1, track 38, 0:40) Lesterson tells the Dalek that the computer detects "meteorite storms." Meteor storms may occur, but meteorite storms cannot.

Episode 4
First Transmitted: Nov. 26, 1966

1:48 (CD-2, track 2, 1:20) Lesterson now correctly refers to the computer as one that will detect "meteor storms." **4:24 (CD-2, track 3, 2:06)** The Doctor seems to be uncertain about how the Daleks can move around without metal floors (as in the original Dalek story); however, this implies that the Doctor has forgotten about their mobility in *The Dalek Invasion of Earth*. One explanation for this is that the Doctor's regeneration causes a memory loss. Memory loss does not seem to be apparent in other places. **6:21 (CD-2, track 4, 0:52)** Ben and the Doctor first notice there are four Daleks and not three Daleks on the base. Some fans consider this a blooper in the story. These fans believe that the Daleks must be incredibly stupid to make this mistake. This is an important plot point and not a blooper. **11:33 (CD-2, track 5, 4:24)** Janley does not realize that this is the fifth Dalek. This is after the Doctor warned Janley and Lesterson that there are four and not three Daleks. **22:20 (CD-2, track 10, 2:06)** The Narrator of the CD version describes the first complete Dalek "animal" in the series.

Episode 5
First Transmitted: Dec. 3, 1966

4:28 (CD-2, track 13, 2:25) One of the Daleks proves that the earlier claim of incredibly stupid Daleks was not a true error. The Daleks know about the problem of too many Daleks. The Dalek says, "No more than three Daleks to be seen together at any one time." **5:39 (CD-2, track 15, 0:45)** Janley has trouble saying "power cable." **17:35 (CD-2, track 21, 2:59)** There is the sound of a falling pencil in the background. This may be a Collector addition.

Episode 6
First Transmitted: Dec. 10, 1966

6:07 (CD-2, track 34, 0:46) The Daleks receive orders to begin exterminating humans. **14:17 (CD-2, track 44, 0:51)** The Doctor is very callous about sacrificing Bragen's guards. This is out of character for the Doctor. **18:37 (CD-2, track 49, 1:10)** Why do the Daleks not immediately exterminate Lesterson? The Daleks already received orders to exterminate humans. **21:55 (CD-2, track 52, 0:29)** Valmar (Richard Kane) is more concerned with the damage to the power supply than with the lives saved.

Comments: The Doctor defeats the Daleks and saves the planet Vulcan.

Pause to Consider: Audio Tapes

The BBC released some of the missing episodes on audio tape. *The Power of the Daleks* is the earliest of the stories released as a commercial audio tape. There is editing for length of the episodes — in this case the episodes range in length from over 25 minutes to about 19 and a half minutes. Splitting of some of the episodes left part of the episode on one side of the tape and the remainder on the opposite side of the tape. The collector's audio recordings are often significantly longer than the commercial audio tape. This is also true for the commercial CD versions.

(FF) THE HIGHLANDERS

Writer: Elwyn Jones and Gerry Davis; **Director:** Hugh David

Media: Commercial 2 CD set — episodic version — 96 minutes (used); Collector's audio recording — episodic version — 95 minutes

Highlights: The Doctor is in drag. Jamie McCrimmon (Frazer Hines) joins the series. Frazier Hines narrates the story.

Questions: Is the Doctor's treatment of the wounded Laird due to newly acquired medical knowledge, or just first aid?

Errors and Other Points of Interest

Many fans believe the basis of this story to be an Anglo-Scottish conflict, and not on an attempt the reestablish the Stuart dynasty. They believe this to be a blooper. This depends on your personal interpretation. There were Scots on both sides. It is possible that some individual Scots were simply anti–English, and not just pro–Stuart.

Episode 1
First Transmitted: Dec. 17, 1966

8:01 (CD-1, track 6, 1:23) How is the Doctor able to treat the Laird (Donald Bisset)? The Doctor claimed no medical knowledge in other stories. **10:57 (CD-1, track 8, 0:52)** When the Doctor first meets Lieutenant Ffinch (Michael Elwyn) the following exchange takes place: the Doctor introduces himself as "Doktor von Wer...." The Lieutenant replies, "Doctor Who?" to which the Doctor answers, "That's what I said."

Episode 2
First Transmitted: Dec. 24, 1966

2:16 (CD-1, track 16, 0:20) Some observers claim that Ffinch's threat of 300 lashes is a blooper. The use here, and in other places, makes it seem more like a figure of speech instead of a real threat. **16:07 (CD-1, track 23, 0:35)** Ffinch now threatens his men with 500 lashes each. If the preceding 300 lashes was a blooper so is this one. **21:20 (CD-1, track 30, 0:05)** The Doctor is in drag.

Episode 3
First Transmitted: Dec. 31, 1966

2:00 (CD-2, track 3, 1:08) Mackay (Andrew Downie) wants to kill Ben because Ben is English. This may be where some observers came to believe this is incorrectly an Anglo-Scottish war. This could simply be depressed and defeated prisoners lashing out at anyone. **7:12 (CD-2, track 7, 1:04)** Now it is the Sergeant (Peter Welch) with the threats. The Sergeant threatens his men with 500 lashes each. Are these threats bloopers or figures of speech? Viewers often cite Ffinch's 300 lashes as a blooper, and then ignore the Sergeant's 500 lashes.

Episode 4
First Transmitted: Jan. 7, 1967

2:01 (CD-2, track 18, 0:31) The Doctor is now a Redcoat. **19:14 (CD-2, track 31, 0:44)** The Doctor is again Doktor von Wer. **22:42 (CD-2, track 32, 2:28)** Polly asks the Doctor to allow Jamie to join them on their travels. Jamie would spend more episodes in the TARDIS than any other companion would during the series.

(GG) THE UNDERWATER MENACE

Writer: Geoffrey Orme; **Director:** Julia Smith

Media: Commercial DVD —*Lost in Time*— Episode 3 — 24 minutes (used); Commercial tape — with *The Edge of Destruction* in the tape *The Missing Years*— Episode 3 — 24 minutes; Collector's audio recording — 98 minutes (used)
Highlights: The Doctor appears as a gypsy with a tambourine.

Errors and Other Points of Interest

Some viewers have claimed that the actor playing Zaroff (Joseph Furst) has such a fake accent that it should be a blooper. This is not a blooper since the actor is speaking normally, for him, and not trying to create an accent.

Episode 1
First Transmitted: Jan. 14, 1967

10:15 The Time Lord's ability to understand other languages fails when the travelers meet the first Atlantean. This is apparently the only Atlantean who does not know English. **12:05** Polly seems surprised that the Atlantean speaks modern English. On this occasion, it is apparently not the Time Lords' Gift. **13:31** The Doctor has trouble with his lines saying "producing feed ... food from the sea."

Episode 2
First Transmitted: Jan. 21, 1967

0:27–0:49 The audio only version sounds obscene. This is not the only occurrence of these sounds. **4:44** The Doctor says the crust of the Earth is more than 100 miles thick. Zaroff agrees, but goes on to add that there is a fissure near the island making the crust only 15 miles thick. The problem with this description is that the distances are wrong. The Mohorovicic discontinuity defines the bottom of the crust. The crust has a maximum thickness of 70 kilometers (43.5 miles) below the continents and an average of 5 kilometers (3.1 miles) below the sea floor. **4:50** The Doctor says "a white-hot molten core" is beneath the crust. Apparently, the Doctor forgot there is about 1800 miles of mantle between the crust and the core.

Episode 3
First Transmitted: Jan. 28, 1967

0:34 We can hear a PA in the background. **3:19** Why are the Atlanteans not surprised that Amdo speaks in English instead of Atlantean? **11:35** Ben and Jamie's mock German salutes are almost comical. **15:23** This is one of the better instances with an obvious supporting wire on some of the Fish People. **16:37** Some fans have found fault with Zaroff saying, "My nuclear reactor is activated, and when the desired figure is reached, fission will take place...." This is technobabble and not a blooper. However, one must remember that until fission begins the nuclear reactor produces no energy. **20:54** Many viewers comment on Zaroff's "Oooh," when hit over the head by Polly. One particularly astute viewer saw through all the make-up and noted that it was Victoria with the boulder. Others have described the rock, smaller than a soccer ball, as being enormous. **23:01** Zaroff "fires" his gun, but the lack of recoil or smoke clearly indicates that the gun did not fire, and the sound was only a sound effect.

Episode 4
First Transmitted: Feb. 4, 1967

0:34 Some viewers object to Zaroff's line "Nothing in the world can stop me know!" **1:58** The Doctor stumbles over his line. **13:33** Some observers object to the fact that Zaroff has a plunger with which to destroy the world.

Comments: The Doctor saves the Earth.

(HH) THE MOONBASE

Writer: Kit Pedler; **Director:** Morris Barry

Media: Commercial DVD — *Lost in Time* — audio only for Episodes 1 and 3, video for Episodes 2 and 4 — 98 minutes (used); Commercial 2-CD set — 99 minutes (used); Commercial tape — *Cybermen — The Early Years*, episodes 2 and 4 — 48 minutes total (used); Collector's audio recording — 96 minutes
Highlights: This is the return of the Cybermen. These are not the same Cybermen from *The Tenth Planet*. Frazier Hines is the Narrator of the CD version.
Questions: Why are the control units left next to the patients in the hospital?

Errors and Other Points of Interest

In the tape, *Cybermen — The Early Years* (8:14), Colin Baker notes that Jamie has contracted the same disease as other members of the Moonbase. This is incorrect; Jamie has a concussion not an infection.

Some fans propose a question: Why did the Cybermen not make more laser holes? If they were trying to capture the Moonbase intact, they obviously did not want to make too many holes. Each hole would weaken the entire dome; too many holes could cause the complete destruction of the dome, which might also damage the contents.

Episode 1
First Transmitted: Feb. 11, 1967

1:59 (CD-1, track 4, 0:41) Ben exclaims that the Doctor missed Mars by about 200 million miles. This would mean the Ben knows that the Earth and Mars are nearly on opposite sides of the Sun. How does Ben know that the Earth and Mars are not on the same side of the Sun? **2:09 (CD-1, track 4, 0:52)** Polly refers to the moon as the "move." **8:55 (CD-1, track 6, 3:28)** Hobson (Patrick Barr) says the year is 2070. This is before the Dalek invasion, thus future anachronisms are possible bloopers. The use of magnetic tape would qualify as a future anachronism. **21:25 (CD-1, track 16, 0:27)** It is not obvious from the audio only version, but it is possible that Polly sees, but does not recognize, a Cyberman. Polly says, "Something just went out the door." This is a problem if Polly actually saw what went out the door, because she saw the Cybermen in *The Tenth Planet*.

Episode 2
First Transmitted: Feb. 18, 1967

1:25 Polly brings an empty glass of water to Jamie. **1:38 (CD-1, track 18, 1:01)** Polly now calls the creature a "Cyberman." **5:13 (CD-1, track 18, 4:46)** The Doctor says he studied with Lister at Glasgow in 1888; however, Lister was in Edinburgh at that time. **9:19 (CD-1, track 21, 1:25)** The Earth Controller (Denis McCarthy) hears, and responds to, the discussion about shutting down the Gravitron. **9:37 (CD-1, track 21, 1:43)** Why does the Earth Controller not respond to the sarcastic comment? The Controller heard the earlier discussion about shutting down the Gravitron. **11:59** We finally see where the Cybermen get the silver lace-up boots they wear, which "everyone" reports as a blooper in *The Invasion*. **12:12 (CD-1, track 22, 0:04)** This is one instance of what fans call the Ben Blooper. The Ben Blooper involves Ben's "sudden" gain in intelligence, for example, his comment "interferon stuff." However, Ben's "knowledge" of interferon may be limited to his finding an empty bottle with interferon written on the label. There is more discussion on the Ben Blooper later. **12:53** The Cyberman's shot at Polly misses her; however, Polly still falls over. **14:39** As a substitute for an airlock, the Cybermen loosely pile some bags in front of a hole in the wall. There is the sound of escaping air when the Cybermen move the bags. Bags would not serve as an efficient means of sealing the hole. There would be a continual leakage of air. It is possible that the Cybermen have an external airlock in place. **16:20** The space suits and "air cylinders" exceed technobabble. **17:27 (CD-1, track 27, 0:07)** The Doctor says all tests are negative. **17:53 (CD-1, track 27, 0:33)** The Doctor has trouble with his line as he says, "Polly, are you suggesting that I am not confident to carry out these tests." **20:06 (CD-1, track 29, 0:13)** The Doctor reports that he has tested the food, amongst other things, and the tests are negative. **20:11 (CD-1, track 29, 0:19)** The Doctor notices that Polly brings coffee into the room — many blooper lists claim she brought tea. Polly proceeds to fill the empty cups from an empty carafe. **21:28 (CD-1, track 31, 1:02)** The Doctor identifies sugar as the problem, even though he tested the food and found the food to be safe. **21:29** The Doctor knocks the cup from the Hobson's hand and sugar, with no coffee, is scattered everywhere. The floor remains dry. **22:09** The Doctor refers to the substance from the sugar as a virus. No matter how large the virus is, it would not be possible to see it under the type of microscope he is using. A much more powerful microscope is necessary to see any virus. **23:44** The anchoring of the hospital beds is very poor. When the Cyberman gets off the bed, the bed nearly falls over.

Episode 3
First Transmitted: Feb. 25, 1967

2:05 (CD-2, track 4, 0:10) The Cyberman knows the Doctor after his regeneration — even though this is a different group of Cybermen. Do the Cybermen, like the Daleks, have the Time Lords' ability to recognize regenerated persons? **2:55 (CD-2, track 4, 1:00)** No matter what Colin Baker states in *Cybermen—The Early Years*, the Cyberman says that Jamie has no infection. **8:18 (CD-2, track 8, 0:33)** Ben knows about thermonuclear power. Ben's gain in intelligence is, in part, due to the addition of Jamie to the cast. Jamie's presence required an adjustment in the lines. This is another appearance of the Ben Blooper. **11:51 (CD-2, track 10, 0:05)** Ben has gained the knowledge of acetone being present in "nail varnish." Some blooper reporters state that it was "nail polish" instead of "nail varnish" that Ben said. This is another part of the Ben Blooper reported by various observers. **16:20 (CD-2, track 12, 0:22)** Polly says she added epoxypropane. This reactive chemical would not be in easily opened containers. Polly might find it in a gas cylinder. **20:48 (CD-2, track 18, 0:56)** The last Ben Blooper appears, as Ben "knows" the solvent mixture would vaporize in a vacuum. **23:02 (CD-2, track 20, 0:35)** Hobson learns that radar detects the Cyberman ship, and it is just over the rim — how could the radar detect it in that position? Radar waves do not bend over rims.

Episode 4
First Transmitted: Mar. 4, 1967

1:18 There is a crack between the doors behind everyone. Through this crack, it is possible to see someone looking into the room. This is not the computer reels on the wall behind the doors. **2:14** The Cybermen destroy the radio aerial. **3:46 (CD-2, track 29, 0:01)** The Cyberman on the Moon's surface opens his mouth and speaks. There is no air on the Moon's surface, so there should be no sound. **3:56** Unlike the other Cybermen, this Cyberman talks without opening his mouth. **7:06** Dr. Evans (Alan Rowe) knocks out the Gravitron operator. Dr. Evans then puts the operator's hat on backwards. **8:27 (CD-2, track 38, 1:06)** There is a comment by one of the scientists that they cannot contact the rescue ship because of the Doppler Effect. However, the Cybermen have already destroyed the aerial, and so contacting the ship is not an option. **8:52 (CD-2, track 38, 1:31)** When discussing the lost rescue ship Benoit (Andre Maranne) mentions that the "Sun's gravity belt" will trap the rescue ship. The Sun's gravity belt traps the entire solar system; otherwise, all the planets would move away from the Sun. What is the "Sun's gravity belt?" **9:33** Dr. Evans has fixed his hat so that it faces the right way, but he has lost his Cyberman control unit. **10:03 (DVD time 9:58; CD-2, track 40, 0:01)** As the scientists are about to be activated by the Cybermen we hear the word "cue." This is not as obvious in the CD or DVD versions. **12:33 (CD-2, track 41, 1:16)** People cite the holes the Cybermen blast into the dome as part of a blooper. They worry about a powerful laser producing only small holes; the slow loss of air through the hole; and how can a small tray fix the problem. However, there are holes in these arguments. First, one of the properties of lasers is that even the most powerful of lasers can focus to a pinpoint. The first blooper, therefore, is that the hole is so large not small. Earlier, the Cybermen only pile some loose bags in front of the entrance they are using. Thus, we know that gas does not escape very fast even through a much larger hole. Maybe they are using a low pressure of pure oxygen instead of air at normal (Earth) pressure. It is possible that the tray is not so flimsy. There is no indication of how tough the material is. Obviously, there were several laser shots. The laser would produce a clean round hole. The odd shape of the hole must be due to several of these holes grouped closely together. **13:33 (CD-2, track 42, 0:44)** Some fans question the strength of the tray. **13:36** The pressure gauge shows the pressure returning to "normal." Normal seems to be about "3." Some fans question this as a blooper, but since this is technobabble, it is not really a blooper. The basis of the fans' argument is that there are many pressure units currently in use — two of which are atmospheres and Pascals. In atmospheres, normal would be 1; while in Pascals normal would be slightly over 100,000. It has been incorrectly reported that normal in Pascals is 500,000. **15:12** The Cybermen spaceships look like paper plates from *Plan 9 from Outer Space* complete with easily seen strings. **21:24 (CD-2, track 51, 0:43)** We can hear the TARDIS take off sound in the vacuum of the Moon's surface. **22:14** The Time Scanner shows a giant claw.

Comments: At least one blooper list has the blooper where Hobson has his name changed to Robson. These Cybermen have two fingers and a thumb. The Doctor and his companions save the Moon and the Earth.

(JJ) THE MACRA TERROR

Writer: Ian Stuart Black; **Director:** John Davies

> *Media:* Commercial CD — episodic version — 93 minutes (used); Excerpts are present in the tape *The Missing Years* packaged with *The Edge of Destruction*; Commercial audio recording — 90 minutes
>
> *Highlights:* The Narrator of the CD and Commercial audio versions is Colin Baker. Tom Baker's first person narration is a better idea.
>
> *Questions:* The cliffhanger to the preceding story shows a claw from a Macra; after seeing this — why is everyone in such a hurry to go outside?

Errors and Other Points of Interest

Anyone who has not seen photographs of the Macra would have trouble picturing them based on the soundtrack. Some people describe them as being crabs or crablike. At other times, the description insect is present. Sometimes the description is as both crabs and insects by Polly, or as insects and bacteria by the Pilot (Peter Jeffrey). The Doctor alludes to their being germs.

Episode 1
First Transmitted: Mar. 11, 1967

3:39 (CD-1, track 3, 1:40) Jamie reminds everyone of what they saw earlier in the time scanner. The warning does not stop them from running outside without checking for danger. **3:43 (CD-1, track 3, 1:43)** Jamie's line is "I'm not being left without nothing to defend ourselves with." Jamie realizes his mistake after he starts this sentence. **17:09 (CD-1, track 14, 0:44)** Medok (Terence Lodge) considers the Macra to be giant insects. **22:00 (CD-1, track 21, 0:19)** The Narrator refers to the Macra as being a crablike creature.

Episode 2
First Transmitted: Mar. 18, 1967

2:30 (CD-1, track 25, 0:24) The Pilot addresses the person making the call by the name "Emergency." **4:04 (CD-1, track 25, 1:58)** The Pilot summons Medok to make his statement. The Doctor tells the Pilot not to believe everything Medok says. The Doctor needs Medok for an alibi, so why did the Doctor undermine Medok's credibility. **4:54**

(CD-1, track 25, 2:48) After Medok makes his statement, the Pilot apologizes to the Doctor. Apparently, the Doctor's crime of being outside after dark is no longer a problem. **7:11 (CD-1, track 26, 0:07)** Some listeners have a problem with the Narrator's line "Jamie is tossing restlessly." **17:05 (CD-1, track 31, 0:32)** Polly says the Macra are insects or giant crabs. **20:03 (CD-1, track 32, 0:46)** Polly now says the Macra is a great insect like a crab.

Episode 3
First Transmitted: Mar. 25, 1967

9:17 (CD-2, track 5, 2:15) The Doctor philosophizes with the comment "Given the answer, what is the question." This did not help Deep Thought. **19:59 (CD-2, track 22, 0:08)** The Narrator refers to the Macra as being crablike.

Episode 4
First Transmitted: Apr. 1, 1967

11:50 (CD-2, track 43, 1:13) The Doctor alludes to the Macra as being germs. **17:03 (CD-2, track 46, 1:07)** The Pilot refers to the Macra as insects and bacteria. **17:40 (CD-2, track 47, 0:22)** The Pilot considers the Macra to be grotesque insects.

Comments: Some viewers claim that the use of two different actors to play Chiki (Sandra Bryant and Karol Keyes) is a blooper.

The Commercial audio tape lists the running time as 150 minutes.

The Doctor saves an unnamed planet.

(KK) THE FACELESS ONES

Writer: David Ellis and Malcolm Hulke; **Director:** Gerry Mill

Media: Commercial DVD —*Lost in Time*— Episodes 1 and 3 — 46 minutes (used); Commercial 2 CD set —145 minutes (used); Commercial recording of episodes 1 and 3 (used); Excerpts are present in the tape *The Missing Years* packaged with *The Edge of Destruction*; Collector video recording of episodes 1 and 3 — 46 minutes (used) A "C" indicates times from this tape; Collector's audio recording —144 minutes

Highlights: Ben and Polly leave the series. Frazier Hines is the Narrator of the CD version.

Questions: Why leave the originals on the Earth where someone may find them?

Errors and Other Points of Interest

Episode 1
First Transmitted: Apr. 8, 1967

6:42 (CD-1, track 10, 0:13) Polly tells the Doctor and Jamie, "I just seen a man killed!" **6:58 (CD-1, track 10, 0:30)** Polly repeatedly describes the weapon the killer used as a "gun." **9:51 (CD-1, track 13, 0:25)** The Doctor describes the gun as "not one developed yet on this planet." **10:33** When the Doctor, Polly and Jamie decide to leave, a large shadow, probably due to a person, covers the top portion of the door in the background. A larger shadow appears on the Collector's tape. **15:53 (CD-1, track 23, 0:08)** From Polly's description and the Doctor's analysis, Jamie develops the idea "ray gun." This is a great jump for this Scotsman. The term "ray gun," unimaginative as it is, remains throughout the story.

Episode 2
First Transmitted: Apr. 15, 1967

1:44 (CD-1, track 33, 0:14) "Polly's" name is Michelle Leuppi. The incorrect name Michelle Lopez appears in some sources. 3:10 (CD-1, track 34, 0:05) We learn that raw state Chameleons suffocate in an Earth-type atmosphere. 18:47 (CD-1, track 48, 0:30) Why is Polly not with the other bodies?

Episode 3
First Transmitted: Apr. 22, 1967
2:18 It appears as if the control panel is about to fall off the wall. 7:29 (CD-1, track 65, 1:51) There is a noise off set after the Commandant (Colin Gordon) says "For what!" 11:41C What appears to be a boom mike appears above Detective Inspector Crossland's (Bernard Kay) head. This only occurs on the Collector's tape.

Episode 4
First Transmitted: Apr. 29, 1967
8:38 (CD-2, track 12, 0:13) Spencer (Victor Winding) demonstrates the superior intelligence of the Faceless Ones. After he and Jenkins (Christopher Tranchell) see the Doctor on the monitor, Spencer says he tried to kill the Doctor, but "he must have escaped." 19:47 (CD-2, track 24, 0:19) Even though this is Jamie's first time on an airplane, he has no trouble quickly finding the "emergency" facilities.

Episode 5
First Transmitted: May 6, 1967
2:07 (CD-2, track 36, 0:49) The Narrator describes "two raw state Chameleons." We learned earlier that raw state Chameleons suffocate in an Earth-type atmosphere. Since Jamie is not suffocating, this must be an Earth-type atmosphere. 3:51 (CD-2, track 37, 0:56) The presence of miniaturized "dolls" may indicate either help from the Master, or where the Master got his original TCE (Tissue Compression Eliminator). 7:07 (CD-2, track 38, 2:51) Meadows (George Selway) tells the Doctor the Faceless Ones are taking 50,000 people.

Episode 6
First Transmitted: May 13, 1967
17:22 (CD-2, track 76, 0:36) Most of the bodies of the people converted by the Faceless Ones remain on Earth. Why is Polly on the ship and not on the Earth like the other originals? Recall that the conversion of Polly took place on the Earth and not on the space station. 18:14 (CD-2, track 78, 0:29) Many fans have questioned why the Faceless Ones got off so easily. They are guilty of 50,000 admitted kidnappings and an unknown number of murders (the killings in this story are probably not the only deaths).

Comments: The Doctor saves 50,000 kidnapped victims, but he does not seem to worry about the murder victims and their murderers.

(LL) THE EVIL OF THE DALEKS

Writer: David Whitaker; **Director:** Derek Martinus and Timothy Combe

Media: Commercial DVD — *Lost in Time* — Episode 2 — 25 minutes (used); Commercial 3-CD set — 191 minutes (used); Commercial audiotape — 165 minutes (used); Commercial tape — *Daleks — The Early Years* — Excerpts and Episode 2 — 25 minutes;

Excerpts are present in the tape *The Missing Years* packaged with *The Edge of Destruction*.

Highlights: Victoria Waterfield (Deborah Watling) joins the Doctor and Jamie. The Fourth Doctor (Tom Baker) gives a first person narration on the commercial tape, and Frazier Hines is the Narrator on the CD version.

Questions: Why does Maxtible have a picture of Waterfield's wife in his house?

Errors and Other Points of Interest

Episode 1
First Transmitted: May 20, 1967

7:10 (CD-1, track 8, 0:11) This is one of the few cases where the Doctor is carrying money. **9:05 (CD-1, track 9, 1:42)** The Doctor says, "it is a lot for what we ... he had to do." **15:06 (CD-1, track 12, 0:54)** Where did Waterfield (John Bailey) get a photograph of the Doctor and Jamie? Jamie was not with the Doctor during the last encounter with the Daleks. An alternative question would be — Why did Waterfield not have a photograph of the Doctor, Jamie, Ben and Polly? Why use the names Doctor Galloway and Jamie McCrimmon?

Episode 2
First Transmitted: May 27, 1967

1:21 This clock says 9:00 (even though the hour hand seems slightly off). All the other clocks seen at this time appear to be near this time. **1:47** Even though all the clocks seen a few seconds earlier were near 9:00, this one clock is at 9:30. **9:16** The Daleks effectively capture Jamie and the Doctor once Jamie triggers the trap. Some fans question why the Daleks follow this with such an elaborate scheme. These fans consider this a potential blooper. One explanation is that the Daleks did not want Jamie to know about them so that concern about the Daleks would not taint his actions. Waterfield seems to confirm this later. **11:59 (CD-1, track 32, 2:12)** Maxtible (Marius Goring) says the date is June 2, 1866. **14:09** When the view switches from a close-up of Victoria's face to the Dalek and Victoria, there is a quick glimpse of a camera lens behind the Dalek before the camera backs away. **15:33 (CD-1, track 34, 0:40)** While talking to the Doctor in the laboratory Maxtible calls Waterfield "Whitefield." **16:14 (CD-1, track 34, 1:21)** Maxtible has a problem with the English language as he says to the Doctor, "Everything you see about you here was constructed by us two." **16:37 (CD-1, track 38, 2:05)** Maxtible's, and later Waterfield's, time travel theory exceeds technobabble. **22:28 (CD-1, track 35, 2:09)** Some fans question why Toby (Windsor Davies) kidnaps Jamie for Terrall (Gary Watson). **23:06 (CD-1, track 36, 0:03)** Waterfield tells the Doctor the Daleks do not want Jamie to know about the situation. **23:06** There is an unusual noise as the Doctor and Waterfield talk. There is a repeat of this sound later.

Episode 3
First Transmitted: June 3, 1967

1:25 (CD-1, track 44, 0:26) We learned that Toby apparently misunderstood what Terrall wanted. Thus, the kidnapping was a mistake. It is possible that Terrall did not know what he really said. In another state of mind, Terrall may have planned to take a hostage to exchange for Victoria. **12:16 (CD-1, track 50, 1:47)** The Daleks reinforce Waterfield's earlier assertion that Jamie should not learn what is happening. **23:29 (CD-1, track 57, 1:01)** If the metal spikes killed Jamie — what would happen to the Daleks' plan? If they wanted to make sure their program was a success, the Daleks should have used less lethal traps. This applies to the other traps.

Episode 4
First Transmitted: June 10, 1967
    4:34 (CD-2, track 4, 0:22) The ax, like the spikes, is part of a lethal trap. The Daleks' experiment nearly ends a second time. **13:04 (CD-2, track 12, 0:16)** Another trap nearly ends the Daleks' experiment.

Episode 5
First Transmitted: June 17, 1967
    2:36 (CD-2, track 22, 0:05) The Doctor drinks, and enjoys, wine. This is unlike the norm for the First Doctor. **3:29 (CD-2, track 22, 0:58)** The Doctor says, "You, you, you didn't ... you weren't...." **5:05 (CD-2, track 22, 2:34)** We hear a classic Doctor quote: "I am not a student of human nature. I am a professor of a far wider academy, of which human nature is merely a part." **12:06 (CD-2, track 25, 0:33)** David Whitaker again pays homage to Isaac Asimov with the Doctor saying "positronic brain." This is not the only time in the series.

Episode 6
First Transmitted: June 24, 1967
    2:25 (CD-3, track 2, 1:50) The Doctor names the third Dalek, Omega. The "logical" progression is Alpha, Beta, and Gamma, the first three letters of the Greek alphabet, instead of the first two and the last. Since the story began in London, it is possible the Doctor has Omega (as in "Hand of") on his mind. **11:14 (CD-3, track 4, 0:53)** Maxtible tells Victoria they are on "Skarov." Maxtible should have said Skaro. **22:55 (CD-3, track 14, 1:22)** The Doctor makes another memorable quote: "The Day of the Daleks is coming to an end." **24:21 (CD-3, track 14, 2:49)** How did the TARDIS get to Skaro? The blue box was supposedly behind the shop in London, where it would not fit into the shop. The TARDIS would need to get into the back room where the Daleks' time machine was located.

Episode 7
First Transmitted: July 1, 1967
    The Daleks in the final battle are obviously toys. However, this is not obvious in the audio only version of the story.
    2:06 (CD-3, track 18, 0:34) The Doctor has trouble with his line, "Why are the doo-daleks d-doing this?" The Doctor has been misquoted to say, "I wonder what the doo-daleks are d-doing." **4:27 (CD-3, track 18, 2:56)** The Doctor says, "I might even try to take you to my own planet." This implies that the Doctor now has some control over where the TARDIS goes. **6:16 (CD-3, track 21, 0:26)** Maxtible gives the following values for iron — atomic weight — 55.84 and specific gravity — 7.84. These values are approximately correct. **6:38 (CD-3, track 21, 0:48)** Maxtible identifies a sample as being gold. He has the atomic weight (19.2) and specific gravity (69.4 or sixty-nine point something) wrong. The values should be 197 and 19.3, respectively.
    Comments: The Doctor defeats the Daleks again.

(MM) THE TOMB OF THE CYBERMEN

Alternate Title: *The Tombs of the Cybermen*
Writer: Kit Pedler and Gerry Davis; **Director:** Morris Barry

Media: DVD — episodic version — 96 minutes (used); Commercial audio tape — episodic version — 93 minutes; Excerpts are present in the tape *The Missing Years* packaged with *The Edge of Destruction.*

Highlights: Jon Pertwee narrates the commercial audio tape.
Questions: Why do the Cybermen just open the door from below, instead of staying locked in the tomb?

Errors and Other Points of Interest

The "Parental Guidance" information on the DVD box informs people that there is no "violence," but there is some mild "Sex/Nudity."

Episode 1
First Transmitted: Sep. 2, 1967

1:40 The Doctor tells Jamie and Victoria, "I must be about 450 years old." **2:17** The TARDIS column shakes as it apparently stops suddenly because the column tried to rise too high. **3:17** The tomb is in "The city of Telos." The name of the planet is not given. In later stories, Telos became the name of the planet. **4:42** One of the workers has trouble climbing the path. **5:55** Viner (Cyril Shaps) apparently sees the TARDIS land like a spaceship. **6:14** Victoria picks a very short dress for someone raised during Victorian times. **7:30** The Doctor and Jamie learn that the Cybermen came from Telos and not Mondas. **9:37** First, the Doctor and then Jamie try to open the doors to the Tomb. They would be much more successful if they did not hold the doors closed with their feet. Some reports imply that the Doctor and Jamie hold the doors closed simultaneously, but this does not occur. **10:40** The Doctor explains that the death of the first crewmember was due to drawing all of the electricity from his body. This does not appear to be what happened. **13:50** The members of the expedition learn they need to be back at the ship by 16:30, to do this they are to meet back at the entrance at 16:25. Thus, they will have an hour in case they need to search for somebody. Apparently, there is a new way of keeping track of time. **15:54** A boom mike creeps into the scene at the upper left of the picture. This may be just a shadow. **16:42** There is a reference to Whitehead logic; this is an allusion to an actor who plays one of the Cybermen. **19:44** The Doctor appears in the background waiting for his cue to enter the set.

Episode 2
First Transmitted: Sep. 9, 1967

2:32 As the weapon comes out of its hiding place, the unit hits the side of the doorway. **6:41** The Captain (George Roubicek) tells everyone it will take at least 72 hours to repair the ship. **10:58** Toberman (Roy Stewart) nearly trips on one of the steps. **12:17** We hear the incorrect title of the story referenced as "The Tombs of the Cybermen." **16:21** Klieg (George Pastell) is not aiming at Viner when Klieg shoots Viner. **19:43** In this story, the Cybermen have a thumb and two fingers instead of human hands as shown in *The Tenth Planet*. **21:28** Some observers question Victoria's ability to fire a gun and actually hit the Cybermat.

Episode 3
First Transmitted: Sep. 16, 1967

0:52 Professor Parry (Aubrey Richards) identifies the blooper premise of this story. How could the Cybermen count on anyone finding the right spot or the right planet in the right star system in the right galaxy? Even if they are "rescued," they are still in their tomb. **4:43** Part of the device used to generate the electrical special effect appears below the Cyberman's hand. **4:47** The black hose from around the neck of one of the Cybermen has come loose at one end, and it is dangling behind the creature as he walks. **5:01** When the Cyberman Controller

(Michael Kilgariff) lifts Toberman into the air, a lifting wire is visible. **5:25** The crewmember (Jim — played by Clive Merrison) indicates to the Captain which lever to pull to open the door. **6:18** The Captain stands in front of a switch different from the one before the interruption. After the interruption, the Captain does not pull the lever indicated by Jim. **9:45** The beams from the Cyberman Controller clearly miss Toberman; this is especially true the first time. We can also see the special effects device used to generate the beams. **10:58** As the Cybermen are backing through the hatch; we hear a mysterious voice saying "Ooooooooh." This does not appear to be the voice of anyone on screen. **11:43** The last Cyberman to descend the ladder has a rip in his costume where the sleeve meets the shoulder. **12:43** The crewmember (Jim) pulls the door lever he originally indicated as the correct switch to open the door. Jim does not pull the same lever the Captain did. **13:01** The Captain pulls Klieg's gun from its holster and throws the gun on the table right in front of Klieg. This is clearly not the ideal place to leave the gun. **13:07** The Doctor suggests that they lock Kaftan (Shirley Cooklin) and Klieg in the weapon testing room. This would not be a bad idea, except everyone knows there is a deadly weapon in the room. **13:46** We again see what appears to be the same rip when the Cybermen reach over to pick up the Cybermats. This tear blooper occurs at various other times. **15:35** When Klieg first fires the X-ray laser, the end flies off the weapon. **17:04** We see a string or wire attached to the Cybermat. **17:57** The Doctor "conveniently" falls asleep with the power cable. There was no cable present in this area earlier in the story. **19:57** The Doctor tells Victoria, "There's nobody in the Universe who can do what we're doing." If he is talking about traveling through time and space — what happened to the Monk, Daleks and the other Time Lords? If he is only trying to consol Victoria, some leeway may be allowable and this is not a blooper.

Episode 4
First Transmitted: Sep. 23, 1967

0:50 A boom mike shadow falls across Jamie's face. **2:05** It is obvious that the Cybermen returning to their tombs is simply running their emergence backwards. **5:21** There is an excellent boom mike shadow on the wall behind the Doctor. **10:16** The trajectory from the laser clearly would not have hit Kaftan in the neck. **10:56** Toberman lifts what is obviously an empty costume instead of the actual Cyberman Controller. **11:03** The head of the "Cyberman Controller" falls off. **11:06** The Cyberman Controller's head is back in place. **15:29** The Captain says that they are ready to take off. Apparently, his minimum of 72 hours is really only overnight. **18:15** Again, it is obvious that the Cybermen returning to their tombs is simply running their emergence backwards. **18:42** Jamie stumbles as he exits the hatch, and Victoria simply puts out her hand to steady him. He does not "nearly" knock her down as has been claimed by other observers. **22:18** During the story, the survivors removed all of the bodies of killed people. The survivors left no one lying on the ground. Why leave Toberman's body where it fell?

Comments: The Doctor defeats the Cybermen again.

(NN) The Abominable Snowmen

Writer: Mervyn Haisman and Henry Lincoln; **Director:** Gerald Blake

Media: Commercial DVD—*Lost in Time*—Episode 2—23 minutes (used); Commercial 2-CD set—episodic version—142 minutes (used); Commercial tape—*The Troughton Years*—Episode 2 only—23 minutes; Collector's audio recording—139 minutes

Highlights: We meet the Yeti and the Great Intelligence. Frazier Hines is the Narrator of the CD version.

Questions: Is Padmasambhava (Wolfe Morris) a Time Lord?

Errors and Other Points of Interest

Some observers report that snow appears on the TARDIS scanner, but there is no snow when the travelers exit the TARDIS. This is not in any of the extant material, so no confirmation is possible.

Episode 1
First Transmitted: Sep. 30, 1967

1:08 (CD-1, track 3, 0:00) The landing sound of the TARDIS is slow. **1:39** (CD-1, track 3, 0:31) Some viewers claim that Jamie thought they had only traveled down the mountain on Telos. Jamie asks the Doctor if they are on Earth, and the Doctor tells Jamie they are on Earth, so Jamie knows they are not on Telos. **17:28** (CD-1, track 20, 0:03) Travers (Jack Watling) has trouble saying "Yeti." **19:36** (CD-1, track 21, 1:07) Some viewers find fault with Sapan (Raymond Llewellyn) being of Welch descent. Maybe Sapan is simply a pilgrim from Wales.

Episode 2
First Transmitted: Oct. 7, 1967

0:32 (CD-1, track 24, 0:00) The cliffhanger and the reprise do not overlap as they do in most stories. **3:00** (CD-1, track 26, 0:58) Thonmi (David Spenser) and the Doctor discuss the "stranger" taking the holy ghanti for safekeeping in 1630 (about 300 years earlier). This citation is present because of a potential inconsistency in the time of the event. **8:08** (CD-1, track 29, 0:52) Padmasambhava says the holy ghanti has been missing for "200 years or more." Some fans cite this as being in variance with the 300 years arising from Thonmi and the Doctor's conversation. The phrase "or more" could mean 300 years is a possibility. **17:17** The spheres reflect the studio lights. This is not the only time. **17:34** (CD-1, track 35, 0:18) Travers and the Doctor discuss the Abominable Snowmen saying the beasts are shy elusive creatures that would not attack anyone. This does not agree with the behavior of the Abominable Snowman in *The Five Doctors*.

Episode 3
First Transmitted: Oct. 14, 1967

8:31 (CD-1, track 48, 2:47) We learn that the Second Doctor must battle "The Master." **13:12** (CD-1, track 54, 0:35) We hear a classic Doctor line: "They came to get their ball back."

Episode 4
First Transmitted: Oct. 21, 1967

6:36 (CD-2, track 10, 0:07) We hear another classic Doctor quote: "Bung a rock at it." **12:42** (CD-2, track 17, 0:28) While they are in the cell, Thonmi tells Victoria that the holy ghanti disappeared 300 years earlier. This agrees with the earlier discussion between the Doctor and Thonmi. **20:29 (CD-2, track 23, 0:36)** Khrisong (Norman Jones) has trouble with his lines.

Episode 5
First Transmitted: Oct. 28, 1967

12:43 (CD-2, track 35, 0:59) The Doctor realizes that Padmasambhava is the same person he met 300 years earlier. Supposedly, the Great Intelligence kept Padmasambhava alive. **14:35 (CD-2, track 38, 0:17)** Padmasambhava recognizes the Doctor. This means that the Doctor has not regenerated since his last visit or Padmasambhava has the Time Lords' ability to recognize even regenerated Time Lords.

Episode 6
First Transmitted: Nov. 4, 1967

14:50 (CD-2, track 60, 1:31) The Doctor uses a phrase later made famous from *The Hitchhiker's Guide to the Galaxy* with "Don't Panic." **18:13 (CD-2, track 64, 0:28)** Travers fires one shot from his rifle. Yet the Narrator says Padmasambhava catches bullets (not a bullet). **22:04 (CD-2, track 67, 0:55)** Jamie refers to the Doctor's outfit as a "homemade Yeti kit."

Comments: Some fans claim many of the names are bloopers. This is due to the use of different names for the characters in the novelization of the story.

The Doctor saves the Earth.

(OO) THE ICE WARRIORS

Writer: Brian Hayles; **Director:** Derek Martinus

Media: Commercial tape, and CD —126 minutes (used)— the tape also contains a reconstruction of Episodes 2 and 3 (an additional 18 minutes)— The CD contains the full audio portion of these two episodes (48 of the 126 minutes).
Highlights: Meet the Ice Warriors.
Questions: Why do the female workers change clothing styles during the story?

Errors and Other Points of Interest

The name ECCO, for the computer, is not in this story. This name comes from the novelization.

Episode 1
First Transmitted: Nov. 11, 1967

5:51 The TARDIS is on its side as it materializes; it will be in a different position when it dematerializes. **6:56** As the Doctor exits the TARDIS he tells Jamie and Victoria that "It's quite a long drop." The Doctor then drops about a foot. **9:02** Why does Clent (Peter Barkworth) immediately assume that Arden's (George Waring) discovery is archeological? It is possible that his assumption relates to Clent's prior experience with Arden's discoveries. **13:22** Walters (Malcolm Taylor) is the first to use the term "Ice Warrior." No "Ice Warrior" uses this term. **17:12** The Doctor cites reversal of the Earth's magnetic field as a possible cause of the ice age. Magnetic reversals are more common than ice ages, so a simple magnetic reversal is an unlikely cause. **17:23** The Doctor says "an excessive burst of sun spock activity" could be a cause of the ice age. Maybe this is so (as technobabble), but sun spot activity is more likely what the Doctor meant to say. **17:47** Supposedly, low carbon dioxide levels caused the ice age. Clent relates the reduction of the gas to the destruction of too many plants (contrary to the reported blooper — Clent never says plants produce carbon dioxide). Later the Doctor says "no plants; no carbon dioxide." Carbon dioxide is a greenhouse gas and low CO_2 levels would give low temperatures. The error is that low CO_2 levels might relate to too many plants, since they would be absorbing this gas. **19:55** This is the first good view of the local map. The distances do not seem to fit from one appearance to the next, or to the travel times to and from the glacier. The travel times may be off, because it is possible that the Ice Warrior's ship, and other points of interest, is not at the nearest point of the glacier. **20:50** Note the boom mike protruding from the alcove on the right. It is there to "hear" the actors coming down the hall. **23:13** Victoria is "upset" about Jamie's suggestion that she dress like the women on the base. She takes a Victorian attitude here (which is to be expected), but this is contrary to her choice of a short dress in *The Tomb of the Cybermen*. **23:25** Varga's (Bernard Bresslaw) helmet changes after the Warrior awakens. Note that the Ice Warrior is very hairy.

Episode 2
First Transmitted: Nov. 18, 1967
1:45 Varga has a new helmet. This time is from the reconstruction. **4:38** As the Doctor and Miss Garrett discuss the revival of the Ice Warrior both agree that a high current and a low resistance would give a great deal of heat. To get a great amount of heat requires a high current and a HIGH resistance. **5:32** Varga tells Victoria he is from "The Red Planet." Victoria responds with "Mars." Varga does not agree or disagree with Victoria. Thus, it is uncertain whether the Warrior is referring to Mars or a red planet in another star system. **7:53** The Computer informs everyone to check the spaceship for fissionable material. **13:38** Arden tells Clent — "they didn't couldn't have come this way."

Episode 3
First Transmitted: Nov. 25, 1967
11:28 The Doctor informs Clent "there is one thing you can do to me for me." **18:04** We are able to hear the interior sound of the TARDIS at the glacier and in the base. **20:08** Penley (Peter Sallis) says that he saw Jamie shot with a ray gun.

Episode 4
First Transmitted: Dec. 2, 1967
3:08 Victoria says there is someone coming before the doors of the Ice Warriors' spaceship opens. **4:25** The Doctor dials once from the lower right (O?) and twice from the lower left (H and H?) to get H_2O. He then uses three different holes to get ammonium sulfide $((NH_4)_2S)$. There are claims that this is a blooper, that the Doctor used the same hole three times to produce both water and then to produce ammonium sulfide. The number of holes dialed works for water (3 atoms) but not for ammonium sulfide (11 atoms). However, this assumes the holes refer to separate elements. **5:02** The Doctor takes a vial of liquid from the machine and Clent calls it ammonium sulfide. Unfortunately, ammonium sulfide is an unstable solid, not a liquid. This substance decomposes to another unstable solid (ammonium hydrogen sulfide) and ammonia gas. The liquid in the vial cannot be ammonium sulfide. **5:13** Some fans claim that the observation about the atmosphere of Mars being mostly nitrogen is a blooper. These fans consider this a problem because the atmosphere of Mars is mostly carbon dioxide with very little nitrogen. The question arises: does the use of the most up-to-date information available really constitute a blooper? In 1967 when "The Ice Warriors" was written and filmed, astronomers believed the atmosphere of Mars to be mostly nitrogen with a little carbon dioxide. During the mid–70s, well after the writing of this story, the Viking Landers found the atmosphere to be mostly carbon dioxide, with

little nitrogen. **8:14** The Ice Warrior searching for Victoria walks right past her (within a few inches), and does not see her. **8:57** Penley expresses his concern about the peculiar weapon used on Jamie. **12:43** As Penley and Storr (Angus Lennie) discuss Jamie's condition, a shadow repeatedly passes back and forth. This occurs at other times on the same set. **12:46** There are reports claiming that Penley did not understand Jamie's paralysis, because he did not know someone shot Jamie. First Penley says it must be something to do with the weapons used, and later he says he does not understand the cause (how did the ray gun work?). There are earlier observations to refute the claims of these reports. **13:43** Apparently, the camera hits something as there is a thunk and the picture jumps. **15:03** There is a boom mike near the upper left of the screen. **20:18** There is a large boom mike shadow on the tabletop. **20:40** We see the local map again, and it does not match the earlier map very well. **20:54** Clent mentions cobalt radioactivity. There is no basis for this. Cobalt is a non-radioactive element. Radioactive cobalt can form in nuclear reactors by adding the appropriate materials, but this only occurs if there is intentional addition of the materials. There is a radiation problem associated with nuclear reactors, but normally not due to cobalt. Some people claim this as a blooper, even though it is really technobabble. Why is Clent worried about cobalt? The people need to worry about fissionable material, and cobalt, radioactive or not, is not fissionable. **22:45** The view screen primarily shows Varga's mouth. **23:07** Varga gives the Doctor an ultimatum — the Doctor must answer the question in ten seconds, or the Ice Warrior will reduce the air pressure to zero. The pressure begins to drop, assuming the gauge beside the monitor is a pressure gauge, before Varga begins to count. **23:34** The pressure gauge has dropped to the second mark from the bottom and the Doctor has not surrendered.

Episode 5
First Transmitted: Dec. 9, 1967

1:05 Unlike the cliffhanger, much more of Varga's face may be in the view screen. **1:47** The Doctor surrenders as the pressure gauge nears the third mark from the bottom (it stops before it reaches the second mark). In the cliffhanger, the gauge showed a lower reading than this and he had not surrendered. **3:33** This is a good place to compare the audio with Varga's lip movements. **11:20** This is another view of the map. Compare this to other views, along with Clent's comments on the distance. **13:15** The door in the Ice Warrior ship does not completely close. **17:14** The camera shakes as Penley talks to Clent. **19:50** Note Miss Garrett's costume; this is for later reference. **22:10** The Doctor says that stink bombs are harmless to humans. However, the "ammonium sulfide" he has in the vial is a stink bomb because it releases ammonia gas and hydrogen sulfide gas. The threshold limit values (TLV) for these gases (the level where their toxic effects begin to become apparent are 50 ppm for ammonia (the same value as for carbon monoxide) and 10 ppm for hydrogen sulfide (the same value as for hydrogen cyanide). These toxic gases are far from harmless to humans.

Episode 6
First Transmitted: Dec. 16, 1967

1:30 Miss Garrett's costume is not the same as the one she wore a few scenes earlier. **4:53** The last Ice Warrior bumps his head when entering the door. **7:20** There is a clunk offstage as if a door is slamming closed. **10:44** The Doctor says he believes that the ice warriors have a far greater fluid content than human beings do. Humans are 70 percent water; does this mean that the Ice Warriors, with far greater water content, are jellyfish? Besides the effect of the sonic gun on the Ice Warriors is apparently very much like that on the humans. This indicates a similar fluid content. **12:10** When

Miss Garrett pushes the off switch, one of the other switches slips. **12:46** Why does Penley turn the oxygen down? Is he trying to kill the humans? **13:43** Note the position of the unconscious female in the lower right. **14:37** The unconscious female in the lower left has moved. **14:52** As the Ice Warrior grabs the gun control unit, he nearly knocks the unit over since this console is not sessile. **22:56** The TARDIS is no longer on its side when it dematerializes.

Comments: At several points in the story, it is stated or implied that Penley left the base about six weeks before. Blooper hunters have cited his short beard as a blooper against this. It is a blooper if Penley stopped shaving at the same time he left; there is no confirmation of when he stopped shaving through anything in the story.

The episodes are indicted by numbers as "ONE" instead of numerals as "Episode 1."

The times come from the four episodes (1, 4, 5, and 6), and the two episodes on the CD (2 and 3). The only exception is the new helmet blooper from the beginning of second episode.

The Doctor meets and defeats the Ice Warriors.

(PP) THE ENEMY OF THE WORLD

Writer: David Whitaker; **Director:** Barry Letts

Media: Commercial DVD—*Lost in Time*—Episode 3—23 minutes (used); Commercial 2-CD set—episodic version—145 Minutes (used); *The Troughton Years*—Episode 3—23 minutes; Collector's audio recording 141 minutes

Highlights: Patrick Troughton has dual roles. Frazier Hines narrates the CD version. Reg Lye's portrayal of Griffin is excellent.

Questions: Why, in the one extant episode, does Jamie change in and out of uniform?

Errors and Other Points of Interest

Several money saving measures are present in this story. Examples include the imprisoning of Denes in a corridor instead of building a new set, and Bruce saying he has more guards with him instead of actually showing them. These are not true bloopers, and, as such, do not belong on this list even though some fans believe otherwise.

Some people have a blooper problem with the Doctor's /Salamander's variable Spanish, really Mexican, accent. Actually, Salamander is from the Yucatan region of Mexico, and Mexican "Spanish" is different from Spanish "Spanish."

Some observers claim there is poor editing of this story.

Episode 1
First Transmitted: Dec. 23, 1967

0:38 (CD-1, track 2, 0:03) The TARDIS landing sound is too slow. **10:43 (CD-1-, track 9, 0:41)** The Doctor tells Astrid (Mary Peach) that he is not a Doctor of any "medical significance." What happened to his answer in *The Moonbase* or *The Highlanders*? **21:11 (CD-1, track 13, 4:10)** Victoria notes the Doctor's out of period clothing.

Episode 2
First Transmitted: Dec. 30, 1967

7:40 CD-1, track 18, 0:30) We learn that the volcanoes in the Central European Zone have been "dead" since the sixteenth century. While it is not certain how large the Zone is, it apparently includes Hungary. There are no volcanoes in or near Hungary. **10:44 (CD-1, track 20, 0:44)** Astrid tells Kent (Bill Kerr) that they have landed in Hungary (in the Central European Zone). Apparently, Salamander is in a city in Hungary.

Episode 3
First Transmitted: Jan. 6, 1968
0:39 (CD-1, track 27, 0:00) There is no reprise. **3:29 (CD-1, track 30, 0:26)** Some fans consider keeping Denes (George Pravda) in the corridor a blooper. **4:15** As Griffin is asking Victoria about a menu, a boom mike shadow falls on Fariah's (Carmen Munroe) face. **9:58** Benik (Milton Johns) fails to destroy Kent's portrait. Some viewers claim this to be a blooper, but it seems to be an excessive claim. **10:18** Some fans report, as a blooper, that many of the sounds in this episode seem poorly redubbed. These fans claim an example occurs when the plates are broken in Giles Kent's trailer; where there seems to be a 3-second lag between the breaking and the sound. This problem does not appear in these video releases. **13:51** As Griffin is talking to Jamie and Victoria the door behind Griffin opens; apparently Fariah got there before her cue. **20:02 (CD-1, track 40, 0:18)** Jamie fires the first of three shots. **20:56** How could Jamie fire three shots from his gun? There is no hole in the barrel.

Episode 4
First Transmitted: Jan. 13, 1968
1:36 (CD-2, track 3, 0:36) When the Doctor is talking to Giles Kent about Astrid contacting them, he says "contess" instead of "contact." **5:52 (CD-2, track 9, 1:37)** The Doctor flubs his lines when he tells Fariah he will return the Fedorin (David Nettheim) file to her. The Doctor explains, "I'll give it to you back." **15:52 (CD-2, track 16, 0:39)** Donald Bruce (Colin Douglas) asks the correct questions in the wrong order and the other actors meet this with confused silence.

Episode 5
First Transmitted: Jan. 20, 1968
There is significant tape print-through in this episode.
4:33 (CD-2, track 27, 0:11) Some observers have a problem with Bruce only saying he has guards with him instead of showing them. Cost cutting measures are not really bloopers.

Episode 6
First Transmitted: Jan. 27, 1968
7:06 (CD-1, track 48, 0:15) The Narrator relates to the viewers that the underground inhabitants have "sticks and objects." Where do the inhabitants get sticks if they are underground? Are there underground trees? Of course, the sticks could be wood from shipping crates. **21:08 (CD-2, track 68, 1:09)** Salamander seems to know a lot about the TARDIS even though this is the first time he has seen the ship.

Comments: This is Doctor Who's tribute to James Bond.
The Doctor saves the Earth.

(QQ) THE WEB OF FEAR

Writer: Mervyn Haisman and Henry Lincoln; **Director:** Douglas Camfield

Media: Commercial DVD—*Lost in Time*—Episode 1—25 minutes (used); Commercial 3 CD set—episodic version—147 minutes (used); Commercial tape of Episode 1—

25 minutes (used); Collector's tape of Episode 1— 25 minutes; Collector's audio recording—147 minutes

Highlights: We find what Sergeant Benton was doing before he joined UNIT. We meet Colonel Lethbridge-Stewart. Frazier Hines narrates the CD version.

Questions: Disguising robots as Yeti in the Himalayas is acceptable, but why go to the extra work to disguise them in London?

Errors and Other Points of Interest

Not all the Yeti move about with the characteristic noise from the control spheres. One of the Yeti is John Levene.

Episode 1
First Transmitted: Feb. 3, 1968

0:29 (CD-1, track 2, 0:00) To some viewers it sounds as if the Doctor calls Victoria "Debbie." **2:12** There is a bandage on the Doctor's cheek. **6:25** The Yeti appears to change shape in the museum. The sphere reactivating the mechanism could cause some changes. Changes in the Great Intelligence may be responsible for some of the changes. Part of the change is due to changes in the lighting. The Yeti in this story have glowing eyes. **7:23** The bandage on the Doctor's cheek is no longer present. **7:40** Jamie suddenly jerks his hand off the TARDIS console as if the console was burning him. **7:51** If the TARDIS has "landed," why is the light on top still flashing? **10:56** There seems to be something like a boom mike above Professor Traver's (Jack Watling) hat as he finishes talking. This only appears in the taped version and not on the DVD. It may be the result of a defect in the tape. **11:42** It is possible to see the reflection of the studio lights or the TARDIS lights in the scanner. This is not the only time. **14:11 (CD-1, track 12, 1:15)** The Doctor explains to Victoria about the underground. He says that the underground was after her time. Since her time was 1866, and the London underground first opened in 1863, some fans cite this as a blooper. The Doctor's quote is "little after your time, I think, Victoria." To the Doctor's credit, he did qualify his assumption about Victoria's time with "I think," thus, this may not be a true blooper. **14:20 (CD-1, track 12, 1:24)** The Doctor thinks that it is unusual to keep landing on the Earth. What about *The Hand of Omega*? **20:42** The Yeti in this story carry weapons. **21:27 (CD-1, track 23, 0:04)** There is the sound of a pencil dropping on the floor. **22:58 (CD-1, track 25, 0:05)** Staff Sergeant Arnold (Jack Woolgar) has trouble discussing the use of the common room during World War II. **24:10 (CD-1, track 29, 0:00)** We see and hear the same explosion repeatedly.

Episode 2
First Transmitted: Feb. 10, 1968

6:31 (CD-1, track 39, 1:00) Professor Travers refers to the events in *The Abominable Snowmen* as being over 40 years ago. **8:44 (CD-1, track 41, 0:17)** We learn the events of *The Abominable Snowmen* were in 1935 (over forty years ago). Thus, the events in this story must take place in 1975 or later.

Episode 3
First Transmitted: Feb. 17, 1968

1:46 (CD-2, track 3, 0:12) Victoria finds the Doctor and Colonel Lethbridge-Stewart. Relating this to earlier dates in this story leads to the conclusion that Lethbridge-Stewart's promotion to Brigadier must be after 1975. **11:20 (CD-1, track 11, 0:52)** The Doctor notes that the appearance of the Yeti is different. This may partially correlate with the change in the Yeti during the first episode. **22:09 (CD-1, track 25,**

0:57) Why is the Doctor worried about the TARDIS — are the doors not locked?

Episode 4
First Transmitted: Feb. 24, 1968
    8:21 (CD-2, track 39, 1:41) Colonel Lethbridge-Stewart learns from the Doctor that the TARDIS looks like a police box. This may partly refute the supposed blooper in *The Spearhead from Space*. 12:20 (CD-2, track 42, 0:17) The Colonel leads an expedition to find the "police box."

Episode 5
First Transmitted: Mar. 2, 1968
    4:24 (CD-3, track 2, 3:50) Jamie has trouble with his lines. 9:49 (CD-3, track 8, 0:12) The Doctor exclaims "Success!" before we hear any sound indicating success. This may be due to the limitations of an audio only version. 13:37 (CD-3, track 10, 1:33) The Yeti in this story can roar. This is another difference from the Yeti of *The Abominable Snowmen*. This is not the only occurrence.

Episode 6
First Transmitted: Mar. 9, 1968
    17:41 (CD-3, track 37, 1:37) Jamie enters the hall. The Doctor tells Jamie to do what the Intelligence says. The Doctor does not tell Jamie anything else. 20:04 (CD-3, track 37, 4:01) Jamie orders the "tame" Yeti to attack. The Doctor still has not told Jamie about the "fixed" helmet. 21:23 (CD-3, track 37, 5:20) The Doctor complains about Jamie "saving" him. The Doctor incorrectly says that he had warned Jamie.
    Comment: The Doctor saves the Earth.

(RR)   Fury from the Deep

Writer: Victor Pemberton; **Director:** Hugh David

Media: Commercial 2-CD set — 143 minutes (used); Commercial audio tape — 135 minutes (used), times indicated with a "T"; Excerpts are present in the tape *The Missing Years* packaged with *The Edge of Destruction*.
Highlights: Victoria leaves the series. Frazier Hines narrates the Commercial CD version. The first person narration of the audio tape version of the story by Tom Baker is memorable.

Errors and Other Points of Interest

Episode 1
First Transmitted: Mar. 16, 1968
    1:40 (CD-1, track 3, 0:17) Victoria and Jamie note that the TARDIS "always" lands in England. We learn the reason for this in *The Remembrance of the Daleks*. 3:30 (CD-1, track 3, 2:08) The sonic screwdriver makes its first appearance. 12:21 (CD-1, track 8, 1:48) Harris (Roy Spencer) explains that something in the pipeline would be the only way to lower the pressure. A leak would also lower the pressure. 21:09 (CD-1, track 19, 0:06) Why is Victoria choking on oxygen?

Episode 2
First Transmitted: Mar. 23, 1968
    6:11 (CD-1, track 29, 0:07) Price (Graham Leaman) and Jamie discuss the fact that the plant supplies all the gas for southern England and Wales. This must be the Southern Region referred to later. 17:43

(**CD-1, track 38, 0:11**) Harris says that natural gas is not toxic.

Episode 3
First Transmitted: Mar. 30, 1968

17:19 (**CD-1, track 61, 0:42**) The Doctor says this seaweed is different, "It is ... alive." Apparently, all other seaweed in the world is dead. How does normal seaweed grow if it is not alive? **17:30** (**CD-1, track 61, 0:53**) The Doctor stumbles over his lines. **17:48** (**CD-1, track 61, 1:11**) The Doctor stumbles over his lines.

Episode 4
First Transmitted: Apr. 6, 1968

13:22 (**CD-2, track 16, 0:14**) Megan (Margaret John) informs Harris, "throughout the Southern Region, receiving stations are working on emergency supplies." This sounds like a regional if not a national emergency. **13:40** (**CD-2, track 16, 0:32**) Megan now tells Harris this is not a national emergency.

Episode 5
First Transmitted: Apr. 13, 1968

10:14, 8:24T (**CD-2, track 36, 0:49**) There is a claim by some viewers of Robson (Victor Maddern) attacking a guard from behind and covering the guard's nose and mouth with his hand. If the guard's nose and mouth were covered, how could the guard inhale the gas? There is no mention of Robson covering the guard's mouth in either the CD or audio tape versions. According to the narrator of the CD version, Robson attacks the guard from behind. According to the narrator of the tape version, Robson leaves his room and Robson's expression surprises the guards into inaction, then Robson's gas overcomes the guards. **21:54** (**CD-2, track 53, 0:55**) The Doctor scolds Jamie because there is no longer any element of surprise. This is after the Doctor and Jamie landed in a noisy helicopter. The helicopter would eliminate any possible surprise.

Episode 6
First Transmitted: Apr. 20, 1968

2:48 (**CD-2, track 58, 0:02**) The Doctor flies the helicopter as he flies the TARDIS. **8:01** (**CD-2, track 59, 1:44**) Victoria's screams are finally useful. Too bad the Doctor had not met Mel yet.

Comments: The Doctor saves the Earth.

(SS) THE WHEEL IN SPACE

Writer: David Whitaker, based on a Story by Kit Pedler; **Director:** Tristan de Vere Cole

Media: Commercial DVD — *Lost in Time* — Episodes 3 and 6 — total 47 minutes (used); Commercial 2-CD set — episodic version — 142 minutes (used); Commercial tape — *Cybermen — The Early Years*, episodes 3 and 6 — total 48 minutes; Excerpts are present in the tape *The Missing Years* packaged with *The Edge of Destruction*; Collector's audio recording — episodic version — 140 minutes

Highlights: Zoe Heriot (Wendy Padbury) joins the Doctor and Jamie. Wendy Padbury narrates the CD version.

Errors and Other Points of Interest

Episode 1
First Transmitted: Apr. 27, 1968

The Doctor and Jamie are the only actors for most of this episode.

8:36 (CD-1, track 8, 0:39) The Doctor has trouble with his line to Jamie. **15:22 (CD-1, track 18, 0:22)** Simply opening the inner and outer doors would lead to an explosive decompression. This does not appear to be the case. **20:11 (CD-1, track 23, 0:49)** We learn that the ship the Doctor and Jamie are on is the Silver Carrier.

Episode 2
First Transmitted: May 4, 1968

8:53 (CD-1, track 40, 1:56) Leo (Eric Flynn) has trouble with his line. **10:59 (CD-1, track 42, 1:04)** Jamie tells Doctor Gemma Corwyn (Anne Ridler) the Doctor's name is "Doctor John Smith." **13:50 (CD-1, track 44, 0:07)** Zoe reports a star in M13 is entering the nova phase. Therefore, the star is not a nova at this time. **14:22 (CD-1, track 44, 0:44)** Zoe apparently informs Jamie "Pre-century history is my field." Zoe may be saying, "isn't." It is not clear in the audio version what she actually says, but Jamie's comments agree with Zoe saying, "isn't."

Episode 3
First Transmitted: May 11, 1968

1:19 These Cybermen have three fingers. **2:46 (CD-1, track 55, 0:08)** Leo (Eric Flynn) observes that the star is about to go nova. The star is in the Hercules Cluster, and not just in the direction of the Hercules Cluster. **3:23 (CD-1, track 56, 0:30)** The Cybermen's control device says that the Cybermen are aboard the wrong ship (Voyager) instead of the one they are on — the Silver Carrier. It is possible that the Cybermen do not know the real name of the ship, or the Cybermen changed the name of their captured ship. Another explanation is that these Cybermen has recently visited the Star Trek Universe. **4:57 (CD-1, track 58, 1:01)** Doctor Corwyn explains the situation with "the radiation flux will swing the Perseid shower straight in on us." The Perseids are near the Earth; thus, there is no need for material to travel from the Hercules Cluster to the Wheel. **5:16** Bill Duggan (Kenneth Watson) may have a hole in the seat of his pants. **7:35 (CD-1, track 62, 0:12)** Meteors due to the predicted nova are nearing the Wheel. This would be difficult, as it would take years for material from outside the Solar System to reach the Wheel even if it were traveling at the speed of light. How did the Cybermen aim them at the Wheel? The Hercules Cluster is about 30,000 light years from the Earth, thus, it would take 30,000 years, at a minimum, for any affects noted in the region of the Earth. This should include "radiation flux." The time would be significantly longer for anything traveling at less then the speed of light. **9:56 (CD-1, track 64, 0:00)** Doctor Corwyn does not comment on the Doctor's double hearts. **11:50 (CD-1, track 64, 1:53)** Zoe explains that the Silver Carrier only had fuel for 20 million miles, and the ship would need to refuel to make it the 87 million miles to the Wheel. In space, it would take the same amount of fuel to travel 20 million miles or 87 million miles or 1000 million miles. Some fans have a problem with this because spaceships require fuel for accelerating, decelerating or maneuvering, but not for actual travel. These fans overlook the fact that Zoe says the ship got to the wheel too soon. To get there so soon it must have used extra fuel for acceleration. **13:04 (CD-1, track 65, 0:13)** Some observers have a problem with the Cybermen "ionizing" a star. Since this is technobabble, this is not a true blooper. **23:31** There is a major reflection of the studio lights from one of the Cybermen's chest units.

Episode 4
First Transmitted: May 18, 1968

1:03 (CD-2, track 3, 0:08) No one knows who the Cybermen are. This would indicate that this story occurs before the events in *The Tenth Planet*. **7:51 (CD-2, track 10, 0:13)** Zoe complains that Jamie is on her tape. The use of tape recorders between the present time and the Dalek invasion of the Earth is an anachronism.

Episode 5
First Transmitted: May 25, 1968

13:30 (CD-2, track 36, 0:03) We should pay close attention to the distance to the meteors. The meteors must be traveling at least 5000 miles per second (8000 km/s). Even matter ejected from supernovas does not travel this fast, so meteors only "influenced" by the nova should be moving slower. Supernova material travels at about 2000 miles per second (3200 km/s). **15:21 (CD-2, track 36, 1:55)** We learn that the "meteorites" are not from the nova but are meteors deflected from their near Earth orbits. **20:23 (CD-2, track 43, 0:21)** Gemma tells the Doctor "switch over to the sectional supply unit" to avoid being poisoned by the Cybermen. This explains the Doctor's later blooper, and explains to those people who do not know what the Doctor was trying to say.

Episode 6
First Transmitted: June 1, 1968

1:27 We can see Jamie's supporting wire. **2:25 (CD-2, track 48, 0:51)** The Doctor says, "Switch over to sexual air supply." Some viewers wonder what the Doctor was trying to say. The Doctor is passing along the information given by Gemma when she warns the Doctor to shift to the "sectional supply unit." **2:52** We finally hear the correct word (meteor). The narration covers this on the CD version. **4:26** Something is hanging onto the Cyberman's arm. **5:56 (CD-2, track 51, 0:40)** The Cyberman hits something with a clang. **8:50 (CD-2, track 57, 0:06)** These Cybermen recognize the Doctor. This would indicate that this story takes place after the events in *The Moonbase* and/or *The Tomb of the Cybermen*. **11:26** It must be very cold on the Wheel. The vial the Doctor picks up, and calls mercury, contains a solid. If it is solid mercury the temperature is around -40°C, or lower, as this is the freezing point of mercury. **11:47** The camera jiggles as the Doctor starts across the room. **12:02** This is one of the shots where Doctor Corwyn's "body" looks more like a picture of Doctor Corwyn's body. **15:21** The fact that the Doctor did not place his trap closer to the door leads some observers to cite this as a blooper. These observers believe the Doctor should have caught both Cybermen. The fact that the second Cyberman only watches his companion suffer seems to be the real problem. In any case, how did the Doctor know that two Cybermen would enter the room instead of one? **16:24** Flannigan (James Mellor) walks into the door as he leaves the room. **17:54** The Cyberman opens the airlock doors. However, there has not been sufficient time to evacuate the airlock (but this is technobabble). The air rushing out should affect the Cybermen, but there is no noticeable effect. There is a noticeable lack of an explosive decompression. Some fans claim these two items are bloopers. The Cybermen outside are not affected until the neutron force field is turned on to repel them. If there were no air remaining, there would be no out-rushing of air. **19:55 (CD-2, track 73, 0:13)** Zoe utters, "Time And Relative Dimensions In Space." **20:21** The mercury has warmed and melted so the Doctor is now able to pour it into the funnel. The original vial contained a solid and not a liquid. **20:50** Compare the TARDIS wall behind the chest to the remainder of the TARDIS walls. **21:25** The "cliffhanger" is a lead into a repeat of *The Evil of the Daleks*. **21:31 (CD-2, track 74, 1:10)** Zoe demonstrates her knowledge of pre-century history when she fails to recognize the word Dalek.

Comments: There are many references where the actors use "meteorites" in place of the correct term "meteors." Meteors are in outer space, meteorites are on the surface of a planet. This is also an example to illustrate why multiple bloopers normally appear on this list only once in a story. These times are from the Collector's audio recording to avoid possible covering narration. The narrator on the Commercial CD introduced other uses of meteorites. Here are thirty-two examples of using meteorites blooper to illustrate why this limitation is appropriate:

Episode 1, 21:47; **Episode 1**, 22:15; **Episode 2**, 7:09; **Episode 2**, 15:20; **Episode 3**, 6:00; **Episode 3**, 7:42; **Episode 3**, 8:11; **Episode 3**, 10:57; **Episode 3**, 11:03; **Episode 3**, 13:10; **Episode 3**, 13:25; **Episode 3**, 21:16; **Episode 3**, 21:48; **Episode 4**, 6:07; **Episode 4**, 6:12; **Episode 4**, 6:43; **Episode 4**, 15:34; **Episode 4**, 16:12; **Episode 4**, 17:03; **Episode 4**, 17:39; **Episode 4**, 19:37; **Episode 5**, 6:47; **Episode 5**, 7:58; **Episode 5**, 9:51; **Episode 5**, 12:30; **Episode 5**, 15:16; **Episode 5**, 16:50; **Episode 5**, 21:06; **Episode 6**, 0:40; **Episode 6**, 1:56; **Episode 6**, 5:19; **Episode 6**, 8:26.

These Cybermen have two fingers and a thumb.

The Doctor saves the Wheel, and indirectly the Earth.

(TT) THE DOMINATORS

Writer: Norman Ashby (pseudonym for Mervyn Haisman and Henry Lincoln);
Director: Morris Barry

Media: Commercial tape — episodic version — 121 minutes (used); Collector's tape — movie version — 116 minutes

Questions: What happened to all the material removed from the new tunnel in the side of the shelter? How many ways can you make three Quarks look like twelve? (One blooper lists cite ingenious solutions to this question as bloopers.) Why does Toba (Kenneth Ives) sometimes reply to Rago (Ronald Allen) with "Command accepted," and, at other times, with no response?

Errors and Other Points of Interest

The inhabitants of the planet Dulkis also called Dulcians; this is in variance to some blooper lists, which label the inhabitants Dulkians.

The Dulcian costume that Zoe is given has a faulty zipper. The zipper comes loose in many scenes.

Some viewers incorrectly report that the "skirt" to Zoe's costume actually falls off during the cliffhanger to Episode 2.

The costumes for the female characters consist of a bathing suit with a flimsy see-through skirt. Many observers report this "skirt" coming up and allowing the viewer to see the female's underwear. Since the "skirt" is already see through, it is always possible to see the characters "underwear." Anyone reporting seeing underwear is a victim of an overactive imagination.

The Dominators do not seem to know what they control. Sometimes they control ten galaxies, and sometimes they control only one.

Some people have reported seeing the arms of the Quark operators. Cloth is visible in some scenes, but not the actual arms.

Episode 1
First Transmitted: Aug. 10, 1968

8:03 The light on the top of the

TARDIS does not flash during the landing. **8:16** The back interior of the TARDIS is visible as the Doctor exits. **8:52** There is a boom mike shadow on Zoe as the Doctor re-enters the TARDIS. **12:37** Some viewers report that when Kando (Felicity Gibson) is sitting at the console, it is possible to see her underwear. This is not possible. **22:21** The positioning of the Quark footprints is not correct. Notice how the Quarks walk relative to the footprints.

Episode 2
First Transmitted: Aug. 17, 1968

6:50 The receptionist announces Cully (Arthur Cox) as "Curly." **13:58** Teel says, "There has been a steady uniform decrease in radiation," but the graph shows a rapid decrease followed by a long slow decrease. The long slow decrease is uniform, but the rapid decrease before does not fit the description. In any case, the decrease should follow a smooth curve with no linear portions. **18:42** The shadow of a boom mike appears on the Council Room wall as Cully and Zoe are planning to return to the island. **19:46** The reflection of one of the stage-crew appears in the panel next to the door. **20:46** There is a boom mike shadow on Rago as he prepares to examine Teel (Giles Block). **21:34** The Quarks are on the left side, following Rago; in the next view they are on the right side following Toba. Finally, during the next shot, they are back on the left side behind Rago. **22:30** Some viewers report that Zoe struggles with the Quarks as she exits the Travel Capsule, and that it is possible to see her underwear. What Quarks? What struggle? What underwear? **22:43** The Survey Building is above the viewers with the sky in the background. **22:56** The Survey Building is now below the Dominator and Quarks. **23:06** Zoe's zipper comes loose during the attack. We also see this in the reprise.

Episode 3
First Transmitted: Aug. 24, 1968

0:53 The caption "Episode 3" is missing from the opening to the episode. **1:14** For some unknown reason some people think that Zoe's strap falling down is a major blooper. Some fans incorrectly credit this to Episode 2. Zoe has trouble with her straps at other times. **2:13** As the Doctor and Jamie enter the Council Chamber, something gets on the camera lens. This happens again at several other times. **2:51** A camera enters the set from left of center. **9:17** Toba tells Zoe and the other prisoners that the Dominators are "masters of the ten galaxies." **13:10** Zoe is still having zipper problems. **20:33** Cully complains that Balan (Johnson Bayly) is still in the way of Cully's shot at the Quarks. However, in the preceding shot Balan passed the Quarks, and was no longer in the way. **23:20** Some observers think that Jamie's destruction of the distant Quark to be a blooper because he should have shot at the nearer two. From the camera angle it is impossible to see if Jamie even had a chance a shooting the nearer Quarks.

Episode 4
First Transmitted: Aug. 31, 1968

1:08 Toba moves to the right faster than the camera. **1:34** The Dominator tells the Quarks to keep behind the "inferior types." The Doctor and Zoe are to remain in the ship. The Doctor had been tested and found to be "inferior," but Zoe, through her endurance, had demonstrated herself to be superior to the Dulcians. **1:36** You can see part of the studio ceiling above the set. **2:35** Toba repeats his ten galaxies reference to Rago. **10:26** The travel capsule has now moved to a position next to the ruins. **10:48** There is rubble on top of the hatch. **10:57** Most of the rubble on top of the hatch disappears. **13:54** Jamie draws a Quark away from the drilling site. Cully rolls a rock down onto the Quark. The Quark transports back to the drilling site. This assumes that Cully rolled the rock onto the Quark chasing Jamie and not onto the second Quark at the site. Balan indicates later that there may be two drilling sites involved. **13:55** The Quark chasing Jamie begins firing. The first shot shows that Quarks can shoot around corners. **14:18** The drilling site has no large boulders near the drill, Cully rolls one boulder down the hill, so zero plus one gives two boulders. This is further evidence that two drilling sites may be involved. **19:20** Rago tells the Council "we control an entire galaxy." He apparently forgot about the other nine.

Episode 5
First Transmitted: Sep. 7, 1968

10:32 Jamie's solution to the problem is very similar to the solution from *The Dalek Invasion of Earth*. Some fans consider this a blooper because of the similarity. **11:42** The Doctor uses his sonic screwdriver to cut through the wall. Note that the hole dug by the shelter inhabitants should have produced nearly enough material to fill a significant part of the shelter. **14:24** Two Quarks approach a disabled Quark. In the next scene, one of the Quarks explodes, and the other two have disappeared. **16:58** Zoe's faulty zipper appears several times in the shelter after she leaves the tunnel. **21:52** We can see the face of the Doctor's stunt double as he runs with the Dominator's bomb. **22:57** Another supposed blooper is the firing of rockets down narrow drill holes into the planet. This is technobabble, not a blooper. **23:29** Jamie's last words are "Maybe so, but we happen to be on the island!" This does not compare to the opening of the next episode.

Comments: Some observers question the Dulcian and Dominator use of years as a time measurement. What other term should they use for the period of revolution about the planet's sun? There is no indication that it is the same length of time as a year on Earth. Maybe the Dulcian "year" is similar to a Martian year, or a Venusian year, or …. Along the same lines, ten revolutions could be a decade without it being the same length of time as a decade on Earth. These should not be bloopers. The Dominators may be using Dulcian revolutions because they are on Dulkis, and not because of their own "special" time unit. If the Dominators are the "Masters" of so many planets, they may adjust time to local time.

There is a similar "blooper" about Zoe using feet as a measurement. This is an anachronism, not a true blooper.

Rumors to the contrary — no part of this story is in color.

The Doctor saves the planet of Dulkis.

(UU) THE MIND ROBBER

Writer: Derrick Sherwin and Peter Ling; **Director:** David Maloney

Media: Commercial type — episodic version — 100 minutes (used); Collector's tape — movie version — 93 minutes
Highlights: We meet the Master but not "The Master."
Questions: How much of this story is real, and how much is in the characters' minds?

Errors and Other Points of Interest

The average length of these episodes is only 20 minutes.

Episode 1
First Transmitted: Sep. 14, 1968

0:28 There is no on screen credit for the writer of this story. This is the only episode of Doctor Who with no writer given on-screen credit. **0:34** Jamie's new line is "Doctor, come on, will you look!" This is different from the preceding cliffhanger. The Doctor's lines are different also. **1:07** If there is a very large amount of mercury vapor coming from the console, Jamie and Zoe, and maybe the Doctor, should be dying. *The Power of the Daleks* lightly touches on the hazards of mercury vapor. Persons from Gallifrey may not be as susceptible to mercury as Earthlings are. **4:02** The Doctor tells Zoe they are "Nowhere." **7:55** At least one viewer, who supposedly has been there, believes that "nowhere" should be black. The appearance of "nowhere" is technobabble. **16:10** Look at the TARDIS scanner as the Doctor pushes Zoe and Jamie back into the TARDIS. The scanner shows: "PRODUCER PETER BRYANT." **16:10** The Doctor pushes Zoe so hard that he leaves a handprint on her jumpsuit. There are claims that this remains visible for several minutes. **19:59** Zoe is in different positions in the distant shots and the close-up shots. In the distant shots, she is on her right side with her legs pointing clockwise. However, in the close-ups, she is on her left side and her feet are going counterclockwise. There is a repeat of this in the reprise.

Episode 2
First Transmitted: Sep. 21, 1968

0:25 There is on-screen credit for Peter Ling in this and later episodes. **4:20** Even before the Doctor "creates" the new "Jamie" (Hamish Wilson), we hear the new actor's voice calling to the Doctor. The new voice was supposed to begin when the Doctor reassembled Jamie's face. This does not occur at the very beginning of the episode as has been claimed. **8:27** Gulliver (Bernard Horsfall) informs the Doctor that the "Master" is in charge. **8:35** The Doctor learns there will be a charge of treason. The Doctor then mutters "treason again." This sounds as if the Doctor has faced treason charges before. **12:08** Fraser Hines' features are not present on the board, so it is impossible for the Doctor to re-assemble it correctly. **16:25** The arrangement of the letters in "Jamie's" view does not seem to correspond with the letters around which the group is walking. **21:13** The surnames of two of the child actors (Christopher and David) are "Reynolds" at the end of this episode, but they are "Reynolds" at the end of Episode 5. This is not a blooper at this time.

Episode 3
First Transmitted: Sep. 28, 1968

3:23 The Doctor can now get Jamie's face right, since the appropriate pieces are present. **4:31** The door creaks shut after the Doctor, Jamie and Zoe enter. The creaking sound effect cuts off while the door is only partially closed, and then starts again and continues beyond the physical closing of the door. **4:42** Note, for future reference, that Zoe recognizes the candles in the house. **5:32** Some viewers claim that the map of the maze is incorrect. Zoe claims that the pattern is "one left turn; two right turns, three left turns; four right turns and so on." Using the map shown it should only take the group two right turns. This may not be a true blooper since we do not see the entire map. It is possible, for example, that only the portion showing the last two of Zoe's four right turns is present. **15:48** Look to the right as Jamie enters the building. There is no electric eye alarm at the bottom of the doorway. **16:54** The first time Jamie reads the tickertape, he does so correctly. You can tell from the way he is holding the paper that he does not always read the paper from the same side. **17:25** Someone is hiding behind the cave wall next to The Medusa (Sue Pulford). **17:35** The Doctor tells Zoe that the unicorn turned into a statue, when it really turned into a cardboard backed picture. **18:01** Jamie reads the tickertape incorrectly this time.

Episode 4
First Transmitted: Oct. 5, 1968

1:05 Jamie reads the tickertape correctly. **2:38** Jamie trips the electric eye alarm. **2:48** We see the electric eye alarm, which was not present earlier, is now present. **13:59** The Master (Emrys Jones) tells the Doctor that "For twenty-five years I've delivered five thousand words every week!" A few seconds later Zoe replies, "Why, that's well over half a million words!" Zoe is apparently a master of understatement; the total is indeed over half a million words, it is 6.5 million words. This, of course, assumes that weeks and years have the same meaning in this world. **15:33** It is obvious that the books on the shelves are not real books, but pictures of books. **16:17** The Master makes an interesting, but unfounded (?), observation about the Doctor, when he says the Doctor is ageless since he exists outside of time and space.

Episode 5
First Transmitted: Oct. 12, 1968

4:20 Rapunzel's (Christine Pirie) hair is thinner on the roof than at the bottom. **10:50** If the Master "sees" from the lights in the soldiers' hats, how can he see the soldiers' faces?" **12:38** Notice the diameter of the hair before Jamie and Zoe begin to descend, and its diameter when they reach the bottom. **13:42** The Master spits as he shouts the line, "Change robot weapon to destructor beam!" **13:48** The plastic around the robot guns opens as the guns extend. **15:18** Plastic surrounds the robot guns. This plastic opens as the guns extend. Shots of the robots shooting show the plastic closed except in close-ups of the guns. The plastic is open in the close-ups. **16:32** The disappearance of the Master, without the Doctor taking him to Earth, appears to be a blooper according to some fans. In truth, the Doctor thinks that the destruction of the computer will return them all, including the Master, to reality. **17:12** The surnames of two of the child actors (Christopher and David) appear as "Reynalds" at the end of this episode instead of "Reynolds." This time it is a blooper.

(VV) THE INVASION

Writer: Derrick Sherwin, from a story by Kit Pedler; **Director:** Douglas Camfield

Media: Commercial tape — episodic version, missing episodes 1 and 4 — 144 minutes (used); Commercial 3-CD set — Episodic version — 195 minutes (used); Collector's audio recording — episodes 1 and 4 — 48 minutes
Highlights: We meet the Brigadier, *Corporal* Benton and UNIT.
Questions: This story takes place before the events in *The Tenth Planet* so why do the people in the Antarctic base not recognize the Cybermen? What happened to the magazine that bought Isobel's pictures?

Errors and Other Points of Interest

The Cybermen have regained their fingers. They now have five digits as in *The Tenth Planet* instead of three digits as in *The Tomb of the Cybermen*, *The Moonbase* or *The Wheel in Space*.

The Cyberman voices are different from other stories.

Some fans believe it to be a blooper that Vaughan (Kevin Stoney) does not fire the inefficient Packer (Peter Halliday).

Frazier Hines narrates the Commercial CD version.

Episode 1
First Transmitted: Nov. 2, 1968

Most sources consider this story to take place in the late sixties. The Collector's recording of Episode 1 contains a comment before the episode by a BBC announcer telling the audience "the TARDIS lands in England in the year 1975."

4:08 (CD-1, track 5, 0:04) The TARDIS becomes invisible after the Doctor removes the visual stabilizer circuit. **23:09 (CD-1, track 23, 0:29)** The Doctor tells Jamie that Vaughan blinks far less than once every 10-15 seconds. This is noteworthy because this is an unusually slow rate.

Episode 2
First Transmitted: Nov. 9, 1968

5:39 (CD-1, track 33, 0:26) The Brigadier (Nicholas Courtney) is now officially the Brigadier. **5:45 (CD-1, track 33, 0:32)** Upon reflection, the Brigadier recalls the Yeti attack was four years earlier. **5:57 (CD-1, track 33, 0:45)** The Brigadier says that Travis told him all about the Doctor's TARDIS. This could be another reason why the Brigadier already knows about the appearance of the TARDIS without having seen it. **6:39 (CD-1, track 33, 1:25)** The Doctor first hears of the existence of UNIT. **8:41 (CD-1, track 36, 0:47)** The Cybermen recognize the Doctor and Jamie from an encounter on Planet 14. Where is Planet 14? This would indicate an untelevised meeting between the time Jamie joined the Doctor and the present story. For these Cybermen to recognize the Doctor and Jamie the Planet 14 adventure must be at a point in time before this story. **10:17 (CD-1, track 37, 0:51)** When Zoe is talking to the reception computer, she mispronounces integer. **15:54** Vaughan blinks rapidly. This is at variance to the Doctor's earlier observation. **23:37** Pay attention to the corner the Doctor and Jamie run around to escape the guards.

Episode 3
First Transmitted: Nov. 16, 1968

0:49 The Doctor and Jamie do not run around the same corner as in the climax to Episode 2. **6:16** Vaughn sends Packer to see Professor Watkins (Edward Burnham). Packer gets into the lift and pushes "3." Apparently, the Professor is on the third floor. **16:26 (CD-1, track 73, 0:08)** When the Doctor and Jamie escape after seeing the Professor, Jamie is concerned as the Doctor disables the lift and says, "but we're six floors up!" The Professor is not on the third floor. **17:54** The guards run into each other in their haste. **18:01** The chains holding the lift are very slack — they obviously do not look like they are supporting the weight of the lift. Some viewers incorrectly report that there are cables instead of chains present. **18:47 (CD-1, track 78, 0:08)** Packer, who has been waiting outside the lift, has the repaired lift sent to him on the sixth floor. The Professor must be on the sixth floor — so why did Packer originally push three? See the comments at the end of this story for the answer.

Episode 4
First Transmitted: Nov. 23, 1968

16:34 (CD-2, track 19, 0:20) The Phone Operator (Sheila Dunn) reports to the Major-General Rutlidge (Edward Dentith) that there is an outside call — he asks her "male or female?" to which the Phone

Operator does not reply "male"; she replies "Mr. Tobias Vaughn." **21:03 (CD-2, track 22, 1:00)** The Brigadier has difficulty with the word map.

Episode 5
First Transmitted: Nov. 30, 1968

4:52 (CD-2, track 30, 0:19) The narrator refers to the Major-General by the much lower rank of "Major." This is not the only occurrence. **9:23 (CD-2, track 33, 0:39)** The Cybermen seem to have contracted laryngitis. **12:13** After the Cyberman exits the box, some of its cocoon is stuck to its side. When the camera switches to a rear view — someone pulls the material away from the Cyberman. **18:03** Vaughan, after his talk with Cyber Control, turns to talk to Packer — during their conversation, the door behind Vaughan has trouble closing. **19:27 (CD-2, track 40, 0:32)** The Brigadier pays premature homage to *Scooby Doo Where Are You?* with the line, "I think those crazy kids have gone off to the sewers to get photographs of the Cybermen." Scooby Doo first aired in September 1969. **22:48** There is a report that the name of the Cyberman actor Carrigan is misspelled as "Carrigon" in the closing credits to this episode. No Cybermen actors receive credit in the video release of this episode, thus, this problem cannot occur here. This is an Episode 6 problem.

Episode 6
First Transmitted: Dec. 7, 1968

3:53 These Cybermen have five digits on each hand, like those in *The Tenth Planet*. **13:33 (CD-2, track 57, 0:00)** Gregory (Ian Fairbairn) reports to Vaughan and Packer, that UNIT has rescued Professor Watkins. This leads to Gregory's execution. Why not execute Packer also? **14:29** The Cybermen kill someone, whom we are to assume is Gregory. The person killed does not look very much like Gregory. Some fans consider this a blooper. **20:35** Isobel (Sally Faulkner) leans against the window and the entire window wobbles. **21:28** After the pedestrian stops, you can still hear his footsteps. **22:21** Some observers pose the question, "Where do the Cybermen get silver lace-up shoes?" This is supposedly a blooper. However, they have been wearing lace-up shoes at least since *The Tomb of the Cybermen*. We found out in *The Moonbase* where the Cybermen get their shiny lace-up boots. **23:59** Cyberman Ralph Carrigan has his name misspelled as Ralph Carrigon in the closing credits of this episode. His correct name appears at the end of each of the following two episodes.

Episode 7
First Transmitted: Dec. 14, 1968

7:32 The Brigadier starts to close the door to the safe before he finishes removing the file. **9:57** The Captain is apparently leaving the aircraft in a jeep so he can get to Russia faster. In reality, Jimmy is driving to the "hypersonic" jet. **13:54 (CD-3, track 16, 0:07)** Vaughan tells the Doctor he has been working with the Cybermen for five years. Some fans feel this may lead to bloopers with other stories. **21:01** The soldier on Zoe's right does not seem to be overly concerned with what Zoe is writing. **24:20** The spelling of Carrigan is correct.

Episode 8
First Transmitted: Dec. 21, 1968

8:41 The launch of the Russian rocket appears to be stock footage of a V-2. **12:38** It is obvious that the falling Cyberman is really an empty costume. **17:14 (CD-3, track 42, 0:35)** Zoe has trouble saying fifty thousand miles. **17:55 (CD-3, track 42, 1:01)** The Brigadier and the others learn it will take twelve and a half minutes to reach the Cybership. They all look at the clock and it reads "2:20." The missile should hit at about 2:32. **20:13** When the missile hits the Cybership, the clock in the missile-launching center reads "9:45," not "2:32."

20:21 The Cyberman warship has no defensive weapons. How does it fight? It is possible the rockets took the Transports by surprise, but they have had plenty of time to prepare for the Russian missile. **22:38** Captain Turner (Robert Sidaway) sees the TARDIS, and no doubt reports its appearance to the Brigadier. This is yet another place where the Brigadier can learn about the appearance of the TARDIS.

Comments: The Doctor defeats the Cybermen and saves the Earth.

The answer to the question in Episode 3 is that the WC is on the third floor.

(WW) The Krotons

Writer: Robert Holmes; **Director:** David Maloney

Media: Commercial tape — episodic version — 91 minutes (used); Collector's tape — movie version — 85 minutes

Questions: Vana recovers from the Kroton treatment in the third episode. If the Gonds recover so quickly — why do the Krotons not recycle them as in *The Savages*? If the Krotons need more intelligent Gonds, why do they eliminate the most intelligent ones?

Errors and Other Points of Interest

Some observers report that the *one* time we see a whole Kroton (it is leaving the machine), it is possible to see the operator's legs moving. It is not clear if the "one" time referred to is Episode 2 — when the two Krotons are talking, or Episode 2 — when the Kroton is reflected in the door after Jamie enters, or Episode 3 — when the Kroton leaves the machine, or Episode 4 — as the Kroton is leaving the machine. All of these show leg movements. These occurrences and others are in the following list.

Episode 1

First Transmitted: Dec. 28, 1968

0:32 The story gets off to a great start — one of the sliding doors sticks closed. **3:04** The Doctor says the atmosphere is safe, and that it has ozone and sulfur in it. He does not specify if the sulfur is present as sulfur dioxide or as hydrogen sulfide (unless the temperature is above the boiling point of sulfur, 445°C or 833°F). All of these substances are very toxic. Jamie mentioned a rotten egg smell earlier — this is indicative of hydrogen sulfide — which equals hydrogen cyanide (used in gas chambers) in toxicity. **3:09** When the Doctor, Jamie and Zoe enter, Jamie trips and almost knocks Zoe down. **3:25** The Doctor picks up a piece of rock and identifies it as magnesium silicate. There are dozens of magnesium silicates; however, without looking at the sample, Zoe immediately tells Jamie that it is mica, and not one of the other possibilities. Both the Doctor and Zoe should know that no mica is a simple magnesium silicate. **7:58** The Doctor says "Joey" when he is trying to say "Jamie, Zoe." **11:47** Zoe starts to say, "Doctor, I think I can hear something," before the sound starts. **11:52** Someone else is apparently just inside the door as Vana (Madeleine Mills) comes out of the machine. **11:59** Some observers consider that Vana losing her cloak as she raises her arms is a blooper. At this point, she is in a trance, and she would not notice the cloak falling off her shoulders. **12:39** The Doctor has again forgotten that he studied with Lister. He no longer considers himself a doctor of medicine. This may be because he remembers the details a little better — in *The Moonbase* he thought he must be, not that he definitely was. **14:50** Some viewers consider that fact that Selris (James Copeland) is Scottish to be a blooper. These viewers apparently know that the ancestors of the Gonds did not come from Scotland. Unfortunately, these viewers do not tell us which country they believe to be the original home of the Gonds. The Gonds should have accents related to their ancestors. If the Gonds originated on this planet, any accent is possible, and they may or may not sound like Earth accents. **19:03** When one of the Gonds hits the learning machine, a faceplate falls off showing the double-sided tape that was holding the part onto the machine. Later we see that the machines are empty.

Episode 2
First Transmitted: Jan. 4, 1969

4:40 The camera shakes as the scene switches to Jamie and Selris. **6:31** The meter to the right of the monitor appears to be an "intelligence meter." **9:12** Jamie gives Vana a cup to drink, but forgets to give her the pills the Doctor left. **13:47** Jamie is supposed to be running to see the Doctor; however, when he first appears, he is standing still, and only "continues" his running after he is on camera. **14:09** The shadow of the person opening the door for the Doctor and Zoe appears to the right of the opening door. **18:48** We can see the "legs" of a Kroton while the Krotons are talking. **18:49** Blooper hunters claim that sometimes there is a reversal of the Krotons' hands. Sometimes the right is a pincer, the left is spade shaped, and at other times, it is the reverse. In this scene, one of the Krotons has the reverse arrangement of the other. Some fans report this as an Episode 1 blooper; however, the Krotons did not take form until Episode 2. **21:28** We can see the "legs" of a Kroton reflected in the door after Jamie enters.

Episode 3
First Transmitted: Jan. 11, 1969

0:51 Both Krotons now have identical right "hands." In the next shot, we see both hands, and they have the same arrangement of "hands." It is possible that the Krotons have interchangeable hands. **0:54** An object comes into view above the monitor showing the Doctor and Zoe. **1:41** We can see the "legs" of a Kroton. **5:54** We can see the "legs" of a Kroton as it leaves the machine. **9:05** We can see the "legs" of a Kroton. **12:19** The Doctor mentions the smell of hydrogen telluride. Hydrogen telluride smells like horseradish. Jamie mentioned the smell of hydrogen sulfide (rotten eggs) not horseradish in Episode 1. **12:23** Zoe refers to hydrogen telluride as the worse smell in the world — obviously, she has not smelled methyl isocyanide (or any isocyanide). **13:12** When asked about tellurium, Zoe says the atomic weight is 128, and the atomic number is "fifty...." (She stops as she sees a Kroton nearby.) The fact that she simply rounded the atomic weight to 128 instead of giving the exact value of 127.60 is a blooper in the eyes of some viewers. Another explanation (technobabble — so it does not count) is that 127.60 is the average on Earth, but by the time of Zoe's training, a new value is in use. Minor revisions in the atomic weights have occurred many times in the past. Values for many elements may change when Universe averages replace Earth averages. The persons citing this as a blooper are listing the late twentieth century value for the atomic weight of tellurium. If these persons had used the early twentieth century value, it would be 127.5 instead. Unlike atomic numbers, accepted atomic weights can change. **14:33** As the Kroton is looking at the scanner and giving directions to the other Kroton the "intelligence meter" is registering. **15:06** When the Kroton fires on the TARDIS, initially smoke only comes from the gun, then another source starts sending out smoke. **19:38** The

Doctor and Zoe leave Beta (James Cairncross) in his laboratory where Beta is making sulfuric acid, and Beta continues talking to Vana and Thara (Gilbert Wynne). **20:12** Beta is now in the room of the learning machines. **20:32** The Doctor and Zoe enter the learning hall. How did Beta get there before the Doctor? Apparently, Gonds have developed transmat technology.

Episode 4
First Transmitted: Jan. 18, 1969

0:40 The large "rock" next to Zoe is very wobbly — not like a rock of its size. **1:20** Vana enters with a plastic vial that she later claims to be acid. Some viewers consider the presence of sulfuric acid in a plastic container to be a blooper. Other people seem to believe this to be an incompatible combination. Depending on the concentration of the acid, there are many useable plastics. Even a few plastics can handle any concentration of sulfuric acid. In this case, the acid cannot be very concentrated because pure sulfuric acid is colorless. **2:04** The Doctor and Zoe must remove a "rock" from the legs of Thara. The rock is supposed to be heavy, but it moves easily when Thara moves his legs. Zoe and the Doctor have some trouble making the rock seem "heavy." **4:02** Zoe smells the liquid in the bottle the Doctor has, and identifies the liquid as sulfuric acid. Sulfuric acid is odorless, so what does she smell? The liquid is not clear, like sulfuric acid, but the Doctor explains that other things are present in the acid. **4:43** Jamie picks up a piece of slate from inside the machine where the Doctor left it, and identifies it as the Doctor's mica. This is obviously not a piece of mica. **6:31** We can see the "legs" of a Kroton as it leaves the machine. **10:27** Beta and Jamie accidentally bump into each other while working in Beta's laboratory. Beta's mask falls from over his nose to below it. In the next shot, it has levitated back into its original position. **13:22** We can see the "legs" of a Kroton. **13:39** We see a tear in Zoe's jacket at the shoulder. **20:05** The Doctor and Zoe have escaped to safety, and are calmly standing beside Jamie and the others. Jamie's exclamation on seeing the pair is, "Did you get out all right?" **21:11** When Thara proclaims, "we are free at last," the camera shakes. **21:15** How did Thara know his father was dead?

Comments: The Doctor saves the planet of the Gonds.

Pause to Consider: Accents

Many of the actors in the series do not have accents that fit their roles. In *The Massacre of St. Bartholomew's Eve*, Anne Chaplet's Cornish accent is an example. If there were a blooper, it would have to be due to the person who did the casting for the role. Bad accents are not bloopers, and are not part of this list except when the actor breaks accent in mid-scene. There are instances, such as in *The Underwater Menace*, where there is an accusation that an actor speaking in his normal voice has a fake accent. On other planets, there are two explanations. First, non–Earth descendents could have any accent, even an accent similar to an Earth accent. Earth descendents could come from any region of the Earth with an accent from that region.

(XX) The Seeds of Death

Writer: Brian Hayles and Terrance Dicks; **Director:** Michael Ferguson

Media: DVD — episodic version — 147 minutes (used); Commercial tape — movie format — 136 minutes; Collector's tape — movie format — 136 minutes
Highlights: The Moonbase, and its equipment, seems to be falling apart. A few instances are in this list, but not all.

Errors and Other Points of Interest

Some fans propose that hairy Ice Warriors are bloopers. They specifically refer to the Ice Warriors approaching the weather station in Episode 5. However, hairy Ice Warriors appeared earlier. More importantly — The original appearance of the Ice Warriors (in *The Ice Warriors*) showed several shots of hairy Ice Warriors.

There are questions concerning the Ice Warriors versus human susceptibility to high temperatures. The first Ice Warrior passes out at slightly above 40°C. The next Ice Warrior stumbles at slightly above 50°C. Finally, Slaar enters the control room when the temperature is slightly below 60°C. Supposedly, these temperatures would have the same effect on humans. This is only partly true — humans can withstand these temperatures for short periods. The highest temperature recorded on the Earth was slightly below 60°C (57.7°C to be exact); this report was in 1922, before remote recording was possible. This means that someone on Earth survived that temperature for at least part of a day. The unusual part is that none of the people works up a sweat at these high temperatures.

Episode 1
First Transmitted: Jan. 25, 1969

2:06 The side of the console wobbles. **5:21** The dying crewmember falls across the control council. The console is obviously not very substantial — it wobbles significantly. **9:54** Eldred (Philip Ray) has the First Doctor's Astral Map in his museum along with other props. **9:57** Some viewers incorrectly claim that the Doctor leaves the TARDIS with his braces unclipped. There is a loose end after the clip making it look unclipped, but his braces are not unclipped. **12:15** As the technicians talk to the Ice Warriors, the reflection of a man in a sweater appears on one of the wall panels by the door through which the crew entered after the attack by the Ice Warriors. **14:51** A shadow appears in the doorway as the Doctor is talking to Eldred. **14:56** There is another shadow in the doorway. **16:41** Eldred refers to "neutral cesium ions." This is a contradiction in terms. An ion is, by definition, a particle with a charge, thus it cannot be neutral. **21:46** One of the Kroton's "intelligence meters" is on the wall next to the monitor. **21:57** Locke (Martin Cort) tells Radnor (Ronald Leigh-Hunt) and Gia Kelly (Louise Pajo) that Osgood (Harry Towb) is dead.

Episode 2
First Transmitted: Feb. 1, 1969

2:31 This is one of many instances where a boom mike shadow appears in the museum. In this case, it falls on Radnor. **8:08** Some observers make a questionable call that Zoe is losing her pants at this time. **8:46** It is a pity that one of the more than a dozen boom mike shadows did not appear in this scene near Kelly. If it did appear, it might be easier to hear what she says, as the microphone is too far away from her. This is not as bad on the DVD version. **8:58** During the discussion about traveling to the Moon the sound of something, apparently a pipe, clatters on the floor. **9:58** Kelly repeats the information that Osgood is dead. **19:23** Fewsham (Terry Scully) now reports that Osgood killed Locke, and then killed himself. This is a claimed blooper. It could be that Fewsham is telling Miss Kelly an obvious lie as a clue that something is wrong. **20:12** The Ice Warrior is hairy.

Episode 3
First Transmitted: Feb. 8, 1969

3:23 The two technicians accompanying Miss Kelly quickly succumb to STACS (Star Trek Additional Cast Syndrome). **6:59** At least some aspects of solid-state technology must have been lost during the Dalek invasion. Transmitters have been set back to using vacuum tubes. **7:17** Zoe has trouble with her line about getting back into orbit. **8:03** During the jumble as the rocket lands on the Moon, one must wonder just how far Jamie's hands go toward the left side on the screen. **12:46** The wall of the Moonbase shakes as the Doctor and Phipps (Christopher Coll) run away from the Ice Warrior. **13:55** Again, we see hairy Ice Warriors. **14:58** If the Ice Warrior is looking for the escapees, why does he not look around instead of simply walking pass Jamie and Zoe? **15:20** Jamie, and a few seconds later an Ice Warrior, nearly knock one of the walls down. **15:22** The steel girder is another sub-standard part of Moonbase construction. **19:30** It would help to synchronize the lip movement and the voice of the Ice Warrior. This is due to the dubbing of the Ice Warrior voices in after filming. Sometimes this is well done, but this is not one of those times. **20:25** Notice the Doctor's sideburns. **20:47** When Zoe opens the storeroom door after saying, "I think I heard something," an Ice Warrior is right there looking in the door. In the next shot, the Ice Warrior transports down the hall and has turned around to face the other way. **21:43** It is no wonder the Ice Warriors always lose — no real soldier would simply walk into a room that might house an enemy and leave his flank exposed.

Episode 4
First Transmitted: Feb. 15, 1969

1:47 The "dead" Brent keeps moving his finger. (We will ignore his obvious breathing.) **3:51** A boom mike shadow appears on Kelly's head while she is working on the unit. **7:46** We see the face of the Doctor's stunt double (Tommy Laird). **8:58** The T-Mat requires reprogramming to "kill" the Doctor. Why does Slaar (Alan Bennion) still insist on using the machine to kill the Doctor? There are much easier and faster ways to kill the Doctor. **12:19** As the camera pans back, it is obvious that Slaar turns and stares directly at Phipps without seeing the man. **13:05** The Ice Warrior seems to be practicing the latest Martian dance after the Warrior leaves the T-mat booth. **17:45** A boom mike shadow passes over Eldred's head as he is telling Radnor that the Ice Warriors must have come to Earth for some purpose. **19:38** A boom mike shadow adorns Eldred's back. **22:52** Zoe hits her head as Phipps lifts her too high. This comes from viewers reports, but it is a questionable call. **23:46** The temperature gauge is up to 40°C.

Episode 5
First Transmitted: Feb. 22, 1969

1:18 The temperature gauge has dropped to 35°C. **1:24** The first Ice Warrior passes out at slightly above 40°C. **2:23** During the battle in the storeroom, the Ice Warrior knocks Jamie into the wall. Jamie nearly knocks the wall down. **2:42** The second Ice Warrior stumbles. Now the temperature is slightly above 50°C. **2:56** Notice the Doctor's sideburns now. They are much longer than when he lost consciousness. **4:46** When Radnor talks about Miss Kelly leaving by T-mat, he mistakenly uses the phrase "soon after take-off." **4:53** The Weather Control Bureau is not on the part of the map towards which Eldred is pointing. **5:37** We see another hairy Ice Warrior. **6:26** The technician (Peter Whitaker) falls on the catwalk—dead. **9:31** Slaar enters the control room when the temperature is slightly below 60°C. **12:51** Miss Kelly answers Zoe's inquiry about there being no rockets by saying, "we do send up satellites for communications." This implies that they routinely launch satellites. **13:10** The Doctor describes the molecule as having five atoms. The model he is holding has more than five atoms. If each of the individual units is supposed to represent an individual molecule, why are they not all the same? For any compound, all the molecules would be identical. **16:50** Some of the prop plants fall over as Jamie and Zoe pass. **17:31** The dead technician is still on the catwalk. **19:05** Kelly says, "It's been years since we sent up satellites." This appears to be in variance with her earlier comment. **20:46** You can see where Slaar's makeup ends and the actor's neck begins. **21:50** The Doctor has long hair. **22:15** The Doctor now has a new haircut. He was hairy in the T-Mat Control Center and now he is much less so.

Episode 6
First Transmitted: Mar. 1, 1969

3:18 Both the Doctor and Zoe have trouble walking and running after the Doctor enters the Weather Control Bureau. **3:47** Zoe still has trouble with the foam on the floor. This time the foam causes her to run in the wrong direction. **4:10** Someone moved the dead worker's body since the preceding episode. **6:57** This is where the reported blooper where the Doctor calls the high-tension cable the "HTK." The quote is, "There's some more HT cable." **7:26** The security guard has his gun aimed at the Ice Warrior, and there are a few branches behind the guard. **7:34** Now, as the security guard is bringing his gun up to aim it, there is a tree behind him. The guard now appears to be on the opposite side of the same tree seen earlier. **8:09** Someone is trying to keep out of sight in the corridor to the left of the screen. You can see the edge of his arm move just before the light in the Doctor's right hand gets in the way. **12:52** Even though she did not hear Slaar's name, Zoe knows his name. **13:42** The reflection of a boom mike appears in the upper part of the door to the T-Mat cubicle. **19:20** One of the lenses in Slaar's helmet appears to be cracked. **19:40** During their conversation, Slaar tells the Grand Marshal, "Use your retroactive rockets to change course." **19:51** This is the first time we hear Slaar's name, except when Zoe said his name. In addition, the names "Lord" or "Ice Lord" do not occur. **19:55** The Grand Marshal tells Slaar that the fleet is now in the orbit of the Sun. **21:13** Fortunately, for the Doctor, the control console has been re-enforced since the first episode. **23:44** The closing credits misspell Grand Marshal as "Grand Marshall."

Comments: Some viewers have trouble with people giving up other forms of transportation in favor of trans-mat.

The Doctor saves the Earth.

(YY) THE SPACE PIRATES

Writer: Robert Holmes; **Director:** Michael Hart

Media: Commercial DVD—*Lost in Time*—Episode 2—25 minutes (used); Commercial CD—episodic version—148 minutes (used); Commercial tape—*The Troughton Years*—Episode 2 only—25 minutes; Collector's audio recording 146 minutes.
Highlights: Milo Clancey (Gordon Gostelow)
Questions: Why not give Home Planet a more creative name than "Home Planet?"

Errors and Other Points of Interest

At several points in this story, it is possible to hear clearly an explosion in space. It is not possible to hear explosions clearly in space.

Episode 1
First Transmitted: Mar. 8, 1969

2:50 (CD-1, track 2, 2:17) There is a clear noisy explosion of Beacon Alpha 2. **11:26 (CD-1, track 6, 0:50)** There is a clear noisy explosion of Beacon Alpha 7. **23:21 (CD-1, track 24, 0:00)** We clearly hear the explosion of Beacon Alpha 4. Sound does not travel well in space, thus, explosions will not be clear in space. This time it may not be a blooper if we are supposed to be hearing what the Doctor and the others are hearing. Inside the beacon, it would be possible to hear the sound clearly.

Episode 2
First Transmitted: Mar. 15, 1969

1:18 Where are the stars? This continues throughout the episode. **1:56** General Hermack (Jack May) pretends to get coffee, but nothing comes out of the machine. However, it is fortunate that nothing came out of the machine; the General did not hold his cup under the spout. **4:28** As Milo enters the cabin, a large boom mike shadow appears next to the door. **11:47** As the General and the crew are talking to Milo Clancey about the loss of Beacon Alpha 4, Milo looks up and a boom mike shadow adorns his forehead. **14:15 (CD-1, track 35, 1:37)** For no apparent reason, there is a close-up of Zoe looking as if she is about to cry. This occurs after the Doctor says, "Now, what on Earth is that?" The Doctor has been misquoted to say, "What's that noise?" **16:49** The Major (Donald Gee) must have gotten his helmet from Ice Warrior War Surplus. **18:18** Zoe asks the Doctor how he knows if the next section has the opposite pole. Originally, magnetic forces connected the two sections, thus neighboring sections must have the opposite pole to the one the Doctor, Jamie and Zoe are occupying. This makes the later movement of the section incorrect. **21:48** The Doctor increases the power of the solar magnets on the section of the beacon and the section shoots off into space leaving the other sections unmoved. Apparently, in the future Newton's Third Law of Motion no longer applies. The section with the opposite polarity that propelled the Doctor's section off into space would travel equally in the opposite direction. If the section was truly being repelled, it should have moved directly away from the ring instead of moving into and through the ring.

Episode 3
First Transmitted: Mar. 22, 1969

7:08 (CD-1, track 51, 2:21) Milo Clancey describes argonite as "the most expensive mineral in the galaxy." This means that the beacons are made of "gold." If argonite is so valuable, why not protect the beacons better? **7:18 (CD-1, track 51, 2:34)** After the Doctor simply informs Clancey that they are only visitors, Clancey seems to know all about the travels of the Doctor and companions through time and space. **9:40 (CD-1, track 52, 0:23)** Major Warne (Donald Gee) tells the General that his sonar is not working. How can sonar work in space? Sonar relies on sound waves, which do not travel through the vacuum of space. **23:22 (CD-1, track 61, 1:30)** The Doctor and the others fall over a cliff, repeatedly screaming for several seconds indicating a long fall; the reprise does not substantiate this. The reported, by some viewers, term "several seconds" may be an exaggeration.

Episode 4
First Transmitted: Mar. 29, 1969

0:48 (CD-2, track 2, 0:19) In the

reprise, we find that the Doctor and the others did not fall as far as their screams would indicate. **2:27 (CD-2, track 7, 0:21)** The Doctor finds Lieutenant Sorba (Nik Zaran). Why did the pirates even bother to keep the Lieutenant alive? The pirates killed all the other soldiers.

Episode 5
First Transmitted: Apr. 5, 1969
3:50 (CD-2, track 26, 1:24) Why did the General wait until now to determine the course of the Beacon sections? **5:34 (CD-2, track 27, 1:19)** The Doctor must explain to Zoe how a candle works. Zoe has apparently forgotten what she knew in *The Mind Robber*. **17:34(CD-2, track 33, 0:16)** Miss Issigri (Lisa Daniely) complains to Caven (Dudley Foster) with "If you think if you think for one moment...."

Episode 6
First Transmitted: Apr. 12, 1969
1:49 (CD-2, track 47, 0:14) Zoe tells Jamie that the Doctor's pulse is weak. She does not say his pulses are weak. **22:19 (CD-2, track 81, 0:26)** We hear the final clear explosion in space as the pirate ship explodes.
Comments: The Doctor leads to the downfall of the Space Pirates.

(ZZ) THE WAR GAMES

Writer: Terrance Dicks and Malcolm Hulke; **Director:** David Malony

Media: Commercial recording — episodic version — 241 minutes (used); Collector's tape — movie version — 234 minutes
Highlights: The Doctor has his first kiss. Meet the Doctor's son Moor (David Troughton). This is the only situation where replacement of the Doctor and all the companions occurs at the same time.

Errors and Other Points of Interest

There is a hole in the Doctor's right pants leg that disappears, reappears, and varies in size. Some times are present for comparison.

Episode 1
First Transmitted: Apr. 19, 1969
4:45 When the blanket moves aside so Lieutenant Carstairs (David Savile) can see Major Barrington (Terence Bayler), it is possible to see two people in the background quickly scrambling out of the way. These unknown persons do not appear to be wearing soldier's uniforms. **19:58** After many serious situations, and near death experiences, the Doctor kisses Zoe goodbye.

Episode 2
First Transmitted: Apr. 26, 1969
3:15 The Redcoat (Tony McEwan) tells Jamie that the year is 1745. When we see the map later, there is no 1745 area. **3:26** After the Doctor and Zoe have been watching the troops through a telescope, the picture remains as the telescope cropped circle for a brief instant after the action switches back to the tree where Zoe and the Doctor are hiding. The Doctor and Zoe are hiding behind the tree, not in the tree as erroneously reported. **10:26** The door and the wall sway as the guard and Jamie enter. **23:45** In the climax to the episode, the Doctor and the others find they have driven

from World War I to an attack by Roman soldiers. This clearly indicates that the World War I (1917) Zone is adjacent to the Roman Zone.

Episode 3
First Transmitted: May 3, 1969

1:38 The Doctor and the others drive into the Roman Zone from the 1917 Zone. **5:57** The shadow of the entering soldier appears on Lieutenant Ransome's hat while he is bending over the Captain. If the soldier was so close, why did the soldier not see the Captain, or hear the Captain's cries a few moments earlier? **7:28** The explosion does not even blow the fuse out. In addition, it does not appear as if the flame has reached the lock, or the explosives. **8:02** We get a view of the entire map. It is not easy to read it, but according to the map, the World War I Zone is not adjacent to the Roman Zone, so how can people travel directly from one to the other? The Doctor indicates that the 1917 Zone is adjacent to the American Civil War Zone. Where is the 1745 zone? **9:34** The Doctor gives his name as "Dr. John Smith." **11:47** The Doctor uses his sonic screwdriver. **14:42** Positioning of the map in the control center is different from the map the Doctor found in the General's safe — it apparently has only nine areas instead of twelve. The map the Doctor found has triangular zones. The map in the control room has square zones. **16:31** The ambulance enters the American Civil War Zone instead of the Roman Zone from the World War I Zone. Thus, both the American Civil War Zone, and the Roman Zone must be adjacent to the World War I Zone. **16:58** Zoe reads "America 1962" from the map, sits back to reflect, then recalls that this would put them in the American Civil War. However, when the Doctor read the map earlier, and you can read it as the Doctor reads, "American Civil War Zone." Clearly, the Doctor and Zoe were not reading the same map.

Episode 4
First Transmitted: May 10, 1969

3:19 The same ten Roman soldiers march by twice. **9:01** Jamie calls to the soldier with the blonde hair — none of the soldiers appears to be blonde. **9:39** We hear a voice off set after the soldier sets his gun down. This blooper may be the result of the print-through during duplication of the tape. **15:02** Just before the Scientist (Vernon Dobtcheff) puts the machine around Lieutenant Carstairs's head — something falls off the backside of the machine. **19:33** When the fighters fall against the wall of the barn, the wall wobbles significantly. **19:52** Why does the Captain (David Garfield) fire his second shot towards the floor? **21:14** The Doctor and the War Chief (Edward Brayshaw) recognize each other, as Time Lords usually do.

Episode 5
First Transmitted: May 17, 1969

4:14 A boom mike shadow falls on Russell's (Graham Weston) chest when he grabs the two fighting soldiers (Spencer (Michael Lynch) and Harper (Rudolph Walker). **6:48** Zoe says, "Time and Relative Dimensions in Space." **8:27** The reflection of what appears to be a camera is on one of the balloons in the back of the room. **10:35** When the technician pushes the button, we see the entire console tremble. **12:34** The butt of Lieutenant Carstairs gun does not come near the guard's head; however, the gun does knock out the guard. **12:34** The sound of the blow does not correspond to the delivery of the blow. **14:27** Zoe tells the Doctor she will memorize the faces, names and the like of all the resistance leaders. This includes Arturo Villar (Michael Napier-Brown). **16:06** The timing of the SIDRAT noise is a little late. Jamie stops because he "hears" the machine; then after a pause, we hear the sound. **20:43** Jamie shouts about the door closing before it begins to close, or even the sound of closing begins.

Episode 6
First Transmitted: May 24, 1969

1:30 As the Security Chief (James Bree) is talking to the Scientist, who is standing still in front of him, the reflection of moving legs appears in the panel on the front of the desk. **2:24** The Scientist says "Time Lords" for the first time in Doctor Who history. **3:13** The guards are not very observant—the Doctor and the others are "hiding" behind a transparent screen, yet the guards do not see them. **12:35** Zoe reconfirms the fact that she has memorized the names and other information about the resistance leaders. **16:01** The Doctor sends Zoe and Russell to the 1917 Zone. **16:51** The inside frame of the central board can be seen. The frame has no back and nothing inside. **17:20** Russell and Zoe arrive in the American Civil War Zone instead of the 1917 Zone. Some fans incorrectly report this as occurring in Episode 7. **22:02** There is a hole in the Doctor's right pants leg.

Episode 7
First Transmitted: May 31, 1969

1:00 Before there is any indication, the Security Chief has a premonition and says, "Wait!" **2:35** The Doctor reaffirms with Jamie that Zoe went to the 1917 Zone. Too bad, the companions landed in the American Civil War Zone. **3:03** The War Chief mentions the name SIDRAT. This is the only use of the name in this story. **3:51** The hole in the Doctor's pants leg has regenerated. **4:19** The Security Chief is observing the map—the numbers "1," "2" and "3" are in front of him—he is nearest the number "1." The Security Chief says, "Alert the Roman Zone Commanders in Sector "5." This indicates that on this planet a five appears as "1." **4:28** This is one of the points on the commercial recording where it is difficult to hear the dialog. It is very difficult to hear the Security Chief say, "These resistance people must be captured...." **6:19** The War Chief indicates, on the map, that the escapees are going from area "1" to area "2," which means they have not left sector "1," but they have left sector "5," since "1"="5." **8:16** The fleeing Doctor, Jamie, and Lieutenant enter from the front left, then instead of continuing on away from the Roman Zone—they exit front right, which should bring them back into the Roman Zone (at a different point). **8:42** The Doctor, Jamie and the Lieutenant enter the 1917 Zone, after leaving the Roman Zone. **14:43** The War Lord (Philip Madoc), War Chief, and Security Chief have been watching the video from the 1917 Zone—and area "1" on the map. Thus while it has already been established that area "1" is the Roman Zone—this is the point where the 1917 Zone is viewed. Alternatively—the designations of the zones randomly vary. **16:44** The hole in the Doctor's pants is back. **21:32** The Security Chief has several top members of the Resistance cornered. Instead of capturing them all, the Security Chief only takes the Doctor and the machine. **21:32** The order of entry into the SIDRAT is Doctor, Guard, Security Chief, and finally a Guard.

Episode 8
First Transmitted: June 7, 1969

0:55 During the reprise, the people enter the SIDRAT different from the cliffhanger—they enter the SIDRAT in the following order: Doctor, Guard, Guard, and finally the Security Chief. **4:07** Zoe again reaffirms that she knows the names of the resistance leaders. **4:56** The Civil War Soldier has apparently watched too many American Western Movies—he makes sure his hat does not fall off as he falls. **8:11** During the conversation between the Doctor and the War Chief there is the reflection, on the monitor in the back wall, of a camera moving into position. **10:27** Zoe has apparently forgotten all the names and faces of the resistance leaders—she does not recognize Arturo Villar. **15:58** The War Chief tells the Doctor that he plans to control the

Universe. Is the War Chief a relative of the Master? **16:11** Some observers claim that in one scene, Zoe is having trouble holding up her pants — this may be the scene. **17:50** The alarm sounds, and light number "1" flashes. (Number "2" flashes also.) The Security Chief announces a failure of the communication circuit in the Roman Zone. This means the Roman Zone is number "1." Earlier, the Security Chief referred to the Roman Zone as "Sector 5," thus, "1" still equals "5." **19:09** The Crimean War Zone is apparently number "3." **19:27** We again see the map of the zones. **21:45** A boom mike shadow appears on Arturo Villar's hat.

Episode 9
First Transmitted: June 14, 1969

5:10 The War Lord asks the War Chief where the resistance groups are located. The War Chief indicates area "3" on the map and says the resistance people are in this area — the American Civil War Zone. **14:12** Villar shoots two guards. However, the bandit is only aiming at the first guard, neither of Villar's guns point at the second guard. **14:18** The table is not very stable; this becomes obvious as the operator pushes buttons on it. Russell reinforces this fact. **14:19** The operator falls on the table and demonstrates how flimsy it is. **17:55** The SIDRAT control panel is now set at an angle to prevent viewers from seeing the interior framework as happened during the earlier view. **19:02** There is another reflection in a wall panel. This time it is in the panel beside the guards at the top of the ramp. **19:08** The War Chief dies, but we do not see his regeneration. **19:45** Villar again kills people without firing in their direction. The bandit is shooting at the floor of the room (you can see the direction the smoke travels after one shot), and people at the bottom of the ramp are falling.

Episode 10
First Transmitted: June 21, 1969

0:34 The TARDIS key is a normal key. **1:44** The TARDIS column stops moving and no one notices. **2:05** The Doctor tells Jamie and Zoe that Time Lords "live forever — barring accidents." **2:50** The TARDIS console starts to move again. **5:30** The Doctor finally returns to his home planet. We do not hear the name Gallifrey. **6:55** The map appears again — it is still the same map. **7:10** It would seem that the evidence shown should be entirely of photographs or entirely line drawings. **10:28** Two bodies are on the floor. **11:26** One of the two bodies is no longer on the floor. **13:40** During his trial, the Time Lords seem to have forgotten Susan. **19:03** The Time Lord tells the Doctor that Zoe and Jamie will remember their first adventure together. **22:42** There is a flash behind the Doctor — apparently from a light. **22:54** The regeneration begins, but we do not see the results. This is a Time Lord induced regeneration, so it may not be appropriate to compare this to other regenerations.

Comments: We see the zone map several times. Each time it seems the same. The map consists of triangular zones with the triangles pointed alternately up and down. The triangle in the upper left is pointing up. There are five zones along the top of the map, left to right; they are 1917 Zone (World War I), American Civil War Zone, Crimean War Zone, Roman Zone, Mexican Civil War Zone. The second row has the first triangle pointing down, and from left to right the areas are English Civil War Zone, Thirty Years' War Zone, Control Base, Boer War Zone, and Peninsular War Zone. The bottom row only has three triangles with the first one, on the left, pointing down. Thus, as we go from left to right the zones are Russian-Japanese War Zone, blank, and The Greek Zone. This map confirms and refutes some bloopers. Which of these is the 1745 Zone?

The War Chief, as a Time Lord, apparently has technology to make people not see "impossible" things. The Scientist is developing a machine to enhance this ability. This may be a means of explaining why other people do not "see" different clothing on the Doctor and the Companions.

III
The Third Doctor

(AAA) SPEARHEAD FROM SPACE

Writer: Robert Holmes; **Director:** Derek Martinus

Media: DVD — episodic version — 97 minutes (used); Commercial Tape — movie version — 91 minutes; Collector's tape — movie version — 91 minutes

Highlights: The "new" Doctor (Jon Pertwee) enters the series. Liz Shaw (Caroline John) and Brigadier Lethbridge-Stewart (Nicholas Courtney) replace Jamie and Zoe. The credits now list "Doctor Who" instead of "Dr. Who." The Doctor has a nude scene. The new Doctor's face first appears in the opening credits to the second episode. The Doctor is now in color.

Questions: If the Autons in the museum were able to watch the Doctor and Liz, as he comments on their eyes following Liz and he, why did the Autons simply file out without looking for the Doctor and Liz?

How did the Doctor know where the TARDIS was located? (He did not have his "watch.")

Errors and Other Points of Interest

Some observers question General Scobie's epaulets.

Episode 1

First Transmitted: Jan. 3, 1970

1:40 The cluster of fifty meteorites is five aircraft flying in close formation. **3:03** The TARDIS obviously materializes in front of a painted backdrop. **3:10** There are reports that the new Doctor begins his regeneration by nearly pulling off the left-hand or right-hand TARDIS door, depending on the report. This is a matter of prospective — it is the door on the Doctor's right, which is the left side of the screen. **3:10** When the Doctor falls out of the TARDIS, he leaves the doors open. **4:24** Notice the file behind the Brigadier — it is an "X" file. **5:14** Liz tells the Brigadier, "Most meteorites don't even reach the Earth's surface — they usually burn up in the atmosphere." Meteorites are the meteors that do not totally burn up in the atmosphere — a meteor becomes a meteorite when it reaches the Earth's surface. **6:38** The Brigadier tells Liz, "Since UNIT was formed...." Some fans suggest that this is not the Brigadier's voice. On the DVD, it sounds like a bad recording of the Brigadier's voice. **7:30** It has been brought to question — how did the Brigadier know the TARDIS looked like a Police Box? In the two previous adventures with the Doctor (*The Web of Fear* and *The Invasion*), the Brigadier did not see the TARDIS. In *The Web of Fear,* the Doctor told the Brigadier (then Colonel) that the TARDIS looked like a Police Box. The Colonel then mounted a major project to retrieve the blue police box.

In *The Invasion,* Captain Turner did see the TARDIS (as a Police Box) and no doubt reported this fact to the Brigadier. Also in *The Invasion,* the Brigadier tells the Doctor that Travers told him all about the TARDIS. **8:28** We learn that the Doctor has two hearts. **12:48** There are claims that the appearance of the spotlights during the Brigadier's interview is a blooper. However, this often occurs in "normal" interviews. These are studio spotlights, not news crew spotlights. **17:54** The UNIT soldiers are guarding the TARDIS. Someone closed and apparently locked the doors. The Doctor did not leave them this way. **18:56** The Doctor's heartbeat slows to ten beats per minute. Is this for each heart, or is this the total for two hearts? **21:04** Some viewers question where the Doctor keeps the TARDIS key during the chase scene. When the kidnappers load the Doctor into the ambulance both of the Doctor's hands are limp and open, thus he cannot be clutching a key in either hand. Later, as the Doctor flees in the wheelchair, he is wearing shoes, or at least socks, so it is possible that he put his key in them instead of in his boots. After the Doctor leaves the wheelchair, he could have then clutched the key in his hand. **22:10** The Doctor's hand is not on his head before he is shot.

Episode 2
First Transmitted: Jan. 10, 1970

0:33 Many people cite a blooper at the beginning of this episode. Supposedly, the Doctor grabs his head before the shot. However, because of the foliage this is at best a questionable blooper. There is the possibility of editing in the movie version to remove the error. In addition, the Doctor could have his hand up to move branches. **1:21** Dr. Henderson (Antony Webb) tells the Brigadier that the Doctor's EEG shows no activity. Any other doctor would have considered his patient to be "brain dead," not unconscious. **2:08** The TARDIS key is a normal key. **2:29** Some viewers question the cleverness of the Nestene intelligence. It seems to some that it is a blooper for the Nestenes to split into fifty separate units, especially since one of the units gets broken. There is a discussion of the broken Nestene unit at this time. **7:37** Another reported blooper is that Liz calls meteorites comet debris. This is not completely an incorrect statement. Some meteors, particularly those in meteors showers such as the Perseids, are definitely associated with comets and are, therefore, comet debris. Other meteors may or may not be associated with a comet. A group of fifty meteors would definitely qualify as a meteor shower and could be candidates for comet debris. The use of the terms meteor and meteorite would not be applicable after it has been determined that the objects are not natural. **8:42** Channing says, "Two energy units are still missing." This continues the question of the Nestene intelligence. **9:34** Some fans question — why make the Autons so ugly, when it is possible to produce more realistic units, such as Channing and Scobie. This may be due to production problems. The "ugly" Autons may be mass production units — made quickly with minimal extras. They could reserve a few special units for replacing important individuals. **13:45** The Third Doctor has a tattoo on his arm. **14:12** The UNIT troops unearth one of the energy units. This unit, along with the unit Seeley has, constitutes the two missing units. The broken pieces must not be from a missing unit, but from a unit already collected. This shows the question of the Nestene intelligence is not entirely a blooper. **17:58** The first time the Doctor speaks to the guard everything is all right. However, in later shots the same footage repeats with different words dubbed. Try reading the Doctor's lips. **18:02** The Doctor tells the guard/attendant (Derrick Sherwin) that he will not say his name, and the attendant should immediately contact the Brigadier. The Doctor does not even say that he is "The Doctor." When the action shifts to the Brigadier, who is apparently talking to the attendant, the Brigadier's first words are, "The Doctor." **23:20** In the cliffhanger, the Auton approaches Ransome (Derek Smee) and no "hand" gun is seen. There is no audible sound associated with the gun.

Episode 3
First Transmitted: Jan. 17, 1970

0:55 The reprise shows the Auton approaching Ransome—the "hand" gun quickly emerges and a click sounds as the gun appears. **1:34** Channing (Hugh Burden) does not see Ransome escaping. Channing does not even look in Ransome's general direction. **2:26** Channing tells Hibbert (John Woodnutt) that he saw Ransome. One explanation could be the fact that all the Autons are one mind, and as long as one of the units saw Ransome, all of the units could report seeing him. **9:28** A man's shadow moves along the TARDIS door behind the Doctor. **14:26** A dog is barking at Seeley's house. The dog sounds more like a barking man. An Auton or a disgruntled neighbor silences the dog. **15:21** When Mrs. Seeley (Betty Bowden) first sees the Auton in the house, there are two close-ups of the Auton's face. During the second and longer close-up, the actor is blinking his right eye.

Episode 4
First Transmitted: Jan. 24, 1970

1:45 Some observers question how Channing managed to build his own body. These observers claim this to be a blooper. The Doctor explains this ability by saying that once on Earth the unit can build a suitable shell. Channing may have built a series of more and more complex bodies with his current body being the result. **3:21** During the Doctor's first visit to Madame Tussaud's museum, the woman in the blue dress forgets not to move. She looks up, then down again. **3:30** People have questioned why would Madame Tussaud's use someone else's models, and if the models were so good, why did people not question the process? The explanation is that an "entirely new process" produces the models. A "new" process could result in the use of other models and could explain a lack of knowledge about the process. In addition, this could be a temporary exhibit, or the staff could be Auton replacements. **3:36** The woman in the blue dress again forgets not to move. **7:02** The Doctor partially clears up the movements of the woman in the blue dress during his second visit when he says to Liz, "Funny how their eyes seem to follow you...." This indicates that the exhibits are capable of motion. **12:28** People have cited the trick of not showing the breaking glass is a blooper. When the Autons leave the store, it is possible to see a break in the lower window line where the doorstep, not the windowsill, is. **12:59** Notice the positions of the actors. **13:11** Blooper hunters have complained about this being the same shot as the earlier one, but from a different angle. **13:12** When the Autons begin shooting people at the bus stop—people are in different positions in different camera angles. **13:14** The "dead" man in the gray coat keeps moving his hands. **17:05** It has been claimed that the General (Hamilton Dyce) should have been killed instead of sent to the Wax Museum. However, the destruction of the General's facsimile results in the General regaining consciousness, thus there must be a mental link. Apparently, the facsimile requires the General's memory. This means that they need to keep the General and others alive at least for the time being. **20:05** The sound effects and some of the Doctor's facial expressions as the tentacles wrap around him are, at best, "interesting." **23:37** The Doctor gives his name as "Doctor John Smith."

Comments: The Doctor saves the Earth.

110   III. The Third Doctor

(BBB) DOCTOR WHO AND THE SILURIANS

Writer: Malcolm Hulke; **Director:** Timothy Combe

Media: Commercial Tape — episodic version — 167 minutes (used); Collector's tape — movie version — 154 minutes
Highlights: The Brigadier calls the Doctor — Dr. Watson. Bessie joins the series.

Errors and Other Points of Interest

Liz ties her belt on the left in the first and fifth episodes, but in the second episode, she ties it on the right.

Episode 1
First Transmitted: Jan. 31, 1970

2:57 Liz says, "It would make a nite nice trip for us" as she talks to the Doctor. **3:12** Liz snags her belt on her skirt as she stands after talking to the Doctor. **8:36** The Doctor says, "Your nuclear reactor would turn into a massive atomic bomb." This is good for the plot even though it is scientifically impossible. **16:14** After discussing the files with the Brigadier, Major Baker (Norman Jones) puts the files into a briefcase that will not close.

Episode 2
First Transmitted: Feb. 7, 1970

1:28 The Doctor is apparently following the dinosaur's trail. Some observers question what the Doctor is doing. **5:40** How did the dinosaur get through the small doorway that the Doctor came through? **8:40** It is possible to hear the wounded Silurian breathing at the beginning of the following scene when the Doctor and Liz are in the laboratory.

Episode 3
First Transmitted: Feb. 14, 1970

4:34 When Dr. Quinn (Fulton MacKay) enters the barn, his coat is very wet. **4:51** Dr. Quinn's coat is completely dry. **10:42** The Doctor tells the Brigadier the footprints are not the ones he saw in the cave, as these are the footprints of a biped. This means the dinosaur that attacked him in the cave was not a biped. We only see the dinosaur that is a biped. **16:22** There are some time discrepancies; the Doctor refers to the globe he found in the cabinet and then picked up by Liz, as representing the Earth 200 million years ago (mid–Triassic). **16:35** Now, the Doctor says that Dr. Quinn's notes refer to the Silurian period (395–430 million years ago). The Doctor misses his earlier estimation by about 200 million years.

Episode 4
First Transmitted: Feb. 21, 1970

1:15 The Doctor first refers to the "Aliens" as Silurians with no reason given. **12:48** The dinosaur looks like an allosaur. Some viewers claim a blooper here; they say the dinosaur is a tyrannosaur. The identi-fication as a tyrannosaur is from the novelisation and not from the show. This dinosaur is a biped. **16:35** Permanent Undersecretary Masters (Geoffrey Palmer) speaks to Dr. Lawrence (Peter Miles) without any sound for a few words.

Episode 5
First Transmitted: Feb. 28, 1970

7:35 The Silurian to whom the Doctor is talking has a loose mask. The tape used to hold the edge of the mask down is apparent where the mask meets the left of the actor's chest. **16:28** As the Silurian walks away from Major Baker, it snags a wire on the floor of the cave. **17:02** As Major Baker arises, the polystyrene "boulder" he is leaning against wobbles in an un–boulder-like manner. **19:23** As everyone is moving away from Major Baker, a boom mike shadow appears on the map to the right of the screen.

Episode 6
First Transmitted: Mar. 7, 1970

2:44 The Doctor says he needs a scanning microscope (scanning electron microscope?). **5:40** The scanning microscope that appears is a light microscope (albeit a fancy one); such a microscope costs a fraction of a scanning electron microscope. **6:57** The rebellious Silurian also has a loose headpiece. You can see a piece of tape at the back when he orders the dead Silurian taken away. **8:21** Dr. Lawrence complains to Liz about how easily the Doctor can get expensive equipment. This implies an expensive scanning electron microscope instead of a much less expensive light microscope. **8:29** Dr. Lawrence insists on complaining to the Brigadier, but complains to Liz instead. **9:10** Dr. Lawrence, after being belligerent to Liz, storms out of the room without saying a word to the entering Brigadier. This is at odds with Doctor Lawrence's earlier insistence on complaining to the Brigadier.

Episode 7
First Transmitted: Mar. 14, 1970

7:01 The Brigadier tells Liz, "I've just sent the last of my men into these caves." **8:00** Even though the Brigadier has sent the last of his men to the caves, just before the Brigadier and Liz come down the hall, Captain Hawkins walks across the set. **9:18** Carefully note the door through which the Silurians enter. **9:24** The Doctor intervenes to stop the Silurians from killing everyone in the cyclotron room. Even though the Silurians stop killing, the red light on the Silurian to the Doctor's left continues to flash. Some fans incorrectly list this as an Episode 6 blooper. **10:20** There are reports that a blooper is present along the line that it is not the Van Allen belt which protects the Earth from radiation but the ozone layer. This is not exactly a blooper. The Silurians refer to the Van Allen belt as the "Filter belt"; this is a more accurate description. Very harmful radiation from the Sun and from cosmic rays is "filtered" by the Van Allen belt, leaving the ozone layer to "filter" the less harmful ultraviolet (UV) radiation. **14:18** Some viewers claim a blooper at this time. The blooper goes like this — with the reactor on overload the Silurians must leave the room and seek safety. The fact that they walk off towards the left instead of towards the door by the control panel is supposedly a blooper. The real answer is that this is not a blooper — they left by the door they entered through earlier. **17:47** Some fans report seeing the zipper on one of the Silurian costumes.

Comments: This is the only BBC story with *Doctor Who* in the title. The Doctor saves the Earth.

(CCC) The Ambassadors of Death

Writer: David Whitaker, Trevor Ray, and Malcolm Hulke; **Director:** Michael Ferguson

Media: Commercial tape — episodic version — 172 minutes (used); Collector's tape — movie version — 161 minutes (used) — an "M" indicates these times
Highlights: Benton becomes a Sergeant.

Questions: Why do the aliens consider kidnapping the astronauts as a positive diplomatic step?

Errors and Other Points of Interest

Episode 1
First Transmitted: Mar. 21, 1970

1:31 The ceiling of the control room is high with large flat panels. **2:01** The image of the astronaut on the screen (a CSO image) stays on too long, and then just disappears. **2:36** Some observers question how the Doctor manages to get the TARDIS console out the doors. **4:58** Van Lyden (Ric Felgate) tells the base "changing attitude of capsule." The astronaut's image should remain fixed relative to any camera inside the capsule. The image rotates on the viewscreen; this could not happen. **6:00** Some fans report the nose cone of Recovery 7 changes color between scenes. The color changes beginning in these shots may be due only to differences in lighting. **14:10** Beginning with "Cambridge" the map shifts significantly when the Brigadier marks a point. **15:10** Liz gets some information from "France." The Brigadier marks a different region of the map. There is no point on the map in or near France. **21:15** An object falls as the window opens. **22:10** The video screen with Taltalian's (Robert Cawdron) image on it retracts; however, the image does not retract.

Episode 2
First Transmitted: Mar. 28, 1970

8:35 The panel seems rather flimsy. **11:31** The nose cone of Recovery 7 is a different color on Earth. It is possible that the paint burned off or changed color during re-entry. The black paint could be more heat resistant than the other paint. **13:20** Just before the Brigadier enters the truck, he talks over his shoulder to some of his men. Some fans cite this as a blooper because there is no one in the direction he is talking. Two soldiers did walk in that direction, but they were probably out of earshot by the time the Brigadier gives his instructions. It is possible that there is someone directly behind him, as the camera does not show that area. If this were true, then this would not be a blooper. The reason why he did not look in the direction out of camera view could be simply that the Brigadier is not Linda Blair.

Episode 3
First Transmitted: Apr. 4, 1970

16:58 Some observers claim a blooper when Reegan (William Dysart) touched one of the Ambassadors and was not killed. This may not be a blooper for two reasons. First, Reegan is wearing insulated gloves. In addition, we already know that the radiation levels are much lower — leading to the collapse of one of the Ambassadors. Reports incorrectly place this "blooper" in Episode 4. **17:08** When the Ambassador knocks Reegan against the wall inside the cubicle ("recovery room") the wall shakes as if it is not much of a wall. **17:54** Lennox (Cyril Shaps) flees up the stairs pursued by one of the Ambassadors. The Ambassador starts back down the stairs, and Reegan jumps out of its way. Reegan hits the brick wall, which behaves like something other than a brick wall. There are reports incorrectly citing this to be an Episode 1 blooper.

Episode 4
First Transmitted: Apr. 11, 1970

2:34 The Doctor uses his loupe incorrectly. He should keep both eyes open. **10:36** Taltalian's accent changes when he confronts Liz in the car. **15:39** The Doctor tells Cornish (Ronald Allen) that he can withstand a greater G-force than the other astronauts can. This implies that Cornish can use more M-3 variant in the rocket. **20:57** One of the guards (Max Faulkner) apparently dies because he is touching the gate when the Ambassador also touches the gate. **23:22** As the Ambassador opens the safe, it is obvious that it is not much of a safe. **1:31:41M** There is editing in the movie version of the program so that the cliffhanger at the end of Episode 4 and the reprise at the beginning of Episode 5 are both present. There is about one minute of duplication beginning when the Doctor tells the Brigadier that he is going to see Sir James Quinlan (Dallas Cavell).

Episode 5
First Transmitted: Apr. 18, 1970

1:15 The soldier running after the Brigadier is "zapped" by the Ambassador and thrown against the back wall. The back wall is not very substantial. **1:24** When the Brigadier tries to open the door, we find that the sidewall is not very sturdy. **13:03** Controller Cornish tells the Doctor that if there is too much M-3 variant, the rocket may explode. **15:34** The valve for the M-3 variant says "M3 varient." **18:22** The ceiling of the launch room has a high ceiling with girders showing. **18:22** The nose cone of Recovery 7 has regained its color. Maybe it has a fresh coat of paint. **19:03** The first stage of the rocket has 48 percent M-3 variant. **20:29** The first stage of the rocket explodes because 48 percent M-3 variant is too much for its systems. **23:02** We learn that the unidentified object is traveling at about 7000 miles per hour (with its speed decreasing) towards the Recovery 7. The UFO then stops in front of Recovery 7. The problem is that the orbiting Recovery 7 should be traveling at nearly 18,000 miles per hour. Both Recovery 7 and the unidentified object need to be traveling at the same speed to appear stationary relative to each other. If the 7000 miles per hour is relative to Recovery 7, there would be no blooper, but no such explanation is present.

Episode 6
First Transmitted: Apr. 25, 1970

2:20 The color of Recovery 7 appears to change again. **8:34** The Brigadier tells Cornish that Lennox died because someone put an isotope in his cell. Only a radioactive isotope (radioisotope) would pose a threat. A non-radioactive isotope would not be a threat. **14:08** The guard, apparently killed in Episode 4, is back on duty at the gate. This is the Reincarnated Guard Blooper. **23:04** There are two phones on the desk. They are about two feet apart with a folder between.

Episode 7
First Transmitted: May 2, 1970

1:01 The phones have moved the folder to the side so the phones can move close together. **7:42** Watch one of the police officers at the gate. The police officer at the gate is "killed." **7:57** We see that the Reincarnated Guard Blooper is not a true blooper. The police officer who is "killed," gets up without any apparent major ill effects. **9:56** In order to display the abilities that earned him his Sergeant stripes — Sergeant Benton correctly identifies an SOS message before it is completed. **22:41** When the Doctor is trying to transport the aliens back to their ship on board a rocket, he suggests using pure M-3 fuel as the G-force will not effect the Ambassadors. If 48 percent, exploded what will 100 percent do? This may be a belated response to the kidnapping of the astronauts. **23:17** The control room now has a ceiling like the launch room instead of the original control room.

Comments: The Doctor saves the Earth.

The commercial tape is a collection of color (Episode 1), and black and white (both from the original tapes). In addition, color portions from Collector's tapes have been interspersed. There is post-transmission enhancement of the video and sound for the entire story in the commercial version.

(DDD) INFERNO

Writer: Don Houghton; **Director:** Douglas Camfield and Barry Letts

Media: Commercial tape—episodic version—167 minutes (used); Collector's tape—movie version—154 minutes
Highlights: Liz Shaw (Caroline John) disappears from the series.
Questions: If everyone has a double in the parallel Universe—where is the doppeldoctor? If the Doctor wanted to convince the people in the parallel Universe, why does he not let them know about his two hearts?

Errors and Other Points of Interest

Bessie's tires are dirty outside the Doctor's laboratory, but clean inside.

Episode 1
First Transmitted: May 9, 1970

5:47 When the scene switches to Sergeant Benton driving a nail into the wall, some observers suggest that the wall wobbles significantly. This is an exaggeration. **8:58** The drill head is at 20-miles. **10:36** The time now reads 59:28:48. **15:08** After the Doctor tells Liz "we already know," a cough sounds in the background. **16:15** The Doctor says he will switch the "nuclear power through." How is this possible? Nuclear reactors produce heat (usually as steam) which becomes electrical energy. The Doctor can use the heat (steam) or the electricity, but not direct nuclear power. This error occurs many times throughout the story. **17:23** The power gauge in the Doctor's "Lab" reads "MEGGA VOLTS" instead of the correct spelling of Megavolts. There are, incorrectly, reports giving the spelling as "Megga Volts" and "MEGGA VOLTS."

Episode 2
First Transmitted: May 16, 1970

2:51 This is one of the best instances of a general problem. If the "monsters" are so extremely hot, that leaning against the wall causes scorching of the wall—why are their clothes not scorched? There are incorrect reports that this particular scene is in Episode 1. Other reporters have questioned the fact that there is no singing of his hair. An explanation may be that the change causes an alteration of the person's normal hair along with the rest of his body. The old hair could have fallen out or been burned off to be replaced by fast growing heat resistant hair. **5:14** The Doctor and the Brigadier climb the steps and pass a fire extinguisher. **6:14** Sergeant Benton comes up the stairs past the same fire extinguisher. **6:25** The Brigadier and the Sergeant descend the stairs, but there is no fire extinguisher present. **6:40** The fire extinguisher returns by the time the Doctor goes to the stairs. **13:35** Stahlman (Olaf Pooley) tells Petra (Sheila Dunn) that in 25 minutes, they will accelerate the drilling—at which point there will be exactly 49 hours to penetration. **14:54** The time is now 59:32:24. Time has apparently reversed itself. **14:58** The Doctor flips a switch on the red box to obtain power for his experiments. **19:25** Liz does not have a "door opener" to leave the Doctor's lab.

20:59 Liz now has her own "door opener" to reenter the building. 21:07 Note the relative positions of the console and Bessie.

Episode 3
First Transmitted: May 23, 1970

1:15 The time is 49:18:33. 1:19 After the Brigadier quickly walks across the room, the time is 49:15:01. Apparently, the room is much larger than it appears. 1:55 Stahlman says there is an acceleration of the drilling. Acceleration was supposed to begin at exactly 49:00:00 (see earlier). 4:06 The Doctor arrives in the parallel Universe. The TARDIS console and Bessie have accompanied him. The transition causes Bessie to turn around and face the door. No items closer to the console than Bessie join the Doctor. 11:42 Notice the Section Leader's wig. 13:02 The Section Leader's wig is different. 13:26 The Doctor gives his name as, "Doctor John Smith." 13:42 This is one of many instances where the Doctor says "continny-um" instead of "continuum." 15:13 The Doctor reads the time to penetration as "3 hours 22 minutes." 15:29 Some people consider *Petra's* eyelashes a blooper. 16:06 At this point *Stahlman* starts to call the Brigade Leader the Brigadier, but he catches himself part way through, and ends correctly. 16:52 The camera jostles as *Sutton* is talking to *Petra*." 22:09 As the Doctor escapes from the Brigade Leader's office, he and others walk pass the console with a red box attached. The red box is the switch sending power to the Doctor's workshop. If there is no parallel universe counterpart to the Doctor, why is this box present? 22:34 After seven minutes, the time has changed from "3 hours 22 minutes" to "3:22:58." These are alternate Universe times.

Episode 4
First Transmitted: May 30, 1970

15:32 Back on Earth, the time is now 48:49:52. The accelerated drilling began slightly more than 10 minutes earlier. This means that either the times at the beginning of Episode 3 were correct or the accelerated drilling by Stahlman began at an incorrect time. 18:40 If the "monster" is so exceedingly hot that holding a wrench makes it red hot — how is the sergeant able to push against its bare skin without burning his hand.

Episode 5
First Transmitted: June 6, 1970

2:31 The tag on Stahlman's radiation suit in the parallel universe has his name spelled "Stahlmann." This may or may not be a blooper. 10:47 The reports that the desk calendar shows 23 July are not confirmable in the video release. The calendar is on the desk in the Brigade Leader's Office. 14:10 People have reported that the Doctor preformed a blooper when he did not attempt to escape while demonstrating the TARDIS to the *Brigadier* and *Liz*. He only sent the TARDIS a few seconds into the future instead of leaving the parallel Universe. This is not a blooper since the Doctor has already explained that there was only enough residual power to move a few seconds in time. 17:22 Stahlman appears to be lifting the door. Why does the door continue to rise after he stops lifting? A possible explanation, and why this may not be a blooper, is that the door was only temporarily stuck. 23:16 As noted earlier, the tag on Stahlman's radiation suit in the parallel universe has his name spelled "Stahlmann." If this is not a blooper, due to slight differences between the two universes, then the blooper is in the closing credits (later time) where his name is spelled "Stahlman."

Episode 6
First Transmitted: June 13, 1970

3:39 Stahlman is wearing a radiation suit. A suit designed to keep out the heat would also be insulating enough to keep out the cold. This suit is not effective in protecting Stahlman from the cold of the fire extinguishers. **22:11** As the Doctor prepares to leave, Bessie is facing toward the console.

Episode 7
First Transmitted: June 20, 1970

0:59 Notice that the Doctor's tie is loose. **1:10** We learn another one of the abilities of the TARDIS console—it is able to tie ties. The transfer not only transports the Doctor, but it also ties his tie neatly. **1:20** Bessie remains facing the same direction after transportation between Universes. This is not the same as before. **4:54** As Liz says, "some sort of coma," to the Brigadier, there is a noise off set. **10:50** The Doctor's normal pulse rate is 170. **18:30** How does the Sutton from this universe know that fire extinguishers are effective against the transformed Stahlman? Sutton grabs a fire extinguisher and begins to use it almost as fast as the Doctor does (if not faster). **19:57** The drill stops with 35 seconds to go. The final scenes of the story are suspenseful, but there is a potential blooper. At least one observer points out that since the drill-hole was to be 25 miles deep and the drilling was to go on for 60 hours, the final stopping distance of the drill would only be about 21 feet short of penetration. This would really be an insignificant distance to prevent the pressure from blowing through and causing the catastrophe observed in the parallel Universe. The 21-foot estimation is relative to a constant drilling rate, which may or may not be true (it cannot be true). There is a blooper in this estimation. The 21-foot estimate assumes 60 hours were necessary to drill the entire 25 miles. However, at the point where we see the 60 hours time, the well is already 20 miles deep. Thus, 5 miles require 60 hours. Using this distance, the drill stopped with slightly more than 4 feet to go. Thus, the blooper in the story does not go away, and the blooper in the calculation is still open.

Comments: Parallel Universe characters are designed with asterisks, for example, *Sutton*. The Doctor saves the Earth.

(EEE)   TERROR OF THE AUTONS

Writer: Robert Holmes; **Director:** Barry Letts

Media: Commercial tape—episodic version—95 minutes (used); Collector's tape—movie version—89 minutes

Highlights: Jo Grant (Katy Manning) replaces Liz Shaw as the Doctor's companion. The Master (Roger Delgado) makes his appearance.

Questions: Why do the invading Nestenes not build a larger force of Autons?

Errors and Other Points of Interest

There are many complaints about the CSO in this story.

Episode 1
First Transmitted: Jan. 2, 1971

2:15 The Master demonstrates another Time Lord special ability—he is able to snap his fingers while wearing leather gloves. **2:20** The Nestene sphere is bluish in color instead of reddish as in *Spearhead from Space*. Later the sphere is reddish in color; then it changes back to bluish. Some viewers cite this as a blooper. It is not a blooper because between the times it changes from bluish to reddish the Doctor explains that there is an energy transfer into the unit. Thus, the reddish color appears after the unit has been re-energized. Later the Master is seen transferring energy out of the sphere to animate the Autons. After the energy transfer the reddish unit becomes bluish again. **3:01** Jo does not completely close the door behind her — it slowly swings open during the first part of the scene. **5:05** Jo reads the description of the Nestene sphere as having a diameter of 8½ inches. This gives a volume of over 5000 cubic centimeters. **7:28** We see the first use of the Master's weapon. This weapon goes through more reincarnations than the Master does. **11:00** The Doctor, the Brigadier, and Jo arrive at the radio telescope facility. Captain Yates is there to meet them. **11:09** Captain Yates says the sabotage took place in the control cabin. How could the Captain know this without examining the room? It is possible that someone reported the sabotage to Captain Yates. Does this mean that after examining the cabin, Captain Yates or the others reset the Master's trap? **11:57** The Time Lord (David Garth) notes his trip was 29,000 light years. Some people feel this means Gallifrey and Earth are in the same galaxy. This distance is too small to allow travel from another galaxy. However, the Time Lord does not say he came directly from Gallifrey. **14:32** Why does the Doctor not enter the control room the same way the Master left the room? If the Master could get out — the Doctor could get in the same way. The Doctor can see the trap by looking in the window. **16:21** A boom mike appears near the Director's (Frank Mills) head in the control room. **19:08** The energized sphere switching from bluish to pinkish may allay the complaints of some viewers. **20:23** There are claims that the hypnotized Jo's response to the Master's question is a blooper. The Master asks Jo who accompanied her to the radio telescope. Jo tells the Master, "Myself, the Brigadier, and the Doctor." The blooper is supposed to be because she did not mention Captain Yates. Jo correctly named the people who went with her; Captain Yates was already there, he did not go with her. **23:29** Some viewers question how the Doctor realizes there was a bomb.

Episode 2
First Transmitted: Jan. 9, 1971

1:21 This is one of the many scenes throughout this story where the empty interior of the TARDIS is visible to the viewers. **1:27** The Doctor and Captain Yates have trouble with their lines. Captain Yates begins, "But I understood that under hypnosis, it was impossible for…." The Doctor interrupts with "You thought that under hypnosis … [Embarrassed pause] it was impossible for a subject to be … [Another embarrassed pause] persuaded to do anything that was against nature?" **15:12** When the Doctor is examining the door to the Master's TARDIS, he grasps the door handle. The door is obviously unlocked as it begins to open. Thus, the Master apparently forgot to lock the door to his TARDIS. **17:29** Professor Philips (Christopher Burgess) needs a key to open the door that the Doctor found open. **21:40** The key to the Master's TARDIS is a "normal" key. **21:56** Now the Doctor also needs a key to open the door.

Episode 3
First Transmitted: Jan. 16, 1971

1:17 As Jo is running after the Doctor, she trips with a loud "Ooof!" **3:05** The scene where the Auton falls down the embankment was not the original plan. The car did not stop short, as intended, so the stuntman went all the way down the hill instead of just a few steps. The camera operators did a good job of covering, even though they were not ready. There are incorrect reports that this is an Episode 1 blooper. **3:37** Some viewers observe that even though neither Auton police officer "dies," only one officer reports to the Master. They question the disappearance of the other officer. In this version of the story, neither officer reports to the Master. **12:47** Some fans question why the Master should bother to disguise himself. **12:52** Some observers question how the Master is able to disguise himself as someone of a different height. **13:04** After checking the technician's credentials, Captain Yates seems to be inordinately interested in the technician's bottom. **18:28** Jo is on the phone near the end of the bench furthest from the window. **18:47** Jo is by the lab-bench near the window after finishing her phone call. The doll attacks Jo while she is at the bench. **21:10** Jo tells the Doctor that the doll attacked her while she was on the phone. **21:14** Captain Yates tells the Doctor, "Fetch some cocoa." The Doctor replies, "Fetch a tin of what?"

Episode 4
First Transmitted: Jan. 23, 1971

6:00 It seems too much of a coincidence that the radio Jo uses has the correct frequency to stimulate the daffodil. There are a multitude of frequencies from which to choose. The frequency must be specific otherwise all radio transmitters would work and there would be more than just the few sporadic incidents reported. **12:25** The sphere is bluish again. **19:13** The Master goes behind the coach, enters, changes clothes with Farrel, and Farrel exits the coach in only nine seconds.

Comments: The Doctor saves the Earth.

(FFF) THE MIND OF EVIL

Writer: Don Houghton; **Director:** Timothy Combe

Media: Commercial tape — episodic version — 147 minutes (used); Collector's tape — movie version — 136 minutes
Highlights: The creature in the machine shows us that the Master's greatest fear is the Doctor laughing at him.
Questions: Why is a UN force (U.N.I.T.), even if composed of British soldiers, guarding a Top Secret British missile?

Errors and Other Points of Interest

The creature is supposed to be growing inside the Keller machine throughout the story. The size of the creature inside the machine is sometimes large, and at other times small. The creature is not continuously growing.

The creature in the machine is supposed to show the Doctor's fears. The first fear apparently is fire, as shown the first time the Doctor is affected. Later we learn that the Doctor also fears: Daleks, Cybermen, Silurians, the War Machines, Ice Warriors, Koquillion, the Zarbi and the Sensorites. Thus, he is more afraid of the Sensorites than either Autons or Yeti, or many of the other enemies he had to battle. The problem is — he befriended the Sensorites. He also did not fear the Zarbi once they were no longer under the control of the Animus. These appearances occur during the climax of Episodes 1 and 3 (and the reprises).

Episode 1
First Transmitted: Jan. 30, 1971

3:44 The Doctor accidentally tosses his cloak on one of the observers. **11:22** Why does no one notice the Master's control device that is obviously present behind Captain Chin Lee's (Pik-Sen Lim) ear? **12:39** Why did Chin Lee wait so long to destroy the stolen papers? **14:41** The Doctor's comments seem to indicate that he is several thousand years old. **22:53** Dr. Summers (Michael Sheard) states that the drowned man had water in his lungs. The man died because of his fear of drowning, not by immersion in water, thus there should be no water in his lungs. This problem does not apply to the man killed earlier because of his fear of rats. The scratches on his skin could be self-inflicted.

Episode 2
First Transmitted: Feb. 6, 1971

8:01 The Master's shadow is on the door to his left; so what produces the shadow to his lower right? In three consecutive shots from the same angle, the shadow is present, then it disappears, and finally it reappears. **16:50** If Mailer (William Marlowe) is such a dangerous prisoner, why do the guards sit with their backs to him? **17:04** The guard on the right does not follow the rules when he moves his piece. He should have taken the piece the other guard just finished moving. **17:39** Captain Yates explains to the Doctor that they are moving a nuclear powered missile loaded with nerve gas. After this point, some fans consider all references to the missile as a nuclear missile to be bloopers. However, since the missile is nuclear powered, it could be correctly referred to as a nuclear missile.

Episode 3
First Transmitted: Feb. 13, 1971

6:05 The only way a missile the size of Thunderbolt could be nuclear powered is if it dropped small atomic bombs out of its tail, and these bombs blew the missile in the direction it wanted to go. There is a reason why nuclear powered transportation is limited to large ships — the reactor, shielding, and steam conversion units weigh many times more than Thunderbolt. **11:38** Jo apparently hurts herself when she disarms Mailer. She appears to favor her arm for the remainder of the scene. **19:11** The Master refers to Thunderbolt as a nuclear missile. Some observers consider this a blooper; see the earlier explanation. **19:50** The Doctor tips over a water carafe and then the table; as the Doctor escapes, the Master repeatedly slips on the pool of water. Some viewers incorrectly consider this a fistfight. Not to be outdone, other viewers incorrectly state that the Doctor slipped. **21:33** When placing the handcuffs on the Doctor's right hand, we hear the characteristic clicking sounds; however, there is no characteristic sound when attaching the handcuffs to the Doctor's left hand.

Episode 4
First Transmitted: Feb. 20, 1971

4:27 The entire wall shakes when the cell door opens for the Doctor to enter. **11:31** The Master shows Mailer a slide of Thunderbolt, then switches to a slide of a map before turning off the projector. **11:32** The Master refers to Thunderbolt as "a gas missile; nuclear-powered." **14:34** Jo turns the projector back on and the first slide has miraculously moved back into place. There should be the picture of a map. **18:45** Captain Yates is running across an open area — maybe some of the hijackers are not looking in his direction, but the ones coming around the back of the truck are looking directly at the Captain. **20:39** While the Doctor and Jo are discussing what to do about the alien creature there is a female sneeze offstage.

Episode 5
First Transmitted: Feb. 27, 1971

4:30 The back part of the Thunderbolt control panel looks suspiciously like the upright part of the control panel for the Keller Machine. **7:48** The game board the Doctor and Jo are using is not in the correct orientation for the pieces. **12:48** After the Master picks up the control box, one of the controls moves. Some viewers consider this a blooper; however, the Master moves the control back before switching on the box. **21:06** The soldier's gun clearly fires before the prisoner is in front of the gun barrel, yet the bullets hit the prisoner anyway.

Episode 6
First Transmitted: Mar. 6, 1971

1:25 Some observers claim the resolution of the cliffhanger is a blooper. **1:34** Some viewers find fault with the Doctor's comment "Do you think for once in your life you could arrive *before* the nick of time?"

16:55 As Sergeant Benton is closing the doors to the Processing Room, the camera operator obviously hits something as the camera shakes. **16:59** The Brigadier tells the Doctor they tried, unsuccessfully, to destroy the missile. Apparently, they consider it a good idea to release radioactive material and nerve gas over southeast England. This appears to be more an attempt at population control than an exercise in common sense. **21:19** The Brigadier orders the missile destroyed. This releases nerve gas and radioactive material over southeast England.

Comments: The chandelier in the Prison Governor's office is one of the objects that give false boom mike shadow bloopers. The Doctor saves the Earth and defeats the Master.

(GGG) THE CLAWS OF AXOS

Writer: Bob Baker and Dave Martin; **Director:** Michael Ferguson

Media: Commercial tape — episodic version — 97 minutes (used); Collector's tape — movie version — 92 minutes
Questions: Why do the Axons leave Filer (Paul Grist), even if in a coma, at the reactor facility to recover and warn everyone?

Errors and Other Points of Interest

Episode 1
First Transmitted: Mar. 13, 1971

0:38 The stars show through the Axon ship. **0:55** We learn that the mass of the Axon ship is variable. Is this supposed to be in the sense that the mass of an automobile is variable because as the gasoline burns the vehicle gets lighter? Otherwise the mass should be constant unless the ship is decelerating from near the speed of light — the maximum speed reported is "25 mps" (m= meters or miles). **4:52** The Doctor agrees that the ship has a variable mass. **8:29** Watch the screen to the upper left during the destruction of the missiles. It goes from blank, to a brief flash of the un-launched missile show earlier, to a different missile (apparently un-launched also). **9:51** Chinn (Peter Bathurst) wants to assume the UFO is hostile because it landed near the power complex. How does he know this? Contact with the UFO was lost; no one knew where it landed, or even if it did land. **10:36** Pigbin Josh (Derek Ware) looks very dry after his dunking. **11:28** The sky outside the window of Filer's car does not look like the outside sky in other scenes. This is due to the blue CSO screen without a backdrop. **13:00**

There is a blooper call because the UNIT HQ van looks like a BBC outside broadcast van. Just what does a UNIT HQ van look like? **18:05** The ship opens its door to let Jo in; then the ship allows Jo to wander through the ship as if Axos did not know Jo was in the ship. **21:59** Some fans object to the "sonic injection of axonite." How could anyone inject an element by sound? This is technobabble, and, as such, it does not constitute a blooper.

Episode 2
First Transmitted: Mar. 20, 1971

1:06 The "unconscious" Jo moves her thumb. **6:34** There is a large shadow on Captain Yates. **8:30** Some viewers claim that the replication of Filer is a blooper because there is no purpose for having a replicant. The answer to this claim appears later. **10:43** The following is a technobabble blooper, and its inclusion here is because of its report as a blooper. The accelerator in the Nuton Power complex is either a "Light Accelerator" or a "Particle Accelerator." Winser (David Savile) claims to be able to accelerate particles "up to the speed of light." The unit has a meter reading "LIGHT X/1." The Theory of Relativity does not allow acceleration of light beyond the speed of light. Thus, the accelerator could not be a Light Accelerator, and theory will not allow the acceleration of any other particles to the speed of light because they would acquire infinite mass and require infinite energy to accelerate — thus the accelerator could not be a Particle Accelerator. Another problem is that the graduations on the meter are apparently in multiples of the speed of light. **14:02** Some fans have objected to the Master using a "Laser Gun." Apparently, these fans believe that the Master's weapon requires a more sophisticated name. **14:26** The guard is not very alert. The viewers clearly hear the doors open, but the guard, only a few feet away from the doors, apparently hears nothing. **14:48** The soldier killed by the Master loses his beret as he falls. In the next shot, the "dead" soldier again has the beret on his head. **14:48** The Master kills one of the soldiers. One of the Axon creatures will kill this same soldier in the next episode. **16:59** We learn that the need for a duplicate Filer is because the Axons needed someone to infiltrate the complex; that does not look like one of the Axon creatures. **21:40** The "brick wall" outside the room where the Brigadier, Jo and Filer are imprisoned sways outward as the prisoners initiate their escape.

Episode 3
First Transmitted: Mar. 27, 1971

1:14 There is a continuity blooper during the capture of the Doctor and Jo. Jo is standing behind the Doctor when one of the creatures impales Filer. After the Doctor and Jo back away, Jo is standing beside the Doctor as the Axons receive the order to "repersonalize." In the next shot, from a different angle, Jo is about a foot in front of the Doctor instead of beside him. There are claims that Jo is a yard in front of the Doctor. Judge the distance for yourself. **4:20** The Axos Spokesperson's image shows through Jo. **6:51** Sergeant Benton should get an "excellence in acting award" for keeping a straight face while talking to the rubber-mask disguised Master. **14:55** The "dead" guard from the preceding episode reappears and dies again. **19:10** Hardiman claims, among other things, that a chain reaction would change the station into a "gigantic nuclear bomb."

Episode 4
First Transmitted: Apr. 3, 1971

2:21 In order to distract Jo, the Doctor presents her with some simple math problems. The conversation goes as follows:

Doctor: "three sevens" Jo: "21"
Doctor: "times four" Jo: "84"

Doctor: "minus 35" Jo: "49"
Doctor: "twice that" Jo: "88"
Doctor: "plus 10" Jo: "108"
Doctor: "divide by 9" Jo: "12"
Doctor: "divide by 4" Jo: "3"
Doctor: "three sevens" Jo: "21"

Clearly, Jo needs some math lessons. **2:51** The Doctor trips and nearly falls on his face while escaping from the Axon ship. **4:25** Hardiman's (Donald Hewlett) head shield would work better if the faceplate were in place. **6:35** Captain Yates carefully aligns the camera towards the Axon ship. While tightening the setscrew, the camera moves out of alignment. **8:37** The TARDIS doors loudly slam shut and do not completely close. This occurs at other times also. **9:25** As the Doctor and the Master are discussing leaving Earth, the TARDIS doors start to swing open. **10:34** The doors of the TARDIS swing open to allow the Doctor to leave. No one touched any switch to open the door. **11:50** There is another CSO problem. The shots inside the jeep clearly have a dark blue background. This begins just before the Axons attack. **14:48** The TARDIS leaves the Nuton Complex. **15:20** When the Doctor and the Master exit the TARDIS, while inside Axos, outside the door is another TARDIS wall that is not a part of Axos. **17:59** The TARDIS doors have not closed completely. This is visible as the Doctor says, "Come on, you must take the load." This is not the only instance. **18:11** The TARDIS appears briefly during the battle, even though it left the area earlier. **20:16** As the Brigadier stands beside the door during the evacuation of the room, the brick wall shakes. **20:58** It is possible to see the inside wall of the TARDIS. **22:00** There is a claim that there is an involved blooper concerning the Nuton Power Complex. This follows Hardiman's statement about the complex becoming a nuclear bomb. Some observers claim this is what occurs at the end of the story, and not only is there no loss of life, but also the Brigadier and the others immediately return to the scene of the explosion with no regard for the radioactivity. There are holes in this argument. The claim of a "gigantic nuclear bomb" is good for suspense, but scientifically unsound. An atomic explosion cannot occur in a nuclear power plant. An excellent example of this is Chernobyl. Essentially the worst set of conditions yielded only a meltdown and a chemical explosion. Radiation from Chernobyl was due to damage to the containment building. The explosion at the end of this story occurs in the accelerator room not the reactor, and the explosion is obviously not a nuclear explosion. Since the explosion is not near the reactor and not nuclear — there is no radiation hazard to avoid. With no radiation hazard, it would be acceptable for the Brigadier and others to return to the vicinity of the explosion.

Comments: The Doctor saves the Earth.

(HHH) Colony in Space

Writer: Malcolm Hulke; **Director:** Michael Briant

Media: Commercial tape — episodic version — 146 minutes (used); Collector's tape — movie version — 136 minutes (used) an "M" indicates these times

Questions: How do so many people manage to sneak up behind the telepathic Primitives?

Errors and Other Points of Interest

Episode 1
First Transmitted: Apr. 10, 1971

0:15M Even though this is the movie version, it still says Episode One. **2:35** There is a claimed blooper questioning why Jo does not think the TARDIS can move when she saw it move in the preceding story. The explanation is that Jo knows the TARDIS can move, she just does not think it can travel to other planets. Jo demonstrates that she believes the TARDIS could move when she says to the Doctor, "You don't seriously think that you'll get that thing working again, do you?" Her later "surprise" is when she sees an alien planet. **4:00** The TARDIS instantaneously disappears instead of fading. **5:44** The TARDIS simply appears instead of fading into the picture. The quick disappearance and reappearance supposedly indicates Time Lord Control of the TARDIS. **4:07** Both at the beginning and at the end the Brigadier enters the room and says, "Come back at once." Fortunately for the Brigadier, the TARDIS returns to a different corner of the room. **4:26** The Doctor still has trouble with the word "continuum" when he says to Jo, "We're outside the space-time continnyum." **7:25** The Doctor and Jo leave the TARDIS doors wide open. **8:38** When the Primitive gets to the TARDIS, the doors are only slightly ajar. **12:23** Someone has closed the TARDIS doors completely by the time the Primitives tip the TARDIS over. **13:41** Mary Ashe (Helen Worth) says they left Earth "back in '71." If this is '72, why does she make a year sound as if it has been so long? Given the conditions they were living under, maybe it just seems like a long time. **13:47** The calendar says Monday 2 March 2472. Too bad 2 March 2472 is really a Wednesday. It is possible that at some time in the future there will be another adjustment in calendars (see *Silver Nemesis*). **17:30** Mary Ashe says, "There is no animal life, just a few birds and insects." Check out any zoology textbook — birds and insects are animal life. **19:27 (19:21M)** There are reports that two of the colonists suddenly switch places. Either both viewed versions have a bad splice (post BBC?) at this time or two of the colonists in the background suddenly move after Winton (Nicholas Pennell) walks past them to address Ashe and the Doctor. They do not actually switch position. **22:49M** The editing of the separate episodes into a movie has the robot entering through the same door twice. One time is from the climax of episode one, and once is in the reprise from episode two.

Episode 2
First Transmitted: Apr. 17, 1971

2:27 Why does Caldwell (Bernard Kay) simply allow the Doctor, a total stranger, to get into the IMC vehicle and drive? **6:28** Morgan (Tony Caunter) sees Caldwell and the Doctor approaching. While they are so far away it is still not possible to see the riders clearly, Morgan not only identifies the Doctor (as a colonist), but he also can distinguish the Doctor's "fancy dress." **7:46** The monitor screen behind Caldwell sometimes is correctly showing an image, and in others, it is showing a blank CSO (blue screen). This occurs while Dent (Morris Perry) is questioning Caldwell, and in later scenes. The effect is most obvious during close-ups.

Episode 3
First Transmitted: Apr. 24, 1971

2:51 Pat Gorman plays IMC crewmember Long in this episode, switches sides and is a Colonist in Episode 5, and is a Primitive in the remaining episodes. Some observers incorrectly report that he was an IMC crewmember in Episode 2. **13:09** When Winton arrives at Caldwell's camp, dirt covers his face and hair. **13:57** Inside Caldwell's quarters, Winton's face and hair are suddenly clean. Contrary to other reports, Caldwell's base is not a tent. **15:21**

Something falls over directly behind Winton's back. **17:37** Some fans claim that the use of tape spools by the IMC is a blooper. This just dates the time the stories was really made, unless the persons claiming this to be a blooper have examined recording devices made circa 2472 and know that tape has not made a comeback. This is an Anachronism Blooper discussed elsewhere.

Episode 4
First Transmitted: May 1, 1971

1:46 Why does a ship with landing gear designed for a horizontal landing swing up and land on its tail instead? The ship is not of a style to be capable of balancing on its tail. The Master apparently wanted the landing of his TARDIS to look like a real spaceship landing, but by landing on the tail instead of the skids, the Master fails. **5:28** The Doctor confirms that the Primitives can read his mind. **10:06** The Doctor shows one of the Primitives some magic tricks. How is it possible to fool a telepath into believing something you are thinking about is really magic? How do you hide your intentions of attacking a telepath from him?

Episode 5
First Transmitted: May 8, 1971

1:57 A boom mike shadow falls on the Master's head as he and others come out after the battle. Normally this is too minor to be present in this list, but the shadow attracts the Master's attention. **6:30** After the Doctor discovers the position of the alarm, he tells Jo "this doesn't give us much room to get under—about a foot." When the Doctor and Jo crawl under the beam, it looks more like two feet (especially since the Doctor can fit under the beam while on his side). **6:38** Some observers have questioned the behavior of the doors to the Master's TARDIS. The claim is that the "massive" doors easily move when bumped, unlike truly massive doors. There is an incorrect report that this occurs in Episode 3, when the correct report is Episode 5. However, even though the TARDIS doors are thick, the indentations would significantly reduce their mass. It is also possible that all the remaining material of a TARDIS door is a shell and not solid. **8:20** Jo mispronounces "duralinium," and the Doctor corrects her. Jo's facial expression as she turns away lets everyone know a blooper has occurred. **9:16** There is a proposed blooper: if the Master wanted to kill the Doctor why use a nonlethal gas in his TARDIS? Reason 1: how would the Master know who would gain entry to the TARDIS. Reason 2: the Master wanted to be present so he could gloat over the Doctor's death. Reason 3: the Master's reason was, as indicated—that he needed the Doctor alive (assuming that he could remotely alter the type of gas used). **13:49** The door does not stay closed as Winton leaves. **13:54** A shadow appears on the back of one of the Colonists as Winton (Nicholas Pennell) is talking to him. The shadow appears to be the IMC attacker. Why did Winton not warn the Colonist? **14:05** Pat Gorman makes his reappearance. Now he is a Colonist. **1:51:16M** There is a glitch in the editing or transmission between what would be episodes five and six of the movie version.

Episode 6
First Transmitted: May 15, 1971

0:36 An error in some Blooper Lists occurs at this point. The error goes as follows: The Doctor kicks the Master's weapon away. The weapon goes one way and the Master another. Since they went in different directions, the Master could not pick up the weapon while he was on the ground. A short time later, inside the Primitive's city, the Master again has his weapon. The real story is that the Master does lose his weapon, but one of the Primitives picks it up and carries it into the city. **4:56** The Master takes his weapon from the hands of one of the Primitives. Thus, the Master's possession of his weapon inside the city is not a blooper. **6:16**

Captain Dent tells Morgan to put a man with a communicator on the hill overlooking the dome. **7:29** The ship is next to the dome. Thus, anyone on a hill overlooking the dome should also be looking down on the ship. **8:00** Why does the guard appear to be looking up, not down, to see the ship and dome? **19:55** Even though the IMC guards are at the bottom of the hill some of the colonists are initially aiming at a target above the guards. **21:04** The Master's TARDIS console is very shaky. **23:28** This is the point where the Brigadier is lucky not to be standing where the TARDIS materializes. **23:36** A large shadow falls on the Brigadier as the TARDIS returns.

Comments: One or more members of the special effects crew must have recently seen a rerun of the movie Zardoz, while creating the Primitive's masks. The Master's TARDIS key, like the Doctor has, is just a normal key. The Doctor saves the planet, the Universe, and defeats the Master.

(JJJ) THE DAEMONS

Alternate Title: *The Demons*
Writer: Guy Leopold (Robert Sloman and Barry Letts); **Director:** Christopher Barry

Media: Commercial tape — episodic version — 122 minutes (used); Collector's tape — movie version — 113 minutes

Errors and Other Points of Interest

Episode 1
First Transmitted: May 22, 1971

1:40 The reflection of a boom mike appears on the top of the car. **3:32** You can see the face of the hidden driver just before the "driverless" Bessie disappears towards the left side of the screen. **11:59** Some viewers claim that Miss Hawthorne's (Damaris Hayman) clothes rearrange themselves between shots as she calms the wind. All apparent changes could be due to the wind. **12:57** A strong wind will cause a sign to shake or to blow over — wind will not cause a sign to spin. **21:42** The Doctor and Jo do not turn Bessie's headlights off when they leave the car. **22:39** Jo apparently trips. This may have been done on purpose, and not be a blooper.

Episode 2
First Transmitted: May 29, 1971

5:07 Yates and Benton appear in uniform as Captain Yates is talking to Jo on the phone and Yates says he will come to Devil's End at first light. Yates does not say he will immediately leave. **7:27** Some observers suggest that Captain Yates and Sergeant Benton did not have time to change from their uniforms into "civvies." The Captain and the Sergeant have several hours to change clothes between the Captain's telephone conversation and the present. Even though the scenes are close together, there is significant time in between the scenes, and it is not a blooper. **12:35** Miss Hawthorne reports the repeal of the last witchcraft laws occurred in 1951, instead of the correct date during the 18th century. **12:50** Garvin (John Joyce) appears to be holding the shotgun together during part of his fight with Sergeant Benton. **15:20** The milk van runs into a signpost and bursts into flame. The signpost says "Devil's End 1." Thus, the heat barrier is at a distance of one mile from the Devil's End. Some viewers report that the next scene states the barrier is at five miles from town. The signpost could be one mile from Devil's end and five miles from the town. **19:15** Even though Bessie remained overnight with the headlights on, she starts up immediately with no evidence of the battery being dead. The headlights have turned themselves off in the meantime.

Episode 3
First Transmitted: June 5, 1971

5:36 Some fans incorrectly state that the barrier has a "five-mile radius." No one says this; the actual description by the Brigadier is "ten miles in diameter." This is apparently the scene erroneously reported to be immediately after the scene in the middle of the preceding episode. The center may not actually be in town but may be at Devil's End. **7:04** There is a characteristic sound as the Doctor shows each of the first three slides. This sound is not present before the fourth slide. The position of the slide holder in the projector has clearly moved. **8:03** The Doctor pronounces "Daemons" as "Day-mons" from "Day-moss." **9:11** The Doctor explains that a loss of mass would release energy. This is true. However, the shrunken spaceship found earlier apparently retained its mass. **9:42** The Doctor mispronounces "Daemons" a second time. **10:14** From this point onwards, the Doctor says "Dee-mons." **14:47** Listen as the Master says, "The whole world can be ours." Clunk. Clunk. The lights behind the Master do a lot of shaking at this time. **19:45** To demonstrate his medical expertise, the Doctor lifts and jostles Jo's head to see if she has a broken neck.

Episode 4
First Transmitted: June 12, 1971

1:03 When the Master summons Azal, he says, "Go back to the mark!" The next shot shows the Brigadier and the Doctor at the heat barrier—however we can still hear the voice of the Master. **1:21** There are reports that a production crewmember appears behind the Master as the Master summons Azal (Stephen Thorne). This may be the occurrence referred to in other lists. However, the "crew-member" may be a figure in the display shown in the background in Episode 1. Some lists report this blooper to be in Episode 3. **5:02** Azal says, "Remember Atlantis." This is referring to an apparent "failure" of the Daemons. This listing is a cross-reference to *Fury from the Deep*, and *The Time Monster*. **10:23** Watch the cable on the floor move like a snake. **11:16** We get a view of the Doctor's stunt double. **12:29** The energy exchanger interferes with radio communication. **15:36** Sergeant Benton says, "There's the Doctor." In the next shot, the Doctor is not in sight and it takes several seconds before the Doctor appears. This appears to be a demonstration of Sergeant Benton's X-ray vision. **22:52** Azal "grows" without a cold wind.

Episode 5
First Transmitted: June 19, 1971

0:57 When the Master summons Azal for the last time, there is a white object at the lower right of the screen as Azal begins to grow. This can also been seen at the climax of the preceding episode. **7:38** The energy exchanger has miraculously stopped interfering with the radios. In all fairness, the earlier interference was during testing of the apparatus, which may be different from actual operation. **10:42** The Doctor slams the door shut and nearly pushes the entire wall section over. **11:50** This is a classic Brigadier line: "Five rounds rapid!" Some viewers have a problem with this line. **15:50** Watch Azal drool on himself. **18:37** There are claims that Jo left her own clothes behind when she left the cavern so she could not change back into them. At this time, it is obvious that she is carrying her own clothes when she leaves the cavern. **19:34** At this point, as Jo goes to change her clothes, she no longer has the old clothes she carried from the cavern.

Comments: You should try saying the Master's incantation backwards. The Doctor, with Jo's help, saves the Earth. The Master is defeated.

(KKK) Day of the Daleks

Alternate Titles: *The Day of the Daleks*
Writer: Louis Marks; **Director:** Paul Bernard

Media: Commercial tape — episodic version — 96 minutes (used); Commercial tape — movie version — 88 minutes (used) — an "M" indicates these times; Collector's tape — movie version — 88 minutes

Highlights: We hear the "new" Dalek voices. The Doctor and Jo ride on a motorized tricycle.

Errors and Other Points of Interest

Some observers question the apparent coincidental location of Auderly House to the Controller's base. This may not be exactly true for two reasons. It is possible that the time machine used by the rebels and the Daleks will change not only the time coordinates, but also the positional coordinates of the travelers. If the positional coordinates change, then the Controller's base could be anywhere. An alternate explanation is that there are many regional bases, and the one in this story happens to be the one nearest Auderly House. The story does refer to other regional bases.

Episode 1

First Transmitted: Jan. 1, 1972

0:17 The title is not a blooper. It really is "Day of the Daleks," even though others have erroneously called the story "The Day of the Daleks." **1:55** The Brigadier answers the phone. The male secretary tells the Brigadier that the Minister is calling. When the secretary finishes speaking the Minister says "Hello." The Brigadier is talking at the time and apparently does not hear the Minister. He apparently does not hear the Minister's second hello, as the Brigadier does not respond until the third hello. **3:16** The Doctor hands Jo a clipboard with a pen on it. The pen falls onto the TARDIS console where the pen just sits. **3:23** The Doctor and Jo meet themselves; however, there is no scene in the show where Jo and the Doctor go back to meet each other. The returning Doctor and Jo are dressed the same as the "present day" people they meet. **4:20** When Jo returns the clipboard to the Doctor, the pen that fell earlier has miraculously moved to Jo's hand. **5:16** Some viewers object to the Brigadier calling Auderly House a government-owned country house and Sir Reginald Styles treating it as his own private residence. This objection continues when the Brigadier asks permission to search the house. **6:43** The braille wire supporting the chandelier makes its appearance as Styles (Wilfrid Carter) enters the room. This wire is a requirement to support such objects on sets. **7:42** Some viewers say the Brigadier asking permission to search the grounds epitomizes the problem of Sir Reginald's treatment of this house as his own. These viewers probably think that the Brigadier should be able to search any government owned building without needing to ask permission from the temporary resident (apparently these viewers feel that searching Number 10 Downing Street would not require permission). **8:07** The Brigadier has trouble standing as he runs through the mud on his way to the tunnel. **8:57** Some fans question the Controller's shiny face and the unusual behavior of the female staff of the base. All the male administrators have shiny make-up indicating that this is intentional. The female behavior is still unexplained. **9:12** The Ogron's first lines are halting and slow. He follows this with a much faster "normal" line. **10:54** There is a thin, black arc curving up behind the Brigadier. The line disappears when the Doctor fires the gun. **12:25** The Guerilla's time machine behaves differently the first two times it is used. At this point, it sends the Guerilla back to the future even though he is quite some distance away in the ambulance, and the machine does not affect the person holding it. **12:53** There is a crash off-stage. **13:06** As the camera zooms back when the Controller (Aubrey Woods) contacts the Daleks a boom mike appears over the Controller's head. **21:30** The "monitor," with the Controller's image on it, is swinging while the Controller is talking to the Daleks. This is especially noticeable at the edges of the image.

Episode 2
First Transmitted: Jan. 8, 1972

1:41 The Daleks are reciting "Exterminate..." as in the climax to the preceding episode. Unlike normal reprises, this ends with the climax closing theme music and a black screen before going to the new episode material. **15:20** The Guerilla's time machine now sends the person holding it (Jo) to the future. The Dalek device only changes the point where the person "lands." **20:58** The Doctor and Boaz (Scott Fredericks) fight in Styles's house. During the struggle, Boaz loses his hat and then he runs outside. **21:16** Boaz has regained his hat. Some observers incorrectly attribute this to Episode 1.

Episode 3
First Transmitted: Jan. 15, 1972

1:10 The reprise again ends with the start of the closing theme music. **5:37** According to the Controller, the Doctor is Jo's companion, not vice versa. **5:44** It is possible to see the head of the Dalek operator. **11:37** It is possible to see walking feet reflected on the side of the ramp as Jo and the Controller are talking about the guard. **15:36** A boom mike shadow moves back and forth on the Manager's (Peter Hill) head while he is talking to the Controller in the interrogation room. **22:58 (1:04:54M)** The screen of the Dalek's mind-probe produces the same graphics as the Doctor Who credits. There are reports that this includes the words "Doctor Who — Jon Pertwee" even though by this time in the series the credits read "Dr. Who — Jon Pertwee." This takes place at the juncture of Episodes 3 and 4 in the movie version. The editing into a movie has apparently edited out the credits part of this blooper. In the episodic version, the initial credits appear below the Dalek screen instead of on the normal closing graphics.

Episode 4
First Transmitted: Jan. 22, 1972

2:02 The Doctor learns that since the Daleks discovered the secret of time travel they have invaded the Earth again. Thus, this story does not relate to the invasion in *The Dalek Invasion of Earth*. **12:04** Some observers question the use of the word dalekanium for the explosive. This name appeared in *The Dalek Invasion of Earth* to describe the material used for the Dalek casings. **15:19** A "click" sounds off-stage. This occurs just after the Doctor says to the Controller, "You spoke of the war...." **19:12** One of the emerging Ogron's has a bad mask — part of his face sneaks out from under the mask. **21:15** Some fans comment on the military expertise of the Daleks. They attack one side of Auderly House while their targets casually walk out the door on the opposite side. **1:27:49M** The character Monia (Valentine Parker) is misspelled Monica in the closing credits. This does not occur in the episodic version.

Comments: The Doctor defeats the Daleks and saves the Earth.

(MMM) THE CURSE OF PELADON

Writer: Brian Hayles; **Director:** Lennie Mayne

Media: Commercial tape — episodic version — 98 minutes (used); Collector's tape — movie version — 92 minutes
Highlights: David Troughton

Errors and Other Points of Interest

Episode 1
First Transmitted: Jan. 29, 1972

4:24 Note Jo's hair. **6:00** When the Doctor opens the door, it is possible to see the interior wall of the TARDIS. **6:24** When Jo steps out of the TARDIS, the doors are open, but the falling TARDIS has its doors closed. **7:58** King Peladon (David Troughton) says Earth is many light years away — Alpha Centauri agrees with this. Earth is about 4.3 light years from Alpha Centauri and over 30 light years from Arcturus. Why does Alpha Centauri consider Earth remote given the distance to Arcturus? Maybe the Vogon fleet has not completed the bypass in the area of Earth. **9:04** Some fans suggest a blooper in that that Jo's hair becomes straighter as she and the Doctor climb towards the citadel. Observing Jo's hair at this time makes this a questionable call. The high wind may flatten, not straighten, her hair temporarily. **15:41** The opening door of the secret passageway hits the Doctor. **18:46** Izlyr (Alan Bennion) introduces himself by name. No one refers to Izlyr as an Ice Lord, just as Lord or as Izlyr.

Episode 2
First Transmitted: Feb. 5, 1972

0:50 Izlyr talks over part of Jo's lines. **9:02** The Doctor refers to Centauri (Stuart Fell) as a hexapod. A hexapod is a creature with six limbs. These are obvious as the "arms" on Centauri. Since all six limbs the Doctor ascribes to Centauri are so obviously arms, on what is Centauri walking? **15:20** The Bed Blooper appears in this episode. According to this blooper, there is a problem with there being only one bed in the Ice Warrior's room. There are three simple explanations: 1. Since the Ice Warriors are a warrior race at least one of them is awake at all times. Therefore, they use the bed in shifts. 2. It is possible that the Ice Warriors are like the warriors of Ancient Greece. 3. Does anyone know what a female Ice Warrior looks like? Maybe Izlyr and Ssorg (Sonny Caldinez) represent a husband and wife team. **16:11** Pay close attention to Jo's shoes. **16:20** Jo's hair blows in the wind. **16:21** As Jo creeps along the ledge, the "stone" walls behind her are very shaky. **16:31** Jo has managed to change her shoes on the narrow ledge. **17:06** Jo's hair is again combed and neat. There are no apparent wind effects. **18:18** Jo talks over Izlyr's lines as payback. Earlier, the Ice Warrior talked over her lines. **18:20** We learn the true explanation of the Bed Blooper. When Izlyr and Ssorg (Sonny Caldinez) recapture Jo, Izlyr says, "How did you escape my room?" If he and Ssorg were both using the room he should have referred to it as "our" room. Since Izlyr is apparently not sharing the room, he only needs one bed.

Episode 3
First Transmitted: Feb. 12, 1972

9:47 The studio lights reflect in the mirror the Doctor is holding. This happens later also. **12:30** The Doctor moves the torch to open the secret entrance. We see that the torch angles out from the wall as the Doctor gets there, and he leaves it in a down position. **12:47** As the Doctor is passing through the hidden door one of the strings used to open and close the door appears. There are erroneous reports that this occurs in Episode 2. Some viewers incorrectly report that Jo accompanies the Doctor. **13:41** When Jo gets to the secret entrance, the torch has returned to the angled out position instead of remaining the way the Doctor left it. The door opening–torch position involves other inconsistencies. **15:50** The Doctor allows the wheel to stop spinning and Aggedor does not notice. **16:23** Some observers claim a blooper concerning what Jo appears to be saying in the sentence apparently ending with "off." Jo says to the Doctor, about Aggedor (Nick Hobbs), "I'll scare him off!" The quality of this particular recording may cause this blooper claim. **21:47** As the combat changes to hand-to-hand, it appears that the Doctor has forgotten his Venusian Karate. The Doctor used this method of defense so effectively in the past.

Episode 4
First Transmitted: Feb. 19, 1972

10:32 When the various delegates are discussing the lack of radios to contact their ships, no one remembers to ask about Arcturus's (Murphy Grumbar) radio. **14:45** For a second time, the Doctor allows the wheel to stop spinning and Aggedor does not notice. **16:34** Some viewers claim that Aggedor does not notice that the hypnotic wheel stops as the Doctor is trying to calm the beast down after attacking Hepesh (Geoffrey Toone). However, on earlier occasions the Doctor allowed the wheel to stop spinning and Aggedor did not notice. **22:20** The real Earth Delegate, Amazonia (Wendy Danvers) says, "Doctor, Doctor who?"

Comments: There are reports that the residents of Peladon are Pels. Neither the name Pel, nor any other appears in this story. The name Pel occurs in *The Monster of Peladon*.

(LLL) THE SEA DEVILS

Writer: Malcolm Hulke; **Director:** Michael Briant

Media: Commercial tape—episodic version—148 minutes (used); Collector's tape—movie version—136 minutes

Errors and Other Points of Interest

Watch the clock in the Master's cell. Episode 2 is a day after Episode 1 (the Doctor discusses being overnight on the Fort), and the clock reflects this. Later in Episode 2, the time reads about 2:50; however, at the beginning of Episode 3, the clock has gone back to 12:08. There are other problems.

The closing credits list the director as Michael Briant whereas other sources list the director as Michael Bryant.

Episode 1
First Transmitted: Feb. 26, 1972

1:18 Some viewers incorrectly report that the Doctor uses a telescope, but his view appears as through a binocular. The actual blooper involves the Doctor looking through his binoculars and seeing a telescope's view. **4:02** Trenchard (Clive Morton) says, "Send that new man, Wilson, in to see the prisoner." **4:31** Wilson (Brian Justice) says, "Mr. Trenchard sent me to see sir, if you want your book changed." This quote does not exactly match the previous quote. Trenchard said nothing about a book. **5:47** If this is supposed to be a prison, what is a rack of swords doing just outside the Master's cell? **14:03** Some viewers claim that the Master did not understand that the "creatures" in the Clangers episode "The Rock Collector" were puppets. However, it is obvious from his subsequent comments and his facial expression that the Master was being sarcastic. **21:05** It is bad enough that a stuntman is substituting for Jo, but they could have at least gotten him a wig of the correct color.

shot since it did not hit the Doctor. If it is not a warning shot, this may be why the Doctor uses the phrase "completely hostile." **4:33** After a hole is melted in the metal door and well before the metal has had time to cool, one of the Sea Devils sticks him are through the door and does not get burned. **5:39** The rescue helicopter appears to be all one color with the number 50; when it reaches the Fort, the helicopter is not entirely one color and the number is 56. This assumes there was only one rescue helicopter. **6:45** The Doctor says that the name Silurians was wrong; the name should be Eocenes. **6:50** Jo describes the Silurians as "that race of super reptiles that had been in hibernation for billions of years." Billions of years would place their origin well before the development of life on the Earth. **7:24** The Doctor re-wires the radio to make it a transmitter. Will this alteration still allow it to receive? **7:24** The Doctor's radio transmitter has a battery clip with no battery. This is visible several times, but it is acceptable until the Doctor uses the radio. **8:17** Some observers wonder how the helicopter could arrive so soon. The observers believe this to be a blooper. Captain Hart (Edwin Richfield) had already sent sea rescue out to the fort much earlier. **21:39** The time reads about 2:50.

Episode 2
First Transmitted: Mar. 4, 1972

0:57 There are reports about the movement of shadows in the background. This takes place while the Doctor and Jo are helping the worker back to the radio room. This may not be a true blooper as one of the Sea Devils immediately enters from the side; it could be the creature's shadow. **3:51** The Doctor's assertion that the creatures are "completely hostile" appears on some blooper lists, because the Doctor has not had time to gather sufficient data. The shot by the creature may have been a warning

Episode 3
First Transmitted: Mar. 11, 1972

2:46 The clock has gone back to 12:08. **6:25** The Captain says the submarine is fitted with new experimental sonar equipment. This, in part, may explain why the Sea Devils capture the submarine instead of destroying it like the other ships. What better way to determine the fighting abilities of a foe then to capture one of their advanced weapons systems (not just the sonar). This explains the Submarine Blooper. **7:05** Some observers note the time on the clock when the guard handcuffs the

Doctor. Then look again as the Master tells the Doctor he is going to contact his "friends." Time in the Master's cell seems to be passing at an accelerated rate. **8:58** The Master says he found out about the Sea Devils from the Time Lord files. The Master then adds that the Sea Devils were once rulers of Earth. **13:38** As Jo comes through the doorway a large shadow (camera?) shifts position. **19:11** When Jo leaves the Master's cell, she forgets her handbag. **19:52** There are blooper claims that as the submarine falls to the seafloor — first, we see the sub falling, then we see the crew falling about, next the sub actually hits the seafloor, and finally we see the crew again falling about. The supposed blooper being that the crew was falling about before the sub actually hit the seafloor. This is not a blooper because the descending sub's bow hits a rock immediately before we first see the crew stumbling, and before the sub finally settles onto the seafloor. **20:58** Jo miraculously recovers her handbag as she and the Doctor are running across the open field. **22:13** The Doctor tells Jo to come down the rope. This implies that he has reached the bottom and the rope is no longer supporting his weight. This explains the question of why the rope is slack as the Master reaches the lifebelt post. This is not a blooper as people have claimed.

Episode 4
First Transmitted: Mar. 18, 1972

3:12 If a land mine goes off in the close proximity of another land mine, both will explode. The first and fifth explosions (behind the sign) and the third and fourth explosions (in front of the sign) refute this. **5:07** A Sea Devil goes through, and touches, the melting door. Why does the hot metal not burn the creature? **7:31** Some observers question why the Sea Devils capture the submarine. This is the Submarine Blooper. **9:40** The Captain calls off the search because of nightfall. Some fans assume that this is part of a time blooper since it seems to be light too soon. If we consider the following scenes to occur the next morning — then it may not be a blooper. **10:39** The first time the Master signals the Sea Devils he presses several keys. Watch the keys closely; the last time he presses the blue key it sticks. **11:45** Some viewers have a problem with the time of the attack. They assume it is an evening attack. If the Sea Devils were actually attacking in the morning instead of in the evening, this would explain many of the time inconsistencies. This is consistent with the Captain's later comment, "It'll be light soon." If the attack were at dawn, then it would be daylight when the Doctor and the others arrived. This also means the Captain and the others were only watching the radar screen for a few minutes instead of overnight. This does not entirely explain the time inconsistencies, such as Trenchard's call to the Minister. **14:20** The prison guards must be very poor shots. With pistols at point blank range and on the beach with rifles, they inflict no apparent damage. Trenchard with his pistol does have some effect since one of the three Sea Devils flinches and begins to fall. The damage to the Sea Devil must not have been significant since all three Sea Devils enter the Master's cell. **15:33** The Captain notes that it will be light soon. **15:51** The Naval personnel arrive at the prison. This is a blooper if the attack is in the evening, but not a blooper if the attack is in the morning. Earlier the Doctor and Jo took half an hour to get between the prison and the naval base. **21:37** Normally a ship will pull a diving bell up very slowly. If a bell rises too fast, the diver will develop the bends. (This may not be a problem, as the speed of ascent depends on the depth and the time spent at depth.) Fortunately, the Doctor was not inside the bell. **22:04** The water spots on the camera lens move significantly between shots. This indicates that more time took place between the shots than what appears on the screen.

Episode 5
First Transmitted: Mar. 25, 1972
   3:24 The Sea Devil tells the Doctor that they ruled the Earth "when man was only an ape." If this is true then the Doctor's earlier supposition about the creatures being Eocenes is incorrect. **17:29** The submarine stops before the force field appears. **20:02** Some fans question why the Sea Devils do not attack the escaping submarine. The Sea Devils are concerned with the information the crew are carrying back to the base, so the creatures should attempt recapture. This re-creates the Submarine Blooper.

Episode 6
First Transmitted: Apr. 1, 1972
   3:52 The Master refers to "millions of years of hibernation." This is probably where people reporting the Master saying the Time Lord files told him about a race a from few million years ago. **4:49** The Doctor says "dipode" when he should have said "diode." This could be technobabble and not a blooper. **8:00** Why does it take the Master so long to turn off the Doctor's apparatus that is disrupting the Sea Devils? **9:07** The Captain proves to be much better with a gun than the prison guards are. **11:39** Naval personnel either must have better weapons or are better shots than the prison guards are. **11:47** The Sea Devil's weapon kills a man. There is a flash of fire on the dying man's shoulder. **12:02** Another man dies via the Sea Devil's weaponry, but this time there is no flash of fire. **12:41** As the naval personnel are retaking the base, the Master and one of the Sea Devils hear a man approaching and shouting; the Sea Devil pushes the Master behind him and looks like it is preparing to ambush whoever comes through the door. Given all this time to prepare an ambush and to defend itself, why has the warrior not drawn its weapon by the time the creature is shot? **14:19** Some observers claim that the placement of the water-skis is a blooper. The skis are so close to the sea edge that the tide would wash them away. The attack on the base could have resulted in their being forgotten and left too close to the shore. In any case, are these water skis supposed to be Navy equipment? They do not look like they are. What would private water skis be doing on a secret Navy base?

   Comments: The Doctor saves the Earth.

(NNN) THE MUTANTS

Writer: Bob Baker and Dave Martin; **Director:** Christopher Barry

Media: Commercial tape — episodic version — 146 minutes (used); Collector's tape — movie version — 137 minutes; Collector's tape — episodic version — 146 minutes
Questions: Why change cesium to thesium? Was this to help the Doctor?

Errors and Other Points of Interest

Episode 1
First Transmitted: Apr. 8, 1972

0:30 One must assume this is Doctor Who's tribute to Monty Python. **1:28** Some viewers consider Cotton's (Rick James) dialogue to be amongst the worst in the history of Doctor Who. **2:50** Some observers view the entire premise of this story as a blooper. However, in other cases, the Time Lords have attempted to mend past indiscretions. Their possession of the tablets indicates such an indiscretion. In any case, the tablets, and their container, serve as excellent MacGuffins. **3:02** As Jo and the Doctor are examining the container, the Doctor nearly repeats the same line. First he says, "I couldn't even if I wanted to," then a few seconds later he says, "I couldn't open it even if I wanted to." **8:57** In Marshal's (Paul Whitsun-Jones), office there is a boom mike shadow on the wall beside the door. Later this shadow falls on Marshal. **9:53** The chessboard is not orientated correctly. **12:03** As the Mutant comes through the door he nearly knocks the control panel off the wall. **15:40** There is a loud creaking sound as the Administrator (Geoffrey Palmer) enters to room to talk to the Doctor and Jo. There are reports that this occurs in Episode 2; however, the assassination of the Administrator occurs at the end of Episode 1, so it could not possibly occur in another episode. **20:05** Why does the control panel now respond to the Doctor's touch, when he had to break in earlier? It is unlikely that the Overlords programmed the panel to the accept someone whom they did not know. The control panel appears designed to detect a handprint and control which persons can pass through the doors.

Episode 2
First Transmitted: Apr. 15, 1972

0:35 Ky (Garrick Hagon) and Jo enter the transmat with Jo in front of Ky. **0:44** Ky and Jo arrive on Solos; with their relative positions changed. This occurs at other points in the story. If it had occurred every time, it could be an idiosyncrasy of the transmat booth. **2:22** Marshall refers to "a nitrogen isotope unknown on Earth." This is not technobabble; it is bad science, so it is a blooper. **2:52** Marshal tells the Doctor, "Solos is under Marshal Law." This must be Marshal's Marshal Law. **4:34** It is hard to understand the Overlords while they are wearing their oxymasks. **9:20** It appears that the name cesium became thesium to allow Jon Pertwee to pronounce it. **16:29** A boom mike makes its appearance over Stubbs head when the Doctor stops Stubbs from shooting Varan (James Mellor). **16:52** Some viewers have a problem with Marshal uttering lines like "I'm surrounded by incompetents!" **18:44** Professor Jaeger (George Pravda) draws several arrows that appear on the screen above the Doctor. These arrows quickly begin to shift their positions.

Episode 3
First Transmitted: Apr. 22, 1972

4:16 Some observers question the severity of a storm that is capable of throwing debris all the way to Skybase. At no point in the story is it stated that a firestorm is entirely an atmospheric phenomenon. Meteors could be responsible for this, just as there are certain meteors showers occurring yearly as the Earth revolves around the Sun. Earlier the Doctor implied a partial atmospheric involvement, but so are the trails left in Earth's atmosphere by meteors. **4:23** Skybase is in the vacuum of space. Sound does not travel through a vacuum. How is it possible to hear the firestorm on Skybase? **15:16** One of the guards stumbles and falls.

Episode 4
First Transmitted: Apr. 29, 1972

6:53 One of the cameras seems to be recording bad images. This occurs at several times. **13:33** Some observers have a problem with much of the CSO. **14:22** This is one of the points in the story where it is obvious that the vertebrae of the Mutants simply stick to the backs of their cloaks. **18:52** As Stubbs and Cotton, approach the guard from the only entrance to the transporter room. A Solonian still manages to hit the guard from behind. How did the Solonian get behind the guard when the guard is watching the only door? **22:44** Varan disappears through the wall of Skybase. This would result in an explosive decompression. The safety system of Skybase should close all the doors. When Jo and the others escape the room, the door is standing open. The hole in the outside wall would draw a gale force wind through the door. No significant air movement is apparent.

Episode 5
First Transmitted: May 6, 1972

3:23 When the third guard first stops, he is facing the wrong way. **9:27** The Doctor opens a door with his gloved hand; he removes his glove later. **9:35** After ordered to capture the Doctor unharmed — these guards seem a little overzealous. **10:14** The Doctor now removes his glove to open the door. **13:55** Jo asks the guard for the key. The guard complies by pulling the key out of his pocket. The guard pulls his pocket completely inside out and there is a long string left dangling. **17:06** Marshal, or one of the guards, drops something as the group comes around the last corner. It may be part of one of the guns. **17:09** Ky's gun comes apart as the guard kicks the weapon. **18:33** As the Doctor and Jaeger lower the top onto the apparatus, a boom mike shadow appears on the side of the cover.

Episode 6
First Transmitted: May 13, 1972

3:44 Cotton asks Jo if she knows the plan, and Jo responds to the affirmative. **4:08** When the probe opens, Jo acts as if she does not know what to do, and Cotton must again tell her what to do. Why did Jo forget the plan so quickly? **6:18** There are apparently guards outside the room to interfere with Jo, Ky, and Cotton entering. **9:03** There are still guards, well at least one guard, outside the room to interfere with Sondergaard (John Hollis). **10:40** Why is there no guard outside to interfere with the Mutt entering? **12:11** There are numerous, apparently distant, weapon discharges. At whom are the guards firing? **18:14** A gun, dropped by a falling guard, breaks. **21:37** The Investigator (Peter Howell) says, "Doctor Who…?"

Comments: The Doctor saves the planet of Solos. This title was also the title of the first Dalek story.

Pause to Consider: CSO

Color Screen Overlay, CSO, is a special effects technique used not only in *Doctor Who* but also in numerous other programs. The basic method involves recording images of the actors in front of a monochromatic, usually blue, background, and superimposing this onto another image. This technique makes it appear as if the actors are part of the second image. A short presentation of this technique, by Barry Letts, is included with the DVD release of *Carnival of Monsters*.

CSO is present in many episodes of *Doctor Who*. In some cases, the results are good, while in other cases the technique creates additions to this list. Usually a CSO image is discernible by an outline around the actors. There are cases where the blue screen background substitutes for a blue sky. Unfortunately, when a blue screen is used for the sky, an evenly blue colored, cloudless sky results. This is particularly disconcerting when interspersed with scenes of normal sky.

This list contains many CSO listings. The three main problems are bad outlines of the actors, including the disappearance of parts of their bodies or objects (see *The Green Death*), an unrealistically blue sky (see *The Claws of Axos*), and the actors apparently walking through solid objects (see *The Underworld*).

(OOO) The Time Monster

Writer: Robert Sloman and Barry Letts; **Director:** Paul Bernard

Media: Commercial tape — episodic version — 148 minutes (used); Collector's tape — movie version — 136 minutes — there are editing breaks corresponding to the end/beginning of each episode.
Highlights: Sergeant Benton's diaper

Errors and Other Points of Interest

Episode 1
First Transmitted: May 20, 1972

0:40 Some viewers have a problem with the Doctor's dream. **2:37** Some fans wonder why volcanic activity in modern day Thera is significant. **2:56** Some viewers question the Master's intelligence, because he stays in England where UNIT can capture him. The Brigadier has repeatedly reminded the Doctor that all UNIT posts have orders concerning the Master. Since UNIT is worldwide, just where can the Master go on the Earth? The real question is, why does the Master remain on the Earth? **2:56** The Master temporarily has a Greek accent. **5:37** There is something moving off to the right of the screen as a large square shadow moves across the table to the left of the Doctor. This occurs as the Doctor bends over the map and asks Jo to contact the Brigadier. **12:49** The TARDIS appears to be an empty Police Box. It is possible to see into the TARDIS and through a side window. **12:51** It is possible to see Jo's finger moving to operate the "TARDIS sniffer-outer." **24:01** The sequence of events here is: Stuart Hyde (Ian Collier) clutches his head. Then, Stuart is calmly holding his clipboard and watching the crystal. Finally, the Master shouts, "Come, Kronos! Come!" A different order occurs in the reprise.

Episode 2
First Transmitted: May 27, 1972

1:18 The order of events now is the Master shouts, "Come, Kronos! Come!" Stuart Hyde clutches his head, but does not hold a clipboard. **9:49** Some viewers object to Chronovore as a poor combination of Latin and Greek. **15:59** Jo demonstrates another of her many talents. While talking to Jo on the telephone, Sergeant Benton places his hand over the receiver so he can talk to the Doctor. Even though the receiver is covered, Jo still hears the conversation. This is evidenced by her comment, "It's all right, I heard." **23:53** When the Master brings Krasis (Donald Eccles) from Atlantis, the crystal, in front of Krasis, remains behind.

Episode 3
First Transmitted: June 3, 1972

0:58 The Master says, "You watch the crystal!" The crystal appears to be uncovered. **1:20** There is now a cover over the crystal. **8:02** The Master, like Sergeant Benton earlier, places his hand on the crystal. **8:08** Hippias (Aidan Murphy) tells the King (George Cormack) that both Krasis and the crystal disappeared together. This is not what happened at the end of Episode 2. **9:46** At this point, at least one viewer has pointed out an apparent inconsistency. The claim is that the scene where the King opens the door to the chamber with the Minotaur (Dave Prowse) and the scene where Jo enters the room are simply different camera angles of the same side of the door instead of different sides of the same door. From the outside, the hinge is on the right side, and the door opens away from the Minotaur's chamber. This viewer says the key is the statue beside the door. Note that the statue is immediately next to the door. There is a second, apparently identical, statue a little further away on the opposite side of the door. **12:59** Dr. Ingram (Wanda Moore) finds one cork — after searching. The Doctor uses two corks to construct his apparatus. Where did the second cork come from? **13:16** The Master removes the "time energy" from the crystal. Now it is possible to move the crystal. **15:04** Some viewers are very upset by this series of events. These viewers claim a blooper along the lines that the Master must convince Krasis the crystal is safe to the touch. Thus, they believe the crystal is dangerous. This "problem" continues when the Master picks up the crystal and unit. **16:12** The Master picks up the unit containing the crystal (not the crystal itself), and first carries the assembly into the outer lab, and, in the next episode, carries the unit into his TARDIS. This is not a blooper since both the Master and Sergeant Benton proved that it was safe to touch the crystal. In addition, since the Master has removed the "time energy" from the crystal, there should be no problem with transporting the crystal. Even though the Master can lift and move the crystal assembly alone, it is obvious, from its size, that it would be easier for two people to move it, thus there is justification to convince Krasis to help. **18:31** Why does the Roundhead-UNIT battle take so long with no apparent casualties? **19:52** Some fans suggest that the Doctor said something obscene to the Brigadier as the two of them are getting into their cars. It sounds more like "Do buck up." This could be simply a Freudian problem on the part of these fans. **21:14** The footage of the V-1 is black and white in an otherwise color episode. **22:23** Why does it become more difficult for the Brigadier and Captain Yates to communicate by radio as they get closer together?

Episode 4
First Transmitted: June 10, 1972
   2:04 If the Master transported the V-1 from the past before it crashed, how can the Farmworker (George Lee) remember it exploding? When the Master transported the V-1 from the past, it could no longer crash in the past. **2:46** The Farmworker attempts to help move the TARDIS. He drives a tractor and says, "One, two, six, heave! One, two, six, heave!" **4:02** The Master carries the crystal and unit into his TARDIS. **5:55** One of the TARDIS doors does not completely close. **6:58** The light on the top of the TARDIS is not flashing during dematerialization. **11:41** The console in the Master's TARDIS is just as unstable as the one in the Doctor's TARDIS. The console moves when the Master operates a switch. **11:54** Jo falls over and we see that she is wearing white underwear. The glimpse of her underwear is not a blooper, but the color sets a blooper. **11:56** A boom mike appears above and to the right of Jo. **14:02** Doctor Ingram turns off the machine. **16:36** Sergeant Benton asks Doctor Ingram, "But why, I mean, if you turned it on the Brig and company should have speeded up again." Benton should have said, "Turned it off." **18:44** The Doctor's speech is just as much gibberish backwards as forwards. It is not simply English in reverse. **20:30** As the Doctor and Krasis are introducing themselves something hits the floor off-stage.

Episode 5
First Transmitted: June 17, 1972
   0:50 The stick holding the TARDIS is obviously present after the Master "throws" the Doctor's TARDIS out of his TARDIS. **1:19** We again have the opportunity to see Jo's underwear, but now they are yellow instead of white. **1:58** Surely, the Master knows about the ability of the TARDIS to rescue the Doctor. So why does the Master eject Jo with the TARDIS to allow the Doctor's rescue? **2:09** This is one of the times

where we can see a white power cable on the floor of the Doctor's TARDIS. **6:36** When the Master's TARDIS lands in Atlantis, it is apparent that the Master's chameleon circuit, like the Doctor's, is also faulty. **8:48** Someone forgot to turn the TARDIS light on during landing. **19:09** While the Master is talking to Queen Galleia (Ingrid Pitt), someone coughs off-stage. **23:30** Jo "falls" into the room with the Minotaur. The door, from the outside, opens to the left (into the Minotaur's chamber), not the right as in Episode 3. Facing the door the statue is still on the left, as in the preceding episode. However, the statue is now several feet away (not immediately beside the door), and there is a torch between the statue and the door. The statue is, as some viewers claim, the key; there has been more than a simple switching of camera angle. The placement of the hinge is the only problem.

2:15 The Minotaur throws Hippias through a "glass" window. The window looks like cellophane and sounds like glass. **8:10** A boom mike shadow adorns Jo's new clothes. **13:12** Atlantis is being destroyed—where are the Daemons? **13:53** The Master fastens Jo to the console of his TARDIS; however, after Jo forces the time ram to occur she is loose. **16:18** A white power cable appears on the floor of the Master's TARDIS. **17:27** Jo manages to move the entire TARDIS console when reaching for the Time Ram Switch. **17:44** Jo is now free of the TARDIS console. **21:44** The "Baby" Benton is wearing a small diaper. It does not appear to be made of expandable material. **23:58** Just what is the "Adult" Benton wearing? It seems unlikely his diaper "grew" with him.

Comments: The Doctor saves the Universe, and defeats the Master.

Episode 6
First Transmitted: June 24, 1972

(RRR) THE THREE DOCTORS

Writer: Bob Baker and Dave Martin; **Director:** Lennie Mayne

Media: Commercial DVD — episodic version — 98 minutes (used); Commercial tape — episodic version — 99 minutes; Collector's tape — movie version — 93 minutes
Highlight: The Doctor regains his freedom to time travel.
Questions: How do the fleeing Doctors know they are not leaving Jo, Sergeant Benton and Doctor Tyler locked in the cell? Why do the Second and Third Doctors look to the younger First Doctor as if he is more knowledgeable?

Errors and Other Points of Interest

Many fans complain that in the First Doctor stories, William Hartnell was always having trouble with his lines. Listen to his delivery in this story.

The doors to Omega's "home" supposedly appear textured from the outside. Outside views, such as in Episode 3, show the doors but it is not possible to determine if any texture is present, or if they are smooth with a design. Persons claiming this to be a blooper say there is texture, but when people are exiting, Episode 3 and Episode 4, the outside is smooth and only the inside has texture.

Episode 1
First Transmitted: Dec. 30, 1972

3:08 Why does Doctor Tyler (Rex Robinson) contact a military group (UNIT) instead of a scientific group? Doctor Tyler indicates that the missing Ollis (Laurie Webb) was his final incentive. **3:31** Some viewers question Doctor Tyler's comment, "We may not be NASA." They wonder what happened to the Mars program in *The Ambassadors of Death*. These viewers seem to have forgotten that even NASA still uses balloons for cosmic ray research. **4:13** Doctor Tyler refers to giving information to "Yanks and the Other Lot." The Brigadier seems upset with this. In *The Invasion*, we learned that UNIT could contact the Soviet Union with a simple phone call, so why should the Brigadier worry about shared information? **4:55** The Doctor asks the Brigadier to pass him "a silicon rod." The Brigadier passes the Doctor what appears to be a glass rod (silicate rod). Silicon is opaque and metallic looking, not transparent. **5:59** The Brigadier claims that UNIT HQ is a "top-secret security establishment" (misquoted as "top-secret establishment"). However, there is a large sign outside making it anything but a secret. **6:40** Doctor Tyler begins to unfasten the lid to his instrument box. Transportation to Omega's world occurs before he finishes getting the lid off the box. The next shot of the box shows the lid completely unfastened. **8:08** The sign outside UNIT headquarters has Brigadier Lethbridge-Stewart misspelled in that it does not contain a hyphen. To be fair, the closing credits do not use a hyphen in the Brigadier's name. **8:20** The rain washes Bessie's tires clean after driving through a storm. **8:22** Jo places a large umbrella in the back of Bessie. Then the car leaves for Omega's world. **8:57** The camera operator must have been afraid of the blob. As the blob is disappearing down the drain, the camera is shaking a lot. This is less obvious in the DVD version. **9:04** The box Doctor Tyler was beginning to open is entirely open. **10:26** Why is there not more radiation in the box where the blob was hiding? It spent much more time in the box then when passing through the sink. This is less obvious in the DVD version. **13:30** The creature has a cord attached to its front. This is an ignition wire for the explosion. The explosion occurs as the cord makes its appearance. **14:40** This is one of the many scenes showing the remains of the wall of the Doctor's laboratory. It is possible to see the bright white of the polystyrene walls. **17:23** We learn the First Law of Time is a Time Lord Law, not a Physical Law. If it were a Physical Law, the Time Lords could not break it. **17:53** It is possible to see the Second Doctor's recorder before it supposedly materializes. However, this is after the Doctor heard the materialization sound effect. **17:55** The Second Doctor's reflection appears in the time rotor before he "appears." **20:06** Remember — for future reference — the Time Lords appear to have at least partially updated the Second Doctor. This and later scenes confirm that the Time Lords know at least part of what is happening to the Doctors. **21:34** There is a boom mike shadow on the Third Doctor's left shoulder. **22:28** As the Second and Third Doctor go to look at the monitor, a boom mike shadow appears on the back wall to the left.

Episode 2
First Transmitted: Jan. 6, 1973

0:49 The scanner should be looking out from the TARDIS the same way you look out from your eyes. Without a reflecting surface, you cannot see yourself. So how can the TARDIS see itself? Some observers report this is in all four episodes, but it only occurs in Episode 2 and Episode 3. **9:00** The door to the Doctor's lab has a sign reading "Staff Only: No Admittance." Some fans consider this a blooper because only staff would be present at a "top-secret security establishment." **9:41** The umbrella has disappeared from Bessie. **9:41** Bessie has very dirty tires. They are no longer the rain-washed tires from before transporting, but they are the dirty tires of a car driven to its present position. **13:39** The Second Doctor offers the Brigadier a jelly baby. **13:53** What makes Doctor Tyler so certain he traveled faster than the speed of light? At the speed of light, or even much less, he could have traveled to any one of several quarries on the Earth. **15:01** This is one of many instances where it is possible to see the edge of the television screen that Omega is using. This also occurs in the next two episodes. **19:39** After the escaping Doctor Tyler nearly runs into one of Omega's creatures; Doctor Tyler grabs a wall and it shakes a little. More importantly to this list, as the creature chasing him, the creature walks into the wall. **21:05** The TARDIS monitor not only shows the First Doctor, but also the camera crew. This also occurs at other times. **23:22** A well-groomed lawn appears after transportation of UNIT HQ. What is a well-groomed lawn doing beneath a building?

Episode 3
First Transmitted: Jan. 13, 1973

3:20 It is possible to see the actor's lips and jaw moving beneath Omega's (Stephen Thorne) mask. **3:22** A boom mike is visible at the top of the screen. **3:47** It is possible to see the top of the wall in the back of the set. **6:59** This is another instance of the TARDIS seeing itself. As in the previous occasion, the scanner seems to be in the far corner of the room from the TARDIS. **7:24** As everyone exits the TARDIS, it is possible to see the entire interior including the "secret" doors in the back to allow an unlimited number of people to enter or to leave. **7:48** Notice the view outside the door. It is a CSO image. **9:17** The Second Doctor and Sergeant Benton quickly leave. They leave the TARDIS doors wide open. **11:14** Notice the "texture" of the doors. **20:41** Notice the "texture" of the doors both inside, and later from the outside. **22:32** Some observers cite the fact that the Time Lord President (Roy Purcell) knows about Omega is a blooper. The Time Lord's knowledge of the Doctors' activities has been repeatedly demonstrated beginning with the appearance of the Second Doctor.

Episode 4
First Transmitted: Jan. 20, 1973

6:20 Omega has no head — so how did we see his lips and jaw earlier? **7:38** Notice the "texture" of the doors, both from inside, and from further away as the Doctors run away. **7:39** Even though we are in a completely different part of the "planet," the view (CSO) is identical to the outside UNIT HQ. **8:11** How does the Second Doctor know who Bessie is? **8:24** The Brigadier complains about the locked TARDIS doors. The Second Doctor and Sergeant Benton left the doors wide open. **12:42** The First Doctor reports to the Time Lords. This is apparently not the first time, so this explains the claimed blooper questioning how the Time Lord President knew about Omega. **13:54** There is an excellent view of the cast and crew reflected in the TARDIS monitor after the image of Omega (not the First Doctor this time) fades. **14:16** The view out the laboratory window is the view from Earth, not a view of Omega's "planet." **14:25** The light on top of the TARDIS is not flashing during dematerialization. **16:50** The companions need to learn how to walk more quietly. As they are passing through the singularity to return to Earth, it is possible to hear them not only walking up the front steps, but also walking down steps in the back.

Comments: The Doctors defeats Omega and saves the Universe.

(PPP) Carnival of Monsters

Writer: Robert Holmes; **Director:** Barry Letts

Media: DVD — episodic version — 98 minutes (used); Commercial tape — episodic version — 102 minutes (used), the second episode present is the extended version (about five minutes longer) with the Delaware synthesizer arrangement of the theme music — Commercial tape times, where used, as designated CT; Collector's tape — movie version — 93 minutes
Questions: Why did the other Drashigs stop chasing Jo after the first one died?

Errors and Other Points of Interest

Boom mikes appear in many scenes in the DVD version, but not in the taped versions.

Episode 1

First Transmitted: Jan. 27, 1973

0:55 The workers (Functionaries) apparently have the same tailor as the Time Lords in the preceding story (*The Three Doctors*). **4:23** The Miniscope has a power cord attached. Many fans claim the presence of a power cord on the Miniscope is a blooper. This cord appears at other times. **5:36** For future reference — the Doctor tells Jo they are on Metebelis 3. **9:19** to **9:56** Claire (Jenny McCraken) and Andrews (Ian Marter) complete a circuit of the deck between these times. Andrews claims that twenty laps is a mile. They complete the lap in 37 seconds. This corresponds to slightly less than 5 miles per hour. This is a good running pace, but not a leisurely stroll. **10:25** After Major Daly (Tenniel Evans) dozes off, Jo begins to sneak across the room. It is possible to hear the sound of a pencil falling, then rolling across the floor. **10:41** The date on the paper is Saturday, April 3, 1926 — this is a correct date. **11:12** After seeing the newspaper, Jo says they have "slipped back about forty years in time." This would mean that the UNIT stories with Jo take place in the mid-sixties. **11:34** The Doctor says the plesiosaurs have been extinct for 130 million years. Plesiosaurs survived until near the end of the Cretaceous (65 million years ago). **13:26** Unlike the norm for the First Doctor, the Third Doctor orders a large scotch. **16:03** The calendar in Major Daly's cabin is supposedly for June 1926. The calendar shows June 1 to be on a Saturday, thus it must be either 1924 or 1929. Some viewers incorrectly report the calendar to have the days of 1925. **17:48** Shirna (Cheryl Hall) explains entertainment. **19:18** Pletrac (Peter Halliday) takes the micrograph to confirm its validity. **20:44** to **21:04** Claire (Jenny McCraken) and Andrews (Ian Marter) complete another circuit of the deck. They complete this lap in 20 seconds. This is about 9 miles per hour. This is even a faster running pace than earlier. Obviously, this is not a leisurely stroll. The clock on the wall indicates that the time interval may have been longer. If the beings inside the Miniscope are supposed to be reliving exactly the same experiences, why are the times required for the two laps different? **23:51** When the Doctor opens the TARDIS doors it is possible to see the inside wall of the TARDIS. **23:55** The Doctor quickly leaves the TARDIS and does not close the door. When Vorg (Leslie Dwyer) picks up the TARDIS the doors are closed, and remain closed until the Doctor opens them much later. This appears again in the reprise.

Episode 2
First Transmitted: Feb. 3, 1973

1:20 (1:48CT) Vorg pulls the TARDIS out of the Miniscope. It is about three inches high. The mate, John Andrews, told Claire Daly that twenty laps around the ship is a mile. Based on the true dimensions of the TARDIS and the ship — if the TARDIS was reduced to three inches, then the ship should have been reduced to about seven or eight feet. How does an object compressed to seven feet fit into the Miniscope? **(3:53CT)** Shirna (Cheryl Hall) explains entertainment again. There are two identical segments in both Episode 1 and Episode 2. This may be in part due to the fact that Episode 2 is an extended version. The second explanation only appears in the extended version in the commercial tape. This only appears in this list because of its presence on some blooper lists. **(5:27CT)** Pletrac (Peter Halliday) takes the micrograph to confirm its validity. There are claims that the second appearance of this scene is a blooper. Only its appearance on other lists warrants its inclusion on this list. This only appears in the extended version. **2:56 (6:36CT)** Vorg introduces the Drashigs. **3:16 (6:57CT)** Some viewers claim that Vorg's inability to control the Drashigs and his ability to control the plesiosaur are in conflict, and therefore a blooper. Plesiosaurs have brains, albeit small ones, and Vorg says that Drashigs have "no intelligence center," so he cannot control them. This averts a blooper. **8:03 (8:56CT)** Even though Vorg appears completely human, he describes humans as if they appear alien when he says that all humans look alike. This occurs when Shirna pulls Vorg aside to tell him about the Doctor and Jo. **9:34** A boom mike appears in the upper left of the screen. **11:52** There is a boom mike above Vorg. **14:42** A boom mike appears above Pletrac and the others. **17:46** A boom mike appears above Orum (Terence Lodge) and Kalik (Michael Wisher). **22:09 (27:04CT)** Vorg introduces the Drashigs again. This is not a repeat of the earlier introduction.

Episode 3
First Transmitted: Feb. 10, 1973

3:06 Note the color and style of the sonic screwdriver. Compare this to the sonic screwdriver seen in *Planet of the Spiders*. **3:13** Jo is nearly up to her waist in muddy water. She is also wet and muddy as she runs towards the cave. **3:57** Jo is still very muddy. **4:05** After Jo enters the cave, she is dry and no mud is present, but a few seconds earlier, she was nearly up to her waist in water because she was stuck in the mud. She was also muddy while running up to the cave. **4:48** Jo asks the Doctor about Miniscopes. During the subsequent conversation, the Doctor tells Jo of the banning of Miniscopes; this one must have slipped through the cracks. How does the Doctor know that they have traveled to a point in time after the ban? This also shows that the other Time Lords interfere with other planets. The Doctor did think the TARDIS had landed on Metebelis 3, so he could have the time wrong. **15:49** This is one of many examples of a wig coming loose. It is Kalik's this time. **21:43** Vorg says the Miniscope has its own power circuit, so why did the machine need the power cord seen earlier.

Episode 4
First Transmitted: Feb. 17, 1973

2:10 There is a boom mike above and behind Pletrac. **2:31** The Doctor learns that Vorg is in charge of the Miniscope. **6:05** The Doctor must be told a second time that Vorg is in charge of the Miniscope. **10:05** There is a boom mike in the upper left. **10:22** The Doctor learns that Vorg won the Miniscope and does not know how to operate the machine. Since he does not know how to operate the machine, he did not collect the specimens in the machine. There are claims, as part of a blooper, that Vorg collected the specimens. If Vorg collected the specimens, this would mean that Vorg needed time travel capabilities. An alternative would be that the plesiosaur was a modern "sea monster." **10:59** Some viewers claim that when the Doctor refers to the omega circuit it appears as if he is just saying the first thing that popped into his mind. **11:07** The Doctor begins to explain his two purposes with "It will enable me to get Jo out of here in time and get her out of this retched contraption." **13:13** Orum exclaims to Kalik that the Drashigs will need to get out of the Miniscope, but they cannot get out because the plates are molecularly bonded. If the Drashigs cannot get out without help, how did the Doctor get out? **13:44** The Doctor needs a rubber band to hold the Phase One switch in position. **15:56** When Kalik first bends down behind the Miniscope, it moves easily. Some viewers cite this as a blooper because the machine should be too heavy to move so readily. In Episode 1, the Miniscope moved easily during its unloading. **17:08** Claire, Andrews and Major Daly pass out from the heat. There are claims that Claire remaining pale, while the others turn red, is a blooper. This report also promotes the Major to a Colonel. This may be due to Claire's "real life" make-up covering her "red" skin. **19:08** Vorg throws the Phase Two switch, returning everyone and everything to its original time and space. The return of Harry's grandfather to 1926 Earth gives the Fourth Doctor one of his companions.

Comments: The Doctor saves Inter Minor.

(QQQ) Frontier in Space

Writer: Malcolm Hulke; **Director:** Paul Bernard and David Maloney

Media: Commercial tape — episodic version — 145 minutes (used). Collector's tape — movie version — 134 minutes

Errors and Other Points of Interest

The incidental music for episode five is different.

Watch the ship's clock (the black numbers on white) during Episode 1; it goes back and forth in time. The earliest time shown is 22:01 and the latest time shown is 22:55. The ship's officers confirm two of the times.

Episode 1
First Transmitted: Feb. 24, 1973

3:34 Some observers claim a blooper: if the Master's device makes people see what they fear, why does Jo see a Draconian spaceship when see does not even know what a Draconian is? Jo sees the ship and then hears the sound and the image blurs, but when it clears, she still sees the same spaceship, not something she has never seen before. **15:49** Watch carefully between the time Hardy (John Rees) says, "They'll be through any minute!" and the time the Doctor appears with his sonic screwdriver. There is a single frame of the Ogrons cutting through the door — a case of bad editing. **16:21** As the action first shifts back to the Doctor and Jo in the cell, the reflection of one of the production crew appears on the cell door. This crewmember quickly moves. **16:24** A studio light appears just outside the cell door. This could have been one of the ship's lights, if it stayed there; however, the production crew removes this light later. **16:32** When the Doctor opens the door and discovers Hardy outside there is another editing blooper. A black frame separates the shot from the back of the Doctor and the shot of the front of the Doctor. **20:36** Jo is not wearing tights.

Episode 2
First Transmitted: Mar. 3, 1973
   4:13 Jo is wearing dark blue tights. The problem is that she was not wearing tights earlier. She may have been wearing tights during the rescue of the cargo ship. **23:43** There was an accidental substitution of one of the credit slides from Episode 1 for one of the slides from the end of Episode 2. This gave Louis Mahoney and Roy Pattison extra credit and no credit for Lawrence Davidson and Timothy Craven.

Episode 3
First Transmitted: Mar. 10, 1973
   1:25 When the Doctor and Jo hide behind the wall during the kidnapping attempt, a rip in the seat of Jo's pants peeks out. This may not be an actual rip but a weak seam. **5:44** Some viewers considers Jo's new outfit to be a blooper. Apparently, it does not seem likely that she would have the opportunity to change while incarcerated. This may not be a blooper because there evidently has been some time between her last appearance and the Doctor's return. **9:32** Professor Dale (Harold Goldblatt) makes his appearance. There are claims that Harold Goldblatt is always interrupting the other actors. Count the times. **15:40** Watch the woman behind the Doctor and his co-conspirators. She apparently chokes on the contents from the cup. Maybe she is just guilty of overacting to the Doctor's earlier comment on how bad the liquid tasted. This has been incorrectly reported to be in Episode 4, and the woman supposedly has a pony tale. **17:13** If General Williams (Michael Hawkins) is so distrusting of the Doctor and Jo, why not bug the cell? If he had, he would have heard the Master's admission of guilt.

Episode 4
First Transmitted: Mar. 17, 1973
   1:06 Airlocks need to be very sturdy, they are holding back a lot of air pressure (15 pounds per square inch is over one ton per square foot), and the walls should not shake easily. The Doctor's banging on the wall with the gas cylinder makes the entire wall shake. **7:55** We learn that the Doctor's sonic screwdriver is on the moon. Thus, he must have several. **8:37** Is that supposed to be the Earth on the monitor? It cannot be the moon since they have not taken off yet. **13:41** This is one of the times where the strings supporting the Doctor are obvious. **14:37** There is a combination of bloopers arising when the Doctor disconnects the hose to his oxygen cylinder. The suit does not depressurize, and the hose only pushes in one direction. The gas tube should start moving the Doctor immediately and continuously. **16:18** As the Doctor begins to re-enter the ship you can see a person's hand as the door first opens, and his shadow on the exterior wall. There are incorrect reports that this occurs in Episode 6.

Episode 5
First Transmitted: Mar. 24, 1973
   14:31 The Master says, "Release the first missile." The Ogron pushes one button. We see two missiles fired. **20:46** General Williams says all ships for the peace talks were to be unarmed. If this is true, how did he manage to destroy the Draconian ship and start the war? **21:37** Some fans claim that the Master lending a helping to Jo is a blooper. There are many cases where the Master has been polite. This could be another one. These fans also claim that the Master was holding Jo's hand, when in reality he was holding her arm. **23:17** In order

to prevent the Master from hypnotizing her, Jo cites nursery rhymes. She starts with "Mary had a little lamb...," but has trouble when she continues to say "... and everywhere that Mary lamb...." This has been incorrectly assigned to Episode 4. Jo's second quote has been reported as, "and wherever Mary lamb...."

Episode 6

First Transmitted: Mar. 31, 1973

4:59 Another claimed blooper is that a squarish cabin could not fit in a cylindrical spaceship. Apparently, the reporter forgot that in geometry any shape, including a square, can be circumscribed by a circle, and hence a cube by a cylinder. **11:19** The Master turns on the homing signal. **12:31** Why does the homing signal stop? The Master behaves as if the approaching rescue ship turned it off. **13:44** The General notes that there is "one dominant life-form, a large and savage reptile." Apparently, the General does not consider the Ogrons to be dominant life forms. **14:55** Some observers consider the Ogron "Monster" to be a blooper. **15:17** As the Ogrons flee back into the base and see the Master, there is a large boom mike shadow on the right wall. **18:32** The Master must give the last Dalek a push so that it heads in the correct direction. **23:17** Jo has a gun in her right hand as she helps the Doctor. She is not carrying a gun when she enters the TARDIS.

Comments: The Doctor defeats both the Master and the Daleks. The Doctor saves the Earth and Draconia.

(SSS) Planet of the Daleks

Writer: Terry Nation; **Director:** David Maloney

Media: Commercial tape — episodic version — 141 minutes (used). Episode 3 is in black and white; Collector's tape — movie version — 104 minutes — no episode 3

Errors and Other Points of Interest

Episode 1

First Transmitted: Apr. 7, 1973

0:28 Jo helps the Doctor to stand and enter the TARDIS. She has a gun in her right hand while she is outside the TARDIS. The gun disappears as Jo enters the TARDIS. **0:56** The Doctor tells Jo they need to "get out of here." He does not specify where they are going. **2:35** Jo enters the console room carrying a coat. How does she know she will need a coat? The TARDIS has not landed yet. **3:06** If the TARDIS Log that Jo is holding is supposed to be a tape recorder (as some people surmise), why are the tape reels not turning while Jo is recording her entries? **4:55** The Doctor's body temperature drops below zero, and his hearts slow to about one beat every ten seconds. **9:38** After the Doctor awakens and walks over to the TARDIS console, watch the central column. You can see one or more of the production crewmembers reflected in the silver strip. **9:55** Some observers object to the style of handles on the Thal spaceship. **11:05** Some fans point to the loss of air in the TARDIS as indicating a link between the interior and the exterior of the TARDIS. The TARDIS can survive in outer space, so it cannot leak air too easily. A more likely explanation is that a piece of fungus was stuck in the door when Jo left, and this prevented the doors from closing completely. **11:52** The Doctor is stuck in the TARDIS and he is running out of air. Why does the Doctor take time to change his clothes? **15:03** Some fans object to the presence of a cordless telephone on a Thal spaceship. Apparently, these fans are experts on the level of development of Thal technology. **17:01** The volume of air enclosed in the TARDIS would support one person for several days (there is a lot of air in the TARDIS besides that in the console room). If the Doctor went into a trance, as on other occasions, he could extend this time. **18:01** The Doctor and the Thals leave the TARDIS doors open. **21:34** The Doctor tells the Thals that he is on a special mission. **23:46** The Doctor and the Thals spray paint the invisible Dalek. Apparently, each can contains multi-colored paint, as the painted Dalek is not just one color.

Episode 2
First Transmitted: Apr. 14, 1973

0:30 Now that the paint is dry, the Dalek is more evenly colored. **1:24** Some viewers claim that Vaber (Prentis Hancock) does not finish his discussion about the Spiridons' invisibility. Codal (Tim Preece) supplies the explanation. **8:29** Taron (Bernard Horsfall) says to the Doctor, "There's our ship, your friend's inside." **9:21** Some viewers report that a blooper occurs because the Thals had not told the Doctor that Jo was in the ship. Thus, it would be impossible for the Doctor to say, "Jo Grant's in there!" This is not true as the Doctor learned earlier of Jo's presence. **11:26** The Dalek escorting the Doctor audibly bumps into the edge of the door as it passes through. **15:55** While Wester (Roy Skelton) is treating Jo, it is possible to see the shadow of the person holding the bowl. How does an invisible Spiridon cast a shadow?

Episode 3
First Transmitted: Apr. 21, 1973

3:15 Taron tells Rebec (Jane How) that the liquid is an allotrope of ice. Allotropes are different forms of the same element. Ice is not an element so it cannot have allotropes. Ice has polymorphs. **9:42** As Jo is climbing out of the crate there is a Dalek staring directly at her. The Dalek could not help but see Jo. **9:55** The dial on the wall moves as if someone is turning the hand from behind. **12:08** In the elevator, the Doctor first pushes the center button for down, then he pushes the bottom button for stop. After the elevator stops the doors open. **12:42** In the same elevator, the Doctor pushes the center button to stop and the bottom button to open the doors. **16:22** How do the Daleks manage to search Marat's (Hilary Minster) body? In reality this is not a blooper since it was done out of view of the camera. How do the Daleks know what the purpose of the map is? **20:45** The Daleks are shown cutting through the door. They have cut along the top of the door and part of each side. This includes the upper right. **21:00** In this shot, the Daleks finish the cut in the upper right of the door. The Daleks cut this area earlier. **21:11** There are fans who object to the use of toy Daleks.

Episode 4
First Transmitted: Apr. 28, 1973

2:31 There is tape on the back of the map. Tape must be present to keep the map from falling off the Dalek's "hand." **3:00** While they discuss the destruction of the explosives, the right hand Dalek seems about to lose its top. **4:01** A very large "rock" hits Jo on the head. A rock that large would have done much more than stun her for a few minutes. Jo is obviously preparing for the blow as she begins rapidly blinking just before the "rock" hits her. **4:47** The Dalek following the Doctor and the others up the ventilation shaft has a wire attached to its top. There are incorrect reports that this is in Episode 3. **7:59** Codal and Rebec have difficulty when moving some obviously polystyrene "boulders." Some fans claim that Jo, who is not present, helps with the "boulders." **11:56** The Daleks refer to their disease as being due to bacteria. **12:36** Some viewers claim that the Doctor has forgotten that he followed the Daleks to Spiridon. This is not exactly true. At this time, the Doctor explains that he asked the Time Lords to send him after the Daleks. Since the Doctor did not actually program the TARDIS flight, he would not necessarily know where he was. Thus, he has not forgotten why he is there. **16:10** In many scenes, the pots for the jungle plants are obvious. One of the better shots is directly in front of Jo after the Doctor asks, "Did you notice anything peculiar about the Daleks, Jo?" **16:46** A dark shadow appears on the backdrop as the group takes refuge on the Plain of Stones. Apparently, this is a person, but this is not definite. **19:58** The second time we see the glass case holding the bacteria, it is possible to see the reflection of one of the production crew. This person moves around.

Episode 5
First Transmitted: May 5, 1973

1:11 Instead of being scared off by the shots, the jungle animals simply "close" their eyes (the lights are turned off). It is possible to see the silhouettes of the cardboard cutouts representing the animals. Do not overlook the one-eyed "monster." **3:24** The face of the "invisible" Spiridon appears as Codal begins to struggle with the Spiridonian he thought was Taron. **3:34** Look through the disturbed foliage as Taron knocks out the Spiridonian. A BBC camera appears. **13:21** The first Dalek knocks over a potted plant. **13:39** There seems to be a light missing behind the backdrop as Jo and Latep (Alan Tucker) return to the Plain of Stones. A large dark area or shadow appears in the background. **13:52** As the pursuing Daleks enter the rock circle, the first Dalek runs into a rock and it is possible to hear the Dalek scraping against the polystyrene rock. **14:00** The Doctor stands to leave his hiding place behind the boulder. As the Doctor stands, Jo grimaces as if he just stepped on her foot. **15:58** Why is the Doctor no longer concerned about the automatic distress signal when opening the Daleks? **16:31** Wester is trying to hide his presence so he can move around freely. Why does he not take off his fur? **19:00** The Dalek containing Rebec bumps into the camera it is passing with a thunk. **20:30** Some viewers have a problem with the sealing of the Dalek laboratory to keep the virus from escaping, and they wonder what occurs when the Doctor and the Thal blow up the base. Apparently, these people were watching a different program. There is no virus in this story, and the laboratory containing the bacteria survives the attack. The Supreme Dalek and others leave the base after the attack. **20:46** We see the now visible Wester — though "dead" his eyelids flutter.

Episode 6
First Transmitted: May 12, 1973

2:39 In the time since the Doctor was last in the Dalek's stronghold they have redesigned the elevator controls. The door now has a four button control: bottom — open/close and next to bottom — down. **3:48** As the Doctor and Rebec are looking at the "stored" Daleks, it is possible to see the shadow of a Dalek in the corridor behind them as they start to move away. Some fans report that Taron, the leader of the Thals, was with the Doctor instead. **4:26** Jo acquires a new hairdo, even though there appears to be no beauty salon on the entire planet. Maybe this is one of Latep's special skills that qualified him for this mission. **5:13** Being able to see the strings used to lower the door to the spaceship is supposedly a blooper. The door is of the drawbridge type — this type of door used would require cables to open and close. **8:24** The Supreme Dalek has trouble with its eyepiece and the lights on top. The lights should work when it is talking; however, they also work when other Daleks are talking. **16:58** The last Dalek nearly knocks the console over. **17:41** The Doctor says to Taron, "Throughout history, you Thals have always been known as one of the most peace loving peoples in the galaxy." Obviously, Taron has forgotten the part of their history experienced by the Fourth Doctor in *Genesis of the Daleks*. **20:21** Who closed the TARDIS doors? The Doctor and the Thals left them open in Episode 1. **20:41** The Doctor runs up to the console and makes the entire unit shake.

Comments: In many ways, this story is a continuation of *Frontier in Space*.

The Doctor defeats the Daleks, and saves the planet Spiridon.

(TTT) The Green Death

Writer: Robert Sloman and Barry Letts; **Director:** Michael Briant

Media: Commercial DVD — episodic version —154 minutes (used); Commercial tape — episodic version —154 minutes; Collector's tape — movie version —143 minutes
Highlights: Jo Grant leaves the series. The Doctor is in drag again. The Doctor leaves to ride off into the sunset.
Questions: Since they already know that there are other entrances, why is the Doctor concerned about the Brigadier closing the mineshaft?

Errors and Other Points of Interest

Episodes 2, 5, 6 at 25:04, 24:29 and 25:17 (respectively) — the background for the closing credits of these three episodes appear upside down and backwards.

Episode 1
First Transmitted: May 19, 1973

0:43 Some fans question why the mine is being checked when it is closed. This could be an inspection prior to reopening, or, more likely, the BOSS wants to know what is happening in the mine. **1:48** The miner rings to signal he wishes to ascend. Who is controlling the lift? **2:42** Some of Professor Jones' (Stewart Bevan) vegetarian followers are wearing sheepskin coats. Some observers claim this as a blooper because the group members are vegetarians. At no time do Professor Jones or any of his followers profess that they are animal rights activists or vegetarians. Notice that when Jo reaches Professor Jones' compound, the cow in front is not a milk cow. **3:52** The miner must sound the alarm as no one else is around. Who controlled the lift that brought him to the surface? **4:17** Jo has forgotten what a dematerialization circuit looks like. **4:28** There are claims suggesting that the browning of Jo's apple is a blooper. Initially the apple is still white, after an undetermined amount of time, it is light brown, and about two minutes later, it is a little darker brown. Supposedly, the change is too rapid; note the changes for yourself. **7:02** After an undetermined amount of time, the apple is still mostly white. **9:18** The apple now appears to be brown. **9:50** The TARDIS light does not flash during dematerialization. **10:52** The steer in front of the house is a Hereford. Hereford's are excellent sources of meat, but they are poor sources of milk. This would indicate that the residents are not pro-animal rights. **11:22** The Doctor finally makes it to Metebelis 3, but the TARDIS light does not flash on landing. **11:41** Some fans suggest that a blue sun giving a red sunset is a blooper. Do not be confused by the later "blue" scenes. If this is after the sunset—then the blue scenes are during the night not under a blue sun. **18:53** Jo's coat knocks a clay triangle off the tripod as she goes over to Dr. Jones. **20:14** The Doctor nearly knocks the TARDIS apart as he exits. **20:38** Dai Evans (Mostyn Evans) signals Dave (Talfryn Thomas) to lower the lift. **20:45** Dave operates the lift. This shows that someone must be present at the top of the shaft to raise or lower the lift. This is not in agreement with earlier operation of the lift. **23:29** Watch the bottom right of the screen as Evans receives his cue to begin speaking.

Episode 2
First Transmitted: May 26, 1973

2:16 Jo's lamp temporarily disappears from her helmet. Before the fall, she has it, right after the fall she does not, and then she has it again as she stands. **5:12** Professor Jones tells the Brigadier that he tried to borrow the cutting equipment from Global Chemical "a few weeks back." Stevens gives a different story later. **7:43** Stevens (Jerome Willis), unlike Professor Jones, tells the Brigadier "They tried to borrow ours yesterday." Some observers cite this as a blooper; however, this could be proof that Stevens is lying. There is misquoting of this statement and Professor Jones' statement on some lists. **11:27** This is 1973 (and filming took place in 1973), so why is a 1972 (leap year) calendar on the wall? **14:56** The Doctor's stunt double needs to get a wig that not only is the same color as the Doctor's hair but also the same length. **18:51** Even though the cable is cut, a different motor is connected, and only one car is to be lowered (not a counterbalanced member of a pair), the wheels at the top of the shaft move exactly as they did previously when it was counterbalanced. **21:17** After the sludge infects Bert (Roy Evans), Jo must help him through the mine. Bert and Jo come around a corner and bump one of the fallen timbers. Fortunately, this is a fallen timber in the disused portion of the mine instead of a supporting timber.

Episode 3
First Transmitted: June 2, 1973

3:23 The bad CSO causes the bottom of the cart to disappear. **6:55** The "egg" the Doctor picks up makes many balloon-like sounds (it is a balloon). **11:01** Here is a question posed by some viewers: "Why is there a camera in the pipeline?" Obviously, since there is a ladder present, there should be a surveillance camera to watch the ladder. **11:58** The first time Elgin tries to open the door he pulls on the top dog; this will not open the door. The second time he tries to open the door he correctly pushes the dog to open the door. **16:26** The removal of Fell's (John Rolfe) "headphones" leaves his hair mussed. He is still in a trance. A few seconds later, when Fell walks past the Doctor, Jo and Elgin, his hair is neat. Who combed Fell's hair? **23:31** Some fans claim the Doctor's line "postulate the active nuclei" is a blooper. Even though this is babble, it is technobabble, and, as such, it is not a blooper.

Episode 4
First Transmitted: June 9, 1973

1:32 Hinks (Ben Howard) has to stick his arm into the maggot's mouth so he can be "bitten." **3:31** Nobel Prize or no Nobel Prize — Professor Jones does not know how to use a microscope. Apparently, he has spent too much time writing papers and too little time in the laboratory. **6:57** There is a boom mike shadow on the uniform of one of the UNIT soldiers as Jo says, "no you can't." **14:39** The Doctor has trouble with the word "chitinous" (referring to the "shell" on the larvae). He pronounces the first syllable as "chit" instead of the correct pronunciation "kite." **16:09** The calendar indicates that Monday is April 28. This is not a 1972 or 1973 calendar. **19:33** Professor Jones hits the microscope with his face. **25:24** The closing credits contain the grammatical blooper: "Yate's Guard" (Brian Justice).

Episode 5
First Transmitted: June 16, 1973

5:35 Jo tries many times to call Greyhound One (though she never says "Calling Greyhound One" as claimed). This time, as Jo tries to contact the Brigadier, her line is "Hello Brigadier, this is Jo, Greyhound One." There seems to be some confusion about the Greyhounds. **7:37** Jo now calls "Greyhound One. Come in." **8:44** The Doctor tells BOSS he is working out sums — then he says "Pi — 3.1416," and appears to be continuing on to list other digits in the value of pi. However he should have said 3.1415(92654...). **11:51** As the maggots are approaching the tunnel, a click sounds and a person's shadow moves on the lower part of the vertical beam. **13:07** This begins the Day Night Blooper. At this time, we see the Doctor escaping during the day. Later, the guards supposedly catch Captain Yates at night. Finally, we see the Doctor in daylight. The claim is that all of these should be during the day (or all during the night). The claim that the capture of Captain Yates was at night is questionable. His capture takes place in front of a window hidden by a blind. During the struggle, it is possible to see blackness behind the blind. There is no evidence that this is an outside window. It is possible that the blind conceals a room with its lights out. Factories and laboratories do have internal rooms with windows and blinds. **13:36** The Doctor destroys the Global Chemical gate. **13:51** The Day Night Blooper continues with the supposed capture of Captain Yates at night. **13:54** Jo calls "Brigadier Hello, Greyhound One, Greyhound Four." **14:30** The Day Night Blooper ends with the Doctor appearing in daylight. **14:47** Sergeant Benton replies to Jo saying, "Station calling Greyhound One." **15:18** The model crossing the set is not very convincing. **16:25** Many old mines have loose boards on the ground in front of the entrance. Thus when Sergeant Benton jumps over the maggots and lands on the boards they behave like boards. Since boards are often in front of old mine entrances, this is not a blooper as reported. **21:16** Some viewers have found fault with the small change in the New York numbers (7203 to 7580) as opposed to the Moscow change (10003 to 110098). Without knowing, the exact meaning of the numbers this is uncertain. It could mean that there has been more work in Moscow than in New York. **23:58** Captain Yates manages to break James' (Roy Skelton) conditioning. James falls against the wall, which wobbles. This also occurs in the reprise.

Episode 6
First Transmitted: June 23, 1973

1:21 Unlike Professor Jones, the Doctor uses the microscope correctly. **12:39** The gate destroyed by the Doctor has regenerated. **14:09** The console unit is not very substantial; it moves around every time Stevens gets on the unit. **16:44** Stevens does not always mime the BOSS's words correctly. **25:08** The sun is too far above the horizon to be dusk. It is apparent there is a filter present to make it appear later. The removal of the filter as the closing credits begin spoils the effect, and makes this a blooper.

Comments: The Doctor saves the Earth.

(UUU) The Time Warrior

Writer: Robert Holmes; **Director:** Alan Bromly

Media: Commercial tape — movie version — 90 minutes; Collector's tape — episodic version — 97 minutes (used)
Highlights: Sarah Jane Smith (Elisabeth Sladen) becomes the Doctor's new companion.

Errors and Other Points of Interest

Episode 1
First Transmitted: Dec. 15, 1973

2:40 Bloodaxe (John J. Carney) has horse trouble as he and the others are riding towards the spaceship. **4:26** Linx (Kevin Lindsay) exits his spaceship and plants the Sontaran flag. After this Irongron (David Daker) and Bloodaxe quickly turn their heads to look to the right (offstage). **8:51** Irongron's gun goes off before he fires it. **9:25** The Doctor uses the alias "Doctor John Smith."

Episode 2
First Transmitted: Dec. 22, 1973

2:51 This story takes place in the 12th century. Unfortunately, after the Norman Conquest English counties such as "Wessex" no longer existed. The use of Wessex is an anachronism. To be fair, some names probably did persist among local residents, also this specific reference is to "Wessex Castle," and not to the county. **4:44** This Sontaran has three fingers. **18:02** When Linx questions the Doctor about his origins, the Doctor uses the name Gallifrey for the first time in the series. **18:38** We learn that the Sontarans also have time technology. Linx partially explains Sontaran time technology at this point.

Episode 3
First Transmitted: Dec. 29, 1973

1:15 The Doctor grabs Bloodaxe's hand and pulls him down in front of Irongron. The Doctor then escapes into the yard, but touches no one while running about. **1:38** Irongron claims the Doctor struck him. The Doctor did not strike Irongron.

Episode 4
First Transmitted: Jan. 5, 1974

1:24 We learn that the probic vent of the Sontarans is their weakness. Compare this probic vent to the ones seen in *The Two Doctors*. **4:15** Sarah Jane picks up what appears to be a potato in the kitchen. If it is a potato, it is a few years too early, and an anachronism. **6:21** During the battle scene, the Doctor's neck and chin are visible. **8:53** Sarah Jane learns that the serving wenches will eat the oatmeal. Thus, the serving wenches will also get the drug. **18:20** The Doctor shows Professor Rubeish (Donald Pelmear) a three-step sequence to send the other scientists back to the twentieth century. After the Doctor illustrates these three steps and Professor Rubeish looks away, the Doctor flips another switch not previously indicated. **21:13** Sarah Jane repeats the three-step sequence, apparently without the final switch step. **21:51** One of the "unconscious" men keeps moving his hand as Hal (Jeremy Bulloch) rises and approaches the table. The hand is at the far left of the table. **21:58** Many fans consider the failure to warn the serving wenches to leave the castle to be a blooper. **23:01** The explosion of the castle is obviously the explosion of a rock cliff (possibly in a quarry).

Comments: Some blooper lists incorrectly refer to Irongron as Irongrod. The Doctor defeats the Sontarans, well at least one Sontaran.

(WWW) INVASION OF THE DINOSAURS

Alternate Title: *The Invasion*
Writer: Malcolm Hulke; **Director:** Paddy Russell

Media: Commercial — episodic version — Episode 1 in black and white — 147 minutes (used); Collector's tape — movie version — no Episode 1 — 115 minutes; Collector's tape of Episode 1 — black and white — 25 minutes
Highlights: #177781 and #177782.
Questions: The Minister's explanation to Sarah Jane in Episode 5 opens a time travel paradox. If the Earth returns to before the parents of the people on the "spaceship" were born, that is — if their parents never existed — how could the "spaceship" people have been born?

Errors and Other Points of Interest

Episode 1
First Transmitted: Jan. 12, 1974

0:21 The name of this episode is not a blooper; the use of the name "Invasion" was to keep the appearance of the dinosaurs a "surprise." **1:49** As Sarah Jane and the Doctor emerge from the TARDIS, a light colored vehicle drives by in the background. Supposedly, no vehicles should be present; however, this could be a looter. **11:03** When the Doctor opens the vehicle door, the far wall reflects a bright light. Since the solid doors are closed — where is the bright light coming from? Obviously, it is from a studio light. **11:19** A supporting wire appears against the ceiling beam as the Pterodactyl first flies towards Sarah Jane. **11:35** The cloth the Pterodactyl is holding is a poor way to disguise its operator. **14:38** The Doctor again uses his "Doctor John Smith" alias. **16:54** The Tyrannosaurus rex has the wrong number of fingers on its hands. Three are present instead of two. **24:01** Where is the looter who was to accompany the Doctor and Sarah Jane?

Episode 2
First Transmitted: Jan. 19, 1974

1:16 The Tyrannosaurus rex simply says, "Roar" sometimes. **1:26** There is a bad CSO alignment. It appears as if the UNIT troops are firing at the building next to the monster instead of at the monster. **1:59** The Doctor identifies the dinosaur as a Tyrannosaurus rex (two fingers on hand); he does not call it an Allosaur (three fingers on hand). **6:11** Sergeant Benton points to the map and notes the color-coding: red — Tyrannosaurus, blue — Triceratops, green — Stegosaurus, pink — Pterodactyl. Apparently, there have been no Brontosaurs. **11:18** This is one of the times where switching back and forth between the actors and the CSO of the Stegosaurus leads to obvious differences in the color of the sky. **20:13** Benton tries to say Apatosaurus. The Doctor comes to his aid and adds that the more common name is Brontosaurus. Either this is the first appearance, or Sergeant Benton forgot to plot the largest of the dinosaurs appearing in London on his map. Before anyone claims the use of Brontosaurus as a blooper, it is still an accepted name. **20:40** This is one of the "floating" dinosaurs created by the CSO. **21:14** When the Doctor's gun first appears, it is in the back of the jeep. It appears as if the sabotage device Captain Yates is to attach is already present. **22:11** Captain Yates attaches the sabotage device. The device was in place earlier.

Episode 3
First Transmitted: Jan. 26, 1974

8:11 General Finch (John Bennett) must "click" the pen twice before the pen will write. **11:06** The Tyrannosaurus rex defies gravity. It arises through an impossible movement. This happens again later. **11:30** Some viewers have questioned the appearance of the Doctor's hair. They feel his hair only appears this way in this scene in this episode. This is the Hair Blooper. **12:24** A beam hits Sarah Jane on the back of her head. Later we see the scratches and bruises on the front of her head, and she does not say anything about a bump on the back of her head. **16:16** The door behind Sergeant Benton starts to open. **18:53** We hear very clearly the sound of the lift starting; however, Sarah Jane neither hears the start nor notices the motion.

Episode 4
First Transmitted: Feb. 2, 1974

0:39 Some observers claim the interspersed scenes of Sarah Jane on the "ship" and Earth scenes give the plot away. It is already obvious that Sarah Jane is not on a real ship. The wound on her head already "gave" the plot away. **1:52** When the Brigadier approaches the "Whomobile," a metal tube passes across the bottom of the screen. Some fans claim that the Doctor could not have moved the tube since his hands were down. However, the movement of the clipboard by the Doctor a few seconds later indicates that he may have been responsible for the movement of the tube. **3:23** Mark (Terence Wilton) introduces himself as "John Kryton." **3:26** Sarah Jane mentions that Mark made a 2.362-meter jump during the last Olympics. Records are measured to two, not three, decimal places. **7:58** As Butler (Martin Jarvis) enters the hidden lift in the tube station, he bangs his head. **9:01** When the Doctor enters/leaves the "closet" in the underground, there are hooks, some with coats on them, on the wall to the left of the entering Doctor. There are claims that the hooks and coats disappear when he leaves/enters the underground shelter. This may in part be due to a different camera angle. **10:01** The Doctor leaves the lift. It is not possible to see the left wall because of the camera angle. However, part of a coat peeks out from the very edge of the door. **10:18** The zoom towards the security camera is very wobbly. **10:56** A right-hand wall wobbles as the shutter-like doors close. **11:13** A different wall section wobbles this time. **12:11** The Doctor enters the lift, and again the left wall is out of view of the camera, so it is not possible to see if anything is hanging there. **13:02** The items are again visible on the walls of the lift. When the Doctor returns with the Brigadier it is possible that changes occurred.

Episode 5
First Transmitted: Feb. 9, 1974

5:30 When Butler raises the cup to smash it for the demonstration, he hits the red flashing top of the apparatus with a "thunk." **7:16** As Sarah Jane turns around; there is a "freeze frame" of the back of her head. **10:11** This is the point where some observers think the shots for the Hair Blooper originated. **11:49** Sarah Jane apparently needs to lose weight because as she leans against the "brick" wall beside the door, her weight makes the wall shift. **22:33** The Minister (Noel Marcus) tells Sarah Jane that the people on Earth and their ancestors will vanish. This leads to a time paradox for the survivors.

Episode 6
First Transmitted: Feb. 16, 1974

2:02 Some fans consider this the most

outlandish scene for Tyrannosaur special effects. This is because of how far the dinosaur leans over when attacking the Brontosaurus. This is another incidence where a dinosaur defies gravity. **3:41** As Butler pushes Sarah Jane into the storeroom, there is a boom mike shadow on the right wall below the vent. **6:24** The entire wall shakes as Sarah Jane struggles to remove the grating, and again as she enters the vent. **16:52** The smoke from the flare the Brigadier is holding disappears into the CSO of the Triceratops.

Comments: The Doctor saves the Earth.

(XXX) DEATH TO THE DALEKS

Writer: Terry Nation; **Director:** Michael Briant

Media: Commercial tape — episodic version — 98 minutes (used); Commercial tape — movie version — 93 minutes; Collector's tape 92 minutes

Questions: If making it to the center of the city does not reward the people entering, what is the purpose of the city? Why were the Daleks' guns the only thing affected?

Errors and Other Points of Interest

Episode 1, 24:09; Episode 2, 23:50; Episode 3, 24:08; Episode 4, 24:09

The credits misspell the name of Dalek operator Murphy Grumbar as Murphy Grunbar at the end of each episode. This does not appear in the movie version, as only John Scott Martin and Cy Town receive credit as Dalek operators.

Episode 1

First Transmitted: Feb. 23, 1974

1:59 The TARDIS lands without the light on top flashing. This could be due to the power failure. **11:10** Some fans have questioned the fate of the Exxilon in the TARDIS after Sarah Jane knocked the creature unconscious. Since Sarah Jane left the door open when she left, the Exxilon could simply leave through the open door when it awoke. **19:29** Jill (Joy Harrison), the geologist, describes what parrinium is. Some fans wonder about the similarity between the words parrinium and perineum. The similarity between alien terms and Earth terms should not be bloopers. There are many instances where the alien terms sound similar to Earth terms. For example, consider the similarity in the name Myrka, *Warriors of the Deep*, and merkin. **21:12** The Captain (John Abineri) is not looking in the same direction as the other actors when he shouts "landing in the next valley." **23:32** Some observers feel that making it obvious that the Dalek guns do not work spoils the cliffhanger.

Episode 2

First Transmitted: Mar. 2, 1974

Some viewers report that Sarah Jane is absent from the cell in some scenes. You should count the times Sarah Jane is absent. **0:44** This is one example where only three Daleks carry on the action even though four are present. One Dalek remains motionless. **1:53** There are many scenes where the Dalek's head seems about to fall off or at least to move with difficulty. **3:34** This is another example where only three Daleks carry on the action even though four are present. **5:44** The attachment of the arrow to the back of the Captain's jacket is obviously only superficial. **13:26** Some fans wonder why the Daleks carry a model TARDIS for target practice. **13:55** This is one of the times where the Daleks' new guns do not appear to be working. The natives "die" anyway.

Episode 3
First Transmitted: Mar. 9, 1974

3:56 The wire holding the "root" guardian makes its appearance as the Dalek explodes. This wire appears many times. **9:10** During the conference in the Dalek ship, the head of one of the Daleks wobbles. **11:19** In some of the scenes at the mine, the tracks the Daleks need to move on are visible. **11:41** As the Daleks discuss setting the explosive charges, another Dalek head wobbles. **11:52** As the "root" guardian comes out of the water, we can see the wire support. **12:56** The Dalek guns now appear to be working. **23:31** The cliffhanger for Episode 3 is not very effective since no one knows why it is a cliffhanger.

Episode 4
First Transmitted: Mar. 16, 1974

11:49 Either we are seeing the Doctor's reflection in a mirror and he leans in front of the camera or someone else's head leans in to the right of the screen. **14:48** Hamilton (Julian Fox) slams the explosive against the beacon and nearly causes the structure to fall over.

Comments: The Doctor defeats the Daleks and saves the planet of Exxilon.

(YYY) THE MONSTER OF PELADON

Writer: Brian Hayles; **Director:** Lennie Mayne

Media: Commercial tape — episodic version — 146 minutes (used); Collector's tape — movie version — 133 minutes
Question: Why does the Queen's handmaiden not talk?

Errors and Other Points of Interest

The light on the top of the TARDIS flashes a lot faster on landing and take-off than is normal.

The positioning of the torches for opening and closing the secret doors is still a problem in this story. The Doctor apparently remembers from *The Curse of Peladon*. Sarah Jane finally learns how to work the door.

Episode 1
First Transmitted: Mar. 23, 1974

8:38 Some viewers report that the door nearly knocks the Doctor over as he opens the secret door in Episode 1. This is the only time in Episode 1 where the Doctor opens a secret door. It opens away from him, he and Sarah Jane go through, and the door closes. The door neither hits nor nearly knocks down anyone. This is really a blooper from *The Curse of Peladon*. **16:20** Some observers question the "sudden" importance of trisilicate to all areas of technology. Peladon has only been a source for fifty years. Only Mars was a source before this time. There are similar situations occurring in Earth history. These observers apparently forgot about the invention of the transistor, and the time involved for its widespread use. **23:58** Lip-readers have come up with different conclusions as to what the Doctor says. This repeats in the reprise.

Episode 2
First Transmitted: Mar. 30, 1974

4:54 Sarah Jane opens the secret door and leaves the torch in the down position. **7:18** It is possible to hear the sound of dripping water. This is a sound effect from the mines. Unfortunately, this is not a scene in the mine. **13:10** Alpha Centauri (Body—Stuart Fell; Voice—Ysanne Churchman) refers to the natives as "Pels." **13:48** Alpha Centauri makes the statement "Natives of primitive planets are forbidden access to sophisticated weapons." Why is there an armory full of sophisticated weapons? There are not enough Federation personnel to use all the weapons. **14:43** Some fans question the efficiency of having the armory door controlled by a switch in the control room. This system worked until the Doctor let slip the location of the control. **15:46** As Alpha Centauri is going to wake Eckersley (Donald Gee), a shadow appears and goes around the corner behind Eckersley. **17:53** The Doctor arrives at the door Sarah Jane entered. Sarah Jane left the torch in the down position. The torch is back in the up position. **21:30** The Doctor and Sarah Jane fall on a mat at the bottom of the pit. In the next scene, the mat has disappeared.

Episode 3
First Transmitted: Apr. 6, 1974

3:37 Watch the left center of the screen. There is a plume of smoke or "heat waves" in front of the door. A few seconds later, the smoke becomes easier to see. This also occurs later. **8:43** Some viewers claim that Sarah Jane nearly bursts out laughing. This may be the place, but it is uncertain. There are other possible occurrences. **18:39** Some observers question Gebek's (Rex Robinson) ability to knock out the guard. The helmet does not protect the guard's chin, so it would be possible. The physiology of the Pels may allow this to work easier than for humans. Observers should not mistake human behavior for alien behavior. **19:33** The Doctor and Gebek hide behind a moving rock. **21:10** The Doctor and Gebek begin examining the alarm. **21:38** When Eckersley checks the monitor, the first shot is of the refinery alarm. The Doctor and Gebek are not present, even though the two of them arrived earlier. The second shot of the alarm shows the Doctor and Gebek. **23:33** Watch the size of the flame in the torch above the miner.

Episode 4
First Transmitted: Apr. 13, 1974

0:45 As the Doctor turns to face the door, the sonic screwdriver is on top of the control box. After the door opens, the screwdriver disappears. **9:17** Some viewers object to the refinery being "shut down." However, there has been no mining since before the beginning of this story. **12:09** The Doctor refers to the residents of the planet as "Peladonians." This is to refute reports that they are only Pels or Peladonians as both names appear in this story. **15:43** Ettis (Ralph Watson) tells Preba (Graeme Eton) the sonic lance overlooks the Citadel. Overlook means to look down on something. **16:59** Some fans report that when one of the Ice Warriors asks about the heat in the mine, the Ice Warrior to Gebek's right has no mouth. Later we see its mouth in a frontal shot. **20:31** The sonic lance is lower than the Citadel. It does not overlook the Citadel.

Episode 5
First Transmitted: Apr. 20, 1974

1:09 We see the face of the Doctor's stunt double (Terry Walsh) during the Doctor's fight with Ettis. This also happens in the cliffhanger. **2:26** Some observers question the presence of central heating in the mines. **21:22** In previous stories, various viewers object to the appearance of hairy Ice Warriors.

Episode 6
First Transmitted: Apr. 27, 1974

1:43 The Ice Warriors burn a hole in the refinery door. **1:51** Just before the Doctor sends Aggedor, the hole in the door disappears. **2:09** The hole in the door is still missing when Aggedor returns. **2:13** The hole in the door reappears. **8:36** Azaxyr (Alan Bennion) walks down the corridor positioning the Ice Warriors for an ambush. A studio light shines through a crack in the wall as he passes. **9:17** Max Faulkner dies in the ambush. **12:17** Max Faulkner dies a second time. A three-minute reincarnation has apparently occurred. **15:37** Eckersley's blow to Alpha Centuari's head lifts the front of the headpiece. This is one of many instances where a lifting of the headpiece occurs. **18:50** Viewers question how the Doctor was able to get Aggedor out of his pit. The answer is — the same way Aggedor got into the pit. **19:33** If Aggedor is following Eckersley, how did the trackers get into the lead? **20:01** When Aggedor (Nick Hobbs) dies and falls, you can see the actor's leg. **20:06** The dead Eckersley is still breathing. Not a normally reported blooper, but someone else reported it.

Comments: The Doctor saves the planet of Peladon.

(ZZZ) PLANET OF THE SPIDERS

Writer: Robert Sloman and Barry Letts; **Director:** Barry Letts

Media: Commercial tape — episodic version — 148 minutes (used); Collector's tape — movie version — 134 minutes
Highlights: We say goodbye to Jon Pertwee. Two regenerations appear in this story.
Question: At the end, the Doctor says the TARDIS brought him home (=UNIT Headquarters). Does this mean the Doctor considers Earth his home instead of Gallifrey?

Errors and Other Points of Interest

Episode 1
First Transmitted: May 4, 1974

12:54 The Doctor addresses the Brigadier as Alistair. **13:10** Why does Clegg (Cyril Shaps) associate the sonic screwdriver with the Drashigs? It is obvious from the views of the Doctor confronting the Drashigs that the screwdriver Clegg is holding is different from the one the Doctor used. Compare the one that Clegg is holding with the one he "sees" the Doctor holding. You should review *Carnival of Monsters*. **15:00** Sergeant Benton brings an envelope in and announces that it is from South America. The envelope does not appear to have a customs stamp, and the Sergeant does not mention having to pay a high duty on a valuable gemstone. Apparently, Jo and UNIT are parts of a smuggling ring. **22:46** While Professor Clegg is holding the blue crystal, a force disrupts the Doctor's laboratory. This "major" disruption leaves the equipment on the lab-bench in place and does not knock the hat-stand over.

Episode 2
First Transmitted: May 11, 1974

10:19 The Doctor says the moonlight on Metebelis 3 is blue — not the sun. This, at least in part, refutes the complaint from *The Green Death* about a blue sun giving a red sunset. **12:16–24:09** The climax to an 11-minute chase is Lupton simply disappearing. If he could do this, why wander about for so long and allow the Doctor and others recognize him? **12:53** If the spider is on Lupton's (John Dearth) back, what happens when Lupton sits in various vehicles? **13:42** Pay attention to the color of the Whomobile. **17:58–19:34** During the time the Whomobile is in the air, the color is gold. While on the ground, it appears silver. **19:48** The Whomobile has returned to its normal color. **20:46** Lupton shoves a man (Terry Walsh) into the water and then zaps another man. **21:10** Lupton is now trying to keep a dry man from getting into the boat. The dry man is the same man Lupton shoved into the water seconds before. **22:12** The Doctor's stunt double makes his appearance as the hovercraft passes onto the shore and back into the water.

Episode 3
First Transmitted: May 18, 1974

11:45 The camera starts to follow Tommy (John Kane) into the room, but the camera hits something with a "thunk." **17:00** Look at the spots near the top of the screen to the left of Lupton. **21:47** Neska (Jenny Laird) says, "No, I shan't you shan't take him."

Episode 4
First Transmitted: May 25, 1974

2:19 This is one of many cases where the support controlling the Queen Spider appears under her. **11:04** The new TARDIS key makes an appearance. **16:43** The "considerate" spiders give the victims in the larder pillows. Some viewers consider this a blooper.

Episode 5
First Transmitted: June 1, 1974

19:02 The light on top of the TARDIS does not flash during dematerialization. **19:14** As the TARDIS appears, the split screen partially cuts off one of the conspirator's leg. **19:50** As Sarah Jane exits the cellar, the wall to her right begins to wobble. This continues as Tommy locks the door. **20:12–23:12** Compare the cliffhanger to the reprise. **20:47** K'anpo (George Cormack) notes that the Doctor speaks Tibetan.

Episode 6
First Transmitted: June 8, 1974

0:33–5:19 Compare this reprise to the cliffhanger from the preceding episode. The sequence is different. **3:57** K'anpo tells the Doctor to see through his eyes — the Doctor not only sees through his eyes, he can see through Sarah Jane to the spider behind her. **8:37** K'anpo refers to "regeneration" for the first time in the series. **11:44** As the Doctor reappears in the cellar both sides of the split screen have different lighting levels. This is very noticeable again as the TARDIS disappears. **11:57** Each time the backdrop appears there are dark spots in the sky. **11:59** The light on top of the TARDIS stays on instead of flashing. **16:27** Some of the controlling strings on The Great One are obvious. These may represent spider webs. **19:21** The light on top of the TARDIS is already on when the Doctor returns. **23:39** It is possible to see into the empty TARDIS.

Comments: The Doctor saves the Earth and Metebelis 3.

IV
The Fourth Doctor

(4A) Robot

Writer: Terrance Dicks; **Director:** Christopher Barry

Media: Commercial tape — episodic version — 98 minutes (used); Collector's tape — movie version — 90 minutes
Highlights: The new Doctor appears.
Questions: Why does the virus cease to be active after destroying the Robot?

Errors and Other Points of Interest

Sergeant Benton receives a promotion to Warrant Officer. He is appropriately dressed as such throughout the story. He even "clarifies" this to Sarah Jane. The closing credits for each episode still list him as "Sergeant Benton."

Episode 1
First Transmitted: Dec. 28, 1974
5:50 The "brick" the Doctor breaks is obviously made of wood. Listen for the sound it makes when it hits the floor. **13:46** Miss Winter's (Patricia Maynard) views do not seem to be SRS views. She is a feminist, and other SRS members do not appear to be feminists. **17:59** The Doctor bumps Harry's arm as he raises his hand.

Episode 2
First Transmitted: Jan. 4, 1975
12:43 Some observers question the use of the disintegrator gun. The SRS has spent one and a half episodes stealing the gun and its parts and then used the weapon to break into only one safe. These observers believe that K1 (Michael Kilgarriff) should have been able to break into the safe without the ray gun. Sarah Jane refutes this argument later when she says the safe was made of a special metal. The "special metal" might require the ray gun. **14:07** As the Brigadier and the Doctor are talking, there is a long thin rope (light cord) between them this appears after the camera angles shifts to exclude Sarah Jane. **20:36** The Doctor types out a letter to Sarah Jane. While he is typing, the letter looks single spaced and only covers a small part of the page. He then pins the letter to the side of the TARDIS. **21:02** Benton points out to Sarah Jane that he is now a Warrant Officer. He has been dressed appropriately since the beginning of the story. **21:20** Sarah Jane finds the Doctor's letter; it looks double-spaced and fills most of the page. Some observers claim that the letter Sarah Jane finds is handwritten. **23:20** While pursuing the Doctor the Robot knocks down one of the concrete pillars supporting the roof. Obviously, the pillar was not doing a very good since the roof did not fall. This also occurs in the reprise.

Episode 3
First Transmitted: Jan. 11, 1975

3:40 Some fans complain about the apparent changes in K1's motives from scene to scene. A partial explanation occurs at this point when K1 tells Sarah Jane he is confused. **4:28** The Robot stumbles while fighting the UNIT troops. **6:57** Sarah Jane tells Professor Kettlewell (Edward Burnham) there is an SRS meeting that night. **14:21** Even though Sarah Jane reported a night meeting, it is daylight when everyone exits the building. **14:37** During the escape from the Meeting Hall, Jellicoe (Alec Linstead) hides behind the Robot. As they move away from the door, several UNIT troops have a good chance to shoot Jellicoe, but, even though the troops fire many shots, they repeatedly miss Jellicoe. **19:42** The Warrant Officer stumbles against the side of the UNIT vehicle. **23:09** Some observers object to the Action Man Tank.

Episode 4
First Transmitted: Jan. 18, 1975

2:59 Jellicoe is supposedly following Miss Winters. However, just before the doors close we see her walking off to the left. After the doors close, it is still possible to see through the crack between the doors. Jellicoe heads to the right instead of following Miss Winters. **5:28** Here is a further explanation of the fan question about K1's motives appears here. When K1 kills Professor Kettlewell, the action clearing affects the robot's sanity. **6:55** The first zoom towards the screen showing the countdown is off-center. **8:35** K1 informs Sarah Jane "the bunker is cleared." **9:06** A classic Brigadier quote: "Just once I'd like to meet an alien menace that wasn't immune to bullets." However, the Robot is an Earth menace, not a true alien menace. **10:08** Earlier the Robot said the Bunker was empty — so where did the soldier come from? **14:41** The Robot's legs keep disappearing from the point just before it begins to grow until its destruction. The CSO could be better. **15:35** When the Robot is holding "Sarah Jane," it is obvious that it is holding a doll. Using a doll with realistic looking hair would help. **17:05** The giant Robot "crushes" one of the soldiers under its foot. After the foot falls, the soldier's head comes up on the far side of the foot. **19:06** The bucket of virus the Doctor is carrying disappears into the CSO on the way to the giant Robot. **21:09** This is the first time the Fourth Doctor says, "Would you like a jelly baby?" **23:20** The shadow to the left of the TARDIS changes before the TARDIS disappears.

Comments: The Doctor saves the Earth.

(4C) THE ARK IN SPACE

Writer: Robert Holmes; **Director:** Rodney Bennett

Media: DVD — episodic version 98 minutes (used); Commercial tape — movie version (used); Collector's tape — movie version — 93 minutes
Highlights: There is no one other than the Doctor and his companions in the first episode. Harry (Ian Marter) is now a companion.
Questions: Why is there an empty cubicle available for Sarah Jane?

(4C) The Ark in Space

Errors and Other Points of Interest

Episode 1
First Transmitted: Jan. 25 1975

0:00 To date, this is the only pink and green opening title sequence. **1:06** Dune (Brain Jacobs), the cryogenically frozen man, is blinking when the Wirrn first opens the door. It is possible that the Wirrn Queen revived Dune before "infecting" him. If Dune revived, he could be blinking. **3:40** As the Doctor is talking to Harry he mentions the "Bennett Oscillator." This is an inside joke about the director of this story. **5:31** Harry not only presses the switch, he also moves the entire wall panel. **14:14** The Doctor tells Harry he is going to distract the Autoguard. What the Doctor meant is that Harry's shoe is going to distract the Autoguard. **15:50** The Doctor and Harry leave the bottom panel of the trans-mat couch open. **16:19** Orac (Peter Tuddenham) appears to have some influence over the Ark. **19:52** A slime trail is clearly visible on the floor. **22:28** Some viewers consider the fact that it takes so long for someone to notice the slime trail to be a blooper. **22:51** The person occupying the cubicle next to Dune's (D4) empty cubicle is very short.

Episode 2
First Transmitted: Feb.1, 1975

0:57 The Doctor does not quite stand out of sight as he waits for his cue. **3:19** The Doctor says, "My doctorate is purely honorary." **23:23** Apparently, the weapon has multiple settings ranging from stun to kill. Some viewers believe it should only have one setting.

Episode 3
First Transmitted: Feb. 8, 1975

15:02 Everyone leaves the "revival" room without closing the doors. If they are so concerned about the Wirrn in the room, they should immediately close the doors. **15:04** Notice the reflections of the stagehands in the yellow panel beside the door. **15:52** The doors are no longer open. **20:34** The bottom panel of the transmat couch is back in place. A potential blooper, but Rogin has had time to replace the panel.

Episode 4
First Transmitted: Feb. 15, 1975

0:49 Vira (Wendy Williams) has a gun in her hand. **0:53** Vira no longer has a gun. It is possible she dropped the gun. **13:26** Cubicle D4 now has a very tall person inside it. **18:19** The space-walking Wirrn look quite different from the Wirrn inside the Ark. **18:32** Vira reports the Wirrn are in the cargo hold. **20:30** The engines start before Rogin (Richardson Morgan) pulls the last lock. **21:31** Some viewers question how all the Wirrn can fit into the cockpit. Vira has already stated there are Wirrn in the cargo hold. The rocket is to transport everyone from the Ark to the Earth, thus there must be room for many passengers. Not all the Wirrn need to be in the cockpit. **22:28** There is a supposed blooper concerning the matter transmitter. Some observers postulate that the ability to transport only three people at a time is inefficient. If the transport ship had not been lost, an inefficient method would be unnecessary. **22:28** Some fans believe the Doctor should go to the Earth in the TARDIS, not in a possibly faulty transmat. How could the Doctor test the transmat if he went in the TARDIS?

Comments: Noah's head only splits open in the novelisation of this story. There was no filming of such a scene.

The Doctor saves humanity.

(4B) The Sontaran Experiment

Writer: Bob Baker and Dave Martin; **Director:** Rodney Bennett

Media: Commercial tape — episodic version — 49 minutes (used); The Commercial version comes packaged with *The Genesis of the Daleks*; Collector's tape — movie version — 48 minutes
Highlights: The return of the Sontarans.
Questions: Who throws the rocks down on Harry when he is in the trap?

Errors and Other Points of Interest

Episode 1
First Transmitted: Feb. 22, 1975

4:37 Some observers report a farm cottage in the background. This is questionable. **11:28** The reflection of a member of the production crew appears on the back of the "head" of the Sontaran robot. **15:10** Notice that these Sontarans have five fingers. **17:47** The Doctor reaffirms that the Earth is uninhabited.

Episode 2
First Transmitted: Mar. 1, 1975

1:35 If the Sontaran G3 Military Assessment Survey is so important — why send only one Sontaran? **2:02** Styre does not use the "normal" Sontaran gun. This may indicate a greater time difference between this story and other Sontaran stories. **5:33** Styre states that the Sontarans know the Earth to be uninhabited. Why should there be such an extensive survey before the invasion of a barren planet? **10:48** The Doctor appears shot before Styre fires his weapon. **19:29** During the Doctor's fight with Styre — notice that the Doctor is crouched over in close-ups and standing straight in long shots. **20:26** Obvious stand-ins are involved in the fighting. **21:05** The Doctor manages to knock Styre's head sideways. **23:22** This may be the car some observers report seeing.

Comments: The Doctor defeats the Sontarans.

(4E) Genesis of the Daleks

Writer: Terry Nation; **Director:** David Maloney

Media: Commercial tape — episodic version —143 minutes (used). The Commercial version comes packaged with *The Sontaran Experiment*; Collector's tape — movie version —133 minutes
Highlights: We get to meet Davros (Michael Wisher).
Questions: Why do none of the escaping Thal prisoner's take the unconscious guard's weapon?

Errors and Other Points of Interest

It seems hard to believe that a war has been going on for a thousand years with the opposing cities so close together. People are able to walk back and forth between the two cites, and people can sneak in and out of either city undetected.

Episode 1
First Transmitted: Mar. 8, 1975

1:56 The Doctor says, "Whatever I've done for you in the past I've more than made up for." Some observers cite this as a blooper; however, it may have been intentional. **2:35** During their discussion, the Doctor says to the other Time Lord, "Do you mean avert their creation?" The Doctor receives permission to commit genocide. Compare this to the events in the *Trial of a Time Lord*. Why did the Doctor not use this in his defense during his trial? **3:45** Sarah Jane refers to Nerva as a Beacon. How did she know this? **9:39** A shell explodes outside the trench (back center of the set), but the gas is vented inside the trench (lower left). **9:54** The Doctor loses his hat in the trench outside the Kaled door. **11:56** The Doctor is still wearing his overcoat. **12:06** The Doctor's overcoat disappears, and he is wearing the short red jacket that he will be wearing for most of the remainder of the story. The overcoat is not present in the background.

Episode 2
First Transmitted: Mar. 15, 1975

1:23 Tane (Drew Wood) tells the approaching party to announce "name, rank, and serial number." Nyder (Peter Miles) only gives his name and rank. **7:10** Notice the reflection in the card Ronson (James Garbutt) is holding. **12:59** Sarah Jane learns that the nose cone of the rocket is to hold the explosives. **14:48** The cell door does not close completely. **23:58** Sarah Jane falls outside the scaffolding.

Episode 3
First Transmitted: Mar. 22, 1975

1:26 Sarah Jane falls outside the scaffolding (as shown in the climax to the preceding episode), but she falls onto a landing inside the scaffolding. **5:32** The Doctor grabs a stalactite. While trying to dislodge it, he causes a boulder next to it to wobble in an unboulderlike manner. **9:26** Why load the explosives into the bottom of the rocket (where the engines are located)? There are small rocket engines next to the door, but they could not lift the rocket. The smaller engines must be steering rockets. **15:20** The Kaleds get the Doctor and Harry into the Thal Dome. If the Kaleds can get into the Dome so easily, why do they not invade and end the war? **21:02** The soldier on the right has trouble with his gun. This could be a blooper or an attempt to illustrate how broken down the equipment is after so many years. **21:31** There is a blooper claim that there is a single frame showing the Doctor's back while the guard is crawling towards the switch. This is supposedly an example of bad editing. If so, more editing removed it from these tapes. This is not present in the reprise either. Reports also incorrectly list this as occurring in the climax of Episode 2 and the reprise in Episode 3.

Episode 4
First Transmitted: Mar. 29, 1975

7:59 The reflection of a moving camera appears on the wall behind the Doctor and Bettan (Harriet Philpin). **9:54** One of the Muttoes picks up the same rock that the Doctor used on the "clam" in the cave. **17:11** Gharman (Dennis Chinnery) makes an unusual sound when Nyder (Peter Miles) hits him.

Episode 5
First Transmitted: Apr. 5, 1975

1:18 The Doctor says that the Dalek invasion of Earth happened in 2000. Apparently, he saw the trailer to *The Dalek Invasion of Earth* and not the story itself. **3:30** It is possible to see through a crack beside the door and see a stagehand or an actor moving. **16:13** The Doctor pulls both explosives and detonators from the same cabinet. No one ever stores those two items together. **16:30** The Doctor is going to commit genocide.

Episode 6
First Transmitted: Apr. 12, 1975

9:46 The Doctor loses the time ring during the struggle; the ring lands next to the wall. **15:22** The Doctor returns to look for the time ring. It is no longer where it fell; it is in the middle of the corridor. **16:03** The Doctor is wearing his short red coat. **16:50** The Doctor emerges from the incubator room wearing his overcoat and his hat. We do not see him enter at this time; however, the last thing he was wearing was his short red jacket. There are incorrect reports that the Doctor was seen entering the incubator room at this point also. The Doctor lost his hat during the trench battle outside the Kahled door in Episode 1. The Doctor was wearing his overcoat just before questioning in the first episode. **20:12** This is one of the scenes where the voice-lights of the Daleks are out of sync with their voices. An explanation could be that these are not fully developed Daleks. **20:38** Some fans question how long it will take to open the blocked tunnel. If the humans are dead and the Daleks do not care — it could take centuries. Only a concerted effort could excavate quickly. **22:20** The Doctor is wearing his overcoat when he, Sarah Jane and Harry grasp the time ring. **22:29** The Doctor is no longer wearing his overcoat.

Comments: The box containing the commercial tape lists the wrong title. The reported name of the story is *The Genesis of the Daleks*.

The Doctor and the Daleks struggle to a draw on the planet Skaro.

(4D) REVENGE OF THE CYBERMEN

Writer: Gerry Davis; **Director:** Michael E. Briant

Media: Commercial tape — episodic version — 97 minutes (used); Commercial tape — movie version — 91 minutes (used); Collector's tape — movie version — 90 minutes

Errors and Other Points of Interest

Some Blooper Lists contain a blooper calling the space station Nerva Beacon. This story takes place during the time when the space station was Nova Beacon. We learn that the name Nerva Beacon came later.

There are many occasions where the "emotionless" Cybermen show emotions.

Episode 1
First Transmitted: Apr. 19, 1975

0:55 Some fans consider the fact that the Doctor arrives at the Beacon not wearing his brown overcoat (that he was wearing at the end of *Genesis of the Daleks*) to be a blooper. This problem first appeared in *Genesis of the Daleks*— when last seen (holding the time ring) the Doctor is not wearing his overcoat. **2:28** The second body, and most of the others, is obviously a manikin. **5:46** The "stars" showing through the hallway windows are holes in pieces of paper taped to the windows. In this scene, one of the pieces of paper is waving in the breeze. **6:35** The Doctor explains that events in *The Ark in Space* take place far in the future. This is when it gained the name Nerva Beacon. **11:47** Apparently, the victim must hold the cybermat in position before the machine can "bite." **12:30** The tape makes noise even when it is not going pass the playback head. **17:15** To forestall the claim of a new blooper — the Doctor mentions that Voga is Jupiter's thirteenth satellite. The fact that Jupiter has more satellites was unknown during writing of this episode. **18:31** The transmitter that Kellman (Jeremy Wilkin) uses to send his message starts before he does. In addition, the sound does not match his finger movements. **19:25** The Doctor says that the matter transmitter will only transmit human tissue. He uses this to "cure" Sarah Jane, because the poison, being non-human, is not transmitted. If the matter transmitter can only transmit humans, how can the Cybermen or the bombs travel later? By the way — how do they transmit the character's clothing? (The clothing would not be a problem if the clothing were made of human tissue.)

Episode 2
First Transmitted: Apr. 26, 1975

4:47 This is one of the instances where Lester (William Marlowe) appears to be wearing an upside-down Interplanetary Space Command badge. Compare his insignia to the other crewmembers and to logo on the sides of the equipment. **5:23** Some observers object to the presence of gravity and air on the small asteroid. We never see any openings to the outside, so air could be inside the asteroid with no way to exit. This could explain the presence of air. These observers apparently forgot that Lord Cavendish proved, in 1798, that everything, including asteroids, has gravity. It is the magnitude of the gravity that is questionable. A large quantity of gold would result is an asteroid with a greater mass, and hence a greater gravitational attraction than a normal asteroid. **11:21** Some viewers have a problem with Tyrum's (Kevin Stoney) excellent dialogue. **16:01** Some fans question how the Vogans found a NASA rocket to use against the Cybermen. **17:21** The Commander (Ronald Leigh-Hunt), on Nova Beacon, notes the Cyberman ship and reports, "It's coming directly towards us!" **45:58M** Bad editing in the movie version leaves a black section between Episode 2 and Episode 3. The transmitting station may be guilty of creating this problem. **19:18** When we first see the ship, it is not moving towards Nova Beacon. The Commander made a mistake earlier. **19:31** The Cyberman ship finally begins to turn in the direction of the space station.

Episode 3
First Transmitted: May 3, 1975

1:17 This Cyber Leader (Christopher Robbie) does not recognize the Doctor. **7:09** This is one occurrence where the Cyber Leader appears to be giving the Doctor a massage. **8:06** A Cyberman sneaks up behind the Doctor in order to prevent the Doctor from using the bomb as a threat. Then two Cybermen bring over the other prisoners to the Doctor. One of the latter Cybermen has a "rocking" head. This problem occurs again later. **9:54** The Cyber Leader tells the Doctor, "You will have ... to reach your surface, and save your lives...." He pauses after "your"; he apparently caught his mistake. **13:35** One of the Vogans reports that their weapons have no effect on the Cybermen. If the Vogans use gold for everything, why do their bullets not hurt the Cybermen? Why do the Vogans not know of the susceptibility of the Cybermen to gold? Why do the Vogans not use the "glitterguns" developed to defeat the Cybermen the last time? **17:19** Sarah Jane gets out of the boat and stumbles about the beach.

Episode 4
First Transmitted: May 10, 1975

1:44 A classic Doctor quote, "Harry Sullivan is an imbecile!" **6:21** Lester finally appears to have his insignia correct. **18:19** In this view of the Vogan rocket, it appears as if it is going to one side of the target. **18:47** The Vogan rocket is now coming directly towards Nova Beacon. **19:21** Sarah Jane yells, "But we're still heading for the biggest bang in history." It seems a similar expression described Zaphod Beeblebrox. **19:49** An explosion is space should not produce so much noise. **20:51** It is obvious that Nova Beacon is about to "crash" into a rotating cylindrical drum instead of an approximately spherical asteroid. **21:44** The TARDIS light flashes during its landing. **21:53** As the Doctor enters the TARDIS, the paper printout from the space/time telegraph is hanging on a hook beside the door. **22:24** The TARDIS takes off without the light on top flashing.

Comments: The Doctor defeats the Cybermen, and saves the Earth and Voga.

(4F) TERROR OF THE ZYGONS

Writer: Robert Banks Stewart; **Director:** Douglas Camfield

Media: Commercial tape — episodic version — 96 minutes (used); Collector's tape — movie version — 91 minutes
Highlights: This is Harry Sullivan's last adventure with the Doctor.

Errors and Other Points of Interest

Episode 1
First Transmitted: Aug. 30, 1975

3:09 "Sergeant" Benton is still a Warrant Officer. This time he receives credit as such at the end of each episode. **6:44** The Doctor seems a little perturbed when he asks why the Brigadier called him. The Doctor says, "Have you brought me 270 million miles…." The distance from the Earth to Jupiter (Nova Beacon is near Jupiter) ranges from about 365 to 415 million miles (assuming they are on the same side of the Sun. This distance would be much more if the two planets were on opposite sides of the Sun. **6:51** The "space-time telegraph" from the previous story has evolved into a "psionic beam." **15:35** The Creature does not look like the Borad (see *Timelash*).

Episode 2
First Transmitted: Sept. 6, 1975

14:25 Between the time the Brigadier says, "Exactly what could have caused injuries like that Doctor?" and the Doctor's response, the "dead" soldier moves one of his fingers. **14:46** "Harry's" wound has only a faint color when he first steals the transmitter from Sarah Jane. **15:12** After pushing Sarah Jane back and rushing out the door, "Harry's" wound becomes much darker. This may be due to differences in Zygon versus human physiology. **21:09** The Doctor drives off to lead the Skarasen away. How does he know that he is not driving directly towards the beast? **24:06** Broton (John Woodnutt) quotes the Master: "Die! Doctor! Die!"

Episode 3
First Transmitted: Sept. 13, 1975

8:46 There are reports that the name of the town is Tulloch and that Tullock is a blooper. The sign outside The Fox Inn reads Tullock. **14:47** Why do the Zygons leave Sarah Jane unsupervised in the library where she can find the secret entrance? The entrance is easy to find since she opens the secret door almost immediately. **16:21** At least one viewer considers the ability to see the outline of Sarah Jane's undergarments through her clothes a blooper. **18:36** Harry's cell door sticks slightly when Sarah Jane opens the door.

Episode 4
First Transmitted: Sept. 20, 1975

6:47 Everyone seems to forget about the Zygon fleet. Apparently, the fact that it will be "centuries before the fleet arrives" placates them. **13:03** The shadow beneath the Zygon spaceship is wavering—or the Sun is vibrating.

Comments: The Doctor saves the Earth.

(4H) Planet of Evil

Writer: Louis Marks; **Director:** David Maloney

Media: Commercial tape — episodic version — 94 minutes (used); Collector's tape — movie version — 87 minutes

Questions: Why would anyone transport an unknown object, the TARDIS, to their ship after they have said it might be booby-trapped?

Errors and Other Points of Interest

Before someone claims the lack of stars is a blooper, they should remember that Zeta Minor is at the edge of the known Universe. Stars are apparently sparse in this area. If you were looking outward there would be no stars.

Episode 1
First Transmitted: Sept. 27, 1975

1:09 The year is 37,166. **5:54** The central column of the TARDIS is quite wobbly. **6:11** As the Doctor moves around the TARDIS console, a boom mike shadow appears on the wall behind him. **6:42** The Doctor tells Sarah Jane they are 30,000 years too late. This would place the events of *Terror of the Zygons* about the year 7166. **7:05** As the Doctor and Sarah Jane leave the TARDIS, it appears that someone forgot to turn off the flashing light on top. **13:26** When Sarah Jane returns, the TARDIS light is no longer shining.

Episode 2
First Transmitted: Oct. 4, 1975

11:21 Sorenson (Frederick Jaeger) explains that six pounds of antimatter will produce energy equivalent to what their sun produces in three centuries. Six pounds of antimatter will consume six pounds of normal matter to produce about 5×10^{17} Joules. This implies that the Morestran Sun produces about 5×10^{7} Joules per second. (This assumes that the Morestran year is about the same length as an Earth year.) This compares to our Sun, which produces about 4×10^{26} Joules per second. The Morestran Sun must be between Venus and the Earth's Moon in brightness as seen from the Earth. **15:01** We again see the TARDIS key.

Episode 3
First Transmitted: Oct. 11, 1975

1:15 Notice the Doctor's image on the

view screen. **1:57** Notice the Doctor's image on the view screen at this time. **7:57** Sorenson's glowing eyes could be better. They seem closed and probably painted. **14:46** While Sorenson and Salamar (Prentis Hancock) are talking, the camera wobbles. **14:48** There is a boom mike shadow on Salamar as he and Sorensen walk down the hall. **19:57** Some observers question Sarah Jane's apparent knowledge about Morestran ships. **22:26** The camera wobbles as Salamar begins to speak. This also occurs in the reprise. **22:58** Notice how far Sarah Jane and the Doctor have moved down the tubes.

Episode 4
First Transmitted: Oct. 18, 1975

1:31 Some viewers report that the Doctor and Sarah Jane were much further down the tubes in the climax of the preceding episode. **7:04** Salamar removes the neutron accelerator from its receptacle. **13:50** Vishinsky (Ewen Solon) places the neutron accelerator into a different receptacle from the original. **16:22** There are reports that there is a blooper during the take-off of the TARDIS. Supposedly, the Doctor leaves the doors open. We can hear a sound similar to the doors closing. Open doors would cause the same problem as occurred at the end of *The Enemy of the World*. We clearly see, from the outside, that the doors are not open as the TARDIS dematerializes. **18:21** The sign on the door to the Force Field Generator Room seems to be a poorly attached piece of cardboard. **18:41** Vishinsky tells Sarah Jane to position the force field units "in a line straight across." **19:25** The force field units are in a compact triangle. It is possible that this is Sarah Jane's concept of a straight line. **19:44** The Doctor nearly falls after tossing Sorenson into the pit. **19:53** The Doctor falls through the set as he is walking around the Well at the End of the Universe. **21:59** Why is the guard by the back wall keeping his weapon aimed at Sarah Jane?

Comments: The Doctor visits the planet Zeta Minor and saves the Universe.

(4G)   Pyramids of Mars

Writer: Stephen Harris (Robert Holmes and Lewis Griefer); **Director:** Paddy Russell

Media: Commercial DVD — episodic version — 98 minutes (used); Commercial tape — episodic version — 98 minutes (used); Commercial tape — movie version — 90 minutes; Collector's tape — movie version — 93 minutes
Questions: Why attack and kill the servant and then ignore the Doctor and Sarah Jane?

Errors and Other Points of Interest

The knot on Professor Marcus Scarman's tie varies from scene to scene. Two examples appear in this list. Pay close attention to the stripe on the knot. This gives a red triangle. Sometimes the red triangle is to the upper left and sometimes to the lower right (to the viewer).

Some fans consider it a hole in the plot to bury Sutekh with the means of his rescue. At no point do we learn that the intention of the Osirans was life imprisonment. The Doctor even notes that the Osirans did not want to sink to Sutekh's level by killing him.

(4G) Pyramids of Mars

Episode 1
First Transmitted: Oct. 25, 1975

1:29 Marcus Scarman (Bernard Archard) says that the contents of the tomb are First Dynasty, but we see items from later periods. An observer reports seeing King Tutankhamen's throne (not First Dynasty). **3:04** Sarah Jane demonstrates one of her remarkable abilities — precognition — she is wearing an Edwardian dress before she learns they are in 1911. **3:47** Pay close attention to Sarah Jane's hair-clips. **3:49** The Doctor says he is something like 750 years old. **4:13** The time disturbance not only causes Sarah Jane to fall down, but also causes her hair-clips to disappear. **9:18** Note the distance from the bottom of the window to the ground. **9:58** Note that not all windows are the same distance from the ground. **10:43** The Doctor and Sarah Jane cannot be standing on the ground by the window they jumped from earlier. **12:24** It is possible to see the wire on Ibramin Namin's (Peter Mayock) hand that supplies power to his ring. **18:37** Sarah Jane says that she is from 1980. **21:03** The Doctor begins to translate the Osiran message by looking for the letter E. This implies that he assumes the Osirans sent a message in English. Giving the final message in English is not a blooper, as claimed, because he would no doubt translate it for the other people present. **22:16** Sarah Jane opens the door, and it is obviously dark outside. **22:10** If it is night outside, why are the candles not lit? **22:54** Ibramin Namin is playing the organ. Then he stops playing and walks over to the sarcophagus. This may be a way of indicating that Sutekh is taking over the house.

Episode 2
First Transmitted: Nov. 1, 1975

2:59 Many people seem to believe that Sutekh was an Osirian; the Doctor clearly calls Sutekh an Osiran. **6:48** Note the elastic tied to the branch. **12:00** There is a bulge in Marcus Scarman's back for the special effect bullet to "hit." **14:22** Some viewers report a blooper at this point. The blooper goes something like this: when Sarah Jane exits through the window after she removed the control ring from Namin's finger, she bumps the backdrop and causes it to move. At this time, the Doctor, not Sarah Jane, removes the ring. Sarah Jane could still bump into the backdrop. **15:08** Everyone exits into the TARDIS. Sarah Jane still does not bump into the backdrop. **16:37** The Doctor shows Sarah Jane a time travel paradox — alternate time. **19:06** Everyone exits through the window. This is Sarah Jane's last chance to bump the backdrop and cause it to move. **19:06** This is obviously not the window Sarah Jane and the Doctor jumped from earlier, even though they are in the same room. From the outside, Sarah Jane's head would barely reach the window. **19:06** Sarah Jane jumps from the window, but it sounds as if she lands on a floor instead of on the grass. **22:25** There is a strange scream as Sarah Jane runs into the house.

Episode 3
First Transmitted: Nov. 8, 1975

0:44 The mummy destroys Laurence Scarman's instrument. **0:47** Laurence Scarman's instrument has reincarnated. **3:02** The Doctor is wearing his hat. Pay close attention to this hat. It will disappear. **3:12** The Doctor no longer has his hat as he enters the house. **4:18** The Doctor leaves his hat on a chair as he leaves to go get the explosives. **4:41** While walking through the woods, the Doctor again has his hat. **11:08** Look at the knot in Professor Scarman's tie. **12:26** Look at the knot in Professor Scarman's tie. **14:22** Upon returning to the house, we see the hat still waiting for the Doctor. However, there was time for the Doctor to throw his hat onto the chair after entering the room and before the hat appears on camera. **15:09** The Doctor refers to four murders. Unfortunately, there is a miscount. The murders to this point are:

Collins (Michael Bilton), Namin, Dr. Warlock (Peter Copley), Ernie Clements (George Tovey) the poacher, and Laurence Scarman. The Doctor increases his number by adding Marcus Scarman, but this still gives a bad total. **15:57** Some viewers believe that Marcus Scarman is in telepathic rapport with the mummies. If this were true, why would he need the mummies to signify their understanding of their instructions? **17:09** The smoke from the canister (coordinate selector) rises from the floor before the canister begins its journey. **17:10** The screw heads on each side of the sarcophagus were not appropriately painted. The badly painted screws do not "disappear" when the CSO image is present. This occurs most, but not all, times. **17:10** Note the wires holding the cylinder. **19:22** Some observers believe that if Marcus Scarman controls the mummies telepathically, then he should notice the Doctor in disguise. Marcus Scarman asks the "mummy" if there is any damage to his relays. This could cover the possible error.

Episode 4
First Transmitted: Nov. 15, 1975

 0:32 The explosion destroys two of the mummies. This, combined with the destruction of one of the mummies in Laurence Scarman's home, means that no mummies remain. **3:35** There should be no mummies remaining. Where did these mummies come from? **4:06** There is a cushion on the floor for Sarah Jane's head. **5:27** We get to see the TARDIS key and strings. **6:02** The dangling TARDIS key has trouble making it into Marcus Scarman's hand. The three supporting threads appear at times. **6:12** Sutekh (Gabriel Woolf) refers to the "Pyramid" not "Pyramids." **6:24** The Doctor tells Sutekh that the TARDIS is isomorphic (only the Doctor can operate the TARDIS). Sutekh is in the Doctor's mind, so this must not be a lie. Other people, before and after, have operated the TARDIS, so it is not isomorphic. **8:11** Two mummies follow Marcus Scarman and the others. **8:22** One of the mummies following Marcus Scarman and the others has vanished. **9:50** Marcus Scarman signals the door to slide open and stands in the doorway. Another door seems to be closing before he and the robot enter followed by the original door sliding shut. This could be due to the camera angle. **10:15** There is the reflection of a studio light from the base of the mummy's neck behind the mummy. **15:05** Some viewers have a problem with Sarah Jane looking at the Eye of Horus and telling the Doctor it "reminds me of the city of the Exxilons." The problem is that during *Death to the Daleks*, she never entered the city of the Exxilons. This quote occurs while she and the Doctor are looking at the puzzle on the wall. This puzzle is comparable to the symbols on the outside wall of the city of the Exxilons. Sarah Jane did see these symbols. **15:10** Some fans object to the Doctor's mumbo jumbo while solving the puzzle. As with the symbols outside the city of the Exxilons, all he must do is to pick the symbol that does not match. **15:19** The Doctor tells Sarah Jane, "120.3 multiply by the binary figure ten zero zero" is 162.4 centimeters. This multiplication gives 962.4 not 162.4. The first value should have been 20.3 not 120.3. **15:30** When the Doctor is trying to decode the pattern on the wall, he comes up with the solution "162.4 centimeters." He goes on to equate this with "seven stitches" on his scarf. Finally, he measures a few inches on his scarf and uses this distance. This would be okay except that 162.4 centimeters is not the few inches he measured but over five feet. **17:26** The switches on Sarah Jane's trap appear as if held in place by tape. **20:40** When Sutekh stands, a hand appears withdrawing from where it was holding a cushion in place. This is the Hand of Sutekh blooper. **22:42** The Doctor explains that it takes two minutes for radio waves to travel from Mars to the Earth. In two minutes, radio waves travel about 22 million miles. The closest approach of Mars to the Earth is about 56 million miles.

Comments: Many blooper lists do not distinguish between bloopers involving Marcus Scarman and bloopers involving Laurence Scarman. The lists just use Scarman.

The Doctor saves the Earth.

(4J) THE ANDROID INVASION

Writer: Terry Nation; **Director:** Barry Letts

Media: Commercial tape — episodic version — 97 minutes (used); Collector's tape — movie version — 90 minutes
Questions: What happened to the Kraal invasion fleet?

Errors and Other Points of Interest

Episode 1
First Transmitted: Nov. 22, 1975

1:38 Sarah Jane tells the Doctor she does not like ginger pop. **2:57** While the Doctor walks through the forest his scarf tangles in some bushes. **2:58** The Doctor almost manages to hit Sarah Jane in the face with a tree branch. This is really her fault since she is not watching. **6:09** There does not appear to be anything on the ground in front of the "meteorite." **6:38** The Doctor and Sarah Jane jump behind the "meteorite" to avoid being shot by the mechanics. There is something on the ground for them to land on and not get dirty. There are reports that the item on the ground is both a tarpaulin and a piece of cardboard; it looks more like a cushion. Obviously, it has nothing to do with keeping their costumes clean, since the Doctor does not stay on it. **13:29** Just before reactivation of the androids, someone says something offstage before the clock starts. **13:39** There is a noise off-stage. **14:28** The Doctor gives Sarah Jane the TARDIS key. **16:26** Why go to the effort to make androids with human hands and no faces? This could be because hands needed more work to perfect them, or because the development of hands preceded the development of faces. Hands are necessary for delicate manipulations; faces are not necessary for such actions. **17:20** Some viewers believe that the behavior of the stone-faced guard towards the Doctor to be a blooper. These viewers describe the guard as being "abashed." **19:44** The sign on the door says "Brigadier Lethbridge-Stewart." Finally, the Brigadier's name has proper hyphenation. This is another inconsistency between the Kraal duplicate and the Earth. On the Earth, the Brigadier's hyphen is routinely absent (see, for example, *The Three Doctors*). **22:53** While walking down the hall, after the Doctor's capture, one of the androids steps on the Doctor's scarf.

Episode 2
First Transmitted: Nov. 29, 1975

1:43 As Sarah Jane opens the door to the Doctor's cell, the door hits something — is it the Doctor? **4:21** Benton is a Warrant Officer. **4:54** The doors do not completely close. Note the opening and closing sound. **5:20** How do the Doctor and Sarah Jane get back in without the door opening sound? **12:40** Some viewers consider the Doctor hitting three double bulls to be a blooper. They feel he should have hit the higher scoring triple twenty since this would amount to more points. However, the Doctor was not playing against anyone, so why does the score matter? The double bull is a smaller target, indicating a better player. **13:23** Some viewers wonder why the Kraals want to leave a perfectly suitable home planet and conquer another. Apparently, these persons believe that other planets do not have their own Hitlers. Another reason appears later. **15:24** The Doctor removes pages from the calendar and finds that they all say Friday, July 6, with no year. During the 1970s, this would refer to 1973 or 1979. **17:36** If everything from Crayford's (Milton Johns) mind is from two years earlier — why is Harry there, why is Benton not a Sergeant, and why is the Brigadier missing? **18:14** The Kraal android machine is not very good. To begin with, it makes a bad duplicate of Sarah Jane by creating a scarf she was not wearing at the time of her capture. **18:32** We find that the android machine made another error in that it misread Sarah Jane's mind. The machine missed Sarah Jane's dislike for ginger pop. **21:56** Some viewers claim that the Kraals consider the androids indestructible. At this point Styggron not only demonstrates the fallacy in this but also says the androids are not indestructible. **23:58** Some fans object to the flaws in the Kraal invasion plan. **24:00** The Doctor throws "Sarah Jane" to the ground. The special effects people should have gotten a wig that was a better match in texture and color to Elisabeth Sladen's real hair.

Episode 3
First Transmitted: Dec. 6, 1975

1:23 Some viewers pose the question — What is the purpose of destroying the village? Even if the Kraals no longer need the village, why waste their time destroying it? Of course this is using Earth psychology to explain alien psychology. **10:25** The Doctor explains to Sarah Jane that radiation will soon make the Kraal planet uninhabitable. This is another reason why some viewers are wrong in questioning why the Kraals want to invade other planets. **13:10** Crayford says, "Space shells with the androids inside ... just be taken for meteorites." He meant to say meteors not meteorites. **16:40** The Doctor tells Sarah Jane, "Don't waste the water. Remember, it is an excellent conductor." Any scientist knows that water is a very poor conductor. This is why electrocution occurs to wet people — the water does not conduct the electricity away. **18:28** Some observers ask the question of why do the Kraals need androids when they have the virus. At this time, we learn that they need the androids to spread the virus. **18:58** Styggron tells the Doctor that the Kraal fleet is ready to land. **23:10** We see the rocket — it does not look like a Saturn V. **23:47** The rocket taking off (stock footage of a Saturn V) does not resemble the Kraal rocket shown earlier.

Episode 4
First Transmitted: Dec. 13, 1975

0:56 The Doctor says, "It's all right it's not activated." Note that activation of the androids has not occurred at this point. **1:46** If there has been no activation of the androids, how is the "Doctor" able to open the pod and look out? **5:07** This is the beginning of several references about "meteorites" and "meteorite showers." Meteors should replace meteorites. **9:22** Does the programming of the androids include chivalry? The "Doctor" lends a hand to "Sarah Jane" as she gets out of her pod. **10:36** The Doctor enters through the automatic doors. The doors open correctly, but they do not completely close. **11:53** You hear someone pulling on the mike cord the Doctor is holding. It is also possible to see that someone is tugging on the cord. **12:24** The "unconscious" Benton's eyes are moving. **13:36** Why does the Doctor wait until now to use his robot detector? **14:57** The rocket still does not look like a Saturn V, and no gantry is visible. **15:21** This time as the

Doctor enters, the doors "bounce" back into an open position. **15:40** Sarah Jane climbs a bright red gantry; this gantry was not next to the rocket seen earlier. **17:30** Why has Crayford never looked under his eye patch? **17:36** When the Doctor and the "Doctor" are in a fight, we again see the inefficiency of the Kraal android machine. The Doctor's hair does not look like the "Doctor's" hair. **20:05** How can the Doctor use his own android against Styggron? The radar neutralizes all the androids. The radar is still transmitting. **20:42** The death of the "Doctor" results in the disappearance of its skin. This exposes the "skeleton" underneath. The head of the skeleton is larger than the Doctor's head. **20:56** Where is the Kraal fleet? They supposedly can conquer the Earth without the androids. Earlier in the story, the fleet was ready to land.

Comments: The Doctor saves the Earth.

(4K) THE BRAIN OF MORBIUS

Writer: Robin Bland (Terrance Dicks and Robert Holmes); **Director:** Christopher Barry

Media: Commercial tape — episodic version — 100 minutes (used); Commercial tape — movie version — 59 minutes; Collector's tape — movie version — 93 minutes
Questions: Why not place the brain of Morbius directly into the Doctor's body?

Errors and Other Points of Interest

Episode 1
First Transmitted: Jan. 3, 1976

5:59 The Doctor explains that he was born "within a couple of billion miles." This is too great a number to be in the same solar system unless the star is very large, and too small a number to refer to different solar system. **7:44** It sounds as if Maren (Cynthia Grenville) calls the silent gas dirigibles Hoothi and not Muthi. There appears to be some disagreement as to the name used.

Episode 2
First Transmitted: Jan. 10, 1976

4:02 The Doctor tells Maren he is 749 years old. **9:55** As Solon (Philip Madoc) and Condo (Colin Fay) walk along the tunnel a red shape (possibly the costume of one of the Sisterhood, as Sarah Jane is still behind them) appears beside them to the left. This is a reported blooper. **13:41** The red costume reported as part of the costume of one of the members of the sisterhood is really a curtain.

Episode 3
First Transmitted: Jan. 17, 1976

9:56 While the Doctor is talking to Maren, a boom mike shadow appears on him. This boom mike shadow appears during other scenes in the cave. **17:24** Solon says to Morbius, "There would be severe pain. There would be sear seizures." **19:43** Condo appears to be partly metallic inside.

Episode 4
First Transmitted: Jan. 24, 1976

4:01 The death of Condo is an exercise in overacting. **13:10** The Doctor tells Sarah Jane that Solon must have used hydrogen cyanide (HCN), and he and Sarah Jane begin looking for the material. Sarah Jane finds a vile of a colorless liquid labeled HCN. Hydrogen cyanide boils slightly above room temperature (78.1°F or 25.6°C), which is why it is stored in metal cylinders instead of glass bottles. It would quickly evaporate from the bottle Sarah Jane found.

If the liquid in the bottle were to evaporate, there would be enough HCN to kill a roomful of people. **13:57** The Doctor wants to convert the HCN to cyanogen. Cyanogen is slightly less toxic to humans than is HCN. One good whiff of either vapor would kill Sarah Jane. It is possible that cyanogen is more toxic to non-humans than hydrogen cyanide. **14:42** Sarah Jane asks the Doctor, "How do we tell if it has worked?" The Doctor begins, "If we are still here in a month…." The implication seems that if Solon and Morbius do not die, they will leave the Doctor and Sarah Jane locked in the room. However, if Solon and Morbius did die, the Doctor and Sarah Jane would still be in the room because there would be no one to let them out of the room. The Sisterhood would not enter the building without a good reason. **15:38** Morbius identifies the gas as cyanide instead of cyanogen. **17:59** In the Doctor's brain battle with Morbius, there are several images shown. The implication is that these are the Doctor's past lives. However, not only do the three previous Doctors appear, but also nine other images. Many observers consider the additional images to be bloopers. However, it is more likely that some of the images are earlier lives of the Time Lord Morbius. **20:16** As Morbius tumbles over the cliff, his artificial head falls apart. The next shot shows a reassembled head. **20:17** As Morbius falls over the cliff, he hits the camera. **23:05** When the TARDIS doors open, it is possible to see the lit side window. **23:08** The take-off of the TARDIS is very fast and unusual.

Comments: Note that one of the commercial tapes is very short, and significant material was removed to produce this very short version. The Doctor visits the planet Kara.

(4L) The Seeds of Doom

Writer: Robert Banks Stewart; **Director:** Douglas Camfield

Media: Commercial tape — episodic version — 145 minutes (used); Collector's tape — movie version — 135 minutes

Errors and Other Points of Interest

Episode 1
First Transmitted: Jan. 31, 1976

11:48 The Doctor says, "I'm only seven hundred and forty-nine." **16:46** The "snow" looks realistic until the Doctor digs the Krynoid pod out of the "snow." **20:13** This is one of the last shots in this episode showing the chessboard propped against the back wall. Notice that the upper rightmost square is dark.

Episode 2
First Transmitted: Feb. 7, 1976

1:44 Even though it has only been a few minutes, someone appears to have played a game of chess and put the board back against the wall. The upper rightmost square is now light instead of dark. **7:48** Scorby (John Challis) has some difficulty operating the base radio. He must toggle the switch between "send" and "receive." In many places, Scorby toggles the switch while he or someone else is talking instead of waiting until he or they finish. **18:09** Why does Scorby take Sarah Jane to find the power plant? It would be easier to shoot everyone. If he really needed to take a hostage, Scorby should have taken someone stationed at the base instead of a visitor like himself. **23:10** We have Doctor Who to thank for making everyone aware of a serious threat to everyone's safety. If someone destroys the power plant that supplies your house — your house will explode!

Episode 3
First Transmitted: Feb. 14, 1976

2:29 Scorby has trouble opening the case. **8:43** Mrs. Ducat (Sylvia Coleridge) has a boom mike shadow on her head. **10:52** The Doctor substitutes the chauffeur's hat for his own. **15:14** The Doctor now has his old hat, and discards the chauffeur's hat. **19:35** The Doctor's scarf tangles in the bushes. This is complicated when Sarah Jane stoops down on the scarf.

Episode 4
First Transmitted: Feb. 21, 1976

12:52 Harrison Chase (Tony Beckley) tells Mrs. Ducat that it is autumn. Many of the trees do not reflect the season. The large number of evergreens may make this misleading. **21:11** The Doctor spits on himself while thanking Sarah Jane. **23:31** Sarah Jane's scream when looking up at the Krynoid appears dubbed in later. This scream occurs in the reprise also.

Episode 5
First Transmitted: Feb. 28, 1976

3:50 Sarah Jane grabs an axe to attack the Krynoid tentacle. She is very careful not to hit the prop tentacle with the axe; she only hits the tentacle with her hands. **11:45** The shots of the Krynoid in the morning show a blue CSO which doubles for the sky. The trees in many, but not all, of the CSO images have no leaves. This does not entirely reflect what appears around the house. There is a more consistent lack of foliage in the next episode.

Episode 6
First Transmitted: Mar. 6, 1976

1:16 The Sergeant beats on the air in order to "hit" the door. **4:39** The entire wall moves as the Doctor closes the door. **17:24** The Doctor manages to hit Sarah Jane's chest as he says "Steam! Steam!" This occurs in front of the door. **17:47** A wind machine whips about the foliage. The wind also blows the Doctor's and Sarah Jane's hair about. **19:04** It appears as if Sarah Jane has been standing in a wind tunnel. **20:20** The TARDIS travels to Antarctica and the Doctor and Sarah Jane exit. Why did the TARDIS go to Antarctica? The Doctor agrees to Sarah Jane's statement "You forgot to cancel the coordinate program, didn't you? When was the coordinate program set?

Comments: The BBC is not the only source of bloopers. In the late 1980s KERA, a television station in Dallas, Texas, showed the movie version of this story with the tapes in the wrong order. The very first scene (no opening credits) shows the Doctor and the Sergeant entering the mansion with the defoliant tanks (Episode 5), and the very last scene shows the Doctor grabbing the sword off the wall as he and Sarah Jane leave the cottage. There is one impressive sequence where Sarah Jane wakes up after the power plant explosion to find herself in the mulching machine about to be ground into mulch.

The Doctor saves the Earth.

(4M) The Masque of Mandragora

Writer: Louis Marks; **Director:** Rodney Bennett

Media: Commercial tape — episodic version — 99 minutes (used); Collector's tape — movie version — 92 minutes
Highlights: We get the first tour of the TARDIS halls and see the second Control Room.
Questions: Where is the other follower of Mandragora?

Errors and Other Points of Interest

Some observers claim there is a mixing of evening and daylight scenes, which would create one or more bloopers. This does not appear to be the case, as the times noted for each transition from day to night show. The scenes in Italy before the Doctor arrives may be from different days. Once the Doctor arrives the other scenes do not appear random, and the daylight or nighttimes coincide with the story. Confusion may arise because even at night it does not seem to get very dark outside.

Episode 1
First Transmitted: Sept. 4, 1976

4:50 The Doctor slams the door so hard that the entire TARDIS shakes. **10:01** The TARDIS lands in Italy during a brightly lit day. **12:33** Some fans consider the random killing by the ball of helix energy to be a blooper. The ball appears disorientated, else it would not be hitting the ground and the water and expending energy. **13:34** The helix hits the water. Thus, the helix is having problems. **13:45** The helix hits a peasant. Disorientation of the helix is still present. **19:06** Some viewers claim it to be a blooper when no one notices the out-of-period clothing worn by the Doctor of Sarah Jane. This is not true because at this point Count Federico (John Laurimore) comments on the Doctor's strange garments. **20:42** Why is there a curfew being called? It is obviously broad daylight. **20:55** An apparently disorientated helix hits a soldier.

Episode 2
First Transmitted: Sept. 11, 1976

2:48 The Priest appears to be reading from a blank book. **3:18** The soldier tells his friend, "I ain't goin' in there, Giovanni" with a most unconvincing Italian accent. **7:20** This is the first time since the Doctor landed where it appears to be dark outside. The following scenes are at night. **19:23** After several nighttime scenes, daylight now appears through the window, and the following scenes are daylight.

Episode 3
First Transmitted: Sept. 18, 1976

7:01 Hieronymous (Norman Jones) tells the High Priest (Robert James), "The great god's dwelling place must not be defiled by unbelievers in these last hours." **10:19** Why is Giuliano (Gareth Armstrong) carrying the torch with his injured arm? **11:20** Sarah Jane questions how she can understand other languages and the Doctor says he will explain later. **14:12** Consistent with the passage of time it has now become night again. **17:46** Hieronymous tells the Doctor that another emissary of Mandragora is coming. The other follower never appears nor do we hear of him again. **19:45** The fact that the Doctor says he knows that Sarah Jane is under Hieronymous's influence (drugged) when she becomes unduly curious causes some observers to claim a blooper. **19:50** The Doctor explains to Sarah Jane about languages: "It's the Time Lord's gift I allow you to share." This explains many things except how we hear other languages at times.

Episode 4
First Transmitted: Sept. 25, 1976

0:47 Why does the glowing face not shine through the eye slits of the mask? **1:07** After Hieronymous kills Count Federico, we see the Duke's body (cloak) on the floor. **1:14** In the long shot, the Count's body is no longer present. **5:08** The Doctor tells Sarah Jane that in 50 years he could use Galileo's telescope. This story takes place in the late fifteenth century, thus the Doctor is referring to the middle of the sixteenth century. Galileo developed his telescope in the early seventeenth century. The Doctor should have said something like 100+ years. **5:14** It has appropriately become daylight again. **6:12** We learn about the planning of the masque. **8:51** Some viewers report that the Doctor calls Sarah Jane "Lis." The Doctor really says, "Miss" not "Lis." The actual quote is "Nonsense? It isn't nonsense, Miss!" Watch the Doctor's lips; he is definitely saying a word beginning with an "M" not an "L." **10:07** Giuliano (Gareth Armstrong) says everything is ready for the masque. **11:45** If wires were capable of conducting the energy away, then wearing armor would be equivalent to the Doctor grasping a lightening rod. **12:58** The Doctor has not met Leonardo Da Vinci. **14:25** The masque begins. Some viewers believe it not to be possible to arrange the masque so quickly. Plans for the masque probably began as soon as the Prince sent the invitations. **14:30** In anticipation of the lunar eclipse, it has again become night. **18:14** We can see Hieronymous's neck beneath his mask. This is not the glowing image from earlier. **18:22** The hood of Hieronymous's cloak is not visible around the glowing mask. **22:34** Finally, the Doctor and Sarah Jane leave as they arrived — in broad daylight. **23:09** The Doctor still has not seen Leonardo Da Vinci.

Comments: The Doctor saves the Earth.

Pause to Consider: The "Time Lords' Gift"

The Fourth Doctor's comment, "It's the Time Lord's Gift I allow you to share," may placate Sarah Jane Smith, but it opens the door to many other potential problems. On the surface, it seems to indicate that anyone near a Time Lord is able to comprehend what any other person is saying. The Doctor does not place any limits on the Gift. There are three aspects of the Gift that may create or resolve some bloopers.

If the Gift allows anyone near a Time Lord to comprehend anything said in any language, then all instances where we hear an incomprehensible language should be bloopers. For example, in *The Leisure Hive*, the Foamasi ambassador speaks in his own language, which neither the Doctor nor the viewers understand. There is no reason given why the Time Lords' Gift fails at this time. There appear to be no restrictions concerning accents. It is also possible that the Gift leads to translation of an alien language into heavily accented English.

There are many instances throughout the series where the Gift seems to extend beyond vocal language to include written language. People from many different planets are able to read and write messages that are understandable to others. An example of this is the message Peri receives in *Timelash*. This also applies to the viewers. For example, the viewers are able to read the entries in the TARDIS Databank in *Castrovalva*. These entries should be in Gallifreyan. The words appear to be in English, which not only the viewers and Tegan read, but also Nyssa who is a Traken. However, in *Remembrance of the Daleks*, the Doctor shows the viewers his card, which contains non–English symbols, presumably Gallifreyan. Thus, Gallifreyan sometimes appears as English, and sometimes it does not. Either the Time Lords'

Gift is not infallible, or one set of occurrences (translated or not translated) should be bloopers.

Translation, through the Gift, should not only include simple vocabulary, but also more complicated concepts. Thus, when a Dalek utters something completely incomprehensible to a non–Dalek speaking person, we may hear "Exterminate." Many viewers object to some translations. For example, these viewers object to the translation of Dalek measurements into Earth equivalents. If what the Dalek says translates to "Exterminate," then whatever the Dalek says could translate to "miles." The bloopers should be when non–English measurements appear — for example, the use of "rels" in *Dalek Invasion Earth 2150 AD*.

(4N) THE HAND OF FEAR

Writer: Bob Baker and Dave Martin; **Director:** Lennie Mayne

Media: Commercial tape — episodic version — 99 minutes (used); Collector's tape — movie version — 93 minutes
Highlights: Sarah Jane leaves the series.

Errors and Other Points of Interest

Some viewers object to the Kastrians using Latin terminology since their culture is much older. This could be a simple Kastrian to English supplied through the Time Lords' Gift.

Episode 1
First Transmitted: Oct. 2, 1976

4:37 The Doctor and Sarah Jane do not seem to realize that the sirens and man waving represent danger. That would make them like the rocks in the quarry (very dense). **6:45** Abbott (David Purcell) tells some of the workers to come and help with the others going to get an ambulance. No one goes back for an ambulance. An ambulance appears anyway.

Episode 2
First Transmitted: Oct. 9, 1976

2:31 A fly lands on Professor Watson's (Glyn Houston) forehead; supposedly, Sarah Jane swallowed the fly during an outtake. **3:41** Professor Watson says to the Doctor, "Who the devil are you?" The Doctor does not tell him, and no one addresses the Doctor as "Doctor" in the Professor's presence. **11:09** Professor Watson says, "Is that you Doctor?" No one told the Professor who the Doctor was. **13:17** In the decontamination room, a boom mike shadow falls on Miss Jackson's (Frances Pidgeon) shoulder and head. **14:26** The shadow under the moving hand, on the floor, is not always in the correct direction. The best shots are with the hand seen on the monitor. Some fans report this to occur in the first two episodes. When seen in the first episode the hand is in the plastic box; it is not on the floor until the Episode 2. Thus, the Episode 1 report is incorrect. **20:54** Driscoll (Roy Boyd) leads everyone through the facility from the decontamination room. Why is the decontamination room so far from the site of potential contamination (the reactor)? Is a contaminated person supposed to walk through the entire facility contaminating people?

Episode 3
First Transmitted: Oct. 16, 1976

2:06 Professor Watson says that Driscoll entering the core would cause a nuclear explosion. This could only occur if Driscoll was composed of fissionable material (uranium-235 or plutonium, for example). **3:43** No one would order an air strike on a nuclear facility, especially with tactical nuclear missiles. Such an attack would be true if they are attempting to devastate the countryside. **4:38** When seen from the ground, the sky is hazy. **4:59** Some observers consider that hiding behind the jeep for protection from the missile attack a blooper. Since the group is very close to the facility either side of the jeep would be equally effective against the blast from a nuclear missile. **5:04** The planes are flying through a blue sky with a few scattered clouds. Where is the haze? **5:45** Why fire two nuclear missiles? One missile would totally destroy the facility and spread large amounts of radioactive debris over the area. **18:51** The Doctor says, "Your weapons won't work in here. We are in a state of temporal grace." **19:23** The Doctor tells Sarah Jane, "I want to see Kastia." This is one of the times he uses "Kastia" instead of "Kastria." **20:08** The TARDIS light is not flashing during take-off.

Episode 4
First Transmitted: Oct. 23, 1976
6:50 The Doctor helps Eldrad I (Judith Paris) by holding her breast. **8:28** The control panel the Doctor is using is not very substantial. Every time he pushes a button, the entire panel flexes. **13:22** Sarah Jane's reply to the Doctor's comment "A recording from the past. The King obviously knew there was a chance that Eldrad would return" is cut off. Eldrad II's (Stephen Thorne) tirade interrupts Sarah Jane and she waits patiently until she can deliver her line. **13:48** There is a boom mike shadow on the back wall as the Doctor talks to Eldrad after they find the dead king. This occurs while Eldrad is talking to the Doctor and Sarah Jane. **15:47** The front of a camera appears in the doorway next to Sarah Jane as Eldrad says, "I created this world." **17:12** The entire set beside the bridge across the chasm shakes as the Doctor and Sarah Jane jump on the set. **17:22** The Doctor bumps one of the "rocks" while he is setting the scarf trap for Eldrad. The "rock" wobbles significantly. **17:49** The Doctor tosses the ring into the chasm. **18:18** The Doctor tells Sarah Jane that Eldrad is probably not dead. This is after the Doctor threw the ring into the chasm were Eldrad fell. Thus, the Doctor gave Eldrad the ring that Eldrad needed to reclaim his power.

Comments: The Doctor visits the planet Kastria, but is too late to saves its inhabitants.

(4P) THE DEADLY ASSASSIN

Writer: Robert Holmes; **Director:** David Maloney

Media: Commercial tape — episodic version — 95 minutes (used); Commercial tape — movie version — 89 minutes; Collector's tape — movie version — 88 minutes
Highlights: The Master (played by Peter Pratt) is back. The Doctor solves a problem with the aid of no companions. This is the first time in many seasons where the Doctor visits Gallifrey. This is the only story to feature the Doctor with no companions.
Questions: If Chancellor Goth created the world in the matrix, why would he, a resident of Gallifrey, imagine a world with Earth clothes, weapons, equipment and plants?

Errors and Other Points of Interest

Episode 1
First Transmitted: Oct. 30, 1976

3:57 When the Castellan (George Pravda) is speaking into the wrist communicator, his eyes are looking directly at the camera. When we see Commander Hilred (Derek Seaton) from the side, he is looking directly at his wrist communicator. When looking at the Commander through the Castellan's communicator the Commander is looking down instead of straight at the camera. **5:15** One of the guards has trouble getting into the TARDIS. **5:32** As the Doctor is sneaking out of the TARDIS one of the guards turns around and looks directly at the Doctor but does not see the Doctor. **5:55** The guard acts shot before he is actually shot. **6:52** The CIA is part of the Doctor's past. In this story CIA=Celestial Intervention Agency.

Episode 2
First Transmitted: Nov. 6, 1976

4:27 The Doctor's arms are up next to his face. **5:04** It is not possible to see the Doctor's arms next to his face. **23:25** The Doctor's foot is clearly not between the rails, yet the rails are able to trap his foot. The explanation may lie in the Doctor's comment about everything in the matrix being an illusion. This also occurs in the reprise.

Episode 3
First Transmitted: Nov. 13, 1976

9:38 Why does the "soldier" need a map to the reality he has created? **20:05** We see Solis (Peter Mayock) shot in the shoulder. Some viewers claim that he dies clutching his stomach. Solis does not really grasp his stomach. In any case, it is possible that the weapon causes muscle contractions including abdominal pains. These viewers also report the name of the guard is Sorris; however, this name does not appear in the closing credits. **23:13** In some video versions of this story, the Doctor's drowning scene is not present. This may also be true in the reprise.

Episode 4
First Transmitted: Nov. 20, 1976

8:59 Coordinator Engin (Eric Chitty) mentions that Time Lords have twelve regenerations. **15:59** The Doctor refers to "stellar system." It is nice not to hear blooper terms such as constellation. **16:38** In this story, the Great Key (of Rassilon) appears to be an ebonite rod. **17:29** We get our first look at the "Eye of Harmony." Compare this to the Eye of Harmony in the Eighth Doctor's TARDIS. **22:20** Some viewers claim that the Master's TARDIS appears to be a board held up by planks of wood. **22:30** There are claims that Coordinator Engin calls the Master "Baster" when he says, "It's we who should thank you Doctor for destroying the Master." It is not obvious in the different versions exactly what he said. It could be either "Master" or "Baster."

Comments: The Doctor defeats the Master and saves Gallifrey.

Many aspects of Time Lord Culture and Gallifrey first appear in this story.

(4Q) THE FACE OF EVIL

Alternate Title: *The Day God Went Mad*
Writer: Chris Boucher; **Director:** Pennant Roberts

Media: Commercial tape—episodic version—99 minutes (used); Collector's tape—movie version—93 minutes
Highlights: Leela (Louise Jameson) becomes the Doctor's new companion.

Questions: How did the members of the Sevateem find their way through the "stone wall" in the cave?

Errors and Other Points of Interest

Episode 1
First Transmitted: Jan. 1, 1977

6:21 Leela, when talking to Tomas (Brendan Price), pronounces Calib's (Leslie Schofield) name as "Kal-lib." She pronounces his name differently later. **9:37** Some viewers cite, as a blooper, the ability of invisible creatures, composed of pure energy, to leave footprints. Apparently, the persons making this observation never saw *Forbidden Planet* with its Creatures of the Id. **22:39** The paralyzed guard recovers from his paralysis long enough to use his left arm after Neeva (David Garfield) pushes him over.

Episode 2
First Transmitted: Jan. 8, 1977

6:35 When talking to the Doctor, Leela now pronounces Calib's name as "Kay-lib." **10:56** The sound of the motor ejecting the strip continues after the Doctor has removed the strip. **14:00** A wire is obviously pulling the horda along. This happens *before* the Doctor says, "So that's a horda," not *after* as has been indicated in other sources. **23:03** There is a large boom mike shadow on Leela's face as she enters the "Doctor's" mouth. **23:43** There is another tie-in to *Forbidden Planet* when the Creature of the Id appears. In the movie, the invisible creature became visible in weapons fire.

Episode 3
First Transmitted: Jan. 15, 1977

0:50 Even though Tomas moves the gun barrel about, the beam remains in a fixed position. **8:04** The Doctor comments to Jabel (Leon Eagles) that the entire control room is disconnected. **8:12** A monitor, showing Leela, comes on in the completely "disconnected" control room. **14:49** The Doctor ties this story to *Forbidden Planet* when he says "from the dark side of Xoanon's Id." **17:41** The Doctor and Leela fight with a Tesh guard. During the ensuing struggle, they fling the guard's weapon down the hall. **17:58** Leela picks the weapon up from next to the guard's body, not down the hall where it landed earlier. **20:56** It is possible to see the lights on one of the guns flashing (firing) when the Tesh guards are grouped together getting ready to attack Leela.

Episode 4
First Transmitted: Jan. 22, 1977

2:10 Leela moves the gun about while firing, but the beam does not move with the barrel. She does not move the barrel as much as some people would indicate. The emitted beam never comes from very far from the gun barrel, as others report. **6:36** After Xoanon takes over Leela's mind, she fires her weapon at the Doctor. The Doctor jumps up as Leela fires again. Leela is behind the Doctor when she fires; however, the beam appears in front of the Doctor. This gives a bad special effect. **15:05** Leela, while under Xoanon's control, attempts to stab the Doctor. She is shocked unconscious and the Doctor helps her to a nearby chair. Just what does the Doctor have in his right hand while he is helping Leela? Some people might call it a blooper some might call it.... **15:40** Neeva slips on the floor. **22:47** The Doctor swings the usual TARDIS key on a chain.

Comments: The Doctor saves the people of an unnamed planet.

(4R) THE ROBOTS OF DEATH

Writer: Chris Boucher; **Director:** Michael E. Briant

Media: DVD — episodic version — 96 minutes (used); Commercial tape — movie version — 90 minutes; Collector's tape — movie version — 90 minutes
Questions: Why is V.9 and not D.84 listening outside Uvanov's quarters?

Errors and Other Points of Interest

Episode 1
First Transmitted: Jan. 29, 1977

6:05 The Doctor exits the TARDIS wearing his scarf. The scarf disappears and reappears at times. **8:39** If Chub's (Rob Edwards) dying scream is not a blooper, it should be. **13:12** The corpse markers are bicycle reflectors. **17:06** The Doctor is not wearing his scarf on his way to Uvanov's (Russell Hunter) quarters. **17:32** After V.9 locks the Doctor and Leela in Uvanov's cabin the robot stands outside the door and listens. It is possible to see the actor's neck between his sweater and the mask. **20:58** The Doctor left the cabin without his scarf, but he is wearing it as he walks down the hallway.

Episode 2
First Transmitted: Feb. 5, 1977

7:29 Uvanov tells Poul (David Collings), "If we could have got her to tell her what those corpse markers were; we'd be halfway to a confession!" The second time he said "her" he should have said "us." **12:00** We can now identify the villain in the story because his feet and lower trousers are in view. **16:11** When talking about bumblebees the Doctor says "Tehran" (capital of Iran) instead of "Terran" (Earthling). **18:25** The robot's fingers miss the keypad. **18:25** The movements of the robot's fingers do not coincide with the sound effects.

0:54 The second cable explodes just before Dask (David Bailie) touches it. **2:28** Some fans claim that someone is visible at the edge of the set when Leela is bandaging Toos' (Pamela Salem) arm. This appears to be Poul. **4:25** A studio camera operator appears in the background when Toos says, "There's a strict legal code covering the disposal of robots." **5:54** V.35 is in the "morgue" awaiting repairs. **9:20** It is possible to see the actor's throat moving when D.84 is talking. **9:55** Some observers report that the silver gloves on the agitated hands of the robot clearly have a "Marigold" logo. Apparently, these observers can see the future, as they know that a different company will be manufacturing gloves for the robots of the future. **14:22** Leela is pounding on the door to the crew's quarters. A moment after the scene begins the gold statue near her becomes illuminated. Apparently, someone was late turning on a studio light. **16:39** The sound effects accompanying Leela's knife throw at the robot are very cartoon-like. **16:39** The knife that Leela throws is obviously heading for the floor. The knife still manages to stick in the robot's chest. **19:20** Toos shuts the door to her quarters on the robot's arm. When seen from inside the door it appears to have the robot trapped about mid-arm. When seen from outside, the door traps the robot at the wrist. **20:42** V.35 is still in the robot "morgue."

Episode 3
First Transmitted: Feb. 12, 1977

Episode 4
First Transmitted: Feb. 19, 1977

1:18 Uvanov sticks a probe into one of the robot's heads. In the struggle, the head nearly comes off the robot. Some observers erroneously report this to be in Episode 3. **5:49** V.5 tells V.6 that V.35 through V.40 have checked the ore lockers. V.35 is in the "morgue" and unavailable. **7:09** The deactivated robots have trouble not moving. **8:55** Robophobia is referred to as "Grimwade's Syndrome" as an in-joke, not a blooper. This is in reference to Peter Grimwade who complained about always working in stories with robots in them. **12:42** V.35 is still in the "morgue"; it is behind Leela. **13:09** The Doctor removes the top of the communicator. **13:22** The top of the communicator is back in place. **19:15** Taren Capel's (David Bailie) voice slowly responds to the increase in helium gas in the room. The Doctor's voice does not change. **22:02** After the struggle, the body of S.V.7 (Miles Fothergill) is on the floor breathing heavily in a most un-robot-like manner. **22:06** At the end of the story, Leela yells, "Will somebody let me out?" The helium changes her voice. The helium also changes the Doctor's response ("Ha"!). The Doctor's voice was not to change. The changed voices of both Leela and Taren Capel are from post-production editing; however, one word from the Doctor was also changed. **22:29** The Doctor tells Leela his voice did not change because he is a Time Lord. **22:35** The Doctor is still 750 years old.

Comments: The Doctor defeats the Robots on Storm Mine 4.

(4S) THE TALONS OF WENG-CHIANG

Writer: Robert Holmes; **Director:** David Maloney

Media: Commercial DVD — episodic version —144 minutes (used); Commercial tape — movie version —134 minutes; Collector's tape — movie version —134 minutes

Errors and Other Points of Interest

To illustrate the problem with some blooper reports try this one: There is a boom mike shadow on the curtain in the final fight scene. There is no further information to narrow this down to a specific time.

Jago's (Christopher Benjamin) accent varies from scene to scene.

Episode 1
First Transmitted: Feb. 26, 1977

3:52 The Doctor and Leela leave the TARDIS with the door open and walk away. A few seconds later, they walk by the TARDIS on their way to the theater and the door is no longer open. **4:28** Some viewers incorrectly report that the Doctor and Leela hear a fight and run, not walk, past the TARDIS. **6:25** There are only four attackers gathered around Buller's (Alan Butler) body. **7:07** The four attackers are now five attackers. **9:26** It is possible to see the dark pedestal holding the woman. **12:33** Why is the corpse not wearing shoes? There has not been enough time for anyone to rob the body, and the murderers did not seem to be interested in shoes.

Episode 2
First Transmitted: Mar. 5, 1977

0:53 Watch the lower left of the screen as the "ground" shakes. **8:04** This is one of the times when tape-covered modern electrical outlets can be seen on the walls of Litefoot's (Trevor Baxter) lab. **14:03** If you have X-ray vision, you can see the car beneath the mound of hay. **15:05** The Doctor must help the prop spider move its legs.

Episode 3
First Transmitted: Mar. 12, 1977

5:47 The teeth of the giant rat are obviously made of rubber. Watch how the teeth flex when the rat bites on the meat. Pay attention to the rat's fur. Even though the rat is crawling through the sewers, its fur is clean, with no evidence of slime. **6:23** Some observers wonder why Weng-Chiang needs only young girls. The explanation is not present due to editing. **7:45** The Doctor calls the Thames the Fleet, and he calls the Fleet the Thames. **8:15** The Doctor says he caught a salmon in the Fleet and shared it with the Venerable Bede (673?–735). The Venerable Bede apparently spent his entire life in Northumbria and was never near London. **8:25** There is a 1970s newspaper in Litefoot's laundry basket; it has a Denis Healey headline. **13:12** During the inspection—why is the cleaning girl partly undressed while Leela is not? **14:46** While Weng-Chiang is preparing the cleaning girl, Leela miraculously becomes partially dressed to match the other girl.

Episode 4
First Transmitted: Mar. 19, 1977

1:14 The Doctor kills a giant rat. Some observers wonder what happened to the other rats. **21:16** We see that there is at least one additional giant rat in the sewers.

Episode 5
First Transmitted: Mar. 26, 1977

12:02 This is one of the cases where the Doctor's lips are not moving with the sound. **15:50** Notice the set behind Jago and Litefoot. **16:05** The set behind Jago and Litefoot is no longer the same. **19:10** Another classic Doctor quote: "Eureka is Greek for this bath is too hot."

Episode 6
First Transmitted: Apr. 4, 1977

10:58 When the Doctor begins to regain consciousness, he quotes: "There's a one eyed yellow idol to the North of Katmandu. There's a little marble cross below the town." Litefoot asks "Kipling?" to which the Doctor replies, "Harry Champion, 1920." J. Milton Hayes wrote the lines in 1911. **12:50** Leela must throw her knife away since her attackers fail to knock the weapon out of her hand. **14:48** The Doctor drops (breaks) the first Lucifer (match) after he lights it. **15:55** The Doctor saves Leela after Magnus Greel (Michael Spice) puts her in the distillation machine by damaging the machine with an ax. The distillation machine stops, thus saving Leela. Obviously, the ax damaged the machine sufficiently to stop it from working. **17:20** Notice the primer wire on the left under the table. The primer wire is for the small explosive charge. **18:42** Watch the curtain open so a hand can come through to overturn the bowl. **19:42** The wires and spent flash charges fall down the front of the idol. **19:58** When Magnus Greel falls into the destroyed machine, the machine regenerated, even to the extent of making the ax disappear. The repaired machine works perfectly to Magnus Creel's detriment. **20:37** Watch the left edge of the screen—slightly above the center. **20:40** In the final shot of the Doctor holding Mr. Sin over his head, it is obvious that he is holding a dummy.

Comments: Weng-Chiang—Magnus Greel.

The Doctor saves the Earth.

(4V) Horror of Fang Rock

Writer: Terrance Dicks; **Director:** Paddy Russell

Media: Commercial tape — episodic version — 95 minutes (used); Collector's tape — movie version — 88 minutes

Highlights: The one, and only, sighting of a Rutan during the series ("If you've seen one Rutan you've seen them all").

Errors and Other Points of Interest

Episode 1
First Transmitted: Sept. 3, 1977

8:27 Why is the lamp swinging? No one bumped the lamp and there is no apparent breeze inside the lamp room. **13:58** Leela trips while running to the Doctor.

Episode 2
First Transmitted: Sept. 10, 1977

6:18 As the Doctor puts his feet on the table in the crew room there is a boom mike shadow on Lord Palmerdale's (Sean Caffrey) face. **18:44** Two of the actors do an excellent job partially covering a blooper. Lord Palmerdale shakes Harker (Rio Fanning) awake. Lord Palmerdale begins the exchange with "Can you use a Morse apparatus?" Harker replies: "Of course I can — can I what?" (He should have just said, "Can I what?"). Palmerdale then follows, ignoring the distraction, with "Use a Morse telegraphic apparatus, like that one over there." Finally, Harker finishes with the correct line: "Of course I can."

Episode 3
First Transmitted: Sept. 17, 1977

2:59 "Reuben" makes his debut at this time. Some viewers claim there is a continuity flaw in the story. They claim that the Rutan alters its form to impersonate the dead Reuben (Colin Douglas) at the start of the episode and then "Reuben" stands in the crew's bedroom for some time. These viewers question how the alien could scale the exterior of the lighthouse to kill Lord Palmerdale during this time. The Rutan apparently is in two places. The Doctor is apparently only concerned with one Rutan from the scout craft; therefore, it must be the same Rutan both inside and outside the lighthouse. It is possible that the Rutan could shift out of the "Reuben" form, scale the wall, and shift back to "Reuben." This is not a blooper. **4:08** Some observers claim a blooper at this point. These observers claim that when Colonel Skinsale (Alan Rowe) opens the door to the crew's quarters he does not see "Reuben" climbing the stairs. Skinsale ignores "Reuben" and looks away from "Reuben," downstairs, and says "Doctor? Harker?" Some observers claim that Skinsale purposely ignored seeing "Reuben." Palmerdale then asks, "What was that cry? Did he say?" The Colonel obviously could not answer this. This is not a blooper. Skinsale says, "Doctor? Harker?" as he is opening the door, then looks downstairs, and then he looks upstairs and sees Reuben and says, "Oh," thus he notices "Reuben" as soon as he looks in "Reuben's" direction. **7:23** "Reuben" is in the bedroom and beginning to turn green. (Is he changing back to his Rutan form?) **9:02** We now see the Rutan climbing the lighthouse wall above the bedroom window (the same window the Doctor will hang from later). **12:27** "Reuben" is back in the bedroom with a green glow fading. (Is he changing from his Rutan to his "Reuben" form?). **14:05** Vince

(John Abbott) trips as he reenters the lamp room.

Episode 4
First Transmitted: Sept. 24, 1977
1:47 One of the "dead" Reuben's fingers moves. **2:51** Leela nearly bursts out laughing. **5:00** Some viewers claim yet another blooper. These viewers claim that after "Reuben" comes back down the stairs and re-enters the bedroom, he moves a curtain aside to expose a closed window with open shutters. Then in the exterior shot, we see the Doctor hanging from a windowsill beneath a window with closed shutters. The window is unlit and there are *no* shutters. **5:10** The Doctor's hands seem to move back and forth on the windowsill. **5:48** The Doctor re-enters the room by opening the window, which still has no shutters.
Comments: The Doctor saves the Earth.

(4T) THE INVISIBLE ENEMY

Alternate Title: *The Enemy Within*
Writer: Bob Baker and Dave Martin; **Director:** Derrick Goodwin

Media: Commercial tape — episodic version — 93 minutes (used); Collector's tape — movie version — 96 minutes
Highlights: K9 joins the TARDIS crew. Hairy beach balls attack Leela.
Questions: Why kill the crew of the Titan base instead of "making contact?"

Errors and Other Points of Interest

Episode 1
First Transmitted: Oct. 1, 1977
2:33 The computer "knows" that the obstruction is an "un-identified organism" and not a meteor or some other non-living object. This may be technobabble or a blooper. **3:14** The TARDIS column wobbles more than usual. **4:02** The Doctor tells Leela that they are between Jupiter and Saturn. **5:47** Captain Safran (Brian Grellis) fails to move all of the switches to the "off" position. The Captain moves one switch only halfway down. **6:18** Some observers believe that some of the guns do not have triggers. None of the guns has a hole in its barrel. **7:15** There are fans who question the killing of the men on Titan. Why not infect the crew? The virus later "recruits" people on Bi-Al. **9:03** Lowe (Michael Sheard) pushes the blue distress signal button. **9:22** The "blue" button is flashing red and green. **9:26** The flashing "red and green" button is non-flashing blue again. **9:41** Now Safran pushes the same button as Lowe did earlier; it is again flashing red and green. When Safran presses the button the alarm stops but the button continues to flash. **10:04** The Doctor tells Leela that the message took thirty minutes to arrive. This places the TARDIS about 335 million miles from Titan. **15:10** The sign outside the Cryogenics Section reads "Kryogenics Sexshun." There are other similar signs. **18:12** When Lowe first emerges from the Cryogenics Section, there is very little frost on his cheeks, but quite a bit on his forehead. **18:59** The frost on Lowe's face moves from his forehead and to his right cheek. **20:32** There is a plastic dish on the table, partially hidden by some leaves of the bush. **21:02** Some viewers claim that when Lowe first crouches down by the bush on the table, there is no

other object near him on the table. These viewers claim it was necessary to place an object on the table for Lowe to knock it off and alert the people in the hall. This is not a blooper. The dish appeared earlier. **21:36** The knife Leela throws at the crewmember does not seem to be stuck very solidly in his back. The subsequent wobble is amusing to some fans.

Episode 2
First Transmitted: Oct. 8, 1977
0:29 There is supposedly a member of the production crew in the background during the first scene. **1:09** The places where the Doctor's shots hit appear not to bear any relation to where he is aiming. **3:13** There is a hole on Safran's inside left pant leg as he starts to rise. **4:01** There is a claim of a blooper in that the crash damage is present in the first shot of Bi-Al (before the crash). This does not seem to be the case. **10:55** Some observers claim a blooper is present because Marius (Frederick Jaeger) seems so willing to give up his "best friend." An explanation appears later. **13:12** There seems to be some discrepancy as to Leela's immunity to the virus. K9 says the Leela is not immune and later Marius says that she is immune. Since Leela is a descendant of the people in this story, she should be immune. **14:41** The explosion takes place just before the shuttle hits Bi-Al. **16:25** It is not very likely that Professor Marius would find an undamaged body in the wreckage of the shuttle. **18:49** Marius reports that Leela is immune to the virus. Marius apparently did not get K9's report. **19:43** The cloning technique used by Professor Marius is remarkable. The cloning machine not only re-creates the person, but also the clothes they were wearing. Apparently, this avoids a naked Doctor and Leela. **22:28** Some fans wonder why parts from the TARDIS are interchangeable with equipment from other technologies. In this case, the dimensional stabilizer simply fits into the wall unit.

24:02 Professor Marius not only injects the cloned Doctor and Leela into the Doctor, but also a significant amount of air. The air would kill a human. This repeats in the reprise.

Episode 3
First Transmitted: Oct. 15, 1977
2:10 A question has arisen — why does the Doctor's clone not have the infection, while the Lowe clone remains infected? **5:48** There is an obvious crack in the wall before K9 fires to break away a section. This occurs after the shuttle crash, so the damage (cracks) could be from the crash and K9 takes advantage of the weakness. Some viewers erroneously report this to occur in the Episode 4. **6:50** Two supposedly different blood samples have all the cells aligned identically, and moving in the same direction. This is not a very likely situation. **10:22** Watch the beam K9 uses to shoot the attacker; it does not reach the appropriate position (K9's nose) until late in the shot. This occurs just before the person infects K9. **10:33** Some fans question the ability of the virus to take over K9. The reason being, how can a virus infect a machine? The persons bringing up this question must have forgotten that the Doctor caught the virus from an infected machine. **11:36** Leela drops unconscious before K9 even fires. **13:03** This is one example showing that Marius's operating room has no ceiling. **14:59** You can see someone reflected in the mirror on the nurse's (Elizabeth Norman) head. **16:06** Some observers wonder about Lowe's continued infection, versus the Doctor's lack of infection. The virus had not taken the Doctor over completely, but Lowe was completely under the control of the virus. **21:15** The camera pans in on the clone of Leela's knife. (How is it possible to clone a knife?) **22:06** The macro-virus does not look like the micro-virus.

Episode 4
First Transmitted: Oct. 22, 1977

3:51 The Doctor and Leela enter the TARDIS and apparently close the door. Everyone outside stops shooting so apparently they believe the door is closed. K9 rolls up to the outside of the TARDIS. **4:10** K9 is now inside the TARDIS; apparently he enters through the closed doors. **4:55** The Doctor opens the TARDIS doors for K9. Outside the TARDIS is a black void instead of a well-lit hallway. **5:28** The damage caused by the crashing shuttle appears to have disappeared. This view shows an undamaged Bi-Al with a shuttle still on the launching platform. **14:33** The Doctor approaches the incubation chamber carrying the box of antibodies from Marius. **14:42** The Doctor no longer has the box of antibodies. He is still outside the incubation chamber, and the box is nowhere in sight. **16:04** The Doctor says he lost the antibodies with no further explanation. **19:58** Marius says he must return to Earth. Marius already mentioned the weight problem. This explains the question some people have posed about Professor Marius being willing to give up his "best friend."

Comments: The Doctor saves the Solar System.

K9 is also K.9 and K-9.

(4X) IMAGE OF THE FENDAHL

Writer: Chris Boucher; **Director:** George Spenton-Foster

Media: Commercial tape — episodic version — 94 minutes (used); Collector's tape — movie version — 90 minutes

Questions: How can someone with a time machine ever be late for anything?

Errors and Other Points of Interest

Episode 1
First Transmitted: Oct. 29, 1977

4:34 The width of the skull is greater than Thea Ransome's (Wanda Ventham) head. The skull is nearly as wide as Thea's face plus her hair. **7:22** The TARDIS shakes violently. This could knock items over. **8:28** The violent shaking of the TARDIS was sufficient to throw things about; however, the hat stand remains upright. **12:36** Now the Doctor must pick up the hat stand from where it fell. The hat stand was still standing earlier. **12:55** The light on top of the TARDIS is no longer present. **15:20** Ted Moss (Edward Evans) reportedly says to the Doctor and Leela, "No, I were sent by the council to cut the verges." The actual quote is, "No, I was sent by the council to cut the verges."

Episode 2
First Transmitted: Nov. 5, 1977

6:39 A question has arisen: How did the Doctor get out of the locked room? At this time, the guards place the Doctor in the room and the door is closed. There is no sound indicating the locking of the door. **8:58** An answer to the question of the locked room — we hear a sound and the door opens; apparently, everyone except Max Stael (Scott Fredericks) is in the kitchen. **13:38** After Max tells Ted Moss, "I will deal with them. Now go, quickly," they begin to walk across the room. The camera operator bumps into a table with accompanying noise and shaking of the camera. **19:25** Thea goes looking for the Doctor and finds the room empty. Thus, Thea did not let the Doctor out of the room. Thea is not the answer to how the

Doctor escaped from the locked room. **21:15** When Thea tells Max she wants the Doctor's help, Max already knows of the Doctor's disappearance. Max does not appear to be surprised. Apparently, Max opened the door for the Doctor. This explains how the Doctor got out of the locked room. **23:10** The Doctor uncovers the skull, and then he says, "Would you like a jelly baby?" The Doctor is not holding a jelly baby. This is also in the reprise.

Episode 3
First Transmitted: Nov. 12, 1977

1:56 When Leela opens the door, we see a good example of the wobbling wall syndrome. This also happens at other times. **18:44** Leela tells the Doctor that they are going to be late and the Doctor agrees. How can anyone be late in a machine capable of arriving before it leaves?

Episode 4
First Transmitted: Nov. 19, 1977

2:21 The Fendahl's eyes appear painted on Thea's eyelids. **3:26** The Doctor discusses the fact that the Fendahl "killed the hiker and Mitchell." The Doctor saw Mitchell, but how did he know the other person was a hiker? **5:08** The movement at the edge of the screen just before the Doctor talks to Max is the Fendahl's fingers and not a blooper. **5:43** Just before the Doctor passes behind the Fendahl, the camera operator bumps into something and shakes the camera. **8:08** The Doctor explains that the Fendahl is made of twelve Fendahleen and a Core. The Doctor then continues with his shooting of a Fendahleen, and Stael killing himself. The Doctor concludes there are only ten remaining. The Doctor apparently did not see Fendelman's body. There are nine remaining not ten. **9:44** The Time Lords committed genocide. The Doctor should use this in his upcoming trial. **11:35** The Doctor tells Adam Colby (Edward Arthur), "The Fendahl fed into the RNA of certain individuals...." Adding information to the RNA of individuals would not make any long-term changes. The information would need to become part of the DNA, unless the Fendahl employed a virus. **12:16** Watch the Doctor's right hand as he helps the fallen Leela. **17:31** Part of the explosion footage repeats, and part runs backwards. Running the explosion backwards makes it appear to be an implosion. If it is an implosion, the "BOOM!" of an explosion should be a "MOOB!"

Comments: Due to a miscommunication, there is an incorrect reference to this story as *The Island of Fandor*.

The Doctor saves the Earth.

(4W) THE SUN MAKERS

Writer: Robert Holmes; **Director:** Pennant Roberts

Media: Commercial tape — episodic version — 100 minutes (used); Collector's tape — movie version — 94 minutes
Highlights: Villa is in character before he even met Blake.
Questions: How do you play one-dimensional chess?

Errors and Other Points of Interest

Episode 1
First Transmitted: Nov. 26, 1977

4:03 At least one viewer has found fault with the following conversation between Cordo (Roy Macready) and Gatherer Hade (Richard Leech). Cordo finds out how much he must pay the Gatherer and says, "But, Your Honor, I already work a double shift now! I have only my three hours sleep time away from the foundry!" The Gatherer replies, "Twenty-one hours a week! Well, you must manage without sleep time until the debt is paid." This viewer feels, incorrectly, that the Gatherer should have said "Twenty-one hours a day!" **4:50** The Doctor and K9 are playing two-dimensional chess (normal chess), and the Doctor says, "Even simple one-dimensional chess exposes the limitation of the machine mind." Why mention one-dimensional chess? **6:05** A boom mike shadow appears on the wall of the TARDIS as Leela bends to talk to K9. **6:17** Some viewers question the Doctor referring to Pluto as a "lifeless rock." They feel that Pluto is a ball of ice with no rock present. The composition was, and is, uncertain. Observers can only suggest that it is a ball of ice, which may or may not have a rocky core. **7:17** A car park sign is visible from the rooftop. **7:47** Leela yells to Cordo, "Come down!" "Down" is exactly what Cordo was planning to do. She does a better job next time when she cries, "Come back!" **8:30** The "jelly baby" the Doctor holds up for Cordo to see is definitely not a "jelly baby." Maybe it is a humbug. **9:20** Leela, and the others, are standing in front of one of the viewers. It is possible the camera took her picture at this time. **21:49** K9's ears move differently in close-up and distance shots. This may be an optical illusion.

Episode 2
First Transmitted: Dec. 3, 1977

1:00 The shadows of the guards are not moving. These guards are waiting for their cue instead of hurrying to the alarm. **2:27** Many fans consider the "boing" made by the Collector's (Henry Woolf) computer to be a blooper. **3:12** The backdrops in the correction center (and later in other places) are photos of memory chips produced by AMD (Advanced Micro Devices, Sunnyvale, California). In some cases, the "AMD" logo appears. Some fans incorrectly refer to this room as the rehab center. **8:43** There is a boom mike shadow on the person behind Mandrel after Mandrel says, "What palace?" This becomes a real blooper because this person looks up at the boom mike. **8:55** When Mandrel (William Simons) says to Leela, "They've got things called guns, and what have we got?" The camera shakes as the camera operator stumbles or hits something. **13:55** Leela could have her picture taken here. **18:03** The Doctor offers the Gatherer a "humbug" to indicate that he knows the Gatherer is lying to him. (He explains this later.) It is not a blooper for jelly baby as some viewers suggest. **23:28** Leela could have her picture taken at this time also.

Episode 3
First Transmitted: Dec. 10, 1977

2:04 After K9 shoots the second guard there is a close-up of K9's gun retracting. A longer shot follows with K9's gun retracting a second time. **3:23** Leela's wound is on the right side of her forehead. **4:55** The Doctor explains that he did not believe the Gatherer's story. This explains the Doctor's "humbug." **18:04** Notice the "AMD" logo above Cordo's head. **19:05** Some viewers believe the mug shots of Leela without a wound on her forehead constitutes a blooper. The viewers also cite that Leela could not have had her picture taken earlier because there were no cameras in the area of her capture. This is not a blooper. There are several places where an unwounded Leela could have had her picture taken. Some of these places appear in this list. The scanners are continually operating, thus there would be stored pictures for sorting when they are not specifically tracking someone. It is also possible that modification of the picture occurred before the officials allow the populace to see the pictures. **20:37** If the pressure is so high within the system, how can anyone open the vent without the pressure blowing out? The workers would need an airlock. **21:32** Watch the object pulled towards the ceiling behind the Gatherer as he says, "We could have offered more victims."

Episode 4
First Transmitted: Dec. 17, 1977

15:23 The facial expressions on the Gatherer as he is about to be thrown off the top of the building are not the most convincing. **20:16** The Collector is in front of the open cabinet preparing to open the switch. Watch where the Collector is the next time we see him. **20:51** The Collector is moving towards the closed cabinet to open it so he can throw the switch. **21:37** It is possible to see the outline of the Collector's bald wig. **22:34** The Doctor hands Leela the TARDIS key on a chain.

Comments: The Doctor visits Pluto and saves mankind.

(4Y) Underworld

Writer: Bob Baker and Dave Martin; **Director:** Norman Stewart

Media: Commercial tape — episodic version — 89 minutes (used); Collector's tape — movie version — 81 minutes
Highlights: This story is a case of too much CSO and too little tunnel.
Questions: The TARDIS and the ship can escape from a planet. Why would a planetary nebula have a greater gravitational attraction than a planet and pose a greater threat of trapping them?

Errors and Other Points of Interest

The story's ideas about the formation of planets and the effects of gravity are bloopers according to some observers and technobabble according to others.

Episode 1
First Transmitted: Jan. 7, 1978

0:44 This is another case of an exceptionally wobbly TARDIS column. **4:51** Captain Jackson (James Maxwell) wonders if the sound they heard came from outside the ship. How could he think the sound came from outside the ship? The Captain should know that sound does not travel through the vacuum of space.

Episode 2
First Transmitted: Jan. 14, 1978

2:22 K9 begins a countdown to impact. He reaches zero while the ship is still well above the surface of the planet. **6:56** No wonder the Doctor has to help Herrick (Alan Lake) fire his weapon — Herrick is not looking where he is shooting — either directly or through the view plate above the barrel. **11:47** The Doctor and Leela rearrange the tarp with three guards looking at them. However, none of the guards notices. **13:55** Herrick puts a marker on a very distinctive rock formation, and the other Minyans say they will stay there. **14:32** A guard walks by the rock formation with the maker, but no Minyans remain.

Episode 3
First Transmitted: Jan. 21, 1978

5:10 Leela shouts, "Revolution!" This startles Idas (Norman Tipton) so much that he runs through a rock. Leela chases after him and runs through the same rock — so much for the CSO. **7:32** The Doctor explains to Leela that there is no gravity. If there is no gravity, what holds them down?

Episode 4
First Transmitted: Jan. 28, 1978

2:50 As Jackson and the others mount their attack, the Doctor, Leela and Idas go down another path. Leela and Idas' legs keep disappearing as they move along the path. **8:05** As the Oracle addresses the Doctor, a person is apparently skulking in the background to the Doctor's right. This happens before Leela's shield gun enters the picture. **12:51** When K9 blasts into the cavern trapping the Doctor, Leela and Lakh (Richard Shaw), K9 is still behind a rock after the explosion. Then the rock disappears. **14:00** The Doctor runs out of the ship with the fission grenades. Leela runs after the Doctor with a shield gun. **14:07** Leela has no shield gun so she draws her knife. **14:50** Leela has sheathed her knife and recovered the shield gun. **16:49** The Doctor lifts a small girl and she flashes the world. Her behind is not bare as has been suggested. This is just one of the mooning incidents in the series. **20:54** The Doctor leaves the Minyans to make their 370 years' journey to Minyos II. The question has been posed — why does the Doctor not give everyone a ride in the TARDIS? This is not a blooper as suggested. The Doctor does not normally just give people rides to where they can go without his aid.

Comments: There are many CSO problems in addition to the ones listed.

The Doctor saves the Minyans.

(4Z) THE INVASION OF TIME

Writer: David Agnew (Graham Williams and Anthony Read); **Director:** Gerald Blake

Media: Commercial tape — episodic version — 150 minutes (used); Collector's tape — movie version — 140 minutes
Highlights: The Doctor becomes President of Gallifrey. There is another tour of the TARDIS.
Questions: The Sontarans claim reinforcements cannot join them. Why do reinforcements not enter through the hole in force field where the first ship entered? (This might be slow, since the hole is small.)

Errors and Other Points of Interest

Some viewers report that the TARDIS light remains on throughout the story. This is true for Episodes 1 and 2. We do not see the top of the TARDIS in Episodes 3 and 6. The light is out when the TARDIS appears during Episodes 4 and 5.

Episode 1
First Transmitted: Feb. 4, 1978

0:44 The Doctor's scarf appears around his neck. **0:55** The Doctor's scarf is no longer around the Doctor's neck, it is on the hat-stand inside the TARDIS. **3:25**

The Doctor leaves the Vardan ship wearing his scarf, and enters the TARDIS without the scarf. **5:15** The Doctor is traveling to Gallifrey — however, the center column of the TARDIS is not moving. **8:20** The TARDIS light remains on after it lands. **8:44** The TARDIS light is still on. **8:47** Some fans wonder why Leela can go to Gallifrey when Sarah Jane could not. Sarah Jane could not accompany the Doctor when the Time Lords called the Doctor. The Doctor takes Leela without hearing from the Time Lords. The circumstances are different. **20:02** The two Time Lords (Lord Gomer (Dennis Edwards) and Lord Savar (Reginald Jessup)) bump into each other as they turn around.

Episode 2
First Transmitted: Feb. 11, 1978

5:37 As Castellan Kelner (Milton Johns) says, "I'll see that she is driven out of the Citadel," someone out of camera range apparently drops something. This is hard to hear because of the alarm. **8:03** Another Doctor quote: "Even the sonic screwdriver won't get me out of this one." **9:34** The Doctor leaves Borusa's quarters wearing the Sash of Rassilon. **11:32** The TARDIS light remains lit. **12:59** The TARDIS light is still on. **17:21** The TARDIS doors are open into the console room. **17:36** The TARDIS doors are not open on the outside. **20:04** K9 leaves the TARDIS doors open — later the doors are closed. **20:34** When the Doctor returns he apparently is not wearing the Sash. You need to look closely because in other scenes the Doctor's coat hides the Sash. **22:30** It must be very cold in the studio. It is possible to see Rodan's (Hilary Ryan) breath as she says, "dare!" **22:52** The guard drops his gun after K9 shoots him, and the gun breaks. K9 is momentarily stuck as K9 drives over one of the gun pieces.

Episode 3
First Transmitted: Feb. 18, 1978

22:17 It is not possible to see if the TARDIS light remains lit. **22:27** The "lost" Sash makes a definite reappearance.

Episode 4
First Transmitted: Feb. 25, 1978

0:50 Initially the Doctor attempts to place the crown on the back of K9's head. The Doctor must place it over K9's ears instead. The crown remains on K9's ears for a time. **2:14** Why did Andred (Christopher Tranchell) not know his weapon would not work inside a TARDIS? **2:35** The TARDIS light is no longer shining. **2:55** As the Doctor says to K9, "I am going out for a few moments," a person size shadow moves behind the Doctor. No one on the set is moving so the persons in front of the camera do not cause the moving shadow. **5:10** The crown is still over K9's ears. **7:30** The crown materializes on the back of K9's head. Some observers incorrectly report this movement as occurring in two subsequent scenes. There are four scenes in between the crown being over K9's ears and this scene. **9:06** The crown has caused K9's ears to be misaligned. **11:08** K9's ears are back in alignment. **17:01** There is a reported blooper. The inside of the door the Doctor opens is smooth. The inside of the door in his office has a relief design. These would seem to be two views of the same door. Later we see that there are two sets of doors.

Episode 5
First Transmitted: Mar. 4, 1978

0:38 This group of Sontarans has three fingers. **0:50** Some fans think that Stor's (Derek Deadman) cockney accent is out of place. The question is — how many Sontarans have they personally met who did not have a cockney accent? **3:06** Twice after Borusa tests his receiver, we hear a voice in the background. While the receiver is on only static sounds, the voices come after switching the receiver off. This may be a fault on the tape. The second time is the more obvious of the two. **10:30** The Sontarans struggle to open the doors to the Doctor's office. The Doctor eventually unlocks the doors and the Sontarans pull the doors, with smooth interiors, open (outward from the office). When seen from inside the office—the doors are opening into the office. If you look back through the doors—we see that there are two sets of doors. **10:55** As everyone escapes into Borusa's quarters, K9's motor is running on high. When the camera pans back, we see that K9 is not even moving. **17:52** The TARDIS light is still off. **22:48** Rodan and the Doctor discuss the Sontaran Battle Fleet they see on the scanner. **23:20** The bottom of the control panel swings away from the wall as the Castellan touches the panel.

Episode 6
First Transmitted: Mar. 11, 1978

2:10 There are claims that there is a blooper because three Sontarans enter the TARDIS and the story only accounts for two. This is not true as illustrated by these instances. Two Sontarans enter at this time. **5:04** During the "tour" of the TARDIS, Leela steps on the Doctor's scarf. The Doctor says, "Would you get off my scarf please." Contrary to blooper reports—the Doctor does not stop in mid-speech (no one is talking at this time), and he does not say "and stop standing on my scarf!" **7:31** Two Sontarans enter the lower part of the TARDIS. **8:36** Deep inside the TARDIS, there are still only two Sontarans. **11:14** The Sontaran running after the Doctor jumps on a chair next to the swimming pool and falls. **11:19** The Sontaran, from the previous blooper, tries to "fall" into the swimming pool, but he starts too far away. **21:28** The Doctor may have lost his memory about the Castellan's collaboration, but why did everyone else forget? **22:29** Some viewers wonder why everyone is so happy with a Sontaran Battle Fleet, seen by Rodan and the Doctor, overhead. A likely explanation is that with the return of the force field, there was no reason why they should stay. **22:46** Some observers believe that two people like Andred and Leela cannot fall in love so quickly.

Comments: There are publicity photos apparently showing the Sontarans kneeling before the Doctor. This has been mistaken as part of the story.

The Doctor saves Gallifrey.

The Search for the Key to Time

(5A) THE RIBOS OPERATION

Alternate Title: The Rebose File (mistake)
Writer: Robert Holmes; **Director:** George Spenton-Foster

Media: Commercial DVD — episodic version — 99 minutes (used); Commercial tape — episodic version — 99 minutes; Collector's tape — movie version — 95 minutes
Highlights: The Search for the Key to Time begins. The Doctor's lip has a problem.
Questions: Is the White Guardian (Cyril Luckham) really the person who gives the quest to the Doctor?

Errors and Other Points of Interest

Episode 1
First Transmitted: Sept. 2, 1978

0:54 There is a light shining between the TARDIS doors into the console room.

2:46 Notice the Doctor's lip. **7:40** Some fans question how it is possible to detect the change in coordinates of the segment while the TARDIS is in flight. This would not be the first time something like this occurs. This occurred in *The Chase*. In any case, this is technobabble. **8:03** There is a flap, or clamp, on Garron's (Iain Cuthbertson) wrist-communicator, which keeps swinging about as he moves his arm. **11:40** Romana I says the Doctor is 759, but the Doctor claims he is only 756. **11:58** The Doctor apparently snags or steps on something. **15:50** The Doctor and Romana I leave the TARDIS doors open when they depart. **21:42** It is possible to see the wire used to power the tracer.

Episode 2
First Transmitted: Sept. 9, 1978

2:09 The Guard looks through the door as the Doctor leaves his hiding place to pick up the sonic screwdriver. The guard does not see the Doctor. **2:46** There is a feather on the floor from Romana I's cloak. The feather is near the spot where the Guard Captain (Prentis Hancock) kneels.

Episode 3
First Transmitted: Sept. 16, 1978

0:37 The Graff's soldiers are supposedly very loyal and obedient. If they are so good, why do they stop when the Doctor, not the Graff, orders them to stop? **4:56** K9 must open the door to the TARDIS so he can leave. The Doctor and Romana I left the doors open. This would indicate that the door is self-closing. **22:28** Binro (Timothy Bateson) tells Unstoffe (Nigel Plaskitt) that since the Shrivenzales can live in the catacombs there must be another way to leave. This apparently refutes the claimed blooper asking how the Doctor gets out of the catacombs after they are sealed.

Episode 4
First Transmitted: Sept. 23, 1978

10:13 As Unstoffe leaves his hiding place on Garron's approach, the "ground" is obviously dirt on top of cardboard or plywood. **20:44** Some viewers wonder how the Doctor escapes from the catacombs. Binro already covered this when telling Unstoffe about the Shrivenzales. **20:44** The TARDIS door is still open. Unlike earlier, this would indicate that the doors are not self-closing. **22:54** The tracer does not make a sound as the Doctor holds the device near the jethrik. A few seconds later as Romana I holds the tracer near the jethrik, the tracer sounds loudly.

Comments: The Doctor visits Ribos.

(5B) The Pirate Planet

Writer: Douglas Adams; **Director:** Pennant Roberts

Media: Commercial DVD — episodic version — 102 minutes (used); Commercial tape — episodic version — 102 minutes; Collector's tape — movie version — 96 minutes
Highlights: You should watch for the spinning K9. The Doctor sums up his purpose in the entire series with the words: "I save planets, mostly."
Questions: Why does Romana I question the Doctor's ability to land the TARDIS after he successfully landed on Ribos?

Errors and Other Points of Interest

Episode 1
First Transmitted: Sept. 30, 1978

5:16 Romana I says the Doctor has been operating the TARDIS for 523 years.

She implies it has been the same TARDIS for the entire time. This would indicate that the Doctor was about 250 when he began using the TARDIS. **6:02** The "collision" gives the Doctor an excuse to have a sore lip. This slowly heals throughout the story. **8:04** We meet K9's stunt double. Notice the collar. **8:55** As a future reference — look for K9 spinning around. **11:43** The Doctor and Romana I leave the TARDIS door open. **12:31** The Doctor steps on the end of his scarf. **13:56** There is a large boom mike shadow on the side of the hallway as the citizen exits with the Doctor saying, "Excuse me. What I'd like to know...." **21:28** The next to the last Mentiad slips in the mud.

Episode 2
First Transmitted: Oct. 7, 1978

2:47 K9 tells the Doctor "5347.2," but the Doctor repeats it as "543.72." K9 agrees that this is the correct number. **4:53** After the coin toss, Mula (Primi Townsend) walks around the Doctor while discussing the consequences. A production crewmember is standing outside, just look through the doorway. **6:12** The Doctor throws a bag of jelly babies onto the front of the air car; most, if not all, of the jelly babies stay in the bag; yet when the guard gets out of the air car, candy is scattered all over the ground. **6:26** The bag of "jelly babies" on the street contains many things that are not jelly babies. Some observers incorrectly report this to be in Episode 1. **16:24** The Doctor tells Romana I: "I just put 1.795372 and 2.204628 together." Romana I asks, "What does that mean?" To which the Doctor replies, "Four!" These values add to 4. Some viewers have misquoted these two numbers, and they get an answer that does not add to 4. **18:24** Notice the ascot around the Doctor's neck. **18:51** When the Doctor, Romana I, and the guards pass along the Corridor the white ascot the Doctor is wearing disappears. He is wearing it before and after being in the Corridor. However, the Doctor keeps his hand over his neck so it is not a definite blooper. **19:33** The Doctor is again wearing his ascot.

Episode 3
First Transmitted: Oct. 14, 1978

2:01 Mula, to K9: "You mean they slammed him to the wall with good vibrations?" Apparently, Mula is a Brian Wilson fan. **5:44** Look for the sign on the chair behind the Captain (Bruce Purchase) that says, "FRONT SEAT." **10:28** The Doctor again throws a bag of jelly babies onto the front of the air car. All of the candy stays in the bag; yet when the guard gets out of the air car candy is scattered all over the ground. **15:10** We can see the strings holding the planets. This occurs at other times. **19:30** The Doctor trips as he is fleeing from the bridge. He apparently trips over the crowbar on the floor. **20:18** If the Time Dams slow things down why can Xanxia (Vi Delmar) move, breath and, later, blink at a normal rate?

Episode 4
First Transmitted: Oct. 21, 1978

1:42 Carefully watch the Captain's chair as the Doppeldoctor appears. **3:09** The guards fall as if hit by rocks before the rocks actually hit them. **7:32** Why should it be so difficult to find the mineral PJX18 (quartz); it is one of the most common minerals in the Universe (at least according to current theories)? **8:21** Mr. Fibuli (Andrew Robertson) responds to the nurse's (Rosalind Lloyd) question with "Yes, Sir!" **11:14** As the Doctor says "Newton's revenge," he stops leaning against the wall — the entire wall moves. **11:48** It sounds as if the Doctor tells Romana I to "cover your heads!" **16:23** It is surprising that the writer of this story did not have Romana I and the Doctor awaken with towels under their heads (or feet). **16:43** The TARDIS door seems partly open during materialization. The

Doctor does not close the door completely when he leaves. **19:32** There is a large shadow moving behind Romana I.

Comments: The Doctor saves the planet of Zanak.

(5C) THE STONES OF BLOOD

Writer: David Fisher; **Director:** Darrol Blake

Media: Commercial DVD — episodic version — 96 minutes (used); Commercial tape — episodic version — 97 minutes (used); Collector's tape — movie version — 91 minutes
Questions: Why does the segment detector work outside the circle, but only works sporadically within the circle?

Errors and Other Points of Interest

Episode 1
First Transmitted: Oct. 28, 1978

1:54 There are reports of a boom microphone in the first scene in the circle. This is a questionable call. **2:35** One of the most common bloopers cited for the story is the number of Ogri. The reports go that there are three Ogri, one falls off a cliff, and there are still three Ogri. There are several notations about the Ogri in this list. At this point, we see only two Ogri feeding from two bowls of blood. This is the Ogri blooper. **4:52** Romana I finds out that the President of the Supreme Council did not send her on this mission. The Doctor tells her it was the White Guardian. Romana I should not forget this important fact. **6:02** If you look through the doorway into the control room, it is possible to see the shadow of a ladder on the roundels in the TARDIS wall. **8:20** Pay attention to the trees. **14:22** The weight of a landing crow causes a large rock to shake. **14:22** Compare these trees to the earlier trees around the circle.

Episode 2
First Transmitted: Nov. 4, 1978

0:30 There is no reprise of the ending of the preceding episode. This is a real cliffhanger. **2:11** Someone forgot to turn on the rear bicycle light. **4:28** The Doctor apparently left the TARDIS doors open. **6:27** Why is the sea so calm now? **6:29** If it is still night, how can there be a sunset? **7:00** When did the Doctor and Romana I learn the properties of the individual segments? **10:27** The Ogri blooper continues with one of the Ogri. **10:52** K9 warns the Doctor about "Unidentified aliens." Not just the one we saw earlier. **11:24** Apparently, there had been some problem during rehearsal. The Doctor subtly lifts up the front left corner of K9 so K9 can make it across a crack in the floor. **11:31** There is a cord attached to the front of K9 to help him move. **12:18** Only one Ogri attacks the Doctor and K9. Where are K9's "aliens?" **16:11** K9's stunt double plays this. The double is wearing a different collar. **20:48** The collar shows that this is the real K9.

Episode 3
First Transmitted: Nov. 11, 1978

1:53 There appears to be a trolley under the Ogri. **1:54** Look behind the Ogri attacking through the doorway. There are production crewmembers in the room behind the Ogri. One is clearly pushing the

Ogri through the door. Some fans incorrectly report this to be in Episode 2. **2:11** After the Doctor closes the door and turns around, the camera shakes. **3:48** One of the Ogri falls over the cliff. **5:38** The Doctor says three stones are missing from the circle. This is apparently where the concept of three Ogri and the Ogri blooper arose. The Doctor also notes that one of the Ogri fell over the cliff. At no time do more than two Ogri ever appear together. **6:28** The Doctor asks Professor Rumford (Beatrix Lehmann) if she has any tritium crystals. She apparently finds some in Vivian Fay's cottage. The problem is that tritium is a radioactive form of hydrogen gas. How can the Doctor expect Vivian Fay or Professor Rumford to have crystals of a radioactive gas? **7:05** Professor Rumford is referring to a needle and dial. Where are they? **12:18** The Doctor must remove some left over fire from the explosion. **12:30** K9 reports two Ogri approaching from the south-southwest. We see only two Ogri. **17:46** Two Ogri attack the campers. **23:03** Vivian Fay (Susan Engel) appears in the spacecraft with two Ogri. **23:55** The closing credits contain an error. Dick Mills (special sound) should be Elizabeth Parker.

Episode 4
First Transmitted: Nov. 18, 1978

2:55 Look at the section of the Doctor's scarf on his right next to his top-buttoned shirt button. **6:21** One of the two remaining Ogri is destroyed by the Magora. From this point onwards no more than one Ogri is apparent. This finishes the Ogri blooper. **16:49** Vivian Fay sits while waiting for the Doctor's execution. At the moment of the execution, she is standing and holding her hand out to the Doctor.

(5D) THE ANDROIDS OF TARA

Writer: David Fisher; **Director:** Michael Hayes

Media: Commercial DVD — episodic version — 98 minutes (used); Commercial tape — episodic version — 98 minutes (used); Collector's tape — movie version — 92 minutes
Questions: At the end — how did Romana I know to ask about K9?

Errors and Other Points of Interest

Episode 1
First Transmitted: Nov. 25, 1978

0:25 The opening credits are in a different order. The order is title, part number, writer instead of title, writer, and part number. This order appears in all four episodes. This consistency makes this not a real blooper. **1:43** Romana I reminds the Doctor that the Guardian sent them on their quest. Again, Romana I should remember this important fact. **11:15** Some viewers consider the appearance of the Taran beast to be a blooper. How do these viewers know that this does not look exactly like a Taran beast? **12:40** Notice that the foil has a blunt tip instead of a point. Apparently, the soldiers do not want anyone to get hurt during a battle. The foils do not carry enough charge to electrocute anyone — otherwise the Doctor would be dead. **15:34** Romana I's restraints do not look very convincing. The restraints are obviously for an android, not a person. They could be, for example, magnetic to interfere with an android's circuitry. Romana I could not escape at this point because there are either other people in the room or because of the drug. **17:59** Prince Reynart (Neville Jason) loses his grip as he first attempts to lift the cloth. **22:38** The tray and everything on it appear to be made of metal. **23:28** It sounds as if a plastic object falls on the floor. In the long shot, we see that it was a "metal" cup.

Episode 2
First Transmitted: Dec. 2, 1978

3:45 The shadow of a person rising appears on the side of K9 as K9 "wakes-up." **4:09** Unlike other times, we both see and hear the TARDIS door open for K9. **10:12** If the android prince has low batteries, why make it walk to the capital? **15:23** Zadek (Simon Lack) tells the Doctor that nine tenths of the population perished in a plague. This is why there are not very many people left on the planet. **16:30** There are fans that recognize the Taran throne to be Tim's chair from *The Goodies*. **20:59** Some viewers object to the British Government sending a general as its representative to the coronation.

Episode 3
First Transmitted: Dec. 9, 1978

4:59 There are claims that K9 has more in common with a dog than simple outward appearance. K9 illustrates his similarity to dogs when he asked to investigate the android — K9's probe seems to extend to the appropriate region for a dog to investigate. **12:11** When the Doctor starts to close the door to the Pavilion of the Summer Winds there is a movement of one of the shadows and a hand appears from outside and pulls the door shut. **12:11** Some viewers incorrectly report that the Pavilion door slowly swings open after the Doctor first closes it. This does not happen. **18:49** The Doctor knocks out the escape panel before K9 finishes cutting — but the entire hole shows that the cut is complete and smooth. **22:26** Count Grendel (Peter Jeffrey) crosses in front of the set instead of going through the doorway. Some viewers claim that it was the Doctor who committed this blooper. **22:50** Farrah (Paul Lavers) aims at the fleeing Count, but the Doctor runs up to him and knocks the weapon from Farrah's hands. How could the Doctor see outside and know about Romana I's kidnapping?

Episode 4
First Transmitted: Dec. 16, 1978

15:17 The Doctor begins to cross himself but covers it up by moving his fingers through his hair. This is a claimed blooper — it is up to the viewer to make the call. **18:29** Some observers ask the question — If Prince Reynart (Neville Jason) is the ruler of a planet, why does he have such a small army? Obviously, the force must be small because they are trying to keep the kidnapping of the Prince a secret. In addition, we learned earlier that most of the people on the planet had died in a plague, thus any army would be small.

Comments: The Doctor saves the planet Tara.

(5E) THE POWER OF KROLL

Writer: Robert Holmes; **Director:** Norman Stewart

Media: Commercial DVD — episodic version — 91 minutes (used); Commercial tape — episodic version — 91 minutes (used); Collector's tape — movie version — 82 minutes
Highlights: We see the biggest of the Doctor Who monsters.
Questions: Why are there no female Swampies?

Errors and Other Points of Interest

Some viewers claim that the Doctor switches from wearing to not wearing galoshes. There are no confirmable instances. The Doctor switches from wearing his galoshes up to wearing them folded over. When folded over we can see characteristic light and dark green stripes. This list contains a few examples of each occurrence.

Episode 1
First Transmitted: Dec. 23, 1978

2:58 Whatever Fenner (Philip Madoc) drank must have left a bad taste in his mouth. **3:45** The Doctor is wearing his galoshes "up." **4:59** Thawn (Neil McCarthy) and Fenner leave to look for Rohm-Dutt (Glyn Owen). Even though there should only be two people, Thawn and Fenner, in the boat—three people are present. **5:58** The music and the Doctor's playing of the reed flute do not match. **11:15** Thawn incorrectly refers to the solar system they are in as a "constellation." **14:11** The Doctor puts his drink into his pocket. **14:30** The Doctor asks, "Just the six of you here?" Thawn replies, "No, five." The Doctor implies that he believes there are six people in addition to himself. Thawn replies to indicate that he does not consider the Swampie, Mensch (Terry Walsh), a member of the crew. The problem arises when the Doctor counts the six people—he counts himself as one of the six. If he considered himself part of the group why did he not say, "Just the six of us here?"

Episode 2
First Transmitted: Dec. 30, 1978

2:11 Skart (Frank Jarvis) dresses as Kroll in order to kill Romana I. The Doctor pulls the top off the Kroll costume and knocks Skart down. Skart falls wearing the remainder of his Kroll costume. **2:36** Now, Skart is wearing normal Swampy clothes instead of his Kroll costume. **10:56** The Doctor is wearing his galoshes folded down. **11:01** Some observers question how the primitive Swampies developed bookbinding. It is not clear if they are the ones who bound the book. **13:04** We see the boat with Thawn, Mensch and another person. Mensch dies, and Thawn returns to base. **14:27** Thawn tells Fenner and Harg (Grahame Mallard) about his experiences with Mensch and the other person. When he finishes they wake Dugeen (John Leeson), who is on his break. Fenner and Harg are at the base, and Dugeen is on break. Who accompanied Thawn and Mensch? **16:13** Thawn asks about Dugeen and learns that Dugeen is on a break. **21:34** There is a boom mike shadow on Dugeen's lap in the control room.

Episode 3
First Transmitted: Jan. 6, 1979

0:31 Some fans wonder if Fenner's first line is a comment about Kroll or the plot. **8:30** In the close-up of Rohm-Dutt talking, the camera shakes. **13:52** Some viewers claim that when the Doctor breaks the glass the rainwater only gets the vines wet, and nothing else. This is not true—they all get wet below their knees (except possibly Rohm-Dutt). **16:39** The Doctor is wearing his galoshes all the way up, as the characteristic stripes are not visible. **18:23** Thawn (Neil McCarthy) has trouble saying, "Swampies most certainly do have some problems."

Episode 4
First Transmitted: Jan. 13, 1979

1:38 Notice the line between the swamp grass and the image of Kroll. **6:52** The ladder the Doctor is using is not very stable. We see the Doctor open the control panel, and this causes the ladder and the entire rocket to shake. **7:56** Some observers claim that a hammer blow can make the side of the rocket silo wobble. This appears to be an overstatement. **7:59** The ladder the Doctor is standing on is still not too stable. **11:55** The "dead" Dugeen's legs move. **15:58** The Doctor says he is nearly 760.

Comments: Some lists incorrectly refer to Rohm-Dutt as Roam Dutt.

The Doctor saves the natives on the third moon of Delta Magna.

(5F) THE ARMAGEDDON FACTOR

Writer: Bob Baker and Dave Martin; **Director:** Michael Hayes

Media: Commercial DVD — episodic version — 148 minutes (used); Commercial tape — episodic version — 148 minutes (used); Collector's tape — movie version — 137 minutes
Highlights: We get our first glimpse of Romana II. Drax (Barry Jackson) gives another of the Doctor's names.
Questions: The White Guardian sent the Doctor and Romana I on their quest because of an impending problem. What is the White Guardian going to do about this problem after the Doctor disperses the segments?

Errors and Other Points of Interest

Episode 1
First Transmitted: Jan. 20, 1979

7:19 The TARDIS materializes without its light flashing. **7:26** This is one of the times we hear the noisy column of the TARDIS. **13:42** The rocket enters the radar screen from the bottom. The rocket launches from the planet's surface. The center of the radar screen gives the location of the radar. The Atrios radar is in space with the TARDIS and the missile converging toward it. The radar (satellite?) survives a nuclear explosion. **14:56** The light on top of the TARDIS appears to flash much faster than normal. **19:29** This is the first view of K9's left side — there is no additional panel. **19:33** We hear the sound of falling polystyrene. **21:52** Astra (Lalla Ward) loses her circlet.

Episode 2
First Transmitted: Jan. 27, 1979

1:32 The Doctor reports the burial of the TARDIS. **2:31** The TARDIS appears behind Romana I as K9 begins cutting the door. The Doctor and Romana I previously reported its burial. Some viewers incorrectly report that the TARDIS had already left. **3:26** Merak (Ian Saynor) picks up Astra's circlet. **6:01** Instead of simply following the red design down the tunnel, K9 passes through, or under, the design. **22:19** K9 drives over the end of the Doctor's scarf, and the Doctor must pull the scarf from beneath K9. **22:44** The door does not completely close.

Episode 3
First Transmitted: Feb. 3, 1979

2:34 K9 now says the TARDIS is missing. **4:32** The door to the transmat is completely closed. **16:11** The Doctor pats K9 so hard that he knocks K9's ears out of position. **18:33** The Doctor says he has never seen K9 spin. The Doctor saw K9 spin in *The Pirate Planet*. **21:56** Shapp (Davyd Harries) drops his gun on the floor and the weapon breaks.

Episode 4
First Transmitted: Feb. 10, 1979

17:45 Merak says that only the Doctor

and Romana I are able to open the TARDIS. How did Merak know this? **19:17** Romana I meets the future Romana II. **20:50** K9 has the additional panel installed on his left side; this panel is not supposed to be installed until later. Installation and use of the panel is to be in Episode 6. Some observers incorrectly state that installation of the panel is in Episode 5.

Episode 5
First Transmitted: Feb. 17, 1979

9:31 Drax (Barry Jackson) demonstrates the ability of the Time Lords to recognize one of their own, even after regeneration. **9:39** Drax reminds the Doctor of the Doctor's nickname (Theta Sigma).

Episode 6
First Transmitted: Feb. 24, 1979

1:19 Some fans worry about Earth Capitalism. These fans object to the export and sale of Earth shoes to the Mutes. **3:22** How can Schapp understand a time-loop without getting any explanation? **3:28** Merak appears to know much more about the sixth segment that what he learned in passing from Romana I and the Doctor. **5:37** Princess Astra says she is the sixth Princess of the sixth Dynasty of the sixth Royal House when she should have said she is the sixth Princess of the sixth Royal House of the sixth Dynasty. In either case, it makes her the six-six-six. **6:44** The mute guarding the TARDIS kicks up the carpet on the floor as The Shadow (William Squire) is about to enter the ship. The carpet stays on top of the mute's foot until the mute starts walking. **8:32** K9's weapon retracts faster than normal. **9:01** We see K9's new panel for the "first" time. **9:18** Merak uses Astra's circlet to distract the guard. **11:38** The Princess changes before touching the detector. She was closer while in the TARDIS, and she did not change at that time. Why is it different this time? **14:45** The Doctor says he cannot replace the segment of the Key to Time in a second. Why not begin to change it at the beginning of the loop and get a full 10 seconds? **17:29** The doors of the TARDIS are open while the Doctor is explaining about the deflected missiles. Through the open door, wooden paneling can be seen (part of another set?), and what appears to be some sheets of black foil. **19:16** Romana I says they are to give the Key to Time to the White Guardian. **19:39** Romana I has forgotten that in *The Stones of Blood*, she learned that it was not the President who sent her with the Doctor. She seems surprised that they are not meeting the President. **22:44** Princess Astra again has the circlet she lost earlier. Merak had the circlet last, and did not return it to her.

Comments: The box containing the DVD gives a playing time of "Approx. 91 minutes." Apparently, the last two episodes take zero time.

While visiting the planets Atrios and Zeos, the Doctor saves the Universe.

(5J) Destiny of the Daleks

Writer: Terry Nation; **Director:** Ken Grieve

Media: Commercial tape — episodic version — 100 minutes (used); Collector's tape — movie version — 93 minutes
Highlights: We see the many faces of Romana. Romana I becomes Romana II. Davros (David Gooderson) returns.
Questions: Why do androids have breasts?

Errors and Other Points of Interest

Many of the characters in the story incorrectly refer to the Daleks as robots. The Daleks are cyborgs. This list contains several instances.

There are many Earth-like luggage trolleys and spotlights. Some observers consider the presence of these items to be bloopers.

Episode 1
First Transmitted: Sept. 1, 1979

4:17 The planet Skaro still has high radiation levels. To combat the radiation the Doctor gives Romana II some pills, which she takes immediately, and a beeper. Some viewers incorrectly state that the Doctor gives Romana II no pills. **4:41** K9 spins around again. **13:09** The Doctor and Romana II are at the top of the hill. The Doctor comes down the hill alone — he is the only one seen descending and there is only one set of footprints. Romana II is already at the bottom of the hill. How did Romana II get down? **17:46** When the Doctor's pill beeper sounds, he says, "Must remember to give Romana hers." **21:39** One of the many Earth-type spotlights looms over Romana II.

Episode 2
First Transmitted: Sept. 8, 1979

3:56 During her interrogation, Romana II shouts, "I don't know anything about the Daleks!" The lie detector accepts this statement. **5:39** Commander Sharrel (Peter Straker) learns of the capture of a prisoner. Sharrel may know the Doctor is looking for Romana II. The Commander tells his subordinate to "bring him in at once." How did he know the prisoner was a he? **7:45** When talking to the other prisoners, Romana II says, of the Daleks, "They used to be humanoid themselves." Apparently, she was able to fool the lie detector. **10:52** Here is one of the Earth-type luggage trolleys. **17:40** The second Dalek to enter runs over something. **18:49** A Dalek hits the doorframe. **20:30** The Doctor and Romana II reunite. The Doctor does not offer Romana II a radiation pill. **21:51** If the Daleks do not know about this part of the complex, who turned on all the lights?

Episode 3
First Transmitted: Sept. 15, 1979

1:01 This is the first time Davros moves across the floor. It is obvious that he is waddling like a duck. This occurs throughout this episode and into the next episode. Some observers incorrectly report that this also occurs in Episode 2, where he only moves his hand and "lights" his eye. **3:35** Either this point, or one a few seconds later, is where some fans claim Davros sways as the Doctor is pushing him. **7:44** Commander Sharrel apparently does not know the difference between a "mutant humanoid," and a "humanoid mutant." The computer, when reporting on Davros, displays "humanoid mutant" but the Commander says "mutant humanoid." **11:54** The Doctor says, "Now spack off." **15:12** One of the Daleks says "Self-sacrifice illogical, therefore impossible." **17:08** When the Doctor uses the sonic screwdriver to detonate the explosives, not only is the sound of the sonic screwdriver heard, but we also hear the interior sound of the TARDIS. **17:33** Davros "runs" down a corridor and hits the wall. **17:36** After the explosion, the Daleks file off the set. As the last Dalek begins to move its entire, top section jumps. **17:43** Davros again hits the wall of the corridor. **17:50** Commander Sharrel refers to the Daleks as robots. **17:55** As Commander Sharrel gets up there is a boom mike shadow behind him. **21:20** It is the Doctor's turn to call the Daleks robots, when he says the Movellans are "another race of robots, no better than the Daleks." It is possible that the Doctor is not actually calling the Daleks robots.

Episode 4
First Transmitted: Sept. 22, 1979

2:53 Watch for the production crewmembers reflected in the panel beside Davros. **3:10** This is a second instance where we see the production crewmembers' reflection in the panel beside Davros. **4:21** The Doctor now states, "One race of robots fighting another." In this case, the Doctor is obviously referring to the Daleks as robots. **5:15** Davros gets into the robot controversy with "another race of robots." **6:47** Some observers consider the trapping of the Movellans in "scissors cut paper" to be a blooper. The entire plot of the story rests upon the trapping of both the Daleks and the Movellans in a situation where there is no superior choice. **12:26** The Daleks have already stated that self-sacrifice is impossible. Why are the Daleks so willing to indulge in self-sacrifice at this time? **13:07** The first Dalek jumps as it begins to move. **13:16** After the bomb-laden Daleks leave, we see a very shaky and incomplete Dalek standing next to Davros. Note the errors in the construction of this Dalek. **14:01** How did the ex-prisoners get into the spaceship so fast since the door only allows one person to enter at a time? The attack begins with the door closed. **14:10** As the attacking ex-prisoners are attacking the Movellens, one of the Movellans just stands by and watches. **14:41** After the attack, the spaceship door remains open to the inside of the spaceship. Thus, Commander Sharrel could not have escaped that way. **15:24** We see where the attackers must have hidden earlier. There is insufficient space for all the attackers to be out of sight. **17:47** The group of Daleks moves across the ground with their bases obscured. From their gait, they appear to be walking cardboard Daleks. **18:48** The Daleks are not looking where they are going as they walk, not glide, along. **20:16** It is a good thing that the Movellens are not human; if they were human, Romana II is grabbing Commander Sharrel where it really hurts. **21:51** It appears that at least some shots of the two exploding Daleks are just shots, from a different angle, of the same Daleks exploding. **21:55** Three of the five Daleks disappear immediately before the explosion. These three must be the "real" Daleks. The explosions come from the ground, not from the Daleks. Slow motion is the best way to view this. **23:39** Why is the Movellan ship taking off with so much extra weight (dirt and rock on top)? Their engineers would not develop such an inefficient system. The ship should have a means of cleaning the top before liftoff. **24:16** Each time Romana II leans back the TARDIS door partly opens. Why do the Doctor and Romana II insist on moving all the debris when it is obvious they could already get into the TARDIS? **24:57** There appears to be no flashing light on top of the TARDIS. The long shot shows a flashing light. **24:57** It looks as if the bottom part of the TARDIS door is still open.

Comments: The Doctor defeats the Daleks and the Movellans.

(5H) CITY OF DEATH

Writer: David Agnew (Douglas Adams and Graham Williams); **Director:** Michael Hayes

Media: Commercial tape — episodic version — 100 minutes (used); Collector's tape — movie version — 92 minutes
Highlights: Paris
Questions: Why does the Egyptian scroll not show the hands of the Jagaroth?

Errors and Other Points of Interest

Episode 1
First Transmitted: Sept. 29, 1979

1:13 The glove on the wrist of Scaroth (Julian Glover) does not fit well. **1:40** The dust blows up as a stream from the ground towards the ship instead of down and away from the ship. **3:49** There is a classic quote here — when Romana II asks the Doctor where they are going the Doctor says, "You talking philosophically or geographically?" **8:05** Romana II and the Doctor examine the sketch Romana II picked up from the floor of the café. **9:34** This is a different sketch. Romana II did not pick up this particular sketch earlier. **11:59** Just before the time-slip in the Louvre, the tour guide attempts to get the Doctor's attention. She must walk around the Doctor when he turns the other direction. After the time-slip, it should be the same, but the tour guide does not walk around the Doctor. **20:48** There is a boom mike shadow on Hermann's (Kevin Flood) head as Hermann says to the Count, "The Detective and his friends, Excellency?"

Episode 2
First Transmitted: Oct. 6, 1979

0:40 During the reprise, and in the climax, the Doctor, Romana II, and Duggan (Tom Chadbon) leave the restaurant as a group. **1:12** Duggan is no longer part of the group going to the Count's house. **1:55** Duggan reappears inside Count Scarlioni's house. **6:31** Hermann (not the Count as reported) locks the Doctor, Romana II and Duggan in the basement. The Doctor is standing facing the lamp as Duggan lights it. The light brightens the Doctor's back instead of his side towards the light. **16:34** When Duggan hits the wall of the hidden room — not only does the wall to the hidden room shake, but the "solid" wall also shakes. **20:39** The Countess (Catherine Schell) has trouble not moving her eyelids.

Episode 3
First Transmitted: Oct. 13, 1979

4:43 Scaroth (the Count) tells the Doctor that his people died "400 million years" ago. The characters indicate that life began on Earth at this time. The time stated, 400 million years ago, would make it about the beginning of the Devonian (The Age of Fishes). The time should be between 4,000 and 5,000 million years ago. **8:16** We now find that the Doctor met Leonardo. This must be after the events in *The Masque of Mandragora*. The Doctor and Leonardo must have met in an untelevised adventure since the Doctor's previous televised visit to Italy. **14:03** Scaroth first hears of the Time Lords. It is apparent that the Doctor is the first to tell the Count. **20:11** It is unusual that one of the most famous sites in the world, the Louvre, does not have a crowd outside. This is especially true after the news about the theft of the Mona Lisa became public.

Episode 4
First Transmitted: Oct. 20, 1979

2:21 The Count continues with his assertion that his people died 400 million years ago. This continues throughout the remainder of the episode. **5:49** Romana II fixes Professor Kerensky's (David Graham) time machine using a British (3-pin) electric plug instead of a French plug. **9:22** The Doctor warns the Count not to try to change history. The Count replies, "What else do you ever do?" This is very extensive knowledge from a person who first heard of the Time Lords in the preceding episode, and the Count does not know the Doctor's history. However, we do not know the extent of the earlier discussion. **17:32** The Doctor throws the end of his scarf over his shoulder and hits Romana II in the face. **17:53** Before the advent of plants, the atmosphere would be unbreathable. At the beginning of the Devonian (400 million years ago) it might be breathable. It would not be breathable before life developed as indicated in the story. **19:06** The Doctor picks up some mud and tells Duggan it is "the amniotic fluid from which all life on Earth will spring...." This confirms that 400 million years ago are supposed to be before life developed on Earth.

Comments: The Doctor saves the Earth.

(5G) THE CREATURE FROM THE PIT

Writer: David Fisher; **Director:** Christopher Barry

Media: Commercial tape — episodic version — 97 minutes (used); Collector's tape — movie version — 90 minutes
Highlights: K9's new voice (David Brierley).
Questions: If Erato can force the bandits to bring the translator to the pit, why did he wait 15 years?

Errors and Other Points of Interest

Episode 1
First Transmitted: Oct. 27, 1979

3:28 The control console shakes as the Doctor asks where the TARDIS has materialized. **6:58** The soldier on the left starts to lower his weapon before Madame Karela (Eileen Way) commands, "Wait!" In the next shot, the soldier hits the ground with his sword. **19:53** After K9 shoots Torvin (John Bryans), the bandit turns to look for a good place to fall — then falls. **21:45** The guard attacking K9 and Romana II stops and is "hurt" before K9 fires. This occurs again in the reprise.

Episode 2
First Transmitted: Nov. 3, 1979

3:01 Why does the Doctor need a book to learn Tibetan? See, for example, *Planet of the Spiders*. **16:27** The first good view of K9's left side since *The Armageddon Factor* shows that the extra panel has disappeared. **19:17** K9 explains that TARDIS means "Time And Relative Dimensions In Space."

Episode 3
First Transmitted: Nov. 10, 1979

12:04 Note the size of the piece of shell the Doctor steals with his scarf. **12:32** Romana II tells Organon (Geoffrey Bayldon) the Doctor was born "about 750 years ago." **16:23** The Doctor says, "Time Lords have ninety lives." This could be analogous to saying a cat has nine lives, but it makes one wonder.

Episode 4
First Transmitted: Nov. 17, 1979

10:17 The photon drive that the Doctor shows Romana II is larger than the piece he stole from the pit. **14:06** Unlike other times, the alien time units are not minutes and seconds. The Doctor must do the conversion. **14:50** If Erato spun a shell of aluminum, or a shell of anything, around the star, the total mass would increase. The increase in mass would increase, not decrease the gravity. **21:20** The Doctor looks over his shoulder to pick a place to fall when the TARDIS console explodes a few seconds later. **21:40** It is surprising that the hat stand remains upright no matter how much the TARDIS shakes. However, unlike other times the hat stand does lean over and straighten up as the TARDIS does likewise.

Comments: The Doctor saves the planet Chloris.

(5K) NIGHTMARE OF EDEN

Writer: Bob Baker; **Director:** Alan Bromly and Graham Williams

Media: Commercial tape — episodic version — 96 minutes (used); Collector's tape — movie version — 88 minutes
Highlights: "East" in Eden.

Errors and Other Points of Interest

Episode 1
First Transmitted: Nov. 24, 1979

3:26 The TARDIS doors open — the Doctor and Romana II exit close together. Romana II immediately closes the doors. How did K9 get outside? **3:38** The TARDIS doors seem partially open. **5:05** The Doctor tells Captain Rigg (David Daker) that he represents "Galactic Insurance and Salvage." **5:52** The Doctor has trouble saying "recreate." **6:54** The Captain reads the computer screen, which shows "Galactic Salvage and Insurance." He does not notice that the Doctor gave him the wrong name for the company. **8:33** The Doctor finds the vraxoin vial and pours some into his left hand to allow K9 to identify it. Since his left hand is now contaminated, anything he touches with it — such as his left pocket — will receive contamination. **9:09** The Doctor now places the vraxoin vial in his right coat pocket; if it is tightly sealed, minimal contamination should come from it. **9:13** Tryst (Lewis Fiander) undergoes a variety of accent changes — you need to pick your favorite spot. **12:11** The Captain informs the Doctor "Galactic went out of business twenty years ago." He does not tell the Doctor about the incorrect name. **15:29** Eden appears on the dial in the NNW position on the CET machine, by the red pointer. **18:42** Stott (Barry Andrews) removes the vraxoin from the unconscious Doctor's right pocket. **21:57** Notice that Romana II turns the dial to "Eden" in the upper right (ENE) position. **22:24** The line is already present showing where K9 will cut out the wall panel.

Episode 2
First Transmitted: Dec. 1, 1979

1:46 When K9 seals the wall panel, a hand comes up from the bottom to hold the panel in place. **3:39** The Doctor asks the Captain if there is any way to shield against the scanner. The Captain answers, "Any shield would be too small to hide any useful quantity of the stuff." The Captain pauses for a second as he realizes what he just said. **6:21** The Doctor leaves the TARDIS doors open. **7:04** The CET machine is not set on Eden. However, it should be since Eden is the last place projected. **8:51** As the Doctor prepares for his first attempt to separate the ships, he says, "Ready for another try?" **20:52** Some viewers often cite as a blooper the fact that Costa's (Peter Craze) scanner detects vraxoin in the Doctor's left pocket after the Doctor placed it in his right pocket. If the Doctor put his contaminated hand in his left pocket and kept the sealed (non-leaking) vial in his right pocket—then the scanner should have found the vraxoin in the Doctor's left pocket as it did. This scene also occurs in the reprise. **21:34** Does Romana II turn the CET machine to the correct position?

Episode 3
First Transmitted: Dec. 8, 1979

2:13 In the reprise of the preceding episode, Romana II turns the dial to a N-S position. She does not turn it to NNW. **9:35** Stott has trouble saying "expedition." **10:32** Stott points a nearly invisible gun at K9. **13:27** The Doctor says the Mandrel is "quite dead" and kicks the body. The next shot shows the "dead" Mandrel breathing heavily. **17:00** The "quite dead" Mandrel moves, then gets up and attacks the Doctor. **20:20** The TARDIS doors are still open.

Episode 4
First Transmitted: Dec. 15, 1979

1:54 No one knows how to pronounce Hecate. Compare this pronunciation to later. **2:59** The TARDIS doors are still open. **8:29** Fisk (Geoffrey Hinsliff) accidentally calls Tryst "Fisk" while they are talking. Some observers erroneously report this to be in Episode 3. **9:44** Dymond (Geoffrey Bateman) leaves his ship, and then Romana II and Della come around the corner. Where did K9 come from?" **10:13** The crewmember falls after K9's shot; this causes the crewmember's gun to break. **11:02** We get another example of how to pronounce Hecate. **14:05** The console explodes before the beam from the gun hits the console. **14:17** After the shot, Della (Jennifer Lonsdale) falls clutching her stomach. This would be okay, but the shot hit her in the shoulder. **18:07** The seam in the back of the last mandrill's costume opens and shows white as the beast enters "Eden." **22:47** After remaining open for nearly the entire story, the TARDIS doors are now mysteriously closed.

Comments: The Doctor saves the passengers and crew on the Empress.

(5L) THE HORNS OF NIMON

Writer: Anthony Read; **Director:** Kenny McBain

Media: Commercial tape—episodic version—101 minutes (used); Collector's tape—movie version—93 minutes (used)

Errors and Other Points of Interest

Some people consider the use of the metal grid panels on the floors to be a blooper.

Episode 1
First Transmitted: Dec. 22, 1979

3:04 The ship is definitely falling apart; the entire control console of the spaceship is very unstable. **7:24** K9's ears are not in alignment. This is not a blooper at this time. **9:33** K9's ears are back in alignment. This is still not a blooper. **9:46** No matter what Newton said—the Doctor and Romana II fall in opposite directions during the collision. **14:26** The Doctor interrupts Romana II's speech on singularities. **18:46** The Co-pilot (Malcolm Terris) steps on the Doctor's scarf as he is leaving. The scarf stretches, then pops loose. **19:29** K9 says, "Defense shields are inoperative" (shields plural — not "except on door"). How did the Doctor extrude the inoperative defense shield to leave and reenter the TARDIS? **24:36** The Doctor exclaims to K9, "That's not an asteroid; that's a planet."

Episode 2
First Transmitted: Dec. 29, 1979
   3:04 After the TARDIS hurls to safety, K9 falls over on his side, but the hat-stand is still standing. **3:23** The Doctor demotes the planet back to an asteroid. **9:56** Some people consider the sound effects of the broken TARDIS to be bloopers. **12:41** The bad CSO allows us to see part of the Co-pilot after he enters the Nimon's abode. **13:30** Soldeed's (Graham Crowden) crowd has difficulty in knowing when to cheer. **16:26** The view-screen in the TARDIS shows the Nimon's complex to have two very short and fat antennae. **20:48** There is a blooper reported that after the Doctor is pushed into the Nimon's abode, he can still be seen (especially his shoes) due to the bad CSO. There are bloopers in this observation — the Doctor jumps into the maze, he is not pushed, and the Doctor is wearing boots, not shoes. **46:48M** Bad editing or bad transmission leaves a black segment between the two episodes. This is not present in all Collectors' copies.

Episode 3
First Transmitted: Jan. 5, 1980
   2:20 There is a rip along the seam in the seat of the Co-pilot's pants. **2:48** The rip in the Co-pilots pants is gone. **4:21** One of K9's ears is backwards. They were both backwards after the collision with the asteroid, but they are both in position by the time the Doctor, Romana II and K9 had entered the other spaceship. Now, this is a blooper. **16:08** The antennae on the Nimon's complex are now long and thin. **19:10** Romana II refers to the invaders as "Nimons." Thus the plural of Nimon is Nimons.

Episode 4
First Transmitted: Jan. 12, 1980
   19:27 Seth (Simon Gipps-Kent) shoots Soldeed as the leader is pulling the lever to destroy the complex. Soldeed crumples to the floor and apparently dies. Does the weapon have a "stun" setting? **19:40** When told to rescue the others, Seth replies, "But they're dead!" The Doctor tells Seth they are still alive, but paralyzed. At this time, one of the "paralyzed" or "dead" prisoners indicates that he is still alive by moving his leg. **23:52** Just before the complex explodes, a shot of the lever shows that Soldeed's body is no longer on the floor. This is a problem unless the weapon has a "stun" setting. **25:27** The Doctor tells Romana II that he is glad he reminded them to paint the ship white. **26:06** There is a claimed blooper that the plural of Nimon is Nimon. This is clearly not the case when listening to the actors and reading the closing credits. The plural is Nimons.

   Comments: The Doctor saves the planet of Skonnos.

(5M) SHADA

Writer: Douglas Adams; **Director:** Pennant Roberts

Media: Commercial tape — episodic version — 106 minutes (used)
Highlights: Tom Baker, as the Doctor, narrates the missing sections. This is a Fourth Doctor story with Seventh Doctor music.
Questions: If it takes Skagra three months to reach the Earth by ship — why are the scientists he left behind so old?

Errors and Other Points of Interest

Episode 1
First Transmitted

0:00 Timing begins with the Doctor Who opening, and not with the opening narration by Tom Baker. **0:55** We see the countdown on the monitor; each number change has a sound effect. Keep track of the sound effects. **1:25** Based on the sound effects the number on the monitor should read "VI." **11:08** Wilkins (Gerald Campion), the porter, reminds the Doctor of his degree from Cambridge in 1960. **16:33** The man walking down to street to his car stops walking as if waiting for his cue to continue.

Episode 2
First Transmitted

3:33 Professor Chronotis (Denis Carey) exclaims that it was "Young Parsons" who borrowed the book. No one mentions Parsons' first name. **7:40** After the sphere emerges from the bag, the Professor appears to be wearing disappearing glasses. Views from the front show him not wearing glasses, and in views from the side, the Professor is wearing glasses. **8:40** Romana II addresses Parsons (Daniel Hill) as "Chris Parsons." Romana II has never heard Chris's first name. **10:36** Romana II explains to Parsons that the collar will take over for the autonomic brain. The collar, not the Professor's brain, will control his hearts and breathing. **11:02** The Doctor learns that the book is 20,000 years old. This dates the Time of Rassilon. **13:16** It appears as if Romana II is leading up to "forty-two." **13:32** Some viewers report a blooper — they claim that after K9 pronounces the Professor dead, the Professor appears to be breathing. This is not a blooper because the collar that Romana II put on the Professor is to keep him breathing, even though he may be brain dead.

Episode 3
First Transmitted

1:46 The TARDIS leaves with the Doctor's scarf caught in the door. This is probably intentional, but some people believe it to be an error. **2:55** Romana II tells the Doctor the Professor warned her about Shada. The Doctor seems to forget about this warning. **5:24** The lighting changes from before the TARDIS appears to alter after the ship appears. **10:56** Clare Keightley (Victoria Burgoyne) drops her books before, not after, she runs into Wilkins. The porter is not the cause of her dropping the books. There are incorrect reports that this is in Episode 1. **13:46** Skagra (Christopher Neame) forces Romana II into the TARDIS. In his haste, he leaves the TARDIS key in the door.

Episode 4
First Transmitted

2:26 The Narrating Doctor says he ordered the ship back to its last destination.

The ship was already at its last destination. He should have sent the ship to its last embarkation point. **4:08** Clare hits her head on the table as she begins to rise. This may not be a blooper.

Episode 5
First Transmitted

8:14 The Doctor must again learn about Shada. **12:34** Why does Skagra need to drain the Professor's mind a second time? K9 said the extraction was complete the first time.

Episode 6
First Transmitted

1:34 The Doctor, Romana II and Clare enter the Professor's room (his TARDIS), and the Doctor tells K9 to enter, but there is no sound of K9's motor. Later K9 is in the room. **4:14** There is something sticking out of the bottom of the TARDIS model.

Comments: This is much shorter than a normal six-part story, and is present in this list even though not transmitted.

The Doctor saves the Universe.

(5N) The Leisure Hive

Writer: David Fisher; **Director:** Lovett Bickford

Media: DVD — episodic version — 87 minutes (used); Commercial tape — episodic version — 87 minutes; Collector's tape — movie version — 77 minutes
Highlights: The Doctor told Sarah Jane about Time Lords understanding other languages in *The Masque of Mandragora*, so why are the Doctor and Romana II unable to understand the Foamasi?

Errors and Other Points of Interest

Episode 1
First Transmitted: Aug. 30, 1980

2:18 Wires pull K9 along the beach. **7:06** Brock (John Collin) declines membership on the Board and any further investment. Brock seems definite. **8:24** No one seems surprised by Brock's sudden appearance and his acceptance of a position on the Board. In light of Brock's earlier refusal, this seems unlikely especially given how suspicious some of the Argolins are. **13:45** The green cut in the wall seems to "growing" from both ends. **16:11** Some observers question Brock's interest in Hardin's (Nigel Lambert) experiments. They feel he should be interested in stopping the experiments instead. However, this is incorrect; he should be interested in this potential threat to his plans. On the other hand, if he knows the experiments to be fakes, he should encourage further work to stretch Argolin finances beyond the breaking point. **17:47** The holographic projection of Hardin's experiments begins. Watch the woman's necklace. Some observers claim this to be a blooper, while it is really a plot point. **18:40** The holographic show ends. **18:46** The Doctor and Romana II enter the conference room. **19:11** The Doctor claims to have seen part of the holographic projection even though he and Romana II entered the room after the show was over. **19:31** Romana II and the Doctor discuss the experiment they did not see. **20:10** The Doctor and Romana II observe that they recognized that the experiment was a fake because the necklace changed.

Episode 2
First Transmitted: Sept. 6, 1980
2:39 The end of the sonic screwdriver is extremely bent. Did the Doctor use it as a hammer to knock a hole in the back wall? **5:11** The Doctor refers to radon-222 decaying rapidly. This is true, but irrelevant after forty years. Radon-222 decays too rapidly to be a significant problem after a month or two unless continuously re-supplied. **12:30** Stimson (David Allister) hurries down the hall wearing his glasses. The glasses, for no apparent reason, simply fall off unnoticed.

Episode 3
First Transmitted: Sept. 13, 1980
1:50 During the reprise, the Doctor emerges from the booth much older and much hairier. **11:18** Pangol (David Haig) is the first to mention The West Lodge. **17:03** The Doctor is temporarily "1250 years old." **13:55** Romana states that if she ages 500 years she will be 650. This implies that she is 150. Some viewers consider this an inconsistency, since she was 140 in *The Ribos Operation* and 125 in *City of Death*. This assumes the stories are sequential and in real time. **17:25** Why does the Time Lord's Gift not work?

Episode 4
First Transmitted: Sept. 20, 1980

3:02 Just how did Brock and Klout (Ian Talbot), his assistant, manage to fit their bulky Foamasi bodies into the smaller Earth clothes? **3:07** The Foamasi (Andrew Lane) informs everyone, "I'm the Foamasi Government," instead of saying, "I'm from the Foamasi Government." Later he says that he is an ambassador. **5:07** Why are Mena's (Adrienne Corri) attendants following the Doctor and the others instead of staying with Mena? **13:21** If all persons exiting the generator are supposed to be identical, why are their heights different? **16:39** The Doctor emerges from the booth a second time. Now he has returned to his original age. However, his hair ("dead" matter) should not have returned to its original style and length. Dead matter would not become youthful again. **16:39** The Doctor is dressed as Pangol. The Doctor does not appear to be wearing his regular clothes underneath. **17:15** Where did the Doctor get his own clothes? If they were under the yellow clothes, the Doctor would not need to be changing into them. **17:36** Where did all the extra helmets on the floor come from—the Doctor was only wearing one (the others disappeared with his other selves). **19:48** It is possible to see the light through the window in the side of the TARDIS as the Doctor opens the door.

Comments: The Doctor saves the planet of Argolis.

(5Q) MEGLOS

Writer: John Flanagan and Andrew McCulloch; **Director:** Terence Dudley

Media: Commercial tape—episodic version—87 minutes (used); Collector's tape—movie version—77 minutes
Highlights: We see the return of Barbara.

Errors and Other Points of Interest

Some viewers report a blooper that during Episode 1 it is possible to see a wire holding one of the planets in place while the ship carries Meglos and the others through space. There are no views of any planets, at any time, from the ship. Thus, no wires or planets make an appearance as described.

Episode 1
First Transmitted: Sept. 27, 1980

6:07 We learn the solution to the mystery of why the TARDIS hat stand resists falling. K9's manual is helping to support it. **8:37** The ruffian on the Earthling's left trips. **10:22** General Grugger (Bill Fraser) expresses a question posed by many fans — "Why would you send across the galaxy for a thing like that?" Why does Meglos need an Earthling when both Tigellans and the Captain's crew are readily available? **15:29** The Doctor says that he did not see the Dodecahedron on his earlier visit because of religious objections. **18:17** The reflection of another person appears in the glass in front of Meglos. **19:58** Some of the words on the screen below the Doctor's picture do not make sense. What is a "DATEB?" Either all the words should make sense, or none of them should make sense. (Apparently, DATEB is date of birth, but this coding does not match the format of other items on the screen.) **22:33M** The Doctor says, "That's the third time."

Episode 2
First Transmitted: Oct. 4, 1980

0:43 Meglos traps the TARDIS in a "chronic hysteretic loop." **23:19M** The Doctor again says, "That's the third time." This is due to a problem in editing the climax and reprise parts of the first two episodes into a movie. **1:33** The Doctor tells Romana II that they are in "chronic hysteresis." Romana II agrees. Either the Doctor or Meglos got the name wrong. This could be two technobabble phrases for the same thing. **12:02** Romana II goes back to close the door of the TARDIS. When the Doctor, Romana II and K9 walk away, you can see that the door is still partially open. **17:04** This is one of the times, the cactus gloves appear on Meglos' wrists (as he appears mimicking the Doctor). **17:52** As Meglos (appearing as the Doctor) backs out of sight, the wall to his left wall wobbles.

Episode 3
First Transmitted: Oct. 11, 1980

4:18 Romana II goes off screen to the left, all the people "following" her go off screen to the right. **4:55** Even though the Doctor previously says that he did not see the Dodecahedron before, now he recalls seeing it. **9:18** Some observers wonder what Caris (Colette Gleeson) is looking at as she exclaims, "That's impossible!" **16:32** Three apparently dead crewmembers are on the floor. **18:30** We hear a cough offstage as Meglos shows Brotadac (Frederick Treves) and says, "This ought to replace the odd torn jacket." **19:29** For the most part the ropes do not burn — so why use the torch? The ropes "break" as if they have been roughly cut.

Episode 4
First Transmitted: Oct. 18, 1980

3:48 General Grugger complains to Meglos about losing 50 percent of his crew on Tigella. Meglos says that three men are not important. This indicates that the original crew was six men and that three remain. **5:05** Upon their return to Zolfa-Thura, we find that there are at least six crewmembers present, not three. Some observers incorrectly list this as an Episode 1 blooper. **8:59** The "Doctor" gives away his coat. **10:12** The Doctor takes his coat off to give it away after seeing the "Doctor." **11:29** The Doctor gives his coat away. **15:06** Why not let K9 stun the guard in the first place, instead of waiting until after Deedrix's (Crawford Logan) unsuccessful attempt? **17:50** The Doctor still has his coat even though he gave it away. This may not be a blooper even though there are reports to the contrary. This is not the first destruction/disappearance of the Doctor's coat (for example in *Nightmare of Eden*), and he still has one in the next episode. The TARDIS wardrobe must have many coats.

Comments: Some lists spell Zolfa-Thura as Zolpha-Thura.

The Doctor saves the planet of Zolfa-Thura.

The E-Space Trilogy

(5R) FULL CIRCLE

Writer: Andrew Smith; **Director:** Peter Grimwade

Media: Commercial tape — part of the E-Space Trilogy Collection — episodic version — 93 minutes (used); Collector's tape — movie version — 84 minutes
Highlights: Adric (Matthew Waterhouse) joins the TARDIS crew.

Errors and Other Points of Interest

Episode 1
First Transmitted: Oct. 25, 1980

1:30 Romana II is concerned that the Time Lords want her to return. The Doctor reminds Romana II that she "only came to help with the Key to Time." This implies that the Time Lords know about the White Guardian sending the Doctor and Romana II on their quest. **18:03** When Romana II asks the Doctor, "What was that noise?" there are reports that there is a fly buzzing around the Doctor's head.

Episode 2
First Transmitted: Nov. 1, 1980

1:14 There is a hole in Adric's left pants leg. **2:13** This is one of the many times where we see that the Marshmen have sleeves with cuffs. **7:40** This is one of the few times where we see the hat stand actually fall. **8:55** Why have a "doorbell" if no one will answer the door? **12:29** Romana II says the TARDIS weighs "five times ten to the sixth kilos" (5×10^6 kilos). One source has translated this to 50,000 tonnes. However, 50,000 tonnes is 5×10^7 kilos. This is how false bloopers begin. For the physicists — Romana II uses kilo(gram)s, then specifies "in your gravity." Kilogram is a mass, not a weight, unit, and hence is independent of gravity. **12:46** How can the Marshmen move an object weighing 5×10^6 kilos? **13:13** It is possible to see the back wall inside the TARDIS as Romana II begins to close the doors.

Episode 3
First Transmitted: Nov. 8, 1980

6:54 Adric crosses his fingers after the Doctor tells him to do so. The first two views of Adric crossing his fingers show him using one finger from each hand before he gets it correct. Some viewers report that in one shot, Adric crosses his fingers in one way and from a different angle, he crosses them differently. **15:48** As the Doctor pulls the manuals from the shelf, he nearly knocks out the back panel of the console.

Episode 4
First Transmitted: Nov. 15, 1980
  2:47 The TARDIS door, to the right of the screen, is ajar. **4:37** We see a closed right door of the TARDIS, but now it appears that the left door may be ajar. **5:35** The Doctor puts one of K9's "ears" on backwards (both "ears" are on correctly later). **16:23** Romana II says 4,000 generations. This or what the Doctor says later is a blooper. **18:59** The Doctor says 40,000 generations. Was it the Doctor or Romana II who made the blooper? **17:01** The "dead" Tylos (Bernard Padden) moves his head with all the gas blowing on him. **22:14** Many fans question why the technology of Gallifrey is interchangeable with that of Alzarius and/or Terradon. It is possible that one or more Time Lord Ships entered E-Space in search of vampires (see *State of Decay*), and they brought Time Lord Technology to E-Space.
  Comments: The Doctor saves the inhabitants of Alzarius.

(5P) STATE OF DECAY

Writer: Terrance Dicks; **Director:** Peter Moffatt

Media: Commercial tape — part of the E-Space Trilogy Collection — episodic version — 95 minutes (used); Collector's tape — movie version — 87 minutes
Questions: If the fuel tanks are still full of blood, what has the King Vampire been using for food?

Errors and Other Points of Interest

Episode 1
First Transmitted: Nov. 22, 1980
  4:32 There is a crack at the top of K9's left side panel. A light flashes through this crack. The crack is there later but not the flashing lights. **9:37** The hole in Adric's pants has developed a patch.

Episode 2
First Transmitted: Nov. 29, 1980
  2:21 There is a claimed blooper in that the Doctor says the décor is rococo when it is Saxon/early Romanesque. The Doctor's actual quote is, "Would you call it rococo?" Romana II replies that it is not. Since the Doctor asked a question instead of making a statement — it is not a blooper. **10:02** Romana II runs through the names of the Hydrax officers. The Doctor tops off the list with "Very good!" Apparently, Romana II had a lot of trouble with this list during rehearsal. **13:40** We cannot hear the heartbeat while the Doctor and Romana II are climbing to the control room. **15:32** We still cannot hear a heartbeat while the Doctor and Romana II are climbing to the control room. **17:01** While in the cabin of the scout ship, the Doctor and Romana II first hear the heartbeat of the King Vampire. Why could the Time Lords not hear the heartbeat while ascending to the control room? **17:46** The descending Time Lords can now hear the heartbeat of the King Vampire, even though they could not hear it when ascending the same ladders.

Episode 3
First Transmitted: Dec. 6, 1980
  7:01 Something flies out of their hands as Camilla (Rachel Davies) and Zargo (William Lindsay) pull their hands apart. **10:47** Tarak (Thane Bettany) breaks into the cell

imprisoning the Doctor and Romana II. At this time, Tarak hits the Doctor in the face. There are erroneous reports that this is in Episode 1. **14:39** This is the first of several shots of the boom mike shadow on the TARDIS console while the Doctor and K9 are talking. **18:22** The Doctor removes the printout much faster than the printer is printing. **20:11** This is a better example of the Doctor removing the printout too fast. **22:39** According to Rassilon (as read by the Doctor), a steel "arrow" through the heart of a vampire will kill the vampire. **22:47** If a steel arrow through the heart kills a vampire, why does the steel knife Adric throws not kill Zargo (William Lindsay)? Note: there is no blood on the extracted knife.

Episode 4
First Transmitted: Dec. 13, 1980

12:28 K9's "ears" are out of alignment. **12:30** Some of the "dead" guards move so K9 can get pass them. **15:14** We can no longer hear the heartbeat in the upper shafts or in the scout ships. **18:18** As the rebels exit the throne room one of the rebels kicks a "dead" guard; the guard then repositions his leg. **19:27** As the scout ship turns to drop back down it seems to suspend the laws of physics. When the ship is horizontal, with the engines still firing, there should be a significant horizontal movement. The ship should make an arc instead of going straight up and straight down. If the engines stopped and a side thrust flipped the ship over then the flight path shown could result. **23:11** There are blooper claims because some fans wonder why Kalmar (Arthur Hewlett) would want to "get back" to Earth when neither he nor his people have been there. The Doctor states that the Great Vampire brought Kalmar's ancestors to the planet. Apparently, they were the crew of the Earth ship serving under the three officers. The survivors apparently have so many bad memories of the planet that they want to go anywhere else.

Comments: The Doctor saves the Universe.

(5S) WARRIOR'S GATE

Writer: Steve Gallagher; **Director:** Paul Joyce

Media: Commercial tape — part of the E-Space Trilogy Collection — episodic version — 94 minutes (used); Collector's tape — movie version — 84 minutes
Highlights: Romana II and K9 leave the series.

Errors and Other Points of Interest

Episode 1
First Transmitted: Jan. 3, 1981

10:41 Adric's pants share his healing powers. The hole, which became a patch in *State Of Decay*, is now completely "healed." **19:20** The metal manacle around Biroc's (David Weston) left arm can easily be seen. **19:48** The manacle is no longer around Biroc's arm. This allows him to drop it on the floor. **20:21** Captain Rorvik (Clifford Rose) appears to read the back of the printout. There are no (other than in the reprise) later scenes with the mass detector producing a printout.

Episode 2
First Transmitted: Jan. 10, 1981

3:42 Romana II has trouble pronouncing her name. **7:48** After the two Gundans attacking the Doctor destroy each other, the one on the right of the screen drops his axe on the Doctor's back, and it simple bounces off with no damage. **11:03** Adric takes one of K9's ears to triangulate better. The two of them separate before Adric has an opportunity to replace the ear. There are incorrect reports that this occurs in Episodes 3 and 4. **14:57** K9's ear has regenerated. **20:41** The mirror does not seem to be very steady — the stage crew should find a better way to attach it to the wall.

Episode 3
First Transmitted: Jan. 17, 1981

3:16 Some fans propose a blooper concerning K9's application of Newton's Third Law. The argument is that Newton's Third Law would not be applicable in a contracting system with a mass instability. The contracting system would produce an additional acceleration on anyone not at the center of mass. It is possible to bypass this by saying — the difference in acceleration, and hence the variations from Newtonian physics, depend on the relative differences in the distances of the two objects from the center of gravity. At this point, the center of mass may be sufficiently distant so the deviation is still minimal. However, this is irrelevant since the storyline establishes that K9 is not working properly, and therefore anything he says may be wrong. **6:48** K9 appears to have lost his ear again. **8:58** K9's empty interior is visible when Packard (Kenneth Cope) swings K9 up to throw him out of the ship. The Doctor and Adric do this to K9 later. **10:13** A boom mike makes its appearance. Apparently, with crewmembers on the stairs and at the foot of the stairs there was no convenient position to place the boom mike out of sight. The boom mike appears in the lower screen — from behind the cloth covering the weapon. **10:13** Some observers report a blooper concerning the appearance of a boom mike while Adric and Romana are hiding beneath the cover of the weapon. While this is included as a blooper separate from the above on some lists, it really appears to be a re-listing of the preceding blooper. **14:29** Romana II learns the ship is made of dwarf star alloy. Some fans consider this a blooper. In reality, this is technobabble. In addition, this is not pure dwarf star material — it is an alloy. **20:10** One of the Tharils is supposed to hit the serving girl on the shoulder; he manages to hit her left breast on the way to her shoulder. **20:18** A Tharil at the table strikes a serving girl in the shoulder. The chivalrous Doctor jumps to her side. The camera follows the Doctor but overadjusts and must correct its position. This overshooting of the camera is a common though minor blooper.

Episode 4
First Transmitted: Jan. 24, 1981

7:22 As Biroc leaves, the reflection of another person moves onto the glass in front of the Doctor. **9:54** When everyone ducks, the entire TARDIS console shakes. **10:11** The Doctor seems to have a problem with his leg as he walks past the hat stand. **13:48** There is a boom mike shadow on Royce's shoulder while he is in the "storage" room getting ready to revive another Tharil. This repeats later. **21:31** Why does the back blast come from the back of the ruins and not from the back of the spaceship?

Comments: The camera overshooting in Episode 3 is an extreme example of a very common blooper. This type of situation normally occurs two or three times per episode. Such minor bloopers are normally not in this list. Only extreme or previously reported occurrences, such as this one, are present in this list.

(5T) THE KEEPER OF TRAKEN

Writer: Johnny Byrne; **Director:** John Black

Media: Commercial tape — episodic version — 98 minutes (used); Collector's tape — movie version — 89 minutes
Highlights: We see a new Master (Anthony Ainley), and the first appearance of Nyssa (Sarah Sutton).
Questions: The Doctor describes the Traken Union as being populated by kind and caring people — where are these people during the Doctor's visit?

Errors and Other Points of Interest

Episode 1
First Transmitted: Jan. 31, 1981
12:53 The Doctor gives Adric a time log to examine; however, most of the pages are blank. Besides, when did Adric learn to read Gallifreyan? Is this another example of the Time Lords' Gift? **20:24** The set partially rearranges as the TARDIS disappears. Do not mistake the elimination of the TARDIS shadow as rearrangement of the ground.

Episode 2
First Transmitted: Feb. 7, 1981
5:53 The camera shakes as Kassia (Sheila Ruskin) starts to move the second dead Foster. **20:51** Kassia's has her eyelids painted as red eyes.

Episode 3
First Transmitted: Feb. 14, 1981
9:24 Watch the end of the Doctor's nose while he, Adric and Tremas (Anthony Ainley) are imprisoned. Some observers incorrectly report that the Doctor and the Master were in the cell, but the Master is still inside the Melkur (Geoffrey Beevers and Graham Cole). **11:29** The escapees are in plain sight of the pursuing Fosters, yet the pursuers turn down another corridor. **11:58** As the escapees run down the corridor, the shadow of another person moves over the unconscious Fosters. **21:18** The Master's teeth appear painted on his lips.

Episode 4
First Transmitted: Feb. 21, 1981
16:32 There is a very large shadow on Nyssa that moves shortly before she stands. **18:52** As the Master approaches the Doctor, the camera shakes. **19:25** The Master regenerated at the end of *The Deadly Assassin*, but now he appears to have had a relapse. He states that he is nearing the end of his twelfth regeneration. **21:06** The Doctor tells Adric to enter the number "3-3-7," apparently to finish unlocking the door. Adric pushes one button twice and the wind blows him away, but the doors open anyway. The Doctor enters the seven after he escapes. **23:14** The reflection of a camera and several members of the production crew appear in the front of the clock door as the Master opens and closes the door. **23:33** We see the "new" Master — supposedly his thirteenth incarnation. **23:52** The Doctor and Adric are in the TARDIS and Nyssa is still on Traken looking for her father. They did not leave together.

Comments: The Doctor saves the Traken Union and defeats the Master.

(5V) Logopolis

Writer: Christopher H. Bidmead; **Director:** Peter Grimwade

Media: Commercial tape — episodic version — 98 minutes (used); Collector's tape — movie version — 92 minutes

Highlights: Tegan (Janet Fielding) and Nyssa are added and the Fourth Doctor is subtracted. We get a glimpse of the Fifth Doctor.

Questions: Tegan sees and enters a "Police Box" — how does she know it is a ship and not a Police Box that is being transported on another vehicle?

Errors and Other Points of Interest

There are many noted discrepancies about which lever opens the TARDIS door.

Episode 1
First Transmitted: Feb. 28, 1981

0:55 Some viewers find fault with the counterproductive sign by the trash receptacle — "Take Your Litter Home." **8:46** Adric and the Doctor discuss that the TARDIS chameleon circuit became stuck in "Totter's Yard." **10:04** The dubbing of the Doctor saying "But since we left Traken..." is very bad. **11:21** The Doctor is preparing to move the TARDIS to examine the police box. Adric reaches toward the usual red lever. The Doctor says, "No, no, no — don't open the door." Adric replies, "Aren't we going out there to measure it?" This confirms that the lever controlling the TARDIS doors is still the red lever. **12:02** There is a creak and the camera shifts position. **12:18** This is the first appearance of the Watcher (Adrian Gibbs) in the distance. Unfortunately, Peter Davidson does not play the Watcher. **15:16** Upon hearing a noise, the Doctor goes to the TARDIS console and uses the red lever, moving it up and a little later down, with no effect on the doors. **15:40** The Doctor uses the black lever with the green handle to open the door. **19:37** Tegan says, "My neem — my name's Tegan Jovanka."

Episode 2
First Transmitted: Mar. 7, 1981

0:49 Some viewers question why the police think that the dolls are corpses without any proof that they were not dolls. This is not entirely true — the police officers never indicate that the dolls are corpses; they are investigating an unusual situation. **1:26** Adric leaves the TARDIS with wet pants, even though they are not supposed to get wet until the bicycle "accident." **7:35** When the Doctor and Adric are shutting everything down the Doctor uses the black and green lever with no noticeable effect on the doors. **8:40** When the Doctor materializes "underwater," Adric opens the doors by putting his finger into the green and gray hollow button and later closes the doors the same way. **12:22** The green and gray hollow button closes the door. **14:50** Tegan — "Doctor Who-ever you are?" **22:07** Nyssa appears and joins the TARDIS crew. **22:15** Tegan sounds jealous when asking Adric — "Who's Nyssa?"

Episode 3
First Transmitted: Mar. 14, 1981

0:43 The shrinking TARDIS has only one door handle instead of the two handles on the full size TARDIS. The full size TARDIS has one of the handles on the main door and the other is on the telephone door. This handle discrepancy occurs at other times. **1:09** This TARDIS has an extra door handle on the backside — no notice is present on the door. **1:45** The model the Logopolitans are carrying has only one door handle instead of the two handles as on the full size TARDIS. **3:19** When Adric and the Monitor (John Fraser) enter through the doors, it is obvious that the room and the people behind them are only a picture. **11:19** As the Master pulls his hand away from the bracelet he gives Nyssa, a part falls on the ground. **22:54** It is possible to see light through one of the TARDIS interior windows.

Episode 4
First Transmitted: Mar. 21, 1981

3:39 The Master nods a cue to Tegan for her to notice the dying Monitor. **3:44** When the Monitor, like many other people, finds out his world is about to end — he goes to pieces. **6:45** The Master's TARDIS must have a faulty chameleon circuit also, as it does not blend in with its background. **11:41** Adric uses the red lever again. It still has not recovered its door opening function, but now Adric uses it to send the TARDIS back to the Universe. **11:43** Adric pushes the red lever up, but it begins to fall back — he covers this by moving it back down. Adric does this after saying, "Hold on, we're going back!" though there are misquotes. **12:03** There are several tall bushes in close proximity to the TARDIS. **12:14** Adric again uses the green and grey hollow button to open the door. **12:22** The TARDIS has landed in an area surrounded by bushes and weeds. The TARDIS is in a different locality in *Castrovalva*, and different from a few seconds earlier. **12:29** Nyssa leaves the TARDIS door open. **20:19** The Doctor leaves the control room of the radio telescope, and the Master follows. The Doctor sets a trap with his scarf, and trips the Master. Then the Doctor is wearing his scarf. The Doctor does not really have time to set his trap, nor time to recover and put on his scarf. **20:42** The image of the Master looking from the control room is obviously not a person but a picture. **21:38** The Doctor removes the plug and the sparks go sideways instead of "down." This is because of tilting of the camera — not the telescope. **22:27** When the Master enters his TARDIS, the shadow remains after dematerialization. The shadow could be due to other objects in the room. **22:48** The Doctor dies with his boots on. **23:55** The Doctor's boots have regenerated into shoes, or much shorter boots.

Comments: The Doctor defeats the Master and saves the Universe (at least most of it).

The light on top of the Master's Police Box does not flash.

V

THE FIFTH DOCTOR

(5Z) Castrovalva

Writer: Christopher H. Bidmead; **Director:** Fiona Cumming

Media: Commercial tape — episodic version — 96 minutes (used); Collector's tape — movie version — 85 minutes
Highlights: The New Doctor takes over.

Errors and Other Points of Interest

Some observers consider the fact that the Security Guards do not descend from the telescope to be a blooper. Count the number of Guards ascending.

Episode 1
First Transmitted: Jan. 4, 1982

0:00 This is not a blooper — the start of Episode 1 is a reprise of the end of Logopolis before the normal title sequence. The Fourth Doctor is wearing his boots. This is also where timing of the episode starts. **1:37** The Doctor's boots have regenerated into shoes. **1:44** The TARDIS is no longer in the same field as in Logopolis. The field the about the TARDIS is mostly grass. **2:04** There are different security guards pursuing Adric, Nyssa and Tegan in this story than in Logopolis. **3:54** Nyssa uses the red lever to close the TARDIS doors, and says, "This works the doors. That's all I know about these controls." Compare this to the lever blooper cited in Logopolis. **4:01** There is a blooper report concerning the presence of Tegan and Nyssa's handbags on the TARDIS console. Only Tegan's handbag is present. **7:16** The Doctor has question mark symbols on each of his collars. These are facing in the "correct" direction as "??." **12:14** There are reports citing the Doctor looking into the mirror as a blooper. The claim is that in order for the Doctor to be looking into the mirror, he must be staring at a wall behind him. This is a blooper, if it is correct, or at least a bad presentation. To accomplish this effect you must remember, "The angle of incidence equals the angle of reflection." **17:31** Some fans consider the levitating of the Doctor's coat tails in the zero room a blooper. Why is this a blooper? **18:24** There is a reversal of the question mark on the Doctor's collar. **19:53** Some viewers find fault with the Master telling Adric, "If escape were that easy Adric, we could all be free of this nasty world." These viewers feel that universe or some other large unit should replace "world." This would be out of character for the Master; he has repeatedly referred to the Earth in this way. **20:45** The question mark symbols on the Doctor's collars have now returned to the "correct" orientation. **21:45** The information for the TARDIS Databank refers to hydrogen in terms of the periodic table, and gives additional correct information. The screen goes on to refer to the Big Bang as "Scientific Mythology." Really?

Episode 2
First Transmitted: Jan. 5, 1982

8:08 The Doctor tells Tegan and Nyssa that they will jettison 25 percent of the TARDIS. **11:56** For some reason a few viewers find a problem with the first references to Castrovalva. The TARDIS Databank says: "Castrovalva, the central habitation of the planet that forms the Andromedan Phylox Series." These viewers report that Nyssa reads "One of the planets that forms the Andromedan Phylox." Nyssa's quote should read: "Dwellings of Simplicity — Castrovalva. Where's that?" **12:33** The false quote earlier may be from Nyssa's explanation to the Doctor when she tells him about Castrovalva — "It's in Andromeda — a small planet of the Phylox Series." **20:06** As Nyssa passes under a branch, while helping to carry the zero cabinet, she catches her tiara in a branch, and she loses her tiara. Neither Nyssa nor Tegan notice the loss of the tiara.

Episode 3
First Transmitted: Jan. 11, 1982

17:22 Some observers consider Nyssa's use of the term "telebiogenesis" to be a blooper. This is a technobabble term, so this is not a blooper. The word may have a different meaning in Traken. **17:48** Some viewers have found fault with the Doctor referring to the tapestry as "some form of fast particle projection." These viewers argue that light is made of photons not particles; therefore, the Doctor should not have used the term particle. The problem with this argument is that, simplistically, photons are particles of light. **22:46** Neil Toynay plays the Portreeve. Neil Toynay is an anagram for Tony Ainley. An anagram is present to disguise the fact that the Master is still in the story. To aid in this charade, we also see a separate listing for The Master in the credits.

Episode 4
First Transmitted: Jan. 12, 1982

4:33 There are claims that the clothes the people are washing are not wet. This may not be a blooper — the main purpose of their actions concerns concealing the zero box, not cleaning clothes. **4:41** Mergrave (Michael Sheard) enters and tells the Doctor, "Here are the other fifteen volumes." The two people carrying the books are not carrying fifteen volumes. **7:37** We hear the sound of Nyssa knocking on the door before she actually knocks on the door. **15:24** Mergrave and Ruther (Frank Wylie) go and search for the broken window. Just before the camera switches to a different shot, the back wall begins to collapse. **15:33** Pay close attention to the edge of the broken glass near the Doctor's head. **15:42** When Mergrave and Ruther go to see the cause of the noise, the camera wobbles. **20:09** As the group is attempting to escape Castrovalva, Adric cries, "I can see!" He then shouts, "Over there — the hillside!" Adric then points to the left, and the group starts in that direction. This is supposedly a blooper. The first quote may refer to the fact that since Adric created Castrovalva, he can see within its confines. Adric's comment illustrates this: "What exactly am I looking for, Doctor?" Adric may or may not need to look in a particular direction to "see." **21:40** Some fans consider the appearance of a fence on the deserted planet to be a blooper. It appears in the background and the Doctor, Tegan, Nyssa, and Adric are jogging down the path. It is never been proven that this is a deserted planet. There are other signs that this is not a completely uninhabited planet. **21:55** The Doctor acquires his celery stalk.

Comments: The New Doctor defeats the Master.

(5W) Four to Doomsday

Writer: Terence Dudley; **Director:** John Black

Media: Commercial tape — episodic version — 97 minutes (used); Collector's tape — movie version — 89 minutes
Questions: If the Urbankans have not been to Earth for 2500 years, how do they know modern English and French?

Errors and Other Points of Interest

Episode 1
First Transmitted: Jan. 18, 1982

2:18 Adric saying "Galaxia Kyklos" is not a blooper; it is Greek for the Milky Way. **6:22** Some fans question what could possibly increase the density of something. The statement is technobabble. For example, one answer to this question is a refrigerator. Cooling water from the boiling point to 4°C (39°F) increases the density of the water. An increase in the density allows additional mass to be stored in the same volume. **7:27** The spare TARDIS key is a "normal" key. **9:06** The Doctor demonstrates that there is a magnetic shield around the monopticon (at about 12 to 18 inches). **9:57** The doors of the TARDIS are not open; as shown later this sometimes means locked. (Why would the Doctor bother to give Tegan a key if the doors were unlocked?) The Doctor takes Tegan with him — now no one left behind is able to get into the TARDIS, since the Doctor and Tegan have the only keys. **11:54** Adric opens the TARDIS doors. This means the closed doors are unlocked. Why did the Doctor worry about giving Tegan a key to the TARDIS? This time the closed doors are locked and not unlocked. **13:23** We learn that the Urbankans were last on Earth about 2500 years ago. **14:16** Tegan begins sketching. **15:38** On leaving, Adric simply pulls the doors shut. If pulling the doors shut does not lock them, what will keep Monarch out later? If pulling the TARDIS doors shut locks the doors, then how did Adric get into the TARDIS? **17:13** Tegan finishes her sketch. If Tegan can produce fashion sketches so quickly, and so well — why does she want to be a stewardess? Some observers cite this as an Episode 2 blooper. **18:22** Monarch (Stratford Johns) enters the storeroom to examine the TARDIS. The head of a production crewmember pokes up to the left side of the instrument in the foreground. **18:26** Monarch cannot open the TARDIS doors — "proof" that simply pushing the doors closed, as Adric did, causes them to lock. **19:52** If Bigon (Philip Locke) and the others speak English, why does Kurkuyji (the Aborigine played by Illarrio Bisi Pedro) not speak English also? Kurkuyji has had more time, and besides, he is a robot. **19:59** Some fans pose the question — out of thousands of Aboriginal languages how can Tegan speak one that is at least 35,000 years old? Apparently, the persons submitting this question never saw *The Masque of Mandragora*. Some persons incorrectly attribute this to Episode 2. Why does the Time Lords' Gift not allow everyone to understand Kurkuyji? **21:08** Bigon identifies Villagra (Nadia Hammam) as being from the Mayan civilization. Later the Doctor surmises the "Mayans" are from 8000 years ago; this would make Villagra pre–Mayan.

Episode 2
First Transmitted: Jan. 19, 1982

1:33 A noise (cough?) sounds in the background after Enlightenment (Annie

Lambert) says "frightened." **2:36** Various sources have questioned why Monarch keeps returning to Earth. Monarch would need many recognizance missions if he were planning to move his entire civilization to Earth. **5:52** In spite of the magnetic shield around the monopticon, the Doctor is able to place his hat on the unit. **8:19** We find that Monarch visited the Earth not only 2500 years ago but also 4000, 8000, and 12,000 years ago. The Doctor surmises these times. **8:32** The Doctor says that 4000 years ago (2000 BC) was the Futu Dynasty. He should have said Xia Dynasty (2100–1600 BC). **8:36** The Doctor supposedly commits a blooper when he refers to the civilization of 8000 years ago was Mayan instead of pre–Mayan. **10:24** Tegan and the Doctor descend a very flimsy set of stairs. **14:24** The Chinese dancers under the dragon costumes are not dressed in historically accurate Chinese garb. Jeans and T-shirts seem to be inappropriate attire. **15:51** When going down the steps Nyssa's air regulator pops up and she needs to pull it back down. **19:14** The light from the induction furnace suddenly gets brighter after Adric touches the window. Obviously, the person controlling the brightness was a little late. **22:07** Bigon corrects the visitation time of 12,000 years to 35,000 years. Bigon continues by saying the 35,000 date was after a 20,000-year trip (one-way), and that with each trip Monarch doubled his speed. This means it would take 20,000 to return to Urbanka and 10,000 years to get back (speed doubled). Thus Monarch's second visit would have been 5000 years ago, followed by a 10,000 + 5,000 (doubled speed) return trip. This would place his third visitation 10,000 years in the future. The alternative is that there is a doubling of the speed during each one-way trip — this results in bad dates also.

Episode 3
First Transmitted: Jan. 25, 1982

4:19 Monarch says they have been receiving messages from Earth for 50 years. This places Urbanka within about 50 light years from Earth (depending on whether or not this time refers to the first radio waves transmitted). This means his home planet is within the Milky Way Galaxy and makes it impossible for the planet to be in any other galaxy. A supernova supposedly destroyed Urbanka's sun — there were no supernova explosions within 50 light years of Earth during the last 50 years. This proves that Monarch is lying. **5:16** The Doctor seems to think that one reason why Monarch wants to go to Earth is the high silicon content. Since silicon is one of the most abundant elements in the Universe, there are numerous sources available in addition to the Earth. **8:10** Enlightenment refers to a Galactic legend of Rassilon and the "Eye of Harmony." **8:49** Adric refers to the TARDIS as meaning "Time And Relative Dimensions In Space." **11:14** This is the first time the Doctor uses the sonic screwdriver to cause a monopticon to rotate in a counter clockwise direction. This is one of the "two" times claimed by some viewers that the Doctor uses his sonic screwdriver to cause a monopticon to rotate in a counter clockwise direction. **12:10** The monopticon view on one of the monitors in the control room shows the views rotating in a clockwise, not counter clockwise, direction. **12:39** This is the second time the Doctor uses the sonic screwdriver to cause a monopticon to rotate in a counter clockwise direction. This is the second of the "two" times cited by some viewers. **16:10** This is the third time the Doctor uses the sonic screwdriver to cause a monopticon to rotate in a counter clockwise direction. This is the third of the "two" times cited by some viewers. **16:20** The monopticon view on one of the monitors in the control room shows the views rotating in a clockwise, not counter clockwise, direction. **17:53** There are two incorrectly rotating monitors at this time **22:22** Some observers question Monarch's lack of concern about the TARDIS leaving. However, Monarch has yet to realize he wants to steal the TARDIS.

Episode 4
First Transmitted: Jan. 26, 1982
1:12 How did Monarch know that pencils contain graphite? Pencils did not exist the last time he visited Earth. In any case, the Doctor gives Nyssa a mechanical pencil made of conducting metal. **5:57** The Doctor again bypasses the defenses of the monopticon by removing his hat. **10:32** One of the cast members in the background is caught relaxing. **11:01** For a second time the Chinese dancers, under the dragon costumes, are not dressed in typical Chinese garb. **18:46** The spacewalking Doctor bends the laws of physics. The ball does not have sufficient momentum to cause the Doctor to move so fast towards the TARDIS. The throw, over the shoulder, should have caused him to rotate backwards. You cannot get only the momentum you want—you will get all types of momentum. The Doctor catches the returning ball on his left side; this should impart a momentum causing him to not only go backwards, but also to cause him to rotate. **19:50** Some viewers claim there is a blooper arising because the Doctor tells Tegan to grab helmets before they know the life-support stops. **20:03** The Doctor and Tegan rush away leaving the TARDIS door open, and Monarch does not take two steps forward and enter. **20:14** The Doctor says that he expected Monarch to stop the life-support. This means that the earlier claim of a blooper is invalid. The Doctor did "know" about the life-support system. **20:26** The Doctor says that he can go into a trance to reduce his need for oxygen. Then he proceeds to hyperventilate by taking deep breaths; this will increase his oxygen requirements. To go into a trance the Doctor would need to take shallow breathes such as in *Spearhead from Space*. **22:06** Now we see closed TARDIS doors, even though the doors were open when the Doctor and Tegan left. **23:12** The Doctor enters with the metal collar from the helmet, and Adric enters carrying a helmet. **23:22** The Doctor's collar and Adric's helmet have disappeared inside the TARDIS.

Comments: The Doctor saves the Earth.

(5Y) KINDA

Writer: Christopher Bailey; **Director:** Peter Grimwade

Media: Commercial tape — episodic version — 99 minutes (used); Collector's tape — movie version — 91 minutes

Errors and Other Points of Interest

Some observers comment on the preponderance of wobbly camera shots. The number of camera jostles in this story is not much different from other stories.

Episode 1
First Transmitted: Feb. 1, 1982

1:28 Adric and Nyssa are reportedly playing draughts on a board that is 90 degrees from its proper orientation. **1:37** Adric initially moves to a white square and then quickly shifts to a black square. **2:36** Look through the TARDIS doors as the Doctor enters and Tegan leaves. A pink area appears near the floor inside the TARDIS. **5:42** The explorers are not from Earth, they are from "Home World." This is similar to *The Space Pirates*. **6:07** This is one of the camera jostles. **7:55** The Kinda accept Tegan sleeping alone under the chimes as if that is entirely normal. **11:41** We learn about the unexplained disappearance of Roberts and two others. We do not learn for sure what happened to the missing people. Some people consider this lack of an explanation to be a blooper.

Episode 2
First Transmitted: Feb. 2, 1982

18:13 We met the "new" Saunders (Richard Todd). His behavior may explain what happened to the missing crewmembers. **22:05** As the Mara moves onto Aris's (Adrian Mills) arm, he opens his mouth and screams. There are modern fillings in his teeth.

Episode 3
First Transmitted: Feb. 8, 1982

10:28 Saunders explains he has six charges placed in two overlapping equatorial triangles. **10:52** Observers have commented that the charges seen during Adric's wanderings are not at the corners of equilateral triangles. This may not be a valid blooper. This conclusion depends on the meaning of "overlapping equilateral triangles," or it may be an attempt to emphasize that Saunders is no longer in touch with reality.

Episode 4
First Transmitted: Feb. 9, 1982

2:34 Some viewers feel that a fire extinguisher outside the Dome is a blooper. **4:26** Hindle (Simon Rouse) backs up and twice kicks a box on the floor. It is possible to hear the sound, and one of the cardboard tubes begins to wobble. **5:27** Karuna (Sarah Prince) tells the Doctor that dreaming under the chimes is "forbidden." We also learn that "There is great danger in dreaming alone." If this is true, why did the Kinda not help Tegan when they found her sleeping alone? **10:58** Some observers claim that Tegan talks of Hindle as if she had met him even though she had not. She only talks of Hindle twice. In this, the first time, she is agreeing with Adric to calm Adric. **12:01** Sanders loud "boom" during Hindle's close-up seems misplaced. **13:58** This is the second instance where some observers claim Tegan talks about Hindle as if she has met him. In this situation, Tegan's reference to Hindle is a hysterical respond to the situation. She is not responding as if she knows Hindle. **18:24** High angle shots of the mirrors reveal a gap in the circle. This gap was for the ground level shots into the circle. **19:06** Everyone comments on the blooper of the bouncing snake — what else is there to say? **19:29** When the Mara's head rises above the mirrors, the snake could avoid seeing its reflection. **20:36** Just what is Tegan doing when the Doctor walks over to Aris's body (you can also see her reflection a moment before this). Apparently, she is examining Aris's wounded leg. **20:40** Power lines appear on the "ground" in many places. Apparently, they are supposed to represent tree roots.

Comments: Some lists refer to Aris as Ariss.

The Doctor saves the planet of Deva Loka.

(5X) The Visitation

Writer: Eric Saward; **Director:** Peter Moffatt

Media: Commercial DVD — episodic version — 97 minutes (used); Commercial tape — episodic version packaged with Black Orchid — 97 minutes; Collector's tape — movie version — 89 minutes

Errors and Other Points of Interest

There are various reports about the recovery times after deactivation of the control bracelets. The times on this list include a short description of the consequences. This is to address the claimed blooper that Mace and Tegan do not lose consciousness like "everyone" else.

Episode 1
First Transmitted: Feb. 15, 1982

4:49 This is one of the appearances of the console power cord. It is on the floor to the left rear. **6:33** While Tegan and Nyssa are talking there is a shadow moving behind Nyssa's reflection in the lower left of the mirror. **11:13** Adric falls to the ground, and when he rises — his knees are dirty. **11:50** Adric's knees are now clean. **11:54** Adric's stumble is not very convincing. **13:59** The Doctor does not have his celery stalk. **14:20** The Doctor now has his celery stalk in his hand. Where did he get it? **14:57** Some viewers have found fault with Nyssa asking Richard Mace (Michael Robbins) if he saw a meteor or a comet. This only demonstrates her lack of knowledge about Earth science. These viewers also describe a meteoroid as becoming a meteorite immediately upon entering the Earth's atmosphere. Why would Mace know the difference? **14:58** Some viewers claim that what Mace saw should be a meteorite not a meteor. There is no mention of the object hitting the Earth, thus the terms comet and meteor are acceptable. An object does not become a meteorite until it hits the Earth or some other planet. **19:08** Still other viewers report a reoccurring blooper concerning the Doctor's disappearing hat. The hat seems to disappear then reappear later. The hat is not disappearing — the Doctor is simply folding it and putting it in his pocket. This is one example showing the Doctor folding his hat and placing it in his pocket. **20:01** The Doctor and Nyssa are exploring the house. The Doctor finds some gunpowder on the floor but does not notice anything else. Nyssa leans over and picks up a power pack from about the same spot — how did the Doctor miss it? **22:40** The android (Peter van Dissel) wears poorly disguised cricket gloves.

Episode 2
First Transmitted: Feb. 16, 1982

1:35 Some fans question the camouflaging of both sides of the secret entrance. The reason may be technobabble. **5:46** The unconscious Tegan lifts her head to avoid hitting the doorframe. **7:10** Tegan says the Doctor is from Guilford. **11:22** The escape pod buried itself in the ground at an angle. **11:42** The floors inside the escape pod are not at the angle indicated by the outside views; the floors are level. **16:31** Notice how green the foliage is. **16:37** Notice how "green" the foliage is. **16:39** Watch the cloth backdrop, with the "trees," sway in the breeze. **19:52** The Doctor, Nyssa and Richard Mace are heading towards the TARDIS. They stop and talk for a time, and decide that Nyssa will continue on to the

TARDIS. Nyssa begins walking off along the path the group had just come down — back towards their pursuers. **21:21** The android receives an order to destroy the people in the house. **22:14** If the android is attempting to destroy Tegan — it is a very poor shot. In any case, it received an order to destroy, not to take, prisoners.

Episode 3
First Transmitted: Feb. 22, 1982

3:59 When Nyssa is moving the "anti-robot" machine, not the robot, into her room, she stops and makes a show of pulling her pants back up. Some observers claim this is a blooper; however, they also claim that she is moving the android, not the machine, towards her room. **6:51** The Headman (Eric Dodson) does not lose consciousness immediately upon having the control bracelet deactivated. He passes out a few seconds later and then quickly recovers. **7:02** The Poacher (Neil West) immediately loses consciousness after deactivation of his bracelet. He remains unconscious. The Headman responded differently indicating individual differences are important. **9:15** We hear the sound of a pencil dropping. **10:54** The ends of the pieces are straight; a saw cut the pieces, not an ax. **14:07** Something or someone is moving by the doorframe behind the Doctor. **20:37** The Terileptil (Michael Melia) destroys the sonic screwdriver. **23:03** Why is the Doctor concerned about Tegan opening the cage door? The real problem would be fleas, which could easily escape through the closed door. Fleas were the problem with the Black Death. If the disease is airborne instead, then breathing the same air as the rats could cause infection. The air the rats are breathing can easily exit the cage.

Episode 4
First Transmitted: Feb. 23, 1982

1:54 Mace quickly loses consciousness after deactivation of his bracelet. After a short time, he regains consciousness. This may not be a fair comparison because deactivation of his bracelet was by being "zapped" by the Doctor. **1:57** When the Doctor and Tegan begin to struggle, Tegan's bracelet has a power pack. The power pack disappears during the struggle. When the Doctor removes the power pack, we do not see the actual removal of the power pack; the Doctor could have palmed the unit. **2:05** Tegan passes out but quickly recovers after the Doctor deactivates her bracelet. **5:44** We hear the sound of the machine before Nyssa activates the switch. **7:24** Deactivation of his bracelet causes the Miller (James Charlton) to pass out. The Doctor states that he is "Just stunned." We do not see the Miller later, so we do not know how quickly he recovered. **7:42** The Doctor asks Richard Mace, "Which is the nearest city?" At the beginning of the story, they had landed at "Heathrow." Why does the Doctor need to ask which seventeenth century city, not town or village, is in the locality of modern Heathrow? **12:35** Watch the person's image moving on the reflective surfaces behind Adric. **13:01** Nyssa tells Adric "It's beginning to get dark." **13:23** Nyssa was correct — it is dark outside. **13:36** Nyssa informed Adric that it was getting dark. Then we see that it is dark outside. Now, inside the house, bright sunlight shines through the window. **16:44** The image of London seems like an old print instead of a TARDIS generated image.

Comments: The Doctor saves the Earth.

(6A) BLACK ORCHID

Writer: Terence Dudley; **Director:** Ron Jones

Media: Commercial tape — episodic version packaged with The Visitation — 50 minutes (used); Collector's tape — movie version — 47 minutes

Errors and Other Points of Interest

Episode 1
First Transmitted: Mar. 1, 1982

4:09 We clearly hear the sound of someone hitting a cricket ball. The umpire signals a wide. This is impossible. A cricket ball is wide when it is not possible to hit it. **8:57** Lady Cranleigh (Barbara Murray) queries "Doctor Who?" **9:30** In many stories, some observers find fault when people do not notice the "unusual" clothes worn by the Doctor and his companions. This is obviously not the case in this story.

Episode 2
First Transmitted: Mar. 2, 1982

1:29 We can see Ann's shoulder as she lies unconscious. Her mole has disappeared. This was in the climax to the preceding episode also. **14:55** Some viewers question the ability of a 1925 police officer to recognize a 1929 police box (TARDIS). Why should it be so strange that a police officer can identify an object with a sign saying "Police Box" as a Police Box? **15:05** The Doctor holds up the TARDIS key — it is a normal key. **21:18** Notice how far the wall extends above the roof where George (Gareth Milne) and Nyssa are standing. **22:31** George apparently falls over the low wall seen earlier. **22:33** George does not fall over the wall; he climbs on top and jumps.

Comments: The Doctor solves a murder mystery.

(6B) EARTHSHOCK

Writer: Eric Saward; **Director:** Peter Grimwade

Media: Commercial DVD — episodic version — 98 minutes (used); Commercial tape — episodic version — 98 minutes; Collector's tape — movie version — 89 minutes
Highlights: We say good-bye to Adric.

Errors and Other Points of Interest

Painting of the chin-pieces of the Cybermen began after the filming had begun. In the first scenes filmed, the Cybermen had clear chin-pieces, and in later scenes, the Cybermen had paint on the chin-pieces. Since filming of the scenes was not in viewing order, scenes with clear chins are interspersed with painted chins. Some examples are present on this list. There also seems to be some variation in the painting.

Some fans suggest that the "power failure" caused by the Cybermen is counterproductive, since they want to go to Earth. However, the Cybermen do not generate a complete power failure and it is only temporary.

Episode 1
First Transmitted: Mar. 8, 1982

4:22 When the rescue party is moving along the caves, the last soldier hears a noise and turns around. On the far cave wall, the moving shadow of one of the androids appears. Even though the soldier is looking directly at the moving shadow, the soldier does not see the shadow. **6:45** As Kyle (Clare Clifford) and Scott (James Warwick) are talking, the camera wobbles. **9:20** The Doctor tells everyone the time is in the "twenty-sixth century." Adric refines this to "2526." **13:18** The Doctor refers to the dinosaurs as an "amazing species." Science currently knows of hundreds of species, not just many examples of one species. The Doctor compounds this error a few seconds later by saying, "They were also the most successful creature ever to inhabit the Earth." **16:29** One of the "boulders" moves quite easily when kicked by a running soldier. The "ground" is not too stable either. **19:22** The scanner shows the soldiers strung out along the tunnel instead of lying in ambush in one "room." This is in addition to the dying group. **22:33** As the Doctor ducks out of sight, the rock to his right side moves. **23:04** The Cyberman's chin-piece is clear plastic.

Episode 2
First Transmitted: Mar. 9, 1982

5:26 Why does the android have breasts? Maybe they are beam locators. **9:42** There is a shadow moving on the rock behind Adric. **11:36** The Doctor asks Adric the fundamental questions that most observers have: "Why a bomb ... and why these particular caves?" **12:03** The Cyber Leader (David Banks) recognizes the TARDIS, and later the Doctor. This implies there is only one group of Cybermen, not multiple unrelated groups. **12:08** The power cords to the TARDIS console are visible at the Doctor's feet. The cords have tape covering for most of their length. **13:02** When the two Cybermen are looking at past images of the Doctor, there are inserted frames of the Cybermen looking at their own images. **13:27** When the Cybermen are viewing past encounters with the Doctor—there is an insert from Revenge of the Cybermen showing the Fourth Doctor. How do the Cybermen in the twenty-sixth century know about an encounter with the Doctor in the twenty-ninth century? **15:09** Some blooper hunters have a problem with the Cybermen being able to detect the moving TARDIS. Detection of the moving TARDIS is not unique to this story. For example, in *The Chase*, detection was possible. **15:17** Why do the Cybermen have a complicated contingency plan, when they can sneak bombs into hidden sites on Earth? The Cybermen got one bomb into the cave, why not other bombs in other caves? **15:21** Notice the Cyberman's chin. **16:40** The Doctor pushes the lever up instead of down to open the TARDIS doors. **17:57** Ringway (Alec Sabin) says, "I just happen to think that the disappearance of three crewmembers rather important." There are incorrect claims that Captain Briggs (Beryl Reid) said this; also it should be "two" instead of "three" crewmembers. **20:09** The Cyber Leader misses the button he is trying to press; however, we still hear the sound effect. **22:42** As Ringway is running down the corridor, he slows down before going out of the shot. It is possible that a turn in the corridor or a door is present. **22:50** The "dead" crewmembers are clearly breathing; this leads some observers to claim a blooper. This is probably a BBC cost-saving measure. It certainly saved a trip to the local mortuary to find some non-breathing extras. **23:02** The camera wobbles as the Doctor and Adric stand.

Episode 3
First Transmitted: Mar. 15, 1982

1:38 Captain Briggs says, "What's the

Deday?" **2:23** The Cyberman's chin-piece is now dark. **4:30** Why does the Doctor not strengthen his case by introducing the military personnel in the TARDIS? **7:55** Nyssa moves the red lever down to open the TARDIS doors. This is not what the Doctor did earlier. **8:46** We learn why the Cybermen planted a bomb and did not use a missile. How did the Cybermen get the first bomb to the Earth? **11:31** One of the Cybermen stumbles as the group is climbing the stairs on the ship. **12:02** The second beam from the woman's gun does not come from the end of her gun. **13:23** The Doctor talks about the vulnerability of the Cybermen to gold and says that gold "clogs up their chest units, suffocates them...." Some viewers misquote the Doctor as saying, "clogs their respiratory system." This misquote led to a blooper report about Cybermen and respiratory systems. Suffocation could result from interference with a self-contained recycling system. **14:51** The Captain says they are carrying 15,000 silos. This implies there are 15,000 Cybermen on the ship. This may or may not be true. Some of the silos may be for equipment like a thermolance. **15:17** When Tegan tells Scott she is exhausted, an object, apparently a stick, is waving in the background. **15:23** There is a member of the production crew holding a clipboard in the background as Scott and the others climb the steps. **15:44** Berger (June Bland) asks the Doctor about evacuating the hold. The Doctor replies, "Unfortunately, Cybermen don't need it [air]." This refers to the Doctor's earlier comments on the vulnerability of the Cybermen, and misquoted. If the Doctor had said "respiratory system," it would have implied that the Cybermen needed air. **16:01** Two of the Cyberguards appear to be chatting away with hand gestures. This occurs at other times. **16:09** Scott explains to Tegan that their rifles are the same weapons the ship's crew was using. Scott also notes that these rifles are ineffective. **18:44** Why do the previously ineffective weapons now begin to work against the Cybermen? **20:04** Note the position of the charges. **20:08** The "identical" and superior Cybermen have apparently spawned a midget. **20:15** The four explosives set around the edges of the door do not damage the edges of the door—just the center. **20:20** Earlier there was only activation of the Cyber Leader's personal guard. Soon all of the Cybermen (including the Cyber Leader) walk down a corridor. There are eight Cybermen. Later we see one Cyberman destroyed and one injured. The remaining Cybermen, still eight of them, walk onto the bridge. The Cyber Leader gives the command to activate the other Cybermen later. **21:32** Look at the Cyberman's chin. **23:05** If you watch carefully, it is possible to see that the three rows of Cybermen are multiple images of one column. When a Cyberman gets close to the edge of its image, his hand will disappear.

Episode 4
First Transmitted: Mar. 16, 1982

2:52 Another Cyberman with a clear chin-piece appears. **5:13** Four soldiers approach the TARDIS—Scott, two males and one female. Just before the female enters, the Cybermen grab her, so only the males enter. The three soldiers making it into the TARDIS are Scott, one male, and one female. **5:23** The TARDIS is no longer in temporal grace. Weapons work inside the TARDIS. **5:42** When Scott fires the Cyberman's gun, he misses (based on the special effect glow)—but the Cyberman falls anyway. **7:39** Scott leaves the TARDIS with one male and one female trooper. **7:44** Some fans suggest that leaving the crew alive is a blooper. **8:18** Just where are the evacuating Cybermen going? If they are landing on the Earth, they will have a long wait. **8:29** Soon after the soldiers leave the TARDIS, the female soldier has returned to being male. **10:45** The Cyber Leader learns about the complete evacuation of the ship. **11:11** We see the revival of more Cybermen. All the Cybermen were supposedly to be evacuated. Why are there any left to revive? This occurs again. Why not evacuate these Cybermen? Are they to remain aboard the exploding ship? **11:28** When descending the stairs the Cyber Leader stumbles on the last step. **17:20** The Doctor tells everyone that the "freighter ... [is] ... still locked onto the same spatial coordinates." It is difficult to believe that the Earth occupies the same spatial coordinates at two times separated by 65 million years. **18:12** We do not see the actual continents of 65 million years ago. **21:42** Adric apparently has a premonition about the exploding keyboard. He taps a few times and jerks back. Adric keeps pulling away before the explosion. **22:30** We see the freighter exploding before it actually hits the Earth.

Comments: The Doctor saves the Earth. There is no closing music.

These Cybermen have five fingers.

(6C) TIME-FLIGHT

Writer: Peter Grimwade; **Director:** Ron Jones

Media: Commercial tape — episodic version — 98 minutes (used); Collector's tape — movie version — 90 minutes

Highlights: The "bad" CSO after the Doctor and the others land at the ancient "Heathrow" actually reinforces the fact that they are in an illusion.

Questions: Why does the Master (Anthony Ainley) not fix the chameleon circuit in his TARDIS so it does not continue to represent a column?

Errors and Other Points of Interest

There are claims that Kalid includes people's names and the names of Earth objects in his chants.

Episode 1
First Transmitted: Mar. 22, 1982

2:17 Does Heathrow Airport really have an air traffic control center in a small room with only two people? **2:58** Nyssa notes, "Cyber fleet dispersed." This partially answers one of the questions passed on by some viewers about Earthshock. **4:49** The console power cord, covered with tape, is visible on the floor near the Doctor's feet. **5:35** The TARDIS seems only a short distance above the runway. **5:50** The TARDIS must be much higher than it was in the previous view. **17:08** Tegan appears to get her heal stuck in the steps. **18:36** The Doctor surmises that they have traveled back about 140 million years, and are now in the Jurassic period. This goes along with the remainder of the story. However, his comment about the cold, "we can't be far off the Pleistocene era," presents a problem. The Pleistocene epoch began about 2 million years ago; this is a 138 million year error. In addition, it should be the Pleistocene Epoch not the Pleistocene era. **19:22** Captain Stapley (Richard Easton) fails to see the Concorde, yet Tegan easily sees the plane. Some fans question the Captain's eyesight. However, an explanation of this may be a residual effect of the hallucination the Captain had. The residual effects are demonstrated later when the flight crew sees a highway. **23:37** The Doctor receives his warning about the attacking Plasmatons before the attackers become visible. The Doctor's expression also seems premature. This also occurs in the reprise. **24:08** Leon Ny Taiy is an anagram of Tony Ainley to keep the presence of the Master a secret.

Episode 2
First Transmitted: Mar. 23, 1982

12:18 You should pay close attention to Kalid's teeth. **22:36** Why did the Master bother to use a disguise? Why does the Master decide to remove his costume at this time? Why did the Master bother to disguise his voice? **22:41** Compare the Master's teeth to Kalid's teeth. **22:44** The Master experiences some difficulty getting out of his disguise. This occurs in both the cliffhanger and in the reprise.

Episode 3
First Transmitted: Mar. 29, 1982

2:36 The Master activates his TCE (look at the tip), but this does not kill the flight crew. **2:40** The TARDIS key is a normal key. The Doctor gives it to the Master, and the Doctor never gets it back. **6:04** Captain Stapley and Bilton (Michael Cashman) enter the TARDIS — the doors are open and the red lever is down. This begins a series of observations about the red lever and the doors. **6:49** The red lever is still down and the doors open when the Master enters the TARDIS. **7:18** It is possible to see inside the room the passengers are breaking into through a crack between two of the plates. **8:38** The Master stands, the lever is now up, and he moves it down with the accompanying sound of the doors closing. How did the lever get back up? Why does down now mean closed? **10:31** The lever is back up and the Master must move it down to open the doors. **12:30** The Master moves the red lever up to close the TARDIS doors as he leaves. **13:53** The Doctor refers to the central object as both a casket and as a sarcophagus within a few seconds. **15:26** It appears as if a hand emerges from the sarcophagus (aka casket) and then falls back down. This is probably not a hand. **18:46** Angela Clifford (Judith Byfield) disappears into the Master's TARDIS and never leaves. **21:40** A boom mike shadow appears on the wall behind Nyssa as she says, "I think we're winning." Nyssa has been misquoted.

Episode 4
First Transmitted: Mar. 30, 1982

6:21 As the Doctor and Tegan walk past the rock, the camera wobbles. **7:55** The Master apparently takes the Concorde with him as he dematerializes. **13:05** The red lever is up and the TARDIS doors are open. **16:32** As the Concorde takes off you can see many buildings in the background. These are not the ruins seen earlier. **16:48** Some viewers cite the appearance of a crow size bird during the stock footage of the Concorde taking off as a blooper. The claim is that no birds should be present during the Jurassic era. The problem with this assertion is that birds first developed during the Jurassic period, and early birds were about the size of crows. As an alternative, maybe the Doctor was correct when he said the Pleistocene was close. **23:06** The Doctor leaves Tegan behind.

Comments: The Doctor defeats the Master.

Pause to Consider: Boom Mike Shadows

This story includes boom mike (boom microphone) shadow bloopers. Boom mike shadows are common occurrences in many Doctor Who stories. Lights are required to see the actors and boom mikes are required to hear the same actors; however, the two do not always act together. On some sets, such as inside the Dominator's spaceship in

The Dominators, there are boom mike shadows in nearly every scene. In a few stories, the actual boom microphone appears. Seeing the actual boom mike is a greater error than just seeing the shadow.

(6E) ARC OF INFINITY

Writer: Johnny Byrne; **Director:** Ron Jones

Media: Commercial tape — episodic version — 98 minutes (used); Collector's tape — movie version — 91 minutes

Highlights: A future Doctor appears. Tegan is out of uniform. Omega (Ian Collier) returns.

Errors and Other Points of Interest

Episode 1
First Transmitted: Jan. 3, 1983

1:08 We learn that the choice must be the Doctor and not just any Time Lord. This explains the fan question about why choose the Doctor. However, if the fans are correct, it would create another question — why do the Time Lords think that killing the Doctor is the solution? If the Doctor dies — the "Renegade" would simply bond to another Time Lord. **4:10** Nyssa reminds the Doctor that the TARDIS is no longer in a state of temporal grace, and therefore the firing of weapons inside the TARDIS is possible. **5:58** Colin (Alastair Cumming) carefully closes the gate, which immediately proceeds to swing open again. **8:10** There are three parallel controls apparently with slide controls. However, one of the slides is missing. **9:12** The console power cord is near the Doctor's right knee. **9:46** Many more stars appear through the apparition than appear after the apparition moves out of the way. **15:28** The Doctor now claims, "Quantum magnetism is the only way to shield antimatter." This is not exactly as claimed in *Earthshock*. **16:30** Some people think the first guard to come through the door is a blooper. **23:32** To keep Omega's identity as the villain a secret, the credits list him as "The Renegade" in the first two episodes.

Episode 2
First Transmitted: Jan. 5, 1983

1:21 The console power cord is to the right of the screen. It has a masking tape disguise. **9:03** Some observers report that Borusa (Leonard Sachs) stumbles just before he sentences the Doctor to death. This is not present in this tape version; however, there is apparently some editing. **20:59** This is the second time that Borusa passes sentence on the Doctor. Borusa does not have trouble with his speech. Thus, this is not the reported blooper.

Episode 3
First Transmitted: Jan. 11, 1983

15:08 Some fans report that the Doctor's finger movements do not match the numbers he is using to enter the security code. The movements are not as bad as it sounds. The keypad is set up for base twelve, not base ten numbers. The Doctor recites the number: "4553916592." **15:29** Damon (Neil Daglish) asks the Doctor how it was possible for the Doctor to enter the computer room. The Doctor simply replies, "pure luck," and gives no further explanation; he does not mention the presidential code. **18:28** Damon knows how the Doctor got into the room (using the "presidential codes"), even though the Doctor gave him no explanation. **19:13** How did the shot fail to hit Nyssa? **20:16** Borusa has trouble saying "permit" when he says, "Only the gravest emergency would permit me to do as you want."

Episode 4
First Transmitted: Jan. 12, 1983

1:49 Notice the crown on the Doctor's head. **2:55** The crown on the Doctor's head appears different. **5:35** Producer John Nathan-Turner, wearing a sheepskin coat, makes a cameo appearance. There are claims that this is intentional and therefore not a blooper. **5:36** Why is the Doctor looking near the back of the phonebook for the letter J?

Comments: The Doctor saves Gallifrey and the Earth.

The Doctor again defeats Omega.

(6D) SNAKEDANCE

Writer: Christopher Bailey; **Director:** Fiona Cumming

Media: Commercial tape — episodic version — 98 minutes (used); Collector's tape — movie version — 91 minutes

Errors and Other Points of Interest

Episode 1
First Transmitted: Jan. 18, 1983

1:16 Why is Tegan not sleeping in her own room? The furniture and clothes belong to Nyssa. **3:05** There is a guard in the room. In most cases, both Lon (Martin Clunes) and Tanha (Colette O'Neil) appear in the company of guards. **14:05** The Doctor tells Nyssa and Tegan that the device he has made for Tegan will give total exclusion. To do this the device should have earplugs for both ears.

Episode 2
First Transmitted: Jan. 19, 1983

1:15 Even though there are some moments with the red lever, its use (up=closed doors) is far more consistent in this story than in the preceding story. **1:37** Notice the ornate shadow on Tegan. **13:47** There is no guard in Lon's room, and the one at the door does not enter with Dugdale (Brian Miller). This seems inconsistent with the guards' normal behavior.

Episode 3
First Transmitted: Jan. 25, 1983

8:33 Someone stands outside Ambril's (John Carson) office. We can see this person through the translucent glass beside the door just before Ambril and Lon leave. The men see no one in the hall after they leave the room. It is not Nyssa, even though she appears in the hallway after the occupants leave. Nyssa's clothing is the wrong color. **15:25** Nyssa realizes the blue crystals are not natural. This should have been obvious as there are no natural single crystals shaped like regular pentagons. **18:47** There is a plot hole in this story, and a blooper results when the storyline focuses everyone's attention on the plot hole. While imprisoned, Nyssa asks the Doctor why Dojjen (Preston Lockwood) did not destroy the crystal. The Doctor can only answer, "I don't know."

Episode 4
First Transmitted: Jan. 26, 1983

9:18 Again, we receive a reminder of

the hole in the plot. This time it is Lon talking to the Doctor and Nyssa. The Doctor still does not know why the crystal survived. The solution to this problem appears in the *Mawdryn Undead*. **16:45** Lon announces that the fake crystal is glass, then throws it to the ground and crushes the crystal under his foot. When the crystal hits the ground and is being crushed, it makes very unglass-like sounds.

Comments: The Doctor saves the planet of Manussa and again defeats the Mara.

The Guardian Trilogy

(6F) MAWDRYN UNDEAD

Writer: Peter Grimwade; **Director:** Peter Moffatt

Media: Commercial tape — episodic version — 98 minutes (used); Collector's tape — movie version — 90 minutes
Highlights: Turlough (Mark Strickson) becomes a companion. The Brigadier returns.

Errors and Other Points of Interest

Episode 1
First Transmitted: Feb. 1, 1983

5:44 Tegan tells the Doctor if Dojjen (Preston Lockwood) destroyed the crystal they would not have had the problem with the Mara. The Doctor finally explains, "The Mara could only be destroyed during the process of its becoming." This would mean that the destruction of the crystal would accomplish nothing. It would have been better to have this explanation during *Snakedance*. **6:01** The Doctor's reaction to Nyssa coming into the console room is shocking. **6:26** Nyssa describes an object as having a fixed orbit in time. Some viewers consider this impossible, but it really is technobabble, and, hence, immune to blooper claims. **14:57** How did Turlough know where to look before the transmat capsule appeared? **15:07** This is one of many views showing a small hole in the door of the transmat capsule. Many observers object to its presence. This might be a valid argument if these observers could supply a real transmat capsule that does not have a similar hole. **15:18** The Doctor explains that the ship returns to Earth every six years. **18:46** The Doctor causes the TARDIS console to wobble. **19:39** The Doctor believes it to be 1983 on the Earth. **19:58** As the Doctor enters the TARDIS, the camera jumps. **20:38** The Doctor has some difficulty with the door lever. The red lever does not want to stay in place, and it takes the Doctor more than one try to get it to stay in place. **21:02** This transmat capsule, unlike previous capsules, is like the TARDIS — bigger on the inside than on the outside.

Episode 2
First Transmitted: Feb. 2, 1983

1:01 Some fans claim that when Turlough drops the stone, the stone does not bounce like a stone. **3:17** When did Tegan become such an expert on T-Mat systems? **3:47** Some observers do not believe that Nyssa and Tegan would think they are really dealing with a regenerated Doctor because Mawdryn (David Collings) is clearly wearing different clothes. This is a questionable call because of the destruction of most of Mawdryn's clothes. **7:01** Apparently, in 1983 the Brigadier is living as a bachelor. **8:13** The Doctor asks the Brigadier about Sergeant Benton; apparently both the Doctor and the Brigadier forgot about Benton's promotion. **12:06** The Brigadier says he left UNIT "seven years ago." This would make it 1976. This fits with the rest of this story. **13:37** Apparently, in 1977 the Brigadier is also living as a bachelor. **22:23** In this episode, red lever up — open doors. **22:58** The Brigadier says he saw the Doctor regenerate twice. Nyssa says, "So have we." Just when did Nyssa and Tegan see the Doctor regenerate twice. This is also present in the reprise.

Episode 3
First Transmitted: Feb. 8, 1983

1:01 Some viewers find fault with Nyssa running back to the TARDIS. See if you can spot the problem. **4:53** In this episode, red lever up — closed doors. **17:55** The Brigadier assumes that Mawdryn is the Doctor even though his clothes are different. **18:13** Now, in this episode, red lever up — open doors. **20:39** Turlough cries, "I can operate it!" and bangs the console so hard with his fist that the console wobbles. Some observers incorrectly report this to be a blooper in Episode 4 of Terminus. **21:32** Mawdryn says that every seventy years the ship comes within transmat distance of a planet. If this is true, how did Mawdryn go to Earth in 1977, and the Doctor go in 1983?

Episode 4
First Transmitted: Feb. 9, 1.983

1:50 The Black Guardian's (Valentine Dyall) image is slightly larger than the screen. **2:21** In one of the full screen views of the Black Guardian, the Black Guardian spits on himself. **5:29** The console power cord, covered with masking tape, is visible on the floor. **12:04** The Doctor causes the TARDIS console to wobble by pushing a switch very hard. **22:25** The red lever is up — apparently, this is because the doors are open. **22:53** When everyone rushes in through the open TARDIS doors, the red lever is now down.

Comments: The Doctor "saves" Mawdryn and company.

(6G) TERMINUS

Writer: Steve Gallagher; **Director:** Mary Ridge

Media: Commercial tape — episodic version — 99 minutes (used); Collector's tape — movie version — 91 minutes
Highlights: Nyssa leaves the series and her skirt.
Questions: Why did the people who grab Tegan outside the cell door not infect Tegan?

Errors and Other Points of Interest

Episode 1
First Transmitted: Feb. 14, 1983

9:37 Nyssa drops her book near the center of the corridor. **10:36** The Doctor finds Nyssa's book in a different place — closer to the wall. Some viewers report that 10 minutes elapse between the times Nyssa drops the book and the Doctor finds the book. **14:27** At least one fashion conscious fan considers the pirate helmets to be bloopers. **18:08** How can they hear the ship outside? While the ships are in contact the transmission of vibrations from one to the other is possible, but later — sound does not travel through a vacuum. **22:17** The Computer voice announces, "Sterilization procedures will then follow." The computer specifies "procedures," plural.

Episode 2
First Transmitted: Feb. 16, 1983
11:31 The computer voice announces, "This warning is final." This is the last of the Stage 1 warnings. **12:58** Nyssa "loses" her skirt. **13:18** Some viewers cite a blooper here — the computer voice begins giving warnings again even though it has previously announced "this warning is final." This particular announcement it not a blooper; it is the beginning of the Stage 2 warning sequence. This is obviously only another one of the procedures. **21:49** The Doctor and Kari (Liza Goddard) walk across the walkway. Valgard (Andrew Burt) is waiting below the walkway, after the couple passes the Vanir moves towards a stairway. A foot appears at the top of the steps, which disappears almost immediately.

Episode 3
First Transmitted: Feb. 22, 1983
1:55 The beam seems to be traveling at an angle to where Kari is aiming. **16:57** When Olvir (Dominic Guard) first fires his weapon, the beam initially does not come from the muzzle of the gun. **21:36** The ship could not carry enough fuel for an explosion the magnitude of Event One. The fuel could not have sufficient mass to create the Universe. If Event One created the Universe, just what Universe was Terminus traveling?

Episode 4
First Transmitted: Feb. 23, 1983
6:58 Turlough hits the TARDIS console hard enough to make the unit wobble. **11:20** The Doctor summons The Garm (R. J. Bell) to ask for help. The Garm walks out of the forbidden zone and towards the Doctor. The Doctor needs The Garm's help in the control room, which is in the forbidden zone. The Doctor shouts "Let's go" and runs away from not into the forbidden zone. **11:40** Olvir is wearing black pants under his armor and he is not wearing boots. **13:36** Olvir is now wearing white pants and boots, with no armor. When and how did he make the quick change?

Other Observations: Some fans report that in Episode 4 Turlough causes the TARDIS console to wobble after he yells "I can operate it!" This is a blooper from Episode 3 of the *Mawdryn Undead*.

Comments: The Doctor saves the Universe.

(6H) ENLIGHTENMENT

Writer: Barbara Clegg; **Director:** Fiona Cumming

Media: Commercial tape — episodic version — 98 minutes (used); Collector's tape — movie version — 90 minutes
Highlights: The last time the White Guardian (Cyril Luckham) asked the Doctor for help the Doctor did not give the Guardian the Key to Time.
Questions: Considering the Doctor's failure the give the White Guardian the Key to Time, why does the White Guardian bother to ask the Doctor for help?

Errors and Other Points of Interest

Episode 1
First Transmitted: Mar. 1, 1983

1:36 In the reduced lighting, it is difficult, but not impossible, to see the tape covered console power cord. **2:28** If the Guardians are so powerful, why is it so difficult for the White Guardian to contact the Doctor? The White Guardian should be approximately as strong as the Black Guardian (Valentine Dyall). **10:53** As Jackson (Tony Caunter) stands the shadow of the lamp on the sailor behind him could be mistaken for a boom mike shadow. This is to avoid a future blooper report. **18:49** The two saluting officers have respectively two and one stripes on their sleeves. **19:26** The two officers eating with the Doctor, Tegan and Captain Striker (Keith Barron) have three and one stripe. Did one of the officers get a promotion? **19:37** The liquids in the glasses do not move with the rocking of the ship. **19:53** We learn that Marriner (Christopher Brown) is the First Mate. The First Mate should have three stripes on his sleeve, not two. **21:10** One of the sailors running up the steps stumbles. Of course, this is after the sailors have received their rum ration.

Episode 2
First Transmitted: Mar. 2, 1983

3:54 All of Tegan's drink appears to be in the glass. Turlough even picks the glass up later. **4:02** Tegan mutters, "That was a marvelous drink." If she drank it, why is it still in the glass? **4:21** The second time Captain Striker changes the image (from the Greek ship to the "Greek" captain), the image changes before Captain Striker actually pushes the button. **6:52** Watch the shadow flitting about Captain Striker's face as he talks to the Doctor. **7:03** One of the sailors barely sips his rum ration. The next sailor takes the entire ration. All of the sailors should drink it all to get the full effect of the drug. **18:56** Turlough stumbles as he enters the door. **21:39** Mariner tells Tegan there is air on deck. So why did they come to the deck wearing helmets?

Episode 3
First Transmitted: Mar. 8, 1983

5:22 Tegan tells Marriner that she must go to see the Doctor; then she takes off her helmet and sits down. **10:31** It is interesting to note that to turn the vacuum shield on, the Captain moves the lever to the OFF side. The smaller labels, low, medium and high, seem to be in the correct positions. **11:21** When Captain Wrack leaves the room, she first fastens and then unfastens the top dog. **12:52** Tegan trips while walking along the hallway. **14:45** The Doctor changes celery stalks. **15:17** Captain Wrack's ship is not very solid — Turlough "breaking" through the door makes the entire wall shake. **15:18** Turlough enters the airlock and leaves the door wide open. **15:34** At this time, Turlough hears a noise and looks to see the door swinging open, but Turlough left it open. **18:26** When the air is escaping from the airlock, Turlough's vision blurs and begins to spin. This only happens to the stars and not to the rest of the room. Thus, the shield slowly dissipates. **18:57** Tegan is initially "frozen" with her eyes open. The next shot of Tegan shows her eyes are now closed. **19:00** The freezing of Tegan apparently does not affect her earrings. Maybe Tegan is the only thing "frozen."

Episode 4
First Transmitted: Mar. 9, 1983

6:24 What are the lights moving in the background beyond the plank? **6:55** Turlough is wearing a wedding ring. The disappearing/reappearing wedding ring occurs at other times. Some observers erroneously report this as occurring in Episode 3. **10:03** Turlough has "lost" his wedding ring. **13:12**

Why does the Doctor not pick up the entire rug? As it is, they do not pick up all the pieces. **16:43** As Captain Wrack prepares to throw the Doctor into the void, why are the stars spinning? **23:10** Turlough tells the Doctor he wants to go to "My planet. My home." Turlough does not mention the name of his home planet.

Comments: The Guardians face the Doctor again.

(6J) THE KING'S DEMONS

Writer: Terence Dudley; **Director:** Tony Virgo

Media: Commercial tape with The Five Doctors — episodic version — 50 minutes (used); Collector's tape — movie version — 47 minutes
Highlights: Kamelion (Gerald Flood) temporarily joins the TARDIS crew.

Errors and Other Points of Interest

Some observers question why Sir Gilles is the only person speaking French when French was the official language of the English Court in 1215. The answer is that no one actually says anything in French. Sir Gilles' accent is acceptable; however, the explanation for hearing English appears in *The Masque of the Mandragora*.

Episode 1
First Transmitted: Mar. 15, 1983
0:47 Watch the lute player demonstrate the correct method of playing a lute. **1:54** To prevent the public from knowing ahead of time that the Master (Anthony Ainley) was in the story, two anagrams were used for "Sir Gilles Estram" played by "James Stoker" (Estram — Master; James Stoker — Master's Joke). **13:13** Ranulf (Frank Windsor) notices the Doctor's strange clothes; this is one of the cases in the series where a character makes this observation. **18:55** "King John" (Gerald Flood) plays a lute as if it was a guitar — which means incorrectly. The lute player demonstrated earlier the proper way to play a lute. Some observers incorrectly attribute this to Episode 2. **22:22** "King John" hits a plate instead of the table, and he must stop the plate from clattering. **22:49** The Doctor falls back against the wall, and the entire wall shakes as if it is about to fall down.

Episode 2
First Transmitted: Mar. 16, 1983
3:13 The Master's iron maiden TARDIS looks Elizabethan, not early thirteenth century. Apparently, the Master finally repairs his chameleon circuit so that his TARDIS no longer looks like a stone column. **6:40** The guards grab Sir Geoffrey (Michael J. Jackson) before the Doctor points him out. **7:45** The Doctor's cloak catches on something. **13:37** Kamelion cannot fake lute playing as well as "King John." **22:18** Kamelion gets permission to stay aboard the TARDIS.

Comments: The Doctor defeats the Master.

(6K) The Five Doctors

Writer: Terrance Dicks; **Director:** Peter Moffatt

Media: DVD—100 minutes (used); Commercial tape (Collector's Edition—CE) -101 minutes (used); Commercial tape—original commercial release (C)—99 minutes; Collector's tape—90 minutes (used)—times are indicated with an "M"
Highlights: Many many Doctors.
Questions: How can the First Doctor know anything that his "younger" selves do not know?

Errors and Other Points of Interest

Episode 1
First Transmitted: Nov. 25, 1983

2:01 The red lever that has caused so much trouble in the past has, along with the console, regenerated. **3:41** The Doctor attributes the calming influence of the Eye of Orion to a "high bombardment of positive ions." The Doctor compares this to Earth after a thunderstorm. This should be negative ions. **8:17** The Second Doctor tells the Brigadier, "I'm not exactly breaking the rules of time, but I am bending them a little." This may partly explain the discrepancy concerning Zoe and Jamie. Some fans claim the Doctor did not immediately regenerate after his trial at the end of *The War Games*, but came to see the Brigadier before returning to Gallifrey for regeneration. **8:39M** The Time Scoop captures the Third Doctor and Bessie. As the Time Scoop withdraws, it is possible to see Bessie (and the Doctor?) for a split second. This is in neither the DVD nor the CE versions. **10:15** This is the point we see the capture of the Third Doctor and Bessie in both the DVD and CE versions. **18:46** Some viewers question Borusa's (Philip Latham) planning. These viewers feel that Borusa should only need to ask for another regeneration. Since the Master can get another regeneration, the High Council should be able to accommodate Borusa. The answer to this question is that Borusa was not looking for regeneration—he was looking for immortality. Borusa may have been able to convince the High Council of one regeneration, but not perpetual regeneration. **19:27** There is a boom mike shadow on Susan's face as she approaches the First Doctor. **22:51** The Dalek's top tips a little as the creature proceeds along the corridor. **25:06** Through the hole in the wall, we can see the jeans the attacking Cyberman is wearing. **25:26** Sarah Jane has trouble rolling down a gentle slope. **28:23** Why could the First Doctor (William Hurndall) not see the TARDIS from where he was sitting? **31:24** The Master enters the Trans-mat without a cloak. **31:55** The Master is wearing a clock when he arrives in the Death Zone. **37:27** The Third Doctor and Sarah Jane leave Bessie. Bessie somehow reappears on Earth later. **39:56** Some fans object to the First Doctor's pineapple. **40:50** The First Doctor says there are two more traces, and through Turlough's query, the First Doctor notes the tuning of the scanner to him (the Doctor). This means that the scanner is now picking up the Second and Third Doctors in addition to the Fifth Doctor. The problem is that the scanner shows one Doctor alone and two Doctor's together, when all of the Doctor's are still separate (do not forget that there is no way to detect the companions). **44:59** Susan's trip is not very convincing. **46:05** The regenerated console still has a power cord covered with masking tape. **47:16** The Doctor notes the presence of the Cybermen. He goes on to explain that the Time Lords did not use Cybermen in the Zone, thus the Cybermen could not be from the past. The Cybermen must be recent additions. If the Doctors were supposed to succeed, why bring such effective opposition? **50:31** How is Susan able to recognize the Cybermen? **56:54** Why is this Yeti so aggressive? We learned in *The Abominable Snowmen* that the Yeti are quiet and peaceful. The only dangerous Yeti were the robot Yeti controlled by the Great Intelligence. **1:00:17** It is obvious that the Cyberman actor's real arm is inside his suit to allow the loss of his fake arm. **1:01:21** (Collector's and Commercial versions) The First Doctor gives the value of pi as "3.14159265." **1:03:17** The rope from the cliff to the Tower has a low point between the two ends. The rope will sag even lower with a person's weight hanging from it. A person sliding along to rope would end up at the low point and not at the tower end of the rope. **1:06:16** How do the Cybermen fail to see the First Doctor and Tegan? **1:08:57** The Master dances across the floor. **1:09:03** Some viewers question the meaning of the Master's cry "it's as easy as pi!" They claim that it could refer to any irrational number. In any case, why consider this a blooper? **1:09:47** The First Doctor gives the value of pi as "3.14159265" in the DVD version, but on the CE tape, the value given is "3.142857." **1:09:54** The First Doctor simply walks across the floor. There seems to be no logic as to where either the Master or the First Doctor step. The explanation may be as the Master states — the pattern changes each time. **1:15:40** The fact that Jamie and Zoe recognize the Second Doctor is not a blooper, notwithstanding the Second Doctor's claim. The wiping of their memories was to leave them with the memory of their first adventure with the Second Doctor. The actual problem is when Jamie recognizes the Brigadier, whom he has never met (as a Brigadier). Another problem: when Jamie and Zoe had their memories wiped, the Doctor regenerated. Either this story takes place between the memory wiping and the regeneration, or this is part of the "bending" of the rules mentioned by the Second Doctor. **1:22:54M** The Fourth Doctor returns to the point in Shada where he was crawling under the gate to escape the globe. **1:25:35M** Everyone leaves in separate TARDIS's. This occurs only on the Collector's tape. **1:29:06** Borusa freezes the companions. This works on all the companions except the Brigadier who continues turn his head to watch Borusa. **1:31:40** Borusa hits Rassilon's (Richard Mathews) sarcophagus when he lowers his hand. **1:33:43** Both the DVD and CE versions of the story show the Fourth Doctor returning to the river, not the alley. Some observers consider the return to the alley, and not to his point of capture, a blooper. However, the Fourth Doctor was the only person trapped in the Time Scoop, thus it is not surprising that his return is different. **1:34:51** Some viewers question the fact that the Doctors learn details from their own regenerations. **1:35:12** In the DVD and CE version, everyone returns via the Time Scoop. Questions have been posed concerning people leaving together (such as the Third Doctor and Sarah Jane) who did not arrive together. The explanation for this is in Appendix II of the Time Scoop Operation Manual. **1:36:06** Bessie does not appear to return to the Earth. **1:37:21** How does the High Council know they need a new President? **1:38:01** The Fifth Doctor tells Chancellor Flavia (Dinah Sheridan) to return to Gallifrey. How can she return to Gallifrey? She is on Gallifrey. There are other similar references to Gallifrey.

Comments: The Cybermen in this story have five fingers.

The appearance of the Time Scoop in the original Commercial version and the Collector's tape (originally transmitted) is a black triangle. The effect is different in both the CE and DVD versions. In these versions a grayish white pyramid appears.

At the end of the original Commercial and Collector's tape, everyone enters the TARDIS and one by one the separate TARDIS's leave. In the Commercial version, the Time Scoop takes them away.

William Hurndall replaces the First Doctor.

The Fourth Doctor is only present in clips from Shada, which had not aired at the time of this story.

(6L) Warriors of the Deep

Writer: Johnny Byrne; **Director:** Pennant Roberts

Media: Commercial tape — episodic version — 97 minutes (used); Collector's tape — movie version — 89 minutes

Questions: Why does the electric charge from the Myrka only pass through some of the metal walls? (Actually why does the Myrka not short circuit the first time the beast sends a charge through the grounded walls? Are the metal floors non-conducting?)

Errors and Other Points of Interest

Some fans claim a blooper concerning the ability of the TARDIS interior to move around as in Time-Flight. The claim is that even after several minutes the Doctor fails to "level" the interior of the TARDIS. This does not occur in this story.

Special effects bods are supposedly present at some point.

Some people object to the polystyrene doors.

Episode 1

First Transmitted: Jan. 5, 1984

0:43 As the actors walk by the pipes (left center), the pipes wobble significantly. **1:47** As the first Silurian talks, the light on its head flashes along with his words, but it also flashes again when the other Silurian begins talking. **4:54** The Silurians refer to their time in "cold storage" as being "for hundreds of years." Some fans claim the Doctor keeps referring to millions of years. **4:56** The Silurians use the human name "Sea Devil." The Silurians should use their own name for the creatures. It is possible that clarification of this is in the Doctor's explanation in *The Masque of Mandragora*. **5:45** The actor's (Norman Comer) blinking eyes peer through his Icthar mask. **8:08** As the Doctor has trouble when he says "All we need is a ... is a ... bit of time!" **9:52** Just as the missile hits the TARDIS, it is possible to see the console power cord on the floor behind the console. **13:22** Some observers report that the Doctor goofed in leaving the TARDIS doors unlocked. Tegan was the last person to leave the TARDIS, and she, not the Doctor, left the door ajar. **15:56** This is one occasion where Commander Vorshak (Tom Adams) appears to miss, or nearly miss, the button he is pushing. **21:46** Apparently, no one is to leave the reactor room without authorization, but anyone can enter. The sign "No Unauthorized Personnel" is on the inside of the door. **23:10** The walls of the base are not very substantial — during the fight, the Doctor falls against the wall, and the wall shakes.

Episode 2
First Transmitted: Jan. 6, 1984

1:16 Tegan appears not to be wearing a bra. **2:07** The entire keypad depresses when pressed. **2:12** Why is the guard pounding on the wall if he is trying to open the door? The guard should be pounding on the door. **2:21** After the Doctor escapes from the pool, his head and hair are wet, but his clothes are mostly dry. **5:31** Icthar calls himself a "Silurian." Why does he not use his own name for his people and not the human name? I know—the explanation is in *The Masque of Mandragora*. **6:15** The Doctor forgot to fasten the hose to the unit on his back. **6:18** Two vigilant patrolling guards walk right past the body on the floor. **10:18** The TARDIS doors appear closed. **10:23** The TARDIS doors appear open. **11:53** Doctor Solow passes the Doctor after leaving the bridge. Solow continues and encounters the Myrka. The Myrka is heading towards the bridge. Two guards pass the Doctor and find Doctor Solow's body on the guards' way to the bridge. If the guards are going to the bridge they should not find Doctor Solow since she was moving away from the bridge when she met the Doctor. **13:05** The Doctor first uses the name "Silurian" in this story. **13:54** The guards and the Myrka reach the Doctor; they come, not from the direction Doctor Solow left, but from the direction of the bridge (as Doctor Solow did when she first encountered the Doctor). **14:58** Some observers claim that one of the production personnel runs across the set at one point. This is apparently the point, but the person appears to be wearing a uniform like one of the sea-base crew. **17:55** How did Doctor Solow (Ingrid Pitt) know the name Silurian? She was not present when the Doctor mentioned the name. **22:50** Tegan is now wearing a bra (she may have acquired it earlier in this Episode). She did not have a bra earlier in this Episode.

Episode 3
First Transmitted: Jan. 12, 1984

4:24 The Myrka gets a claw cut in its "hair." **7:24** The Sea Devil in back has his helmet on at an angle. This occurs more than once. Later its entire head is at an angle. **12:36** Some fans object to Doctor Solow's karate. **15:32** This is one of many places where the Silurian costumes seem to be falling apart. It is possible to see through numerous tears and other openings. **19:33** The Doctor explains that the technology of the Silurians predates human technology by millions of years—he does not say the Silurians have been "asleep" for millions of years. Some observers claim that the Doctor said the Silurians were asleep for millions of years.

Episode 4
First Transmitted: Jan. 13, 1984

3:10 Two of the Sea Devils behind the Doctor run into each other as they attempt to exit the bridge. **3:25** Another Sea Devil has his head on crooked. **7:02** Tegan enters the air duct before Bulic (Nigel Humphreys). **8:14** The entire wall shakes as Preston (Tara Ward) enters the air duct. **8:57** Bulic has managed to pass Tegan in the narrow air duct so he can help her out the other end. **19:55** There is a rip in the seat of the costume the falling Silurian is wearing. **22:04** Some viewers are not happy with Vorshak's dying moments after he is shot.

Other Observations: Some sources incorrectly refer to Doctor Solow as Doctor Solon.

Comments: The Doctor saves the Earth.

(6M) The Awakening

Writer: Eric Pringle; **Director:** Michael Owen Morris

Media: Commercial tape — with Frontios — episodic version — 50 minutes (used); Collector's tape — movie version — 48 minutes
Questions: Why does the Doctor walk up to the "soldiers" when he is trying to stay hidden?

Errors and Other Points of Interest

Episode 1
First Transmitted: Jan, 19, 1984

3:07 The console power cord is near Tegan's feet. **14:34** Jane Hampton (Polly James) slaps Joseph Willow (Jack Galloway) so hard that she nearly loses her sweater. **23:48** Listen carefully — it sounds as if the closing music begins a little early. This also occurs in the reprise.

Episode 2
First Transmitted: Jan. 20, 1984

8:37 Some observers cite the presence of "stars" in the images to be a blooper. **21:24** As the TARDIS dematerializes, blocks of stone materialize on the top of the pile of stones.
Comments: The Doctor saves the Earth.

(6N) Frontios

Writer: Christopher H. Bidmead; **Director:** Ron Jones

Media: Commercial tape — with The Awakening — episodic version — 98 minutes (used); Collector's tape — movie version — 90 minutes
Questions: Why is the Doctor so worried about interfering this time?

Errors and Other Points of Interest

Episode 1
First Transmitted: Jan. 26, 1984

0:36 Some viewers report that Captain Revere (John Beardmore) is watching the Earth in the opening scene. **0:57** Some object must come up through the hole to make the "dirt" fall. **2:50** The TARDIS has a "boundary error." Apparently, the machine has trouble getting this far into the future. The time appears to be about the same time as in the First Doctor story, *The Ark*. The First Doctor had no trouble getting this far into the future. **3:33** There is an often-cited blooper that when Captain Revere is watching the Earth revolve, the hand of a production crewmember can be seen keeping the globe moving. This blooper has some problems associated with it. Captain Revere dies in the tunnels in the very first scene. Captain Revere has no globe of any type around him to be watching. The globe seen at this time is not the Earth but the planet Frontios. It is Tegan, not Captain Revere, who is looking at the planet. The planet is not rotating, so there is no need for a helping hand. Some observers report this to occur in both Episodes 1 and 2. **5:57** Turlough says, "It's a meteorite storm," instead of "It's a meteor storm." This is one of the many instances during the program where we hear the incorrect term (meteorite) instead of the correct term (meteor). The only meteorites present are the ones the characters pick off the ground. **12:10** Turlough uses the phrase "with some sort of interrupter to raise the voltage." He should have said transformer instead of interrupter. **19:01** A small amount of acid spills from the battery; however, when the battery appears later, much more acid is missing. The loss of acid apparently continues until the battery is light enough for the actors to carry without difficulty. The level changes many times. **22:56** A fragment of a meteorite hits Plantagenet (Jeff Rawle) and he clutches the left center of his chest. Some viewers report the shooting of Plantagenet, and that he grabs the right side of his chest. **23:24** The Doctor laments, "The TARDIS has been destroyed." What happened to Kamelion? Some viewers report that the TARDIS explodes.

Episode 2
First Transmitted: Jan. 27, 1984

5:50 Plantagenet again clutches his chest near the center. Some fans report he clutches his left side. Since he is having heart trouble he should be clutching near his heart, which may or may not be exactly where the fragment hit him. **10:04** We see Plantagenet's shirt removed so he may undergo treatment. The bruise appears to be not very far from where he originally grabbed himself. Some fans claim the times and positions are bloopers. **12:53** There must be a better way of lifting the metal plate than to have Norna (Lesley Dunlop) support most of the weight. **16:08** The Doctor looks at the solutions Norna made and says the rock analysis look like Widmanstatten patterns. Widmanstatten patterns occur on the surfaces of some meteorites, not in solutions. **20:08** Tegan stops her pursuers by inserting a rod through the center of the handles of the doors. **22:03** The rod moves to the top of the handles by the time the pursuers break through the door. This also occurs in the reprise. **22:50** The Doctor enters the chamber from the left while Tegan, who is following the Doctor, enters the chamber from the right a few seconds later.

Episode 3
First Transmitted: Feb. 2, 1984

1:50 The Doctor, Tegan and Norna escape from the chamber by going left. This confirms that Tegan came from the wrong direction in the preceding episode. **5:14** Turlough spits on himself while talking. **10:30** Tegan trips when she misses a step.

Episode 4
First Transmitted: Feb. 3, 1984

5:05 A boom mike shadow appears behind the renegade just before he explains why they are following Cockerill (Maurice O'Connell). **18:10** After the Gravis (John Gillett), switches the spatial distribution circuits out, they look the same as before he touched the circuits. **18:26** The Doctor uses the phrase "Time And Relative Dimension In Space." The word "Dimensions" is not used. **18:38** Immediately after the Gravis says, for the first time, "I will have it," it is possible to see the TARDIS column rise even though it is supposedly inoperative. This occurs at the very edge of the screen. **20:24** The Gravis does a better job on the TARDIS than all the king's horses and all the king's men. (Even Kamelion is happy.)

Comments: Some blooper lists label Plantagenet as Plantaganet.

The Doctor saves the planet Frontios.

(6P) Resurrection of the Daleks

Writer: Eric Saward; **Director:** Matthew Robinson

Media: DVD — episodic version — 98 minutes (used); Commercial tape — episodic version — 98 minutes; Collector's tape — movie version — 91 minutes
Highlights: Tegan leaves.

Errors and Other Points of Interest

Episode 1
First Transmitted: Feb. 8, 1984

1:09 Some fans question who the escaping prisoners are. **1:54** Why does the tramp's body disappear with the others? **2:45** Lytton (Maurice Colbourne) claims the escaping prisoners were "valuable specimens." This may answer the question posed by certain observers about the escaping prisoners. **2:56** The console power cord is near Tegan's feet. **22:53** Kiston's (Les Grantham) name is not in the closing credits.

Episode 2
First Transmitted: Feb. 8, 1984

1:31 The Dalek falling out of the upstairs window has most of its eyepiece missing instead of a little damage. The Dalek also looks partially melted, similar to the two Daleks in the last episode. The falling Dalek has no base either. **6:27** The wreckage of the Dalek is now upstairs instead of on the street below the window. Some observers report this as a blooper. This is not the case, as the Doctor and others went out to get the pieces. The blooper is that they carried in a live Dalek and did not know it. **12:00** Why is Davros surprised by the impasse, and defeat, in the Dalek-Movellan war? He learned about the impasse earlier in *Destiny of the Daleks*. **13:00** During the removal of the dead Daleks, Turlough sneaks aboard the space station. Who removed some of the human bodies? For some strange reason some of the bodies are on the Dalek ship. Why would the Daleks want the dead bodies? **19:36** Three Daleks leave through the time corridor. **20:18** Four Daleks arrive through the time corridor to confront the Sergeant. **23:06** There are fans who believe that Stien (Rodney Bewes) is too good as a Dalek Agent. They also believe that anything showing him to be an unstable duplicate is a blooper.

Episode 3
First Transmitted: Feb. 15, 1984

1:24 The Doctor meets Lytton, but does not learn Lytton's name. **3:51** Some fans question why the duplicates are soldiers and not infiltrators. The Daleks probably want to keep potentially unstable duplicates nearby until they prove themselves. They can always change clothes and infiltrate later. **5:19** The lower body, sealed in the wall behind the Doctor, moves its foot. This is not the only occurrence of a moving body. **5:58** There are reports that Tegan finds the canisters. Tegan does not find the canisters. They are in plain sight, and many people have been examining them. She tosses the canisters around and comments on how light they are. **11:45** Pay attention to the progress the soldiers make when removing the narrow wall panels. They must be taking some panels down and replacing the same panels. **13:34** There is a piece of paper stuck under the front of the first Dalek to enter the room. Maybe this Dalek needed to use the facilities before entering the room. **15:32** We hear the sound effect of the Dalek transporter twice, but only one canister disappears. Professor Laird (Chloe Ashcroft) behaves differently each time, so the purposes of the two sounds may be different. **15:40** Professor Laird's behavior when the canister actually disappears is different from the first time when a canister did not disappear. **16:20** If you watch the background while the Doctor is strapped down, "bodies" are continually moving. In this particular instance, the person to the right moves a hand. This body is next to the bodies of "Tegan" and "Turlough." There are reports that the bodies are corpses. The bodies are not corpses; they are un-animated duplicates. **16:57** It takes two troopers to move the canister that Tegan tossed around and said was so light. Obviously, the troopers need more exercise. **21:51** Leela, amongst others, is not included with the Doctor's past companions. **22:29** The needle is obviously behind the "egg."

Episode 4
First Transmitted: Feb. 15, 1984

1:01 Why is there no "reception committee" waiting for Tegan on the Dalek ship? Do the Daleks expect prisoners to beam aboard and just wait for an escort? **1:41** Again, we have pictures of the companions sans Leela. **4:00** If the Daleks want to invade the Earth, why would they store something on Earth that would lead to their defeat (the Movellan virus)? **5:44** The Doctor, Mercer (Jim Findley) and Stien enter the laboratory where Davros is waiting. It is possible to see a production crewmember push the door shut, stand and walk away. This person shows through the translucent wall to the left of the door. **9:00** One of the falling soldiers nearly knocks over part of the wall. **9:07** Stien leans back and nearly knocks the wall down. **12:04** Colonel Archer's (Del Henney) death is overacted. **12:23** Tegan again demonstrates that she is stronger than two of Lytton's troopers are. **12:53** Three Daleks enter the time corridor. **14:18** Four Daleks exit the time corridor. **16:57** The "egg" begins to release smoke (virus) before hitting the countertop. **18:46** The dead Daleks appear partially melted. **20:39** Who sent the Doctor an image of the space station and the Dalek ship exploding? **21:24** We learn that the duplicates are unstable.

Comments: The video presents four Episodes. The box for the commercial tape advertises the story as being a two-part story.

Originally, the story was four episodes. Later re-editing produced two double length episodes for transmission. The Commercial tape reflects the original recording. This has caused discrepancies in the placement of certain bloopers. The DVD has four episodes and reflects the original intention of the story.

The Doctor defeats the Daleks.

(6Q) PLANET OF FIRE

Writer: Peter Grimwade; **Director:** Fiona Cumming

Media: Commercial tape — episodic version — 98 minutes (used); Collector's tape — movie version — 90 minutes
Highlights: Turlough leaves and Peri (Nicola Bryant) joins the Doctor.
Questions: Where are the tilled fields and animals? Where do the inhabitants get their food?

Errors and Other Points of Interest

The Doctor continually reverses his braces. This can be determined by examining the question marks on the braces. Only two examples of each are present in this list instead of every time. The easiest way to observe this is by watching the bottom-most question mark on both sides in the front.

There is some question about Turlough's age. He looks too young to have fought on Trion. However, he does have a military rank (hereditary?). The explanation may be because people from Trion age differently from Earthlings. Turlough could appear the way he does for many years.

Episode 1
First Transmitted: Feb. 23, 1984

5:40 How did Kamelion survive Frontios? **8:23** Peri, an American, has an English accent when she says, "Elton John." Normally this type of blooper would not appear on this list, but it is present in at least one other source; therefore, it needs to be included. As a reminder—only accent problems listed in other sources will be included here. **16:11** The plastic bag Peri is holding would serve as an excellent float—why does she not use it as such? **19:35** When Peri wakes up, we find that she has dried unusually fast. **20:24** The masking-tape–covered power cord is beneath the Doctor's feet.

Episode 2
First Transmitted: Feb. 24, 1984

2:35 Some viewers find fault with the Doctor's claim that Turlough never mentioned his home planet before. Even though Turlough has mentioned wishing to return to his home planet, this is the first mention of Trion by name. **4:09** Kamelion removes an item from the Doctor's TARDIS. Later we learn this is the Comparator. **4:17** Peri asks Kamelion, "Who is the Master?"—just after she met "him." **7:01** Some viewers are concerned with the Master's command for Kamelion to materialize the Doctor's TARDIS inside the Master's TARDIS. These viewers cite Time-Ram (see *The Time Monster*), but they forget Logopolis. **9:56** The Doctor hears the name Logar. **10:34** The Doctor asks Amyand (James Bate) and Sorasta (Barbara Shelley) about Logar. Some viewers claim no one mentioned the name Logar to the Doctor and question how the Doctor knows to ask about Logar. This is an error on other lists. **17:58** Look at the question marks on the Doctor's braces. The bottom question mark on the Doctor's right is backwards, and the similarly positioned one on the Doctor's left is normal.

Episode 3
First Transmitted: Mar. 1, 1984

13:12 The Doctor discovers that his Temporal Stabilizer (not the Comparator) is missing, and he cannot move the TARDIS. Apparently, the "Master" removed the circuit, so Turlough's return of the comparator was insufficient. **13:32** Look at the question marks on the Doctor's braces. The bottom question mark on the Doctor's right is normal, and the similarly positioned one on the Doctor's left is backwards. **14:57** Some observers feel that the Master's TCE (tissue compression eliminator) should not work on the suits since they are not tissue. There are two problems with this claim. This is the Master's improved model. The Master's TCE has always reduced people's clothes. Why do these observers think this time is a blooper? **22:30** The Master turns and looks up as Peri removes the lid, and then he repeats the same motions again. This also occurs in the reprise.

Episode 4
First Transmitted: Mar. 2, 1984

7:14 Some viewers report a scene where the mountains move relative to the desert floor as the Doctor is walking. Other viewers report this to occur in Episode 1. This is apparently what these viewers are referring to. This is an illusion caused by the moving of the Doctor and the camera at the same time. Note added in proof the Doctor never enters the desert until Episode 2. **10:24** It is interesting to note that Trion spaceships use Earth-type telephone keypads including the symbols "*" and "#" in their "proper" places. **12:27** The Doctor removes the Temporal Stabilizer from the Master's TARDIS. **12:30** The Master's TARDIS also has a console power cord on the floor. **15:12** Kamelion moves the Master's TARDIS (without the Temporal Stabilizer) to just behind the flame jet; this allows Kamelion to carry the box containing the Master out of the TARDIS and into the flame. Maybe the Temporal Stabilizer is only important for time travel. **17:13** The Master's TCE also works on Kamelion — he is not tissue. **19:20** Turlough pushes the last button, says the TARDIS is on a fifteen-second delay, and then the TARDIS materializes. **19:41** The 15-second delay is really a 21-second delay.

Comments: The Doctor defeats the Master and saves the planet Lanzarote.

(6R) THE CAVES OF ANDROZANI

Writer: Robert Holmes; **Director:** Graeme Harper

Media: DVD — episodic version — 100 minutes (used); Commercial tape — episodic version — 100 minutes (used); Collector's tape — movie version — 92 minutes
Highlights: We lose one Doctor and gain another.
Questions: Why is Morgus so determined to have the Doctor and Peri executed?

Errors and Other Points of Interest

Episode 1
First Transmitted: Mar. 8, 1984

0:55 The ground is "shaking." **0:56** The horizon shows through the left mountain. This is less obvious in the DVD version. **1:23** The camera pans to the right, but the right-hand mountain does not come back into view. **1:57** Peri uses the English not the American pronunciation of "glass." **2:56** The camera shakes when the Doctor heads towards the cave. However, the background does not shake. This is less obvious in the DVD version. **3:20** The Doctor claims that the mud bursts occur when the two planets pass close together. This cannot be the case because they are on one of a pair of twin planets. The two planets should orbit about their center of gravity. Each planet should remain on the opposite side of the center of gravity. **4:16** Why do the soldiers simply fire into the air with no target? There are no ricochets. **4:36** Peri falls in the cave, and it appears as if she lands on a trampoline as she quickly bounces back up. **5:18** The Doctor finally explains why he wears a stalk of celery. **8:11** The remote control that Timmin (Barbara Kinghorn) is holding is obviously a television remote control with tape over the logo. **13:37** General Chellak's (Martin Cochrane) image disappears before Morgus pushes the control button. **15:20** Morgus (John Normington) and Timmin descend in the elevator; apparently the walls are not glass (transparent). This is definitely true on one side; the other walls may be glass. **15:58** One of the boxes of guns is stuck when the gunrunners attempt to throw it off the walkway.

Episode 2
First Transmitted: Mar. 9, 1984

1:12 The guns leave no holes or create any other damage to the red clothes over the "Doctor" and "Peri." **1:11** Some fans claim that the sound of the machine gun fire interferes with the image on the screen. This does not occur in the DVD version. **19:44** Salateen (Robert Glenister) appears surprised that the Doctor is an alien. Why should a member of a space-traveling race be surprised? **19:57** The Android's view of the Doctor shows the Doctor's hearts are outside his coat. **21:05** Stotz (Maurice Roëves) has trouble saying the line "All right, then where's the two kilos?" Apparently, he was going to say "spectrox" instead of "two." Some observers incorrectly report this to be in Episode 3.

Episode 3
First Transmitted: Mar. 15, 1984

13:02 When the Doctor rips the handle off the wall of the ship, it sounds as if it clatters across the room; however, the handle is hanging from the Doctor's chain. It is possible that there was an intentional movement of the camera to reflect the Doctor's concern that one of the crew might enter and not an attempt to follow the handle. This is not the case since Stotz later finds at least one of the handles by the door. **17:21** The elevator shaft now has glass walls. One wall is still dark, so this may not be a blooper as reported.

Episode 4
First Transmitted: Mar. 16, 1984

5:27 The Doctor's coat gets dirty during the mud burst. **9:34** The Doctor's coat is now clean. There are other inconsistencies — only some of the times are present. **13:45** The Doctor's coat is dirty again. **17:47** The Doctor is again wearing a clean coat. **18:25** Some viewers claim that the question mark on the Doctor's collar is backwards and thus the image is backwards. This does not appear to be the case. The question mark on the Doctor's right collar is always facing in this direction. **18:28** The Doctor is now wearing a dirty coat. **18:54** The Doctor's coat is now clean. **20:25** From this point until the end, the Doctor's coat is dirty. **24:01** During the Doctor's regeneration small "mouse holes" appear in the TARDIS. This is not the first time they are visible.

Comments: The DVD version of the story is "treated" to remove some of the original problems.

The "New" Doctor actually has a line.

VI
The Sixth Doctor

(6S) THE TWIN DILEMMA

Writer: Anthony Steven; **Director:** Peter Moffatt

Media: Commercial tape — episodic version — 99 minutes (used); Collector's tape — movie version — 92 minutes
Highlights: The new Doctor begins his travels.

Errors and Other Points of Interest

Episode 1
First Transmitted: Mar. 22, 1984

2:11 Some viewers believe that the Twins' father, Professor Sylvest (Dennis Chinnery) is overly melodramatic when talking about the potential dangers of the Twins' mathematical abilities. Apparently, these viewers either did not see *Logopolis*, or forgot Adric's block transfer calculations in *Castrovalva*. **4:36** The Twins (Gavin and Andrew Conrad) are sitting next to each other and then rotate until they are back to back. They are too close together to rotate face to face. This reportedly occurs three times. **6:09** The Twins are now further apart, and they can now rotate to face each other. How did they move apart? **6:16** There are fans that feel the Twins should be intelligent enough to know that Edgeworth's (Maurice Denham) appearance is more than "a simple illusion." **9:39** Mestor (Edwin Richfield) addresses Azmael (Maurice Denham) as Edgeworth. **9:57** Many observers question why the kidnappers stop at Titan 3. Mestor tells Edgeworth to go to Titan 3 so there will be no trail to Jaconda. **12:09** Professor Sylvest finds some dust on the floor. **12:34** The Professor reports that he found zanium, not zanium dust, on the floor. **12:55** Hugo Lang (Kevin McNally) informs the Commander (Helen Blatch) that Professor Sylvest detected "a dust-like deposit on the floor of their [the Twins'] room; he says it was zanium." How did Hugo know the zanium was in dust form? **13:46** The mirror that Peri is holding reflects light onto her neck. **16:51** If you look closely at the display, you will see that this is a computer program written in BASIC. The last line is the "RUN" command, which, when Elena (Dione Inman) hits the return, generates the display about the X.V.773. **16:58** Elena knows much more about X.V.773 than the screen displays. **18:26** As the Doctor walks around the console, it is possible to see the power cord on the floor. **19:07** The Doctor heads for the TARDIS door without touching the console (so the doors do not open); however, we hear the sound of the doors opening. Some observers report that the Doctor returned to the console and opened the door — this does not happen. We never see the Doctor and Peri actually leave the

TARDIS. **19:57** Mestor still addresses Azmael as Edgeworth.

Episode 2
First Transmitted: Mar. 23, 1984

2:02 How did Peri know about the power pack on the gun? **3:06** At least one viewer suggests that the kidnapping was unnecessary, as anyone could have done the calculations. The person suggesting this should try to solve the equations derived by the Twins at this point. **4:41** Azmael is still Edgeworth to Mestor. **4:58** The reflection of someone's leg appears in the plastic in front of the Twins as Mestor is threatening the Twins. It is not Azmael's leg as he is wearing a robe. Mestor is saying, "I see that you have." **7:40** The view screen shows it to be night outside and that the path to the building is level. **8:02** The Doctor again starts to exit the TARDIS without opening the doors. Peri turns a switch controlling the scanner, which generates a sound similar to the sound of the doors opening. **8:58** The Doctor finally pulls the lever to open the doors. There are reports that the Doctor hits the door control. **9:37** When the Doctor and Peri go outside, the view is not the same as seen on the TARDIS view screen — it is daylight and they must go up a hill. **10:43** The Twins realize the circles on their wrists cause their amnesia — so why do they not at least try to remove the circles? **13:14** The console in front of Azmael rocks as he moves his hands. **14:12** The Doctor and Peri enter the base. This is more than 10 seconds before Peri leaves. **15:27** The Time Lords normally recognize regenerated Time Lords — why does Azmael not recognize the Doctor? **15:35** The Doctor recognizes Edgeworth as Azmael. This is the first mention of the name Azmael. **17:56** The Twins hear the Doctor refer to Edgeworth as Azmael. This is where they learn Azmael's true name. They also may have heard Azmael's name earlier when the Doctor first recognized Azmael. **20:28** What are the chances of Hugo picking the one coat in the room with the power pack? **21:08** The computer console wobbles as the Doctor goes to see what Peri has found. **22:58** The Doctor would have had to send Peri back more than ten seconds in time to get her aboard the TARDIS. Peri has been in the base for over eight and a half minutes. **23:28** Peri arrives in the TARDIS.

Episode 3
First Transmitted: Mar. 29, 1984

1:59 The Doctor arrives in an empty TARDIS. **2:18** The Doctor says he overcompensated and was originally ten seconds in the future. If Peri arrived in the past, she should have already been there when the Doctor arrived. **3:46** The Twins tell Edgeworth they know he is Azmael. Some viewers report that Edgeworth tells the Twins his true name, not the other way around. **3:58** We see the TARDIS detected in flight. This leads to many blooper claims in other stories. **6:44** Mestor first refers to Edgeworth as Azmael. It is possible that Mestor read Azmael's mind and realized that deception was no longer necessary. This is before Azmael asks Mestor to stop mind reading. Some observers find fault with the sudden change. **12:30** Azmael and the rest walk down a corridor. An angry Azmael lectures the Twins. After the lecture, they all walk back the way they came instead of continuing down the corridor. **16:59** Azmael wants Mestor to stop reading his thoughts. **17:48** Why does Mestor not leave a slime trail? **18:47** Even Azmael should see the fallacy in Mestor's claim that bringing the planets close together will give them the same atmosphere. The larger planet will retain most of the atmosphere. **19:04** The mathematical delicacy Azmael is talking about is an example of the classic "three-body problem." Modern mathematics still has not found a way to solving this problem exactly. The best modern computers can only approximate a solution. This contradicts the argument that anyone could do the simple mathematics presented in this program. **21:33** Hugo begins to drop before the blow falls. **22:47** A simple error in the calculation for putting the three planets in the same orbit would not, as the Doctor exclaims, "blow a small hole in the Universe." This could be a euphemism for an exploding star. The Doctor has been misquoted. The mass of the planets would have no bearing on the stability of their orbits.

Episode 4
First Transmitted: Mar. 30, 1984
1:29 Noma (Barry Stanton) can easily see Hugo, whom Noma knows Mestor wants, but Noma only takes the Doctor. **7:28** Mestor uses mental energy to open the TARDIS door. **13:40** This should explain the suggested blooper questioning why Azmael did not use the slug poison. Do not forget, Mestor was reading Azmael's mind previously. **22:13** The Chamberlain (Seymour Green) is apparently standing just through the archway behind Peri as she turns to the Lieutenant after sending the Twins into the TARDIS. The Chamberlain seems to be giving a signal.

Comments: The Doctor saves the planet of Jaconda.

(6T) Attack of the Cybermen

Writer: Paula Moore; **Director:** Matthew Robinson

Media: Commercial tape — episodic version — 89 minutes (used); Collector's tape — movie version — 86 minutes
Highlights: We get to see the new forms of the TARDIS.
Questions: Whose time machine did the Cybermen capture? Why would the Cryons contact Lytton for help when he was transmitting a distress signal? Why did the Cybermen not detect Lytton's signal?

Errors and Other Points of Interest

Episode 1
First Transmitted: Jan. 5, 1985
4:35 There has been a blooper claim that the only way the TARDIS could have encountered a gigantic g-force would be for the TARDIS to be in free-fall through an atmosphere. Free-fall would make the inhabitants of the ship feel weightless. The requirement for a gigantic g-force is a gigantic mass, or a gigantic acceleration. **6:31** After the Doctor stabilizes the TARDIS, Peri says, "My heart is where my liver should be." The Doctor looks to see the "problem," but he looks neither at Peri's heart nor at her liver. **7:11** This is one of the better views of the apparent burn in the TARDIS wall; it is above and to the left of Peri. The cause of the burn occurs later. **10:50** There is a discussion about carrying guns. Lytton (Maurice Colbourne) says he is taking only one gun (he may mean one machine pistol). **12:08** A continuity check — the sign says "I. M. FOREMAN, 76 TOTTERS LANE." **15:49** Lytton gives Payne (James Beckett) a gun that is not the same as the "one" gun Lytton said he had. **26:13** The chin of the speaking Cyberman shows through the plastic chin piece of his helmet. This happens in other places. This does not happen in the case of the Cyber Leader (David Banks).

27:58 The prisoner, when shot by the Cyberman, rolls down the hill and hits the camera. **32:26** The Cyberman in the left rear seems intoxicated. **33:52** There are reports claiming a blooper because the Doctor never saw Lytton before, so how can the Doctor recall what Lytton looks like? The Doctor saw Lytton in *Resurrection of the Daleks*. The Doctor did not learn Lytton's name at that time. It is possible that the Doctor learned Lytton's name from one of the other characters off camera. **35:33** The Cybermen in this story have five fingers. **36:55** The explosion caused by the Cyberman's gun seems premature, and not where he is aiming. **38:18** One of the Cybermen apparently says, "It is a fat Controller." (This could be a comment on the Cyber Controller's [Michael Kilgarriff] waistline, and not a blooper.) **42:29** As the Cyberman falls, the plate on the back of his head comes off and you can see the actor's neck. This occurs again in the reprise. **42:36** Russell (Terry Molloy) creates the burn on the wall seen in many earlier scenes. **42:44** Notice the wire to the detonator hanging from the Cyberman in the doorway. **42:51** Three normal Cybermen and one black Cyberman enter the TARDIS. The black Cyberman represents a camouflaged Cyberman for patrolling the dark sewers. **42:59** The TARDIS doors have mysteriously closed, even though there is no door closing sound, and no one touches the door control. **42:59** Four Cybermen are in the TARDIS (excluding those who are dead). **44:04** The credit for the Designer (Marjorie Pratt) seems not to match the other credits. This occurs at the end of the next episode also.

Episode 2
First Transmitted: Jan. 12, 1985

2:18 The Cyber Leader notes that the Cybermen can now time travel. The Cyber Leader then tells the Doctor to go to Telos, but he does not mention any time shift. **3:38** The Doctor refers to the last time he met Lytton. Some viewers claim this is the first time the Doctor ever met Lytton. **9:10** All four Cybermen are normal Cybermen—the black Cyberman has disappeared. We apparently have an abortive attempt at integration. **10:49** Only three Cybermen leave the TARDIS. Some observers cite this as a blooper because one Cyberman must still be inside the TARDIS. This Cyberman is on guard, as noted later. **12:52** The guardrail is not very substantial. **14:12** Some viewers believe that Lytton and the Cryons could not communicate because the Cryons are in Lytton's future. The Cyber Leader did not have the Doctor time-shift, thus Lytton and the Cryons are in the same time. This leads to another problem—how could the Cybermen know of the destruction of Mondas a year before the event? **24:24** Contrary to the claims of some fans, the Cybermen do have a reason for blowing up Telos. **26:00** Some fans wonder how a comet may become a bomb. The referral may be to the damage caused by embedded meteors within the comet. **27:41** There are observers who wonder why the Cybermen would place the Doctor in a cell with explosives. This is where the Doctor learns about the explosives. The Doctor also learns that the explosive is not dangerous at the temperature in the cell. The low temperature may be why the Cybermen do not worry; however, they should make sure he could not increase the temperature. **30:24** The panicking Cyberman attempts to extinguish his burning arm with his gun. **31:23** The Cryons expect there to be guards on the TARDIS. Some viewers believe there should be no Cybermen in the TARDIS and claim a problem earlier when not all the Cybermen leave. **38:06** We see two Cybermen. One was originally on guard outside the TARDIS, and the other exits the TARDIS. The exiting Cyberman should clarify the blooper claim about a Cyberman remaining inside the TARDIS. **41:25** Some of the Cyber Controller's "blood" lands on the camera lens. **41:47** There is a detonator wire hanging from the Cyber Controller. **41:49** During the fight between the Doctor and the Cyber Controller, they kick over and crease a portion of the carpet. **42:38** Just before the bomb is to explode a Cyberman signals another to leave in a very un–Cyberman-like way.

Comments: The Doctor defeats the Cybermen and saves the Earth and Telos.

This story first appeared as two double-length episodes.

(6V) Vengeance on Varos

Writer: Philip Martin; **Director:** Ron Jones

Media: DVD — episodic version — 90 minutes (used); Commercial tape — episodic version — 90 minutes; Collector's tape — movie version — 86 minutes

Errors and Other Points of Interest

Some observers claim the apparent use of a 24-hour clock on Varos is a blooper. This may or may not be a problem. It is possible that residents of planets with Earth descendants simply divide their days, whatever the length, into 24 equal units, which they call hours. Further division of these "hours" into "minutes" and "seconds" is then possible. As an alternative explanation — this could be a simple translation due to the Time Lords' Gift.

Episode 1

First Transmitted: Jan. 19, 1985

4:45 Sil (Nabil Shaban) is using a translator. If he is speaking an alien language, why do his lips move along with the English translation? **11:10** The machine cuffs the Governor's (Martin Jarvis) hands after the vote. **16:06** When Peri and the Doctor first open the TARDIS manual, it appears to have only blank pages. **19:06** It now appears as if at least some of the pages in the TARDIS manual are not blank. **23:02** Some observers question the design of the guns. These observers believe the seven holes should emit bullet-like projectiles. **23:12** The red "bullets" from the gun get larger as they move away from the weapon. **23:16** The Doctor turns off the scanner. Thus, Peri can no longer see what the guard is doing. **23:19** The guard's "bullets" apparently only ricochet the second time the guard fires his weapon. This may be an illusion due to the angle. **23:37** The guard turns away from the TARDIS. **23:48** Peri asks the Doctor, "Why did that man fire at us and then turn away as if we didn't exist?" Peri could not have seen the guard turn away since the Doctor turned off the scanner earlier. **26:25** Sil calls the ore "Zeiton 7." **26:39** Sil says, "When the engineers of every known solar system cry out for this product to drive their space-time craft." This does not strengthen Sil's bargaining position. Sil should have said the opposite if he wished to keep the price low. Sil cannot be positive that the Governor is unconscious. **31:30** The Doctor informs everyone they can escape if they get back to the TARDIS. Peri seems to agree with this. How can they escape in a TARDIS with no Zeiton 7? **37:52** How did the Doctor manage to escape down a side corridor without the guards seeing him? The guards were only a few feet behind. **40:39** This time the machine cuffs the Governor's (Martin Jarvis) hands before the vote. Why does the machine behave differently this time? **41:00** The Doctor simultaneously removes his outer coat and his inner waistcoat (you can see the white inner lining of the waistcoat). There are reports that he did not remove his waistcoat but that it simply disappears. **41:02** Some fans wonder why the desert illusion causes thirst, but the water illusion does not quench the thirst. The Doctor is "inside" the desert illusion, but he is only looking at Peri and the water illusion. **41:27** The Doctor falls and drops his coat and waistcoat. **42:17** The Doctor's coats are no longer behind him as he crawls along the corridor. **43:24** After the Governor says "cut it" the "dead" Doctor moves. This also occurs in the reprise.

Episode 2
First Transmitted: Jan. 26, 1985
1:24 It takes the guards an unbelievably short time to collect the Doctor's body and transport it to the acid room. **2:36** If the acid is so dangerous, why does one of the guards not have his mask over his nose? **4:21** There is a false blooper reported — the Doctor does not "intentionally" push any guards into the acid bath. **4:33** The edge of the acid pool does not seem to be overly stable. **7:32** Peri says the events occur about 300 years in her future. Sil has already stated that the engineers need Zeiton 7 for their "space-time craft." Thus within about three centuries all planets have time-travel technology like the Time Lords. **22:40** As the Doctor releases Peri, one of the buckles slides down the table. **24:43** The energy "bullets" apparently go through, or around, the Doctor without injuring him. **25:04** The Doctor heads back to get Jondar (Jason Connery), and one of the guards apparently fires his weapon and then ducks out of the corridor. We neither see nor hear the guard's "shot." **25:15** The energy "bullets" no longer increase in size as they move away from the gun. **25:18** As the cart turns the corner, the shots from the guards' guns cause an explosion nowhere near where the guards are aiming. **25:55** Sil now calls the ore "Zeiton E." (He may be saying Zeiton A.) **30:37** A studio light shines through the gap near the roof of the tunnel. **32:16** In this case, the machine cuffs the Governor's hands after the vote.

Comments: The Doctor saves Varos.

(6X) THE MARK OF THE RANI

Writer: Pip and Jane Baker; **Director:** Sarah Hellings

Media: Commercial tape — episodic version — 90 minutes (used); Collector's tape — movie version — 87 minutes
Highlights: We meet the Rani (Kate O'Mara).
Question: Why is the absence of birds significant?

Errors and Other Points of Interest

Episode 1
First Transmitted: Feb. 2, 1985
1:06 The camera shakes as the workers push the coal car. **4:03** The Doctor tells Peri that their location, but not their time coordinates, is changing. **4:55** Some observers report that Kew Gardens were not open in the 1820s. This is only partially true. The

gardens did exist, but they were not the home of the Botanical Gardens in the 1820s. The appearance of George Stephenson gives an additional complication. **8:58** The Doctor says he has not changed the course of history. This may just be a ploy — to keep the facts "secret." **12:21** Some observers object to the mention of Thomas Edison since he was born after the events in this story. This is an interesting piece of trivia, but an item with no relationship to this story since no mention is ever made of Edison's name. **13:41** The guard dog lies down in plain sight, but in the next shot, it is partially behind the open door. **15:05** Some viewers claim the dog is not actually barking. **15:18** Some fans cite the use of the tissue compression eliminator on the dog and the guard as a blooper. The blooper is because no body remains in either case. This is apparently the Master's new and improved TCE the Master was working on before the events in *Planet of Fire*. **18:06** Three men attack the Doctor, then one falls down the mineshaft. Later there are still three attackers (at least three pairs of legs) — they appear immediately after we see the Master's face. **20:03** Lord Ravensworth (Terence Alexander) uses the term Luddites. Some viewers cite this as a blooper because the Luddites did not attack coal-mining machinery. The plotline may exonerate this "blooper." This is the Luddite Blooper. **21:57** The Master has a way to open the Rani's latched door. **23:43** The Rani orders Josh and Tom to attack the Master. Josh stops to give the Master time to eliminate Tom, and then Josh stops again before the Rani tells him to stop. **24:39** The man on the floor is clearly conscious. He has his eyes open, and they blink several times. **25:00** There are viewers who claim that the "unconscious" man on the floor raises his leg. He is not unconscious, and he only shifts, not raises, his leg. **25:02** There are reports of a boom mike shadow here. **25:17** Some observers claim that Peri says "Killingsworth" instead of "Killingworth." This does not happen here. This is the only time Peri says either name. **25:33** The Doctor tells Peri they did not come to their present location by accident. **26:15** There is a question about why it is not possible to replicate the brain fluid. This is technobabble, and not a blooper. **27:10** The Master followed the Rani to this area. **27:20** There are those who question the reason why the Rani is so concerned about the planet she rules (Miasimia Goria). Maybe she simply does not want to start over on some other planet. **29:01** The Master refers to his two hearts. He is in his stolen Traken body. Do Trakens have two hearts like the Time Lords? **30:44** The Doctor dirties his face as a disguise. **32:57** The Doctor's dirty disguise has partially disappeared. **33:10** Some viewers question the Master's assumption that simply tossing the blue box down a mineshaft will destroy the TARDIS. The Master's original comment was to "bury" the TARDIS. This may mean that the Master only wishes to keep the TARDIS away from the Doctor, not to destroy the craft. The Master obviously knows how difficult it is to destroy a TARDIS. **35:35** The Doctor alludes to the Luddites as being camouflage. **37:12** Peri sneaks into the bathhouse after the Rani leaves. Peri is very careful to bolt the door behind her. **38:16** The Master and the Rani simply walk into the bathhouse after Peri bolted the door. The Time Lords do not seem to use the Master's door opening device. **39:50** The doors of the TARDIS appear to be about to fall open while it is on the wagon. **41:39** The Master should tell Peri to pull (towards the door) and not push (towards the wall). When the Doctor told Peri to push earlier, she went to the opposite end of the table.

Episode 2
First Transmitted: Feb. 9, 1985

3:23 The Doctor specifically says the troublemakers are not Luddites. In any case, their motivation is due to the Rani's treatment, and not any type of Luddite motivations. This may clear the Luddite Blooper. **4:28** A boom mike shadow appears on George Stephenson (Gawn Grainger) as the Doctor stops Luke before he leaves. **6:30** The list still does not contain the name Thomas Edison. **8:37** The Master has trouble putting the vial into his coat pocket. **10:03** The "dead" Josh is still breathing. **12:06** As Peri stands outside the bathhouse before following the Doctor—the camera goes out of focus twice. **13:07** The Doctor indicates to Peri that the Rani's servants are dead. Josh is still breathing. **15:01** There are those who wonder why the Doctor and Peri do not run out of the room. The Doctor is expecting a trap; he and Peri should be ready to run. **20:18** As the Doctor comes out of the adit, some rain splashes onto the camera lens. **21:21** George Stephenson says "You" to Luke when he should have said "Thee." **24:28** The Rani forgets to camouflage the next to the last landmine as she sets it. **25:37** Some observers believe it to be too much of a coincidence for three Time Lords to appear in the same place. The Master apparently came looking for the Rani, or he detected her TARDIS. We also learn that the Master caused the Doctor's TARDIS diversion to this spot. Thus, the Master's interference makes this not a simple coincidence. **29:56** Peri nearly falls as "Luke" saves her. **35:06** The two trees holding the Doctor's pole deserve the label—blooper. **39:11** The chameleon circuit in the Rani's TARDIS apparently has the same warranty as the one in the Doctor's TARDIS. Her TARDIS really does not look disguised while in the mine. **40:59** Something is stuck under the wall behind the pedestal with the Tyrannosaurus embryo. This tips the pedestal over.

Comments: The Doctor defeats the Master and the Rani.

(6W) THE TWO DOCTORS

Writer: Robert Holmes; **Director:** Peter Moffatt

Media: Commercial DVD — episodic version —134 minutes (used); Commercial tape — episodic version —134 minutes; Collector's tape — movie version —133 minutes
Highlights: We see Spain and Doctors.

Errors and Other Points of Interest

Episode 1
First Transmitted: Feb. 16, 1985

1:09 The story appears to take place between *The Evil of the Daleks* and *Fury from the Deep*. Thus, this story takes place during Victoria's tenure as a companion even though she is not present. It would have been simpler to pick a time when Jamie was the Doctor's only companion. **1:34** The Second Doctor mentions the Time Lords to Jamie. This is much earlier and much more detail than Jamie was supposed to know about the Time Lords. In this story, the Second Doctor is an agent of the Time Lords, even though he was supposedly hiding from them at the time. **2:32** The Second Doctor heads towards the closed TARDIS doors before he remembers the recall disk, and goes back for it. The Doctor forgot to open the doors, so he had to go back anyway. **3:47**

Shockeye (John Stratton) mentions Dastari (Laurence Payne). Dastari is an anagram of "A TARDIS." **9:27** Something falls out of the device as Chessene (Jacqueline Pearce) withdraws it. **11:39** The Sixth Doctor must make the "fish" seem alive by moving it with his fingers. **25:09** This story has tall, "skinny," three-fingered Sontarans. **31:54** Doña Arana (Aimee Delamain) recognizes that the Androgums are speaking English. Where did the Androgums learn English? **32:22** The shape of the probic vent on the back of the Sontarans is different from past appearances of the Sontarans.

Episode 2
First Transmitted: Feb. 23, 1985

17:22 Chessene says the Doña Arana calls the animal a "rat." The Doña should call the animal "rata." Rata is Spanish for rat. The Second Doctor is in Spain so the explanation from *The Masque of Mandragora* may apply. **8:31** The output on the computer screen seems like so much babble. However, on closer examination we see that it also includes the error message "string to long @720." **18:07** The Sixth Doctor tells Peri, "Small though it is, the human brain can be quite effective when used properly." He then pats Peri on the head. In the next shot of Peri, read her lips. **28:29** This is one of the many scenes where the oversized collars on the Sontarans are obviously comical. **32:08** The Sixth Doctor approaches the window of the hacienda to eavesdrop. The window appears open, but it may not be open all the way. **32:23** Chessene hears the Doctor and goes to the window. She must open the window to check on the noise. The window is supposedly already open so the Sixth Doctor could eavesdrop. It is possible the other side of the window is partially open. **35:17** Peri has doubts about her assignment because see does not speak Spanish. The Sixth Doctor replies, "That's all right. Neither do they." If the Androgums do not speak Spanish — how did Chessene understand Doña Arana? **33:07** As the Sixth Doctor and Peri enter the duct, we see that the space station walls are not very stable. **36:30** Dastari tells the Second Doctor he cannot administer "a full anesthetic" because the Doctor must remain conscious. Some observers cite this as a blooper, when in reality it is technobabble. The effect of anesthetic on humans does not necessarily extend to Time Lords or to the present situation. Dastari may be referring to general versus local anesthetics. **37:25** The brain scanner seems to behave differently when viewed at different angles. **40:19** Dastari bumps into the wheel chair. **43:03** When the Sixth Doctor falls on the cables, the supports wobble significantly.

Episode 3
First Transmitted: Mar. 2, 1985

2:41 Stike (Clinton Greyn) has trouble pushing the buttons with his gun. It works the first time, but the second time he hits more than one button, and as for the third time... **6:39** Shockeye prepares to cut Peri's throat as a prelude to butchering her. He does not attempt to "tenderize" her. **8:11** The Sixth Doctor grabs a little too much of Peri and must move his hand. **10:58** The Second Doctor now has orange eyebrows. This would involve dying, as hair is dead matter (except for the roots). It is possible that rapidly growing new eyebrows "pushed" out the old eyebrows to give new orange hair. **13:38** The second Sontaran, like the first, grabs his head too hard and causes the mask to partially cave in. **14:37** Some fans claim that Doña Arana's knowledge of the current restaurants is a blooper. The knowledge Chessene says she gained from Dona Arana's mind includes many restaurants, not necessarily current restaurants. Anita's (Carmen Gomez) earlier comments indicate that the Doña was not always a recluse. **15:31** The Second Doctor has trouble running on the gravel when he tries to signal the lorry. **17:39** The Sixth

Doctor, Jamie, and Peri locate the lorry carrying Shockeye and the Second Doctor into Seville. The Sixth Doctor tells the others "they can't be more than a minute ahead of us." This would mean that the three pursuers had to run nearly as fast as the lorry was driving to be only a minute behind. **25:47** It is possible to see the bag of fake blood through Oscar's (James Saxon) shirt. **26:12** There is no blood on the knife Shockeye uses on Oscar. **26:15** After the stabbing, Oscar covers his wound with his hands — when he moves his hands there is no blood on them. **27:34** The Second Doctor's orange eyebrows "un-grow" and change color. Hair does not grow this way. **27:47** The customers and the staff continue as if Oscar's death was a normal occurrence in a Seville restaurant. **34:43** Shockeye "tenderizes" Jamie before butchering. Why did Shockeye skip this step with Peri? **35:31** Chessene seeks Dastari to tell him a Doctor has escaped. Some viewers believe that for Chessene to know this she must have been in the basement. Why did she not check to see if the Second Doctor and Peri had a key? Was she not suspicious of how the Doctor escaped? Some observers claim that she went to Shockeye instead of Dastari. In explanation — it is possible that she caught a glimpse of the escaping Sixth Doctor without going to the basement. **36:41** Shockeye cuts the Sixth Doctor on the upper inside thigh (the Sixth Doctor holds this area when first going outside). **38:09** The Sixth Doctor's wound has moved to the outside of the thigh, and in some cases lower on the leg. **39:04** What did Oscar have in his canteen? When the Sixth Doctor opens the canteen, the contents are smoking. This would be reasonable if this were a thermos. The smoking is present before pouring the contents onto the cyanide pellets. **41:52** The Sixth Doctor says he always wanted a recall unit for the TARDIS. If he had one as the Second Doctor, he had one.

Comments: In order to mislead people both Doctor's give or imply false information about the TARDIS and time travel. Taken out of context, these may generate false bloopers.

The Doctors defeat the Sontarans and saves the Earth.

Apparently, the Sontarans gave up cloning identical warriors. This has helped their appearance — they are taller and thinner.

(6Y) TIMELASH

Writer: Glen McCoy; **Director:** Pennant Roberts

Media: Commercial tape — episodic version — 90 minutes (used); Collector's tape — movie version — 87 minutes

Errors and Other Points of Interest

Episode 1
First Transmitted: Mar. 9, 1985

0:58 The Doctor tells Peri, "I was contemplating taking you to the constellation of Andromeda." He cannot do this — he could take her to a planet called Andromeda or to the Andromeda Galaxy. A constellation is a region in space visible from a planet. **3:39** Peri mentions the Daleks even though she does not see them until the next adventure. **3:39** Peri forgets her American accent when she pronounces "Daleks." **4:33** The Doctor mentions "time particles." At least one blooper seeker has asked what a time particle is. The answer is a chronon. These appear in various places — see, for example, *Time and the Rani*. **5:03** Some observers cite the timing of the female actor when shot as a blooper. Watch it for yourself and see if you agree. **8:55** Some observers object to the tinsel in the Timelash. **11:49** Both ends of the line Peri is observing are off the screen. **11:56** The Doctor asks Peri to tell him if any part of the line goes off the screen. However, both ends of the line are already off the screen. **15:29** Maylin Renis (Neil Hallett) pulls a knob off the console. He does an excellent job disguising his actions as he replaces the knob. **17:52** The Borad (Robert Ashby) says he has "a life spanning a dozen centuries." Some fans suggest that the creature does not have much to show for all of these years. This lack of progress is supposedly a blooper. This may not be a blooper since we do not know how much of the current technology of Karfel is due to the Borad. **18:13** When the skeleton of Maylin Renis falls to the floor, the string that was holding it up follows the skeleton down. **19:03** Some viewers object to the cause of death being a "fatal seizure." The problem is that there is no such thing as a fatal seizure. This is not a blooper; it is technobabble. Just because people on Earth cannot die from a fatal seizure does not mean that a Karfelon cannot die from a fatal seizure. Medical problems for humans do not necessarily apply to alien races. **23:16** The Doctor apparently visited Karfel as the Third Doctor with Jo Grant. It appears as if there was another companion, though we do not learn his/her identity. Tekker (Paul Darrow) queries the Doctor if Peri is his only companion, to which the Doctor replies that he is "traveling light this time." Since the preceding visit was an un-televised adventure, it is possible that there was another companion besides Jo. There is no mention of any companion other than Jo Grant. **25:28** The Bandril Ambassador (Martin Gower) refers to an Intergalactic Treaty. Thus, it would seem that the two planets are in different galaxies. Could the Bandrils not find a food source in the Bandril's own galaxy? **27:02** There is at least one fan who questions Peri's ability to read the note if it was not written in English. This fan may have forgotten *The Masque of Mandragora*. The Time Lords' Gift may apply to written languages. **28:46** We now learn that the Bandril's Planet is no longer in another galaxy. They will now need to negotiate an Interplanetary Treaty to replace their Intergalactic Treaty. **29:51** The gun the android fires at Peri should hit the door higher. The gun angles slightly upward, so the beam should not have ended at the same level as the gun. **30:54** Note that the teeth on the Morlox are as expected — behind the lips and in the gums. **33:45** Some observers suggest that the ability of Peri to identify Jo Grant is a blooper. However, Peri does say she has seen pictures of Jo before. **39:15** Herbert apparently hits an object with his foot as he whines, "Oh, very well then." **41:05** The Doctor tells Herbert there is no time to take him back. How can this be true — the TARDIS is a time machine; it can arrive before it left. **41:10** The Doctor walks over the console power cord. The power cord appears at other times.

Episode 2
First Transmitted: Mar. 16, 1985

2:24 Some of the special effects lighting shines "through" the Doctor. **2:41** After the attack, one of the fallen guards (supposedly unconscious) moves his legs. Some observers incorrectly report this as an Episode 1 blooper. This may not be a real blooper. **4:01** Some fans consider the physical properties of the crystals to be a blooper. The crystal properties are technobabble. **5:00** When the Doctor removes a small crystal, a patch of adhesive becomes visible. **5:25** We can see the tape holding the end of the large crystal together. We can see other bands of tape at other times. **6:52** Some observers object to the ability of Herbert (David Chandler) and Mykros (Eric Deacon) to enter the Timelash without a rope while the Doctor needed a rope. The Doctor needed a rope so his hands would be free to collect crystals. The Doctor's rescuers did not need to have their hands free to collect anything other than the Doctor. Both Herbert and Mykros did make use of the rope. **7:59** Part of the "Borad's" (Denis Carey) face on the view screen is outside the viewing area. **13:05** The first time the Doctor uses the crystal "he" disappears for 10 seconds and then his image goes through the motions until he switches off the crystal. The different results the second time he uses the crystal leads to the citation of this as a blooper. **13:40** The delay seems to be more than 10 seconds. **15:10** The glowing front of the dormant Timelash shines through Sezon (Dicken Ashworth). **17:09** The guard whose shot exposes the Third Doctor's picture inexplicably falls over as if shot. There is no sound of a shot. **17:33** Apparently, Vena (Jeananne Crowley) knows about regeneration. **21:04** The railing in front of Herbert is not too stable. **23:35** Tekker has the medallion on a chain about his neck. **24:23** The chain is no longer about Tekker's neck. **25:48** The second time the Doctor uses the crystal it gives different results. However, this time Herbert is watching through the special scope. The scope may explain the differences seen by viewers. **26:02** There are those who consider the Borad's knowledge of regeneration to be a blooper. This may not be the case, given the Bandril's knowledge of the Time Lords. Knowledge of the Time Lords may be extensive in this region of space. **27:59** Some observers feel that the image of the star deserves the title — blooper. **29:43** The communication console is not sessile. **30:25** Notice the Doctor's hair. **30:43** Look at the Doctor's hair. It is much longer because shooting of this scene was much later than the remainder of the story. **30:47** When the Doctor opens the TARDIS doors in preparation of ejecting Peri, the TARDIS door opens too far and bounces off the TARDIS wall. **31:08** The tape on the floor is still not capable of disguising the console power cord. **31:39** Look at Peri's teeth while Peri is talking to the Doctor. **33:53** Some observers have a problem with the Doctor saluting another science fiction writer with the line "To be perfectly frank, Herbert...." **34:31** The observer who questioned Herbert's ability to understand the Doctor's reference to the screen (computer monitor) must have forgotten *The Masque of Mandragora*. **35:34** The first time the rocket and the planet appear together, the rocket seems to be going very slowly. It does seem capable of covering great distances in a short time. **36:24** It does not seem possible that the rocket could reach the position where we see it destroyed, between its earlier appearance and now. **37:03** Some observers cite the Bandrils' inability to feed themselves in spite of their technological advancement to be a blooper. The assumption is that anyone who knows about the Time Lords must have a technological development at a level sufficient to prevent famine. **38:33** The Borad's teeth on the Morlox side of his face are in his lips, not in the true Morlox position. **40:48** There are many left over parts on the countertop. Some of the parts are from the Timelash controller. **41:06** How did the Doctor find time to reassemble the Timelash control unit? This would be especially difficult since there are left over parts. Why would the Doctor, or anyone, want to repair the unit? In addition, why would the Doctor bother to repair the unit since he destroys it in the end?

Comments: The Doctor saves the planet of Karfel.

Pause to Consider: Astronomy

There are numerous occurrences within the *Doctor Who* series where various astronomical terms are misused. Some simplified definitions of the commonly confused terms are:

Constellation — a region in space containing stars as seen from a reference point
Galaxy — an exceedingly large group of stars
Light year — the distance light travels in a year
Meteor — a natural object in outer space
Meteorite — a natural object that reaches the surface of a planet from outer space
Star System — Solar System — a star and associated orbital material

Many times, we hear the term constellation or star (solar) system or galaxy where one of the other terms is appropriate. The most flagrant misuse is constellation. If you are looking into the sky at night and pick out a pattern of stars, you have chosen a constellation. This may not be one of the standard constellations such as Taurus, but that is irrelevant. If you could look at exactly the same stars in the night sky on Gallifrey, the pattern would be different. Constellations are a matter of perspective. Unless the actors are looking at star patterns in the night sky, there is no place in Doctor Who for the term, and the constellation would best be translated as blooper.

If the actors are discussing a single star the term "star system" is appropriate, and if an exceedingly large number of stars is involved, then the term "galaxy" may be appropriate. There are other astronomical terms, such as globular cluster, which would be appropriate in certain circumstances, but since these terms are not present in *Doctor Who*, their meanings are irrelevant.

The terms meteor and meteorite, and sometimes comet, are routinely misused. If the object is sitting in or on the ground, it is a meteorite. An object does not earn the name meteorite until it reaches a planet's surface. No object traveling in space is a meteorite. Thus, "meteorite storms," such as in *The Power of the Daleks*, are impossible. Meteors, amongst other things, travel in space. Increasing the size of a meteor gives first an asteroid, and then a planet. Comets, in a loose sense, may qualify as meteors. The characteristic appearance of comets, familiar to most people, occurs only when a comet approaches a star and the star volatilizes some matter. Far from a star, a comet is just an aggregate of rock and frozen matter. The presence of rocks in comets can lead to meteor showers as the Earth, and presumably other planets, the planet crosses the path of certain comets.

Astronomical distances are a common problem in science fiction. Many televised science fiction stories incorrectly use light year as a time unit instead of a distance unit. A light year is a distance a little less than 6,000,000,000,000 miles. Using a light year as a time unit is not a common occurrence in *Doctor Who*. The misuse of light year seems to occur in *The Savages*. The most common distance problem in *Doctor Who* concerns the distance between objects.

In many *Doctor Who* stories, it appears as if the distances between objects are always about the same. Thus, the distance between planets is the same as the distance between stars, which is the same as the distances between galaxies. This leads to nearly equal travel times, with travel from the Earth to Mars taking about the same time as travel from the Earth to Andromeda. Distances between planets are typically less than 0.001 light years, as opposed to distances between galaxies being millions of light years. The travel time from Earth to Andromeda should be about a billion times as long as from the Earth to Mars. Rockets work for travel between planets. Travel to other stars requires faster than light travel (FTL) or a generation ship such as in *The Ark*. Travel to other galaxies requires FTL travel. In *Trial of the Time Lord*, Glitz claims he is "wanted in six galaxies," yet he is seeking FTL. He could not travel from one galaxy to even one other galaxy without FTL. Why would Glitz want something he already has? A TARDIS appears to be acceptable to FTL.

(6Z) Revelation of the Daleks

Writer: Eric Saward; **Director:** Graeme Harper

Media: Commercial tape — episodic version — 90 minutes (used); Collector's tape — movie version — 88 minutes

Errors and Other Points of Interest

Episode 1
First Transmitted: Mar. 23, 1985

0:40 There is a report that a person walks by in the background during the very first scene. This is really an Episode 2 blooper. **8:06** At least one fan questions why Arthur Stengos' body is taken to Necros. Davros (Terry Molloy) answers this question with the comment, "My lure has worked." Apparently, Davros maneuvered the body to Necros to set a trap for the Doctor. **8:11** Davros orders the Daleks not to capture the Doctor. Davros wants to have the "greater pleasure." This is to refute the complaint lodged by some viewers that the Daleks should capture the Doctor upon his arrival. **14:11** We can see the head of the Dalek operator through the grill below the top while checking the security passes of the two employees. **14:11** Lilt (Colin Spaull) has trouble getting his pass out of his pocket. The Dalek moves on before seeing Lilt's pass. **15:28** Grigory (Stephen Flynn) salutes *Star Trek* when he says, "I'm a doctor, not a magician!" **19:29** What is the use of having guards (presumably trained to fire their weapons) when other employees simply take the guns away and use them with the disarmed guard following along behind. **20:14** The Doctor tells Peri he is 900 years old. **23:48** This is one point in the story where it is difficult to hear what Davros is saying. This usually occurs during his monologues. **26:31** The Head of Stengos (Alec Linstead) says he has undergone conditioning to obey a new master. On further questioning, we learn that he cannot remember who his new master is. How can he obey a new master if he does not know who the master is? **32:14** The viewing screen Davros is watching is not very stable, or the landscape is not very stable. There are various other scenes where the special effects landscapes are unsteady. **38:52** Peri sees a Dalek. When the Doctor asks her what she saw, she says she does not know. In *Timelash* (the preceding story), Peri knew what Daleks were, but not necessarily what a Dalek looks like. There is no evidence that she ever actually saw one previously. **41:43** The monument rocks back and forth and no one notices. It does not fall until later. **42:38** Peri should think before she speaks. The Doctor would have to have died before he filled the grave. This "filled" grave would represent the Doctor's death at some other time other than his current visit.

Episode 2
First Transmitted: Mar. 30, 1985

2:27 Some observers wonder about the person walking on the second floor inside the building. Apparently, they believe there are no other employees. **7:25** Orcini (William Gaunt) fires exploding bullets. **14:36** How does the Doctor know Davros is still alive? **21:56** Some observers report, as a blooper, that when Tasambeker (Jenny Tomasin) stabs Jobel (Clive Swift) she does not push the plunger on the syringe. It is true that she did not have her hand on the plunger, but immediately after plunging the syringe into Jobel, she stands between the camera and Jobel. It is possible that she pushed the plunger at this time. When the syringe next appears the plunger is in, and the green liquid is gone. **22:26** The Dalek on the left enters the scene with the plastic strips in his gun firing. This continues until the end of the scene. **25:46** The second time Orcini fires his gun, the weapon no longer has exploding bullets. **26:41** The Dalek weapons continue firing even when there is no beam leaving the gun. **26:41** The beam from the Dalek's weapon does not always exit from the end of the gun. **26:53** There are reports that part of the base of Davros' chair is missing and that you can see the actor's leg. This is a special-effects Davros on a floating base; it may or may not be an opening, or even a leg. It is also possible that it is Orcini's (William Gaunt) leg or Bostock's (John Ogwen) metal encased arm. The base is partially transparent. **27:09** Orcini's leg passes through the base of the special effects Davros. **28:07** The DJ (Alexei Sayle) blows the glass out of the door when he demonstrates his gun to Peri. **29:52** The door glass has regenerated for the Daleks. The DJ blew out this same glass earlier. **31:59** Davros again says Stengos' death and the later events were only a trap for the Doctor. Apparently, Stengos did not choose to come to this planet. **34:48** Through the crack between the doors, we can see someone running. **35:50** Orcini moves the table behind him out of position when he pushes Davros away. **37:00** One of the "dead" guards moves his legs so that Davros can move backwards. **37:06** The Daleks tell Davros, "You are to be taken back to Skaro to stand trial for crimes against the Daleks." When did the Daleks begin this policy? How does this relate to the beginning of the Eighth Doctor movie? **37:43** Look at the back of Davros' chair. It is possible to see the moving reflection of the "dead" guard. **39:00** The lead Dalek apparently goes over a bump that Davros misses. **39:21** The Doctor seems to be aiming too low to hit the Dalek's eyepiece.

Comments: The Doctor defeats the Daleks, at least some of them, and saves Necros.

There are sources that spell Necros as Nekros.

(7A/7B/7C) THE TRIAL OF A TIME LORD

The Mysterious Planet

Writer: Robert Holmes; **Director:** Nicholas Mallett

Media: Commercial tape — episodic version — 98 minutes (used); Collector's tape — movie version — 90 minutes
Highlights: We meet Sabalom Glitz (Tony Selby). This story could also be "The Two Doctors."
Questions: How many Time Lords are in the "jury"?

Errors and Other Points of Interest

There are many different background sounds reported during the trial scenes. Many of these are apparently not present — most of the situations described, such as the announcement "take six," have accompanying loud music — maybe edited in to cover this type of blooper.

It has also been reported that, out of

nowhere, the Doctor is heard saying, "Very Good!" Supposedly, this comes from when the Doctor and Peri were talking about the absence of birds and flowers on Ravolox. The discussion occurs in Episode 1, but the Doctor never says "Very Good!"

Many people have found fault with the arrangements in the trial room. Specifically, the viewing screen should be in front of the viewers, not behind them. The jurors in the back, nearest the screen, would have trouble viewing the screen.

Episode 1
First Transmitted: Sept. 6, 1986

1:17 The TARDIS lands without its light flashing. This could be a consequence of how the TARDIS came to the trial, but we still hear the characteristic sound. **4:39** The Valeyard (Michael Jayston) reports that Ravolox is in the Stellian Galaxy. This indicates that Ravolox is not in the same galaxy as Gallifrey or the Earth. Earth and Gallifrey are in the same Galaxy. **4:44** Much is made of the Doctor entering into situations where he is not wanted. The Valeyard repeatedly makes assertions about the fact that the Doctor should not be on Ravolox; however, the conversation in the TARDIS between Peri and the Doctor leading to the landing is not in evidence. We still do not know why the Doctor and Peri went to Ravolox. **4:55** The Doctor reports that Ravolox has, among other things, the same period of rotation as the Earth. From this, the Doctor postulates that Ravolox is the Earth after about 2 million years. Some observers state that Ravolox could not have the same period of rotation as the Earth because the period of rotation is becoming slower. It is possible that the system used by the Doctor to determine the information about Ravolox corrects for the passage of time. This would be necessary for any instrumentation that would be of any use to a race that travels throughout time. The Doctor does not mention the Moon — something he obviously would look for if he were trying to determine if Ravolox was the Earth. The main reason why the Earth's period of rotation is slowing down is the Moon. If the Moon is still present, the Earth's (Ravolox's) rotation will slow by about 40 seconds in two million years; without the Moon — it would not slow down so much. **5:48** When Peri notices that there are no birds or flowers, the Doctor exclaims, "Exactly." Later in the conversation, the Doctor compliments Peri with "Well done." Some observers report that the Doctor says "Very good" during this scene. **6:02** Peri forgets her American accent when she pronounces "fireball." **6:03** Peri has another accent problem with "sterile." **11:35** The string on Glitz's waist entangles the sight on Dibber's (Glen Murphy) gun. **11:43** Dibber leaves his bag behind on the ground. **12:48** This is another occurrence of the "Constellation" problem. The Doctor reports the moving of Earth's entire constellation. As discussed elsewhere, this does not make sense. **12:51** Moving the Earth a "couple of light years" is not a very great distance in a cosmic sense. Some fans consider this a blooper, since the rescue expedition should not have had trouble finding the Earth after it moved such a "small" distance. A "couple of light years" is only half-way to the nearest star (after the Sun). **20:16** The Doctor argues that he is "only 900 years old." **22:55** Supposedly, one of the stones hits the Doctor prematurely. **23:02** The jury has turned around before the presentation on the screen is over. This occurs at other times.

Episode 2
First Transmitted: Sept. 13, 1986

2:09 Balazar (Adam Blackwood) is required to accompany Merdeen (Tom Chadbon) to answer questions if the Doctor dies. **3:46** The Doctor regains consciousness, and it is obvious that he will recover. Why does Balazar still need to accompany Merdeen? **5:06** The wall of the hut shakes as Peri enters. **5:31** The light-converter pole does not seem too stable. **8:23** Glitz apparently bought a map colored with crayons. Some viewers believe that Glitz would not be so gullible. Later in the trial, we learn that Glitz is working for the Master, not buying questionable maps. **9:04** It is interesting to note that the surface dwellers do not have doors on all their buildings. That is why the guard must enter and the prisoners must leave through the window. **10:44** Glitz says he is wanted in six galaxies. **12:08** It appears as if the Doctor is still passing out jelly babies. **19:28** The lights on Grell's (Timothy Walker) helmet are off. This would be appropriate in a surveillance situation. **20:09** The lights on Grell's helmet are now on; this is inappropriate. **20:40** Obviously, the lead pursuer does not know much about guns. You do not stick the barrel of a gun into the ground unless you want it to explode when you fire the weapon.

Episode 3
First Transmitted: Sept. 20, 1986

1:29 The Doctor sees neither the pursuers nor how they are armed. **1:34** The Doctor tells the fugitives to move on unless they want a spear in the back. The Doctor does not know the pursuers are carrying spears. **3:03** We hear the sound of the switch clicking before the Valeyard touches the switchboard. **6:17** This is a technobabble blooper, and as such should not be here, but... The Doctor says the purpose of the black light converter is "to convert ultraviolet rays to black light." Since ultraviolet rays are black light, the purpose of the converter must be to convert black light into black light — not the most productive process. **7:31** Drathro (Roger Brierley) tells his assistants, Humker (Billy McColl) and Tandrell (Sion Tudor Owen), "only part of the planet was enveloped by fire." Drathro has been misquoted. **8:48** The Doctor observes that Glitz's home is in the constellation of Andromeda instead of the galaxy of Andromeda. **10:14** Drathro and his helpers do not notice the inhabitants until the L1 robot is leaving the village. How did the robot enter the village and not notice any people? **10:16** Drathro contradicts his earlier explanation with "All life perished in the fire!" This could be due to his telling too many lies, or due to the eminent power failure. Again, Drathro has been misquoted. **16:41** The Sixth Doctor attempts a Fourth Doctor impression. **18:59** The warriors salute each of Katryca's (Joan Sims) sentences with their weapons. One of the warriors overdoes this and salutes one extra time.

Episode 4
First Transmitted: Sept. 27, 1986

2:25 Somebody or something is behind the door on the right. **2:40** The doors behind Katryca and her warriors are now closed. The group just entered through these doors. **2:44** Humker and Tandrell flee through doors that are no longer closed. They leave the doors open. **2:56** Someone closed the doors behind the warriors again. **3:04** The guns used by the surface dwellers are not very good; the Drathro causes one of the guns to fall apart by simply touching the weapon. **5:30** The Valeyard states that the Doctor's crime was in being on Ravolox. If the Doctor's presence was being there, why did the Valeyard not include, as evidence, why the Doctor decided to go to Ravolox? The evidence began after the arrival of the Doctor and Peri on the planet. **7:10** Glitz bends over to pick up his gun. He begins speaking before he straightens. **7:59** In a reprise of Glitz picking up his gun, from a different angle, Glitz does not begin to speak until after he has straightened. **8:10** Glitz reports that one of the secrets is faster than light travel. Glitz has apparently been in at least six galaxies since he has already stated so. Why would a person who has been to at least six galaxies be worried about faster than light travel? Intergalactic travel requires faster than light travel or thousands, if not millions, of years. **13:07** Glitz quotes the Brigadier saying, "Five rounds rapid." **14:50** There are various shots showing the walls of the pipe. In some cases, green "food" is on the walls, while in some cases the walls are clean. **15:13** The section of the wall that Dibber is about to destroy is already pre-cut. **16:36** Glitz refers to the "Constellation of Andromeda." Constellation is still not the correct term. **17:14** Drathro has trouble getting through the door. **21:04** The Doctor reminds everyone that the reason for moving the Earth is still unknown. Actually more than the Earth had to move; otherwise, it would have ended as a frozen ball in space. Unless the Sun moved also, the Earth could not be orbiting another star because there is no other star within "a couple of light years." If the Time Lords moved the Sun — why not move the Moon?

Comments: Some lists incorrectly list the name of Ravolox as Ravalox.

The Doctor saves the Universe, including Ravolox.

This represents the return to shorter episodes in place of the double-length episodes.

The title "The Mysterious Planet" was not part of the original transmission. This is a working title, and it is on the commercial tape.

Mindwarp

Alternate Titles: *Mind Warp* and *The Planet of Sil*
Writer: Philip Martin; **Director:** Ron Jones

Media: Commercial tape — episodic version — 99 minutes (used); Collector's tape — movie version — 91 minutes
Highlights: Peri is "killed."

Errors and Other Points of Interest

The working title for this part of the *Trial* is "Mindwarp"; however, the individual tape in the boxed set lists the title as "Mind Warp."

Episode 5
First Transmitted: Oct. 4, 1986

2:44 Some observers believe that a planet in a twin planet system could not have a ring. Saturn, a ringed planet, has planet-sized moons. **3:32** The Doctor tells Peri that the ringed planet is the twin planet. **3:57** There is no information notice on the TARDIS doors. **4:21** Due to the color-tinting the Doctor now has blue hair. Some fans object to this. **5:01** The Doctor quotes, "Send more beams that kill." He says this to Peri while discussing the CD phaser with Peri. Unfortunately, the CD phaser does not emit beams. **7:08** The Doctor clearly pushes then releases the button on the CD phaser. During the trial, the Doctor says the CD phaser was clearly fired by accident. This could be a modified sequence from *Matrix*. **13:57** Some fans find fault with Sil's (Nabil Shaban) new appearance.

Episode 6
First Transmitted: Oct. 11, 1986

4:50 The Doctor says he does not remember the story beginning at this point. Thus, the entire remainder of the story must be suspect from the modified Matrix. This is not a blooper, but it is a reference point.

9:34 As in *Vengeance on Varos*, Sil's lip movements mirror his speaking. If he is speaking English, why does he need the translator on his chest? In addition, why not synchronize the light on the translator with Sil's talking? **17:30** The doorframe in the hallway shakes as the servants enter.

Episode 7
First Transmitted: Oct. 18, 1986

5:12 Crozier (Patrick Ryecart) apparently gives Lord Kiv (Christopher Ryan) an injection using an empty hypodermic needle. **11:45** At this point in the story Crozier's experiment transplants one brain into a different body. **13:23** Crozier takes several drinks from an empty cup. **18:58** Some observers have found fault with the fact that the new Lord Kiv looks and sounds like the old Lord Kiv. Crozier had already commented on the similarity between the appearances of the two.

Episode 8
First Transmitted: Oct. 25, 1986

7:12 There are reports that the Third Mentor (Richard Harvey) appears to be watching *The A-Team* on TV. Viewers could use this to determine how many light years Thoros-Beta is from Earth. It is not obvious what the Mentor is watching. **16:45** It is possible to see the edge of Peri's wig. **18:28** A light bulb apparently blows out as the TARDIS dematerializes. This problem could be due to a shadow. There may be different lighting at different points in the recording of the dematerialization. The change occurs near the left center of the screen. **19:33** Crozier's experimental method now transfers mental information from one brain to another. It now appears as if Crozier was playing with the Lord Kiv earlier. This is in the part of the story where Peri is "killed" so it may be substantially altered. **19:44** Crozier tells Sil that Peri's mind no longer exists. Thus, Peri is dead, and Crozier is her killer. **22:50** The Doctor blames the Time Lords, who, through King Yrcanos (Brian Blessed), killed Peri. However, Peri, according to Crozier, was already dead.

Comments: The title "Mindwarp" was not part of the original transmission. This is a working title, as is "The Planet of Sil." The commercial tape uses "Mind Warp" (*two* words).

The Doctor leaves Thoros Beta before he can save the planet.

The Ultimate Foe

Alternate Title: *Terror of the Vervoids*
Writer: Pip and Jane Baker; **Director:** Chris Clough

Media: Commercial tape — episodic version — 98 minutes (used); Collector's tape — movie version — 91 minutes
Highlights: Mel (Bonnie Langford) becomes the Doctor's new companion.
Questions: The stewardess never seems to be off duty — just what type of labor contract does she have?

Errors and Other Points of Interest

Episode 9
First Transmitted: Nov. 1, 1986

1:24 The Doctor refers to a future adventure — if he is present in the future — does it not mean that he survived the death sentence? **3:04** Professor Lasky (Honor

Blackman) complains about her luggage not being in room 6. This means she had to enter room 6 to learn this. She really has the key to room 9. If she has the key to room 9, how did she get into room 6? Some observers incorrectly report this to be in Episode 8. **6:20** There are fans who question how it was possible to detect the TARDIS using radar. Detection of the TARDIS occurred previously; therefore, this may not be a blooper. In addition, the detection device may not be radar. **7:26** Some fans pose the question: how did Enzu, aka Grenville (Tony Scoggo), know that the Doctor was in the vicinity so that he could send a mayday directed at the TARDIS? The person sent the message to an unidentified ship, and he does not name the Doctor. Both Mel and the Doctor later suppose that someone sent the message to him; we never see any proof that Grenville intended the message for the Doctor. **7:34** The TARDIS lands aligned with the yellow stripes on the floor. This arrangement occurs at other times. **8:47** There are reports of very obvious boom mike shadows during the capture of the Doctor and Mel. They are behind the guard's head at this point, but they are not too obvious. **11:10** The "stars" when viewed from the bridge do not always move in a star-like fashion. **18:37** At least one viewer has questioned the dumping of waste from the ship. A small particle could behave like a meteor and cause a significant amount of damage. The answer is that any system capable of protecting a ship from a true meteor would also protect it from incinerator waste. **20:38** Apparently, there are also changes in the matrix concerning this story.

Episode 10
First Transmitted: Nov. 8, 1986

7:46 The TARDIS light remains lit. **9:09** The Commodore reduces "the diversion to a point naught three safety margin." Compare this to the next order concerning the safety margin. **10:12** The Mogarian on the right turns on his translator — we can see its light. **10:20** This is the first time we see the "fake" Mogarian with the others. Later we see him sitting with the others with minimal interaction before his death. Some observers question why the other Mogarians did not realize the new Mogarian was a fake. The real Mogarians (Sam Howard and Leon Davis) simply did not have sufficient time to detect the imposter. The real Mogarians were probably too busy thinking about the hijacking. **10:25** The light on the left-hand Mogarian fades. Is it off? The Mogarian on the right turns his on as he talks. Its light comes on and does not fade. **10:41** The Mogarian on the left begins talking without a shining translator light. **21:19** Mr. Kimber (Arthur Hewlett) has a Vervoid sting in his neck. **23:03** Even though she is wearing a gas mask, there is no muffling of Mel's scream. This occurs again in the reprise.

Episode 11
First Transmitted: Nov. 15, 1986

1:48 Doland (Malcolm Tierney) enters the room without his mask covering his face. Doland is wearing a mask the next time we see him. **2:55** Some observers pose the question as to how Ruth Baxter (Barbara Ward) became infected. This question rises because it is felt that she should have been wearing gloves. At this point in the story, we find that a grain of pollen entering a scratch in her thumb infected her. Ruth may or may not have been working on the plants when infection occurred, as the pollen could be air born. **4:26** The edges of the inserted image of the black hole are obvious. **4:34** The Commodore tells the pilot to "reduce the margin by a factor of point naught one to naught point two." This sounds like an increase over his previous reduction. **5:45** We hear, but do not see, Rudge (Denys Hawthorne) close the door as he leaves, but Mel enters without opening the door. **5:48** Just before Mel enters the cabin, she causes the wall to shake. **6:28** Compare the view of the "stars" from the bridge at this point to other places. In most other cases the "stars" are moving as the Hyperion III is moving. **6:58** The directional grid changes position between two consecutive views. Note the position of the black hole on the grid. **7:22** This is the second view of the grid; again note the position of the black hole. **9:50** Professor Lasky is wearing grey gym clothes when Doland tells her that Bruchner (David Allister) is down in the hydroponics lab. Some observers incorrectly report that he also tells her that Bruchner is destroying their notes. **12:39** Some fans have considered the incineration of the towels to be a blooper. If incineration is the fate of the waste—why call it a "pulverizer?" **14:20** There are viewers who question the use of a recording tape. We investigated this "future" anachronism previously, and it is not necessary to add anything new at this point. In any case, we do not know if it is anything like twentieth century recording tape. **15:19** Janet (Yolande Palfrey), the stewardess, could use some better training. She is not holding the tray correctly, and manages to spill some of the drink. **15:23** The Mogarian knocks the tray with two cups out of the hands of the stewardess. **15:29** The stewardess only picks up one of the two cups that were on the tray. **15:33** As she is walking away, Janet slips on the wet floor. **17:26** The Vervoid attempting to open the door not only turns the knob the wrong way (understandable for a plant), but also turns it too far for a real doorknob. **18:00** Professor Lasky is wearing a pink outfit when she gets to the hydroponics lab. Some viewers question why she would take time to change her clothes after learning that someone was destroying her notes. Since she did not learn about anyone destroying her notes, this is not a blooper. **20:36** Some people have considered the presence of a 1980s style telephone to be a blooper. It is possible that the ship's decorations represent another nostalgia phase, and items such as telephones, chairs, and the like would be present. **20:50** The ray from the gun does not reach the Commodore (Michael Craig), yet injury occurs anyway. **21:43** The view screen shows the ship heading directly towards the black hole. **21:48** The exterior shot shows the ship traveling at an angle to the black hole, and not heading directly towards it. This view occurs in other places. **21:56** Some viewers claim that the Captain (sic) says the Hyperion is hijack-proof during the hijacking. The Commodore says the ship was "designed to be hijack-proof," not that it is hijack-proof.

Episode 12
First Transmitted: Nov. 22, 1986

2:01 The Doctor describes the gas as marsh gas (methane); Professor Lasky describes it as a methane derivative. Some fans report that the gas smells like methane. The chemical dictionary defines methane as being colorless and odorless. Why compare an odorless gas to methane or any other odorless gas? A methane derivative could have an odor. **2:32** How did the two aliens enter the bridge without letting the gas out of the room? The Vervoids are in the air ducts, so they probably did not go that way. **2:52** The Bridge is smoke-filled. **2:55** What happened to all the smoke? **7:23** The liquid instantaneously penetrates the Mogarian suits. The suits are not very effective for protecting the wearers. **8:24** How did oxygen penetrate the Mogarian suits so quickly? If oxygen, a gas, was the problem, what was the liquid used on them? **8:39** We first see the stars in the window to the far right, they are moving left to right. A few seconds later, they are moving right to left, possibly even stopping. Did the ship suddenly reverse direction? **14:35** Some observers question why the genetically engineered Vervoids were given lethal stingers. There is no specific reference to genetic engineering in this story.

The Vervoids could be from careful breeding of highly developed plants. **17:02** The Doctor and Mel, initially trapped in the lab area, find the "compost" heap and make it up to the bridge in a remarkably short period. **17:19** The Vervoid fails to leave a "stinger" in Professor Lasky. The thorn remained in the other victims. **17:37** Mel and the Doctor find the compost heap. **18:34** Mel and the Doctor reach the bridge. **18:48** Some viewers question the use of the term vianessium. This is technobabble, thus it is not a blooper. **19:04** The Doctor refers to "oxygenated air." Some technobabble goes too far. **21:15** The dying Vervoids are wearing sneakers and, later, tracksuit pants (look for the drawstrings). **21:52** After the destruction of the Vervoids, the Doctor holds a leaf in his in his right hand; in the next shot, the leaf has moved to his left hand. There are reports that the opposite transfer occurs. **22:35** The TARDIS sets at an angle to the yellow lines on the floor. **23:23** The Valeyard assumes that the Doctor has destroyed an entire species. The Doctor was responsible only for those on the ship. What about the parent Vervoids living on their home planet? Where are the Vervoids who produced the original pods?

Comments: The title "The Ultimate Foe" was not part of the original transmission. This is a working title. The commercial tape uses the title "Terror of the Vervoids."

The Doctor saves the crew and passengers of the Hyperion 3.

Time Inc.

Alternate Title: *The Ultimate Foe*
Writer: Robert Holmes and Pip and Jane Baker; **Director:** Chris Clough

Media: Commercial tape — episodic version — 54 minutes (used); Collector's tape — movie version — 52 minutes
Highlights: The Master helps the Doctor.

Errors and Other Points of Interest

Episode 13
First Transmitted: Nov. 29, 1986

2:59 Some viewers find fault with the way Mel and Glitz arrive at the trial. They question why the time scoops do not look the same as in *The Five Doctors*. No one, other than these viewers, identifies the "coffins" as time scoops. **5:19** There is a whistle off set. **6:38** Glitz identifies the bronze metal in the trial room as Maconite. Glitz claims this is a valuable substance. **8:03** The Master is also guilty of the constellation blooper. He also refers to the Earth and its entire constellation moving. **8:05** It has been reported, as a blooper, that the Master uses billion in the European sense (one million million) instead of one thousand million. The actual use appears when he is talking about the Earth moving "billions of miles across space." The actual value of billion is uncertain in this quote. **8:13** The Master now tells us that the recovery ship from Andromeda was a robot ship. This could explain the question of why a "small" movement of the Earth's position resulted in a failure of the rescue ship to find the planet. **11:22** Listen to the bell — it is at least 14 o'clock. It strikes four more times later. **14:36** The harpoon seems to be traveling down a wire. **20:01** The second Mr.

Popplewick (Geoffrey Hughes) apparently does not know who else is working in the office. Initially he refers to the first Mr. Popplewick as the "Very Junior Mr. Popplewick." **20:28** The second Mr. Popplewick he now promotes the Very Junior to "Junior." **20:57** Finally, Mr. Popplewick refers to himself as a "senior clerk." Two people cannot be "very junior," "junior," and "senior."

Episode 14
First Transmitted: Dec. 6, 1986

1:58 Watch the shift in the clouds as the Valeyard appears. This occurs at other times. **5:41** The Master and Glitz "leave" the console room. The next shot, supposedly in a different part of the Master's TARDIS, is really still in the console room. Apparently, this is to avoid the construction of a new set. **5:55** Glitz now refers to Maconite in the context of a strait jacket. It apparently is no longer a valuable metal. **6:29** We must still question the ability of the Master's chameleon circuit to choose an appropriate "disguise." **7:26** The Master's tissue compression eliminator now fires a red beam in addition to all of its previous functions. This could be a result of the Master's continued attempts to improve the weapon. **12:25** Pay attention to the bell — apparently it is 29 o'clock — and all is not well. **18:20** The Doctor says he has lived "over 900 years." **21:37** The Doctor gives Mel the incorrect definition of maser. The Doctor says "microwave amplification and stimulated emission of radiation" instead of "microwave amplification BY stimulated emission of radiation." **27:35** Various fans have considered the Doctor's comment that Gallifrey has no crown jewels to be a blooper. They cite items such as the Coronet of Rassilon. The Doctor may not consider such items to be crown jewels since they have other uses. **28:02** Some viewers question the Inquisitor's (Lynda Bellingham) authority to order the Keeper of the Matrix (James Bree) to repair the Matrix. The Inquisitor probably has other duties when not in court — it is very unlikely that the High Council pulled someone off the street to serve in such an important position. Other observers question why repair has such a high priority. We already know that the Matrix runs Gallifrey — thus its repair should have a very high priority.

Comments: The title "Time Inc." was not part of the original transmission. This is a working title. The commercial tape uses the title "The Ultimate Foe."

The Doctor defeats the Doctor and saves Gallifrey.

VII
The Seventh Doctor

(7D) Time and the Rani

Writer: Pip and Jane Baker; **Director:** Andrew Morgan

Media: Commercial tape — episodic version — 98 minutes (used); Collector's tape — movie version — 89 minutes
Highlights: The new Doctor makes his appearance.
Questions: Why did the Doctor finish repairing the machine after he knew about the Rani?

Errors and Other Points of Interest

Episode 1
First Transmitted: Sept. 7, 1987

0:00 Some observers object to the Rani (Kate O'Mara) appearing simply to shoot the TARDIS out of space. **0:20** There is no flashing light or landing sound when the TARDIS lands. This may be due to the Rani's interference. **0:39** As Urak (Richard Gauntlett) walks across the floor of the TARDIS, it appears that some of his hairs have preceded him. Apparently, these are the leavings from a rehearsal. **0:46** Some fans wonder why a crash that only stuns Mel causes the Doctor to regenerate. It is possible that the Doctor hit his head when he fell. **1:49** Einstein gets into a cubicle without a headset. **3:33** The Rani can check the Doctor's heartbeat simply by placing her hand on his coat. **6:09** Ikona (Mark Greenstreet) finds the TARDIS door unlocked. He removes Mel and apparently does not lock the door. **7:00** The Rani watches Mel scare Sarn (Karen Clegg) into the trap. Thus, the Rani knows that Mel is not in the TARDIS. **8:39** The needle is obviously retracting into the handle. **10:01** The Doctor finds the Rani's Navigational Guidance System Distorter. The Doctor mutters that this device would force any passing spacecraft down. This at least partly refutes the earlier objections by some fans about the Rani shooting the TARDIS out of space. **18:34** The Rani orders Urak (Richard Gauntlett) to go to the TARDIS and remove Mel. The Rani knows Mel is not in the TARDIS, so why does she order Urak to go to the TARDIS? **20:00** When the Doctor and "Mel" return to the TARDIS, they find the door locked. How did Ikona manage to lock the door when he carried Mel out of the TARDIS? **21:02** There is the sound of breaking glass in the background. This appears to be an intentional sound effect. **22:28** The Rani is able to tune in on Urak's vision by making no other adjustments in the TARDIS scanner beyond turning on the instrument. It is possible there was a previous tuning of the instrument to Urak.

Episode 2
First Transmitted: Sept. 14, 1987

3:37 Ikona and Mel stand too close to the explosion and they get wet. **6:10** This begins a discussion some observers consider to be beyond technobabble. **6:31** The Doctor mumbles that he "broke the second law of thermodynamics." This is an error. The Doctor may have forgotten about the second law, and made a mistake, but he could not have broken the second law. **9:04** When "Mel" closes the door, it drops, then starts to rise. **11:26** Mel's shoes are clearly dirty. **13:26** Mel's shoes are now clean. This is the first instance of the Mel's Shoes Blooper. Mel's shoes are dirty in outdoor scenes and clean during indoor scenes. The buildings appear to have automatic shoe cleaners for all those who enter. **15:44** An example of how Time Lord physiology differs from human physiology. The Doctor is able to check Mel's pulse with his thumbs. If a human had done this there would have detected a double pulse — the person's they were checking and their own. **16:13** The Doctor mentions that this is his "seventh persona." **16:29** Apparently, the Rani's TARDIS still has a faulty chameleon circuit. **17:07** There are those who consider the exploding asteroid discussion to exceed the limits of technobabble. **18:09** The Doctor tells Mel he is 953 years old. **18:51** Hypatia is wearing a headset while in the cubicle, but Einstein still appears not to be wearing a headset. Also, note the order of the cubicles. From left to right they are Hypatia, Einstein and the empty cubicle for the Doctor.

Episode 3
First Transmitted: Sept. 21, 1987

1:47 The Rani is still wearing her Mel disguise as she chases the Doctor. **2:34** The Rani is still pursuing the Doctor. However, she has taken time to change her clothes. **4:26** The Doctor hides in the empty cubicle to the left of Einstein's cubicle. This is the cubicle formerly occupied by Hypatia. **11:00** Why does Ikona not know the purpose of the rotating globe? The other people seem to know its purpose. **11:29** Ikona steps on Lanisha's (John Segal) foot. **20:21** When placing the Doctor in his cubicle, he is fitted with a headset. Why do some of the other occupants not have headsets? **21:28** Orac (Peter Tuddenham) appears to have regenerated and joined Doctor Who.

Episode 4
First Transmitted: Sept. 28, 1987

0:00 There are reports that the original transmission of Episode 4 had the wrong opening title sequence. The video release does not have this problem. **2:21** The Tetraps have eyes facing in each direction. Some viewers ask — Why do they need to continually turn their heads to see? The Tetraps have one eye facing in each direction — this does not give any depth perception. The Tetraps must turn their heads to bring two eyes to bear in order to gain depth perception. **7:16** Why place bangles on the legs of the Lakertyans when the insects are available? **10:30** Some observers object to the technobabble concerning "the aftermath of the explosion." **10:34** We again hear the term chronon — the Doctor then tells Mel that chronons are "discrete particles of time." Some viewers have a problem with this term. **12:41** The word "loyhargil" is an anagram of "holy grail." **15:16** Ikona removes a piece of fiber optic "wire" from an ornament, and Mel uses the piece to complete an electrical circuit. Some viewers attribute this blooper to the Doctor. **17:25** We can see Pasteur in his cubicle; he is not wearing a headset. Why did the Doctor need a headset? Neither Pasteur nor Einstein requires a headset, but the Doctor and Hypatia need headsets. **20:08** The end of the rocket ramp is above the top of the cliff. All earlier shots of the ramp show the ramp below the top of the cliff.

Comments: The Doctor saves the planet Lakertya.

(7E) Paradise Towers

Writer: Stephen Wyatt; **Director:** Nicholas Mallett

Media: Commercial tape — episodic version — 98 minutes (used); Collector's tape — movie version — 89 minutes
Questions: Did Kroagnon ask Wotan to design the Robotic Self-Activating Mark 7Z Cleaners?

Errors and Other Points of Interest

Episode 1
First Transmitted: Oct. 5, 1987

1:06 Mel exclaims to the Doctor that the swimming pool is at the very top of the building. **3:54** The positions where the darts are to "hit" the wall are obvious before the darts travel along the wire to stick in the wall. **19:42** As Pex (Howard Cooke) starts breaking down the door, Mel reaches for her cake as if she is preparing to set it on the table. **19:46** After Pex enters the apartment, Mel's cake disappears. **20:12** At least one viewer has a problem with the lift doors. The claim is that "all" lifts have double doors. There is no guarantee that such a situation may occur in the future or on other planets. In addition, this viewer has apparently not ridden on very many lifts, as there are single door lifts currently in use on the Earth. **21:36** One of the Blue Kangs appears to be out of uniform. She is the only one not wearing a navy blue sleeved shirt. Some of the shirts have short sleeves and some have long sleeves. A similar problem is present for the Red Kangs.

Episode 2
First Transmitted: Oct. 12, 1987

9:01 If Mel and Pex are trying to get to the pool on the roof, why are they continually going down the stairs instead of up? Pex may not want to go to the pool, but Mel should be able to tell the difference between up and down. **13:05** The Doctor reads from the coin "Issued by the Great Architect Kroagnon." **13:23** Mel and Pex are going down, not up, the stairs. **15:54** The Doctor again reads from the coin "Issued by the Great Architect Kroagnon." **15:54** The coin we see says, "Issued by Kroagnon." It does not say, "Issued by the Great Architect Kroagnon." Where did the Doctor get "the Great Architect?" The reverse side of the coin may include the longer phrase, and the Doctor's second quote may be from what he remembered from the other side of the coin. **17:23** Does the machine in the basement (Kroagnon) know Audrey, Jr. (aka Audrey II) or Roger Corman? **17:24** Some fans consider the "monster" to be a blooper.

Episode 3
First Transmitted: Oct. 19, 1987

3:39 We can see the wire on which the knife travels. The wire is next to Pex. **4:05** The Cleaner carrying Tilda's (Brenda Bruce) body scrapes against the wall as it goes through the door. **5:25** As the Deputy Chief Caretaker (Clive Merrison) falls, a large shadow appears on the wall to the right. **5:36** The shadow reappears as the Deputy Caretaker climbs out of the room. **6:02** Mel says they are on floor 109, but the room number is 1236. **6:16** Mel again states that the pool is on the top of the building (floor 304), but she points to a lower floor on the map. Maybe this explains her trouble with stairs in Episode 2. **10:32** There is a reflection of the arm of one of the production crew on the reddish TV screen behind the

Chief Caretaker. **11:33** The floor indicator on the lift shows that Mel and Pex have entered on the 48th floor. This means they have gone from the 109th floor to the 48th floor on their way to the roof. They have gone 61 floors in the wrong direction without noticing. **11:42** Pex tells Mel that the Kangs play a game where they push the buttons on a lift. Mel comes back with "we could be stuck in here going up and down for hours!" The lift should stop at each floor that had its button pushed by the Kangs. When stopping, Mel and Pex could simply get off the lift. **14:06** Maddy (Judy Cornwell) apparently decides to move into an apartment where two people have just disappeared down the waste disposal. This is not too intelligent.

Episode 4
First Transmitted: Oct. 26, 1987

4:04 At least one viewer believes that Mel's hair does not appear sufficiently wet after she submerges in the swimming pool. The texture of Mel's hair makes this a questionable call. **7:50** The floor around Mel and the Doctor is very wet as Pex approaches, but it is dry when Pex passes them.

Comments: PEX LIVES

We never learn which planet the Doctor is saving.

(7F) DELTA AND THE BANNERMEN

Writer: Malcolm Kohll; **Director:** Chris Clough

Media: Commercial tape — episodic version — 74 minutes (used); Collector's tape — movie version — 67 minutes

Errors and Other Points of Interest

Episode 1
First Transmitted: Nov. 2, 1987

1:42 At least some of the bodies on the ground appear to be made of rubber. **2:33** This is the first appearance of the "?" umbrella. **5:03** At least one observer objects to Hawk (Morgan Deare) making the comment that the satellite launch is "history in the making." The reason for this objection is that this is not the first American satellite, and, therefore it is not history making. This observer apparently does not know about the early space program in the U.S. Every launch, especially of a new type of satellite, was "history making" in the eyes of the press. **9:01** What is the red planet to the upper left of the screen? Is the satellite supposed to be near Mars? The first satellite near Mars was much later. **11:16** The light on top of the TARDIS barely flashes on landing. **21:33** There are reports that a head pops up from behind one of the shelves while the Doctor and Ray (Sara Griffiths) are talking in the shed. Editing may have removed this from this version.

Episode 2
First Transmitted: Nov. 9, 1987

5:54 Some observers claim a blooper when the Doctor says "high impulse beam." This does not appear to be the case. **9:10** The Doctor says that TARDIS stands for "Time And Relative Dimensions In Space." **9:40** Murray (Johnny Dennis) obviously gets his cheerful attitude from reading *The Hitchhiker's Guide to the Galaxy*. **14:24** The "bees" attacking the Bannermen do not look like bees. The insects are too large. Supposedly, this is stock footage of locusts. **16:04** There is barely any shadow under the Bannerman ship. **17:57** Some observers object to the bus explosion. **22:36** Gavrok (Don Henderson) tells the Doctor he has "traversed time and space." Does this mean the Bannermen can time travel? **23:04** The Doctor and his companions stop before the Bannermen threaten them. They should have waited until the threat became real. This also occurs in the reprise.

Episode 3
First Transmitted: Nov. 19, 1987

1:12 Something, probably a bird, passes over Gavrok's head. **2:22** Weismuller (Stubby Kaye) does not see how the Bannerman attaches the collar about his neck. **2:59** Weismuller tells Ray that she needs a special key to unlock the collar. How can he know this when he was not looking when the Bannerman was locking the collar? **7:14** The Doctor is wearing glasses in the distant shots while driving the motorcycle. The glasses disappear in the close shots. **13:30** The Doctor says an exploding sonic cone would kill everyone — this does not happen. **14:39** Some viewers wonder why the alien food does not poison Billy (David Kinder), and why he becomes a Chimeron after eating the food. This is technobabble and not a blooper. If it were a blooper, then every time in the series where the Doctor, a companion, or another person ate something not from their home planet, they should die. **15:28** Ray asks the Doctor, "What are you doing, Doctor?" The Doctor's response is to put his hand on her chest. **22:59** The light on top of the TARDIS does not flash during dematerialization.

Comments: The Doctor saves the Chimerons and defeats the Bannermen.

(7G) DRAGONFIRE

Writer: Ian Briggs; **Director:** Chris Clough

Media: Commercial tape — episodic version — 73 minutes (used); Collector's tape — movie version — 68 minutes
Highlights: Mel leaves with Glitz (Tony Selby) (is this a blooper?), and Ace (Sophie Aldred) joins the Doctor.

Errors and Other Points of Interest

Episode 1
First Transmitted: Nov. 23, 1987

0:48 If it is so cold, why can we not see anyone's breath? **2:57** In answer to Mel's question, "Where is it?" the Doctor tells her what it is, not where it is. **13:26** At many points in this story, the temperature or the target temperature is -193°C. The problem with this temperature is that oxygen liquefies at -183°C. The lower temperature would cause oxygen to liquefy. There should be liquid oxygen dripping off Kane's "coffin." This would not be a problem if there were no oxygen in the atmosphere of the planet. No oxygen might lead to problems for Mel, Ace, and at least some of the other visitors. **15:51** Belazs (Patricia Quinn) pushes a button on the console — the entire console depresses then rises. **20:09** Kane (Edward Peel) refers to meteorite showers instead of meteor showers. **20:49** Kane places a coin on the console. The wood grain of plywood shows through the paint on the surface of the "metal" console. **22:23** The Doctor nearly sticks his foot through the plastic cliff. **22:45** At the end of the episode, we see that there is a long drop beneath the Doctor.

Episode 2
First Transmitted: Nov. 30, 1987

1:19 Mel's scream seems to cause a major headache to Ace who is only a few inches away. **1:41** In the reprise, we again see that there is a long drop beneath the Doctor. **1:52** The cave "wall" shakes when hit by The Creature's (Leslie Meadows) shot. **1:59** Mel moves the cave wall as she starts to run away with Ace. **3:42** Glitz rescues the Doctor by coming up from below. This makes it appear as if the drop is only a few feet. It is not clear whether the Doctor is still holding onto the umbrella when Glitz reaches him, or if he has descended part way down the cliff to Glitz. Some viewers claim that the Doctor's umbrella repeatedly disappears and re-appears. Thus begins the Saga of the Umbrella. **5:02** Listen for the unusual sound effect as Glitz leans towards the Doctor while discussing the hijacking of the *Nosferatu*. **5:37** Belazs again causes the console to bend when pushing a button. **6:19** Mel finds the umbrella where the Doctor left it. **8:02** It is possible to see the safety wire attached to Mel as she descends. **8:19** Some viewers question the presence of fuzzy dice and seatbelts on the *Nosferatu*. **8:54** The Doctor enters the *Nosferatu* and carries on a conversation with no umbrella in evidence, which is as it should be, since Mel has the umbrella. **9:59** While still on the *Nosferatu*, in a close-up, the Doctor is holding the umbrella while he is talking to Belazs about her debt to Kane. Mel has the umbrella at this time. **11:54** Why does the dragon cut through the door? No one locked the door and no lock is present. The dragon could have gone through the door a lot faster and easier simply by pushing it open.

12:08 Mel is still carrying the Doctor's umbrella. **12:23** It is obvious that the ice walls are simply sheets of plastic. The nitro-9 makes this a little more obvious at this point than at other places in this story. **13:25** Mel has some un-melting fake snow on her lips. **17:17** Mel returns the umbrella to the Doctor. Thus ends the Saga of the Umbrella. **18:05** Pudovkin (Nigel Miles-Thomas) falls back when hit by The Creature's shot. The shot could knock the man down the hall. **19:14** There are observers who question what happened to Pudovkin's body as the group moves down the hall. It is possible that his body is further down the hall. **20:34** Some observers question: Why hide the Dragonfire on the only part of the planet, the polar region, cold enough for Kane to reach? At this point an explanation of why Kane has been imprisoned is given. There is no evidence that it was to be perpetual imprisonment, just permanent exile. Kane is not a prisoner in the polar region; his prison is on the permanently frozen dark side of the planet Svartos (also called Iceworld).

Episode 3
First Transmitted: Dec. 7, 1987

4:39 Kane tells his thawed troops, "We shall be able to leave." Apparently, at this point he is planning to keep them alive. **10:24** Glitz appears to be standing in front of an opaque panel. **10:43** There is a proposed blooper—why did Kane kill his troops after working so hard to collect them? Kane told his troops to drive everyone to the *Nosferatu*. We see troops running towards the ship, but the scene ends before any troops enter the ship. Kane kills the people on the ship, which may include deserters. No mercenaries appear later in the story. **10:45** Glitz can see the exploding *Nosferatu* through the opaque panel. **11:02** Where are the bodies? **13:26** The crystal does not fit through the hole it is supposed to come through. The crystal pushes up the sides of the hole. **18:41** Kane causes the entire panel top to depress. **20:01** What may be the power cable for the TARDIS console appears on the floor. **23:04** Some fans wonder why Stellar's Mother is not upset about the massacre she has just survived. These fans also believe that Stellar is Stella.

Comments: The Doctor defeats Kane.

(7H) REMEMBRANCE OF THE DALEKS

Writer: Ben Aaronovitch; **Director:** Andrew Morgan

Media: DVD — episodic version — 98 minutes (used); Commercial tape — with *The Chase* — episodic version — 98 minutes; Collector's tape — movie version — 90 minutes

Errors and Other Points of Interest

There are many scenes with modern cars and modern buildings present. Only those reported in other sources are included here.

Episode 1
First Transmitted: Oct. 5, 1988

1:25 Not all of the children seem to be wearing 1963 clothing. **4:31** There are burns on the ground in the playground. The question has been posed — why did the first landing not blow out the windows? This may not be a problem as it should be remembered — the Daleks, via their agents, are in control of the school, and the windows could be quickly replaced without question. **6:42** The sign at the front of the junkyard reads "I. M. FORMAN," instead of "I. M. FOREMAN." **8:54** There is a report that one of the soldiers snaps to attention much later than his comrades do. Some observers claim he is five seconds late. The scene does not last long enough after the first soldiers snap to attention for the slow soldier to delay for five seconds. **10:01** Watch the corrugated metal sheets behind the soldier when he dies. The wire attached to him, seen in close-up, moves the metal sheets when pulling on the soldier. **13:16** The Doctor's overdubs his voice during his countdown. **14:47** Modern cars appear through the van windows. **15:04** If you watch the scene very carefully, when the Doctor and Ace change positions, it is possible to see Ace and the Doctor bounce up and down as if they were dropping into their seats. **15:33** There are claims that the Doctor gave the wrong date for the Dalek invasion. The Doctor says the invasion took place in the twenty-second century. **16:14** Rachel (Pamela Salem) uses the word "Dalek" when talking to Allison (Karen Gledhil). Unfortunately, no one told either of them the name Dalek. **16:40** A camera creeps into the edge of the screen as Ace and the Doctor meet the Headmaster (Michael Sheard). **18:40** This appears to be the same book from *100,000 B.C.* **23:04** We see how the Modern Dalek ascends stairs.

Episode 2
First Transmitted: Oct. 12, 1988

10:12 When the camera angle changes the baseball bat disappears from one of the Doctor's hands and appears in the other. **12:29** The Headmaster enters through an open gate. **12:37** Some fans report post–1963 buildings around the cemetery. **12:40** The gate to the cemetery is no longer open. **12:42** A post–1963 bus drives past the cemetery. **18:36** We hear the TV announcer giving the time as a quarter past five and introducing the new science fiction series "Doc...." This is the correct time for the transmission of the very first episode of *Doctor Who*. The date of the first transmission was November 23, 1963. This scene occurs between breakfast and lunch, and it is broad daylight outside (in November). **21:08** The Doctor pronounces "Spirodon" incorrectly. **21:39** Some observers report that the Doctor says "intregal" instead of "integral" in the phrase "plastic explosives with integral detonators." Listen and see if you agree.

Episode 3
First Transmitted: Oct. 19, 1988

4:27 It is possible to see the Doctor's shadow as he waits on the basement steps for his cue. **11:11** Ace trips on a bit of wire for the communication system as she goes around the corner to hear the Doctor explain the Hand of Omega. Some viewers incorrectly report this to be barbed wire. **13:15** A post–1963 skyline appears in the distance. **13:34** The Black Dalek's lights were not working correctly during filming. Addition of the flashing light effect came after filming. **14:23** It takes The Girl (Jasmine Breaks) two attempts to get her helmet to remain in position. **14:31** There are those who wonder why Ratcliffe (George Sewell) displays surprise upon seeing The Girl. They feel he should know her. The surprise may not have been due to her appearance, but her statement. **15:35** The top of one of the Daleks looks as if it is very loose. **19:03** The Doctor's calling card has a "?" symbol. The other symbols must be Gallifreyan. The Greek symbols for theta and sigma are not present as such. There are symbols related to the Greek symbols. **19:57** A post–1963 skyline appears again. **21:19** Ace yells at Mike (Dursley McLinden) for the first time. **22:56** The outside views during the landing of the Dalek shuttlecraft show the laboratory windows to be wide open, but, when seen from the inside, the laboratory windows are closed. If the windows were open, the landing ship might not blow them out. This occurs again in the reprise. **23:11** The wires lowering the Dalek shuttlecraft are in evidence as the ship lands. In addition, the metal eyelets for the wires are visible. This happens again in the reprise.

Episode 4
First Transmitted: Oct. 26, 1988

1:31 Another improbable shot shows the craft landing in exactly the same position as before. It could land close, but landing in exactly the same place is unlikely. **2:54** The second time Ace yells at Mike it appears as if she can barely keep from laughing. She begins with a grin, moves to a smirks, and then exits. **6:45** Some viewers report that when the Doctor, Mike, Rachel and others are looking for Davros, Rachel is suddenly barefoot, and then she miraculously regains her shoes upon leaving the ship. There are problems with this observation. Mike is not with the group as he is under arrest. The group consists of the Doctor, Rachel, Allison, Ace, and Group Captain Gilmore (Simon Williams). Rachel's shoes do not disappear—she has them in her hands. No one knows Davros is present, so the group cannot be looking for him. **9:21** There are no holes in the windows. **11:04** This time there is no shadow under the Hand of Omega. **11:14** A hole now appears in one of the windowpanes. **12:26** There is a better view of the wires on the shuttlecraft as it rises. **12:33** As the shuttle takes off—no blown-out windows are apparent. **14:32** This is the first time the Doctor learns that Davros (Roy Tromelly—Terry Molloy) is present. (The Doctor says he had his suspicions.) Thus, the Doctor could not have been looking for Davros on the Dalek shuttlecraft. **19:46** The stairs move back in a very strange manner when

The Girl kills Mike. **19:58** The dome on the Black Dalek slips sideways as it turns to face the second van.

Comments: The Doctor defeats Davros and the Daleks.

(7L)   THE HAPPINESS PATROL

Writer: Graeme Curry; **Director:** Chris Clough

Media: Commercial tape — episodic version — 74 minutes (used); Collector's tape — movie version — 71 minutes

Errors and Other Points of Interest

Episode 1
First Transmitted: Nov. 2, 1988

1:58 Silas P (Jonathan Burn) hands his card to Daphne S (Mary Healey) with the words "Happiness Patrol Undercover" facing Daphne S. Daphne S must turn the card over to read Silas P's name and then back to be "surprised." **4:41** The Doctor says his nickname in college was Theta Sigma. **14:11** Apparently, someone realized that the original Kandy Man (David John Pope) costume was a problem because you could see the actor's mouth. Later a metal piece appears to cover the actor's mouth. Filming of the scenes was out of sequence, thus the metal piece appears and reappears. **17:04** One of the Happiness Patrol misses her cue and runs onto the set behind the Doctor while he is working on the buggy. **21:01** Silas P repeats his card blooper when he hands his card to the Doctor. **21:31** Some observers question the death of Silas P. The Happiness Patrol knows him, and they know his job.

Episode 2
First Transmitted: Nov. 9, 1988

3:43 The Kandy Man's microphone sometimes picks up the Doctor's voice. **6:25** Ace calls Priscilla P (Rachel Bell), her guard, a killer. Susan Q (Lesley Dunlop) enters from out of earshot and agrees with something she could not possibly have heard. **6:32** The sugar stalactites bend when they should break. This does not occur in Episode 1 as reported elsewhere. **8:52** The alien costumes seem to contain street maps. The Paris streets are supposedly present. **11:38** Trevor Sigma (John Normington) apparently starts to listen to Earl Sigma (Richard D. Sharp) before the latter begins to play. Trevor Sigma says, "That's nice," though he has been misquoted. **16:32** There is a metal piece covering the Kandy Man's mouth. **22:46** Why does the Happiness Patrol not kill the very unhappy box office attendant (Tim Scott)? **23:16** The Doctor sees Ace's picture on a poster saying that she is playing tonight. After reading when she is going to be auditioning, the Doctor knocks on a shutter and asks the attendant who is going to be in tonight's show. This appears in the reprise also.

Episode 3
First Transmitted: Nov. 16, 1988

5:07 Some fans claim that when Helen A (Sheila Hancock) puts Fifi into the pipe the back wall of the hole is visible, and so, these fans believe, it is obviously not a pipe. In reality, the pipe could continue to the left or right, it does not need to go towards the back. **6:53** The Doctor and Ace separated before Ace met Susan Q, and there has been no communication between the Doctor and Ace. So how did the Doctor learn Susan Q's name? **15:38** Kandy Man has no metal parts around his mouth. **18:11** Gilbert M (Harold Innocent) refers to Helen A as "Ellen Hay." **18:59** It is obvious that a wire pulls Daisy K's (Georgina Hale) weapon away.

Comments: The Doctor saves Terra Alpha.

(7K) Silver Nemesis

Writer: Kevin Clarke; **Director:** Chris Clough

Media: Commercial tape — extended episodic version — 84 minutes (used); Collector's tape — movie version — 68 minutes

Errors and Other Points of Interest

Why repeatedly refer to Nemesis as a comet, when it is a meteor (in space) or a meteorite (on Earth)?

Episode 1
First Transmitted: Nov. 23, 1988

5:18 The Mathematician (Leslie French) determines that the Nemesis will return on November 23, 1988 (350 years after 1638). Several observers point out a problem — in 1752, England, amongst other countries, changed from the Julian calendar to the Gregorian calendar. To accomplish the conversion there was an eleven day change, so that the day after September 3, 1752, was September 14, 1752. With this change, Nemesis should have arrived back on Earth on December 4, 1988, and not on November 23. This may not be a blooper because the Doctor covers this problem in Episode 2. **5:51** It would be very unusual for Ace to be wearing a T-shirt and listening to music on a bright sunlit day in November in England. **5:59** The day should be Wednesday — so why is Ace able to read the previous Saturday's football scores in the paper? There is a lot of traveling back and forth in the TARDIS — are all the 1988 scenes on the same day? It is possible that the paper is not for the current day. **7:08** Some viewers claim that the Doctor drops his umbrella on the downstream side of the bridge (right), and then he and Ace jump off the upstream side of the bridge (left). In the next shot, the Doctor and Ace are seen swimming upstream, and the Doctor has his umbrella. This is not a blooper. The direction the stream is flowing is incorrect. The umbrella falls to the right, which is upstream. The Doctor and Ace fall to the left; this is downstream. Finally, we see the Doctor and Ace swimming downstream. **7:14** Some viewers question why the two controlled humans shoot at the Doctor and Ace when the Cybermen know neither of the Doctor's regeneration nor of the Doctor's presence. **10:23** Why does the sudden appearance of two people in a restaurant not cause a greater disturbance? **13:41** Some viewers object to the magnitude of the explosion and the size of the crater caused by the comet. Obviously, they have not seen just how small the crater caused by a meteor of this size can be. Another explanation is that the engines slowed the descent. **17:10** The chess game will reappear in *The Curse* *of Fenric*. **19:32** The gas overcomes the police officer setting in the car, and he falls out of the car. **20:19** Ace is wearing Flowerchild's earring on her jacket. This item comes from the next story (*The Greatest Show in the Galaxy*). This is not a true blooper as transmission of the stories was not in the order of filming. Filming of the story transmitted after this one occurred before this story. **22:22** Lady Peinforte (Fiona Walker) mentions that she "knows" the Doctor's secret. We never learn what the secret is. **23:56** Only the extended version makes it obvious how the Doctor and Ace "escape." In the shorter versions, it appears as if they simply walk away. **24:57** The police officer who fell out of his car earlier is now almost entirely under the car.

Episode 2
First Transmitted: Nov. 30, 1988

0:47 A helicopter simulates the landing of the Cybership. There is a superposition of the ship's image over the helicopter, but the blades are still evident. There appears to be some correction of this in the commercial release. **1:30** The explanation about the Cyberman controlled men shooting at the Doctor and Ace is given. The Cyber Leader (David Banks) says that the Doctor was expected — thus the controlled men were simply looking for anyone suspicious. This would make the previous claim by some viewers not a blooper. **2:06** One of the Cybermen (left of center) has trouble keeping his head on during the first attack. **3:51** The Doctor notes that the arrowheads are made of gold. Some viewers object to the use of gold arrows. **6:02** The Doctor says he supplied information allowing the Mathematician to calculate the date. The Doctor would know about the calendar change. This may cancel the blooper problem with the date of the return of Nemesis. **8:00** There is no shadow beneath the Cybership. **10:12** The Doctor informs Ace that her boom box not only plays, but it also transmits. They then use the jazz tape to interfere with the Cyberman communication system. Some fans report this to be the beginning of a blooper. **12:36** The grave maker says, "Richard Maynarde died 2nd November, 1657. Thus, Richard knows he returned to his time. **19:38** The Cyber Leader and some of the other Cybermen have four fingers instead of three. Sometimes the right hand has four fingers and sometimes it is the left hand. **22:25** Richard throws the arrow to the statue and it lands sticking up with the tip down. When we next see the statue, the arrow is lying horizontal, not vertical.

Episode 3
First Transmitted: Dec. 7, 1988

2:08 The Doctor says to Ace, "You can always go back to your TARDIS." When did Ace get her own TARDIS? **5:06** Some fans have used the stopping of the tape as the root of a blooper. They claim that the Cyber Leader should have immediately called for reinforcements. **5:19** The Cyber Leader does note the end of the interference, but he goes on to say the arrival of the Cyberfleet is eminent, thus reinforcements are on the way — so why call for reinforcements? This partially explains the claimed blooper. **14:58** Since *The Tenth Planet*, it has become easier to kill Cybermen — now only a slingshot is required. The coins, even gold ones, should simply bounce off. In addition, based on the "explosions," not all of the coins hit the chest unit. **17:32** The camera operator following Ace either stumbles or bumps into something. **18:22** It is obvious that the falling Cyberman costume is empty. **20:22** The Cyber Leader's eyes show through the plastic as he gets up after removing the coin. **21:06** De Flores (Anton Diffring) dies and falls next to the comet. **22:12** Lady Peinforte says, "Doctor Who" while addressing the Doctor. **24:40** Watch as the camera shot of the Cyber Leader switches from just before he says, "Launch the Nemesis," to after. We see that his position is not consistent. **25:26** As the "comet" takes off, we see that De Flores' body has disappeared. **27:01** Richard laments about his being marooned in 1988. This happens after he has seen his grave. Richard should know better.

Comments: The Doctor defeats the Cybermen and saves the Earth.

(7J) THE GREATEST SHOW IN THE GALAXY

Writer: Stephen Wyatt; **Director:** Alan Wareing

Media: Commercial tape — episodic version — 98 minutes (used); Collector's tape — movie version — 89 minutes
Questions: The Doctor yells that he has "fought the gods of Ragnarok all through time." When did these occurrences take place?

Errors and Other Points of Interest

Episode 1
First Transmitted: Dec. 14, 1988

5:59 When the Doctor opens the TARDIS door, we can see the light shining through the side window. **13:46** Various observers have objected to the presence of a ringed planet near another planet. The fact that Saturn has moons the size of small planets, but retains its ring system, refutes this claim. **19:54** Ace finds and places Flowerchild's earring onto her jacket. Even though Ace finds the earring here, she was wearing it in the preceding story (*The Silver Nemesis*). **22:19** Astute observers have noted that Bellboy's (Christopher Guard) pants fall down a little too far as he is thrown to the floor. This occurs again in the reprise.

Episode 2
First Transmitted: Dec. 21, 1988

8:42 The Doctor should have been able to see the bars to the cage since the curtains covering them were on the inside of the cage. Some observers claim an enhancement of this blooper when the Doctor leans against the edge of the doorway before entering. Leaning against the side would not necessarily indicate the presence of bars. **9:12** Mags (Jessica Martin) apparently pours a lot of nothing into the Doctor's cup. **22:31** The Doctor drops the club straight down into the well. The shot in the well shows a spinning club. This also occurs in the reprise.

Episode 3
First Transmitted: Dec. 28, 1988

12:14 Whizzkid (Gian Sammarco) misses the saucer when he sets his cup down. **17:24** The Chief Clown (Ian Reddington) enters the workshop, apparently to get Ace, but instead of asking Bellboy, "Where is she?" he asks, "Where are they?" **17:36** The Chief Clown "slaps" Bellboy, but the blow clearly misses Bellboy significantly.

Episode 4
First Transmitted: Jan. 4, 1989

4:52 The Captain's (T. P. McKenna) position relative to Mags dramatically changes between his line, "Come on Mags, you can trust me, you know that, don't you?" and "Once he's out of the way, we can split the proceeds." **7:22** There is a mattress on the ground for the Doctor and Mags to jump on when diving through the rip in the tent wall. **18:23** The Doctor announces "The climate of my act."

Comments: Even though filming of this story occurred before *The Silver Nemesis*, broadcasting occurred later. This leads to some inconsistencies such as Flowerchild's earring.

(7N) BATTLEFIELD

Writer: Ben Aaronovitch; **Director:** Michael Kerrigan

Media: Commercial tape — episodic version — 99 minutes (used); Collector's tape — movie version — 88 minutes
Highlights: The Brigadier and Bessie return.

Errors and Other Points of Interest

The credits at the end of each episode list Keff McCulloch for "Incidental Music" instead of the usual "Incidental Music/Theme Arrangement." Some observers consider this a blooper. This appears not to be a blooper, but the beginning of a new means of listing.

Episode 1
First Transmitted: Sept. 6, 1989

1:22 The Brigadier still does not remember Sergeant Benton's promotion. However, Lethbridge-Stewart has at least retained its hyphen. **3:00** The inside wall of the TARDIS is a sheet instead of a solid wall. The original TARDIS walls no longer existed at this time because the BBC destroyed the set. **13:35** The flash from one of the explosions shines through both the side and front window of the TARDIS. **14:41** The discussion makes the scabbard seem important, and then everyone forgets about it. **17:42** We have another reference to the importance of the scabbard. The writing on the scabbard translates to "The scabbard is worth ten of the sword." **19:47** There is a delay between the explosion of the grenade and the launching of the knight. **19:56** There is a hole in the roof of the brewery. Presumably, the knight made the hole.

20:05 Shou Yuing (Ling Tai) tells everyone she saw someone go through the wall. The rest of us all saw him go through the roof. Some viewers report seeing him go through the ceiling. These viewers were apparently inside the brewery.

Episode 2
First Transmitted: Sept. 13, 1989

6:06 When the scabbard hits the beam, the beam shakes and the glasses begin falling off the shelves. This also reemphasizes the importance of the scabbard. **7:14** Some viewers object to Mordred's (Christopher Bowen) laugh. These viewers compare his laugh to Pee-Wee Herman. **10:14** There are reports that Brigadier Bambera (Angela Bruce) has one eye open as the Doctor enters the room. This appears to be a lighting effect; she does not have either eye open. **14:20** The smoke from the damaged helicopter is not coming from the body but from one of the landing skids. The smoke comes from the left skid. **14:32** The smoke is now coming from the right skid. This could be a reversed image. **15:20** Some observers wonder why the tunnel did not collapse after the nitro-9 explosion. This question arises because the Doctor tells Ace the concrete has gone bad with age. **15:28** Ace mentions that there was no concrete in the eighth century and the Doctor agrees. Apparently, they forgot about the Coliseum in Rome. **21:38** Here and in many other places, this story perpetuates the Arthurian myth where eighth century knights wear twelfth century armor. This includes the body of Arthur who supposedly died, according to the Doctor, in the eighth century. **22:19** Some viewers claim that, in this episode, the Doctor grabs Excalibur by the blade without injury. The Doctor grabs the handle as he helps Ace rise. The Doctor does not touch the sword any other time in this episode.

Episode 3
First Transmitted: Sept. 20, 1989

1:42 The water tank cracks just before Ace goes out the top. **6:26** Some viewers consider it a blooper when Mordred drinks at least four pints with no apparent effects. This would be true if Mordred was from the Earth and not from another dimension with a different physiology. **6:53** Lavel (Dorota Rae), upon entering the pub, says, "Do you have a phun?" **14:34** The residents and their belongings have all been loaded into a truck for evacuation. However, at least two suitcases remain behind. **16:21** Bessie should still be on Gallifrey; see *The Five Doctors*. **19:57** Bessie's license plate now reads "Who 7."

Episode 4
First Transmitted: Sept. 27, 1989

2:54 Mordred (Christopher Bowen) refers to Morgaine (Jean Marsh) as deathless. **5:11** The Destroyer (Marek Anton) labels Morgaine as a mortal. Mordred and The Destroyer cannot both be correct. **6:13** The Doctor falls and his hat rolls quite a distance away from the Inn. **6:19** There are reports of the Doctor saying, "If they dead!" This is a questionable call. **6:35** When the Doctor enters the Inn, he has his hat. How did he have time to go get it? **7:07** This is a clear view of the dark streaks on Ace and Shou Yuing's face after the roof falls on the two of them. **8:50** Some fans cite the disappearance of the streaks on Ace and Shou Yuing's faces as a blooper. It is possible that they could have cleaned there faces by this time. **10:53** If Excalibur is so important, why do people not hold onto the weapon more tightly? It changes hands three times in this scene. **10:55** The Doctor catches Excalibur by the blade. He receives no injury. The blade must be very dull. This could be the problem claimed to occur in Episode 2. **12:06** Morgaine hits one of the light stands with Excalibur. **13:31** Some observers object to the Brigadier's mediocre karate chop. **21:16** Why does the Doctor suggest that UNIT should lock-up Mordred and Morgaine? How can UNIT hope to imprison dimension-hopping beings successfully?

Comments: The Brigadier saves the Earth, as does the Doctor.

(7Q) GHOST LIGHT

Writer: Marc Platt; **Director:** Alan Wareing

Media: DVD — episodic version — 73 minutes (used); Commercial tape — episodic version — 73 minutes; Collector's tape — movie version — 68 minutes
Highlights: This is the last of the Seventh Doctor stories filmed.

Errors and Other Points of Interest

Episode 1
First Transmitted: Oct. 4, 1989

3:42 As the clock strikes six, two maids leave from behind the left panel and one maid exits from behind the right panel. There are a total of three maids. **4:39** Ace is wearing a ring on her left hand. **4:48** Ace has "lost" her ring. **6:33** It is still six o'clock. **7:51** The glass doors on the cabinet reflect the camera operator. This occurs while the Doctor is checking Redvers (Michael Cochrane) for radiation. Some observers report this to be an Episode 3 blooper. **8:07** Some viewers report that some archaeologists believe that Neanderthals could not speak. They consider Nimrod's (Carl Forgione) speaking a blooper. These people probably believe the aeronautical engineers who know that bumblebees cannot fly. **9:53** It is possible to see the box for Ace's radio mike. It is just above her waist on her back. **12:08** Gwendoline (Katharine Schlesinger) tells Ace she can borrow one of her dresses. If the audience is to believe this, then they should have cast someone nearer to Ace's size for the part of Gwendoline. **14:17** It is easy to see that Mrs. Pritchard (Sylvia Syms) controls the flare-up of the candle with her thumb. **14:24** When the door opens, it is possible to see the key dangling in the lock. **23:29** There is a reported misspelling of Katharine as Katherine Schlesinger (Gwendoline) in the closing credits. A correction, if necessary, appears in the video release.

Episode 2
First Transmitted: Oct. 11, 1989

1:42 Inspector Mackenzie (Frank Windsor) is "sleeping" in the bottom drawer. Is the chest deep enough to accommodate a full-grown man stretched-out? The camera angle is set to prevent the viewer from knowing for sure. **3:02** There are still three maids. **3:24** There are now four maids. **20:40** This time, as the clock strikes six, two maids leave from behind the left panel and two maids exit from behind the right panel. Four maids (total) exit at this time. **20:46** Gwendoline has trouble getting out of her chair. **23:30** Another misspelling of Katharine as Katherine reportedly appears in the closing credits. Again, it is not in the video release.

Episode 3
First Transmitted: Oct. 18, 1989

2:31 We see one of the maids die, so we again have three maids. This is the old *Star Trek* ploy — beam down an extra person so there is someone to kill. This maid is another victim of STACS. **6:32** The TARDIS key has regenerated. **12:00** Ace has not gone completely Victorian; her footwear is out of period. **15:27** Some observers object to Josiah's plan to assassinate Queen Victoria and gain control to the British Empire.

Comments: The Doctor saves the Earth.

(7M) THE CURSE OF FENRIC

Writer: Ian Briggs; **Director:** Nicholas Mallett

Media: Commercial DVD — episodic version — 97 minutes (used); Commercial DVD — extended episodic version — 104 minutes; Commercial tape — extended episodic version — 104 minutes; Collector's tape — movie version — 90 minutes
Question: For the story, we may accept that bullets do not affect Haemovores, but why do bullets not affect their clothes?

Errors and Other Points of Interest

Episode 1
First Transmitted: Oct. 25, 1989

3:16 Captain Sorin (Tomek Bork) orders his men to speak only English. In some cases, they follow his orders to the death. Some viewers consider this a blooper. **9:20** We can see a signpost; however, there was a general removal of all signposts during the war years. The sign says "Maidens' Point." Very few other signs appear, unlike the reports listing that they appear in all four episodes. Count the other signs that appear. **9:32** Commander Millington (Alfred Lynch) could not have only a moustache. Royal Navy regulations would require him to be either clean-shaven or to have a beard and a moustache. Maybe he has special permission to look like the picture behind his desk. **17:34** There are those who feel that people in 1943 would not know about Jane Russell. She became famous for her first film — *The Outlaw*. This movie, filmed in 1941, did not receive general release until 1946. These people apparently forgot about the limited releases in 1941 and 1943 along with the extensive pre-release publicity for the movie (beginning in 1941). **19:23** Audrey (Aaron Hanley), Kathleen's (Cory Pulman) baby, holds what looks like a Superted teddy bear. This would be an unfortunate anachronism if true since a Superted is from the early 1980s.

Episode 2
First Transmitted: Nov. 1, 1989

2:03 New runes appear on a blank wall. **3:46** Doctor Judson (Dinsdale Lindens) has been studying the runes for some time in order to translate them. Why do the new runes appearing on a previously blank wall not surprise him? He would obviously have examined the entire area beforehand. The Doctor notices the new runes immediately. **4:40** Some viewers have a problem with using the Ultima Machine to translate Viking inscriptions. There is a coded message hidden within the Viking inscription, so the machine should be able to decode this message. If Doctor Judson and Commander Millington thought an encrypted message was in the inscription, they should use the Ultima Machine. **6:04** The sermon quotation is not from an early 1940s version of the Bible normally in use. **7:47** The camera operator must have realized that Commander Millington was not in the center of the field, and the operator quickly readjusts the camera position. **10:52** Some viewers question how the Russians are going to steal the "huge" Ultima Machine in their small boats. Commander Millington says the Russians want the "mind" of the Ultima Machine. The indicated unit is not "huge," so the Soviets could easily take the unit. **11:38** The stacked "cylinders" are obviously not separate cylinders but a wall with cylinder-like projections. The only cylinders appear to be on the very end of the stack. **13:34** There are claims that Jean (Joann

Kenny) and Phyllis (Joanne Bell) enter the water wearing black shoes or sandals. This is not certain. **13:34** Jean and Phyllis are both wearing pants when they enter the water at this time. Some viewers incorrectly report that they entered the water wearing dresses and exit wearing pants. **14:35** Commander Millington says, "I want all radio transmitters and outside telephone lines disabling." **15:06** The girl climbing into the bunk has a run in her stockings. **16:43** The Russian soldier drops his helmet into the water. Some observers wonder about the irregular movements of the helmet. **17:23** The soldier's helmet has jumped out of the water and is now above the water line. **18:35** Ace says, "and half-time score, Perivale six hundred million, rest of the Universe nil." **19:21** There is a dog running in the background. This is John Nathan-Turner's dog. **19:53** Jean and Phyllis are wearing white shoes. If they entered the water with black shoes, as reported earlier, then this is a blooper. **21:17** Doctor Judson asserts that he is "not an invalid, I'm a cripple!"

Episode 3
First Transmitted: Nov. 8, 1989

1:51 The Reverend Mister Wainwright (Nicholas Parsons) says that in the Dracula legend (according to Bram Stoker), the vampire came ashore in the area. Bram Stoker's account of Dracula has Dracula coming ashore near Whitby. Some observers cite this as a blooper. **2:04** It is possible to hear the rain hitting the Doctor's umbrella. **6:55** Apparently, one of the Haemovores wants more from Ace than blood. **7:50** Some viewers report that Ace's underwear is black at the top of the ladder. This may or may not be true. If this is true, then a blooper results later. It is not obvious that her underwear appears while she is at the top of the ladder. **8:20** When the Haemovores grab Ace, we see her light blue underwear. If she was wearing black at the top of the ladder, then this is a blooper. There are also reports that she is wearing white underwear. **8:23** Some observers think it is a blooper when Captain Sorin does not try to help when he sees the Haemovores trying to break into the Church. Maybe he is simply trying to sneak past so he can continue with his mission. It would be out of character for the Captain not to give top priority to his mission. **8:34** We can see the shadow of someone walking casually by as the Russian soldiers run to the Church. **8:41** It is possible to see the actor's neck when Ace hits one of the Haemovores in the head. **9:27** Can you see someone's finger holding the door open? There are reports that this happens in this episode. **11:48** After the nitro-9 first explodes, the wall is still standing. **11:55** Instead of the nitro-9 blowing the rubble away, the rubble falls towards the explosion. **14:05** The green "box" in the foreground is a post-production addition to cover what happens behind it. **14:37** The pithead the Doctor and the others flee through is slowly sinking in the mud. **21:53** There are reports that it is possible to see someone's finger holding a door open to let the Haemovores through. This may occur here instead of earlier. **22:22** Even though Doctor Judson corrected her earlier, Nurse Crane (Anne Reid) still believes Doctor Judson to be an invalid and not a cripple.

Episode 4
First Transmitted: Nov. 15, 1989

2:25 Some observers object to the numerous rainy scenes with sunny blue skies. **5:45** Some of the debris from the explosion hit the camera. **7:23** One of the "dead" soldiers is breathing rather heavily. **8:10** Captain Bates (Stevan Rimkus) learns that Commander Millington is associated with Fenric, and is planning to destroy the Earth. **8:18** Captain Bates slips in the mud. **8:33** Captain Bates joins the Doctor. Some fans cite this as a blooper since earlier the Captain was trying to kill the Doctor. This is not a blooper since the Captain has learned about Fenric. **10:10** The Haemovore on the right stumbles. **10:51** There are several small holes in the tabletop. These holes are for later events. **11:49** Ace slips in the mud. **12:27** The size of the baby picture is an anachronism. It is too large to be a typical 1940s baby picture. **17:16** There is tape on the bottom of the tipped over king. **21:13** Notice the drop cloth on the ground for the Doctor and Ace to fall upon. **21:15** The Doctor slips and falls. As he falls, he gets mud all over his hand. **21:46** The Doctor no longer has mud on his hand as he touches Ace's face. **22:41** Ace is very wet when she comes out of the water. **22:57** Ace's dress is already nearly dry.

Comments: The Doctor saves the Earth.

Neither the extended VHS version nor the extended movie versions are in this list. Both of these contain additional bloopers, but only the broadcast version is present in this list. Un-broadcast versions do not qualify for this list unless there is no alternative material available.

(7P) SURVIVAL

Writer: Rona Munro; **Director:** Alan Wareing

Media: Commercial tape — episodic version — 73 minutes (used); Collector's tape — movie version — 67 minutes
Highlights: The Master (Anthony Ainley) returns. The Doctor's final monologue.

Errors and Other Points of Interest

Episode 1
First Transmitted: Nov. 22, 1989

2:26 The "garden" the woman is chasing the cats away from looks more like a weed patch. **7:28** The reflection of a boom mike appears in the window next to the door as the Doctor and Sergeant Paterson (Julian Holloway) leave the Youth Club. **22:57** The Master recognizes the regenerated Doctor. This is a trait of nearly all Time Lords, except Azmael.

Episode 2
First Transmitted: Nov. 29, 1989

4:50 The background is not too stable. **11:39** There are reports of the appearance of power lines on the Cheetah Planet as Ace is watching Karra (Lisa Bowerman) approach the water. There should be no power lines on a primitive planet. The power lines may represent a relic of the civilization the Master discusses later. **15:33** The Master implies that an advanced civilization was present on the Cheetah Planet. **18:11** A lone man appears to be walking in the background. He is upper left of center, near the top of the screen. He does not walk like one of the Cheetah People. This person could be one of the other "prisoners" of the Cheetah People. **21:55** The Master's trap snares Midge's (William Barton) feet. The noose may have just tripped him, or be tied around his feet. Some observers assume the tied feet must become mysteriously untied for him to arise. Tied/untied feet would be a blooper. **22:03** Just before Midge rises, the saber-tooth is on the ground next to him. The tooth does not travel to Earth with him. **22:31** Midge is the first to teleport back to Earth and he takes the Master with him. Some observers consider that the failure of the Master to transport like Ace and Midge is a blooper.

Episode 3
First Transmitted: Dec. 6, 1989

7:29 We now learn why the Master did not try to transport himself to safety. The Doctor says that if you teleport you may become like the Cheetah People forever, a fate the Master is trying to avoid at the time. **10:33** Midge appears to have lost his new canine teeth. **13:23** Midge has his canines again. **14:39** The Master gives Midge a saber-tooth. Some fans think it is the one left on the ground on the Cheetah Planet. This may be a different tooth; also, it may be a larger tooth. The Master may have the first tooth or he already had another. **15:11** The colliding bikes would not place Midge where he landed. Run in slow motion — the crash ejects no one. **20:45** The Doctor transports himself back to the Earth. Thus, he must consider Earth to be his home. If he considered the TARDIS his home, he would have transported himself to the console room. **22:51** The Doctor's final monologue is overdubbed.

VIII
THE EIGHTH DOCTOR

DOCTOR WHO [1996 TV MOVIE]

Alternate Titles: *The Enemy Within, Enemy Within,* and *Le Seigneur du Temps* (The Last Time Lords)
Writer: Matthew Jacobs; **Director:** Geoffrey Sax

Media: DVD — 86 minutes (used); Commercial tape — 84 minutes (used); Collector's tape — 89 minutes
Highlights: The Eighth Doctor (Paul McGann) appears.

Errors and Other Points of Interest

There are several questions concerning the time line in this story. To address this issue there are many entries concerning time. The major questions are: Why did the Master wait from 7:45 until the afternoon before going to the hospital? How long did Lee and the Master spend in the TARDIS?

Some observers object to the ending of the story.

0:04 We find that the Master is on trial on Skaro, and that he awaits execution. Later we find out for sure that the Daleks were involved. This leads to many questions concerning the trial, interaction between the Doctor and the Daleks, and previous stories. **0:04** At least one viewer wonders how the Master could have further provoked the Daleks after he tried to start a Dalek-Draconian war in *Frontier in Space*. This member should review that story to find out whom the Master was trying to involve in a war. **0:04** One fan cites an example of a trial occurring between the First Doctor and his Companions and the Emperor Dalek. This person also cites Davros and the Daleks questioning the Fourth Doctor, Harry Sullivan, Sarah Jane Smith, and Romana II together. **0:04** There are those who think that the Daleks should exterminate the Master, not put him on trial. In Episode 2 of *Revelation of the Daleks,* the Daleks tell Davros, "You are to be taken back to Skaro to stand trial for crimes against the Daleks." Thus, there is a precedent. **0:04** Why would the Doctor trust the Daleks and go to Skaro to retrieve the Master's remains? **0:04** At least one viewer wonders how the Master, or anyone, can commit evil crimes against the Daleks. Evil crimes against anyone are from the view of the accusers, and not necessarily evil in the eyes of others. **0:43** The title of the movie is *Doctor Who* not *The Enemy Within*. **1:54** Some fans question why the Doctor did not burn himself on the candles beside the Master's casket. **2:02** The sonic screwdriver returns. **3:24** The record is not of the song we hear playing. The record is only a prop. **3:54** Some observers question how the Master caused the teacup and saucer to jump. **4:07** The Master leaves a slime trail. **4:14** The slime trail the Master left has disappeared. It is possible that the Master, and hence his slime trail, is evolving. **4:18** The Doctor's right hand appears to be in two places at once. He flips some switches on one side of the console, and then appears to be next to the keyboard on another of the console panels. Some observers incorrectly state that his right hand both flips the switches and types on the keyboard. **4:51** Slime remains on the chest. It has not disappeared, unlike the disappearing slime "seen" earlier. **5:01** There are those who question the white blob on the Doctor's chin. **5:08** Some viewers report that the fish is facing two different directions in the short and the long shot. The real cause is a shift in the camera angle. The angle of the cleaver makes it clear the wielder is across the table from the camera; however, in the next shot the camera is behind the cleaver wielder. **6:41** The guns used by Lee's (Yee Jee Tso) gang disappear. They should pull them out when the other gang members pull their weapons. This scene does not appear on the Commercial tape. **6:42** Lee and his friends all run for cover, and at least one of them is shot. There are reports that there is a version of this story where Lee's friends run away from him. This is supposedly in the Commercial tape version. This scene does not appear on the Commercial tape. About a minute of this scene is present on the DVD, but not on the Commercial tape. **7:01** After several shots of Lee running, he makes it to the billboard. There are claims that Lee did not have time to make it to the billboard. This is due to the editing of different versions; we do not see him move to the billboard in the Commercial tape version. The Commercial tape starts with Lee in front of the billboard, after the excised material. **7:23** Initially the gang members do not appear to notice the TARDIS appearing right in front of them. The members do comment on its appearance as they leave. **7:47** We see the front of the TARDIS after the gang shoots the Doctor. The bullets have caused no damage to the front (not unexpected), and none of the Doctor's blood is on the TARDIS (unexpected?). **8:46** No slime trail remains on the ground. Apparently, the Master has evolved into a non-slime form. **8:47** Some observers question why the Master does not take over the Doctor's body at this time. The Master may not have been capable of doing much in his snake form until later. He does seem to be evolving. At this point, it is not definite whether the Doctor will die or regenerate, so the Master may feel that he should wait. **9:16** The Doctor again becomes "John Smith." **10:06** Some viewers question how the Snake-Master got into the ambulance. The actions of the Snake-Master in Bruce's (Eric Roberts) bedroom belie this interpretation. **10:41** We find that one of the bullets went through the Doctor's shoulder. Why was there none of the Doctor's blood on the TARDIS? Earlier stories establish the fact that items such as bullets do not damage the TARDIS exterior, but it does not have a non-stick surface (see *Paradise Towers*). **10:41** There are those who question the Doctor's apparent unconcern as he leaves the TARDIS. They feel he should show concern about the Master being loose inside the TARDIS. **12:21** We learn that the technicians took several X-rays of the Doctor. **13:13** Supposedly, we can see the Doctor's reflection in Grace's (Daphne Ashbrook) goggles, and we hear him talking without his lips moving. This does not occur in this version. **13:24** There are questions as to how the Doctor knows the malfunction requires a part from a special clock. **13:24** Some viewers have forgotten about the Doctor's trip to Varos and the Doctor's first trip to Skaro adventure when they suggest that he should be carrying a replacement unit for any important part of the TARDIS. **14:07** The Doctor has an anesthetic mask covering his face, but the reflection in Grace's goggles shows only his face, without the mask. **14:41** The probe's view does not look too much like real blood. **15:28** There was editing of many of the Doctor's final moments in the operating room for the original BBC1 transmission and the Commercial Tape. This material is present in the DVD version. **15:56** Some fans report that Grace's hands appear to be in two different positions between the Doctor's "death" and Grace removing her goggles. Grace's hands are moving in the right direction. **17:14** Lee learns that the Doctor has "died." **20:21** The Master, in snake form, lifts himself up above the bed — this explains how he could get into the ambulance. **20:57** We see the first view of *Frankenstein* (1931) showing on the television. **22:11** *Frankenstein* appears again. Up to this point, the timing of the movie corresponds with what we see on screen. This is the "It's alive!" speech. This occurs about 25 minutes into the movie. **23:31** The final appearance of *Frankenstein* occurs at this point. We see the point in the movie where the Creature enters room of Frankenstein's bride. This occurs about 55 minutes into the movie. The *Frankenstein* movie has progressed about 30 minutes in little over a minute. Some viewers say that the explanation is in the editing of movies for TV. There are two problems with this explanation. Removing 30 minutes from a 70-minute movie is not too reasonable. Second, most material edited from movies have commercials in place of the excised material. The scenes should remain about 30 minutes apart even with the removal of some scenes. **24:11** Some observers question the presence of an abandoned hospital wing. Apparently, a deleted part of the script explains this, and the wing only awaits money for remodeling. Supposedly, Dr. Salinger's late night tour was an effort to gain donations. **27:00** Lee opens the Doctor's watch. The watch says "7:50." A few seconds later, in Bruce's bedroom, we find that time has flowed backwards. This assumes that both timepieces are reading the "correct" time. **27:13** We see the TARDIS key. **27:19** The alarm clock says "7:46." **27:25** Some fans question why the Master (Eric Roberts) wants to leave Bruce's body so fast. The Master mutters that his new body will not last long, thus he must leave it as soon as reasonably possible. **29:41** The clock in the hospital registers "11:58." **29:51** Dr. Salinger removes his glasses after inspecting the X-ray. The glasses immediately evaporate. **30:02** We now find out what happened to Dr. Salinger's glasses — they have metamorphosed into a lighter. He did not have a lighter in his hand earlier. **30:04** Dr. Salinger destroys one X-ray of the Doctor; where are the others? **32:28** The Doctor opens his shirt and the broken end of the probe wire juts from his chest. The Doctor pulls out a long wire and finally the camera. Some viewers incorrectly report that a camera is present on both ends. **33:04** The Master enters the hospital. Some observers suggest that this is at about one o'clock. The Master could have entered much earlier. **34:25** Grace tells the Doctor that Bryan took all his stuff. Later we find that this is not true. **36:03** The Doctor tells Grace, "I have thirteen lives." That is what we hear, but his lips say "twelve." **36:59** The reflection of the sun on the building in the background makes it appear to be low in the sky. This would occur in the early morning or the late afternoon. **37:12** Lee unlocks the TARDIS door and enters. It is daylight outside. There is a light lit above the TARDIS indicating that it is getting dark (evening), or getting light (morning). **37:50** How did the Master enter the TARDIS without a key? He could not have known about the spare key, because he would not have left it for the Doctor to use. **38:14** The Masters tells Lee that the TARDIS really likes him (Lee). **38:50** Lee gives the Master the bag containing the Doctor's possessions. **39:28** The first view of Grace's home shows that it is getting dark. It is early evening. **39:43**

The Doctor puts on Bryan's shoes. Why would Bryan leave his shoes behind? **40:01** Grace says, of the Doctor's blood, "It's not blood." Some viewers say this is a blooper because the Doctor's blood looked normal to the probe. The blood did not look normal from the probe's view — the real blooper was that no one noticed earlier. **42:45** Why are there bats in the Cloister Room? What do they live on and where do they disappear? **43:48** The Master uses Lee's eye to open the Eye of Harmony. There are those who question this as a potential blooper, but the Master tells Lee, "If the TARDIS really likes you the eye will open." **43:58** Lee looks into the bright light and exclaims, "Arrh, my eye!" There are no lasting effects. **45:10** Where did the Doctor get the jelly babies? At this time, we do not know that they are jelly babies. Why does the Master get this view? The Doctor is with Grace in the park, and the two of them are not eating. **45:30** The Master realizes "the Doctor is half human." Maybe this is why Lee's eye worked on the Eye of Harmony. **46:16** The Doctor describes the Eye of Harmony as the power source of the TARDIS. There is no explanation why the device is in the TARDIS and not back on Gallifrey. Some fans suggest that the Eye in the TARDIS is not the original Eye, but one linked to the main one on Gallifrey. **46:23** The Doctor says, "Time And Relative Dimension In Space." **48:07** The Doctor realizes that they have until midnight. **48:18** Some fans question how the Doctor is able to tap on the glass and then walk through it. The knocking sound appears to come from the Doctor knocking on the wooden frame of the window, and not on the glass. **48:29** The Doctor explains, "The molecular structure of the planet is changing." This would indicate that the change in Grace's window is not a localized phenomenon. This is an argument against those who have attempted to explain some inconsistencies through localized effects. **48:40** The Doctor walks through the glass. **48:54** The clock in Grace's house chimes nine o'clock. **50:06** The Newscaster (Joanna Piros) on the right announces that she will be at the ITAR party. **50:14** Some viewers cite that it is not possible to produce a more accurate clock than a cesium atomic clock. This is from the newscast — there are later references. Since the year of the movie, there has been at least one significant improvement in the cesium atomic clock — thus improvements are possible. The improved clock in the movie is a beryllium clock. This is technobabble, and therefore it should not be a blooper. **50:45** There are claims that the Doctor says he wants to go to the "Institute of Technicological Advancement and Research." **51:04** It is possible to see the Master's normal eyes through the sunglasses. **51:45** The Master is slow replacing his glasses. Some observers cite this as a blooper. **52:07** Grace throws her arms up before the Master vomits. How does she know she needs to protect her face? **52:10** The Master's vomit decolorizes and burns Grace's arm. **52:51** The Doctor offers the police officer jelly babies. The Doctor does not have his own clothes, his bag of personal items, and he has not been back to the TARDIS — where did he get the jelly babies? **53:37** Why did the other officers not respond to the gunshot? **54:08** The Doctor and Grace steal a motorcycle from a police officer, and all the other police officers do nothing. **54:15** This is one of many shots showing the wind playing havoc with Grace's hair. **54:25** What are two big rigs doing on both sides of a two-way street? There is a double yellow line between the trucks. **56:00** There are reports that the railroad cars disappear in the close-up shot. The blue railroad cars are present, then we see the skyline, and finally there is a row of gray cars. When the blue cars are next to the Doctor — we can see that the Doctor is near the end of the line of cars. Thus, there was a break coming, apparently before the gray cars started. **56:29** Grace gets off the motorcycle with neat, not windblown, hair. **57:14** If the Doctor is trying to get into the ITAR building and pass the guards, why does he not simply walk through the glass as he did earlier? The Doctor already stated that the phenomenon is not a local phenomenon. **58:43** The Doctor explains, "I'm half human on my mother's side." This continues the series of questions presented in the later episodes of the Seventh Doctor stories. **1:00:37** The Master's vomit (assumed) neither decolorizes nor burns the guards. The guards are immobilized. Why does the vomit not affect everyone the same way? **1:00:59** The Doctor and Grace use a fire hose to lower themselves to the ground. The hose is not long enough for this purpose. **1:01:24** Why is someone vacuuming the floor during a fire alarm? **1:01:30** The hose is slack even when it is supporting the weight of the Doctor and Grace. In addition, why does it lower the Doctor and Grace so slowly? **1:01:32** Where have all the guests gone? They should be milling about outside. How do the guests get back into the building and seated so quickly? **1:02:30** The Doctor lifts Grace to get the TARDIS key. Thus, the Master did not take it, unless he left it for the Doctor. **1:02:46** A police bike enters the TARDIS and then exits. The two TARDIS doors are open to allow the bike to enter. There are three steps immediately inside the TARDIS door. He was obviously chasing the stolen motorcycle, but why did he simply drive away later? **1:02:47** Some observers incorrectly report that the "Police Public Call Box" sign is missing from the back of the TARDIS. We see the front and one side of the TARDIS, not the back. **1:04:04** Grace informs the Doctor, "It's 11:48, we still have 11 minutes." **1:04:27** The Doctor says he has never opened the Eye of Harmony. **1:04:33** Some fans question how going back in time saves the Earth. **1:05:06** The Doctor places his tool kit on the console but does not open it. When the view switches to Grace, a tool materializes in the Doctor's hand. He had not retrieved anything from the tool kit before this time. In the next shot, the tool kit is open. **1:05:34** The Master is still dressed as Bruce. **1:06:34** Some observers have questioned where the Master found the Time Lord robes. We know from many stories that there is an extensive wardrobe in the TARDIS. The real blooper is how he managed to change so rapidly. **1:06:40** The Master announces that he always dresses for the occasion. When did the Master in the TV series ever dress for the occasion? **1:08:16** We are told the Eye of Harmony was last opened seven hundred years ago. Some fans cite this as a blooper because the Doctor was alive at the time, and he should know about it. The Doctor has already said that he never opened the Eye; he never said the Eye never opened. **1:09:17** In some shots, we can see the Doctor's lower eyelids, but in other shots, they are not in view. This does not occur in the long or medium shots. There are many examples. **1:09:52** Why does it take Lee so long to understand what the Master is? **1:10:14** The Master uses Grace's eye to open the Eye of Harmony. In this case, there has been no foundation set about the TARDIS "really liking" her. This time it is a blooper — why would an item of Time Lord Technology require a human eye to work. **1:10:15** Lee falls on the floor next to the raised area used for the Eye of Harmony. **1:10:33** Compare this view of the Doctor's eyelids to the earlier view. **1:10:45** Why does Grace pull her hair away from her eyes instead of covering her eyes? Does she want to see the light beam better? **1:10:59** The bright light temporarily blinds Grace. Some observers cite this as a blooper because Lee behaved differently. Individual differences could explain these variations. **1:12:06** The overhead shot of the exploding TARDIS console does not show the tool kit that is present in the next shot. **1:12:35** How did Grace gain the ability to rewire the

TARDIS? **1:12:53** The transfer appears to be changing the Master, but it appears to have no affect on the Doctor. **1:13:23** Why does no one in the ITAR building notice the tornado forming? The walls are glass so the tornado should be readily visible. **1:14:04** The time rotor is at an angle, but the special effects are horizontal. **1:14:29** Some observers question — what is a temporal orbit? A temporal orbit is technobabble — not a blooper. **1:14:42** How can it be night everywhere on the planet at the same time? **1:16:01** There are those who question how the Master manages to go unseen from the balcony to the Doctor. **1:16:41** Immediately after the Doctor moves the staff to reflect the light into the Master's eyes, a studio light shines above the staff. **1:16:42** The Master covers his eyes with his right arm, but in the next shot, his eyes are not covered. Some observers incorrectly report that the Master also used his left hand to cover his eyes. **1:16:51** The Doctor first offers the Master his right hand, but in the next shot, the Doctor has his left hand extended? This may not be a real blooper because the Doctor has had time to move. **1:17:43** Note the clock, then note the calendar. The calendar and the clock seem not to be coordinated. **1:17:54** The Doctor places the dead Grace next to Lee's body. Lee has managed to move his dead body to the landing at the top of the first flight of stairs. **1:18:06** Some observers question to whom the Doctor seems to be praying. **1:18:23** There are questions about what the dust is. The dust leaves the Eye of Harmony and goes to Grace and Lee. Apparently, this is supposed to represent their souls. However, many people still question what the dust is. **1:18:51** Lee awakens and tells the Doctor, "Doctor, I have your things." Lee gave the bag to the Master earlier, thus he no longer has the Doctor's things to return. **1:20:09** The Doctor tells Grace and Lee that Gallifrey is 250 million light years from Earth. How can they see a planet that far away? This would place Gallifrey outside the Milky Way Galaxy. **1:20:51** The Doctor must still thump the TARDIS console to make it work. **1:21:28** The Newscaster, who announced she was going to be at the ITAR party, is still in the TV studio. **1:24:20** Some observers consider the fact that the disappearance of the broken cup and saucer to be a blooper. The Doctor had time to clean the mess.

Comments: The Doctor defeats the Master and saves the Universe.

IX

THE FORGOTTEN DOCTOR: THE PETER CUSHING MOVIES

Doctor Who and the Daleks

Writer: Milton Subotsky; **Director:** Gordon Flemyng

Media: DVD — 82 minutes (used); Commercial tape — 79 minutes
Highlights: We see the Daleks in this 1965 movie in color. We see a different Doctor (Peter Cushing).

Errors and Other Points of Interest

The lights on the Daleks in this story behave very differently from those on TV. The lights are continually flashing on any Dalek that is not going to speak. A Dalek that is about to speak does not have flashing lights except when it is speaking.
4:04 Ian addresses Peter Cushing as Dr. Who, not as the Doctor. This is one of the major differences between the TV series and the movie. In general, these differences will not appear in this list. These differences could lead to incorrect bloopers. **4:30** Susan says, "Time And Relative Dimension In Space." **4:49** Ian closes the TARDIS door and the interior light goes out. **7:06** TARDIS (not the TARDIS) has landed, but the light on top is still flashing. **7:09** When Ian closes the TARDIS door, the interior lights do not go out. **8:32** Susan identifies a flower, apparently using an Earth name. What is an Earth flower doing on Skaro? **14:43** The interior light of TARDIS is still on, though Susan may have turned it on when she took the box of drugs in later. **22:12** The cell, as in the TV story, has a bed. Some observers claim that the Daleks should not have a bed in their cells. It is possible the cell was for Thals, even though the Daleks have not seen any Thals for many years. **24:01** A Dalek enters the cell talking very slowly. **24:11** The Dalek that was speaking very slowly is now speaking very rapidly. **25:52** When escorting Susan out of the city, as the left Dalek passes through the doorway, its top jumps up and down as if something goosed the operator. **29:13** Who turned the TARDIS lights out? **29:17** Normally the lights of the TARDIS come on when the doors open; however, as Susan opens the doors this does not happen. **37:27** The Thals are able to read English. **42:58** As in the TV story, we get a glimpse of part of a Dalek. **44:00** Some observers claim that everyone grabbed by the Daleks' claws must slip their hands into the Dalek's claw. Susan does this at this point. Watch for the other occurrences claimed by these observers. These observers also report this particular situation to occur early in the movie. **51:04** If the Daleks plan to exterminate the Thals, why do the Daleks not close the doors after the Thals enter the city? If the Daleks closed the doors, the extermination of the Thals could have been suc-

cessful. **52:57** The TARDIS lights are slow to come on after Dr. Who opens the doors. **1:16:07** The Dalek guard calls and says, "Prisoners escaping...." Ian, Barbara and the two Thals were not escaping prisoners, but attackers. **1:16:55** The Dalek begins to fall apart when it hits the back of the shaft. The Dalek also leaves a significant dent in the back wall of the shaft. **1:18:13** The wall explodes before the Dalek hits it. **1:18:16** The walls, in some cases, wobble as the combatants run into them. **1:21:28** Ian looks out the TARDIS doors and sees an army of giant Roman soldiers marching on the TARDIS. Is this an indication of a problem similar to that in *Planet of Giants*?

1:22:01 The closing credits list Robert Jewell's name as "Jewel." He is one of the Dalek operators.

Comments: Dr. (not Doctor) Who is Peter Cushing. His granddaughter is Barbara (Jennie Linden). Ian Chesterton (Roy Castle) and Barbara are not teachers. Dr. Who apparently lives with Barbara and Susan (Roberta Tovey).

The script is very similar to the original BBC story written by Terry Nation. There are significant differences. Some of the differences were necessary because the movie is significantly shorter than the TV story.

DALEKS—INVASION EARTH 2150 A.D.

Writer: Milton Subotsky and David Whitaker; **Director:** Gordon Flemyng

Media: DVD — 84 minutes (used); Commercial tape — 80 minutes; Commercial tape — *Daleks—The Early Years*— excerpts
Highlights: Again, we see the Daleks, in this 1966 movie, in color.

Errors and Other Points of Interest

5:04 When talking to Tom after he wakes up, Dr. Who specifies that they are going to the year 2150 (as specified in the title). **6:21** Soon after leaving the TARDIS, Susan notes the absence of birds. **8:10** A crowbar suddenly appears in Tom's hand. **10:25** We can see the face of Tom Campbell's stunt double as he falls out the door. **11:21** It is possible to see the wires supporting the flying saucer; this happens in nearly every other flying saucer scene. **12:20** When Susan and Louise are re-united, it sounds as if Susan addresses Louise as Marie. **13:53** What is a Dalek doing in the river? **13:54** Some viewers report that as the Dalek first emerges from the river its bumps are gray-blue. Then the bumps turn black. Finally, the bumps have returned to grey-blue. This is not present either in the 1994 video release or in the more recent DVD release. **13:54** As the Dalek comes out of the river there is a truck moving in the background. **13:54** In spite of Susan's earlier comment, several birds fly by in the background. **25:51** The Dalek stops David (disguised as a Roboman) at the top of the ramp and asks him, "What sector do these prisoners come from?" David replies, "Sector Four." Watch the extra in the dark coat behind David. This person is mouthing the dialogue. **26:11** The rebels roll one of the Daleks down the ramp of the flying saucer. Notice in what position the Dalek lands. **28:51** The last person Tom grabs to ask about the girl immediately falls down after the person frees himself. Which girl is Tom seeking? Whom has he seen? **28:54** The wrecked Dalek at the bottom of the ramp is now in a different position. Some viewers have mistakenly attributed this to the TV story *The Dalek Invasion of Earth*. **31:22** Some observers report that they see Tom descending the ramp. This is in a long shot. The next shot is a close-up showing Tom at the top of the ramp and just beginning his descent. We never see the face of the person in the long shot, so the assumption that it is Tom may not be valid. **34:14** The Roboman next to Tom does not have his helmet on correctly. **38:20** There are claims that a blooper is present when the camera scans across the meal room to the robotizing area. **38:23** Louise's coat catches on a lever and starts the food machine. She turns off the machine with a different switch. **39:08** Some observers wonder how David and the Doctor completely miss Susan's message. **40:33** Susan obviously needs to spend more time in school. The message she leaves for Dr. Who says, "Grandfather we heading for Watford will wait for you there. Susan." **43:37** Contrary to claims, the window to the van is not broken twice. On careful viewing, we see that a reflection is involved. If it had been broken in the long shot, glass would appear to be coming out from the window. **43:42** One of the Daleks knocked over by the van is obviously completely hollow. **47:17** The mystery shot takes place. As the Roboman says "halt," we hear a shot fired. Robomen do not have rifles and David's rifle spews forth quantities of smoke (see the second shot). Apparently the first shot kills one Roboman and he falls into the river (you can see the splash at the edge of the screen) just as David fires and kills the second Roboman. Note that David's rifle is aiming away from the first Roboman when we hear the shot. **47:59** This second shot of the robotizing and meal room indicates that this may not be a blooper. It is possible that the two areas are intentionally different parts of the same room. **1:00:51** Dr. Who learns that the Daleks plan to extract the magnetic core of the Earth so they can pilot the Earth. The choice of the Bedfordshire mine is because of a fracture in the Earth's crust. The purpose of picking the Earth creates many questions and claimed bloopers. There is a discussion about the choice of the Earth in the TV story. **1:02:38** The Daleks confirm what the Doctor learned earlier about their plans. The Daleks then go on to say that they will move the Earth to a location near Skaro. **1:10:26** The eyepiece on the Dalek leading the prisoners suddenly jumps. **1:13:49** The Black Dalek pushes one of the Robomen down the shaft. As the Dalek does this, it loses its claw. The claw is still missing in the next shot of the Black Dalek. **1:14:01** The Black Dalek regenerates a new claw. **1:14:49** The Daleks use rels as time units instead of seconds or minutes. **1:15:59** Notice the arrangement of the timbers placed by Tom. **1:16:12** The timbers are no longer in the same position as Tom left them. **1:18:08** When the red Dalek first starts to fall down the shaft, it nearly loses its eyestalk (apparently, only a small wire holds it). However, in the next shot, as it falls on down the shaft, the eyestalk is back in position. **1:21:47** Some viewers question why the earlier Tom is not visible on the street when the TARDIS returns. The Time Lords have only bent the "Laws of Time" a few times. This situation does not seem worthy of their intervention. Thus, Tom cannot meet himself.

Comments: Constable Tom Campbell (Bernard Cribbins) joins Dr. Who (Peter Cushing), his granddaughter Susan or Susie (Roberta Tovey), and his niece Louise (Jill Curzon).

Many of the scenes in this movie are identical to those in the TV series, except that different characters are involved. It is surprising that more bloopers do not result as false claims from this potentially confusing arrangement.

X
Related Programs

K-9 AND COMPANY

Alternate Title: *K-9 and Company — A Girl's Best Friend*
Writer: Terence Dudley; **Director:** John Black

Media: Commercial tape — 50 minutes (used); Collector's tape — 49 minutes

Errors and Other Points of Interest

First Transmitted: Dec. 28, 1981

9:39 There is an obvious dubbing of the growl of Commander Pollock's (Bill Fraser) dog. **14:22** Classic quote: Brendan (Ian Sears) asks, "Who is the Doctor?" to which K-9 replies, "Affirmative." **14:39** The date is December 18, 1981. **17:25** There are an unusually large number of flowers blooming outside for mid–December England. **19:02** Watch the time on the mantle clock. For many scenes the time is 3:45 (indicating the clock is not working), then the time suddenly changes. Some viewers report the time as being 4:45. This would not be a blooper if the clock were broken. Later the time does change, so the clock is not broken. **24:09** Some observers cite, as a blooper, George Tracey's (Colin Jeavons) description of K-9 as "the goddess Hecate's Familiar ... a dog a dog belching fire." **25:20** The Commander asks Sarah Jane about a "white dog." Who described K-9 as white? **29:29** Brendan's kidnappers leave the door open. **32:00** Sarah Jane states that there was no evidence of a break-in. Apparently, an open or unlocked door was not evidence. **34:37** George Tracy describes K-9 as "the white dog." **36:09** Some fans cite the police officer's "gurning" death as a blooper. **41:24** The clock on the mantel shows a new time as nearly 11; the sudden change in time is a blooper. It is possible that someone finally wound the clock or replaced its batteries. **45:34** The sound and visual effect the first time K-9 fires at the Coven do not coincide.

DIMENSIONS IN TIME

Writer: John Nathan-Turner, and David Roden; **Director:** Stuart McDonald

Media: Collector's DVD — 2 parts — 13 minutes (used); Collector's tape — 2 parts — total time 13 minutes
Highlights: We have a chance to see five Doctors, many of the companions and foes. The Rani (Kate O'Mara) returns.

Errors and Other Points of Interest

Episode 1
First Transmitted: Nov. 26, 1993

1:51 Cyrian (Sam West) states that the Rani requires only an Earthling to complete the collection. **2:41** Ace nearly trips over the rope on the ground. **4:42** Susan Foreman says to the Sixth Doctor, "Who are you?" to which the Doctor answers, "Precisely."

Episode 2
First Transmitted: Nov. 27, 1993

1:28 Bessie's license plate again reads "Who 1." The last time Bessie appeared in *Battlefield*, the plate read "Who 7." **2:24** The Rani plans to land at the center of the Greenwich Meridian. The Greenwich Meridian is a line going from the North Pole to the South Pole. The center of this line would be on the Equator. **2:53** Romana II says, "Doctor Who?" **3:54** Leela tells the Seventh Doctor that the Rani has the "genetic codes and brain prints of every living creature in the entire cosmos." This is a technobabble exaggeration. In addition, to get the information for "every living creature" the Rani would have to capture everyone on Earth, not just one person. The Seventh Doctor agrees with Leela and goes on to say that the Rani can now control evolution. The Seventh Doctor is also guilty of a technobabble exaggeration.

Comments: This was for fun and for charity so everything is very light-hearted.

Too bad the Daleks were unable to join the party.

THE CURSE OF FATAL DEATH

Alternate Title: *Doctor Who and the Curse of Fatal Death*
Writer: Steven Moffat; **Director:** John Henderson

Media: Commercial tape — technically 2 parts, but treated as 1— 21 minutes
Highlights: The Ninth Doctor (Rowan Atkinson) and others make their appearance.

Errors and Other Points of Interest

Episode 1
First Transmitted: Mar. 12, 1999

0:29 The central column on the Master's (Jonathan Pryce) TARDIS needs realignment. **0:31** The Doctor's TARDIS also needs a realigned central column. **2:12** It is possible to see into the TARDIS through the open door. **4:51** Something enters the set behind the Doctor after he finishes kissing Emma (Julia Sawalha). **5:23** The Master spits on himself as he says, "feces". **8:18** As the Daleks file past in their pursuit of the Doctor and Emma, a studio light appears through a break in the line. **9:17** This is the end of the "First" Episode. **14:11** The Tenth Doctor (Richard E. Grant) appears. **14:22** The Tenth Doctor spits on himself while admiring himself. **15:40** The Eleventh Doctor (Jim Broadbent) appears. **16:29** The Twelfth Doctor (Hugh Grant) appears. **16:53** The cushion the Twelfth Doctor is about to "fall" upon pops into view. **18:58** The Thirteenth Doctor (Joanna Lumley) appears. Even though the energy destroyed the Doctor's ability to regenerate, the Doctor gets 12 regenerations.

Comments: The Doctor saves the Master and the Daleks.

As with *Dimensions in Time*, this is very light-hearted.

The commercial release is slightly shorter than the televised version, and this release has two episodes instead of four episodes.

The original transmission of this story was as four episodes.

Index

The A-Team 277
The Abandoned Planet 47
Abbott 180
Abbott of Amboise 48, 49
The Abominable Snowmen 75, 81, 82, 246
Aborigine 227
acceleration 84, 219, 261
accent(s) 20, 48, 52, 64, 94, 95, 112, 185, 195, 209, 253, 274
Action Man Tank 162
adit 266
Advanced Micro Devices 192
Agamemnon 44
Age of Fishes 207
Aggedor 130, 157
Ainley, Tony 226, 237
Air Lock 43
aircraft 107
airplane 70
alien culture 21
alien language 263
alien psychology 174
alien(s) 119, 123, 154, 156, 187, 199, 208, 255, 269, 279, 289, 293
Alistair 157
All Roads Lead to Rome 31
Alliance 47
Allison 291, 292
allosaur 110, 152
allotrope 146
alloy 219
Alpha 72
Alpha Centauri 129, 156, 157
alternate time 171
Altos 18, 19
Aluminum 208
Alzarius 217
Amazonia 130
Ambassador, Bandril 269

The Ambassadors of Death 111, 139
Amboise, Abbott of 48, 49
Ambril 239
The Ambush 14
AMD 192
Amdo 65
American Civil War Zone 101, 102, 103
American Sergeant 57
ammonia 43, 78
ammonium sulfide 77
amniotic fluid 208
Amyand 253
anachronism blooper 124
anagram 226, 237, 244, 267, 286
Andred 195, 196
Andrews, John 142, 143
Androgums 267
android(s) 173, 174, 175, 200, 201, 204, 231, 232, 234, 255, 269
The Android Invasion 173
The Androids of Tara 200
Andromeda 268, 271, 280
Andromedan Phylox Series 226
Anglo-Scottish conflict 63
animal(s) 123, 147, 148, 252
Animus 34, 118
Anita 267
Ann 233
Antarctica 57, 177
antimatter 169, 238
anti-robot machine 232
Antodus 14
Apartment 288
Apatosaurus 152
ape 133
apple 148
aqua regia 33

Arbitan 18
Arc of Infinity 238
archaeologists 299
Archer, Colonel 252
Arcturus 129, 130
Arden 76, 77
Argolin(s) 213, 214
argonite 99
Aridian 38, 39
Aris 230
Ark 163
The Ark 3, 49, 50, 249, 271
The Ark in Space 162, 166
The Armageddon Factor 203, 208
Arnold, Staff Sergeant 81
Arthur 298
Arthurian myth 298
ascends stair 291
Ashe, Mary 123
Ashton 28
Asimov, Isaac 62, 72
aspirin 32
assassin 31
Assassin at Peking 17
assistant 214, 275
asteroid 167, 168, 211, 271, 286
Astra 203, 204
Astral Map 33, 34, 96
Astrid 79, 80
astronaut(s) 112, 113
astronomy 271
Atlantean 64, 65
Atlantis 126, 136, 138
atmosphere 42, 68, 70, 77, 93, 107, 134, 207, 231, 260
atomic number 94
atomic weight 72, 94
Atrios 203, 204
Atropine 22
Attack of the Cybermen 261
Auderly House 127, 129

audio blooper 3
audio tapes 63
Audrey 300
Audrey, Jr. 287
Audrey II 287
Autloc 20
Autoguard 163
automobile 120
Auton(s) 107, 108, 109, 117, 118
autonomic brain 212
The Awakening 249
ax(e) 72, 177, 186, 219, 232
Axon(s) 120, 121, 122
Axon ship 120, 122
axonite 121
Axos 121, 122
Aydan 19
Azal 126
Azaxyr 157
Azmael 259, 260, 261, 302
Aztec costume 20
The Aztecs 20

Babble of Daleks 15
baby 138, 300
Baccu 50
bacteria 68, 147
bad science 64, 65
Baker, Colin 65, 67
Baker, Major 110, 111
Balan 87, 88
Balazar 274
balcony 35, 312
Bambera, Brigadier 297
bandit(s) 103, 208
Bandril(s) 269, 270
Bandril Ambassador 269
Bannermen 289
banning 142
Barclay 57, 58
A Bargain of Necessity 24
barn 110
Barrass 24
Barrington, Major 100
base security 45
baseball bat 291
BASIC 259
Baster 182
Bates, Captain 301
bathhouse 265, 266
bats 39, 310
A Battle of Wits 42
Battlefield 297, 322
Baxter, Ruth 278
BBC 297, 316
BBC1 309
Beacon 100, 165
Beacon Alpha 2 99

Beacon Alpha 4 99
Beacon Alpha 7 99
beam locators 234, 235
Beatles 37
bed blooper 129, 130
Bedfordshire 28, 317
bedroom 187, 188, 308, 309
Belazs 289, 290
Bell of Doom 48
bellboy 296
Ben blooper 66, 67
Benik 80
Bennett 29, 30
Bennett Oscillator 163
Benoit 67
Benton, Corporal 90
Benton, Sergeant 111
Berger 235
Bert 149
beryllium clock 310
Bessie 110, 114, 115, 116, 125, 126, 139, 140, 245, 246, 297, 298, 322
"best friend" 189, 190
Beta 72, 95
Bettan 165
Beyond the Sun 15
Bi-Al 188, 189, 190
Bible 300
Big Bang 226
Bigon 227, 228
Billy 289
Bilton 237
Binro 197
biped 110
Biroc 218, 219
black box 49
black Cyberman 262
Black Dalek 317; lights 292, 293
Black Death 232
Black Guardian 241, 243
Black Orchid 231, 233
Blair, Linda 112
Blake 191
block transfer 259
Bloodaxe 151
blue box 265
Blue Kangs 287
Board 213
Boaz 128
bods 247
Boer War Zone 103
The Bomb 50
bomb, atomic 110, 119
Bond, James 23, 24, 80
boom 230
boom mike shadows 2, 237
Borad 168, 269, 270

Borusa 195, 196, 238, 239, 245, 246
BOSS 148, 150
Bostock 273
Botanical Gardens 265
boundary error 249
box office attendant 293
Boyle's Law 27
Bragen 62
Braille wire 127
brain fluid 265
The Brain of Morbius 175
brandy 56
Brendan 321
Brent 97
brewery 297
Briant, Michael 131
"brick" 161
The Bride of Sacrifice 20
Briggs, Captain 234, 235
The Brink of Disaster 15
British Empire 299
British government 201
broadcast date 27
Brock 213, 214
brontosaurus 152, 154
Brotadac 215
Broton 168
Bruce 79, 308, 309, 311
Bruce, Donald 80
Bruchner 279
Bryan 309, 310
Bryant, Michael 131
Bryant, Peter 89
Bulic 248
Buller 185
butchering 267
Butler 153, 154

café 207
Caldwell 123
Calib 183
California 192
Caligari, Dr. 52
Cambridge 112, 212
Cameca 20
cameo 239
Camilla 217
Campbell, Constable Tom 316, 317
campers 200
candle(s) 89, 100, 171, 299, 307
Capel, Taren 185
capitalism 204
capsule 112, 240
captain 73, 74, 101, 132, 133, 154, 155, 188, 198, 209, 235, 236, 243, 279, 296

carbon dioxide 76, 77
carbon monoxide 78
Caris 215
Carnival of Monsters 135, 141, 157
Carol 22
Carstairs, Lieutenant 100, 101
Cassandra 45
Castellan 182
Castellan Kelner 195, 196
castle 151
Castrovalva 179, 222, 225, 226, 259
catacombs 197
cat(s) 208, 302
cave(s) 37, 142, 165, 183, 234, 254, 290
The Cave of Five Hundred Eyes 17
The Cave of Skulls 12
Caven 100
Cavendish, Lord 167
cavern 126, 127, 194
The Caves of Androzani 254
CD phaser 276
celery stalk 226, 231
Celestial Intervention Agency 182
The Celestial Toymaker 51
The Celestial Toyroom 51
cellular dissemination 46
cemetery 291, 292
Centauri 129
Centauri, Alpha 129, 156, 157
Central European Zone 79, 80
The Centre 34
cesium 133
cesium atomic clock 310
CET machine 209, 210
Chal 53
chamber 137, 250
Chamberlain 261
chameleon circuit 138, 221, 222, 236, 244, 266, 281, 286
chameleons 70
Champion, Harry 186
A Change of Identity 23
Channing 108, 109
Chaplet, Anne 48, 49
Charlie 52
The Chase 3, 36, 54, 197, 234
Chase, Harrison 177
chasm 181
Chatterton 49
chauffeur 177
Checkerton 49
Checkmate 42
Cheetah People 303

Cheetah Planet 302, 303
Chellak, General 254
chemical formula 19
Chen, Mavic 45, 46
Chernobyl 122
cherub 56
Cheshireman 14
chess 191, 192, 294
Chessene 267, 268
chief caretaker 288
chief clown 296
Chiki 69
children 291
Chimeron 289
Chin Lee, Captain 119
Chinese dancers 228, 229
Chinn 120
chivalry 174, 219
Chloris 209
chocolate 33
Christian names 24
Christmas 46
chronic hysteresis 215
chronon 269, 286
Chronotis, Professor 212
Chronovore 136
Chub 184
Chumblies 43
church 301
churchwarden 56
CIA 182
circlet 203
circuit, chameleon 138, 221, 222, 236, 244, 266, 281, 286
citadel 129, 156
city 124, 154, 165, 172, 315
city administrator 22
City of Death 206, 214
civilization 228, 302
Claire 141, 143
Clancey, Milo 98, 99
Clangers 131
Clanton, Billy 52, 53
Clanton, Ike 52, 53
Clanton, Phineas 52, 53
The Claws of Axos 120, 135
cleaner 287
Clegg 157
Clements, Ernie 172
Clent 76, 77, 78
cliffhanger 21, 42, 75, 78, 85, 88, 89, 109, 113, 120, 154, 155, 156, 158, 199, 200, 237
Clifford, Angela 237
climax 165, 170, 215, 233
clock 71, 92, 131, 132, 141, 143, 173, 263, 299, 308, 309, 310, 312, 321; atomic 310;

beryllium 310; cesium atomic 310; mantle 321; TARDIS 12
clock door 220
cloister bell 15
cloister room 310
cloning 189, 268
close-up 99
closet 153
closing credits 150
coach 118
coal car 264
coal-mining 265
coat pocket 266
cobalt 78
Cockerill 250
cockpit 163
Cockylickin 30
Codal 146, 147
coffee 66, 99
Colin 238
Coliseum 298
collaboration 196
collection 322
collector 192, 193
college 293
Collins 172
colonel 107, 143
colonists 123, 124
colony 62
Colony in Space 122
color screen overlay 135
coma 120
comet(s) 108, 231, 262, 271, 294, 295, 296
commandant 70
commander 49, 50, 167, 259, 321
commercial audio tape 5
commercial CD 4
commercial tape 4, 308, 309
commodore 278, 279
common room 81
companion 269
companion leaves: Adric 233; Barbara Wright 37; Ben Jackson 69; Dodo Chaplet 54; Harry Sullivan 138; Ian Chesterton 37; Jamie McCrimmon 100; Jo Grant 148; K-9 218; Katarina 45; Leela 196; Liz Shaw 114; Mel 289; Nyssa 241; Peri 276; Polly 69; Romana I 204; Romana II 218; Sara Kingdom 47; Sarah Jane Smith 180; Steven Taylor 53; Susan Foreman 26; Tegan 251; Turlough 252; Vicki 44; Victoria

Waterfield 82; Zoe Heriot 100; Comparator 253
Concorde 236, 237
concrete 298
condo 175
conductor 174
conference room 213
consciousness 232, 267, 274
consequences 231
Conspiracy 31
conspirators 144
constellation 3, 28, 182, 202, 268, 271, 274, 280
contingency 234
continuity 1, 121
Control Base 103
control bracelet(s) 231, 232
control cabin 117
control device 119
control ring 171
control room 178
control unit 67, 270
controlled humans 294
controlled men 295
controller 128
Controller Cyber 262, 263
Controller Cyberman 73, 74
controller's base 127
Controllers of Morphoton 19
coordinate program 177
coordinate selector 172
Coordinator Engin 182
Co-pilot 211
Cordo 192
core 317
cork 25, 137
Corman, Roger 287
Cornish 113
Coronas of the Sun 46
Coronet of Rassilon 281
corpse marker 184
corpses 221, 252
correction center 192
Corwyn, Doctor 84, 85
Cory, Marc 43, 44, 46
cosmic rays 111, 139
cosmos 322
Costa 209
Cotton 134, 135
Council Chamber 87
Counter Plot 46
countess 207
countryside 181
Coven 321
cow 148
craft 265, 292
Crane, Nurse 301
Cranleigh, Lady 233
crater 294

Crater of Needles 33, 34
Craven, Timothy 144
Crayford 174, 175
crayons 275
creature(s) 118, 121, 131, 140, 168, 245, 247, 269, 290, 309, 322
The Creature from the Pit 208
credit(s) 148, 177, 238, 262, 299
Cressida 44
Cretaceous 141
cricket ball 233
cricket field 47
Crimean War Zone 103
cripple 301
Crisis 25
crow 199, 237
crown 195, 239
crown jewels 281
Crozier 277
The Crusade 34, 35, 46
crust 317
cryogenically 163
Cryogenics Section 188
Cryon(s) 261, 262
crystal(s) 136, 137, 157, 239, 240, 269, 270, 290
cubicle 112, 162, 163, 285, 286
Cully 87
curfew 178
The Curse of Fatal Death 2, 322
The Curse of Fenric 294, 300
The Curse of Peladon 2, 129, 155
Cushing, Peter 26, 27
cut 35
Cutter, General 58
cutting 146
cyanide 176, 268
cyanogen 176
cyber controller 262, 263
cyber fleet 236, 295
cyber leader 167, 234, 235, 236, 261, 262, 295
cyberguards 235
Cyberman(men) 58, 65, 66, 73, 84, 90, 118, 167, 233, 234, 235, 236, 245, 246, 261, 262, 263, 294, 295
Cyberman controller 73, 74
Cyberman hands 58, 68, 73, 84, 86, 91, 92, 236, 246, 262, 295
Cyberman ship 58, 67, 68
Cyberman warship 93
cybermat 73, 74, 167
Cybermen—The Early Years 57, 65, 67, 83

Cybermen defeated: First Doctor 57; Fourth Doctor 168; Second Doctor 68, 74, 86, 93, 296; Sixth Doctor 263
Cybership 295
cyclotron 111
Cyrian 322
Cyril 51

D4 163
D.84 184
The Daemons 125, 126, 138
daffodil 118
Daheer, Ben 35
Daisy K 294
Dako 36
Dale, Professor 144
Dalek(s) 2, 3, 14, 15, 27, 28, 29, 37, 40, 43, 44, 45, 46, 47, 49, 62, 63, 66, 67, 71, 72, 74, 118, 127, 128, 129, 135, 145, 146, 147, 148, 154, 155, 180, 205, 245, 251, 252, 268, 272, 273, 291, 292, 307, 315, 316, 317, 322
Dalek Cutaway 43
Dalek invasion 26, 36, 85
The Dalek Invasion of Earth 25, 37, 46, 62, 88, 128, 165, 317
Dalek Invasion of Earth 2150 A.D. 180
Dalek–Draconian war 307
Dalek-Movellan 251
Dalek saucer 27
Dalek Supreme 47, 147, 148
Dalek–Thal war 15
dalekanium 27, 128
The Daleks 13, 25
Daleks defeated: Fifth Doctor 252; First Doctor 15, 28, 41, 48; Fourth Doctor 206; Second Doctor 63, 72; Seventh Doctor 293; Sixth Doctor 273; Third Doctor 129, 145, 146, 147, 148, 155
Daleks—The Early Years 4, 13, 25, 28, 36, 45, 61, 70
Daleks—Invasion Earth 2150 A.D. 27, 316
The Daleks' Master Plan 35, 43, 44, 45, 61
Dallas 177
Dals 14
Daly, Claire 142
Daly, Major 141, 143
The Dancing Floor 51
Dangerous Journey 25

D'Argenson 24
Dask 184
Dastari 267, 268
Databank 179
DATEB 215
Dave 149
David 27, 316
Davidson, Lawrence 144
Davies, Gerry 58
Da Vinci, Leonardo 179
Davis, Gerry 58
Davros 164, 204, 205, 206, 251, 252, 272, 273, 292, 293, 307
The Day God Went Mad 182
day night blooper 150
Day of Armageddon 45
The Day of Darkness 20
Day of Reckoning 27
The Day of the Daleks 127
The Dead Planet 13
The Deadly Assassin 181, 220
deadly nightshade 22
Deadman's secret key 56
Death of a Spy 45
The Death of Doctor Who 40
The Death of Time 37
Death to the Daleks 154, 172
Death Zone 245
Debbie 81
December 294, 321
decontamination room 180
décor 217
Deedrix 215
deep thought 69
De Flores 295, 296
Della 210
Delos 31
Delta and the Bannermen 288
Delta Magna 203
The Demons 125
Denes 79, 80
Dent, Captain 123, 125
deputy chief caretaker 287
designer 262
Desperate Measures 30
A Desperate Venture 22
des Preaux, Sir William 35
destination 212
Destiny of the Daleks 204, 251
Destroyer 298
Destruction of Time 47
detective 207
Deva Loka 230
Devil's End 125, 126
Devil's Planet 46
Devonian 207, 208
diameter 126
Dibber 274, 276

Dido 29, 30
Dill, Morton 39
dimensional stabilizer 189
dimensions 250
Dimensions in Time 2, 321, 323
The Dimensions of Time 36
dinosaur(s) 110, 152, 234
director 117
dish 189
disintegrator gun 161
distillation machine 186
DJ 273
DNA 191
"Doctor" 215
doctor in drag 63, 64, 148
doctor of medicine 17
"Doctor Who" 12, 52, 54, 55, 63, 130, 135, 221, 233, 295, 315, 316, 317, 322
Doctor Who (movie) 307
Doctor Who and the Curse of Fatal Death 322
Doctor Who and the Daleks 315
Dr. Who and the Savages 53
Doctor Who and the Silurians 110
doctorate 163
Dodecahedron 215
Dojjen 239, 240
Doktor von Wer 63, 64
Doland 278, 279
Dome 165, 230
Dominator 87, 88
The Dominators 86
Doña Arana 267
Don't Shoot the Pianist 52
doppeldoctor 114, 198
Doppler effect 67
Dortmun 27
double pulse 286
Draconian 143, 144, 307
Dracula 39, 301
dragon 290
Dragonfire 289, 290
drashigs 141, 142, 143, 157
Drathro 275
Drax 203, 204
dream 136
drill head 114
Driscoll 180, 181
drug(s) 151, 201, 243, 315
Ducat, Mrs. 177
duck 205
Dugdale 239
Dugeen 202, 203, 207, 208
Duggan, Bill 84
Duke 179
Dulcian(s) 86, 88
Dulkian(s) 86

Dulkis 86
Dune 163
Dutt, Roam 203
DVD 4, 139, 141, 245, 246, 247, 252, 254, 255, 308, 309, 316
dwarf star alloy 219
dwellings of simplicity 226
Dymond 210
Dynasty 204
Dyoni 14

E-Space 217
The E-Space Trilogy 216, 218
Earl Sigma 293
Earp, Wyatt 52
Earth 21, 22, 27, 29, 30, 44, 53, 58, 64, 66, 67, 69, 70, 75, 76, 81, 85, 90, 94, 107, 109, 110, 115, 117, 122, 128, 129, 132, 133, 134, 136, 140, 143, 144, 153, 154, 155, 157, 162, 163, 164, 168, 169, 172, 173, 174, 175, 180, 181, 190, 204, 208, 212, 214, 218, 227, 228, 229, 234, 235, 236, 240, 245, 249, 252, 263, 269, 271, 274, 276, 277, 280, 287, 298, 301, 302, 303, 311, 317, 322
Earth controller 66
Earth saved 302; Doctors 268; Fifth Doctor 229, 232, 236, 239, 248, 249; First Doctor 28, 42, 48, 50, 55, 58; Fourth Doctor 162, 168, 169, 173, 175, 177, 179, 186, 188, 191, 208; Second Doctor 65, 68, 76, 80, 82, 83, 86, 93, 98; Seventh Doctor 296, 298, 299; Sixth Doctor 263; Third Doctor 109, 113, 116, 118, 120, 122, 127, 129, 133, 145, 150, 154, 158
Earth science 231
Earthling(s) 49, 89, 184, 215, 253, 322
Earth's core 26, 49
Earth's crust 28, 317
Earthshock 233, 236, 238
ebonite rod 182
Eckersley 156, 157
Edal, Captain 53
Eden 209, 210
The Edge of Destruction 9, 11, 13, 15, 42, 45, 56, 57, 68, 69, 71, 72, 82, 83
Edgeworth 259, 260
Edinburgh 66

Edison, Thomas 265, 266
Egypt 47
Egyptian scroll 206
eighteenth century 125
eighth century 298
Eighth Doctor 182, 273, 307
Einstein 285, 286
El Akir 35
Elders 53
Eldrad 181
Eldred 96, 97
element(s) 121, 146, 228
Elena 259
elevator 146, 147, 254, 255
eleventh century 44
Eleventh Doctor 322
Elgin 149
Emma 322
Emperor Dalek 307
Empire State Building 39
Empress 210
The End of Tomorrow 27
The Enemy of the World 2, 79, 170
The Enemy Within 307
energy 117, 126, 178, 264
England 14, 64, 65, 82, 120, 136, 151, 171, 179, 227, 253, 254, 263, 267, 269, 277, 294, 300, 315, 321
English Court 244
Enlightenment 227, 228, 242
entertainment 141
environmental issues 25
Enzu 278
Eocenes 131, 133
epoxypropane 67
Equator 322
equipment 111, 181, 235
Erato 208
Ernie Clements 172
The Escape 14
Escape to Danger 33
Escape Switch 47
Estram, Sir Gilles 244
Eternal 51
Ettis 156
euphemism 261
Europe 16, 280
Evans, Dai 149
Evans, Dr. 67
Event One 242
Evergreens 177
evil 307
The Evil of the Daleks 70, 85, 266
Excalibur 298
The Executioners 37
expedition 210

The Expedition 13, 14
experiments 114, 213
The Exploding Planet 43
extraction 213
Exxilon 154, 172
eye 310
Eye of Harmony 182, 228, 310, 311, 312
Eye of Horus 172
Eye of Orion 246

The Face of Evil 182
The Faceless Ones 69, 70
facilities 180, 251
factories 150
failure 242
false blooper 3, 4
false claims 317
fancy dress 123
Fariah 80
farmworker 137
Farrah 201
Farrel 118
Farrow 24
fast return 16
fatal seizure 269
father 259
Faulkner, Max 157
fault locator 15
Fay, Vivian 200
The Feast of Steven 46
feces 322
Federation 156
Federico, Count 178, 179
Fedorin 80
feet 88, 116, 184, 234, 302
Fell 149
female 129, 201, 235, 269
Fendahl 191
Fendahleen 191
Fendelman 191
Fenner 202
Fenric 301, 302
Fewsham 96, 97
fiber optic 286
Fibuli, Mr. 198
field 225
Fifi 293
fifteen 226
fifteenth century 179
fifth dimension 9, 10, 12
Fifth Doctor 221, 245, 246
filer 120, 121
filter belt 111
The Final Phase 36
The Final Test 51
Finch, General 153
fire 133, 189, 200, 235, 254
fire extinguisher 144, 116, 230

fire hose 311, 321
fireball 274
The Firemaker 12
firestorm 134
firework 30
First Doctor 3, 17, 57, 61, 138, 140, 141, 245, 246, 247, 249, 307
First Dynasty 171
First Elder 22
"first" episode 322
first law of time 139
first mate 243
fish 308
Fish people 65
Fisk 210
fission grenades 194
fissionable material 77, 78
fissure 26, 28, 64
The Five Doctors 2, 75, 244, 245, 280, 298
Five Hundred Eyes 2, 17
Flannigan 85
Flashpoint 28
Flavia, Chancellor 246
Flavius 31
fleas 232
Fleet 186
flight crew 236, 237
flight path 218
Flight Through Eternity 38
floor 109 287
floor 304 287
Flowerchild's earring 5, 295, 296, 297
fly 24
flying saucer 316
Foamasi 179, 213, 214
food machine 317
football 294
Forbidden Planet 46, 183
forbidden zone 242
force field 18, 194, 196
force field generator room 170
Ford Prefect 46
Foreman, Doctor 12
Foreman, I.M. 9, 10, 11
forest 173
The Forest of Fear 12
Forester 24
formic acid 32, 33
forty-ninth century 10, 11
forty-two 212
Foster 220
foundry 192
Four Hundred Dawns 42
Four to Doomsday 227
fourth dimension 9, 10, 11, 12
Fourth Doctor 61, 71, 143,

148, 162, 212, 221, 234, 246, 247, 275, 307
The Fox Inn 168
France 112
Frankenstein 37, 39, 40
Frankenstein 309
freighter 236
French bandit 34
French Revolution 9, 10, 12
Frontier in Space 143, 148, 307
Frontios 249, 250, 253
FTL 271
fuel 242
fuel tanks 217
Full Circle 216
functionaries 141
fungus 145
fur 147
furnace 228
Fury from the Deep 82, 126, 266
Futu Dynasty 228
future 115, 249
future adventure 277
future anachronism 3, 279
fuzzy dice 290

G-force 113, 261
G3 Military Assessment Survey 164
Galactic Council 47
Galactic legend 228
Galactic Salvage and Insurance 209
Galaxia Kyklos 227
galaxy (galaxies) 3, 46, 73, 86, 88, 117, 215, 268, 269, 271, 274, 275
Galaxy 4 42
Galaxy of Andromeda 275
Galileo 179
Galleia, Queen 138
Gallifrey 14, 41, 89, 103, 117, 151, 157, 179, 181, 182, 194, 195, 217, 220, 245, 246, 271, 274, 281, 292, 298, 310, 312
Galloway, Doctor 71
game board 120
Gamma 72
Ganatus 14
gang members 308
garden 302
Garm 242
garments 178
Garrett, Miss 77, 78, 79
Garron 197
Garvin 125
gas 83, 124, 144, 217, 279, 295
gas dirigibles 175

Gatherer Hade 192, 193
Gavrok 289
Gebek 156
Gemma 85
gemstone 157
general 109
generation ship 271
generations 217
generator 214
Genesis of the Daleks 148, 164, 166
genetic codes 322
genetically engineered 279
genocide 165, 166, 191
Geoffrey, Sir 244
George 233
German salute 65
germs 69
Gharman 165
Ghost Light 299
giants 25
gift 179, 180
Gilbert M 294
Gilles, Sir 244
Gilmore, Group Captain 292
Giovanni 178
girders 113
girl(s) 186, 292, 293, 301, 316
Giuliano 178, 179
glacier 77
Glasgow 66
glitterguns 167
Glitz, Sabalom 271, 273, 274, 275, 276, 280, 281, 289, 290
Global Chemical 149, 150
globe 110, 246, 249, 286
globular cluster 271
gold 33, 72, 99, 167, 184, 235, 295
gold arrows 295
Golden Death 47
Gomer, Lord 195
Gonds 94, 95
The Goodies 201
Goth, Chancellor 181
government 128
governor 263, 264
Grace 308, 309, 310, 311, 312
Grainer, Byron 57
granddaughter 316, 317
grandfather 143, 317
Grainer, Ron 57
graphite 229
grass 225
grating 154
grave 272, 296
Gravis 250
gravitational attraction 167, 193

Gravitron 66, 67
gravity 154, 167, 193, 194, 208, 216, 219, 254
Great Architect Kroagnon 287
Great Intelligence 75, 76, 81, 246
Great Key (of Rassilon) 182
Great One 158
Great Pyramid 47
Great Vampire 218
The Greatest Show in the Galaxy 5, 295, 296
Greece 129, 136, 227, 243, 292
Greek Zone 103
Greel, Magnus 186
The Green Death 135, 148, 152, 158
greenhouse gas 77
Greenwich Meridian 322
Gregorian calendar 294
Gregory 92
Grell 275
grenade(s) 55, 297
Grendel, Count 201
Grenville 278
Greyhound Four 150
Greyhound One 150
Griffin 79, 80
Grigory 272
Grimwade, Peter 185
Grimwade's Syndrome 185
Grugger, General 215
Grunbar, Murphy 154
guard(s) 98, 102, 108, 113, 119, 121, 125, 132, 134, 135, 156, 164, 170, 173, 182, 183, 193, 197, 198, 218, 225, 238, 239, 244, 248, 262, 263, 264, 269, 272, 273, 275, 278, 293, 311
guard captain 197
guard dog 265
guardian(s) 200, 242, 243, 244; black 241, 243; white 196, 199, 203, 204, 216, 242, 243
The Guardian Trilogy 240
guerilla 128
Guests of Madame Guillotine 23
Guilford 231
guilt 144, 322
guitar 244
Gulliver 89
gums 269
gun(s) 55, 65, 69, 73, 80, 90, 94, 98, 101, 103, 109, 120, 128, 133, 135, 145, 151, 154, 155, 163, 164, 165, 183, 188,

195, 203, 210, 235, 242, 254, 255, 260, 261, 262, 263, 267, 269, 273, 274, 275, 279, 308
gun retracting 192
Gundan 219
The Gunfighters 6, 52
gunfighter's wings 52
gunpowder 231, 235
gunrunners 254
Gurney 56
Gwendoline 299
gypsy 64

hacienda 267
Hade, Gatherer 192
Haemovore(s) 300, 301, 302
hair blooper 153
hairy Ice Warrior 77, 96, 97, 157
Hal 151
half human 310, 311
hall 239, 290
The Hall of Dolls 51
hallucination 236
Hamilton 155
hammer 202, 214
Hampton, Jane 249
The Hand of Fear 180
Hand of Omega 81, 292
Hand of Sutekh blooper 172
handmaiden 155
handprint 89, 134
The Happiness Patrol 293
Hardiman 121, 122
Hardin 213
Hardy 143
Harg 202
Harker 187
Harper 101
Harper, Seth 52
Harris 82, 83
Harrison Chase 177
Harry 143
Harry Champion 186
Harry Sullivan 307
Hart, Captain 131
The Hartnell Years 4, 9, 11, 34, 51
hat stand 190, 197, 208, 211, 215, 216, 219
haunted house 37, 39
Hawk 288
Hawkins, Captain 111
Hawthorne, Miss 125
Hayes, J. Milton 186
HCN 175, 176
Head of Stengos 272
headman 232

headmaster 291
headquarters 157
healing powers 218
heart(s) 22, 84, 108, 114, 145, 212, 218, 250, 255, 261, 265
heartbeat 108, 217, 218, 285
Heathrow Airport 232, 236
Hecate 210
Hecate's Familiar 321
Helen A 293, 294
helicopter 83, 131, 295, 297
helium 185
helix energy 178
helmet(s) 82, 214, 229, 243, 261, 275, 292, 301, 317
Henderson, Dr. 108
Hensell 62
Hepesh 130
Herbert 269, 270
Hercules Cluster 84
Hereford 148
Hermack, General 99, 100
Herman, Pee-Wee 297
Hermann 207
Herrick 193
Hetra 34
hexapod 129
Hibbert 109
hibernation 131, 133
Hickok, Wild Bill 52
Hidden Danger 22
hidden room 207
Hieronymous 178, 179
High Council 245, 246, 281
high impulse beam 288
High Priest 178
The Highlanders 63, 79
highway 236
hijack-proof 279
hijacking 290
hiker 191
Hilred, Commander 182
Himalayas 81
Hindle 230
Hinks 149
Hippias 136, 138
historical accuracy 24, 30, 228
history 134, 288
The Hitchhiker's Guide to the Galaxy 76, 288
Hitler 174
Hobson 66, 67, 68
A Holiday for the Doctor 52
Holliday, Doc 52
holographic projection 213
holy ghanti 75
holy grail 286
home 138, 309
Home Planet 98

Home World 230
homing signal 145
honorary 163
Hoothi 175
horda 183
The Horns of Nimon 210
Horror of Fang Rock 187
Horse (Trojan) 45
Horse of Destruction 45
hospital 309
hovercraft 158
Howard King 34
HQ van 121
Hugo 259, 260, 261
human 167, 189, 247, 248, 251, 267, 286, 310, 311
humanoid 205
humanoid mutant 205
humbug 192
Humker 275
Hungary 80
Hur 12
Hyde, Stuart 136
Hydrax officers 217
hydrochloric acid 33
hydrogen 200, 225
hydrogen sulfide 78, 93
hydrogen telluride 94
hydroponics lab 279
Hypatia 286
Hyperion 279
Hyperion 3 280
Hyperion III 279
hypersonic jet 92

I.M. FORMAN 261, 291
Ian, Sir 35
Ibramin 171
ice age 76
Ice Lord 98, 129
Ice Warrior(s) 76, 78, 118, 129, 156, 157; hairy 77, 96, 97, 157
The Ice Warriors 76, 96
Iceworld 290
Icthar 247, 248
Idas 194
idol 186
Ikona 285, 286
Image of the Fendahl 190
images 176
IMC 123, 124, 125
immortality 245
incineration 278, 279
incubation chamber 166, 190
indoor 286
induction furnace 228
inferior types 87
Inferno 31, 114

Ingram, Dr. 137
inhabitants 252
injection 277
Inn 298
Inquisitor 281
insect(s) 68, 69, 123, 289
Inside the Spaceship 15
insignia 167, 168
instability 219
Institute of Technological Advancement and Research 310
instrument 48, 171, 227, 285
instrument box 139
insulation 116
integration 262
intelligence 75, 76, 81, 82, 246
interferon 66
intergalactic travel 275
Intergalactic Treaty 269
Interplanetary Space Command 167
interplanetary treaty 269
invalid 301
The Invasion 34, 66, 90, 107, 108, 139
Invasion 152
invasion fleet 173, 174
Invasion of the Dinosaurs 152
The Invasion of Time 194
investigator 135
The Invisible Enemy 188
Iran 184
iron 72
iron maiden 244
Irongron 151, 152
island 54
The Island of Fandor 191
Isobel 92
isomorphic 172
isotope 113, 134
Issigri, Miss 100
Italy 178
ITAR 310, 311, 312
Ixta 20
Izlyr 129, 130

Jabel 183
jacket 155, 215, 281, 295, 296
Jackson, Captain 193, 194, 243
Jackson, Miss 180
Jaconda 259, 261
Jaeger, Professor 134, 135
Jaffa 46
Jagaroth 206
Jago 185, 186
Jailer 24
James 150

Jamie 2
"Jamie" 89
Janet 279
Janley 62
Jano 53, 54
Jean 23, 300
jeep 92, 122, 153, 181
Jellicoe 162
jelly baby (jelly babies) 33, 140, 162, 191, 192, 198, 275, 310
Jenkins 70
Jenny 27, 28
jethrik 197
jettison 226
Jewell 316
Jill 154
Jim 74
Jobel 272
jogging 226
John 22
John, Elton 253
John, King 244
Johnny Ringo 52
Jondar 264
Jones, Dr. 149
Jones, Professor 148, 150
Josh 265, 266
Josiah 299
Joules 169
Journey Into Terror 39
Judson, Doctor 300, 301
Julian calendar 294
junior 281
Jupiter 167, 168, 188
Jurassic 236, 237
jury 273, 274

K1 161, 162
K9 and Company 2, 321
Kaftan 74
Kaled(s) 14, 165, 166
Kalid 236, 237
Kalik 142, 143
Kal-lib 183
Kalmar 218
Kamelion 244, 250, 253, 254
Kando 87
Kandy Man 293, 294
Kane 289, 290, 291
Kangs, Blue 287, 288
K'anpo 158
Kara 176
karate 248, 298
Karela, Madame 208
Karfel 269, 270
Karfelon 269
Kari 242
Karra 302

Karuna 230
Kassia 220
Kastria 180, 181
Katarina 45, 46, 47
Kate 52
Kathleen 300
Katmandu 186
Katryca 275
Keeper of the Matrix 281
The Keeper of Traken 220
Keightley, Clare 212, 213
Keller machine 118, 120
Kellman 167
Kelly, Miss Gia 96, 97, 98
Kelner, Castellan 195, 196
Kembel 43, 44, 46, 47
Kennedy, President 11
Kent, Giles 80
KERA 177
Kerensky, Professor 207
Kettlewell, Professor 162
Kew Gardens 264
key(s) 132, 135, 137, 138, 227, 268, 278, 289, 299, 309
Key to Time 204, 216, 242
keyboard 236, 308
The Keys of Marinus 18, 19
Khan-balik 16
Khrisong 76
Kidnap 22
kidnapping 108, 112, 113, 144, 201, 259, 260, 321
Killingworth 265
Kimber, Mr. 278
Kinda 229, 230
king 136, 181, 302
King, Howard 34
Kingdom, Sara 45, 47
The King's Demons 244
Kipling 186
kissing 100, 322
Kiston 251
Kitt 57
Kiv, Lord 277
Klieg 73, 74
Klout 214
knife 18, 184, 186, 189, 194, 218, 287
knight 297
The Knight of Jaffa 35
Koquillion 29, 30, 118
Kraal(s) 173, 174, 175
Krasis 136, 137
Kroagnon, Great Architect 287
Kroll 202
Kronos 136
Kroton 93, 96
The Krotons 93

Krynoid 176, 177
Kryogenics Sexshun 188
Kryton, John 153
Kublai Khan 16, 17
Kurkuyji 227
Ky 134, 135
Kyle 234

L 179
L1 275
laboratory (laboratories) 110, 114, 137, 147, 149, 150, 157, 252, 292
Laird, Professor 63, 252
Lakertya 286
Lakh 194
A Land of Fear 23
landing ship 292
landmine 266
language(s) 178, 179, 213, 227, 263
Lanisha 286
Lanzarote 254
laps 141
Larry 27
larvae gun 33
laser 65, 67, 74
laser gun 121
lashes 63, 64
Lasky, Professor 277, 279, 280
last name blooper 4
The Last Time Lords 307
Latep 147
Latin 136, 180
launch 288, 295
laundry basket 186
Lavel 298
lawn 140
Lawrence, Dr. 110
laws of physics 208, 229
laws of time 317
Lee 307, 308, 309, 310, 311, 312
Lee, Captain Chin 119
leeches 24
legal code 184
The Leisure Hive 179, 213
Lemaitre 24
Lennox 112, 113
Leo 84
Leon Ny Taiy 237
Leonardo 207
Leonardo Da Vinci 179
Les Chen Gris 23
Lester 167
Lesterson 62
lethal stingers 279
Lethbridge-Stewart, Colonel 81

Leuppi, Michelle 70
Levene, John 81
library 168
license plate 298
lie detector 205
life 122
life-support 229
lifebelt post 132
Light Accelerator 121
light-converter 275
light neutrons 3
light year(s) 53, 54, 117, 129, 271, 274, 277
lighter 309
lighthouse 187
lighting 34, 36, 112, 212, 243, 269, 297
lightning rod 179
Lilt 272
limbs 129
limited 300
Linx 151
The Lion 35
liquid(s) 144, 176, 243, 273, 279
liquid oxygen 289
Lis 179
Lister 66, 93
Litefoot 186
lock 117, 227, 285, 290, 299
Locke 96
locked room 190, 191
locusts 289
Logar 253
Logopolis 221, 222, 225, 253, 259
Lon 239, 240
London 27, 28, 42, 72, 81, 152, 186, 232
Long, Hugo 259
Longfoot, Joseph 56
looter 152
Lopez, Michelle 70
Lord 98, 129
lorry 267, 268
lost episode 3
Lost in Time 34, 45, 51, 65, 69, 70, 75, 79, 80, 83, 98
Louise 316, 317
loupe 112
Louvre 207
Lowe 188, 189
Lowery 43
loyhargil 286
Lucifer 186
Luddite(s) 265, 266
Luddite blooper 265, 266
luggage 278
Luke 266

lunar eclipse 179
lunch 292
Lupton 158
Lyden, Van 112
Lytton 251, 261, 262

M, Gilbert 294
M-3 113
M13 84
Maaga 42, 43
Mace, Richard 231, 232
MacGuffin 134
machine 48, 93, 94, 97, 101, 104, 118, 142, 143, 174, 191, 192, 232, 249, 263, 285, 287
machine gun 255
machine pistol 261
machinery 265
Mackay 64
Mackenzie, Inspector 299
maconite 280, 281
Macra 68, 69
The Macra Terror 68
macro-virus 189
Mad Hatters 61
Madame Karela 208
Madame Tussaud's 109
Maddy 288
Madison, Larry 26
maggots 150
magic 124, 272
magnesium silicate 93
magnetic core 26, 27, 317
magnetic field 76
magnetic forces 99
magnetic shield 227, 228
Magnus Greel 186
Magora 200
Mags 296
Maharis 50
Mahoney, Louis 144
Maidens' Point 300
mailer 119
Maitland 21
male 235, 236
Malpha 44
man 302
manager 128, 133
Mandragora 178
Mandrel 192, 210
manikin 166
mansion 177
mantle clock 321
manual(s) 215, 216
Manussa 240
map 22, 77, 78, 89, 92, 101, 103, 112, 119, 136, 146, 152, 275

Map, Astral 33, 34, 96
Mara 230, 240
Marat 146
Marco Polo 16
Marco Polo 17
Maren 175
Marie 316
Marie Celeste 39
Marigold 184
Marius, Professor 189, 190
Mark 153
The Mark of the Rani 264
Marriner 243
Mars 57, 58, 66, 77, 139, 155, 172, 173, 271, 288
marsh gas 279
marshal 134, 135
marshmen 216
martian 88
Martin, John Scott 154
The Masque of Mandragora 2, 14, 178, 179, 207, 213, 227, 244, 247, 248, 267, 269, 270
mass detector 218
massacre 291
The Massacre 48, 49
The Massacre of St. Bartholomew's Eve 40, 48, 95
massage 167
"Master" 89, 90
Master defeated: Eighth Doctor 312; Fifth Doctor 226, 237, 244, 254; Fourth Doctor 182, 220, 222; Sixth Doctor 266; Third Doctor 120, 125, 127, 138, 145
Master TCE 70
Master's Joke 244
Masterson, Bat 52
materialization circuit 148
mathematics 259, 260, 294, 295
matrix 181, 182, 276, 278, 281
matter transmitter 163, 167
Mavic Chen 45, 46
Mawdryn 241
Mawdryn Undead 240, 242
Maxtible 71
Mayans 227, 228
mayday 278
Maylin Renis 269
Maynarde, Richard 295, 296
McGoohan, Patrick 50
McLaury, Frank 53
McLaury, Tom 53
mead 41
Meadows 70

meal room 317
meat 148, 186
mechanical pencil 229
Mechanoids 37, 40, 41
Mechans 40
Mechanus 40
Mechons 40
The Meddling Monk 41
medical degree 30, 66, 79
medicine 126
Medok 68, 69
Medusa 90
meeting hall 162
Megan 83
Meglos 214, 215
Melkur 220
Mellium 50
Mel's shoes blooper 286
Mena 214
Menoptera 32, 33, 34
Mensch 202
mental energy 261
mental link 109
Mentiad 198
mentor 277
Merak 203, 204
mercenaries 290
Mercer 252
mercury 61, 85, 89
Merdeen 274
Mergrave 226
message 167, 278
Mestor 259, 260, 261
metal 131, 175, 201, 218, 229, 273, 281
metamorphosed 309
Metebelis 3 141, 142, 149, 157
meteor(s) 3, 62, 84, 85, 107, 108, 134, 174, 231, 250, 262, 271, 278, 294
meteor showers 174, 289
meteor storm 250, 271
meteoroid 231
meter 94, 121
methane 279
methane derivative 279
Mexican Civil War Zone 103
Miasimia Goria 265
mica 93, 95
micrograph 142
microscope 48, 66, 111, 149, 150
microvirologist 3
micro-virus 189
microwave 281
Midge 302, 303
midnight 310
Mighty Kublai Khan 17
Mike 292, 293

mike cord 174
military 129, 235, 253
milk van 125
Milky Way 227, 228, 312
Millennius 19
Miller 232
Millington, Commander 300, 301
Mills, Dick 200
mind 124, 213, 260, 261
The Mind of Evil 118
mind-probe 128
The Mind Robber 88, 100
Mind Warp 276, 277
Mindwarp 276, 277
mine 148, 150, 266
mineral(s) 46, 198
mineshaft 148, 265
minimal interaction 278
Miniscope 141, 142, 143
minister 127, 132, 152, 153
Minotaur 136, 137, 138
minutes 311
Minyans 193, 194
Minyos II 194
Mira 46
Mire Beast 38
mirror 155, 219, 225, 230, 259
misquote(s) 9, 198, 222, 261, 275, 293
missile(s) 118, 120, 144, 181, 204, 247
missing stories 17
The Missing Years 13, 15, 42, 45, 56, 57, 68, 69, 71, 72, 82, 83
mission 146, 147, 301
Mission to the Unknown 43, 45, 46
mistaken 243
Mitchell 191
model 98, 109, 150, 155, 213, 253
Mogarian 278, 279
Mohorovicic discontinuity 64
mole 233
molecule 98, 143
Mona Lisa 207
Monarch 227, 228, 229
Mondas 58, 73, 262
money 71, 79, 309
Monia 129
Monica 129
monitor 25, 78, 128, 139, 140, 144, 180, 183, 212, 222, 228
Monk 41, 42, 45, 47, 74
Monoid 50
Monoid 1 50
Monoid 2 50

Monoid 4 50
monopticon 227, 228, 229
monster(s) 114, 115, 145, 201, 287
The Monster of Peladon 2, 130, 155
Monty Python 133
monument 272
moon 21, 31, 67, 144, 169, 274, 276, 296
The Moonbase 30, 31, 65, 79, 85, 91, 92, 94, 97
Moor 100
Morbius 175, 176
Mordred 297, 298
Morestran ships 170
Morestran Sun 169
Morgaine 298
Morgan 123, 125
morgue 184, 185
Morgus 254
Morlox 269, 270
Morok 36
Morpho 19
Morphoton, Controllers of 19
mortuary 234
Moscow 150
Moss, Ted 190
motor 183, 196, 213
motorcycle 289, 310, 311
mountains 33, 253, 254
moustache 300
mouthing 316
Movellan virus 252
Movellans 205, 206
movie 108, 183, 300, 310, 315
movie Dalek 38
mud 208
mud bursts 254
Mula 198
mulching machine 177
multiple blooper 2
multi-story errors 2
mummy (mummies) 171, 172
murderers 185
murders 171
Murray 288
museum 107, 109
mutant 134
mutant humanoid 205
The Mutants 13, 18, 133
mutes 204
Muthi 175
Mutt 135
Muttoes 165
muzzle 242
Mykros 270
Myrka 154, 247, 248
The Mysterious Planet 273, 276

myth 298
The Myth Makers 44, 45

nail polish 67
nail varnish 67
naked 189
name(s) 217, 219, 265
name blooper 24
Namin, Ibramin 171, 172
narration 212
narrator 42, 45, 46, 48, 51, 56, 61, 62, 65, 68, 69, 70, 75, 76, 80, 83
NASA 139
Nathan-Turner, John 239, 301
natives 155
Navigational Guidance System Distorter 285
Navy 133
Neanderthal 299
necklace 213
Necros 272, 273
Neeva 183
negative ions 245
Neil Toynay 226
Nekros 273
Nemesis 294, 295
Nero 31, 49
Nerva 165
Nerva Beacon 166
nerve gas 119, 120
Neska 158
Nestene 108, 116, 117
neutron accelerator 170
neutron force field 85
New Companion: Ace 289; Adric 216; Barbara 316; Barbara Wright 11; Ben Jackson 54; Brigadier Lethbridge-Stewart 107; Constable Tom Campbell 317; Dodo Chaplet 48; Emma 322; Grace 308; Harry Sullivan 162; Ian Chesterton 11, 316; Jamie McCrimmon 63; Jo Grant 116; K-9 188; Katarina 44; Leela 182; Liz Shaw 107; Louise 317; Mel 277; Nyssa 221; Peri 252; Polly 54; Romana I 196; Romana II 204; Sara Kingdom 45; Sarah Jane Smith 151; Steven Taylor 37; Susan 316; Susan Foreman 11; Tegan 221; Turlough 240; Vicki 29; Victoria Waterfield 71; Zoe Heriot 83; New Doctor 11, 57, 58, 61, 107, 161, 222, 225, 255, 259, 285, 309, 315, 322

New Villain: Autons 107; Black Guardian 203; Cybermen 57; Daleks 13; Davros 164; ce Warriors 76; Master 116; Omega 138; Rani 264; Sil 263; Silurians 110; Sontarans 151; Yeti 75
New York 150
Newscaster 310, 312
Newton 210
Newtonian physics 219
Newton's Third Law 25, 99, 219
nickname 204
The Nightmare Begins 45
Nightmare of Eden 209, 216
Nimons 211
Nimrod 299
Ninth Doctor 322
nitric acid 33
nitro-9 290, 297, 301
nitrogen 77, 134
Noah 163
Nobel Prize 149
Noma 261
Norman Conquest 151
Norna 250
North 186
North Pole 322
Northumbria 186
Nosferatu 290
nostalgia 279
nova 84, 85
Nova Beacon 166, 167, 168
novelization 110, 163
November 292, 294, 295
nuclear bomb 121, 122
nuclear explosion 180
nuclear facility 181
nuclear missile(s) 119, 181
nuclear power 114
nuclear power plant 122
nuclear powered missile 119
nuclear reactor 110
nude 107
Number 10 Downing Street 128
number(s) 40, 198, 212; atomic 94
Nuton Complex 122
Nuton Power complex 121, 122
Nyder 165
Nyssa 179

object 112, 189
Odysseus 44, 45
office 115
officer(s) 118, 243
Ogri 199, 200

Ogri blooper 199
Ogron(s) 128, 143, 144, 145
O.K. Corral 53
old mother 11
old woman 11
Ollis 139
Olvir 242
Olympics 153
Omega 72, 138, 139, 140, 238, 239
omega circuit 143
100,000 BC 5, 11, 13, 291
opening credits 200
Optera 34
optical illusion 192
Orac 163, 286
Oracle 194
orange 267, 268
orbit 240
Orcini 272, 273
The Ordeal 14
order of filming 295
Organon 208
ornament 286
Orum 142, 143
Oscar 268
Osgood 96
Osirans 170, 171
out-of-period clothing 2
outdoor 286
The Outlaw 300
output 267
overload 111
Overlords 134
overnight 126, 131
Overseer, Road Works 23
oxygen 79, 82, 144, 229, 279, 289
oxygenated air 280
oxymasks 134
ozone 93, 111

Packard 219
Packer 91, 92
Padmasambhava 75, 76
Palmerdale, Lord 187
Pamir Plateau 16
Pangol 214
paper(s) 119, 141, 166, 251, 294
Paradise Towers 287, 308
paradox 152, 153, 171
parallel controls 238
parent 280
parental guidance 73
Paris 45, 293
Parker, Elizabeth 200
Parry, Professor 73
Parsons, Chris 212
particle 226, 278

particle accelerator 121
particle projection 226
particles of time 286
party 310, 312
Pascals 68
passengers 237
Pasteur 286
Paterson, Sergeant 302
path 226, 232
pattern 246
Pattison, Roy 144
Paul 36
Pavilion of the Summer Winds 201
Payne 261
Pedler, Kit 57
Peinforte, Lady 295
Peking 16
Pel(s) 130, 156
Peladon, King 129, 130
Peladonians 156
pellets 268
pen 127, 153
pencils 229
Peninsular War Zone 103
Penley 77, 78, 79
pentagons 239
people 164, 232
perception 286
Perfect Victim 20
Peri 179
period 274
periodic table 225
Permanent Undersecretary Masters 110
perpetual 290
Perseids 84, 108
Petra 114, 115
Pex 287, 288
Phase One switch 143
Phase Two switch 143
phenomenon 310, 311
Phil 27
Philips, Professor 117
Phipps 97
phone operator 91
phonebook 239
photon drive 208
photons 226
Phyllis 301
Phylox Series 226
physical law 139
physician 24
physicists 216
physiology 156, 168, 286, 298
pi 246
Pigbin Josh 120
Pike, Captain 56
pillars 161

pillows 158
pills 205
pilot 15, 68, 69, 278
Pilot 1 9
Pilot 2 10
Pilot: An Unearthly Child 9
pineapple 245
pipeline 82, 149
pirate helmets 242
The Pirate Planet 197, 203
pistols 132
pit 156, 208
PJX18 198
plague 201
The Plague 50
Plain of Stones 147
Plan 9 from Outer Space 27, 68
plane(s) 181, 236
Planet 14 91
The Planet of Decision 40
Planet of Evil 169
Planet of Fire 252, 265
Planet of Giants 24, 25, 316
The Planet of Sil 276, 277
Planet of the Daleks 2, 145
Planet of the Spiders 157, 142, 208
Planet saved: Fifth Doctor 230, 239, 240, 250, 254; First Doctor 19, 23, 34, 36, 54; Fourth Doctor 168, 182, 183, 193, 196, 199, 201, 209, 211, 214, 216, 217, 220; Second Doctor 63, 69, 88, 95; Seventh Doctor 286, 288, 294; Sixth Doctor 261, 263, 264, 270, 273, 276, 281; Third Doctor 125, 135, 143, 145, 148, 155, 157, 158
planet(s) 123, 174, 193, 198, 201, 211, 215, 218, 226, 231, 244, 253, 254, 260, 261, 263, 265, 268, 271, 273, 275, 287, 289, 290, 296, 312
planetary nebula 193
plank 243
plant(s) 98, 147, 181, 207, 278, 279, 280
Plantaganet 250
Plasmatons 237
playground 291
Pleistocene 236, 237
plesiosaur(s) 141, 142, 143
Pletrac 141, 142
pliers 37
plug 25, 222
plunger 65, 272
plural 242

Pluto 192, 193
plutonium 181
Poacher 232
pocket(s) 50, 202, 209, 210, 231, 272
pod(s) 174, 176, 280
poison 167, 261
polar region 290
pole 99, 266, 275
police bike 311
Police Box 82, 107, 108, 221, 222, 233
police officer(s) 117, 221, 233, 295, 310, 321
"Police Public Call Box" 311
police station 46
pollen 278
Pollock, Commander 321
Polo, Marco 17
polymorphs 146
pony tale 144
pool 248, 287
Poppaea 31
Popplewick, Mr. 280
population control 120
porter 212
Portreeve 226
positive ions 245
positronic brain 62, 72
possessions 309
post office tower 54
poster 293
post-production 301
potato 151
Poul 184
power 114, 154, 171, 197
power complex 120
The Power of Kroll 201
The Power of the Daleks 36, 61, 89, 271
power pack 231, 232, 260
power plant 176, 177
The Powerful Enemy 29
praying 312
Preba 156
precedent 307
precognition 2, 171
Prefect, Ford 46
Pre-Mayan 227, 228
pre-release 300
presentation 225
presidential code 238
Preslin 48
Press 288
pressure 116, 144, 193
pressure gauge 67, 78
Preston 248
Priam, King 45
Price 82, 263

Priest 178
Priest of Death 48
primitive planet 302
primitives 122, 123, 124
print 232
print-through 17, 48, 80, 101
Priscilla P 293
prison 131, 290
prisoner(s) 119, 164, 251, 262, 275, 302, 316, 317
Prisoners of Conciergerie 24
Pritchard, Mrs. 299
Probe 135, 185
probic vent 151, 267
process 109
processing room 120
Professor Chronotis 212, 213
Professor Dale 144
Project Degravitate 26
projectiles 263
promotion 241, 243, 297
pseudoscientific 3
psionic beam 168
psychology 174
Pterodactyl 152
pub 298
public 244
publicity 300
publicity photos 196
Pudovkin 290
pulse 100, 116
pulverizer 279
puppets 131
pursuer(s) 232, 275
puzzle 172
pyramid(s) 32, 47, 172
Pyramids of Mars 170

quantum magnetism 238
Quark 86, 87, 88
quarry (quarries) 28, 140, 151, 180
quarters 184
quartz 198
Queen Galleia 138
Queen Spider 158
Queen Victoria 299
quest 203
question 297, 308
question mark(s) 225, 253, 255
Quin 62
Quin, Dr. 110
Quinlan, James 113

A Race Against Death 22
Rachel 291, 292
radar 67, 175, 203, 278
radiation 111, 112, 115, 122, 139, 174, 205, 281, 299

radiation flux 84, 87
radio 118, 126, 130, 131, 137, 176
radio telescope 117, 222
radio waves 172, 173
radioactive 113, 120, 181, 200
Radnor 96, 97
radon-222 214
Ragnarok 296
Rago 86, 88
railroad cars 310
rails 182
ramp 316, 317
Rani 264, 265, 266, 285, 286, 321, 322
Ransome, Lieutenant 101, 109, 190
Ranulf 244
Rapunzel 90
Rassilon 218, 228, 246
Ratcliffe 292
ration 243
Ravalox 276
Ravensworth, Lord 265
Ravolox 274, 275, 276
Ray 288, 289
ray gun(s) 36, 69, 77, 78, 161
reactor 111, 119, 120, 180
reality 230
reasonable 309
Rebec 146, 147
rebels 218, 316
The Rebose File 196
recall disk 266
recall unit 268
recluse 267
recognizance missions 228
reconstruction(s) 5, 58
recovery room 112
Recovery 7 112, 113
recycling 93, 235
red Dalek 317
Red Kangs 287
Red Planet 77, 288
Redcoat 64, 100
Redvers 299
reed flute 202
Reegan 112
reference point 276
refinery 156, 157
refrigerator 227
Refusian 50
regeneration(s) 58, 61, 66, 103, 107, 157, 158, 182, 220, 245, 255, 270
rehab center 192
rehearsal 285
The Reign of Terror 4, 23
reincarnated guard blooper 113

reinforcements 295
relapse 220
relic 302
relief design 195
rels 180, 317
Remembrance of the Daleks 82, 179, 291
remote control 254
Renan, Jules 23, 24
renegade 238, 250
Renis, Maylin 269
replacement 308
replication 121, 265
reprise 80, 128, 136, 141, 156, 158, 161, 165, 182, 189, 199, 207, 208, 214, 215, 225, 237, 241, 250, 253, 262, 289, 290, 292, 293, 296
reptiles 131
rescue 137
The Rescue 15, 29, 30
rescue ship 29
Reserve 53
resistance leaders 102
respiratory compensator 32
respiratory system 235
restaurant(s) 207, 267, 294
Resurrection of the Daleks 251, 262
The Return 50
Reuben 187, 188
Revelation of the Daleks 272, 307
Revenge of the Cybermen 166, 234
Revere, Captain 249
revival room 163
Reynalds 89, 90
Reynart, Prince 201
Reynolds 89, 90
rhymes 145
Ribos 197
The Ribos Operation 196, 214
Richard, King 35
Rider from Shang-tu 17
rifle(s) 76, 132, 235, 317
Rigg, Captain 209
Rill Voice 43
ringed planet 296
Ringo, Johnny 52, 53
Ringway 234
Ringwood 56
RNA 191
Road Works Overseer 23
"Roar" 152
robe(s) 260, 311
Roberts 230
Robespierre 24
Roboman 26, 316, 317

Robophobia 185
robot(s) 123, 164, 184, 185, 205, 227, 232, 246, 275, 317
Robot 161, 162
robot ship 280
Robotic Self-Activating Mark 7Z Cleaners 287
The Robots of Death 184
Robson 68, 83
rock analysis 250
The Rock Collector 131
rocket(s) 88, 98, 113, 165, 168, 174, 175, 203, 270
rocket silo 203
rocking 243
rococo 217
Rodan 195, 196
Rogin 163
Rohm-Dutt 202, 203
Roman Zone 101, 102, 103
Romana II 307, 316
Romanesque 317
The Romans 29, 30
Rome 298
Ronson 165
roof 287, 297, 298
The Roof of the World 16
room 9 278
room number 1236 287
room 6 278
root guardian 155
Rorvik, Captain 218
rotten egg smell 93
Roundhead 137
Rouvray 24
Royal House 204
Royal Navy 300
Royce 219
rubber 288
rubber band 143
rubble 87
Rubeish, Professor 151
Rudge 278
ruffian 215
rug 42, 244
ruins 219, 237
rum 243
Rumford, Professor 200
RUN 259
runes 300
Russell 101, 103, 262
Russell, Jane 300
Russian(s) 300, 301
Russian-Japanese War Zone 103
Russian missile 93
Russian rocket 92
Rutan 187

Ruth 278
Ruther 226
Rutlidge, Major-General 91

S.V.7 185
saber-tooth 302, 303
Sabetha 18, 19
sabotage 117, 153
safe 19, 113, 161
safety margin 278
Safran, Captain 188, 189
Saga of the Umbrella 290
sailor 243
Saladin 35
Salamander 79, 80
Salamar 170
Salateen 255
Salinger, Dr. 309
Sandy 30
Sapan 75
Saphadin 35
sarcophagus 171, 172, 237, 246
Sarn 285
Sash of Rassilon 195
satellite(s) 98, 203, 288
Saturday 294
Saturn 188, 276, 296
Saturn V 174
saucer 296, 307, 312
Saunders 230
The Savages 53, 93, 271
Savar, Lord 195
saw 232
Saxon 217
scabbard 297
scaffolding 165
Scarlioni, Count 207
Scarman, Laurence 171, 172, 173
Scarman, Professor Marcus 170, 171, 172, 173
Scaroth 207
scene(s) 117, 249, 273, 308, 309
Schapp 204
Schlesinger, Katherine 299
school 291, 317
Schultz 57
science fiction 271, 292
Scientific Mythology 226
scientist 101, 102, 104, 212
Scobie, General 107, 108
Scooby Doo Where Are You? 92
Scorby 176, 177
scotch 141
Scotland 94
Scott 234, 235

scout craft 187
scout ship 217, 218
The Screaming Jungle 19
sea-base crew 248
The Sea Beggar 48
Sea Devil(s) 131, 132, 133, 247, 248
The Sea Devils 130
sea monster 143
The Sea of Death 18
The Search 36
The Search for the Key to Time 196
Second Doctor 2, 3, 17, 34, 57, 138, 139, 140, 245, 246, 266, 267, 268
second law of thermodynamics 286
secret 237, 295
secret entrance 130
section leader 115
sectional supply unit 85
Sector Four 316
security chief 102
security code 238
security guards 225
The Seeds of Death 95
The Seeds of Doom 176
Seeley, Mrs. 108, 109
segment detector 199
Le Seigneur du Temps 307
self-sacrifice 205, 206
Selris 94
senior clerk 281
Sense-Sphere 21, 23
Sensorites 19, 21, 118
Sentence of Death 19
September 294
sergeant stripes 113
servant 170
serving girl 219
Seth 211
setisolified 13
Sevateem 183
seventeenth century 179
Seventh Doctor 212, 311, 322
seventh persona 286
Seville 268
sewers 186, 262
sex/nudity 73
Sezon 270
Shada 2, 212, 213, 246, 247
shaft 149, 316, 317
Shapp 203
Sharrel, Commander 205, 206
shed 288
sheepskin coat 239
shelf 216
shell 109, 165, 208

shelter 88
shelves 288
shield 243
shield gun 194
shielding 119
ship(s) 121, 124, 125, 131, 132, 142, 143, 144, 145, 146, 153, 163, 167, 169, 193, 194, 204, 206, 210, 212, 215, 218, 221, 235, 236, 240, 241, 243, 251, 278, 279, 289, 290, 292
Shirna 141, 142
shirt 250, 287, 309
Shockeye 267, 268
shopkeeper 23
short circuit 247
shot(s) 88, 108, 210, 232, 239, 248, 270, 311
shot fired 317
shotgun 125
shoulder 219, 308
shower 108
Shrivenzales 197
shuttle 189, 190
shuttlecraft 292
SIDRAT 101, 102, 103
Sigma, Earl 293
Sigma, Trevor 293
signal 261
signpost 125, 126, 300
Sil 263, 276, 277
Silas P 293
silhouettes 147
silicon 228
silicon rod 139
silos 235
Silurian(s) 110, 111, 118, 131, 247, 248
silver carrier 84
Silver Nemesis 5, 123, 294, 296, 297
Sin, Mr. 186
The Singing Sands 16
sink 25, 139
The Sinking Ship 24
sisterhood 175, 176
sixteenth century 79, 179
Sixth Doctor 267, 268, 275, 322
Skagra 212, 213
Skarasen 168
Skaro 15, 43, 72, 166, 205, 307, 308, 315, 317
Skarov 72
Skart 202
skeleton 175, 269
sketch 207, 227
Skinsale, Colonel 187

Skonnos 211
Skybase 134, 135
skyline 292, 310
Slaar 96, 97, 98
The Slave Traders 31
sleeping 299
slide rule 42
slingshot 295
slips 279
slither 28
slug 261
Small Prophet, Quick Return 44
Smallbeer 56
Smith, John 9, 10, 308
Smith, Doctor John 84, 101, 109, 115, 151, 152
Smith, Sarah Jane 307
Smithers 24, 25
The Smugglers 56
smuggling ring 157
snake 126, 230
snake form 309
Snake-Master 308
Snakedance 239, 240
sniffer-outer 136
snow 57, 75, 176, 290
The Snows of Terror 19
solar magnets 99
solar system 37, 45, 67, 84, 175, 202, 263, 271
Soldeed 211
soldier(s) 112, 118, 121, 162, 165, 168, 178, 182, 200, 208, 234, 235, 249, 251, 291
Solis 182
Solon 135, 175, 176, 248
Solos 134, 135
Solow, Doctor 248
solutions 250
sonar 99, 132
Sondergaard 135
song 307
sonic cone 289
sonic screwdriver 1, 82, 88, 101, 142, 143, 144, 156, 157, 195, 197, 205, 214, 228, 232, 307
Sontaran(s) 152, 164, 194, 196, 267, 268
Sontaran Battle Fleet 196
The Sontaran Experiment 164
Sontaran flag 151
Sontaran hand 151, 164, 195, 267
Sorasta 253
Sorba, Lieutenant 100
Sorenson 169, 170
Sorin, Captain 300, 301

Sorris 182
South Pole 57, 322
Southern Region 82, 83
Soviet Union 139
space 270, 271, 285
The Space Museum 34, 35
The Space Pirates 98, 230
space station 251, 252, 267
spacecraft 200, 285
spaceship(s) 73, 124, 126, 145, 146, 147, 151, 152, 206, 211, 219, 254
space-time craft 263, 264
space-time telegraph 168
Space-Time Visualizer 36
Spain 79, 266, 267
spare key 309
spatial distribution circuits 250
spear 275
The Spearhead from Space 82, 107, 116, 229
special metal 161
species 280
specific gravity 72
specimens 142
spectrox 255
speed of light 121, 140
Spencer 70, 101
sphere 117, 212
spider 33, 158, 186
Spider, Queen 158
spikes 71
spin(s) 203, 205, 243
spinning 197, 198
Spiridon 146, 147, 292
spits 90
splash 317
SRS 161, 162
Ssorg 129, 130
STACS 97, 299
Stael, Max 190, 191
Stage 1 242
Stage 2 242
Stahlman 114, 115, 116
stairs 114, 219, 228, 235, 287, 292, 312
stalactite(s) 165, 293
stalk 27
Stapley, Captain 236, 237
star system 3, 271
Star Trek 62, 272, 299
Star Trek Universe 84
star(s) 99, 166, 169, 175, 238, 243, 244, 249, 261, 279
State of Decay 217, 218
statue 137, 138, 184, 295
steel girder 97
The Steel Sky 49

Stegosaurus 152
Stein 251, 252
stellar system 182
Stellar's Mother 291
Stellian Galaxy 274
Stengos, Arthur 272, 273
Stephenson, George 265, 266
sterilization procedures 242
Stevens 149, 150
stewardess 277, 279
Stike 267
Stimson 214
sting 278
stinger(s) 279, 280
stock footage 174
Stoker, James 244
The Stones of Blood 199, 204
Stor 195
storm 134
Storr 78
story 295
Stott 209, 210
Stotz 255
straight jacket 281
Strangers in Space 21
Striker, Captain 243
stroll 141
stronghold 147
Stuart 63
Stubbs 134
stuck 115, 195
stun 146, 211
Styggron 175
Styles, Sir Reginald 127, 128
Styre 164
submarine 131, 132, 133
submarine blooper 132, 133
substitution 144
suffocation 235
sugar 66
sugar stalactites 293
suit 115
suitcases 298
sulfur 93
sulfuric acid 95
Sullivan, Harry 307
Summers, Dr. 119
sun 31, 66, 134, 157, 168, 169, 232, 274, 276
The Sun Makers 191
Sunnyvale 192
Sun's Gravity Belt 67
sunset 148, 199
supernova 85, 228
Superted 300
Supreme Dalek 147, 148
surface dwellers 275
surveillance 149, 275
Survey Building 87

Survival 302
The Survivors 13
Susan 317
Susan Q 293, 294
Susie 316, 317
Sutekh 170, 171, 172
Sutton 115, 116
Svartos 290
Swampie(s) 201, 202
swimming 294
swimming pool 196, 287, 288
switchboard 275
sword(s) 131, 208, 297, 298
Sylvest, Professor 259
symbol(s) 172, 292
syringe 272
system 193

T-Mat 97
T-Mat Control Center 98
T-Mat systems 240
table 119, 213, 219, 265, 273
tabletop 302
tablets 134
tail 124
The Talons of Weng-Chiang 185
Taltalian 112
tambourine 64
Tandrell 275
Tane 165
Tanha 239
tape, commercial 4, 308, 309
tapestry 226
Tara 201
Tarak 217, 218
Taran beast 200
Taran Throne 201
taranium 46
TARDIS 9, 10, 11, 12, 13, 15, 16, 19, 20, 28, 29, 32, 33, 35, 36, 38, 72
TARDIS Databank 225, 226
TARDIS detected 260, 278
TARDIS key 14, 45, 55, 103, 108, 117, 158, 169, 172, 173, 183, 193, 212, 227, 233, 309, 311
TARDIS lock 21
TARDIS manual 263
TARDIS tracking 53
TARDIS wardrobe 35, 48
Taren Capel 185
target 125, 168, 254
Taron 146, 147, 148
Tasambeker 272
taste 202
tattoo 108
Taurus 271

Tavius 31
taxi 55
TCE 237, 253, 254, 265
technician(s) 97, 118, 308
technobabble 3, 21, 28, 29, 43, 47, 53, 65, 66, 68, 71, 76, 78, 84, 85, 88, 89, 94, 121, 133, 134, 149, 188, 193, 215, 219, 226, 227, 231, 240, 265, 267, 269, 275, 280, 286, 289, 310, 312, 322
technology 146, 151, 155, 217, 248
teeth 186, 220, 230, 237, 270
Tegan 179
Tehran 184
Tekker 269, 270
telebiogenesis 226
telepath 122, 124, 172
telephone 125, 136, 146, 254, 279
telephone door 221
teleport 302
telescope 100, 131, 222
televised version 323
television 140, 254
television station 22
tellurium 94
Telos 73, 75, 262
Temmosus 14
temperature 145, 175, 262, 289
The Temple of Evil 20
Temple of Secrets 44
temporal grace 181, 238
temporal orbit 312
temporal stabilizer 253, 254
tentacle(s) 109, 177
tenth century 41
Tenth Doctor 322
The Tenth Planet 5, 57, 61, 65, 73, 84, 90, 91, 92, 295
Terileptil 232
Terminus 241, 242
Terra Alpha 294
Terradon 217
Terrall 71
Terran 184
Terror of the Autons 116
Terror of the Vervoids 277, 280
Terror of the Zygons 168, 169
Tesh 183
Tetraps 286
Texas 177
thaesium 134
Thal(s) 13, 14, 15, 145, 146, 147, 148, 164, 315
Thal-Dalek War 14
Thal Dome 165

Thames 27, 186
Thara 95
Tharil(s) 219
Thawn 202
Thea 190
theater 185
Theory of Relativity 121
Thera 136
thermolance 235
thermonuclear power 67
thermos 268
thesium 133
theta 292
Theta Sigma 204, 293
Third Doctor 2, 138, 139, 245, 246, 270
Third Mentor 277
Thirteenth Doctor 322
Thirty Years' War Zone 103
Thonmi 75, 76
Thoros-Beta 277
Thoughts 260
threads 172
threat 213
three-body problem 260
The Three Doctors 49, 138, 141, 173
thumb(s) 278, 286
Thunderbolt 119
thunderstorm 245
tiara 226
Tibetan 208
tie 32, 116, 170, 171
Tigella 215
Tilde 287
Time And Relative Dimensions In Space 9, 10, 11, 12, 41, 46, 49, 54, 85, 101, 208, 228, 250, 288, 310, 315
Time and Space Visualizer 36
Time and the Rani 269, 285
time coordinates 264
time corridor 251, 252
time dams 198
time energy 137
Time-Flight 236, 247
Time, Inc. 280, 281
time line 307
time log 220
time-loop 204
Time Lord(s) 9, 15, 58, 61, 62, 64, 67, 74, 75, 76, 101, 102, 103, 116, 117, 123, 132, 133, 134, 139, 140, 141, 142, 165, 176, 179, 182, 185, 191, 195, 204, 207, 208, 213, 216, 217, 238, 246, 260, 264, 265, 266, 267, 270, 273, 276, 277, 302, 311, 317

Time Lord physiology 286
Time Lord robes 311
Time Lord ships 217
Time Lords' Gift 2, 179, 180, 214, 220, 227, 263, 269
The Time Meddler 41, 52
The Time Monster 126, 136, 253
Time of Rassilon 212
time particles 269
Time Ram 138, 253
time ring 166
time rotor 139, 312
time scanner 68
time scoop 245, 246, 247, 280
time shift 262
time-slip 207
time units 317
The Time Warrior 151
Timelash 168, 179, 268, 269, 270, 272
timer 27
Time-Space Visualizer 37
Timmin 254
tissue compression eliminator 253, 265, 281
Titan 188
Titan 3 259
title 52, 163, 280, 281, 307
title sequence 225
Tlotoxl 20
TLV 78
Toba 86, 87
Toberman 73, 74
Toby 71
tocsin bell 48, 49
toggle 176
Tom 265, 316, 317
Tomas 183
tomb 171
The Tomb of the Cybermen 72, 73, 77, 85, 91, 92
Tommy 158
ton 144
tonnes 216
Toos 184
tooth 303
top secret 118
torch(es) 130, 155, 156, 178, 215
torch bearers 31, 36
tornado 312
Torvin 208
Totter's Lane 9, 10, 11
Totter's Yard 221
tour guide 39, 207
towels 199, 279
tower 246
town 232

Town, Cy 154
toy Daleks 72, 146
Toymaker 51
tracer 197
Tracey, George 321
Trafalgar Square 27
The Traitors 46
Traken 179, 220, 221, 226, 265
Traken Union 220
tramp 55, 251
trance 149
transfer 311
transformer 250
transistor 155
trans-mat 163, 245
transmission 134, 163, 203, 240, 241, 242, 252, 281, 286, 292, 295, 309, 323
transmitter(s) 118, 131, 167, 168, 175
transplants 277
transport(s) 97, 169, 303
transportation ships 119
transporter 134
trap 71, 72, 85, 117, 164, 172, 182, 222, 266, 273, 285, 302
Trap of Steel 42
trash receptacle 221
travel capsule 87
travel dials 18, 19
Travers, Professor 75, 76, 81, 108
tray 67, 201, 279
treason 89
tree roots 230
Tremas 220
trench 165, 166
Trenchard 131, 132
Trevor Sigma 293
trial 103, 191, 275, 276, 280, 307
The Trial of a Time Lord 165, 271, 273
The Tribe of Gum 11
triceratops 152, 154
tricycle 127
Trilogic 51
Trion 253, 254
Trisilicate 155
tritium 200
Trojan 44, 45
Trojan War 49, 50
trolley 199, 205
trooper 235
troops 162, 290
troublemakers 265
The Troughton Years 75, 79, 98

Troy 45
truck(s) 112, 119, 298, 310
Tryst 209, 210
tube station 153
Tutankhamen, King 171
tunnel(s) 166, 193, 203, 234, 249, 297
Turner, Captain 93
Tussaud, Madame 109
TV 277, 287, 309, 311, 315
TV announcer 292
TV series 315, 317
TV story 317
TV studio 312
twelfth century 151, 298
Twelfth Doctor 322
twentieth century 94, 151, 279
twenty-ninth century 234
twenty-second century 291
twenty-sixth century 234
The Twin Dilemma 259
twin planet 276
Twins 259, 260
The Two Doctors 151, 266, 273
two-way street 310
Tyler 28
Tyler, Doctor 138, 139, 140
Tylos 217
tyrannosaur 110
tyrannosaurus rex 152, 153, 154, 266
The Tyrant of France 24
Tyrum 167

UFO 113, 120
Ultima Machine 300
The Ultimate Foe 277, 280, 281
ultraviolet rays 111, 275
umbrella 140, 288, 290, 294, 301
umpire 233
The Underwater Menace 64, 95
Underworld 193
The Underworld 135
An Unearthly Child 11
unicorn 90
unidentified ship 278
uniform 125, 149, 248, 287
unit(s) 108, 109, 137
Universe 26, 28, 47, 48, 94, 114, 115, 116, 125, 138, 140, 169, 170, 198, 204, 213, 218, 222, 228, 242, 276, 312
Unstoffe 197
The Unwilling Warriors 21
upstairs 187
upstream 294
Urak 285

uranium-235 181
Urbanka 228
Urbankans 227
Uvanov 184, 185

V-1 137
V-2 92
V.5 185
V.6 185
V.9 184
V.35 184, 185
V.40 185
Vaber 146
vacuum 67, 99, 193, 242, 243, 311
vacuum shield 243
vacuum tubes 97
Valeyard 274, 275, 280, 281
Valgard 242
valley 154
Valmar 63
Vampire, King 217
vampires 217, 218
van 291, 293, 317
Van Allen belt 111
Vana 93, 94, 95
Vanir 242
vapor 176
Varan 134, 135
Vardan ship 195
Varga 43, 47, 77, 78
Varos 263, 264, 308
Vasor 19
Vaughan, Tobias 91, 92
vegetarians 148
The Velvet Web 18
Vena 270
Venerable Bede 186
Vengeance on Varos 263, 277
ventilation shaft 58, 146
Venus 57, 58, 88, 130, 169
version(s) 238, 245, 288, 323
vertebrae 134
Vervoid(s) 278, 279, 280
VHS 302
vial 209, 212, 266
vianessium 280
vibrations 242
Victoria 65
Victoria, Queen 299
video 115, 182, 252, 286, 299
view screen 112, 170, 260
Viking inscriptions 300
Viking Landers 77
Villa 191
village 174, 232, 275
Villagra 227
villain 184
Villar, Arturo 101, 102, 103

Vince 187
Viner 73
vines 202
Vira 163
virus 66, 147, 161, 162, 174, 188, 189, 191, 252
Vishinsky 170
Visians 46
vision 186, 243, 285
visitation 228
The Visitation 231
visual stabilizer 91
Voga 167, 168
Vogon 129
volcanic activity 136
Volcano 46
volcanoes 79
volts 114
vomit(s) 310, 311
von Wer, Doktor 63, 64
Voord(s) 18, 19
Vorg 141, 142, 143
Vorshak, Commander 247, 248
Vortis 34
vote 263, 264
Voyager 84
vraxoin 209
Vrestin 34
Vulcan 61, 62
Vyon, Bret 45, 46

waddling 205
Wainwright, Reverend Mister 301
waistcoat 264
waistline 262
The Waking Ally 28
Wales 75, 82
The Wall of Lies 17
walrus 36
Walters 76
war 165
war chief 101, 102, 103
The War Games 2, 100, 245
war lord 102
war machine 3 55
war machine 9 55
war machines 118
The War Machines 54
War of God 48
war surplus 99
wardrobe 216, 311
Warlock, Dr. 172
The Warlords 35
Warne, Major 99
warning 237, 242
warrant officer 161, 162, 168, 173

warriors 275
Warrior's Gate 218
The Warriors of Death 20
Warriors of the Deep 154
waste 278
waste disposal 288
watch 41
Watcher 221
The Watcher 41
water 34, 78, 119, 132, 174, 227
water line 301
water tank 298
Waterfield 71
Watford 317
Watkins, Professor 91, 92
Watson, Dr. 110
Watson, Professor 180
wax museum 109
weapon(s) 73, 74, 78, 81, 90, 93, 117, 121, 124, 132, 133, 135, 156, 161, 163, 164, 167, 170, 181, 182, 183, 186, 193, 195, 203, 204, 219, 235, 238, 242, 263, 264, 272, 273, 275, 281, 294, 298, 308
Wearp, Mr. 52
Weather Control Bureau 97
The Web of Fear 2, 80, 107
The Web Planet 32, 61
Webster 23, 24
wedding ring 243
weight 132, 153, 206, 216, 246, 311; atomic 72, 94
Weismuller 289
Welch 75
well 296
Well at the End of the Universe 170
Weng-Chiang 186
Wessex 151
The West Lodge 214
Wester 146, 147
The Wheel in Space 3, 83, 91
The Wheel of Fortune 35
wheelchair 108, 267
Whitby 301
White Guardian 196, 199, 203, 204, 216, 242, 243
Whitehead logic 73
Whizzkid 296
Who 1 322
Who 7 298, 322
Whomobile 153, 158
Widmanstatten patterns 250
wife 129
Wild Bill Hickok 52
Wilkins 212

Williams 57
Williams, General 144, 145
Willow, Joseph 249
Wilson 131
Wilson, Brian 198
Wilson, Sydney 30
wine 31, 56, 72
wings 33
Winser 121
Winters, Miss 161, 162
Winton 123, 124
Wirrn 163
woman 109, 144, 302
workers 264
working title 276
workshop 115
world 225
World War I 101, 103
World War II 81
world's end 26
Wotan 54, 55, 287
wound 153, 168, 268
Wrack, Captain 243, 244
wreckage 251
wrench 115
wrist communicator 182, 197
written 179

X file 107
X-ray(s) 186, 308, 309
X.V.773 259
Xanxia 198
Xeron 36, 37
Xia Dynasty 228
Xoanon 183

Yanks 139
Yartek 19
year(s) 123, 164
Yetaxa's tomb 20
Yeti 75, 76, 81, 82, 91, 118, 246
"Young Parsons" 212
Youth Club 302
Yrcanos, King 277
Yucatan 79
Yuing, Shou 297, 298

Za 12
Zadek 201
zanium 259
Zarbi 33, 34, 118
The Zarbi 33
Zardoz 125
Zargo 217, 218
Zaroff 64, 65
Zeiton E 264
Zeiton 7 263, 264
Zentos 50

Zeos 204
Zephon 45
zero 193, 204
zero box 226

zero cabinet 226
Zeta Minor 169, 170
Zoe 2
Zolfa-Thura 215, 216

Zone 246
zoology 123
ZUVDIR 9
Zygon(s) 168, 169

www.ingramcontent.com/pod-product-compliance
Lightning Source LLC
Chambersburg PA
CBHW081536300426
44116CB00015B/2656